OHIO
HANDBOOK

OHIO
HANDBOOK

INCLUDING CLEVELAND, CINCINNATI, COLUMBUS,
AMISH COUNTRY, AND THE OHIO RIVER VALLEY
FIRST EDITION

DAVID K. WRIGHT

MOON
TRAVEL
HANDBOOKS

OHIO HANDBOOK
FIRST EDITION

Published by
Moon Publications, Inc.
5855 Beaudry Street
Emeryville, California 94608, USA

Printed by
Colorcraft Ltd.

Please send all comments,
corrections, additions,
amendments, and critiques to:

**OHIO HANDBOOK
MOON TRAVEL HANDBOOKS
5855 Beaudry Street
Emeryville, CA 94608
e-mail: travel@moon.com
www.moon.com**

Printing History
1st edition—November 1999

5 4 3 2 1 0

ISBN: 1-56691-154-0
ISSN: 1522-3507

Editors: Gina Wilson Birtcil, Gregor Johnson Krause, and Jeannie Trizzino
Production & Design: Allen Leech, David Hurst
Cartography: Chris Alvarez
Index: Sondra Nation

Front cover photo: © Ian Adams Photography. Amish farm near Winesburg, Holmes County OH

All photos by David K. Wright unless otherwise noted.
All illustrations by Bob Race unless otherwise noted.

Distributed in the United States and Canada by Publishers Group West

Printed in China

CONTENTS

MAP SYMBOLS

═══	Superhighway	⬭	U.S. Interstate	⊛	State Capitol
═══	Primary Road	⬭	U.S. Highway	○	City
───	Secondary Road	○	State Highway	○	Town
—·-·	State Boundary	□	County Road	★	Point of Interest
—·-·	County Boundary	✗	International Airport	▪	Other Location
		⚑	State Park		

MAPS

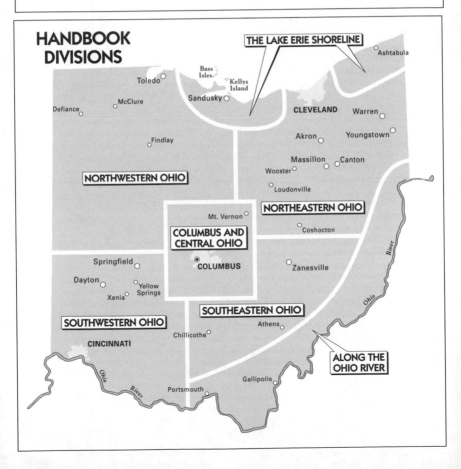

ACKNOWLEDGMENTS

The local tourism folks were consistently helpful, being much too nice to interrogate someone who claimed to be doing a book about Ohio travel. Standouts included staffers in Circleville, Conneaut, Logan County, and several other locales. I consider them Ohio's most valuable players.

HELP MAKE THIS A BETTER BOOK

I went to bed more than one night in Akron or Athens or Belle-fontaine wondering if that great restaurant or insider place to shop would still exist when this book hit the streets. Whenever you find anything I've gotten wrong, missed, or overlooked, or anything that's ceased to exist, please let me know. Is it possible that I sorted all the telephone area codes correctly? I doubt it. I'd also like your criticisms, particularly if you had a bad meal, found directions or maps inadequate, or discovered prices to be out of date. Address comments to:

Ohio Handbook
Moon Travel Handbooks
5855 Beaudry Street
Emeryville, CA 94608
USA

ABBREVIATIONS

Cincy	Cincinnati
CR	County Road
I	Interstate
OSU	Ohio State University
OU	Ohio University
SR	State Route

INTRODUCTION

It takes courage to visit Ohio. Tell friends and neighbors you're planning a vacation in the Buckeye State and frequent flyers to places such as Florida or Las Vegas will recommend a travel agent—or a therapist.

But this is due largely to the fact that ignorance of things Ohioan is awesome. With 11.1 million residents, Ohio is more than twice as populous as the average U.S. state. It's where Thomas Edison was raised, and where Jonathan Winters grew up (or perhaps failed to grow up). It's where Pete Rose both performed for baseball fans and placed the bets that would break their hearts. It's where one Wright brother was born and where astronauts Neil Armstrong, John Glenn, and Judy Resnick found their own right stuff. It's where Sherwood Anderson wrote stunning short stories while aching to trade a middle-class existence (as a successful advertising copywriter) for bohemia. It's where Erma Bombeck discovered that it's okay to be crazy in the suburbs—as long as you can reproduce the craziness regularly in a newspaper column. It's the home of the most successful golfer of all time, Jack Nicklaus. Cincinnati was once the

address of the woman who wrote *Uncle Tom's Cabin,* Harriet Beecher Stowe. And that archetypal Hollywood leading man, Clark Gable, came of age here, too.

But Ohio is much more than a collection of exceptional sons and daughters. It's also a sweeping view of the Ohio River from one of Cincinnati's Rome-like hills. It's a meander down the main streets of places like Miamisburg or Mount Vernon, where visitors realize that small-town America isn't just some long-ago fantasy depicted on Christmas cards. It's gritty Rust Belt neighborhoods in Akron, Cleveland, and Youngstown—as well as the Old World clubs that hang on in the same cities, peopled by aging Italians or Poles, Slovaks or Slovenes, who came to Ohio to roll steel and mold rubber and found freedom. (The state also meant economic freedom to the Appalachian whites and African-Americans who worked alongside the European immigrants.) The state is husky fields of corn that fatten cattle and fill six-year-olds at breakfast. It's the world's largest moundbuilding project, created by ancient people near Chillicothe, and it's the whisper of twilight's tiny waves along a Lake Erie beach

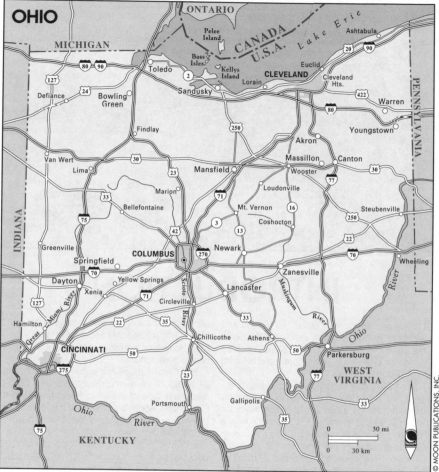

that has seen a lot of pollution until quite recently.

They say rock 'n' roll was invented in Ohio, and the genre's hall of fame lends credence to the claim. Perhaps for balance, there's a polka museum just up the road.

Flights of musical fancy are commemorated here, but so is flight itself: a military museum near Dayton shows where billions of tax dollars have gone for dozens of years. Flight of another type is practiced in the southeastern part of the state, where Wayne National Forest whispers with the flutter of the wings of almost 200 different bird species—and, increasingly, the calls of off-road bikers one to another. North a ways, auctioneers call for bids at livestock auctions attended by clean-living Amish.

Ohioans are well organized in publicizing their attractions. Besides a toll-free number (800-BUCKEYE or 800-282-5393), there are brochure-stuffed kiosks on interstate highways and local visitors' bureaus. Such accessibility is necessary because most travelers arrive in Ohio by automobile and can easily drive completely through the state without ever leaving the wheel. A traveler crossing the state from Pennsylvania on the east to Indiana on the west, or from Michigan on the north to Kentucky on the south, travels less than 230 miles. All but the thirstiest 4-by-4 can cover that much ground on less than a single tank of fuel. Thus, untold numbers of people whistle across Ohio on interstate highways, virtually hermetically sealed against anything of interest. And that is a shame.

No, you really need to immerse yourself in Ohio. Go not only with the idea of being a tourist—heading for the swell cities, great state parks, and authentically preserved history—but also as an observer. You never know what you'll find. In my travels through the state, I found myself witness to several strange and perhaps momentous episodes: teenage employees in Macedonia waging a David-and-Goliath battle in attempting to unionize mighty McDonald's; workers near Cincinnati cleaning away the spillage of thousands of gallons of liquid animal fat on an interstate highway with the timely application of dishwashing detergent; a copyright dispute between two state colleges—one large and the other stupendous—over which should have exclusive rights to the state name on athletic apparel. Nice as the Rock and Roll Hall of Fame and Museum or the Taft historic home may be, the whimsical stuff may best reveal Ohio's kaleidoscopic personality.

THE LAND

Ohio is one of the Great Lakes states (those states whose northernmost residents have taken to calling their border the North Coast). It is only 40 miles from Canada—so close that over the years, many foolhardy souls have started in Ohio and, gambling that the winter is cold enough to keep the ice solid and the Coast Guard doesn't catch them, have walked across the jagged Lake Erie ice to reach the nation to the north. In contrast, only the Ohio River separates the state from West Virginia and Kentucky. Both of those states share Appalachian traditions and flavor with Ohio, and the line separating Appalachia from the Midwest cuts through much of the state, from near Youngstown southwest through Chillicothe.

Ohio's eastern and southern boundaries were established by the outlines of Pennsylvania and colonial Virginia (what is today West Virginia), while to the west and northwest the federal government decided where Indiana and Michigan would begin. In between are 44,828 square miles—most of it Midwest but with bits of both north and south mixed in. Ohio is a bit closer to the equator than to the North Pole (the 40th parallel runs right through Columbus) and the state lies between the 80th and 85th meridians, making it six time zones—almost one-quarter of the globe—west of the Greenwich meridian. It's farther west than anywhere in South America and the same distance north of the equator as Spain or North Korea.

Geography

Ohio has three major geographic areas: the Lake Plains, the Central Plains, and the Allegheny Plateau. (It sounds flat because it *is* flat—the state's highest point is Campbell Hill, 1,549 feet, in Logan County, some 50 miles northwest of Columbus—it's a fair distance from anything that could charitably be called a mountain.) About 15,000 years ago, glaciers ground into the region and covered all but the southeast third of the state in crusts of ice up to 8,000 feet thick. Warmer weather eventually began melting the glaciers, leaving only Lake Erie, low-lying swamps and bogs, and a complex network of streams and rivers. Seventy percent of the state's rivers and streams drain south into the Ohio River. Until the middle of the 20th century, rampaging water tended to wreak substantial havoc each spring. The ambitious construction of earthen dams, widened riverbanks, and sizeable reservoirs has solved much of the problem, though the Ohio River continues to send occasional waves of rising water—and fear—through the populace.

The glaciers left rich soil in their wake, rendering a great majority of the state remarkably fertile. The richest land tends to be in the west-central and northwestern sections of the state, where, until a century ago (before the Great Swamp was fully drained), much of the best cropland—around Findlay and Lima—was underwater. Never covered by glaciers, the south-

*hardwoods along the
Lake Erie shoreline*

east is today much less fertile, forcing agriculture in that quadrant into river bottoms.

The draining of the Great Swamp revealed not only rich ebony earth but also, beneath that, pockets of oil and natural gas. More than half the state sits atop oil and natural gas deposits, and privately owned grasshopper-shaped pumps nodding slowly in rural fields are a common sight. The natural gas they recover is often sufficient to heat an old farmhouse or a new split-level in a sprawling subdivision—which is why ads for Ohio real estate sometimes include the promise "free gas."

Where there's petroleum, there's also coal. Some 30 counties had active mines in place by 1880, and millions of tons of coal are still buried in eastern and southeastern Ohio. Strip mining, with all its environmental perils, proved safer and more efficient than pit mining in the 20th century, though the industry has perpetual pricing and other problems.

Iron was once mined here, too, but it proved no match for vast deposits found later in Michigan and then in Minnesota. Today's most commonly extracted Ohio minerals are crushed stone, construction sand and gravel, and salt.

Climate

"The climate of Ohio is popularly regarded as disagreeable," says a noted historian. Yet he adds that it is ideal for such temperate-climate crops as corn, oats, and soybeans. Neither is it really all that bad for human beings. A typical year might see a few summer days that hit 100°F and a few winter days that plummet to -10°F. Lawrence County in the far south averages 55°F, while Ashtabula, Lake, and Geauga Counties average 48°F. The annual mean is about 51°F. The frost-free season runs from about five months in several northern pockets to almost six months in the Ohio Valley and very near Lake Erie. Is that so bad?

Rainfall ranges from 31 inches near Lake Erie along the northern edge of the state to 42 inches near the Ohio River, along the southern boundary. Prevailing winds come from the southwest, shipping moist and erratic Gulf of Mexico weather up the Mississippi Valley, where it frequently turns right and heads for Ohio. Lake Erie—smallest, most shallow, and most stormy of the Great Lakes—almost seems to suck these storms toward it, often resulting in roiling whitecaps beneath slate skies. Substantial snows, especially in the counties just east of Cleveland, fall when Canadian weather moves in from the west or northwest, picking up moisture as it passes over the lake.

More than half of all precipitation falls during the growing season, with June often the soggiest month of the year. But June's rains are more showerlike than the admittedly depressing, occasionally day-long sieges in March or November. Downpours that are the dying gasps of East Coast hurricanes can also affect the Buckeye State—most often in August and September. And while some southeastern valleys, with their

OHIO BUCKEYE

The Ohio buckeye tree, *Aesculus glabra,* is a tall, handsome tree growing up to 70 feet tall. It is found growing wild along the rich, moist Ohio bottomlands, producing beautiful yellow flower spikes in April or May, later bearing a large chestnut-like fruit about one or two inches in diameter. Though the flower spikes are beautiful, they give off a disagreeable odor—the Ohio buckeye is also known as "fetid buckeye" for this reason.

Native Americans called the fruit *hetuck,* meaning "the eye of the buck," for its dark center. Though not edible for humans (squirrels, however, eat the fruits with no apparent ill effects), Native Americans produced a fish stupefactant from powdered buckeye fruits. They would pour the powder into small pools to stun the fish there, then collect the fish as they floated to the surface. Pioneers used buckeye wood to build cabins and furniture; its wood has also been favored for use in making artificial limbs because of its lightness and workability. Nowadays, many ornamental varieties have been developed from wild native stocks and are found in gardens all over North America and Europe.

buckeye

---

cold-air pockets, are slow to warm, there can be an unexpectedly sunny and uplifting day in even the dankest January or February.

Flora

Only 200 years ago, 95% of Ohio was forest. These stands consisted in large part of hardwoods such as maple, oak, ash, hickory, basswood, beech, and walnut. Where there weren't trees there were grasses such as bluegrass, clover, and wild rye. And in areas too watery for such grasses, stands of cattails, reeds, and other species grew. Most of the hardwoods and virtually all of the wild grasses are gone now, though there remain 7.8 million acres of forest.

There are still many areas, particularly in parks and reserves, that hark back to an era before development. The southeast in particular, with its stubborn soil, is home to acres of wildflowers, trees, bushes, and weeds. There remain only a few stands of original-growth trees—perhaps the most unspoiled is in Belmont County, west of St. Clairsville.

The more travelers look at wild areas, the more they see. Morel mushrooms pop out of the ground in spring or fall. Perhaps most common in Vinton County, they can be found alongside false morels, puffballs, lichen, mosses, wild columbine, purple spiderwort, wild daisies, coneflowers, foxgloves, and more. Morels are also virtually the only growing thing a visitor can legally remove from a state park (even so, do ask first). Dogwood trees mesmerize with their pink-and-white blooms in the spring in southern Ohio, while the ivory flowers of the chestnut and the yellow flowers of the tulip tree aren't all that common but can be found in most parts of the state. The state's namesake buckeye is found along river bottoms and moist areas throughout Ohio, though it is not exclusively an Ohio native.

Fauna

The largest wild animal in any number in Ohio is the white-tailed deer. You're probably most likely to spot these shy creatures, their white tails flicking, as they begin edging into fields from wooded areas at the end of the day. By the end of fall bucks and does are fat and happy from eating corn, oats, apples, and other crops; rutting season begins in November, and the spotted fawns are born in June. Other creatures include rabbits, squirrels, turkeys, pheasants, and par-

OHIO'S ENDANGERED BEAR AND BOBCAT

White-tailed deer, Canada geese, and rock doves (i.e., common city pigeon) thrive in Ohio. Bison and passenger pigeons fared less well, disappearing from the Midwest more than a century ago. The bison are making a comeback under controlled circumstances other parts of the U.S., but the passenger pigeon is gone forever, truly extinct. There are several species that walk the edge of existence. Among them, at least in the Buckeye State, are the bobcat and the black bear.

Bobcats weigh 10 to 30 pounds, are about three feet long, and stand about 15 inches high at the shoulder. More closely related to the common housecat and the Canada lynx than to the mountain lion, they are identified by ear tufts and by a tail that appears to have been bobbed. Their coats are yellowish to reddish-brown, spotted with black. They hunt alone and at night, dining on birds, rabbits, squirrels, and mice. Because so few have been seen, the bobcat currently is on the Ohio Endangered Species List. Their low numbers in Ohio and elsewhere is due to high bounties placed on them in the past and now because of habitat encroachment and environmental degradation.

Since 1970, there have been only 23 verified records of bobcats in the state. Fourteen of these sightings have been reported since 1990; eight of the 16 counties in which they've been seen border the Ohio River. Odds of meeting a bobcat are slim—those with the best chance tend to be turkey hunters and bow-and-arrow deer hunters. The best river counties for bobcat spotting are Jefferson, Belmont, Monroe, Athens, Gallia, Scioto, Adams, and Brown.

Next to white-tailed deer, black bears once were the most common source of food and hides in Ohio. They disappeared from 1850 to the early 1980s, but now the big omnivore is seen on occasion. It's estimated that there are 15 to 20 individual bears, to include sows with cubs, statewide. This small number is no threat to humanity unless and until the animals develop a taste for garbage. A black bear was seen in late May, 1997, at Salt Fork State Park. The bear went on a month-long garbage-eating rampage before it was killed by a wildlife officer as it neared metropolitan Columbus. Once bears get a taste for garbage, authorities explained, they become unpredictable, losing their fear of humans. Proper garbage disposal will do Ohio's tiny bear population a big favor.

Bobcats are endangered and elusive; count yourself lucky if you catch a glimpse of one.

tridges. No wolves have been sighted for some time in the state, but foxes remain plentiful, and coyotes occasionally pop up in incongruous places—such as a grassy strip alongside a Dayton Municipal Airport runway. Smaller mammals and rodents—beavers and muskrats, raccoons and possums, groundhogs and chipmunks, rats and mice, skunks and moles—inhabit all parts of the Buckeye State.

Blessed with sufficient rain, aquatic species of **turtles** and **frogs** thrive. **Treefrogs** are numerous but shy—most evident trilling in woodlands after a summer rain. **Freshwater mussels** are increasingly plentiful—even rare breeds such as the federally endangered purple catspaw, thought to have been absent from state waters for 150 years. Most of the state's **snakes** are harmless, though the farther south one travels the more likely one is to meet an occasional poisonous variety. Copperheads are the most numerous, and there are also timber and swamp rattlers in the southeast.

Birdwatching is alive and well here, with 180 different species common to the state and 350 more moving in and out. Ducks, geese, and other migrants visit on their way south in the fall or north in the spring. Only two federally endangered bird species are found in Ohio, the peregrine falcon and the piping plover; though there is also the airborne and endangered Indiana bat. The native Canada goose population is booming, however, an Ohio Division of Wildlife spokesperson estimated the number at 100,000. Thousands of ring-billed gulls show up every fall along the Cleveland lakefront. But the most punctual birds appear to be the buzzards that are said to return from their wintering grounds in the Smoky Mountains to the village of Hinckley the very same March Sunday, year in and year out. This rite of spring takes place in northern Medina County.

All of the usual seasonal **insects** are here, from potentially dangerous bees and wasps to annoying mosquitoes to harmless beetles and gnats. (There are no so-called "killer" or Africanized honeybees, which would succumb quickly in Ohio's frosty weather.) There are, however, several federally endangered insect species found here—Hine's emerald dragonfly, the Karner blue and Mitchell's satyr butterfly, and the American burying beetle (a.k.a. the giant carrion beetle). The bug population each summer is directly related to the amount of rainfall, the number of birds and bats in the immediate area, and the severity of the previous winter. Monarchs and other butterflies dot fields by day and moths cavort around lights at night. On especially warm summer evenings, look for fireflies in open yards and fields.

Fish

The state's fish population can be separated into four primary geographical categories: the portion of the Ohio River that borders West Virginia; the portion bordering Kentucky; Lake Erie; and inland streams, rivers, and lakes. The distribution of fish species varies slightly in each area. The Ohio River, for example, supports game fish including largemouth, smallmouth and spotted bass; walleye, sauger, and saugeye; striped, hybrid striped, white, and yellow bass; muskellunge; and northern pike. Nonsporting varieties found in the big river include the bottom-feeding carp and channel catfish.

Lake Erie is the home of lake trout and salmon species, plus walleye, northern pike, and perch. Trout and salmon were introduced a couple of decades ago and have taken hold, despite occasionally murky water (the trout and salmon native to the lake don't run in Ohio). Inland bodies of water are more apt to contain the occasional panfish—bluegill, crappie, and sunfish—plus many of the species commonly found in the Ohio River. The Ohio Department of Natural Resources (DNR) has a free Division of Wildlife brochure on current fishing regulations. It carries important information about which game and other fish to refrain from eating. In particular, bottom-dwellers such as carp and channel catfish pose a threat and should not be consumed as river sediments can contain unsafe levels of toxic wastes such as PCBs. The brochure also lists fees and requirements for Ohio and nonresident fishers and is available by calling (614) 265-6300 or (800) WILDLIFE (tel. 800-945-3543).

Environmental Issues

That scourge of asthmatics, the ozone alert, may soon become a thing of the past in Ohio. "You'd think our air would be dirtier than places in Michigan or Wisconsin," allows a spokesperson for the Ohio Environmental Protection Agency. "But that's not the case." Figures from the Public Interest Center in Columbus show all areas in the state to have achieved targeted ozone standards except Cincinnati. Mainly due to cleaner-burning gasoline (a federal mandate), the amount of lead in Buckeye air has decreased by an astonishing 97% in the last 20 years.

Community water systems are monitored for the presence of coliform bacteria, and all other sources of drinking water—primarily wells—are tested quarterly. Officially, 60% of all streams are deemed fit for recreation, while 47% will sustain aquatic life. (Those figures may seem low, but there was a time when virtually every stream in the state was a sinister, soupy mess.) Beaver, eliminated from Ohio by 1830, have returned to several watersheds.

The state is also home to 38 hazardous waste sites (though four of them are only proposed). At 117 million pounds per year, Ohio is fifth among all states in quantity of toxic substances produced. On the other hand, some 215 sites contaminated by past practices have been cleaned up since 1994, many with federal Superfund dollars. Most former mining sites are probably benign and apt to stay that way. Industry has spent some five billion dollars to curb emissions and has devised ways to reduce the use of or recycle hazardous wastes and otherwise meet state and federal standards. Major projects under way at the moment include getting rid of millions of abandoned tires and urging more communities to become interested in residential recycling.

Anyone who believes these are minor accomplishments should corner an aging Ohioan and ask him or her what things were like before 1970. Then, chemical plants kept much of the Ohio River shrouded in toxic mist, while mills in the northeast sent so much debris into the air that a white shirt in the morning would have turned a discomfiting, sooty gray by the end of the day, and clothes hung out to dry could become dirtier than they had been before they'd been washed. At the time, Buckeyes were ponying up millions of dollars for treatment of em-

physema, black lung disease, and reactions to various chemicals. The state had become a place few wanted to live in or even visit—a place people could not see or breathe or drink or swim. Once that realization struck business, industry, labor, agriculture, and state government, the environment began to improve. The improvements were helped along by the decreasing importance of steel mills and coal mines.

Today, Ohio's environmental outlook isn't bad. Current industries that require (and receive) close scrutiny include food processors and companies that coat metal with chromium or other substances. Additional sources of pollution include runoff from farms and from rural septic tanks. Both sources greatly affect water quality and can affect the general health of the populace.

HISTORY

"Ohio" is a French corruption of a Seneca-Iroquois word meaning "beautiful river." The rivers here were indeed pretty. They were also numerous and, when the first humans wandered in as the glaciers receded, not all that old. From about 12,000 to 8000 B.C., these prehistoric people, known today as Paleo-, or ancient, Indians, ranged all throughout Ohio—possibly in pursuit of mastodon and mammoth, buffalo, and deer. These nomadic peoples were followed by groups more inclined to stay in one place, though they, too, were hunters. These were Archaic People. They buried their dead in *kames* (gravel hills created by glaciers) and actively fished and gathered plants. Archaic People disappeared around 1000 B.C.—and left piles of clam shells as evidence of their existence and appetite.

The better-known Adena peoples showed up next. Named for a Chillicothe-area estate on which many artifacts were discovered, the Adena traded widely with other natives, crafted pottery, planted crops, and buried their dead in large, conical hills of their own making. Equally impressive, the Adena built sturdy post-frame dwellings and laid out effigy mounds—such as the Great Serpent Mound in Adams County, some 70 miles east of what is now Cincinnati. The Adena disappeared from southwest Ohio sometime after 100 A.D.

The Moundbuilders

Like the Adena, the Hopewell people were named after an Ohio site where artifacts were discovered. They were a moundbuilding culture, and evidence indicates their presence from river valleys in northern Ohio to points along the Mississippi watershed. The trade network they established was even more far-reaching than that of the Adena—minerals from the Rocky Mountains and silver from Ontario have been discovered in latter-day Ohio. But the best remaining evidence of the Hopewell is the geometrically shaped mounds at Chillicothe, Marietta, Newark, and elsewhere. Like the Adena, the Hopewell also built large structures (one of these had walls measuring 3.5 miles around!).

The Hopewell civilization disappeared about A.D. 600. It was followed by two groups, one from the south and one from present-day Canada. Both groups grew crops but otherwise left the landscape as they found it.

Immediate pre-Columbian Ohio was home to small groups of Delaware and Mingo from the east, Shawnee from the south, Miami from the west, and Ottawa and Wyandot from the north. But these bands did not enjoy seamless harmony. The six Iroquois nations were based in upstate New York and were large, ruthless, and well organized. They swept through Ohio in the process of establishing an empire that would reach the Mississippi River. Besides subduing

pottery pipe from the Moundbuilder culture

the locals, Iroquois made contact with Europeans and then introduced diseases to which other natives had little or no resistance. Between war parties and scourges, life could be dangerous and short.

The First Europeans

Powerful as the Iroquois were, they were no match for expansionist English and French soldiers armed with muskets and swords. And although the Indians sometimes played the Europeans against each other, in the end it was the Indians who usually wound up the losers.

The first European to see the Ohio River apparently was the French aristocratic explorer Robert La Salle. The French knew Ohio and its many rivers from before 1650. They had established a trade in furs with many of the estimated 20,000 natives in the state at the time. They had also constructed wooden stockades along various river routes—but they had not attempted to populate what would one day become the state of Ohio.

The British were apparently less adventurous but more inclined toward long-range planning. Once there were settlements along the East Coast, the English claimed North America from one ocean coast to the other for their own. Soldiers and settlers crept westward, confounding natives with the idea that individuals could *own* pieces of land. Indians in northwest Ohio traded at a French fort built in Detroit in 1701. Meanwhile, English-speaking people were using the Ohio River as a highway, traveling far into the interior, then sometimes heading south on the Mississippi to New Orleans. Exchanging guns, whiskey, and trinkets for furs and other goods, traders from Pennsylvania and Virginia soon influenced Ohio natives, not often for the better.

Inevitably, the English and the French tangled along the frontier. No less a personage than George Washington received valuable training in dealing with the French at Fort Duquesne (in what is now Pittsburgh, Pennsylvania)—a jumping-off point for travelers headed west. Such forts became established targets for British forces, which picked them off. French and Indian forces preferred to kill or capture settlers living in scattered, rustic cabins in eastern and southern Ohio. Following the fall of the French city of Montreal in 1760, French forts in the American territory were handed over to the British—a transfer of power that both angered and confused native tribes.

Warriors such as Pontiac, a member of the Ottawa tribe, fought the British for several years. Sites along the Muskingum River bore witness to pitched battles between Indians and the British, who were aided by colonial frontiersmen. In an effort to stem such fighting (a gesture more economic than humane—Britain's long global battle with Franco had depleted the treasury, and the mother country did not want to find itself obligated to support troops in some distant war), the English Parliament passed an act that forbade colonists to settle west of the Appalachian Mountains. But the act was disregarded, and colonists continued to move westward in search of opportunity.

Of the European arrivals, the Moravian German missionaries co-existed most peacefully with the Indians. They converted a number of Delaware to Christianity, then lived alongside them in farming villages in what is now east-central Ohio. In spite of the fact that other Indians suspected the Christian Delaware of allying with the British and that the British suspected the Moravians of harboring native warriors, the converts and their white spiritual leaders led a peaceful life for a number of years. In contrast, in southern Ohio, frontiersmen from Kentucky and Virginia made life miserable for Shawnee and Delaware tribespeople there—and, despite being greatly outnumbered, the Indians there recipro-

OHIO'S PRAIRIES

Today's visitor can only imagine how the first settlers saw the Northwest Territory, but diaries from that time indicate that much of it was dense forest. Pioneers, moving west through Pennsylvania and Virginia, believed the Midwest to be nothing but trees—and that forests stretched to the Pacific Ocean. Imagine their delight at stumbling upon sunny clearings, some of them vast and filled with grasses and flowers. A modern tourist probably thinks of Illinois and the West when prairie is mentioned, yet there are wonderful examples of prairie remaining in the Buckeye State. A little knowledge will enhance a prairie visit.

Prairies are a mix of perennial grasses and flowering plants. They first appeared in North America 25 million years ago in places where rain was not always frequent. Prairies eventually stretched for miles west of the Mississippi, but in the more rainy Midwest they were slow to develop. Nevertheless, when Europeans arrived in the 17th century, more than 300 small prairies, covering 1,500 square miles, flourished in Ohio. These prairie "islands" were surrounded by forest and many were plowed and planted. Today, some two dozen prairies are preserved. Prairie remnants can be found along railroad rights of way and around undisturbed sites such as cemeteries.

The most common prairie locations are between Dayton and Columbus, but there are examples from Toledo to Portsmouth and places in between. Buck Creek State Park near Springfield has a nice stretch of prairie. Other prairie-prone state parks include Adams Lake, Caesar Creek, and Sycamore. Vegetation includes big bluestem, a grass that can grow to a height of nine feet, plus Indian grass, purple or gray-headed coneflowers, prairie dock, and black-eyed susan. The most common tree on the prairie's edge is the bur oak. That's because the thick, deeply furrowed bark makes it tolerant to drought and fire. Prairie wildlife includes short-eared owls, meadow voles, monarch butterflies, garden spiders, red foxes, coyotes, ground squirrels, bobolinks, horned larks, and red-tailed hawks.

For more information on these rare wild meadows, ask for the free National Audubon Society pamphlet, "Ohio Prairies," at visitor centers.

cated by seeing to it that navigating the Ohio River was a dangerous proposition for whites.

The Revolutionary War

Just as the Indians were adjusting to the British, the Revolutionary War broke out. A three-year border truce ended in 1777 as Delaware and Shawnee moved south across the Ohio River to stage raids on Kentucky and Virginia settlers. Colonists in turn invaded what is now Ohio. Neither side during the conflict acquitted itself honorably; both killed innocent women and children and tortured prisoners, apparently with glee. Perhaps the largest and most shameful massacre took place in 1782 at Gnadenhutten, a peaceful Christian Delaware village west of present-day Uhrichsville. Pennsylvanian farmers, incensed at the slaying of several settlers, marched westward to punish this unarmed band of Delaware. They allowed 96 Gnadenhutten residents to spend a night praying and singing hymns before wiping out the village in its entirety. The incident sparked a cry for revenge even among the Indians who distrusted the Christian converts.

But with the end of the Revolution, in 1783, came the Indian realization that American settlement was inevitable at the very least in what was to become southern and eastern Ohio. Most natives moved west, into the headwater lands of the Miami and Maumee Rivers. Though the Shawnee in particular resisted the influx of settlers, the land was surveyed and divided up—big steps toward statehood. Many of these early white residents were of Scotch-Irish descent, energetic young immigrants who had arrived on the eastern seaboard too poor to acquire land there.

The Northwest Ordinance, proposed by Thomas Jefferson to the Continental Congress in 1784 and adopted in 1787—at about the same time as the Constitution—was to have a marked effect on the area. It defined borders and set land prices over a vast part of what is now the United States, as well as forbidding slavery in the newly organized Northwest Territory and setting requirements for statehood. At the time, the land was a patchwork of parcels dictated by various treaties, purchases, and grants. Near Lake Erie, for example, the Connecticut Western Reserve covered all or part of what would become a dozen northeastern counties. Set aside as payment for Revolutionary War military service, a portion of countryside to the west, known as the Firelands, awaited those Connecticut families whose homes had been burned by British soldiers. The rich land offered a new start.

The Northwest Territory

New settlements were starting up elsewhere. Land speculators calling themselves the Ohio Company founded Marietta at the confluence of the Ohio and Muskingum Rivers. The tiny village became the capital of the far-flung federal Northwest Territory (it was too thinly settled to qualify for statehood), encompassing much of what is now considered the U.S. midwest, including Ohio, Indiana, Illinois, Michigan, Wisconsin, and part of Minnesota. Marietta offered city lots and farmland, some protection from the Indians (who remained angry that their land was being taken), a stopover on the way down the Ohio River, and a place where potential settlers could learn about the company's 1.7 million acres of available land. Arthur St. Clair was the first territorial governor, and under him, Marietta prospered and became an attractive town.

Other settlements included Cincinnati, which was part of the Miami Purchase, plus Gallipolis and Steubenville. Cincinnati was sited where the Miami River emptied into the Ohio. Gallipolis was merely an Ohio River bank where a couple of deceitful speculators persuaded French colonists that life could be good. The French had found themselves between a rock and a sharp object—the guillotine—and were fleeing the French Revolution. Many French settlers who remained in Gallipolis ("city of the Gauls," or, more prosaically, Frenchtown) survived and even prospered. Steubenville was a northern Ohio River fortification from which settlers headed west into (and, with luck, over and through) the rugged Appalachian Mountains.

Such hardy pioneers continued to be harassed by natives. To neutralize the Indian threat, Governor St. Clair ordered a series of forts constructed in a line from Cincinnati northward. Simultaneously, troops and recruits were sent out to punish the Delaware, Shawnee, Wyandot, and other raiding parties—though these met with little success. President George Washington and Congress helped raise a force of 3,000 men,

and several battles took place near the line of territorial forts, which ran parallel to today's Indiana-Ohio state line almost as far as present-day Michigan. Near Fort Recovery (not far from modern Greenville), on snowswept November 4, 1791, some 630 troops and an uncounted number of camp followers under St. Clair were killed in the worst defeat ever inflicted by natives on American settlers.

President Washington sent an old comrade, "Mad" Anthony Wayne, to set things right. Wayne wasn't insane, just highly focused. He realized that the defeated troops had been poorly trained, and he drilled his own men ceaselessly to avoid a similar fate. The war hero then tracked a large party of Indian warriors, catching them near the Maumee River in August 1794. There, at the Battle of Fallen Timbers, natives learned they simply were no match for well-trained, better-armed American forces. In the Treaty of Greenville (named after the town it was signed in) Native American tribal leaders signed a treaty in which the United States agreed to pay each of twelve tribes between $500 and $1,000 a year to give up their claim to certain tribal lands, but were allowed to stay on the land as long as they remained peaceable. The Shawnee leader Tecumseh refused to sign the agreement, having little trust in the fledgling American government.

Statehood

The treaty had a definite effect on whites—they read it as an invitation to inhabit the area north of the Ohio River and west of Pennsylvania in large numbers. A legislature, created by property-owning voters, met in Cincinnati early in 1799. This first group of lawmakers was an assembly for the entire Northwest Territory and so made laws for a vast area. An Enabling Act to create the state of Ohio was signed by President Thomas Jefferson on April 30, 1802. At the time, there were about 50,000 residents of European descent in the area. Chillicothe was designated the first state capital, and the paperwork for statehood was drafted there.

Residents tended to live along the state's several rivers—in Franklinton (now Columbus) on the Olentangy, in Chillicothe on the Scioto, in Dayton on the Miami, or in Cleaveland (later Cleveland), where the Cuyahoga meets Lake Erie. The settlers were mostly farmers, residing together on town lots and working land outside their villages. They were also, though, lumberjacks, traders, blacksmiths, soldiers, chandlers, carpenters, storekeepers, trappers, tailors, printers, laborers, and apprentices in various occupations. Perhaps second- or even third-generation residents of North America, they were overwhelmingly of European descent and disproportionately male. Such people automatically became residents of the 17th state when it was admitted to the Union, on March 1, 1803.

(In 1953, in preparation for Ohio's sesquicentennial, researchers went looking for the original statehood documents. They found that, while Congress had approved Ohio's boundaries and constitution, it had never formally admitted the state to the union. In a ceremony in the original state capital of Chillicothe, the legislature voted for a petition backdating statehood to March 1, 1803. The petition was delivered to Washington, D.C., on horseback. Dwight Eisenhower signed the document, making it the only example of retroactive law on the federal books. Since then, anti-income-tax wackos have seized upon this 200-year-old oversight to insist that the 16th Amendment—the taxing amendment—to the Constitution was approved by a nonstate and is therefore illegal.)

Ohio's state constitution satisfied Congress but contained sections that would resonate locally and nationally for the next 60 years. "There shall be neither slavery nor involuntary servitude in this state, otherwise than for the punishment of crimes," the document decreed. Antislavery sentiment was overwhelming, though the 100 or so free African-Americans within the borders of the new state had not been given the right to vote. That was reserved for white male taxpayers 21 or more years of age. The black residents missed the franchise by the vote of a single lawmaker. They also were denied several routine civil liberties.

Edward Tiffin was the leader of the territorial House of Representatives prior to statehood and became the state's first governor. There were a number of issues facing Ohio, not the least of which was the presence in 1805 of Aaron Burr in the state. Fresh from having killed Alexander Hamilton in a duel, Burr talked of invading Mexico but may have been planning to take control of and create a separate nation somewhere west of Ohio. He found local backing, but Tiffin, in cahoots with President Jefferson, confiscated Burr's boats and supplies. Burr later was captured in the South and tried for treason (he was acquitted).

The War of 1812
Many British agitators had remained just west of Ohio following statehood, and worked to keep the Indians riled and funnel them arms. There were other reasons for the War of 1812, but to Buckeye residents Indians with rifles was cause enough. Part-time Ohio resident William Henry Harrison (and future president of the United States) led troops in an invasion of what would become Michigan—an effort to capture Lake Erie sites and deny British ships access to those ports. A more successful campaign took place on the large lake in 1813. American sailors under Oliver Hazard Perry defeated a British fleet near South Bass Island on September 10. "We have met the enemy and they are ours," Perry told Washington.

The Economy Booms
The war ended early in 1815, and with peace came an avalanche of new settlers. Most were from New York and Pennsylvania, but others came from throughout the United States. The population jumped from about 250,000 residents in 1803 to one million by 1820. Portentously, the $7-million Erie Canal opened in 1825, connecting New York City and the Great Lakes by water and offering an avenue for people and goods between the East Coast and the frontier. No state benefited more from this ambitious waterway than Ohio, as the channel expedited commerce between the new state and the Atlantic coast. Also in 1825, the first steam locomotive began operating in the United States. The state and the nation were on the cusp of the Industrial Revolution.

Buckeye productivity and ingenuity came to the fore, industry by industry. In Cincinnati, the meatpacking business was wildly successful. Youngstown started producing iron ore, and the southeastern portion of the state unearthed tons of coal. Salt was flushed out of the ground with hot water near Akron and became a cash commodity. The main highways of commerce in the early 19th century were in fact not roadways but rather the Ohio and its tributaries. And follow-

OHIO PRESIDENTS

In 1840, William Henry Harrison, a Whig, was elected the ninth President of the United States. Harrison had been born in Virginia, but he had lived in Ohio. Unfortunately, he died in office, of pneumonia, after only a few weeks in office. But he had set the stage for what would eventually total seven Ohioan presidents—and those seven were actually *born* in Ohio. The most impressive streak for this series was from 1869 through 1881, when all three consecutive chief executives—Ulysses S. Grant, Rutherford B. Hayes, and James A. Garfield (who also died the year he was elected)—were elected the 18th, 19th, and 20th Presidents of the United States.

From 1889 to 1893, Benjamin Harrison, a Civil War veteran, presided over the admission of six states to the union. Benjamin Harrison was the grandson of William Henry Harrison and was actually born on his grandfather's farm in North Bend, Ohio. William McKinley served in office from 1897 to 1901, when he was shot by an anarchist and died on September 14.

Large and affable, William Howard Taft was in office from 1909 to 1913. He was the only American ever to serve as both President and Chief Justice of the United States Supreme Court.

Warren Harding's administration was ridden with scandal, but it didn't last long. He took office in 1921 and died of natural causes on August 2, 1923, while returning from an Alaska fishing trip. Harding was the first President elected with the help of female voters.

---

ing the 1811 introduction of steam-powered ships, hundreds of tons of goods and thousands of people sailed at higher speeds.

Canals and Railroads

Ohioans saw the benefits the Erie Canal brought to upstate New York and began digging canals all over the Buckeye State. Legislation for creation of these waterways was passed in 1822, and the Cincinnati-to-Dayton canal served the most populous part of the state. These miles-long canals consisted of 40-foot-wide channels deep enough to accommodate boats to their waterline, with these channels flanked by broad shoulders four feet deep, so canal digging became a major occupation for several years—mostly for Irish laborers who lived in shanties along the routes. (Once the canals were complete, kids sometimes skated on them when they froze in the depths of winter, and families living alongside them sometimes caught malaria from mosquitoes that bred in the still waters.)

Canal prosperity was somewhat short-lived. The first few miles of the Baltimore and Ohio Rail Road were laid in 1830, and the Irish made the transition from shoveling canals to pick-axing road beds. By 1850, some 299 miles of rail were in use; by 1860, the total was 2,974 miles. Though freight was more of a consideration than passenger service, a Buckeye could ride from Cleveland to Columbus in five hours for $4. A web of important public and private roads—such as Zane's Trace, in the southeast, and the National Pike (also known as the National Road) in the east—were heavily used.

The Irish were not the only immigrants who found success through hard work as manual laborers in Ohio. Arrivals from many German states disembarked at East Coast ports and found their way west. Among these were members of the so-called German peace churches—Amish, Dunkards, Brethren, and others. Some, such as the Lutherans, espoused a strong belief in higher education and started colleges. So did numerous Scotch Presbyterians, English Baptists, Congregationalists, Methodists, and others. Oberlin introduced coed education in 1833 and began admitting students regardless of race in 1835. Roman Catholics, mostly German or Irish, also came to Ohio, and adapted to rural and urban areas. Utopians saw in the new land a chance to plant the seeds of a perfect society. Shakers were the most well known among them, though their demise as a sect was virtually assured because men and women slept in separate quarters.

The Civil War

Prior to and during the Civil War, Ohio's many prominent abolitionists strongly supported President Abraham Lincoln. More Buckeyes per capita served in the Union Army, and three different generals—Ulysses S. Grant, William Tecumseh Sherman, and non-native resident Philip Sheridan

—led the blue-clad troops to eventual victory. On the home front, Confederate Colonel John Hunt Morgan headed a band of raiders that invaded and rode all across southern Ohio until forced to surrender at West Point, south of Youngstown, in 1863. No other southern force ever moved so far into enemy territory. Several Ohio sites served as prisons for Confederate soldiers, including Columbus and Johnson's Islands in Lake Erie.

Ohio residents constituted a sizable percentage of the 2.2 million men who died in the conflict. (Not generally known is that approximately 200,000 African-Americans served. More than

OHIO'S CANALS

The speed of a canal boat was nothing to write home about, yet working on packets, as the boats were called, was grueling nonetheless. The position of canal driver—the person who supervised the pulling horses or mules—was the least desirable job on the narrow water routes. A driver's toughest task was the recovery of an animal that had fallen into the canal, something which occurred with regularity. Because the loss of a mule or a team was so expensive, escape holes were provided every so often that prevented the animals from drowning. The hole included a ramp that let the driver lead the animal back to the bank and to work once again.

Drivers walked behind the mules for six hours, rested six hours, walked six more hours, rested, and so on. Fresh drivers were awakened an hour before their walk began so that they could harness, water, and feed the fresh team stabled aboard the boat. Changing teams took about 15 minutes in the spring and summer, which were the canal seasons. Canal employees hurried home in November before the four-foot deep ditches froze over for the winter. Those who were stranded found a rooming house for themselves and a stable for the animals, and they awaited the spring thaw.

One of the most overlooked facets of canal life was the quality of the water. Since it flowed either slowly or not at all, canal water became thick with disease-bearing organisms. As a boy, President James A. Garfield worked one summer on a canal boat. He was promoted from driver to bowman before he developed malaria and was sent home. The canals also were places where everyone threw trash. Boats often hit objects in the water that resulted in costly repairs and lost time. Other damage to the boats, which were as much as 78 feet long and up to 14 feet wide, included hitting a "low bridge." Having just deposited freight made a boat ride higher in the water, with less room to pass safely beneath a bridge. Cabins were sometimes torn off boats, or bridges were ruined.

Canal travel would have been maddening to contemporary Americans. Though the price of a ride was right at a couple of cents a mile, the 1.5 mile-an-hour speed would have driven today's harried traveler to faster forms of transport.

Life on the canals is re-enacted in a park south of Toledo. Before railroads crisscrossed Ohio, mule-drawn barges were the lifeblood of Ohio's canals.

38,000 were killed; 22 earned Congressional Medals of Honor.) As the numerous Union graves all across the state attest, all of Ohio was heavily involved.

Postwar Prosperity

The period from 1865 to 1900 saw industry grow exponentially. The energy industry took advantage of the discovery of oil and gas in northwest Ohio, and a clerk named John D. Rockefeller began an investment in Cleveland that would make his name synonymous with oil wealth. Established East Coast industries were drawn to Ohio by the promise of free gas for new plants. Dr. B.F. Goodrich started a small rubber factory in Akron that was to mushroom into the tire industry within a few years. Other ventures ranged from the use of clay for dishes to glassmaking technology in Toledo.

Industrial Ohio

Business and industry were changing the look of Ohio's big cities, but there were changes to the rural landscape, too. Besides the railroads, Ohio's countryside was the site of "interurbans"—electrically powered cars that ran on rails usually laid beside a road from city to city. Ohio was the center of interurban traffic until the Great Depression. Prior to the advent of the automobile, roads were mostly unpaved and, at the spring thaw, became channels of mud. The first concrete highway was created in Bellefontaine in 1891, due in part to the demands of bicycle riders. That same year, F.W. Lambert chugged around Ohio City in a noisy, three-wheeled horseless carriage of his own design and manufacture—several years before Henry Ford presented his first automobile.

In their Dayton bicycle shop, the Wright brothers were hard at work. In 1903, the brothers flew the world's first working airplane (though they had to go to North Carolina to find the most favorable conditions). In Oberlin at about the same time, Charles Hall, who would eventually become an officer in the Aluminum Company of America (ALCOA), devised a system for reducing aluminum ore. Charles Kettering, born in Loudonville and working in Dayton, along with partner Edward Deeds, invented items ranging from the electric starter motor for cars to the iron lung, eventually forming the Dayton Engineering Laboratories, or

Delco. The Packard brothers of Warren joined others in building a successful automobile, while Springfield's Benjamin Lamme made great strides in the uses of electric power. Ohio's foremost inventor, Thomas Alva Edison, devised light bulbs, motion pictures, and much more, though much of his work took place in New Jersey.

Work was hard at the time, and many laborers attempted to form unions. The big rubber plants in Akron were able to fend off initial attempts to organize its workers, while National Cash Register Company in Dayton beat back an effort to unionize by offering workers the first modern personnel department. Miners were subject to especially dangerous and low-paid conditions, and one of America's most powerful unions, the United Mine Workers (UMW), formed in Columbus in 1890. Despite some successes, union organizers found that the average Ohioan had little interest in unionization.

Ohio was the birthplace of both the National and American Baseball Leagues, as well as the first professional football league. Baseball's Cincinnati Red Stockings started in 1869, and the National League was created in 1886. In 1892, a manager of the Reds began the Western Association, which became the American League. College football's popularity led to the formation in 1920 of the American Professional Football Association in Canton. Besides Canton, early teams hailed from Akron, Columbus, Dayton, Massillon, and Toledo. Perhaps the most famous of the early players was the legendary Jim Thorpe, who had been recruited out of Pennsylvania.

Ethnic Ohio

Cleveland, Toledo, and Youngstown welcomed immigrants from eastern and central Europe. In greater Cleveland, 40 languages were spoken, while parts of Cincinnati spoke almost nothing but German; Columbus and Akron were overwhelmingly English. Churches and coffeehouses proliferated in metropolitan areas along Lake Erie, where news of many homelands was traded and fresh citizens tried to grasp the reform politics sweeping Ohio at the time. Cleveland also was the site of a small but vital middle-class black neighborhood known at the time as Mount Pleasant. African-American males had voted (quietly) in Ohio since 1870.

As reformers were cleaning up local and state governments, the city of Dayton was recovering from the devasting flood of 1913. The Miami River had surged through the town in the wake of heavy rains, rising as high as 20 feet above flood stage. The solution was to hire a renaissance engineer named Arthur Morgan. Morgan designed a series of earthen dams that, when combined with better levees, made Dayton a safer place. Such regional work would become more common as problems arose. As for Morgan, he was later named president of progressive work-study Antioch College in Yellow Springs.

Progressive action was great; socialism was something else. Russia's czarist royal government fell to Communism in 1917, and many Ohioans stereotyped foreigners and trade union organizers as "bolsheviks." Unions increased in power during World War I, but so did the anti-black, anti-Catholic, anti-Jewish Ku Klux Klan a bit later. A brief but intense depression in 1919-1920 saw union and nonunion members alike set adrift. Many tire company employees returned to their southeastern Ohio or West Virginia homes to cultivate parcels of marginal land. Other firms fought the unions by decentralizing — building plants in states where unions were less entrenched.

Ohio's cities had developed personalities of their own by the 1920s. Columbus and Cincinnati were economically diverse, less likely to benefit from boom times but also less likely to collapse during a depression. Since people always have to eat, food processing plants in both cities usually kept things humming. Columbus, with its growing Ohio State University and state government, was especially free of economic woes. Cleveland was the most progressive of the three largest cities, with organized programs to fight illiteracy and poverty. Many people of various nationalities lived in safe, clean, municipal public housing—constructed as much to address a booming population as to make up for low wages. Like their larger counterparts, Akron, Dayton, and Toledo experienced building booms during the decade after World War I.

With passage of the Eighteenth Amendment ordering Prohibition, in 1917, and the subsequent passage of the Volsted Act, in 1919, enforcing it, came organized crime. Looking one direction in a big Ohio town afforded a visitor a glance at a new, high-rise monument or office building. Looking the opposite direction might show gambling, prostitution, speakeasies, and police officers openly on the take. Even the smaller industrial cities, such as Steubenville, could be frightening places. The return of legal alcohol, combined with an unemployment rate that included more than one-third of the work force, caused organized crime to find other illegal activities. Not even "Untouchable" Eliot Ness, the federal agent who successfully battled crime in Chicago, was able to straighten out Cleveland during the 1930s.

Depression, WWII, and the 1950s

When excessive speculation, overproduction of goods, and a lack of regulation brought about the Depression in 1929, the largest of President Franklin D. Roosevelt's public-works projects to put people back to work was the Muskingum Conservancy District. The district was set up to establish permanent reservoirs that helped tame the Muskingum River. These reservoirs make east-central Ohio today a lake-bedecked region enjoyed by boaters and fishers.

The $43 million reservoir project ended just about the time America began to rearm for World War II. At that point, northeast Ohio became "America's Ruhr Valley," crafting every conceivable kind of mechanism for the conflict that seemed inevitable. Aircraft parts, ships, and weapons poured out of the Buckeye State. Women, African-Americans, and Appalachian whites staffed the big industries—and these factions became easy recruits for rejuvenated labor unions. Members of peace churches declined military service but accepted alternative duty, putting in long hours on farms and in hospitals. There was work for everyone, from the thousands of schoolchildren who collected scrap to the elderly, who kept retail shops open.

The prosperity of the war years continued through the postwar recovery period. Ohio was second only to Michigan in the value of its exports as American goods poured out of the Western Hemisphere to a world recovering from war. Republicans rode into many offices with the election of President Dwight D. Eisenhower in 1952 (and stayed in command for two terms), Ohio State University and the Cleveland Browns were consistent winners and sources of state pride in

FAMOUS BUCKEYES

The following notable people were born within the current boundaries of Ohio and does not take into account persons who were not born in the state though lived much of their lives in Ohio, such as John D. Rockefeller or author Harriet Beecher Stowe.

Chief Joseph Brant

Sherwood Anderson, writer, 1876-1941, Camden
Neil Armstrong, astronaut, 1930-, Wapakoneta
Anita Baker, singer, 1958-, Toledo
Kaye Ballard, singer, 1926-, Cleveland
Theda Bara, actor, 1885-1955, Cincinnati
Thomas Berger, author, 1924-, Cincinnati
Halle Berry, actor, 1969-, Cleveland
Ambrose Bierce, author, 1842-1914, Meigs County
Erma Bombeck, newspaper columnist, 1927-1996, Dayton
Joseph Brant, Mohawk leader, 1742-1807, site unknown
Teresa Brewer, singer, 1931-, Toledo
Louis Bromfield, author, 1896-1956, Mansfield
Drew Carey, comedian, 1961-, Cleveland
Tracy Chapman, singer, 1964-, Cleveland
Tim Conway, comedian, 1933-, Willoughby
Hart Crane, poet, 1899-1932, Garrettsville
George A. Custer, soldier, 1839-1876, New Rumley
Beverly D'Angelo, actor, 1954-, Columbus
Clarence Darrow, attorney, 1857-1938, Kinsman
Doris Day, singer-actor, 1924-, Cincinnati
Ruby Dee, actor, 1923-, Cleveland
Phyllis Diller, comedian, 1917-, Lima
Phil Donahue, talk-show host, 1935-, Cleveland
Rita Dove, writer, 1952-, Akron

continues on next page

FAMOUS BUCKEYES
continued

Hugh Downs, TV personality, 1921-, Akron
Paul Laurance Dunbar, author, 1872-1906, Dayton
Thomas A. Edison, inventor, 1847-1931, Milan
Jamie Farr, actor, 1934-, Toledo
James Garfield, 20th President, 1831-1881, Orange
Terri Garr, actor, 1945-, Lakewood
John Glenn, astronaut and U.S. senator, 1921-, Cambridge
U.S. Grant, 18th President, 1822-1885, Point Pleasant
Bob Greene, newspaper columnist, 1947-, Columbus
Joel Grey, actor, 1932-, Cleveland
Zane Grey, novelist, 1872-1939, Zanesville
Arsenio Hall, comedian, 1955-, Cleveland
Warren G. Harding, 29th President, 1865-1923, Corsica
Benjamin Harrison, 23rd President, 1833-1901, North Bend
Rutherford B. Hayes, 19th President, 1822-1893, Delaware
Robert Henri, artist, 1865-1929, Cincinnati
Hal Holbrook, actor, 1925-, Cleveland
William Dean Howells, novelist, 1837-1920, Martins Ferry
Ross Hunter, author, 1921-, Cleveland
Chrissie Hynde, singer, 1951-, Akron
James Ingram, singer, 1956-, Akron
Gordon Jump, actor, 1932-, Dayton
Carol Kane, actor, 1952-, Cleveland
Charles F. Kettering, inventor, 1876-1958, Loudonville
Perry King, actor, 1948-, Alliance
James Levine, actor, 1943-, Cincinnati
Henry Mancini, composer, 1924-1994, Cleveland
Dean Martin, singer, 1917-1996, Steubenville
Maureen McGovern, singer, 1949-, Youngstown
William McKinley, 25th President, 1843-1901, Niles
Marion Mercer, actor, 1935-, Akron
Burgess Meredith, actor, 1909-1997, Cleveland
Howard Metzenbaum, U.S. senator, 1917-, Cleveland
Toni Morrison, author, 1931-, Lorain
Paul Newman, actor, 1925-, Cleveland
Annie Oakley, sharpshooter, 1860-1926, Patterson
Barney Oldfield, race car driver, 1878-1946, Wauseon
Ed O'Neill, actor, 1946-, Youngstown
Jesse Owens, Olympic athlete, 1913-1980, Cleveland
Jack Paar, talk-show host, 1918-, Canton
Sarah Jessica Parker, actor, 1965-, Nelsonville
Johnny Paycheck, singer, 1941-, Greenville
Luke Perry, actor, 1967-, Fredericktown
Tom Poston, comedian, 1927-, Columbus
Eddie Rickenbacker, aviator, 1890-1973, Columbus
Roy Rogers, actor, 1912-1998, Cincinnati
Pete Rose, baseball player, 1941-, Cincinnati
Arthur Schlesinger, Jr., historian, 1917-, Columbus
Martin Sheen, actor, 1940-, Dayton
William Tecumseh Sherman, soldier, 1820-1891, Lancaster

Steven Spielberg, movie magnate, 1947-, Cincinnati
George Steinbrenner, industrialist, 1930-, Rocky River
Gloria Steinem, author, 1934-, Toledo
William H. Taft, 27th President, 1857-1930, Cincinnati
Art Tatum, pianist, 1910-1956, Toledo
Tecumseh, Shawnee chief, 1768-1813, near Columbus
Tenskwatawa (the Prophet), Shawnee religious leader, ?-1834, site unknown
Lowell Thomas, newscaster, 1892-1981, Woodington
Philip Michael Thomas, actor, 1949-, Columbus
James Thurber, writer, 1894-1961, Columbus
Ted Turner, media magnate, 1938-, Cincinnati
Nancy Wilson, singer, 1937-, Chillicothe
Debra Winger, actor, 1955-, Cleveland
Jonathan Winters, comedian, 1925-, Dayton
Orville Wright, aviator, 1871-1948, Dayton
Cy Young, baseball player, 1867-1955, Gilmore

football, and a new state motto, conceived by a Cincinnati schoolchild, summed up the irony-free, hard-working decade: "With God, all things are possible."

Come the 1960s—and Kent State
In the 1960s, the number of state universities in Ohio doubled, from six to 12. Putatively integrated public schools were desegregated in fact—sometimes under federal supervision. Nonviolence gave way to street troubles between black residents and authorities in Dayton and Cincinnati. Rioting and loss of life took place in the Hough section of eastern Cleveland. In 1967, Cleveland's Carl B. Stokes became the first black person to be elected mayor of a major American city. White Ohio residents seemed polarized: either part of the anti-Vietnam War movement or staunch backers of segregationist Alabama governor George C. Wallace. Meanwhile, the environment suffered as coal was torn out of hills that then eroded, streams became so polluted that the fish died, and the waterways began to stink.

But Ohio became most famous in the spring of 1970 as the site of one of the quintessential episodes of the Vietnam War era. President Richard M. Nixon had ordered American troops in Vietnam to invade Cambodia in search of a suspected Communist stronghold. In reaction, college campuses all over the country erupted in protest. On May 4 at Kent State University, outside of Akron, National Guard troops were called out to maintain order in the face of a protest on the campus. A crowd of antiwar activists jeered, swore,

and threw rocks at the troops until, without warning, the guardsmen fired live ammunition into the unarmed crowd, killing four students and wounding nine others. With that, this usually apathetic state school would forever symbolize the divisiveness and futility of the Vietnam War. A modest monument, the May Fourth Site and Memorial, was finally placed at the site in 1986.

If Kent State was a symbol of what was wrong with American foreign policy, Lake Erie epitomized the country's woeful treatment of the environment. Relatively shallow and turbulent, the lake has a long history of having been clouded by sand, but only recently—within the last 100 years—had it become a cesspool. The state joined federal officials in setting aside money and energy to clean the big lake, various rivers, and the air. Mining companies were forced to post bonds that would assure renewal or refurbishment of strip-mined property. Among many benefits was the creation in 1974 of the state's first national park—the Cuyahoga Valley National Recreation Area, comprising some 32,000 acres of still-pristine land between Cleveland and Akron.

The Rust Belt
Between 1970 and 1980 the people of Ohio faced among the most difficult periods they had ever witnessed. Agriculture and manufacturing appeared fit as ever as the 1970s began. But the number of farms and farmers declined steadily during the decade as more counties became urbanized and crop prices failed to keep up with

STATE EMBLEMS

The Great Seal of the State of Ohio was conceived at the dawn of statehood in 1803. "Father of Ohio Statehood" Thomas Worthington and other pols were meeting in the Worthington home near Chillicothe when the founders witnessed the sun rise over Mount Logan to the east. Sun and mountain now grace the seal. Also included are the Scioto River and cultivated fields.

There are several other official Ohio items. They include:

- The State Flower: The red carnation was adopted as the state flower by the Ohio legislature in 1904. William McKinley, a Buckeye who was assassinated in 1901 while serving the country as President, always wore a red carnation in his buttonhole. Consequently, the flower is in memory of the Niles native and 25th President.

- The State Bird: Like several other states, the official bird is the cardinal. Cardinals are permanent Ohio residents and the brilliant red males are easily seen year round in backyards and woodlands.

- The State Stone: Flint has been the state gemstone since 1965. It is found in a variety of colors in several parts of the state, but especially on Flint Ridge, between Newark and Zanesville. Native Americans used the hard rock of sedimentary origin for knives, spearpoints, and arrowheads, while settlers of European origin employed it for flintlock guns and millstones. It is a type of quartz, and when cut and polished, it is considered semiprecious.

- The State Flag: Conceived in the 1880s by a Cleveland resident, this is the only pennant-shaped state banner. It bears 17 stars, indicating that Ohio was the 17th state admitted to the Union; the blue triangle represents hills and valleys, while the three red and two white stripes stand for roadways and waterways. A white circle around a red center represent the "O" in Ohio and the buckeye nut.

- The State Motto: In 1865, legislators added a Latin motto, *Imperium in Imperio* (an empire within an empire), to the Great Seal. Residents disliked the foreign language and, for many years, Ohio was the only state without a motto. Then, in 1958, a Cincinnati sixth-grader petitioned Columbus and his motto, taken from the Bible, Matthew 19:26, was adopted. It reads, "With God, all things are possible."

- The State Song: "Beautiful Ohio" was adopted as the state song in 1969. Written in 1918 by Ballard McDonald and Mary Earl, the song is in fact about the river, not the state. It tells of drifting with the current in a little red canoe, among other imagery.

- The State Tree: You know it's the buckeye, but did you know that it is one of three types of buckeye found in the state? Or that "buckeye" once was a pejorative term for a rural Ohioan? The buckeye leaf is made up of five almond-shaped leaflets and has greenish-yellow flowers. The tree became official in 1953.

- The State Beverage: You may not suspect that the state drink of choice is tomato juice. However, Ohio leads the country in its production and is second only to California in tomato growing. This piece of liquid legislation became law in 1965.

- The State Fossil: Crafty but especially slow moving these days, the *Isotelus* trilobite has been the state fossil since 1985. Residents of inland seas some 500 million years ago, trilobites could reach two feet in length but more commonly were two to three inches long. Their skeletal remains are most often found in the limestone and shale of southwestern Ohio.

- The State Insect: The common ladybug, officially the Ladybird beetle, is the state insect. It has been since 1975, despite tongue-in-cheek votes for the housefly and the mosquito.

- The State Wildflower: The large-flowered or white trillium was designated the state flower in 1987. It's a member of the lily family and more formally is known as the *Trillium grandiflorum*. With age, the petals turn a soft pink and a tiny red berry develops on the plant. Look for it in Cedar Bog, near Urbana, among other places.

- The State Animal: The white-tailed deer is the state animal. Obviously, this 1988 decision was influenced in part because the male of the species is the buck and therefore connects with another symbol, the buckeye.

Taking all this to its logical extreme, Ohio also has a State Rock Song. "Hang on Sloopy," a tune by the McCoys from the 1960s, was made official in legislation passed in 1985. The McCoys hailed from the Dayton area.

the rising costs of raising crops and feeding animals. Only the Amish, who work the land in ways that have not changed for centuries, were able to maintain their independence—though even some of them sold out and migrated to Central America.

The situation for manufacturing was even grimmer. In what seemed like a very short time, Ohio mills and factories became obsolete. They were old and inefficient, and they employed too many people. Further, the companies weren't flexible enough to change to meet the changing demands of the marketplace and the manufacturing environment. Fuel costs increased, materials costs increased, labor was insistent, and foreign competition was producing material more quickly and cheaply that was higher in quality. Having lived in something of an ideal world since the end of WWII, Ohio and other so-called Rust Belt states—states dependent upon long-established manufacturing that had become old or obsolete—were paying the price.

Layoffs hit many cities. Even worse, some manufacturers that were the foundations of their municipalities simply closed—victims of lack of demand, too much competition, or the cost-conscious decision to move operations out of the Midwest.

Happily, by the late 1990s, Buckeye business and industry are back—leaner and smaller, but unmistakably back. The state occupies a favorable location and continues to offer a talented workforce, coal and other resources are available at competitive prices, and manufacturers are making good use of low-inventory, state-of-the-art methods that increase profitability of performance. Farms are fewer but more economically viable, the population is stable, and the hospitality industry is growing. Buckeyes appear ready to greet the new century.

Ohio Today

Approximately 11.17 million people reside in Ohio. Of these, 87.8% are white, 10.6% black, and 1.3% Hispanic. The whites represent a rich stew of eastern, western, and central European heritage, mixed with everyone from persons with Appalachian roots to nth-generation Buckeyes whose family trees are rooted in the Founding Fathers. A number of African-Americans date from the Underground Railroad days of the 1850s, when courageous locals guided runaway slaves to safe havens. The small Hispanic contingent comprises Dominican Republic, Mexican, Puerto Rican, and other heritages.

Slightly more than one Buckeye in five is employed in manufacturing. Service jobs account for more than 26% of the workforce, while trades total 18.7% and government 14.7%. Per capita income is $22,021. There are 264.9 Ohio residents for every square mile of land—about the same density as Florida or neighboring Pennsylvania. That makes the state the seventh most populous in the United States. The population has recently *increased,* reversing the outmigration trend of the late 1970s. The state is 34th in physical size among the 50 states. Ranking 15th among the states in agricultural production, Ohio is losing 70 acres a day to development of various kinds. There is no mainland state smaller than Ohio to the west except Indiana.

Statistics are swell, but they don't provide a living picture of the state. Within a well-defined area west of the Allegheny Mountains, in the eastern Midwest, south of the Great Lakes, and north of the sinuous Ohio River is a land steeped in history and peopled by a variety of resilient Americans The more of it the visitor sees, the more he or she is apt to like.

ON THE ROAD

SIGHTSEEING HIGHLIGHTS

Columbus, Ohio's centrally located capital, is a good place to begin a tour of the state. The big town has an inspiring skyline, which is best viewed from the west bank of the Scioto River (afloat on the river is a replica of Christopher Columbus's *Santa Maria,* permanently moored downtown). Just south of the downtown area lies historic German Village, dense with lovingly restored 19th-century homes. Another important neighborhood, replete with art galleries, is the Short North district, a short walk north (naturally) from the city's big buildings. High Street runs north-south past the vast Ohio State University campus and is home to a wide range of food, drink, and entertainment venues. The Columbus Zoo lies directly north, while a couple of miles northeast are the Ohio State Fairgrounds and the Ohio Historical Center.

Also in the central part of the state—in and near Newark—are the Mound Builders and Octagon Mound State Memorials. Historic US 40, the old National Road (from West Virginia to Indiana), runs through the state capital and is an antiquer's treasure trove.

The **northeastern quarter** of Ohio is the state's most populous region, with three of its seven largest cities: Cleveland, Akron, and Youngstown. But it's also a region of considerable diversity—while Cleveland's University Circle area is thick with outstanding museums, the drive through the Cuyahoga Valley National Recreation Area links Cleveland and Akron in bucolic, rural splendor. Halls of fame are big deals here and include Cleveland's stunning Rock and Roll Hall of Fame and Museum, Akron's clever Inventure Place, and Canton's wildly popular Pro Football Hall of Fame. Southeast of Cleveland, Geauga County is home to Sea World of Ohio and nearby Geauga Lake amusement park. This is also historic country, from villages settled more than two centuries ago by Connecticut veterans of the Revolutionary War to a stretch of sand once part of an important Lake Erie Indian pathway. Of the state's self-sufficient Amish settlements, particularly worth visiting is the area south of Wooster in Holmes County.

Northwestern Ohio, occupying the Lake Erie shoreline, holds attractions such as the Lake Erie Islands, the Cedar Point amusement park in Sandusky, and the busy port of Toledo, the area's largest city. Toledo's municipal parks,

FRANK LLOYD WRIGHT IN OHIO

He didn't spend much time in Ohio, he's been dead approximately 40 years, and his most famous buildings are elsewhere. Yet Frank Lloyd Wright created stunning architecture, most of it residential, that still stands in several Buckeye cities and towns. Among them, with addresses and completion dates:

- Canton: The Dobkins Home, 5120 Plain Center Road, 1955; the Feiman Home, 452 Santa Clara Drive, NW, 1955; the Rubin Home, 518 44th St., NW, 1953.
- Cincinnati: The Boulter Home, 1 Rawson Woods Circle, 1956; the Boswell Home, 8805 Camargo Club Drive, 1958-59; the Tonkins Home, 6980 Knoll Rd., 1955 (?).
- Dayton: The Meyer Clinic, 5441 Far Hills Ave., 1958-59.
- Madison (Lake County): The Staley Home, Lake Road, 1955.
- Oberlin: The Weltzheimer Home, 127 Woodhaven Drive, 1950.
- Springfield: The Wescott Home, 1340 E. High St., 1907.
- Willoughby: The Penfield Home, 2203 River Road, 1955.

The sites generally are in older residential neighborhoods that usually provide a nice contrast to Wright's unique creations. See the respective city or town listing in this book for details on location, hours, admission, etc. If there is no individual listing, assume the home is in private hands and can only be gazed upon wistfully from the street. Happily, a wonderful example of a Wright Prairie Home is open for tours in Oberlin.

A Prairie Home is characterized by a single story, overhanging eaves, built-in accessories, a massive central fireplace, windows and porches that blur the distinction between indoors and outdoors, and a flat roof. Halls are narrow and ceilings low. "It has been said that were I three inches taller (I am five feet eight and a half inches tall), all my houses would have been quite different in proportion. Perhaps," the architect has been quoted as saying. See the Oberlin section for details on paying this fascinating residence a visit.

Frank Lloyd Wright (1867-1959)

zoo, and museum of art all are worth visiting—as are faithfully replicated canal boats south of town, on which visitors may cruise. Down the interstate to the south lie Findlay, with its picturesque Main Street, and Wapakoneta's Neil Armstrong Space Museum. Ohio Caverns and Zane Caverns, plus the highest elevation in the state, are found around Bellefontaine. Heading north, not far from touristy Sandusky, is venerable little Milan, birthplace and boyhood home of Thomas A. Edison.

Northwestern Ohio is undeniably flat, but **Southwestern Ohio** offers gentle pitches and rolls. Tucked amid the hillocks are mighty Cincinnati on the Ohio River, Dayton on the Miami River, Springfield, and more. Cincy is known for its restaurants, major-league athletics in Riverfront Stadium, Museum Center, and the Cincinnati Zoo. Kings Island amusement park is in a suburb, while antique-rich little Waynesville and historic Lebanon are nearby to the north. Northwest of Cincinnati is Oxford, an impossibly pretty college town. And Dayton, also north, is home to the United States Air Force Museum (with an Imax theater). Some 80 miles southeast of Dayton is old Chillicothe, site of the state's first capital, and southwest of Chillicothe is Serpent Mound State Memorial, a most ambitious pre-Columbian Indian site.

Southeastern Ohio is thinly populated, and that can be pleasant. Hocking Hills State Park, near Logan, is one of a number of great parks hereabouts with rock formations, sighing pines, and shady valleys thick with native plants.

Athens, between Columbus and Marietta, is another Ohio college town with brick streets and movie-ready settings. Marietta, situated where the Muskingum River meets the Ohio River, offers the Ohio River Museum and regular stops by paddlewheel riverboats. Up the Muskingum, amid rugged hills near Zanesville and Cambridge, are vendors of colorful and historic glass and pottery, crafted here in the 19th and early 20th centuries. Much of the southeastern sector is occupied by Wayne National Forest, where stands of pines and hardwoods provide a safe, lightly frequented haven for wildlife.

No state has a greater variety of such reserves and preserves than Ohio, with its 72 state parks. Included are forests, beaches, lakes, canals, rivers, meadows, hills, and valleys—and, amid it all, accommodations ranging from rustic to sumptuous. Among the more popular **park destinations** are Headlands Beach east of Cleveland, Maumee Bay near Toledo, Hueston Woods north of Oxford, and Burr Oak near Athens. The parks offer literally something for everyone, with half a dozen golf courses, hiking, horseback, and cross-country ski trails, picnicking, power boating, and canoeing, even lots of fishing and approved hunting. For those who want to understand flora, fauna, and geology, naturalists conduct many summer programs. And parks such as Malabar Farm near Mansfield, in the central northeast, recall the state's rich rural traditions during Ohio Heritage Days (only one of many such special events on the state's 207,000 acres of public park land).

RECREATION

Other, larger states—Idaho, Oregon, Utah—all are lighter on people and heavier on natural wonders than the Buckeye State, yet prudent management has kept parts of Ohio pristine. Virginal tracts remain near even the most populous spots—such as along the Lake Erie shore. Elsewhere, the many covered bridges (there were 130 statewide at last count) accenting rural scenes in Ashtabula County are blessedly free of grafitti. Activities such as off-road bicycling are clearly delineated in many parks all around the state. The *quantity* of outdoor lands may not compare to that in some states, but the *quality* is here—and the territory is extremely accessible.

The most heavily visited recreation area is the Lake Erie shoreline, especially busy in the summer. Dozens of natural and manmade attractions—amusement parks, big cities, sunny beaches, wildlife areas, and more—cluster at the shore. South a bit, in Amish country, the tourist season is longer and just keeps growing. Visitors seem endlessly fascinated by the "plain people," resulting in a parade of everything from motorcycles to motor homes traipsing back and forth past picturesque, manually operated farms. Southeast Ohio offers not only river vistas but the craggy Hocking Hills, a hiker's nirvana. The southwest mimics Lake Erie in its affinity for big cities and amusement parks. Northwestern Ohio, flat of terrain and rich of soil, has an area—near Bellefontaine—where geology has created some nice hills. And pent-up water in the Muskingum Conservancy District of eastern Ohio means that there are numerous sites for fishing, swimming, boating, sailing, and canoeing.

Spectator Sports

Cincinnati and Cleveland both field **major-league** professional sports teams. The River City, Cincinnati, is home to baseball's National League **Reds** and football's NFL **Bengals.** The Lake City, Cleveland, boasts baseball's American League **Indians,** the National Basketball Association's **Cavaliers,** and the NFL **Browns** (which moved into their new lakefront home stadium in 1999).

Cleveland also fields an International League hockey team, the **Lumberjacks** (who skate in Gund Arena) and professional soccer's **Cleve-**land Crunch. Columbus also boasts a pro hockey team—the **Chill**—which calls Ohio State Fairgrounds Coliseum home ice. And Richland is home to the pro soccer **Force,** which plays indoors.

Ohio sites turn up on many professional tours, from cycling to bowling. The **Youngstown-Warren Ladies Professional Golf Association** (LPGA) classic, for example, takes place in July, while the Firestone course in Akron hosts the **World Series of Golf** for men in the latter part of August. The **Professional Golf Association** (PGA) also hosts a match in Dublin in early June, and Toledo and Dayton are home to summertime LPGA events.

Fans of **racing** can choose between horses ridden, horses driven, and motor vehicles ranging from Indy cars to dragsters. The most notable **horse tracks** are Cincinnati's River Downs and Randall's Thistledown Racing Club. Tracks at Beulah Park, in Grove City, Cleveland's Northfield Harness Track, Lebanon's Lebanon Raceway, and Columbus' Scioto Downs host harness and carriage races. A treat for **auto racing** buffs, Cleveland's Burke Lakefront Airport once a year turns into a road-racing course for Indy cars. Mid-Ohio Sports Car Course, near Mansfield, is a true asphalt road-racing course for Indy cars, sports cars, and motorcycles. And **drag racing** fires up regularly in Hebron, Sandusky, Valley View, and West Salem.

Vandalia is the site of a major **trapshooting** event, on the north side of US 40 near Cox Dayton International Airport. Markspersons shoot regularly in contests on Ohio's Lake Erie islands, as well.

In terms of grass-roots spectating, though, it's hard to beat **college football.** More than 50 of Ohio's colleges play on any given Saturday over the last three or four months of the year, and the level of play locally is incredible—many of the participants are top-quality players who are an inch too small or a step too slow to make it on the major university level. The spectating scene at these contests can range from crowds of nearly 90,000 at Ohio State University's Ohio Stadium in Columbus to dog-walkers and parents along the sidelines at a rural community college.

WHO OWNS "OHIO"?

The disagreement began back in 1995, when Ohio University in Athens secured trademark rights to the word "Ohio" for sports and entertainment events and athletic apparel. Because of the trademark, Ohio State University in Columbus was prevented from calling its football field Ohio Stadium. Ohio State is challenging the trademark in court.

This appears to be a lopsided contest. Ohio State University has many more students, alumni, and athletic fans than does Ohio University. The former boasts 48,000 students on its main campus, the latter 19,000. OSU makes $2 million annually off trademark licensing, whereas OU brings in only about $100,000.

The institution in Athens has a couple of things going for it, however. Ohio University was founded in 1804, which makes Ohio State University, founded in 1870, something of a college-come-lately. OU personnel intend to show old photos of people from their school wearing apparel that says simply "Ohio" at least two years before Ohio State University came into existence.

Neither public school seems willing to compromise in the matter. OU has tried to pacify OSU by giving narrow permission to use the word Ohio for the stadium, but with the mandatory word "State" following "Ohio" on all apparel. The folks in Columbus declined the deal. Of 330 OSU items in a licensing catalogue, only two violate OU's exclusivity rights—a doll and a shirt.

This would be much simpler if all of the big schools in the Big Ten, at the very least, were named after the respective state. That's the way it is in Indiana, Illinois, Iowa, and Michigan. But in Pennsylvania, for instance, the megaschool is Penn State; the University of Pennsylvania is a small private school. Adding to the confusion, Penn State is the eleventh school to join the Big Ten.

Ohio State University has petitioned the U.S. Patent Office to cancel Ohio University's exclusivity. OU contends that the lone word is mere shorthand for its more venerable institution, pointing out that universities in Michigan and Florida have patented their state names. The matter should be settled some time in 1999.

In between are crowds numbering in the thousands at state-supported schools and many hundreds at dozens of private four-year colleges. The fun and color can be contagious, no matter the opponent or the outcome.

Another highly enjoyable option is **minor-league baseball.** Spending a warm Ohio summer evening watching a team like the **Akron Aeros,** the **Toledo Mudhens,** or the **Columbus Clippers** practice their craft is the kind of experience that can make a vacation worthwhile all by itself.

National Parklands

Ohio is home to no national parks, but it does have the enjoyable **Cuyahoga Valley National Recreation Area,** between Akron and Cleveland. This incongruously rural, rustic, and peaceful 22-mile stretch along the Cuyahoga River can get crowded—particularly in the fall, when hardwoods in their many hues lure folks out of the cities. (Color-change leaf-peeping peaks first in the northeast and then diagonally across the street to finish in the southwest. The state tourism

hotline—800-BUCKEYE (or tel. 800-282-5393)—starts keeping track in mid-September, but you can expect the peak around mid-October.) Unlike national parks, admission to the Cuyahoga remains free of charge. Activities in this more-than-30,000-acre enclave include hiking, cross-country skiing, artistic exhibits and events, campfire programs, nature walks, scenic rail trips, and more. For more information, call (440) 526-5256.

Ohio's other federal area is **Wayne National Forest,** in the southeastern part of the state. Some 160,000 acres of this big forest's total area of 202,967 acres are open for public use. Park headquarters are sited in Ironton, though the forest really is divided into three units, at some distance from each other. Since the park is entirely undeveloped, activities are all do-it-yourself, from hiking, nature study, and camping to trail riding, picnicking, and enjoying the occasional historic site amid Appalachian Mountains foothills. Two units of the forest lie along the Ohio River, and the third lies north and east of Athens. There are neither formal hours of operation nor admission charges for using the trails on foot or for camping. ATVs are permitted on trails and roads only for $5 per person per day ($25 for a pass for the whole season, April 16-December 15). For more information, call (740) 532-3223.

The state is also home to an international monument and three national historic sites. Just off the Lake Erie shore, **Perry's Victory and International Peace Monument** towers above Put-in-Bay on resorty South Bass Island; **Hopewell Cultural National Park** lies near Chillicothe; the **birthplace of President William Howard Taft** is in Cincinnati; and **Lawnfield,** the home of President James A. Garfield, lies outside Mentor. Modest fees are charged for admission to the monument and each of the historic sites.

State Parks

Ohio boasts some 72 state parks—all free, well kept, and accessible. In 1997, the National Recreation and Parks Association and the National Sporting Goods Association recognized Ohio's parks as the best in the nation. There are many standouts in this park system. **Alum Creek,** north of Columbus, boasts 3,387 acres of water (5,213 acres total), has nice places to ride bikes off-road, and participates in the state Rent-A-Camp program. **Malabar Farm,** near Mansfield, is a unique facility—a utopian farm—with grains, flowers, and the rich scent of just-turned earth wafting through the many well-preserved buildings; it's also home to the only hostel between Columbus and Cleveland. Lightly visited **Nelson B. Kennedy Ledges State Park,** which comprises a mere 167 acres, nevertheless rewards visitors with a serenity amid the huge chunks of mossy rock and thick stands of trees. **Maumee Bay** (MAW-mee) on Lake Erie, is a counterpoint to Nelson, with many amenities. Lake island parks, too—**Catawba, Kelleys,** or **South Bass**—are also well worth visiting. Another watery wonder is **Muskingum River State Park,** which covers parts of three eastern counties in homage to the historic waterway, which feeds into the Ohio River and has boat ramps and campgrounds. In southwestern Ohio, steep and silent **John Bryan State Park,** with adjacent Clifton Gorge, near Yellow Springs, is a green, river-created sanctuary—light on visitors and merchandise.

The parks are far from micromanaged, too: the most closely observed regulations are fishing and hunting license requirements, boating horsepower limits, and restriction to electric motors on various bodies of water, thus preserving some semblance of silence, as well as limiting pollutants. Activities possible within the parks include swimming, fishing, hunting, hiking, sheltered picnicking, boating, golf, tennis, and more—and lodging and dining are also available in many.

The uniformity of signs and services at all the parks makes a visit to any of them easy, for strangers and locals alike, and facilities fully accommodate people with disabilities. Locals love their parks and tend to crowd in on weekends and holidays. Weekday visits are easier—parking or capacity hassles are virtually nonexistent. Check in first at local park headquarters whenever you visit; besides confirming local regulations, you can check schedules of interpretive programs or special events.

The most succinct rundown of what you can do in which park is in the state publication *Ohiopass* (available free by calling the Ohio Tourism Hotline at 800-282-5393). There's also a brochure covering all of the parks. They both have a two-page chart detailing what individual sites have to offer.

Lakes and Rivers

Some Buckeyes would have you think there is only one lake and one river in the state—Lake Erie to the north and the Ohio River to the south. In fact, manmade lakes are a common sight, from **Grand Lake St. Marys** in the west to **Pymatuning Reservoir** on the Ohio-Pennsylvania state line. Almost all offer public access. In-state rivers swell the Ohio River. For decades, south-surging streams and rivers such as the **Miami,** the **Muskingum,** and the **Scioto** drained the state in good years and inundated it in bad years (including 1997), when snowmelt and precipitation were excessive. Careful river and stream management has sometimes sacrificed natural beauty for flood control. On the other hand, visitors will find few, if any, private fences across canoe paths or abandoned washing machines dumped on the banks of scenic waterways.

Canoeing is widespread and popular, in part because most of the rivers and streams are scenic without requiring inordinate paddling skills. The center of canoeing in the state is **Loudon-**

OFF-ROAD BICYCLING IN OHIO

A total of 12 state parks welcome off-road riders, novice to advanced. Five of the parks are in the southwest quarter of the state, making a park-to-park vacation on two wheels an attractive proposition.

The parks include:

Alum Creek State Park, near Delaware, tel. (614) 548-4631. Riders should remember this Alum Creek mantra: "North Trail for advanced cyclists, South Trail for rookies." The former pathway is six miles of creeks, hills, and ravines, and it can be hairy. The latter is two miles and most of the trail is a safe distance from nearby trees.

Beaver Creek State Park, north of East Liverpool, tel. (330) 385-3091, has 15 miles of multiple-use trails, with most stretches suited for the advanced rider. Beaver Creek is so pretty it's a shame to concentrate only on bike control.

Caesar Creek State Park, southeast of Dayton, tel. (513) 897-3055, has a 6.5-mile trail for tough riders and a 1.5-mile trail for normal riders. Bike rental is available.

Deer Creek State Park, south of Columbus, tel. (614) 869-3124, is designed with a 1.2-mile loop for novice to intermediate cyclists. Here and at several other parks, riders are told to be "extra cautious" during hunting season. They don't call it Deer Creek for nothing.

East Fork State Park, southeast of Cincinnati, tel. (513) 734-4323, has a pair of loops, each two miles, and one each for novice and for advanced riders. There are a couple of switchbacks on the advanced trail where a rider can run into himself. Or so it may seem.

Findley State Park, near Wellington, tel. (440) 647-4490, operates a two-mile, multiple-use trail that welcomes off-road bikers. This is novice country, but it's pleasant and not all that heavily used.

Hueston Woods State Park, north of Oxford, tel. (513) 523-6347, has a seven-mile trail with a little of everything for the novice, intermediate, and expert off-road rider. Mountain bikes can be rented at the trail head.

Jefferson Lake State Park, northwest of Steubenville, tel. (740) 765-4459, features a dozen miles of multiple-use trails that include narrow stream crossings, plus moving hazards such as horses. For intermediate and advanced cyclists.

Kelleys Island State Park, on Lake Erie, tel. (419) 746-2546, has two scenic trails. The longer one is five miles and will suit novices and intermediates. The 1.5-mile trail is hilly and rocky, designed with the intermediate rider in mind.

Lake Hope State Park, west of Athens, (740) 596-4938, has just two miles of trail, but the Sandy Loop, as it's known, is for intermediate to advanced bikers. Not for the ravine-impaired.

Mary Jane Thurston State Park, southwest of Toledo, tel. (419) 832-7662, is the novice rider's home, with six miles of gentle, multiple-use trails that wind their way through woods and meadows. Mary Jane Thurston may be the least hilly ride among the bikey state parks.

Paint Creek State Park, west of Chillicothe, tel. (740) 365-1401, has something for everyone. There are four distinct trails measuring three, four, five, and six miles. The three- and five- mile junkets offer single-track excitement, while the four- and six-mile jaunts are more scenic and leisurely.

For pavement riders, the Little Miami Scenic Bikeway offers 47 miles of easy riding on trails that parallel the Little Miami River (see **Yellow Springs** for additional information). While the pavement is for the non-motorized, there are numerous streets and crossroads that call for a full stop. Local bike paths are covered in their respective sections (see **Mansfield,** for example).

---

ville, east of Mansfield, though there are many other sites in northern and southern Ohio. Whitewater is most notable for its absence, yet kayaking, rafting, and tubing are enjoyed wherever water moves of its own accord. Generally, the earlier in the year you put in, the better. By August or September, some streams are so shallow that they are no longer challenging—or even navigable.

Fishing and Hunting

Sixty of Ohio's state parks offer angling opportunities. The Ohio River and Lake Erie both require Ohio fishing licenses if you embark from the state or fish from its shores. Visitors can obtain licenses at sporting goods stores, bait retailers, and similar spots. An annual license (which automatically expires on February 28) costs $24 for a nonresident and $15 for an Ohioan. A three-day nonresident permit is $15. One note of caution: catch-and-release fishing may be healthier for the fisher as well as the fish—many of the fish present in Ohio waters may harbor toxic, possibly carcinogenic, substances in their fat that should not be eaten—bottom-feeders, such as carp and catfish, in particular.

Some form of hunting is allowed in or near 57 of Ohio's state parks. Virtually no two parks have identical rules; 20 offer hunting in season in adjacent state forests or nature preserves. Ohio is a place where a friendly hunter can still ask a

friendly farmer to hunt on the farmer's land and be granted occasional permission. Hunting licenses are $91 for nonresidents, $15 for Ohio adults and $8 for Ohio children (ages fifteen and under). Additional special permits are required for many types of game, and there is a special short-term tourist hunting license available. There is no hunting on Sunday except for coyote, fox, woodchuck, and, in season, waterfowl.

Regulations and fees change, so it's a wise idea to contact the Information Center, Ohio Department of Natural Resources, Division of Parks and

COVERED BRIDGES: A PRIMER

Covered bridges once numbered more than 12,000 in the United States, most of them east of the Mississippi. The first such bridge was erected in Philadelphia in 1805. A total of approximately 3,500, or more than one-quarter of all U.S. bridges, were constructed in Ohio—which makes sense, given the large number of rivers and streams. Today, of the 840 wooden bridges still in existence in this country, 136 are in Ohio.

The United States wasn't the only place where covered bridges were common. Canada and western Europe at one time or another had large numbers. But America had as much wood as anyone, and several designs for the truss or support system were patented in the U.S. in the 19th century. Truss bridges were a series of repeated triangles, some of which were reinforced with steel rods. Trusses let

builders create bridges as long as 200 feet or more. No two bridges were exactly alike, as river or stream width varied and carpenters liked applying individual touches to the big structures.

None of which gives any indication why the bridges were covered. Was it to prevent horses from being spooked? To facilitate stopping with one's beau on a moonlit Saturday night? To provide protection from a snow or rain storm? Actually, the bridges took on sides and tops to protect the trusses from the weather. An uncovered wooden bridge lasted 20 years, whereas a covered truss would last for a century or more. Since none of the remaining covered bridges in Ohio were constructed after 1890, the spans have stood up well.

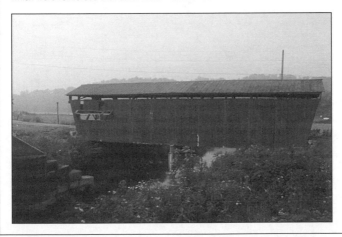

Covered bridges endure, bringing a little bit of the 19th century to the present.

Recreation, 1952 Belcher Dr., Building C-3, Columbus, OH 43224-1386, tel. (614) 265-6561, or go to its Web site, www.dnr.state.oh.us/odnr/wildlife/license/license.html.

Winter sports

Seven ski resorts in five different parts of the state provide decent downhill experiences. Spicy Run Mountain, southeast of Hillsboro, boasts the longest vertical drop (600 feet) in the midwest. The state's longest run, at Mad River Mountain, fives miles southeast of Bellefontaine, totals 3,000 feet. The Mansfield area offers a pair of resorts—Snow Trails and Clear Fork—and so does northeastern Ohio's Cuyahoga Valley National Recreation Area. Brandywine and Boston Mills are convenient to Akron and Cleveland and honor each other's lift tickets. Alpine Valley, 30 miles east of Cleveland near Chesterland, is in the Lake Erie snowbelt and consequently seldom has to worry about exposed patches of grass.

Other winter sports include cross-country skiing, sledding and toboganing, and snowmobiling. A leading destination for all such activities is Punderson State Park, some 25 miles east of Cleveland. Tobogganers especially enjoy Mill Stream Run Reservation in Strongsville, one of the Cleveland Metroparks. Cross-country trails can be found in a number of other state, county, and local parks, as well as on public and private golf courses and near rural bed and breakfast retreats.

Golf and Tennis

Golf is immensely popular in Ohio. Every town of any size has a municipal course, and areas such as Canton-Akron are thick with public and private courses. (The Canton Visitors Bureau, tel. 800-552-6051, offers a brochure pointing out locations of 39 different area courses.) The Department of Transportation and the state's travel information centers have conspired to produce the booklet *Ohio Golf Guide,* which lists 600 courses all across Ohio that welcome the traveling linksperson. Knowing a member is the only way to gain access to the state's several very best private courses, but some are routinely accessible to an out-of-state traveler. Golf is also a very popular spectator sport, featuring some top PGA and LPGA tournaments.

Tennis courts can be found in many city parks and at public schools, and there are private, heated indoor courts in and around larger cities. Professionals make stops in the major cities on at least an annual basis.

ARTS AND ENTERTAINMENT

Music, Dance, and Performance

Entertainment varies widely, from the twang of electric guitars in a neon-lit rural roadhouse to the international renown of the Cleveland Symphony Orchestra. You can partake of varying degrees of sophistication, in all media, for all sorts of taste. Culture is readily available even in many smaller cities (often thanks to the local colleges). A classy example can be found in Wooster, where the **Ohio Light Opera** performs eight operettas each summer in Freedlander Theater on the Wooster College campus. Utterly professional, the productions draw buffs from throughout the Midwest.

Cincinnati was the home of King Records, once a force in the black music scene. It's also the place where **Hank Ballard and the Midniters** invented the Twist (long before Chubby Checker performed on *American Bandstand)*. At the other end of the state, Cleveland is home to an annual **blues festival,** held at the Cuyahoga County Fairgrounds in Berea, and the spring **Tri-C Jazz Fest,** where the likes of Sonny Rollins, Wayne Shorter, and many more perform in half a dozen different locales around town. And at any time or year, you're apt to hear bluesmen such as Robert Cray at places like **Wilbert's Bar and Grille.**

For classical music, you'll be hard pressed to do better than the **Cleveland Symphony Orchestra.** Don't believe it? Check the reviews—or, better yet, try to find a ticket. There are symphonies in other Ohio cities, with seats occasionally available on the day of the performance.

Small local hangouts are great spots to enjoy a wide variety of other types of music, from metal to country, while you quaff a beer and enjoy the friendly atmosphere. The best resource for finding out specifically what's going on is one of the free, alternative weekly newspapers available at city bookstores or music marts.

Another highly enjoyable experience is absorbing a variety of music in a relaxed atmosphere at an outdoor music in the summer. The state's largest is Blossom Music Center, an amphitheater between Cleveland and Akron. The Cleveland Symphony Orchestra makes its summer home there. Another cool place to savor music is at Cincinnati's Riverbend, a favorite summer site for the Cincinnati Symphony Orchestra on the city's far east side.

Dance companies thrive in larger towns, and annual outdoor historical dramas in places like Chillicothe and New Philadelphia add to what's available.

The Toledo Museum of Art opened in 1912 and quickly rose to world-class stature.

OHIO'S AGRICULTURAL FAIRS

County fairs hark back to an America so clean and wholesome it may never have existed. Once a year, kids and adults in every Ohio county display everything from the prizewinning apple pie to the top meat rabbit at fairs all across the state. Some fairs, such as the ones in Darke or Delaware or Fairfield or Mahoning Counties, have longstanding reputations and draw big crowds. In Delaware, for example, the Little Brown Jug trotting race is run on the third Thursday of September during the fair. "People will actually chain folding chairs to the fence beginning in July to 'stake out' their spot for the race," a photographer reports. The race draws 50,000 fans. Other fairs, either because of encroaching urban population or not enough population, are less of a local magnet.

With that in mind, here is a list of fairs, by county, followed by a shorter list of fairs that seem to have just sprung up. All are listed chronologically, but no dates are given because days and dates change from one year to the next. The preponderance of late-summer fairs is due to the fact that there's more of the harvest to display at that time. The list shows the county name, followed by the fair location, followed by the telephone number for directions and information. Note that the fairs do not always take place in the county seat town.

COUNTY FAIRS

JUNE

Pickaway (Circleville), tel. (740) 474-2085
Putnam (Ottawa), tel. (419) 898-1971
Marion (Marion), tel. (614) 382-3558

JULY

Clinton (Wilmington), tel. (937) 382-1741
Lawrence (Proctorville), tel. (740) 533-0106
Madison (London), tel. (614) 852-6346
Paulding (Paulding), tel. (419) 495-2973
Trumbull (Cortland), tel. (330) 637-6010
Harrison (Cadiz), tel. (740) 942-2603
Jackson (Wellston), tel. (740) 988-2631
Crawford (Bucyrus), tel. (419) 683-2711
Franklin (Hilliard), tel. (614) 876-7235
Adams (West Union), tel. (937) 549-3897
Ottawa (Oak Harbor), tel. (419) 898-1971
Warren (Lebanon), tel. (513) 932-2636
Carroll (Carrollton), tel. (330) 739-3524
Logan (Bellefontain), tel. (937) 599-5687
Perry (New Lexington), tel. (740) 342-4142
Clark (Springfield), tel. (937) 323-3090
Butler (Hamilton), tel. (513) 892-1423
Knox (Mount Vernon), tel. (740) 397-5216
Summit (Tallmadge), tel. (330) 633-6200
Clermont (Owensville), tel. (513) 724-7834
Fayette
    (Washington Court House), tel. (740) 335-5856
Lucas (Maumee), tel. (419) 893-2127
Seneca (Tiffin), tel. (419) 447-7888

Shelby (Sidney), tel. (937) 492-5088
Union (Marysville), tel. (937) 358-2931
Pike (Piketon), tel. (740) 947-5253
Preble (Eaton), tel. (937) 456-3748
Greene (Xenia), tel. (937) 767-9463
Auglaize (Wapakoneta), tel. (419) 738-2515
Gallia (Gallipolis), tel. (740) 379-2785
Medina (Medina), tel. (330) 723-9633
Vinton (McArthur), tel. (740) 596-2324
Wood (Bowling Green), tel. (419) 352-0441
Hamilton (Carthage), tel. (513) 761-4224

AUGUST

Champaign (Urbana), tel. (937) 653-2640
Ross (Chillicothe), tel. (740) 634-2921
Richland (Mansfield), tel. (419) 747-3717
Athens (Athens), tel. (740) 594-2771
Cuyahoga (Berea), tel. (216) 243-0090
Scioto (Lucasville), tel. (740) 353-3698
Ashtabula (Jefferson), tel. (440) 576-7626
Erie (Sandusky), tel. (419) 359-1602
Henry (Napoleon), tel. (419) 592-9096
Mercer (Celina), tel. (419) 586-3239
Miami (Troy), tel. (937) 335-7492
Muskingum (Zanesville), tel. (740) 872-3912
Meigs (Pomeroy), tel. (740) 985-4372
Allen (Lima), tel. (419) 228-7141
Darke (Greenville), tel. (937) 548-5044
Huron (Norwalk), tel. (419) 744-2116
Holmes (Millersburg), tel. (330) 378-5572
Jefferson (Smithfield), tel. (740) 765-5156
Tuscarawas (Dover), tel. (330) 343-0524
Defiance (Hicksville), tel. (419) 658-2520
Columbiana (Lisbon), tel. (330) 337-3927

Lorain (Wellington), tel. (440) 647-2781
Monroe (Woodsfield), tel. (740) 472-1465
Lake (Painesville), tel., (440) 354-3339
Portage (Randolph), tel. (330) 325-7476
Sandusky (Fremont), tel. (419) 665-2500
Morrow (Mt. Gilead, tel. (419) 946-2662
Noble (Caldwell), tel. (740) 732-2112
Stark (Canton), tel. (330) 452-0621
Hancock (Findlay), tel. (419) 423-9903
Montgomery (Dayton), tel. (937) 224-1619
Van Wert (Van Wert), tel. (419) 238-9270
Geauga (Burton), tel. (440) 834-1846
Mahoning (Canfield), tel. (330) 533-4107
Fulton (Wauseon), tel. (419) 335-6006
Highland (Hillsboro), tel. (937) 393-1681
Washington (Marietta), tel. (740) 896-2211
Hardin (Kenton), tel. (419) 675-2396
Morgan (McConnelsville), tel. (740) 962-2709
Belmont (St. Clairsville), tel. (740) 425-2263
Wayne (Wooster), tel. (330) 262-800
Williams (Montpelier), tel. (419) 485-3755

Guernsey (Old Washington), tel. (740) 439-2106
Hocking (Logan), tel. (740) 385-4059
Wyandot (Upper Sandusky), tel. (419) 294-4320
Delaware (Delaware), tel. (614) 362-3851
Ashland (Ashland), tel. (419) 289-0466
Brown (Georgetown), tel. (937) 378-3558
Coshocton (Coshocton), tel. (740) 622-2385
Fairfield (Lancaster), tel. (740) 653-3041

INDEPENDENT FAIRS

AUGUST

Hartford (Licking County), tel. (740) 893-4881
Attica (Seneca County), tel. (419) 426-0665
Richwood (Union County), tel. (937) 982-3705

SEPTEMBER

Albany (Athens County), tel. (740) 698-5843
Bellville (Richland County), tel. (419) 886-2687
Barlow (Washington County), tel. (740) 678-2138

Museums and Galleries

For other types of art, Cleveland and Toledo have world-class art museums. Much of the inviting art not only is accessible but it can be purchased—galleries sprout like weeds in Columbus's Short North district, while Cleveland's **Center for Contemporary Art** has a super sale each spring.

Literature

Ohio has been fertile literary ground for some time, and at least a bit of the credit should go to a bookish 19th-century fellow who taught at Miami University in Oxford. Professor **William Holmes McGuffey** created schoolbooks that taught generations of Ohioans—and America itself—how to read. Prized today by collectors, *McGuffey Readers* were used when most schools had one room and kids of many different ages shared modest space in a little building that was by turns frigid and stifling. McGuffey, however, knew how to get their attention and keep it long enough to make them literate. His books sold 122 million copies.

As for actual literature, **Sherwood Anderson** is one of the state's great claims to fame. *Winesburg, Ohio,* a series of sketches of small-town life published in 1919, remains a timeless classic.

Anderson, an Ohio paint company president who ran off to lead a bohemian life in Chicago, used village residents to illustrate meaninglessness and frustration as they surely must have been. A marked influence on Faulkner and Hemingway, he also wrote **The Triumph of the Egg** (1921) and other, less successful, works. Situations in *Winesburg, Ohio* still resonate with modern readers.

Although **Harriet Beecher Stowe** was born in Connecticut, she lived for many years in Cincinnati, near where the courageous runaway slaves in her classic, *Uncle Tom's Cabin,* crossed the Ohio River by moving from one floating chunk of ice to another. That novel was melodramatic (Abraham Lincoln even called Stowe "the little lady who started the Civil War"), but it was an era characterized by high drama—in the actual goings-on of abolitionists, the Underground Railroad, and the like.

For a contrast to such uplifting purpose, read **Ambrose Bierce,** born in Meigs County in 1842. Bierce's writing is bleak, nihilistic, sometimes caustically comic, though also often heavy-handed. Probably best known for his short story "Occurrence at Owl Creek Bridge" (which appeared in the 1891 collection, *In the Midst of Life*), Bierce achieved true fame with *The Devil's Dictionary.*

OHIO FESTIVALS, EVENTS, AND HOLIDAYS

Dates and locations can vary from year to year. You can count on some recurring elements at many festivals—plenty to eat, a parade, perhaps a queen, crafts peddlers, rides, and one or more musical stages. For details on a specific event, turn to the city, county, or region listed.

JANUARY

Collectors' Paradise Record, CD, and Music Memorabilia Show, Columbus. As if to prove that not all the tunes come from the Rock and Roll Hall of Fame, the Veterans Memorial hosts this huge sale.

Winterfest, Chesterland. Alpine Valley Ski Area devises sports such as volleyball in the snow, the snowshoe obstacle race, and the bikini slalom to celebrate winter.

McKinley Day, Canton. This event is held at the McKinley Museum to celebrate the birthday of the man who was president 1897-1901.

FEBRUARY

The River, Portsmouth. The Southern Ohio Museum and Cultural Center exhibits arts and crafts —ceramics, furniture, baskets, decoys, boats—inspired by life on the river.

Evening Owl Walks, Malabar Farm State Park. Four interpretive presentations followed by walks search out Ohio's owls at this popular park near Mansfield.

Winter Campout, East Fork State Park. The venison chili and potluck dinner should keep brave campers warm overnight at the park near Bethel.

MARCH

Cleveland International Film Festival, Cleveland. Some 70 full-length films and 120 short subjects are featured at the theater complex in Tower City, formerly called Terminal Tower, in the heart of downtown.

Book Fair, Columbus. Thirty-five book dealers offer used, scholarly, and collectible books at the Aladdin Shriner's Complex.

Buzzard Sunday, Hinckley. Swallows return to Capistrano, buzzards alight in Hinckley. This long-standing shindig is on the Sunday closest to St. Patrick's Day.

APRIL

Buckeye State Button Collectors Show, Medina. New and antique buttons are on display in what must be one of the smaller art forms.

Geauga County Maple Festival, Chardon. Usually the weekend after Easter, this soiree allows visitors to stir maple candy as they await the start of the bathtub race!

MAY

Dennison Railroad Festival, Dennison. Amusements and vending take place in the vicinity of the venerable depot in eastern Tuscarawas County.

Feast of the Flowering Moon, Chillicothe. Mountain men and Native Americans are celebrated around the original state capital, and there's lots of music and food.

Ice Cream Festival, Utica. A tribute to dessert! The fest includes visiting the local museum of milling and ice-cream making.

Moonshine Festival, New Straitsville. A working still is a historical item on display at this Perry County fete, which has been luring fans of white lightnin' since 1970.

Port Clinton Walleye Festival. There must be walleye in Lake Erie—why else would midway rides and dozens of vendors gather in Water Works Park each year since 1980?

Wild Turkey Festival, McArthur. Vinton County is the unofficial capital of the outdoors during wild turkey season. The calling contest is Saturday afternoon.

JUNE

Commercial Point Homecoming, Commercial Point. This Columbus suburb has been welcoming returning natives since the 1930s.

Deer Creek Dam Days, Williamsport. No fewer than four parades are part of a four-day family festival in south-central Pickaway County.

The Great Ohio Bicycle Adventure. The route varies from year to year on this six-day ride, which usually consists of daily fifty-mile trips.

International Festival, Lorain. Fifty-five different nationalities tempt visitors with ethnic eats, music, and a parade.

Lancaster Old Car Club Spring Festival, Lancaster. Hot rods and antique cars have had folks slicking back their hair at the Fairfield County fairgrounds since 1963!

National Clay Week Festival, Uhrichsville. Everything from the city park to the high school stadium fills up for a salute to the pliable substance.

Stan Hywet Hall and Gardens Antique Car Show, Akron. The Sieberling mansion is a photographer's dream as a backdrop for vintage automobiles.

Vermilion Festival of Fish. This Father's Day Weekend event has been on the Lake Erie calendar since 1965.

JULY

Ashville Fourth of July Celebration. Since 1929, the patriotic "do" south of Columbus includes a parade, a pageant, entertainment, and fireworks.

Crooksville-Roseville Pottery Festival, Ohio Ceramic Center, Crooksville. The people who show up here know and value old and new Ohio-made pottery.

The **Dayton Air Show, Fairborn.** Your tax dollars at work over the years have produced some pretty fantastic aircraft. Many are on aerial display for this event.

First Town Days Festival, New Philadelphia. Five days of merrymaking in Tuscarora Park includes a 5K run, a seniors' day, and a queen pageant.

The **Great Mohican Indian Pow Wow and Rendezvous, Loudonville (also in September).** Camp and gather around a bonfire to cook and eat, paddle and whoop, as in bygone days.

National Walleye Fishing Tournament, Fairport Harbor. This is essentially an "I can catch a bigger fish than you can" contest off the Lake Erie shore.

Ohio Hills Folk Festival, Quaker City. This three-day event has been going on since 1907, proving among other things that Quakers can kick up their heels.

Pro Football Hall of Fame Festival, Canton. Inductees wax nostalgic and the first National Football League exhibition game of the season takes place next door.

AUGUST

Bratwurst Festival, Bucyrus. Bratwurst recipes differ from one butcher to another, so there's sure to be a wide variety. Resist the urge to make "wurst" jokes.

London Marigold Festival, London. If they keep the rabbits out of your garden, they can't be all bad. Marigolds also are known for being the "friendship flower."

Ohio Honey Festival, Hamilton. There's a dash of honey in everything at this three-day fest, from ice cream to Greek pastries to the "living beard" of bees on a beekeeper.

North Ridgeville Corn Festival, North Ridgeville. Festival organizers claim to have a "secret Amish recipe" for their roast corn. Try an ear and learn the secret.

Obetz Zucchinifest, Obetz. They've been worshiping zucchini since the late 1980s at this get-together, which includes Zucchini Burgers and other "Z" recipes.

Ohio Tobacco Festival, Ripley. Some 10,000 Buckeye farms raise the devilish weed, most of which is burley and the rationale behind selection of an Ohio Tobacco Queen.

Parade of the Hills, Nelsonville. Here's an entire week of free nightly entertainment in the northwest corner of Athens County.

Pemberville Free Fair, Pemberville. By definition a bargain, this fair east of Bowling Green is big and growing.

Portsmouth River Days. Ohio and Scioto River activities, from boat races to fish fries, spill over into September at this fest, up and running since 1962.

Sweet Corn Festival, Inc., Millersport. If there really is a secret way to roast corn "Amish style," these people should know how it's done.

Tuscarawas County Italian/American Festival, New Philadelphia. Bocci and *morra* tournaments are only two of many Italian-oriented goings on in New Philly.

Vintage Ohio, Lake Farmpark, Kirtland. Only a couple of years old, this sampling and nibbling fest involves two dozen Buckeye wineries and the Cleveland area's top dining spots.

SEPTEMBER

American Soya Festival, Amanda. There's only one festival anywhere saluting the soybean; this mid-September event west of Lancaster is it.

Galion Octoberfest, Galion. The late-September, early-October social gathering features free big-name entertainment in what the sponsoring Moose Lodge calls the "Heart of Ohio."

Geneva Area Grape JAMboree, Geneva. Grape juice, wine, and grape products are to be sampled, and there's grape stompin' amid a parade and a bevy of queens.

German Village Oktoberfest, Columbus. The usual oompah stuff, but in a particularly nice, legitimately ethnic urban setting.

International Mining & Manufacturing Festival, Cadiz. Features here include a band and a run among Harrison County hills.

Jackson County Apple Festival, Jackson. Southeast of Chillicothe, this apple endeavor is five days of street fair, quilt show, free entertainment, and more. *(continues)*

OHIO FESTIVALS, EVENTS, AND HOLIDAYS
continued

Johnny Appleseed Festival, Lisbon. Activities revolve around the hearty apple here, one of numerous places Mr. Appleseed propagated during the 19th century.

Mantua Potato Festival, Mantua. This toast to America's favorite tuber is in Portage County and there are runs, music, food, games, and a queen.

Marion Popcorn Festival, Marion. They close off the downtown here in what has become one of the state's better parties. All entertainment for thirteen hours daily is free.

Milan Melon Festival, Milan. The square of Thomas Edison's hometown is the backdrop for antique cars, muskmelon ice cream, and watermelon sherbet.

Ohio Swiss Festival, Sugarcreek. Yodeling, Swiss costumes, maybe even Swiss steak, for all we know, put in appearances at this most alpine of all state villages.

The Reynoldsburg Tomato Festival, Reynoldsburg. Stifle the urge to throw tomatoes and instead see and taste their many uses for five days in suburban Columbus.

Slavic Harvest Festival, Cleveland. Did you know that Slavs have a way with gardens, especially veggies? Attend and learn more.

Tiffin-Seneca Heritage Festival. When your heritage involves Tiffin, you evidently want to share it in a mid-September weekend fest that includes food, arts, and crafts.

Wellston Ohillco Festival, Wellston. The hills are alive with the sounds of . . . the founding of Wellston some 125 years ago. High school football is one highlight.

Yankee Peddler Festival, Clay's Park Resort, Canal Fulton. This is one of the state's best fests, with almost everybody selling almost everything.

OCTOBER

Apple Butter Festival, Burton. The intoxicating smell of apple butter wafts through this Geauga County village, where the Cuyahoga River's a mere trickle.

Autumn in the Hills, New Lexington. Perry County's the site for this homecoming festival—there's firefighting competition, a pumpkin show, a bed race, and more.

Circleville Pumpkin Show, Circleville. This granddaddy of all Ohio festivals is a four-day extravaganza in orange and has been for more than ninety years.

Covered Bridge Festival, Ashtabula County. The fairgrounds in Jefferson is the jumping-off point

---

Published in 1906, the book uses some of the blackest imaginable humor to define even seemingly harmless words and phrases. A troubled man, the journalist lived most of his adult life in California before disappearing without a trace in Mexico in 1914.

One of the people most responsible for the characteristic dryly witty tone of *The New Yorker,* Columbus's **James Thurber** wrote wry short stories and urbane journalism and drew his signature peculiar cartoons (whose minimalist lines and sometimes bizarre situations owed something to Thurber's advancing blindness—one famous anecdote tells of his not being able to remember just exactly *what* the object was that he'd drawn up on top of a bookcase in one of the cartoons, so he made it the wife of the man in the drawing) for that publication as a staff member from 1927 to 1933 and principal contributor for many years past that. Collected in books in-

cluding *My World and Welcome to It, The Owl in the Attic,* and *The Thurber Carnival,* the stories captured America's imagination and made the nation chuckle with self-recognition—perhaps most famously at the archetypal Walter Mitty, the mild-mannered little fellow whose fantasy life transforms the elements of his perfectly ordinary life into much grander stuff. Thurber also wrote the classic children's books *The Thirteen Clocks* and *Many Moons* and teamed up with *New Yorker* colleague E.B. White to write the satire *Is Sex Necessary?*

That classic chronicler of the Wild West **Zane Grey** also came from Ohio. Born in Zanesville, he left Ohio to check out the frontier, from where he wrote his stirring tales. Grey's short stories, such as "The Luck of Roaring Camp," are widely anthologized.

Hart Crane, who disappeared at sea in 1932, was born in Garrettsville. A child of the 1920s,

in this visitation to Ashtabula County's many bucolic bridges.

Fall Festival of Leaves, Bainbridge. Those who still like leaves after raking can come to Bainbridge on US 50 in Ross County for crafts, food, and a tractor pull.

Hale Harvest Festival, Hale Farm and Village, Bath. See how they used to ready themselves for winter in the wonderful Cuyahoga Valley National Recreation Area.

Holmes County Antique Festival, Millersburg. This antique show has been on the docket for one-third of a century and it gets bigger with each passing year.

International Doll Show and Sale and Tribute to Teddies, Toledo. Past the many blank stares is great teddy-bear and other workmanship.

The **Ohio Gourd Show, Mt. Gilead.** Fresh gourds and gourdcraft are shown at the Morrow County Fairgrounds on the south edge of town.

NOVEMBER

Downtown Holiday Lighting Program, Public Square, Cleveland. Christmas is great on the farm, but there's something electric about all those big-city lights.

DECEMBER

Christmas at Malabar Farm State Park, Perrysville. One of the state's prettiest places puts on its holiday finery. Bogey and Bacall found Malabar a romantic place—they married here.

First Night, Akron. Among the largest and most ambitious municipal New Year's Eve celebrations anywhere, there is great entertainment everywhere. Limited recently to the first 27,000 who made reservations.

STATE HOLIDAYS

What with four generals who became U.S. Presidents, you'd think there would be some funky or nostalgic holidays peculiar to the state. Not the case. Official state holidays usually mean that state offices are closed and services withheld, but for emergencies.

New Year's Day: January 1.
Martin Luther King's Birthday: January 15, usually observed the third Monday of the month.
Presidents Day: Third Monday in February.
Memorial Day: Last Monday in May.
Independence Day: July 4.
Labor Day: First Monday in September.
Columbus Day: Second Monday in October.
Veterans Day: November 11.
Thanksgiving: Last Thursday in November.
Christmas: December 25.

Crane wrote poems that have been compared to those of T.S. Eliot. **Louis Bromfield** created the farm that today is Malabar State Park, near Mansfield, but until his death in 1956 he was widely admired for his novels.

Brilliant, reclusive **Thomas Berger** was born in 1924 in Cincinnati and has produced more than a dozen darkly comic novels cleverly employing revisionist spoofs of various literary genres to satirize the absurdities of modern life, from the Western *Little Big Man* to the medieval epic *Arthur Rex* and the utopian science-fiction concoction *Regiment of Women*. Berger's hilariously sinister Kafkaesque streak is perhaps on best display in *Neighbors* (made into a greatly inferior movie with Dan Aykroyd and John Belushi) and his private-eye thriller *Who is Teddy Villanova?*

Pulitzer and Nobel Prize–winning novelist (and Oprah-favorite) **Toni Morrison,** too, hails from Ohio. Born in Lorain in 1931, she writes unforgettably of the lives and times of African-Americans in novels including *Beloved,* (which won the Pulitzer in 1988), *Sula, The Bluest Eye* (set in Lorain), *Song of Solomon, Tar Baby,* and *Jazz.* Morrison won the Nobel Prize for Literature in 1993.

Architecture

A 200-year-old dwelling next to freshly hewn ranch houses? It happens in Ohio, where virtually every style of architecture is present, from Vermilion's staid Cape Cod two-stories to the occasional Cincinnati hilltop contemporary. Look, too, for federal, neoclassical, Victorian, carpenter gothic, and other styles. Especially attractive, historic, and carefully preserved older homes can be found on main or near-downtown streets in Findlay, Marietta, Mount Vernon, Piqua, and in big-city neighborhoods such as German Village in Columbus. Ohio is a would-be rehabber's dream, as every municipality has at least a few majestic homes in need of attention. The state's oldest existing residences have been around more than 200 years. Many renovated dwellings open partially for spring garden tours, with proceeds benefiting local charities. Conctact the local convention and visitors bureau or chamber of commerce for details.

Historic and Cultural Tours

In Oberlin, a town steeped in Abolitionist history, three beautifully preserved buildings are stops on the official tour. One, the Little Red Schoolhouse, dates to 1836. A small admission fee is charged. Destinations such as the Cincinnati Art Museum provide a choice of tours. Family Fun Tours are offered on weekends, public tours run six days a week, and group tours are given to those who make reservations. The cost of museum admission also covers the tour itself. These days, the most popular tours appear to be those traversing Amish country—they're offered not only by bus but also by a nostalgic train that departs the depot in Sugarcreek. But these are just a few examples. Both kinds of tours are available widely throughout the state.

Especially for Kids

In no particular order, attractions that prove highlights among kids include **Cedar Point,** the big amusement park in Sandusky; **Paramount's Kings Island,** also an amusement park, this one north of Cincinnati; **Sea World** and **Geauga Lake,** both a few miles southeast of Cleveland;

and more modest but diverting places such as **Wyandot Lake,** a suburban Columbus waterslide complex.

So intriguing for all ages that it hurts to call them "educational" are **Inventure Place,** in Akron, the **Great Lakes Science Center,** on the lakefront in Cleveland, and the **Centers of Science and Industry** in Columbus and Toledo. And for the kid in all of us, there's always Cleveland's **Rock and Roll Hall of Fame and Museum.**

Shopping

Ohio's major cities are ringed with shopping centers. The centers contain all of the big national stores selling the usual brands. For those who like their shopping downtown, Cleveland offers **Tower Center** and the **Galleria at Erieview.** The **Columbus City Center** is in the middle of things, as are shops in the Greater Columbus Convention Center. Down Cincinnati way, check out the **Convention Place Mall.**

Factory outlets also thrive here. One of the biggies is **Aurora Farms** in Aurora, southeast of Cleveland. Another, **Lake Erie Factory Outlet Center,** is midway between Cleveland and Toledo in Milan. Outside of Columbus, look for **Ohio Factory Shops.** There are more **Ohio Factory Shops** north of Cincinnati, and the **Jeffersonville Outlet Center** lies between Cincy and Columbus. The **Libbey Factory Outlet,** in Toledo, and **Rocky Shoes & Boot Outlet,** in Nelsonville, are typical of the many one-brand outlet

A cheesemaker's colorful shop east of Millersburg features a mural and a clock tower.

stores also present throughout Ohio.

Foragers will find antiques everywhere, but especially on display in small towns like Waynesville and Wapakoneta.

Perhaps the most sought-after goods among visitors are anything crafted by the Amish. Amish craftspeople specialize in everything from baked goods to fine furniture. And while Holmes County is the heart of Amish country, they can also be found in the southeast, the southwest, around Columbus, and east of Cleveland. Look for hand-lettered signs along fencerows.

Late summer and early fall is the time for farm produce. In southern Ohio, sorghum offers an alternative to syrup and comes in pint or quart jars. Glass and pottery are for sale year round in the greater Zanesville area, and visitors will run across pockets of everything from bratwurst (Bucyrus) to New Age trinkets (Yellow Springs) along the way.

SLEEPING AND EATING

Visitors who want reserved places to stay but don't want to be tied to a schedule should take advantage of toll-free reservations listings. Many of these lines are open 24 hours a day and often allow vacationers who change plans to cancel as late as 6 p.m. on the scheduled day of arrival. Reserving with a credit card will often ensure that a room or a campsite is held for the entire evening, allowing you to arrive quite late if you need to. However, unless you specify that you'll be arriving for late check-in, some motels and hotels will release the room anyway. Also, should you fail to cancel a reservation in time, the room will be charged to your credit card even though you never show up to fill it.

Those who detest being tied to a schedule can take their chances, or they can make reservations without their credit cards and promise to show up before the afternoon or early-evening deadline. Vacationers might want to get an early start, roll into a motel in the afternoon, then use the rest of the day to explore new surroundings.

Hotels and motels are much less likely to be filled on weekdays than weekends in resort or urban areas. Weekday rates often are lower. You can often further reduce your lodging costs by looking for and using local tabloid coupons and membership cards such as AAA or American Association of Retired Persons (AARP). Unfortunately, such discounts won't do much more than cover the various taxes on a room in a typical town.

Even in Ohio, there are places where travelers must book rooms months in advance. You'll need to do some planning ahead if you want to stay at Cedar Point, Sea World, or King's Island, or attend special events such as the Dayton Air Show (the number of special events is astounding). Midwestern vacationers want to be within a mile or two of their destinations. If you don't mind a drive of 30 minutes or more to and from an attraction, you can usually find a place to stay that's more reasonable and more readily available.

No matter what kind of accommodation you seek, the connection between money and a pleasant experience is pretty solid. If you find an absurdly modest room rate, there's a reason.

As for **bed and breakfast accommodations,** many are delightful. (Not all, however, a friend stayed in an opulent B&B and spent most of the evening listening to a loud teenage boy argue with his parents—the host and hostess—while his sister whined. There is nothing automatically magic about any given bed and breakfast, but word of mouth usually can be trusted.) And if you're traveling on a credit card, make sure the B&B accepts your brand of plastic, or that they will take your check. Bed and breakfast places frequently have a single rate for a room, whether used by one person or two. The average lifespan of a bed and breakfast operation is about five years, so confirm a listing before you arrive.

Ohio has eight great **state park resorts.** Forget about just driving up to them and securing a room (though you might get lucky if there's a last-minute cancellation). The resorts offer good value for the money, being loaded with amenities and things to do. They seem well known only to in-state folks, who come back year after year for vacations, family reunions, or conventions. For more information on staying at any state park, dial (800) AT-A-PARK (tel. 800-282-7275) or go to www.tw-recresorts.com.

There are several great fallback plans for those who want state accommodations but neglected to call months in advance. Vacationers can rent a camp, recreational vehicle (RV), tepee, a houseboat. At **Rent-A-Camp** sites, you need to bring your own sleeping bags and food, but other than that pretty much everything else is provided in 10-by-12-foot lodges, complete with dining canopies, cots, coolers, stoves, foam sleeping pads, and more. Costs vary, from about $20 to $27 per night. The Rent-A-Camp deal is available in 36 different parks, but reserve ahead.

Rent-A-RV charges as little as $45 or as much as $65 daily. Each of these 29-foot travel trailers has its own bath, refrigerator, TV, and sound system (a promotional brochure says that RVs offer vacationers the chance to "experience the pleasure of camping with all of the comforts of home"). RVs are available at Alum Creek near Delaware and at East Fork in Clermont County.

STATE PARK RESORTS

Besides being free to both residents and out-of-state visitors, Ohio's 72 state parks are wonderful vacation destinations—especially the eight with resort accommodations. All eight require two-night minimum stays on summer weekends. Prices are moderate. The resorts include:

- **Burr Oak State Park** in Athens and Morgan Counties in the southeast on SR 78E, northeast of Glouster; tel. (740) 869-2020, has 60 guest rooms and 30 cabins. The resort offers fishing and swimming in a 664-acre lake, plus 28 hiking trails. The lodge sits high above the water, while the cabins, which are not air conditioned, are close to the shore. Two-night minimums on weekends year round.

- **Deer Creek State Park** in Pickaway and Fayette Counties, east of Washington Courthouse and south of Mt. Sterling. The address is 22300 State Park Road, No. 20; tel. (740) 869-2020. Only 30 miles south of Columbus, Deer Creek has 110 guest rooms and 25 two-bedroom cottages. One-third of the park is water, and the resort has a dining room, a lounge/bar, and both indoor and outdoor pools.

- **Hueston Woods State Park** in Preble and Butler Counties, just 4.5 miles north of Oxford. Officially, it's on SR 732 near College Corner, tel. (513) 523-6381. There are 94 guest rooms and 59 cabins. The lodge was reopened in March 1996 after major renovation and is as magnificent as the many hardwoods found in the park. The lake here covers 625 acres and there's a nature center. Lodge prices are the most expensive of the eight resorts, but still barely within the moderate price range.

- **Maumee Bay State Forest,** which was new in 1991. Just outside Toledo at 1750 Park Rd., No. 2, in Oregon, tel. (419) 836-1466, the contemporary facility has 120 guest rooms and 20 cabins on Lake Erie. There are indoor and outdoor pools, golf, an exercise room, whirlpool and sauna, a bicycle trail, a nature center, and more. The nightly tariff applies to single or double occupancy.

- **Mohican State Park,** near Loudonville, tel. (419) 938-5411, Goon Rd. at SR 3, is bisected by a river that's busy with canoes and arched by a covered bridge. The resort has 96 rooms and both the 25 cabins and the campground were renovated in 1995. Midway between Columbus and Cleveland, this parks has a cave and falls and can be overrun with humans.

- **Punderson Lake State Park,** east of Cleveland at 11755 Kinsman Rd. near Newbury, tel. (440) 564-9144, was constructed in the 1920s as a sweeping private residence. The lodge has been offering its 31 rooms to guests since 1948. There are 26 cabins, too. This park is popular for fishing, swimming, hiking, and running in the summer, and for cross-country skiing and tobogganing in the winter. With so few rooms, reservations are a must.

- **Salt Fork State Park,** a this spacious park on US 22E near Cambridge in the southeast, tel. (740) 439-2751, has the largest lodge, with 148 rooms. There are 54 cabins, too. Salt Fork also is near the intersections of I-70 and I-77. Almost 3,000 of the park's 17,229 acres are water. There are two pools, golf, a lounge/bar, a restaurant, and tennis, basketball, and volleyball courts.

- **Shawnee State Park** is three miles north of the Ohio River, west of Portsmouth. Shawnee has a 50-room lodge and 25 two-bedroom cottages. It's at 4404-B SR 125, tel. (740) 858-6621, and is equipped with two pools, whirlpool and sauna, backpack camping, hiking trails, canoe rentals, fishing, an activity director, and a naturalist.

The easiest way to snag a reservation—and reservations are a must—is to dial (800) AT-A-PARK (or tel. 800-282-7275), or one of the above local numbers. Buckeye parks even have a Web site: www.tw-rec-resorts.com. The lodges are open all year and frequently are popular sites for large group meetings. Therefore, never assume a visitor can just mosey up to a lodge and secure a room, even on a winter weekday.

Not that travelers have to stay at a resort to have a good time. Cabins can be found in 16 different parks. They are less expensive, less pretentious, less modern, and much more authentic than the sumptuous resorts—they're the kind of place a kid will remember into adulthood. Amenity levels vary but will be patiently explained. Most are located on or near water and they are in great demand, so call the (800) AT-A-PARK (or tel. 800-282-7275) number early. An informal survey at one park showed all cabins to be occupied by people driving cars with Ohio plates. Obviously, the locals know a good thing.

Indian Lake, Jackson Lake, and Mohican State Parks are the places where you can take advantage of the **Rent-A-Tepee** program. The canvas tepees are anchored to wooden platforms and are a spacious 19 feet in diameter. Each is equipped with a cooler, sleeping pads, lawn chairs, a picnic table, and a fire ring. Indian Lake and Jackson Lake throw in canoes, paddles, and life jackets. Cost of the rental is about $25 per night—not much of a tariff for an exerience the kids may remember the rest of their lives.

Houseboats can be rented at Paint Creek and Alum Creek State Parks. Weekly rental is $700, or $400 for either of two partial-week plans. These floating residences have lots of toys, from air conditioning to VCR's, as well as standard features such as showers, stoves, etc. Each boat sleeps six and has a sun deck and an upper deck, the latter 27 feet wide.

In terms of popularity, not much beats the 16 parks with cabins for rent. All eight of the resorts also offer cabins—and many of these are sprinkled along shorelines, riverbanks, or hillsides. Prices range from $80 at Burr Oak to $130 at Maumee Bay per couple per night. Rentals during the summer are available on a weekly basis only. Some facilities are fully insulated and can be rented any day of the year.

Again, the easiest way to make any sort of reservation—and reservations are smart—is to dial (800) AT-A-PARK (tel. 800-282-7275), or one of the local numbers.

FOOD

You can find every conceivable kind of cuisine in Ohio, from Old World to latest-thing nouvelle/nouveau. Venturing any real distance from a large city will narrow your choices, but the food you find outside city limits is just as tempting and tasty. In fact, places such as Brown's Restaurant in Wapakoneta take a back seat to no one in offering fresh, skillfully prepared meals—and the small-town prices are a revelation.

Top comestible choices throughout the state are seasonal fruits and vegetables, uniformly good beef and pork, and desserts such as sugar-cream or sour cream–raisin pies. In fairness, some stuff takes a little getting used to. Order a tenderloin sandwich off the menu and you usually are served a *pork* tenderloin, deep fried in palate-numbing batter. Scrapple, a fried mush studded with bits of pork, is an acquired taste (and one found on only a few small-town breakfast menus). Biscuits and gravy can be wonderful or a soggy, sorry mess. Be adventurous.

Outside larger towns, vegetarians will be challenged to find much to eat besides french fries in restaurants. Numerous roadside stands sell wonderful fresh produce in season, but dedicated non-carnivores who find themselves in the hinterlands may have to avail themselves of the deli counters at local supermarkets for homemade bean and pasta salads, cheeses, fresh-baked breads, even such standbys as containers of yogurt. Every town of any size has a Chinese restaurant, too. Since most dishes are individually cooked, simply specify tofu instead of beef, chicken, pork, or shrimp.

One of the pleasures of dining in Ohio is the discovery of quality restaurants with numerous sites in the state. Here's a rundown of restaurant chains that got their start and remain tasty destinations in Buckeyeland. Some, such as Donato's Pizza or Mark Pi's restaurants, are in several different Ohio cities. (The list does not include destinations like Bob Evans or Wendy's restaurants, both of which began here but now are everywhere.)

Akron: Fiesta Pizza and Chicken, Parasson's Italian Restaurants, Rizzi's Ristorante & Pizzeria, Rockne's Pub, Swenson's Drive-In.

Canton: Grinders and Such.

Cincinnati: Angilo's Pizza, Barleycorn's, Burbank's Real Bar-B-Q, Empress Chili, Gold Star Chili, LaRosa's Pizza, Mio's Pizza, Skyline Chili, Snappy Tomato Pizza Co.

Cleveland: Angie's Pizza, Antonio's Pizza & Spaghetti, Bella Pizza, Brown Derby Road House, Gepetto's Pizza & Ribs, Great Steak & Fry Company, Hot Sauce Williams Barbecue Restaurant, Marco's Pizza, Pizza Pan, Sakkio Japan, Slam Jams Sports Bar & Grill.

Columbus: Angelina's Villa, Back Yard Burgers, Dino's Pizza, Donato's Pizza, Happy Dragon Chinese to Go, Iacono's Pizza & Restaurant, Mark Pi's China Gate/Mark Pi's Express, Massey's Pizza, Max & Erma's, Pa-Pa Joe's Pizza, Salvi's Italian Eatery, The Spaghetti Shop, Stopwatch Pizza, Tee Jaye's Country Place, Tommy's Pizza.

Dayton: Cassano's Pizza & Subs, Marion's Pizza, Ron's Pizza, The Submarine House.

Toledo: Alexander's the Great Pizza, Bambino's Pizza, Charlie's Coney Island, Marco's Pizza, Netty's, Rosie's Family Restaurant, Salad Galley, Vito's Pizza.

Youngstown-Warren Area: Cornersburg Pizza, Ianazone's Pizza, Inner Circle Pizza, Pizza Joe's.

Finally, great meals or snacks can be found wherever farmers set up roadside stands. (US 2 east of Oregon is especially bountiful.) Apples thrive here—and not only Macintoshes or Jonathans. Sorghum, a yummy syrup squeezed from a cornlike plant, may be too messy for the car, but it keeps well and tastes great back home (or at the motel) on a bagel. Sausage, too, keeps well—either the sagey country variety or the smoky, garlic-tinged, European recipe. Other stuff with some shelf life includes pumpkins and squashes, various kinds of nuts, and jellies and preserves. If you buy perishables such as cider or homemade pie, consume them quickly.

Alcohol

The age at which one can legally consume alcoholic beverages is 21. In Ohio, you can buy alcohol seven days a week. It's sold at carry-out facilities or, in restaurants, over the bar as an accompaniment to food. You also have the option here of drive-through liquor windows. You place your order without leaving the car, pay for it, and an employee comes out and loads the liquor into your trunk.

As throughout the U.S., driving while under the influence of alcohol (or drugs) is a serious offense. You may encounter alcohol-enforcement zones and sobriety checkpoints (they're especially prevalent around the big colleges on Friday and Saturday nights). The simple way to avoid trouble is not to drive if you've been drinking.

TRANSPORTATION, INFORMATION, AND SERVICES

GETTING THERE

By Air

Ohio's three busiest airports are Cincinnati-Northern Kentucky International, Cleveland-Hopkins International, and Port Columbus International. Flying into less-busy commercial airports, such as Akron-Canton or James M. Cox-Dayton Municipal, can result in a less frantic experience, but such ports also, of course, offer fewer flights in and out. Both Cincinnati and Cleveland are major hubs serving international destinations. Of the three majors, only Cleveland has commuter rail service into the downtown area. The Cincinnati airport, as the full name implies, is actually across the Ohio River, in Kentucky. Delta has the largest number of flights in and out of Cincinnati, while Continental offers more flights than any other airline through Cleveland.

By Car

The overwhelming majority of visitors show up in Ohio in automobiles. Being somewhat in the middle of things, the state boasts interstate and national highways headed in all directions. The most heavily traveled stretch includes the Ohio Turnpike (I-80/90) between Pennsylvania and Indiana. This is a heavy-duty truck route. Interstate 71 between Cleveland and Columbus, and I-75 between Dayton and Cincinnati also can be crowded. A pleasant way to enter Ohio is via I-77 from West Virginia. Drivers will find it lightly traveled at least as far north as Cambridge, where it intersects with I-70.

The automobile speed limit on interstate and rural, divided highways is 65 miles per hour. Maximum speed on other rural roads is 55 miles per hour unless otherwise posted. The Ohio Turnpike (I-80/90) is microscopically monitored by the Ohio Highway Patrol, and venturing even a few miles per hour over the 65 mph limit *will* get you noticed. Don't say you weren't warned. Radar-detection devices are legal in the state.

TOURIST INFORMATION CENTERS

Visitors roll into Ohio from all directions. Fortunately for them, the Buckeye State offers a number of convenient Tourist Information Centers. These centers are staffed during business hours, offering a barrage of brochures, maps, booklets, and other information on all parts of the state. If you stop here and can't find what you're looking for, it may not exist.

Tourist Information Centers, starting at 9 and traveling clockwise around the state, are as follows:

I-70: This site is in an eastbound rest area (exit right or south), just a mile or so east of the Indiana-Ohio state line.

I-75: There are centers on either side of the highway just south of Bowling Green.

I-90: Westbound, this center is on the right or north side of the highway near the junction with SR 7 in Conneaut.

I-80: Once you see the sign welcoming you to Ohio from Pennsylvania, look to the right or north side of the highway for the center.

I-70: This center is a dozen miles west of the Ohio River and Wheeling, West Virginia on the right or north side of the road, three miles west of St. Clairsville.

I-77: Three miles north of the Ohio River and Marietta lies the center, on the right or east side of the limited-access road.

US 23: Measured from the Ohio River, the center is 12 miles north, on the left or west side of the highway.

I-71: About 20 miles north of downtown Cincinnati, and just east of Lebanon, there are matching centers on both sides of the road.

I-75: Twin centers serve travelers on the south side of Middletown.

Seat-belt use is mandatory for adults and children. Auto liability insurance is also mandatory.

Overnight parking is not permitted on the shoulder of any road or highway.

By Bus

Greyhound operates interstate buses, stopping in all major Ohio cities. For information on fares, arrivals, and departures call (800) 231-2222.

By Train

Amtrak has two routes through Ohio. The more heavily traveled enters the state from Chicago at Bryan. Cities served on the route east include Toledo, Sandusky, Elyria, and Cleveland. Riders have a choice at Cleveland; they can continue eastward by catching a train bound for Erie, Pennsylvania, or they may head southeast, through Alliance, to Pittsburgh. The second Amtrak route comes from Indianapolis and can be boarded in Hamilton or Cincinnati before it swings east toward Washington, D.C. For times and fares, call (800) USA-RAIL (tel. 800-872-7245).

By Boat

Virtually everyone who enters Ohio by boat does so on a private craft, whether crossing the Ohio River or sailing Lake Erie. There are no regularly scheduled interstate (or international) lake passenger boats. There *is*, however, a toll ferry operating between Augusta, Kentucky, and Higginsport, Ohio, some 40 miles east of Cincinnati on US 52. The Boudes Ferry, as it's known locally, charges $6 per vehicle, which covers the cost of the passengers. No reservations are needed—the boat makes the crossing whenever it's full and the trip takes about 15 minutes. Capacity is about 10 cars.

GETTING AROUND

By Air

There are six major passenger airports: Akron-Canton, Cincinnati-Northern Kentucky, Cleveland, Columbus, Dayton, and Toledo. Flights from Cleveland to Columbus and from Columbus to Cincinnati take less than an hour, as does a Cincy-Cleveland flight, under ideal conditions. There are frequent commuter flights among the three largest airports and at least two daily arrivals and departures among the other three.

By Car

Show up by car and take advantage of a quirk of history. Virtually every major U.S. highway of consequence, except maybe Route 66 and US 101, seems to pass through Ohio. The mother of all such roads is US 40, constructed early in the 19th century and connecting Baltimore and the Mid-Atlantic shore to the Midwest and beyond. The grand old thoroughfare, which has been upstaged by I-70, remains a byway treat, running east-west from Wheeling, West Virginia, to Richmond, Indiana. The most interesting and scenic stretch of this so-called National Road is between Cambridge and Zanesville—a slice of heaven for those interested in old glassware. Antiques are peddled all along the old road.

Other highways with some heritage to them include US 30, which runs east-west north of US 40, connecting Ohio's Allegheny foothill city of East Liverpool on the east with the farm town of Van Wert on the west. US 50 also runs east-west, between Parkersburg, West Virginia, and Cincinnati. And US 20 takes visitors on a trip that roughly parallels the Lake Erie shore before heading west toward Chicago.

US 42 runs south out of Cleveland, skirting the western suburbs of Columbus and then heading into hilly country south of Xenia and on into Cincinnati. US 23 links Toledo and Portsmouth, passing through Columbus on the way. Far to the west, US 127 heads south from the Michigan line, running through historic Anthony Wayne country to Cincinnati, where it crosses the Ohio River.

There are also plenty of strictly scenic roads. State Route 39 from East Liverpool to New Philadelphia displays everything from little old towns to an occasional strip mine. That same route can be picked up a few miles later, west of Dover, on its way into Amish country. A nice road with some Amish atmosphere is SR 83, running south out of Millersburg, through Coshocton, and on to I-70. In the same general area, check out SR 97, between canoe-laden Loudonville and Lexington, or SR 229 between Mount Vernon and New Castle.

For a long stretch of good lookin' road, US 52 is tough to beat. Vistas up and down the 170 miles between Cincinnati and Huntington, West Virginia, are wonderful, despite the occasional high-tension wire, used-car cemetery, and re-

Benny, the first mate, welcomes folks aboard the Boudes Ferry.

finery. The highway changes number to become SR 7, but the riverside trip continues east through Marietta and Wheeling to East Liverpool. The SR 7 portion of the journey runs about 250 miles and is somewhat more industrialized, but just as unpopulated, as its federal counterpart. Another pretty, unpretentious trip south is on SR 13 from Newark to Athens. Elsewhere south of Columbus, almost any rural road can be inviting, even if it leads nowhere in particular. Such roads exist aplenty in Hocking County, for example— though the going is curvaceous and slow, it is most assuredly scenic.

For road conditions and construction within the state, dial (614) 466-7170, 7:30 a.m.-5:30 p.m. weekdays. *The Toledo Blade* daily newspaper offers a helpful weekly column each Friday all summer on local and regional construction and road conditions.

By Bus

Buses are a smart way to get around bigger cities. Bus-stop kiosks provide maps that can be comprehended, and fellow passengers will tip you to times, destinations, fares, etc. Several local bus lines run regular service between suburbs and downtown areas. Laketran, for example, provides passengers parking places near pickup points throughout Lake County, west of Cleveland. Between major Ohio cities, Greyhound is the only significant carrier. For more information, see the section of this book that deals with the specific area in which you're interested.

By Train

Passenger travel is limited to the Amtrak corridors running through Toledo and Cleveland, and to the short stretch of track through Hamilton into Cincinnati. Pending completion of a small depot, Amtrak has promised to begin stopping in Akron on its route between Philadelphia-New York and Chicago. Times are infrequent and trains can be late, but a train ride remains a nostalgic experience. Within Cleveland, the train remains an efficient means of moving betwen Hopkins Airport and downtown. Regularly scheduled public rail transportation also is available between the city and such close-in suburbs as Shaker Heights.

By Boat

Not since the days of canal boats, called packets, were there many scheduled in-state trips by boat. Today, about the only regularly scheduled trips are between the Lake Erie shore and South Bass or Kelley's Islands. There also is ferry service for the short run between Sandusky and Cedar Point. All such services carry passengers only and shut down in the winter.

By Bicycle

But for signs designating that a road can accommodate bicycles, there aren't many amenities for riders. And often, the diamond-shaped bike rider sign is more a clue that the road is scenic than that it has any sort of designated pathway for two wheelers. If you want to ride, take precautions: outfit your bike with a flag on a wispy aerial and wear a helmet. Riding in big cities takes even more skill, as bikers simultaneously must watch for doors opening on parked cars, railroad tracks, potholes, and pedestrians. Determined riders can find many nice suburban and rural streets and roads, and off-roaders are being rewarded with an increasing number of trails. Best bet is to ask at a local cycle shop.

Those desiring highway riding and spoky sociability can join 3,000 other riders for the Great Ohio Bicycle Adventure (GOBA), taking place for a week each June. A different portion of the state is covered every year. During one recent GOBA, riders logged 300-400 miles traveling from Port Clinton to Mansfield and back via such places as Fostoria, Upper Sandusky, Ashland, and Bellevue. For more information on this camping tour, contact GOBA at P.O. Box 14384, Columbus, OH 43214. Cost of the weeklong junket is $100 for ages 16 and over, $55 for children ages 5-16; there is no charge for children under five with parents. One of the treats of this trek is the food, which is prepared by church and civic groups along the route and which is wolfed down in quantity by the riders. Food prices, while most reasonable, are not part of the fee.

TRAVELER INFORMATION

The state publishes *Ohiopass,* a magazine-format annual full of vivid photos and descriptions and dozens of pages of discount coupons to visitor activities and attractions. The publication, which is available free upon request, is of interest and value to any visitor. Call the Ohio Tourism Hotline, (800) BUCKEYE (282-5393), for the latest edition of the visitors information packet.

HEALTH AND SAFETY

Don't blithely go just anywhere in any sizeable city after sundown. Rather, check with your innkeeper or call the nonemergency number of the local police department for advice. Sometimes, a benign club can only be reached by traveling through what seems like a demilitarized zone. The vast majority of blocks in Ohio's cities are safe around the clock, but there are trouble spots in even the most historic or appar-

ently placid locales. In rural areas, if you're not sure whether some specific property is public or private, ask before you trespass.

The usual warnings apply in nature, too. It's not a good idea to hop out of a boat, no matter how inviting unfamiliar water might appear. Nor should you swim in syrupy rivers or along an unguarded Lake Erie shoreline where vicious undertows may be at work. Poisonous snakes, potentially rabid raccoons, stray dogs and cats, stinging insects, field animals, poison ivy, poison oak—all are present in Ohio, but only snake venom and rabies are mortal fears, unless a traveler has an allergic reaction. Persons who have been bitten by any kind of snake should go immediately to an emergency room. Fellow travelers need to keep the patient calm and should never attempt to treat the bite in any way. Any animal bite also should be professionally treated. Having said all that, there really is nothing rational adults need fear.

As for weather dangers, the phenomenon most apt to kill Ohioans nowadays is lightning. Golfers and boaters in particular should get completely off the course (and this doesn't mean hiding under a tree) or the water at the first sign of bad weather. Boaters also run the risk of unexpectedly rough water during a storm, even on shallow lakes and ponds. Tornado season runs from around April 1 to the start of summer, but the dangerous funnels also can occur well into the fall. They're more common in western and southwestern Ohio. By the way, don't attempt to drive away from them. In a severe storm, seek shelter under a highway overpass, or in a ditch or depression, out of the car. If inside, go to a closet or similar windowless room in the middle of the structure.

MONEY

Goods and services cost less in Ohio than on either coast, but more than most places to the south or west. Banks are open early, late, and on Saturday; there are automatic teller machines (ATMs) in grocery and convenience stores, and popular credit cards such as MasterCard and Visa are accepted almost anywhere travelers are served. In fact, the two big cards are so widely honored that exceptions are noted in this book.

Sales tax statewide is 5%. Room taxes vary but almost always total 10% or more of the bill when the sales tax is added. One of the annoying little scams practiced by a few of the newer motels is to tack a dollar onto the bill per night for the use of a small in-room safe—whether you want and use it or not. The front-desk folks don't always mention the added buck until checkout time, so if you discover such a device in your room, call and tell them you don't want to be charged. Unless, of course, you intend to lock up your valuables.

Big-city banks are equipped to exchange any foreign currency in your possession for dollars. Rates are about the same everywhere and there is no bargaining.

COMMUNICATIONS

Telephone
Ohio is home to eight area codes—and more may be coming. The area code in Columbus is 614. A vast area of the southeast uses area code 740. Cleveland uses area code 216, but the area surrounding the city uses 440. Cincinnati numbers are preceded by 513. Dayton and much of the rest of southwest Ohio use area code 937. Toledo and the northwest are in the 419 exchange. And Akron, Canton, and that area employ area code 330. For details on which area code applies where, consult a telephone directory or call the operator.

Internet
Ohio's official Web site is www.state.oh.us. Other pertinent sites are listed throughout this book. Another site to try is www.ohiotourism.com. Both of these sites offer links to other sites on the Web that can be helpful.

Radio
The airwaves are crowded these days. The AM band in Ohio delivers not only powerhouse in-state stations such as WLW in Cincinnati or WTAM in Cleveland, but WWVA in Wheeling, venerable KDKA in Pittsburgh, even WJR out of Windsor, Ontario. Locally, there are the usual oldies, religious, crackpot, "Hi, Neighbor," swap shop, and all-news formats. One pleasant di-

version is WOSU at 820 AM. This is a public radio station operating out of Ohio State University in Columbus. The station emphasizes intelligent talk and is audible over about half the state. Public radio also can be picked up at the low end of the FM band. Elsewhere on FM, you'll find music of varying kinds, from rap to rhapsody. Some of these stations are weak but frequently creative college sites, such as WZIP (88.1 FM) at the University of Akron, or WBWC (88.3 FM) at Baldwin-Wallace College in Berea.

Language Assistance
Ohio is pretty much monolingual. The best bet for help with the language is the International Visitors Council at Port Columbus—the state capital's airport. Volunteers there routinely accommodate speakers of Spanish, German, and French (in that order of frequency). They've even come to the aid of Moldovans, who speak a Romanian dialect. Call them at (614) 231-9610, or visit their airport facility during business hours.

Consulates
British citizens who need assistance in Cleveland can call (216) 621-7674. Should an actual visit be necessary, the British Consulate is at 55 Public Square, downtown. In keeping with the flavor of the city, there is a German Consulate, tel. (513) 621-3447, in the Star Bank Center in downtown Cincinnati. Other foreign nationals may want to consult their respective embassies in Washington, D.C. To find the appropriate number, call (202) 555-1212.

Time Zone
Ohio follows eastern standard time (EST), six hours earlier than Greenwich mean time. From the first Sunday in April until the last Sunday in October, Ohio and all of its neighbors except parts of Indiana adhere to daylight saving time (DST), which advances the clock one hour across most American time zones. If you are traveling east from, say, Chicago or St. Louis, add an hour to the time in eastern Indiana. When it's noon anywhere in Ohio, it's also noon in New York City, 11 a.m. in Chicago, 10 a.m. in Denver, and 9 a.m. in Los Angeles. All surrounding states are on the same time as Ohio except for western Indiana.

Electricity

Electrical power in the U.S. runs on a 117-volt AC system. Which means a transformer may be necessary for a typical European applicance of 200-220 volts to operate properly. Transformers and adapter plugs are available at department and hardware stores, and in some cases can be borrowed at no charge from the front desk or the bell staff.

Weights and Measures

The standard ounces-pounds system of weights and measures is in effect throughout Ohio and the United States, though labels on groceries and other goods usually display metric equivalents. Road signs are in miles only. For specific help with conversions, see the table at the back of this book.

COLUMBUS AND CENTRAL OHIO

This is where the land finally kicks free of the influence of the Appalachians and flattens out. Those who today decry the lack of character in the central Ohio countryside don't realize the elation that overtook the pioneers as they shook off the effects of the apparently endless Pennsylvania and eastern Ohio mountains and hills. Today, the descendants of these pioneers make the Columbus area a beehive of agriculture, business, and industry. Honda chose Marysville, northwest of Columbus, as the site of its North American car- and motorcycle-assembly plant. Ohio State University is located here, too—and folks come from all over the state for the university's hugely popular home football games, which almost invariably are sold out. Several penitentiaries are in the vicinity, too, centrally located. Columbus is Ohio's largest city, growing bigger all the time.

Populations of the region's various cities and towns vary widely. Columbus proper has about 635,000 residents, but 1,020,000 (one of every 12 Buckeyes) live in all of Franklin County. Other central Ohio cities are small in comparison, with Newark the next largest at about 44,000. Lancaster is home to 35,000 people, Delaware has a population of 20,000, Circleville boasts 12,000 residents, Marysville now has a population of 10,000, and London reports approximately 8,000 persons within its municipal limits.

Location

Five major highways run through Columbus, making access in or out of the area to other areas in the state easy. Columbus is linked to neighboring Cleveland to the northeast and Cincinnati to the southwest by I-71, which runs diagonally across the state. Cleveland is about 150 miles away, about two-and-a-half hours, while Cincinnati is closer, only about 110 miles away, about a two-hour drive. Interstate 70 is a major artery linking Ohio to West Virginia and Pennsylvania to the east and Indiana and the central Midwest to the west.

There's not yet an interstate highway between northwest Ohio and Columbus, but US 23 (which becomes SR 15) runs north from Columbus to just south of Findlay, where it intersects I-75.

To the south, US 23 passes through Chillicothe and eventually runs straight to the Kentucky border. Additional roads of significance serving the state capital include US 33, which runs diagonally across the state to Indiana in the northwest and through the Ohio River region to West Virginia in the southeast. Finally, US 62 traverses an opposite diagonal, from Youngstown and the Pennsylvania border in the northeast to the Kentucky border in the southwest.

Orientation

Columbus is the only Central Ohio municipality with enough room to get lost in—and it's hard to do so here. Interstate 270 circles metropolitan Columbus, and there's a tight little circle of limited-access highway all around the immediate downtown area. Important surface streets include Broad Street (US 40), running east-west, and High Street (US 23), running north-south. One landmark that can be invaluable in keeping travelers on track is the Scioto (sigh-OH-toe) River, which runs in a north-south direction. Major manmade landmarks useful for recovering one's bearings include Ohio State University, on the west side of town, and Port Columbus International Airport, on the east. The James A. Rhodes Office Building, at 30 E. Broad St., in the heart of downtown, tel. (614) 466-7361, is the city's tallest building (41 stories and 624 feet tall) with free, panoramic views of Columbus from the 40th floor.

History

For several years immediately following statehood, Ohioans sought a central location for the state capital, which had gone from Chillicothe to Zanesville and back to Chillicothe. Folks in Franklinton, now part of the west side of Columbus, offered to lay out a new capital on the east side of the Scioto River. The legislature accepted the site, which included plans for both a capitol building and a prison, in 1812.

Today's Broad and High Streets, which are main arteries, were part of the original platwork. Delayed by the War of 1812, legislators finally huddled here for the first time in 1816. The town had 700 residents and was a low-lying, insect-infested morass with two mortal exports: cholera and an oft-fatal fever of mysterious (though probably watery) origin. A feeder canal soon con-

COLUMBUS AREA HIGHLIGHTS

Columbus has something for everyone. Consider visiting as many of these attractions as possible—they will give the visitor a vivid cross-section of a state that has seen a lot of history. Most art and historical collections represent all areas of the state.

Columbus Museum of Art
Columbus Science Center
Columbus Symphony Orchestra
Columbus Zoo
Franklin Park Conservatory and Botanical Garden
German Village
Motorcycle Heritage Museum
Newark Earthworks
Ohio Capitol Square Complex
Ohio Historical Center
Ohio State University
Ohio Village
Olentangy Indian Caverns
The *Santa Maria*
Thurber House
Wexner Center for the Arts

nected Columbus to the Ohio and Erie Canal a few miles east, however, and the city began to expand inexorably.

The National Road, now US 40, reached Columbus in 1833. Express coaches thundered east and west every day between the state capital and Pennsylvania or Indiana before the first railroad train chugged into the city in 1850. A few years later, Columbus became a huge marshaling area for Ohio soldiers headed south during the Civil War. Of equal historic importance, the North's largest prisoner-of-war camp was created on the west side of the city. Marking one of the bleakest chapters in the nation's history, there are some 2,260 Confederate graves at Camp Chase Cemetery, which is on Sullivan Avenue between Powell Avenue and Binns Boulevard.

Columbus realized incredible prosperity following the war. Numerous railroads competed for commerce, while nearly two dozen buggy factories made the capital something of a pre-automotive Detroit. The Scioto River's banks

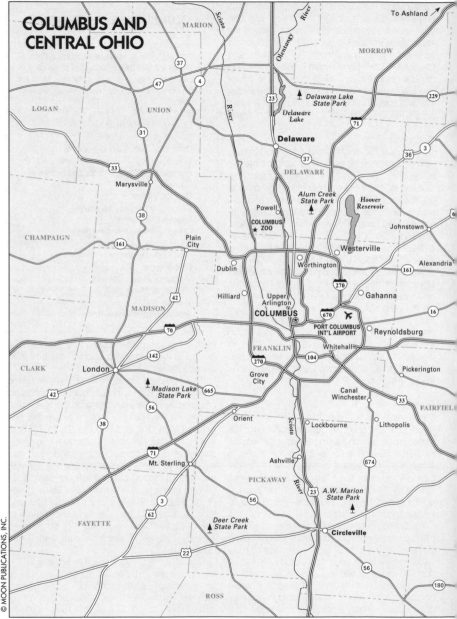

© MOON PUBLICATIONS, INC.

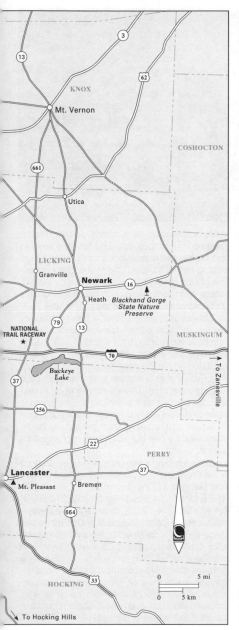

were developed and beautified before the flood of 1913 took more than 100 lives, left 20,000 homeless, and resulted in losses totaling $9 million, an enormous sum in its day. Troops caused the city to swell during both world wars, and the state government, Ohio State University, and the annual state fair all made Columbus the perpetually busy place it remains. From the beginning, the city's mix of businesses and industries was much more diverse than that of other Midwestern locations—a fact, still true today, critical in making Columbus today almost recession-proof.

The Metro Area

But Columbus isn't the only place with a past in central Ohio. Newark, less than an hour northeast, is the Licking County seat. The city was founded in 1802, and is known for its pre-Columbian Indian mounds. It, too, was visited by canal and rail traffic. Transportation enabled the fledgling iron and glass industries to grow, as did the discovery of a local source of natural gas. In a preview of the national prohibition of alcoholic beverages, Licking County voted itself dry in 1910. The resulting visit by Anti-Saloon League detectives resulted in martial law, the shooting death of a bartender, and the lynching of one of the League's hired snoops. Things have since calmed.

Lancaster, some 30 miles southeast of Columbus, is the seat of Fairfield County. The city was founded in 1800 and arose out of the Hocking River Valley. Lancaster got its name from early residents, many of whom came from southeastern Pennsylvania. The familiar canal-railroad-natural gas boom cycle affected Lancaster in the 19th century, as did great advances in farm implements and housing design and construction.

A pair of forts, one a square and the other a circle, stood near present-day Circleville in pre-Columbian times. The structures, together with bones and artifacts, were unearthed during construction of a canal embankment. The city was settled by pioneers of European descent in 1810. Nowadays, the seat of mostly agricultural Pickaway County may be best known for its annual Pumpkin Festival.

Smaller towns and cities serve as Columbus bedroom communities, but they also have a past and a present. London was one of the first and most important areas for raising cattle. The town

the Columbus skyline from across the Scioto River

is surrounded by prosperous farms to this day. Marysville was first known for its grazing land, too, but now is most widely acclaimed for the assemblage of Honda automobiles and motorcycles. Delaware, originally a land office site for farmers wanting to farm in central Ohio, is home to Ohio Wesleyan College and has an attractive and prosperous downtown.

SIGHTS

Considering prison inmates helped build it, the **Ohio Capitol Square Complex,** Broad and High Streets, came out rather well. The Greek Revival building is made of locally quarried limestone and has been in use since 1857. Tours, which are free and last 45 minutes, will reveal the State Seal in the rotunda skylight, not to mention the actual chair in the actual building that Abraham Lincoln was sitting in when he learned that he would be the country's president, as well as various stately lawmaking chambers. The big, old place is open Mon.-Fri. 7 a.m.-5 p.m. and Sat.-Sun. 11 a.m.-5 p.m. Weekday tours begin at 9:30 a.m. and leave every 15 minutes. On the weekend there are only four tours, the first beginning at 11:15 a.m. and spaced about an hour apart. Call (614) 752-6350 for recorded information.

If every famous person's home were as thoughtfully used as the **Thurber House,** 77 Jefferson Ave., Columbus, tel. (614) 464-1032,

more people would come calling. James Thurber grew up in Columbus, spent his teenage years in this house, and used it forever afterward as the setting for his stories. This is the place where the ghosts got in, where the electricity leaked, where the imperturbable dogs lurked in Thurber's 31 books and countless pieces in *The New Yorker*. Nowadays, it serves other writers as a literary center. In warm weather, well-known authors can be found reading their works to eager audiences on the lawn at a literary picnic. In the winter, talented people such as Garrison Keillor or Ann Beattie stop to discuss their words beside a crackling fireplace. There's even a writer in residence holed up on the third floor. The home is open to visitors every day of the year from noon to 4 p.m. and has a modest but quality bookstore inside. Free, but admission is charged for special events.

Just a few blocks from where Thurber grew up is the **Franklin Park Conservatory and Botanical Garden,** 1777 E. Broad St., tel. (614) 645-TREE (or tel. 614-645-8733) or (800) 214-PARK (or tel. 800-214-7275). In an age when inner cities can be frightening places, Columbus has come up with a dreamy, spotlessly well-kept facility that spreads across 28 acres. Outside, in warmer months, look for orderly, English-style gardens ablaze with common and rare floral examples. Inside the vast, glass-enclosed conservatory, wander through flora from the Himalayas, a Pacific island, an arid desert, and a rain forest. Located just a mile or so east of I-71, Franklin

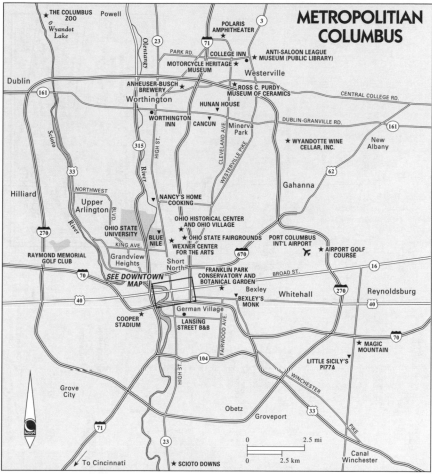

METROPOLITIAN
COLUMBUS

★ THE COLUMBUS ZOO
Powell
⊘ Wyandot Lake
POLARIS AMPHITHEATER
ANTI-SALOON LEAGUE ★ MUSEUM (PUBLIC LIBRARY)
PARK RD.
COLLEGE INN
MOTORCYCLE HERITAGE ★ MUSEUM
Westerville
Olentangy
Dublin
ANHEUSER-BUSCH ★ BREWERY
★ ROSS C. PURDY MUSEUM OF CERAMICS
CENTRAL COLLEGE RD.
Worthington
HUNAN HOUSE
WORTHINGTON INN
CANCUN
Minerva Park
DUBLIN-GRANVILLE RD.
New Albany
Scioto
HIGH ST.
CLEVELAND AVE.
WESTERVILLE PIKE
★ WYANDOTTE WINE CELLAR, INC.
Hilliard
NORTHWEST
Gahanna
Upper Arlington
BLVD
★ NANCY'S HOME COOKING
River
KING AVE.
OHIO HISTORICAL CENTER AND OHIO VILLAGE
OHIO STATE UNIVERSITY
BLUE NILE
★ OHIO STATE FAIRGROUNDS
WEXNER CENTER FOR THE ARTS
PORT COLUMBUS INT'L AIRPORT
✈ AIRPORT GOLF COURSE
RAYMOND MEMORIAL GOLF CLUB
Grandview Heights
Short North
FRANKLIN PARK CONSERVATORY AND BOTANICAL GARDEN ★
BROAD ST.
SEE DOWNTOWN MAP
Bexley
Whitehall
Reynoldsburg
BEXLEY'S ★ MONK
COOPER STADIUM ★
German Village
LANSING STREET B&B
FAIRWOOD AVE.
★ MAGIC MOUNTAIN
HIGH ST.
104
LITTLE SICILY'S PIZZA ▲
WINCHESTER
Grove City
Obetz
Groveport
PIKE
Canal Winchester
To Cincinnati
★ SCIOTO DOWNS

0   2.5 mi
0   2.5 km

© MOON PUBLICATIONS, INC.

Park is open Tues.-Sun. 10 a.m.-5 p.m. and Wednesday10 a.m.-8 p.m. Regular admission is $4 for adults, $3 for students and seniors, and $2 for children ages 2-12.

Olentangy Indian Caverns is between Columbus and Delaware, a mile west of US 23 at 1779 Home Road, tel. (740) 548-7917. This is the real thing—Native Americans rallied here long ago in the safety of extensive caverns. The caves were formed by an underground river washing away solid limestone and leaving behind a maze of subterranean rooms. The Wyandot were the only people who knew of the cave system until 1821, when J.M. Adams went searching for an ox that had wandered and found a cave entrance instead. He carved his name in the soft stone, and his handiwork remains visible. There are four levels here, with three open to the public. Hours are 9:30 a.m.-5 p.m. seven days a week. Admission fees are $8 for adults, $4 for children ages 7-12, and under seven free. Ohio Frontier Land is here, too. After viewing the frontier scene, visitors get the chance to search for gems in a big sluice box nearby.

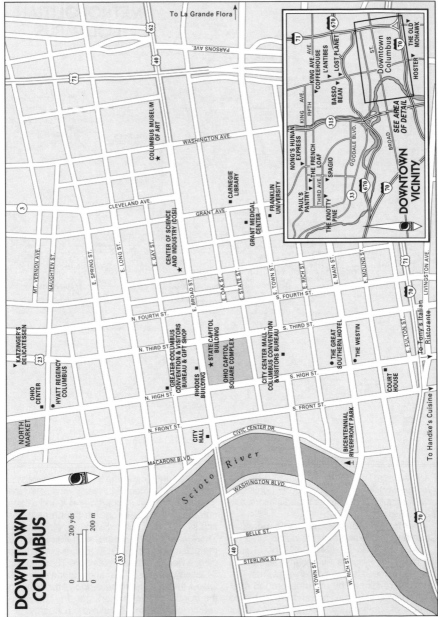

DOWNTOWN COLUMBUS

To La Grande Flora

PARSONS AVE.

COLUMBUS MUSEUM OF ART

WASHINGTON AVE.

CARNEGIE LIBRARY

CLEVELAND AVE.

GRANT AVE.

FRANKLIN UNIVERSITY

CENTER OF SCIENCE AND INDUSTRY (COSI)

GRANT MEDICAL CENTER

MT. VERNON AVE.

NAUGHTEN ST.

E. SPRING ST.

E. LONG ST.

E. GAY ST.

E. BROAD ST.

E. OAK ST.

E. STATE ST.

E. TOWN ST.

E. RICH ST.

E. MAIN ST.

E. MOUND ST.

LIVINGSTON AVE.

N. FOURTH ST.

S. FOURTH ST.

N. THIRD ST.

S. THIRD ST.

E. FULTON ST.

To Tony's Italian Ristorante

KATZINGER'S DELICATESSEN

OHIO CENTER

HYATT REGENCY COLUMBUS

NORTH MARKET

GREATER COLUMBUS CONVENTION & VISITORS BUREAU & GIFT SHOP

RHODES BUILDING

STATE CAPITOL BUILDING

OHIO CAPITOL SQUARE COMPLEX

CITY CENTER MALL COLUMBUS CONVENTION & VISITORS BUREAU

THE GREAT SOUTHERN HOTEL

THE WESTIN

COURT HOUSE

N. HIGH ST.

S. HIGH ST.

N. FRONT ST.

S. FRONT ST.

CITY HALL

CIVIC CENTER DR.

BICENTENNIAL RIVERFRONT PARK

To Handke's Cuisine

MACARONI BLVD.

Scioto River

WASHINGTON BLVD.

BELLE ST.

STERLING ST.

W. TOWN ST.

W. RICH ST.

200 yds

200 m

0

0

DOWNTOWN VICINITY

NONG'S HUNAN EXPRESS

THE FRENCH LOAF

SPAGIO

PAUL'S PANTRY

THE KNOTTY PINE

GOODALE BLVD.

KING AVE.

FIFTH

THIRD AVE.

COFFEEHOUSE

L'ANTIBES

LOST PLANET

BASSO BEAN

KING AVE.

BROAD

ST.

HOSTER

THE OLD MOHAWK

Downtown Columbus

SEE AREA OF DETAIL

© MOON PUBLICATIONS, INC.

James Thurber's childhood home is now a literary center.

The **Columbus Zoo,** 9990 Riverside Dr., Powell, tel. (614) 645-3550 or (800) MONKEYS (or tel. 800-666-5397), is an airy, 400-acre residence for lots of fascinating animals. Three rare and striking white lions are billed as the zoo's "mane attractions," but so are migratory songbirds that chirp in trees above a boardwalk leading to a pool where otters frolic. There are animals from all over the world here, from a baby giraffe to a rare red panda bear. Accessible by bus service from downtown Columbus, the facility charges $6 for adults, $5 for seniors, and $4 for children ages 2-11. From Memorial Day Weekend to Labor Day its hours are 9 a.m.-6 p.m. and 9 a.m.-5 p.m. the rest of the year.

Christopher Columbus must have been quite a sailor. After all, that's The *Santa Maria* riding at anchor in the Scioto River, 109 N. Front St., tel. (614) 645-8760. This 98-foot wooden *nao,* or cargo ship, is a museum-quality representation of Columbus's flagship. It was built from historically accurate plans and is staffed by a helpful crew in period costume. The ship is open Wed.-Fri. 10 a.m.-5 p.m. and Sat.-Sun. 11:30 a.m.-6 p.m., from April-Dec. Admission fees are $3.50 for adults, $3 for seniors, and $1.50 for children ages 5-17.

There's a huge **Anheuser-Busch Brewery** at 700 Schrock Rd. in Columbus, tel. (614) 847-6465. It offers free tours Mon.-Sat. 9 a.m.-4 p.m.

Wineries

The **Wyandotte Wine Cellar, Inc.,** 4640 Wyandotte Dr., Columbus, tel. (614) 476-3624, is available for tours noon-6 p.m. Tues.-Sat. Wyandotte makes 10 to 12 different wines at any one time, all either white or red. Prices are about $8 per bottle for vintages such as Niagara, which also can be found in Columbus-area retail stores. There's nothing but water for children to drink, though they are welcome to a bite of palate-clearing cheese, just like their wine-sipping elders. To sample the wines in a restaurant setting, head for **William Graystone Winery,** 544 S. Front St. (in the Brewery District, just west of German Village), Columbus, tel. (614) 228-2332. The restaurant is affiliated with the winery and serves the products by the glass or bottle.

The **Slate Run Vineyard,** 1900 Winchester-Southern Rd. (SR 674), Canal Winchester off US 33 southeast of downtown, tel. (614) 834-8577, is a newer (since February 1997) and more modest operation. Nevertheless, its 3.5 acres of vines produce 11 wines from both local- and Ohio-grown grapes and vineyards. Slate Run personnel choose from among 45 grape varieties to make their products, and they operate a tasting room and gift shop Mon.-Sat. 1-7 p.m. The bestselling vintage is Winsome, a Lambrusco retailing for $5.99. Slate Run specializes in proprietary blends, with more of the dry wines selling in Columbus area shops all the time.

MUSEUMS

The **Mid-Ohio Historical Museum,** 700 Winchester Pike, Canal Winchester, tel. (614) 837-5573, is a wonderful place to introduce children to the whole museum concept. This attraction has a number of rare and antique dolls and toys used by kids in years past. There are cast iron and tin toys, old-time Lionel trains, rare Shirley Temples and Barbies, GI Joe and Star Wars characters, and a collection of miniature circus toys and wagons. Hours are Wed.-Sat. 11 a.m.-5 p.m. Admission is $2 per person, with kids under six free. There's also a gift shop for children who have become acquisitive after seeing all the toys. The museum is just east of Gender Road and a block north of US 33.

With all the science museums, no wonder Ohio is a high-tech state. Perhaps children become inspired at places like the **Center of Science & Industry (COSI),** 280 E. Broad St., Columbus, tel. (614) 228-6400. Science here is on a continuum, from the streets of yesteryear to space exploration. By far the most intriguing hands-on device is the High Wire Cycle, which lets the rider do exactly what it says. The museum is open Mon.-Fri. 10 a.m.-5 p.m. and Sunday noon-5:30 p.m. Admission charges are $6 for adults, $5 for students ages 13-18, and $4 for youths ages 2-12) and seniors. There's a family rate of $20.

Travelers needn't know the difference between an Ariel Square Four and a Brough Superior to enjoy the American Motorcyclist Association's **Motorcycle Heritage Museum,** 33 Collegeview Rd., Westerville, north of downtown Columbus, tel. (614) 882-2782. Various motorcycles rotate in and out of display as owners of vintage bikes allow the museum to show their proudest possessions. Look for a replica of a wooden 1885 German Daimler, plus a three-quarter size bronze sculpture of an early motorcycle racer. Harley-Davidsons are common here, but so are Hondas—they are constructed a few miles away in Marysville. The gift shop has some nice trinkets and mementos. The museum, just east of the Cleveland Avenue-Main Street intersection, is open every day but for Nov.-Feb. weekends. A donation is requested.

Best "two-fer" in the area is the combination of the **Ohio Historical Center** and **Ohio Village,** tel. (614) 297-2300. Both are at 1982 Velma Ave., two miles northeast of downtown on the west side of I-71. The Historical Center is a large and impressive building, constructed in 1970. It houses four Ohio Historical Society displays: *The First Ohioans, The Nature of Ohio, Ohio: Two Centuries of Change,* and *The Ohio Gallery.* Fascinating one-of-a-kind items make this truly well worth a visit. So is Ohio Village, next door, which displays 16 Civil War–era buildings reconstructed on-site. There's everything from a schoolhouse to an inn to the home of a free black person. Craftspeople in authentic 19th-century attire cook, make cabinets, and sharpen tools in these ancient structures, all of which are connected by clattery wooden sidewalks. Hours are Mon.-Sat. 9 a.m.-5 p.m. and Sunday 10 a.m.-5 p.m. As for the two-fer, admission to one is admission to both. The cost is $5 for adults and $1.25 for children ages 6-12.

There's a museum for everything else, so why not for ceramics? The **Ross C. Purdy Museum of Ceramics,** 735 Ceramic Place, Westerville, north of downtown Columbus, tel. (614) 890-4700, isn't some roundup of crafts but is instead a salute to the slick finish down through the years. Herein visitors will find ceramics used in sports equipment, automobiles, space exploration, heart valves, fire safety, and more. Purdy (1875-1949) *lived* for ceramics as the American Ceramic Society's general secretary and editor. This is a museum for those who like to ingest information without having to play with contrived learning devices or being jostled by crowds. It's just off Schrock Road, east of Cleveland Avenue and north of I-270. It's open Mon.-Fri. 8 a.m.-5 p.m. Admission is free.

Some will applaud it; others may run away in horror. Nevertheless, the **Anti-Saloon League Museum,** 126 S. State St., Westerville, tel. (614) 882-7277, ext. 160, has real fascination. The League's hatchet-swinging role in temperance work is fascinating, marked as it was by personalities at least as strong as the drink they despised. Westerville, north of downtown Columbus, was where the 18th Amendment to the Constitution, which created Prohibition, was formulated early in the 20th century. Located inside the Westerville Public Library, the museum is free and open Mon.-Fri.10 a.m.-6 p.m.

Columbus Museum of Art, 480 E. Broad St., tel. (614) 221-6801, is a marvelous place. There are constantly changing exhibits in all kinds of media. Recently, for example, four distinctive photo exhibits were displayed. Another exhibit covered painting's Years of Expressionism, 1903-1920. The permanent collection features American and European paintings, sculptures, and ethnic art. Artists such as Degas, Renoir, Monet, and Picasso are represented. The facility is open Tues.-Sun. 10 a.m.-5:30 p.m., Thursday10 a.m.-8:30 p.m. Admission is $3 for adults and $2 for seniors and students over 12. Parking is $2. On the first Thursday of each month, admission is free and there is a no-host bar. (Another good art deal takes place along High Street between Nationwide and King Avenues on the first Saturday evening of the month. Private galleries stay open late so that potential buyers can cruise, sip a drink, and view various works.)

For the record, there's a statue of Christopher Columbus—quite a nice one, made of bronze—at State and High Streets. Across the street is **Riffe Gallery,** tel. (614) 644-9624, a free salon operated by the Ohio Arts Council. One recent and impressive show involved the works of artists who had been awarded council residencies. Another was an impressive collection of works by the state's contemporary landscape artists. Media vary widely, from sizeable wooden creations to children's book illustrations. The gallery is open Monday and Tuesday 10 a.m.-4 p.m., Wed.-Fri.10 a.m.-8 p.m., Saturday noon-8 p.m., and Sunday noon-4 p.m.

CULTURE AND ENTERTAINMENT

Wexner Center for the Arts, North High Street at 15th Avenue, Columbus, tel. (614) 292-3535, may be the most versatile cultural site in the entire state. This Ohio State University facility plays host to art and photo exhibitions, films and videos, performing arts, and educational and family programs. It also has a captivating bookshop and a good cafe. There's something of interest here perpetually, be it a collection of silent films with some sort of historic link or a traveling multimedia exhibition making its only stop in Central Ohio. Galleries are open 10 a.m.-6 p.m.

every day but Monday, and admission is free on Thursday, 5-9 p.m. Admission fees at other times are $3 for adults and $2 for children and seniors.

The **Columbus Symphony Orchestra,** conducted by Alessandro Siciliani, is quite well regarded. Playing primarily out of the Ohio Theater at 55 E. State St., tel. (614) 228-8600, the symphony often is sold out but may sometimes be heard for the absurdly low rate of a couple of bucks when playing for students on the Ohio State University campus. Wonderful featured guests, such as violinist Isaac Stern or pianist Andre Watts, are booked whenever possible. There also are pops performances and special holiday concerts. Tickets for the symphony when it plays in the theater are $12-75 for either matinee or evening performances.

There are many other musical and theatrical companies in Columbus. The **Actors' Theatre,** tel. (614) 444-6888, gives outdoor performances during the summer at Schiller Park in German Village, south of downtown. The **Columbus Association of Performing Arts,** tel. (614) 469-0939, presents classical, jazz, folk, country, and pop music, plus comedy, dance, and film in several theaters and in a Rhythm 'n' Zoo series at the Columbus Zoo's amphitheater. The **Contemporary American Theater Company,** 512 N. Park St., tel. (614) 461-0010, has a spring and early summer season, offering such plays as *The Little Foxes.* The **Shadowbox Cabaret,** 236 E. Spring St., tel. (614) 265-7625, combines comedy, theater, and rock 'n' roll in exuberant, original presentations.

A northwest suburb of Dublin resident laughed when she was asked for directions to the big ears of corn. Yet she knew immediately what the visitor was talking about and pointed the way to one of five **Art in Public Places** exhibits. *Field of Corn (with Osage Orange Trees)* is a work by Columbus artist Malcolm Cochran featuring rows of large (six feet or so high), white concrete ears (109 in all) that march impressively across the front yard of an insurance company, framed by the old grove of orange trees. Alternatively, look for *Leatherlips,* a 12-foot high limestone bust of the Wyandot Indian chief constructed in 1990 by Boston artist Ralph Helmick out of pieces of native limestone held together by mortar. The goal of these and other works of art, say Dubliners,

COLUMBUS AREA EVENTS

MARCH

Book Fair, 3850 Stelzer Rd., Columbus, tel. (614) 263-2903, brings together several dozen dealers peddling used, collectible, and scholarly books.

St. Patrick's Day Parade & Celebration takes place in the Dublin Metro Center, tel. (614) 761-6500, ext. 239. There are pancakes early, a 5K run after that, and food, dancing, and music.

Pioneer Crafts Show is set for the Franklin County Fairgrounds, 4100 Columbia St., Hilliard, tel. (614) 666-1512. Here a traveler can purchase all sorts of early American items from costumed craftspeople.

APRIL

Week of the Young Child takes place at the Central Ohio Science Institute, 280 E. Broadway, Columbus, tel. (614) 228-2674. This is a nice idea, as it's a fun way to expose preschool kids to science early, in a series of hands-on activities.

MAY

Medieval & Renaissance Festival is free and takes place at the South Oval of the Ohio State University campus, tel. (614) 292-2324. Medieval performers, crafts, food, and historical performances are included.

Cycling Safari takes place at the Columbus Zoo, 9990 Riverside Drive, Powell, tel. (614) 645-3440. Bicyclists can choose from among three scenic routes, each beginning and ending at the zoo. The rides are labeled Eagle, Rhino, and Cub, which provides an idea of the kinds of challenges to be faced.

The Memorial Tournament is a Professional Golf Association (PGA) event hosted by Columbus native Jack Nicklaus. It takes place at Muirfield Village Golf Club, 5750 Memorial Drive, Dublin, tel. (614) 889-6700.

Herb and Craft Festival, 101 S. High St., in Gahanna off US 62 just east of the I-270 ring, tel. (614) 475-3342, features herbs, crafts, entertainment, and free tours of historic local buildings.

Rhythm & Food Festival shows promise, with blues, jazz, zydeco and world music on two stages, plus food from 25 area restaurants. In Bicentennial Park, Civic Center Drive, Columbus, tel. (614) 645-7995.

Collectors' Paradise Record, CD, & Music Memorabilia Show, Veterans Memorial, 300 W. Broad St., Columbus, tel. (614) 261-1585. Rock, pop, country, jazz, R&B—it's all here in the form of millions of collectible music items for sale. (Also held at other times of the year.)

Antique Flea Market, Powell, tel. (614) 885-6034, mixes local and visiting antique dealers, both of whom have lots to show and sell.

JUNE

Columbus Arts Festival, Downtown Riverfront, tel. (614) 221-CITY (or tel. 614-221-2479). Rated among the country's top juried, outdoor arts festivals, this four-day affair also includes dozens of crafters and no admission charges. A nice preview is the champagne stroll on the eve of the event. It features only strolling acoustic music (as opposed to stage performances) and the atmosphere is lower key.

CC Classic, Town Centre, Grove City, tel. (614) 228-8466, is a weekend of biking events in this suburb southwest of Columbus. There are criterium races and a two-day Columbus-to-Cincinnati ride.

Paper Fair, Veterans Memorial, 300 W. Broad, St., Columbus, tel. (614) 781-0070. More than 100 dealers sell books, post cards, sports cards, historic documents, autographs, and comic books.

Commercial Point Homecoming, though more and more municipalities are playing host to a homecoming weekend, Commercial Point, south of Columbus, has been doing so since the 1920s. Count on a parade, a queen contest, lots of eats (including great fish sandwiches), a beer garden, square dancing, and a midway. Obtain details by telephoning (614) 877-9346.

Rose Festival, Whetstone Park, 3923 N. High St., Columbus, tel. (614) 645-3343, includes entertainment, vendors, and rose-growing information. Best of all, there are thousands of roses abloom here.

German Village *Haus und Garten* Tour, Columbus, tel. (614) 221-8888. Held the last Sunday of June, this is an organized way to visit a number of restored homes. Costs are $10 for reserved tickets or $15 day of tour.

Zoofari, Columbus Zoo, 9990 Riverside Drive, Powell, tel. (614) 645-3400. This fundraiser features food from area restaurants, a nationally known headline act, and lots of local entertainment.

Olde Worthington Art Festival, downtown Worthington, north of Columbus, tel. (614) 964-6078. The village green is the scene of artisans selling their handcrafted items.

Scott Antique Market, Ohio Expo Center, I-71 and 17th Avenue, Columbus, tel. (614) 569-4112. Free but for parking, this is a huge market of antiques and collectibles ranging from fine furniture to military items.

Country Jamboree is at the Hoover Y-Park, 1570 Rohr Rd., Lockbourne, south on US 23, tel. (614) 224-1142. Give it up for local and national country stars, then check out the crafts displays and the activities for children.

JULY

Many communities do themselves up on July 4, but the **Ashville Celebration,** between Columbus and Circleville, given the population, is quite remarkable. This is a place where fish sandwiches are large and plentiful, where the parade is red, white, and blue, and where four days of entertainment ends with fireworks. Virtually everything is free. (No telephone number listed.)

Music and Arts Festival, Towers Hall Lawn, Otterbein College, Westerville, tel. (614) 882-8917. A juried fine arts and fine crafts show and sale has been taking place here annually since the mid-1970s.

"Suitcase Quilts," 1665 W. Fifth Ave., Columbus, tel. (614) 486-4402, is a display of contemporary quilts at the Ohio Craft Museum. The emphasis here is on miniatures, with no quilt exceeding 24 inches in length.

Jazz and Rib Fest occurs at Riverfront/Bicentennial Park downtown Columbus. Nationally known artists bring various kinds of jazz to the fore, competing with the sweet smell and taste of endless racks of ribs, deep in sauce. Place an order at (614) 225-6922.

Ice Cream Social, 160 W. Main St., Westerville, tel. (614) 846-1683, takes place at the Hanby House, a historic stopover on the Civil War-era Underground Railroad.

Senior Expo, 300 W. Broad St., Columbus, tel. (614) 294-8878, is a Veterans Memorial event. Art, entertainment, financial advice, health, goods and services—it all pertains to retirees and those nearing retirement age.

AUGUST

The **Ohio State Fair** takes place at the fairgrounds (717 E. 17th Ave.) in Columbus over 17 days in August. Among the largest and most ambitious fairs in the country, the agricultural and entertainment exposition combines rural and city approaches to having fun. Visitors can telephone (614) 644-4012 for details.

Dublin Irish Festival takes place in Coffman Park, 6665 Coffman Rd., Dublin, tel. (800) 245-8387. The first weekend of August is set aside to fete all things Irish. Activities include step dancing, Irish music, a cultural area, food, and a marketplace.

The Obetz Zucchinifest, tel. (614) 497-2518, is held in the town of Obetz, located on the I-270 ring southeast of downtown Columbus, the weekend before Labor Day and pays homage to the one vegetable that can be grown by anyone. Besides a queen's pageant there is a car cruise-in, a parade, free live entertainment, a midway, and exotic eats such as zucchiniburgers, plus fudgy zucchini and various other zucchini-influenced consumables.

SEPTEMBER

The **West Jefferson Ox Roast** has been firing up in Garrett Park since the 1940s and includes a kiddie tractor pull, the obligatory parade, queen contest, rides, concessions, a car show, and free entertainment. The unfortunate ox produces hearty sandwiches, sold only on Labor Day. West Jefferson, a small town on U.S.-40 seven miles west of the I-270 ring, peddles 7,500 pounds of meat, which is cooked underground. For more information, telephone (614) 879-7373.

A **Sweet Corn Festival** takes place in Millersport at the west end of Buckeye Lake east of Columbus (take I-70 15 miles east of the I-270 ring and head south on SR 237, then head east again on SR 204), and has for more than half a century. This is an especially worthy place to drop a few dollars, since all 80-plus concessions are operated by nonprofit organizations. To find out if the affair is ear-resistible, telephone (740) 467-3943.

Those who look for the messy tomato celebration from Spain will be disappointed, but most will enjoy the **Reynoldsburg Tomato Festival.** There's a largest tomato contest, open to Ohio

(continues on next page)

COLUMBUS AREA EVENTS
continued

growers, plus the usual kings, queens, princes, princesses, talent show, hot-air balloon ride, and more. For particulars, telephone (614) 866-2861. Reynoldsburg is located on US 40 a few miles east of the I-270 ring, at the junction of SR 256.

The geographic center of Ohio seems a swell place for a get-together; hence the **Oldtime Farming Festival** in Centerburg, northeast of Columbus, off US 36, tel. (614) 625-6048. Antique tractors and farm machines are shown threshing, milling, baling, and grist-mill grinding away, and such nostalgic foods as ham 'n'

beans and apple butter are sold.

OCTOBER

All American Quarter Horse Congress, Ohio Exposition Center, 717 E. 17th Ave. (state fairgrounds), Columbus, is one of the world's largest horse shows. Telephone (614) 644-3247 to confirm.

German-American Day, Schiller Park, German Village, Columbus. Events include three-legged races, pony rides, exhibitions, games, and other neighborhood activities. Goose-step to the phone and telephone (614) 221-8888.

---

was to get such stuff out of museums and into public view, where they could be appreciated. A free arts council brochure will locate the pieces for you, but it's almost nicer to stumble unexpectedly on oversize ears or *Leatherlips'* visage. The corn is at Frantz and Ring Roads, while *Leatherlips* is at 7377 Riverside Dr. Telephone (614) 889-7444 for more information, or check this Web site: www.dublinarts.org.

Music

As for music, Columbus offers many, many, rock, blues, jazz, and country spots. A leading site for rock, rap, pop, and country is the **Polaris Amphitheater,** Polaris Parkway, 12 miles north of Columbus on the east side of I-71, tel. (800) 779-TIXX (or tel. 800-779-8499). Recent stars appearing there have included Shania Twain, Phish, Yanni, Spice Girls, Dave Matthews Band, and Boyz II Men. The **Newport,** 1722 N. High St., tel. (614) 228-3582, plays host to the likes of Foo Fighters, Sonic Youth, and Green Day. **Little Brother's,** 1100 N. High St., tel. (614) 421-2025, is another rock and roll palace. They book folks like Southern Culture on the Skids and Big Rude Jake and the Yahoos, usually offering both an early and late show. Their Web site is www.littlebrothers.com. **Red Zone Nightclub** is at 303 S. Front St., tel. (614) 470-4998. Lately, the Zone has been the place to see and hear swing bands.

Jazz has a large and knowledgeable following locally. Musicians play at places like **Hyde Park Grille,** 1615 Old Henderson Rd., tel. (614) 442-3310; **Bexley's Monk,** 2232 E. Main St., tel. (614) 239-6665); **Dick's Den,** 2417 N. High St., tel. (614) 268-9573; **Larry's,** 2040 N. High St., tel. (614) 299-6010; **Oldfields on High,** 2590 N. High St., tel. (614) 784-0477; and **Thirsty Ear,** 1200 W. Third Ave., Grandview, tel. (614) 299-4987. All are Columbus destinations, as is **Columbus Music Hall,** 734 Oak St., tel. (614) 464-0044, which offers music ranging from a 1940s orchestra to salsa to folk.

Blues can be heard all around town. **Brian Boru's Pub House,** 240 N. Liberty St., Powell, tel. (614) 846-1688, books such acts as Cleveland Fats one night and the Blues Drivers the next. **Dolphin Lounge,** 345 Agler Rd., Gahanna, on the eastern side of Columbus outside the I-270 ring, tel. (614) 475-9944, has blues most nights of the week, with open stage nights during the week. **Hilliard Street Blues,** 4704 Cemetery Rd., Hilliard, tel. (614) 771-0062, lives up to its name with blues and acoustic performers most evenings. And **Short North Tavern,** 674 N. High St., Columbus, tel. (614) 221-2432, signs on acts such as Ray Fuller & the Blues Rockers or Shakerman on Friday and Saturday evenings.

Country-western is in the air at **Whiskey Pete's,** 1425 Frank Rd., Columbus, tel. (614) 276-1678. That's where patrons can hear groups such as Whiplash on Friday and Saturday evenings. Another regular CW spot is **Club Dance,** 1987 Brice Rd., Columbus, tel. (614) 866-5920. Folkies will find coffeehouse music at two **Borders Books and Music** stores, 4545 Kennedy Rd., tel. (614) 451-2292 and 6670 Sawmill Rd., tel. (614) 718-9099, both in Columbus; and at **Victoria's Midnight Cafe,** 251 W. Fifth Ave., Columbus, tel. (614) 299-2295, where Vickie offers poetry and an acoustic open stage.

Those who prefer their entertainment on the silver screen can find cineplex theaters primarily in or near major shopping centers. The ultimate Columbus-area movie cineplexes are the **Marcus Cinemas** at 1776 Hill Rd. N. in Pickerington, tel. (614) 759-6500 and its Crosswoods Theater at US 23 and I-270 in Worthington, tel. (614) 841-1600. Both opened in 1998. Each theater has 16 "acoustically perfect" auditoria holding as many as 350 customers. The snack bar sells all of the usual theater fare, plus nachos, cappuccino, and bottled water. Theater personnel, equipped with umbrellas, escort patrons to their cars in the event of rain.

RECREATION

Golf

Why not play golf? Most courses here rent clubs to those who left theirs at home, and golf skills could be karmic—this is, after all, the home town of Jack Nicklaus. **Airport Golf Course,** 900 N. Hamilton Rd., tel. (614) 645-3127, is a par 70, 18-hole facility. Prepare to pay $13.50 weekdays or $15.50 weekends to wage an 18-hole match. A cart is $10 per person at the 5,788-yard, eastside course. On the opposite side of the city, **Raymond Memorial Golf Club** at 3860 Trabue Rd., tel. (614) 645-3276, offers a par of 72 and a total of 6,424 yards for 18 holes. Fees are $13.50 weekdays and $17.50 weekends. Cart rental is $21.

South a ways, try **Grovebrook Golf Club,** 5525 Hoover Rd., Grove City, tel. (614) 875-2497. Costs for the 18-hole, par 71 facility are $15 weekdays and $17 weekends, with cart rental set at about $10 per person. Weekday tee times before noon are just $12. Another nice spot is **Westchester Golf Course,** 1 Bent Grass Blvd., Canal Winchester, southeast of Columbus, tel. (614) 834-4653. Greens fees at the 18-hole, par 72 club are $35.50 weekdays and $45.50 weekends, both with carts. Motorized carts aren't required at most Columbus-area clubs.

Another course, or pair of courses, worth considering is the **Foxfire Golf Club,** 10799 SR 104, Lockbourne (take US 23 north of downtown, a few miles outside the I-270 ring), tel. (614) 224-0399. There are two courses here, Players Club and Foxfire. Fees for Players are $32 weekdays and $36 weekends. Foxfire costs $17 and $21 to walk; add $11 for cart rental at either course. Players is a championship course with bent grass, tight fairways, woods, and a waterfall. Foxfire has four lakes and a meandering creek.

Cycling

Bicycling looks promising, in part because Columbus is flat. But it's also heavily traveled by car. Best bet for riding or walking in the city is adjacent to the lower Scioto River. A total of 18 miles of abandoned rail line and river corridor run along the **Olentangy-Scioto Bikeway.** Built in 1969, the pathway has some sharp curves and narrow bridges but nevertheless is scenic and rewarding. The northern section totals eight miles and passes through suburban communities. The middle stretch is fragmented, with short strips of riverfront trail connected by surface streets. The southern segment parallels the Scioto River and links Columbus with several riverfront parks. A portion of the lower Olentangy Trail runs through the Ohio State University campus. That stretch is bounded by Lane Avenue on the north and Fifth Avenue on the south.

Bicyclists who heed the call of the open road may want to ride all or part of the 52-mile **Dublin Bicycle Loop,** a counterclockwise route on county roads from Dublin to Marysville and back. Parking is available in the public lot at Post and Coffman Roads, Dublin.

On the opposite side of the metro area, check out the 36-mile bike trail that begins in the town of **Canal Winchester,** southeast of Columbus, just west of US 33, and heads in a clockwise direction to Lancaster and return. (The direction taken matters because signs intended for cyclists are on only one side of the road.)

Jogging and Walking

A shady place to jog not far from downtown is the 23-acre **Schiller Park** in German Village. Encompassing streets are City Park Avenue, Reinhardt Avenue, Jaeger Street, and Deshler Avenue. The park's perimeter is much larger than a running track, there are no streets to cross, and the place is thick with shade during warm-weather months. Parking on the street is possible and speedy runners will pass their waiting vehicles every few minutes. As for scenery, there's a statue in a pond of the recently restored Little Umbrella Girl (a Morton Salt-like child fending off a shower with an umbrella) and carefully kept public flower gardens.

Another nice place for a walk or run is **Blendon Woods,** one of several Columbus Metro Parks, at 4625 E. Dublin-Granville Rd. (SR 161), Columbus, tel. (614) 891-0700. There's a 2.5-mile trail through wooded uplands and ravines that make this area just west of Hamilton Road worth a visit. Visitors who tire of foot travel or eyeing waterfowl can play the park's disc golf course or show up at the interpretive center. Call the above number for a free map of the park, which shows locations of other Metro Parks.

Spectator Sports

The biggest show in town takes place on the campus of Ohio State University, where some 80,000 rabid football fans cheer on the red-and-gray Buckeyes five or six Saturday afternoons each fall. Tickets for these games are difficult, if not impossible, to obtain. If an Ohioan asks a visitor to attend a football game in Columbus, the visitor should be honored. The **Columbus Clippers** are the AAA minor-league baseball affiliate of the New York Yankees. They play their home games April through September at Cooper Stadium, 1155 W. Mound St., tel. (614) 462-5250.

The **Columbus Chill,** tel. (614) 791-9999, play minor-league hockey at the Ohio State Fairgrounds, 717 E. 17th Ave. The **Columbus Crew,** tel. (614) 221-2739, plays soccer at Ohio Stadium. The **Columbus Quest,** tel. (614) 873-6556 or (614) 464-2378, plays women's professional basketball in Battelle Hall, adjacent to the Convention Center, 400 N. High St., and won the league championship in 1997 and 1998. For horse racing enthusiasts, harness racing takes place May through September at **Scioto Downs,** 6000 S. High St., Columbus, tel. (614) 491-2515. (The Downs also hosts simulcasts of races from other parts of the country.) The rest of the year

(September through May), quarter horses and thoroughbreds race at Grove City's Beulah Park, tel. (614) 871-9600. The horses are all under the hoods at Columbus Motor Speedway, 1845 Williams Rd., Obetz, tel. (614) 491-1047, a one-third-mile oval that hosts **stock car racing** on summer weekends.

Potpourri

Is it an amusement? Is it a sports facility? **Sports OHIO,** 6314 Cosgray Rd., Dublin, tel. (614) 792-1630, is both. The privately owned park offers the Chiller, a roller- and ice-skating facility; Soccer First, two-and-a-half fields of indoor soccer fields; gymnastics and cheerleading; a golf center; and a fun park that includes minature golf, a heated driving range, batting cages, and a go-kart raceway. Just south of SR 161, west of Dublin and east of Plain City, Sports OHIO is open Mon.-Fri. 11 a.m.-10 p.m. and Sat.-Sun. 11 a.m.-9 p.m. Go-karts are open Mon.-Fri. after 4 p.m. Patrons pay only for the facilities they use.

The younger travelers are, the more they're apt to enjoy **Magic Mountain,** 5890 Scarborough Blvd., Columbus, tel. (614) 863-6400. There is no admission charge to this family fun center, but each attraction costs from $2 to $5 to ride, play, or hit. The attractions include an arcade, bumper cars, a children's gym, a go-kart course, miniature golf, and batting cages. Just south of I-70 on the east side of town, Magic Mountain is open every day except Christmas, Sun.-Thurs. 10 a.m.-10 p.m., Friday 10 a.m.-midnight, and Saturday 9 a.m.-midnight. Similarly, **Wyandot Lake,** next to the Columbus Zoo on Riverside Drive in north suburban Powell, tel. (800) 328-9283, has an oceanlike wave pool, a five-story treehouse, waterslides, and more than 60 rides. Hours are Mon.-Thurs. 10 a.m.-8 p.m., Fri.-Sat. 10 a.m.-9 p.m. The park is open from Memorial Day to Labor Day. Admission fees are $17.99 for adults, $11.50 for seniors, $14.99 for children under 42 inches high, and free for children under 3. Prices are discounted after 4 p.m. each day.

ACCOMMODATIONS

If price is no object, one of the very best places to stay is the **Hyatt Regency Columbus,** 350 N.

High St., tel. (614) 463-1234. The location of this very expensive, amenity-rich hotel is ideal, being equally accessible to the center of town and to the artsy Short North area along High Street. Another large hotel, across the street from the Hyatt, is the **Crowne Plaza,** tel. (614) 461-4100. On the south side of the downtown capital area, look for the very expensive **Westin Great Southern Hotel,** 310 S. High St., at Main Street next to the City Center Mall, tel. (614) 228-3800. This hotel has the reputation of being the city's only historic luxury motel.

Motels, most of them franchises, are at virtually every I-270 exit all around the city, as well as at the airport. Dublin-Granville Road on the city's northeast side also has many places to stay. Some of the local motels heading east along Main Street look seedy and should be personally inspected before staying the night.

The suburbs have some nice accommodations. The one in Worthington that comes immediately to mind is the classy and luxury-priced **Worthington Inn,** High Street and New England Avenue, tel. (614) 885-2600, which also has a worthy restaurant.

Bed and Breakfasts

Bed and breakfast destinations are many and varied in the area. They're also long-lived. "We're steadfast!" says Marcia Barck, proprietor of **Lansing Street Bed and Breakfast,** 180 Lansing St., Columbus, tel. (614) 444-8488 or (800) 383-7839. By that, Marcia means that Columbus-area bed and breakfasts have a nice following and, therefore, are less likely to go in and out of business. The Lansing Street Bed and Breakfast is a moderately priced German Village spot with a reputation for gourmet food. Two newer sources for in-home stays include the **College Inn,** 63 W. College Ave., Westerville, north of downtown Columbus, tel. (614) 794-3090 or (888) 794-3090, and **La Grande Flora,** 820 Bryden Rd., Columbus, tel. (614) 251-0262 or (800) 251-2588.

A couple of others that come highly recommended include **German Village Bed and Breakfast,** 908 City Park Ave., Columbus, tel. (614) 444-7421, where breakfast is served in a garden, and the nearby **Inn on City Park,** 1023 City Park Ave., Columbus, tel. (614) 443-3048. Both are Italianate in style and moderate in price.

FOOD

Visitors are in for an embarrassment of riches when they look for somewhere to dine, because Columbus has a little bit of everything. Making meal decisions more difficult, there seems to be a great new restaurant opening every week. The food here is consistently good, usually inventive, and comes to the table at prices that might amaze coastal dwellers. The casual, modest, hole-in-the-wall places turn out food frequently the equal of the big-deal restaurants. The following represents a range of spots that have been tried and recommended by travelers and local residents. (Incidentally, the *Columbus Dispatch,* the city's big daily newspaper, has a reviewer who approaches most restaurants with his mind already made up. He's known without apologies as the Grumpy Gourmet. His column appears Thursday in the "Weekender" entertainment section.)

L'Antibes, 722 N. High St., Columbus, tel. (614) 291-1666, named for a seaport city on the French Riviera, is one of this city's top meal destinations. The restaurant puts an assured French accent on veal sweetbreads, duck, beef, and fish. If there is a signature dish, it may well be domestic loin of lamb, which comes with a vegetable and potatoes with leeks, for $23. There are a number of desserts, the most popular being crème caramel at $6. L'Antibes is open Tues.-Sat. for dinner. Reservations are recommended and being well turned out is appreciated.

Those who can't do without breakfast will be thrilled to learn of **Basso Bean,** 691 N. High St., Columbus, tel. (614) 221-BEAN (or tel. 614-221-2326) where eggs are served in many tasty ways, from a spicy egg omelet with jalapeños, onions, garlic, and hot sauce, to egg, sausage, and American cheese on a variety of bagels. Other breakfast yummies include fruit oatmeal, a fruit bowl that is governed by what's in season. On weekends, the Short North restaurant's breakfast menu is in force until past noon. An individual breakfast tab is $4-6. For lunch or dinner, try the grilled turkey on a sourdough baguette for $4.50 or chicken salad at $4.95. Open all three meals, every day.

Bexley's Monk, 2232 E. Main St., Columbus tel. (614) 239-6665, is across the street from

Capitol University. Students and the public have been tearing down the doors here for years to get at wood-oven pizzas, elephant-ear garlic, and "the best fish in town." The pizzas are about 10 inches in diameter. With multiple toppings, they sell for approximately $8. A luncheon favorite is a delicious flatbread topped with Caesar salad and smoked chicken baked in a wood-fired oven for $7.25. The Monk is open for lunch Mon.-Fri., for dinner every day of the week, and has a late-night pizza and salad menu, too (until 11:00 p.m. Mon.-Thurs., midnight Fri.-Sat., and 10:30 p.m. on Sunday), should hunger attack while enjoying the bar. Live jazz is scheduled regularly after dinner hours on weekends.

Blue Nile Ethiopian Restaurant, 2361 N. High St., Columbus, tel. (614) 421-2323, intrigues diners with both atmosphere and food just north of the Ohio State University campus (it's very popular with the students). The heart of Ethiopian fare is *injera,* a chewy flatbread made of a fermented grain called *tess* that takes the place of silverware for the adventurous. The bread is used to scoop up mouthfuls of savory stews—here the stew may be chicken, lamb, beef, or vegetarian. The spice combination used in a number of dishes is called *berbere;* Blue Nile uses it judiciously. With a beer, tea, coffee, soft drink, or fruit juice, this is a nourishing and delicious meal. Figure $10 or less per person. The restaurant is open for lunch and dinner every day but Monday.

Cancun, 5701 Maple Canyon Ave., Columbus, tel. (614) 847-1266, is next door to a little Mexican grocery, just south of SR 161 on the city's north side. It serves authentic Mexican food that features such rarely available dishes as *albondigas,* a rich soup filled with meatballs, celery, carrots and onions and *caldo de pollo,* a shredded-chicken soup with avocado. Either is $1.50 per cup or $3.25 per bowl. Main courses include the shredded beef meal for $9.50 or chicken in mole sauce for $8.75. Tortillas, chips, salsa, and side dishes are made fresh on the premises and there is a full bar. Cancun is open every day for lunch and dinner.

The French Loaf, 1456 W. Fifth Ave., Columbus, tel. (614) 488-6843, is a popular, traditional French bakery. Items to covet include croissants, 95 cents with butter and $1.25 filled with chocolate, almond paste, or some other sweet substance. Key lime pie is available two different ways—as a tart for $1.25 and as an entire pie for $8.95. Those who have room can consider baguettes baked in a steam-injected oven, or petit fours or eclairs. Coffee varieties, juices, and other soft drinks are available. It's open Tues.-Sat. 7:30 a.m.-7 p.m. and Sunday 8 a.m.-5 p.m. Dieters are safe only on Monday, when the bakery is closed.

Handke's Cuisine, 520 S. Front St., Columbus, tel. (614) 621-2500, is a landmark for fine dining in the city. Chef Helmut Handke personally supervises the preparation of what he calls "global cuisine." A typical dish might be Wisconsin veal chops accompanied by tomato fettuccini and green-and-white asparagus, for $25.75. Desserts are many and varied, but the crème brûlée draws raves from diners at $6. Handke's is open for dinner Mon.-Sat.

Hoster, 550 S. High St., Columbus, tel. (614) 228-6066, is on the west edge of German Village, known as the Brewery District. It's a brewpub that serves better-than-average food from a menu that changes frequently. Headlining the drinks are a number of lagers, ales, and special brews created seasonally. Those who choose to dine should experience mussels steamed in ale or Texas nachos, both $6.95 and both swell appetizers that complement beer. Sandwiches may be a catfish po' boy at $6.95 or a grilled portobello mushroom on a kaiser roll at $6.75. Up the ladder a bit, the smoked pork chop dinner for $11.95 is a very German meal when accompanied by a frosty mug. Herr Hoster serves lunch and dinner every day.

Hunan House Gourmet Chinese Dining, 2350 E. Dublin-Granville Rd., Columbus, tel. (614) 895-3330, is a popular north-side destination. Emphasizing Hunan and Szechuan cuisines, the House sells lots of shredded chicken with garlic sauce for lunch at $5.75, and General Tso's chicken for dinner at $10.50. There are of course many other dishes from an extensive menu that features chicken, beef, pork, and seafood. Extremely popular as a carryout source, the restaurant is open for lunch and dinner every day.

Katzinger's Delicatessen, 475 S. Third St., Columbus, tel. (614) 228-3354, has at least one claim to fame. No less a person than Bill Clinton chose Katzinger's over every other dining site in Columbus on a visit here—and with good reason. The sandwiches are large and the ingredients are top quality. Try corned beef on rye, a weighty item at $7.75 (half a corned beef on rye is $6.25). There are a number of Jewish and other ethnic foods, as well as a variety of side dishes and salads. Katzinger's also is a popular place to grab a bagel and a hot cup of coffee in the morning. The facility is open Mon.-Sat. 8:30 a.m.-8:30 p.m., and Sunday 9 a.m.-8:30 p.m.

King Avenue Coffeehouse, 247 King Ave., Columbus, tel. (614) 294-8287, bills itself as Columbus's vegetarian restaurant. Between the Ohio State University campus and downtown, a couple of blocks west of High Street, the King is a full-service facility in a coffeehouse setting. Special offerings include an Asian blue plate, featuring several of the facility's most popular items, such as soba noodles, steamed broccoli, snow peas, and special sauces. Another popular item is a veggie gyros with hummus. Meals range in price from about $5 to $8. Having successfully dined without meat, travelers can reward themselves with a range of desserts. Besides many different coffees, there's a full-service juice bar, too. The restaurant is open Tues.-Sat. for lunch and dinner, Sunday brunch, and it offers a special bistro menu on Sunday evenings.

The **Knotty Pine,** 1765 W. Third Ave., Columbus, tel. (614) 488-8878, is a crowded and jolly neighborhood place with an equally busy kitchen and bar. Patrons can order savory meatloaf dinners, priced at $6.95, or chili, which is $3.50 for a bowl and $2.50 for a cup. Ribs fly out of the kitchen, too; half a rack is $10.95, while a whole rack is $14.95. The Pine is open for food weekdays 11 a.m.-10 p.m., Fri.-Sat. 11 a.m.-midnight, and Sunday 11 a.m.-9 p.m. The beer is cold and the people are friendly.

Latin Rooster Rotisserie, 389 Stone Ridge Plaza, Gahanna, on the eastern side of Columbus outside the I-270 ring, tel. (614) 471-4567, is a Peruvian restaurant. Open every day for lunch and dinner, the Rooster makes offbeat dishes such as fried yucca (YOU-ka), a tasty, imported tuber that sells for $2.75. Order it as a side dish with one of the complex, Latin stir-fries, such as *saltado mixto.* This dish has beef, chicken, and

shrimp, along with onions and peppers, over rice for $8.95. Other main dishes range from fish to pork to beef. Desserts include mango ice cream, custard, and a sinful slice of chocolate cake with chocolate frosting for $2.50. The restaurant is open every day for lunch and dinner.

There are a number of sources for pizzas and subs in the Columbus area, but among the very best is a modest place known as **Little Sicily's Pizza,** 2965 Brice Rd., Reynoldsburg, tel. (614) 868-1937 or (614) 864-6020. The "Little Sicily's Famous Sub" includes *cappicola* ham, smoked ham, salami, pepperoni, melted cheese, tomatoes, and hot peppers. It sells right out of the oven for $4.75. A large (15-inch) pizza with the works (anchovies optional) is $17.50. There's a small dining room adjacent, where folks can nibble at an appetizer, admire sports stuff on the walls, and eagerly await the main course. Open every day for lunch, dinner, and until at least midnight, Little Sicily's Pizza would be a credit to any suburb.

Lost Planet Pizza & Pasta, 680 N. High St., Columbus, tel. (614) 228-6191. Not just another pizza joint, Lost Planet is a Short North dine-in restaurant specializing in pizza crusts that are about as thick as a computer diskette. Happily, the pizzas taste a lot better, thanks in part to innovative toppings such as spinach or sweet corn and carmelized onions, chicken Caesar or white chicken, and other variations. Though some distance south of the Ohio State University campus, a few students nevertheless make the trip for the product. Open Mon.-Sat. for lunch and dinner and Sunday from midafternoon.

Nancy's Home Cooking, 3133 N. High St., tel. (614) 265-9012, serves wonderfully homemade-type meals at bargain-basement prices. This is where lots college students come when they want down-home food—including the football team. They order up while admiring walls covered with Ohio sports heroes, past and present. Meat loaf dinner or chicken and noodle dinner is $4, and that includes real mashed potatoes and green beans. In the morning, an omelet with potatoes, toast, and coffee also is $4. Closed on Friday during the summer, Nancy's otherwise is open Mon.-Sat. for breakfast, lunch, dinner, and for breakfast on Sunday.

Nong's Hunan Express, 1634 Northwest

Blvd., Columbus, tel. (614) 486-6630, produces worthy Hunan and Thai dishes, either eat in or take out, on the northwest side. Pad thai, a classic Thai fried noodle dish, a good gauge of Thai food at a restaurant, is rich, with or without meat. It's priced at $4.95 for lunch and $7.95 for dinner. Look, too, for a variety of curries. Those who want to sample a cross-section of Hunan fare should order the combination. It's $6.95 for lunch and $9.95 for dinner. Diners who pay cash or order their food to go receive 10% off the bill. Hours here are Mon.-Fri. 11 a.m-10 p.m. and Sat.-Sun. 3-10 p.m.

North Market, 59 Spruce St., Columbus, tel. (614) 463-9664, is a great place for lunch if you're downtown or in the Short North area. The market features a couple dozen vendors offering food to go. The stuff is consistently good and inexpensive. A curry vegetable sandwich and a milkshake, from separate stands, totals $6. A big slab of pizza and 16 ounces of fruit juice is half that. There's Indian, Middle Eastern, Italian, and other treats, all portable. If the picnic tables inside or those facing High Street are taken, walk around to the west side of the building, where there generally are fewer diners.

The **Old Mohawk Bar & Grille,** 821 Columbus St., Columbus, tel. (614) 444-7204, is alleged to have been a brothel at one time. Now, it's an airy, pleasant bar-restaurant with exposed-brick walls and solid food, including a meatloaf special on Thursday. Other good food, which may be consumed at the bar or at a table, includes turtle soup, burgers, quesadillas, and more. Lunches tend to cost about $5, with dinners twice that. The Old Mohawk keeps its kitchen open quite late—until midnight on Tuesday and Wednesday and even later the rest of the week. Closed Monday.

Paul's Pantry Family Restaurant, W. Fifth Avenue and North Star Avenue, Columbus, tel. (614) 481-8848, is another restaurant in the OSU neighborhood. The students must be well fed, because "we have chefs, not cooks," according to a waitperson. The kitchen talent works all three meals, offering omelets and other items early, a variety of pastas at lunch and dinner, and additional items with an Italian accent. The lunch specials usually are $5.25, while the evening specials are priced from $8.95. Fish and chicken are purchased fresh, with salmon

hand filleted on the premises. The blackened seafood special, $12.95, stars chunks of fresh seafood and scallops and is done here as well as anywhere. Open every day.

Spagio, 1295 Grandview Ave., Columbus, tel. (614) 486-1114, bills itself as an eclectic place. That's evident from one glance at the menu, which may include risotto next to Thai curry which, in turn, is adjacent to a complex Japanese fish entree. Lobster tail is offered occasionally, and the wood-burning oven here turns out a terrific pizza. Among many favorites, try Nicole's pasta at lunch. It's a chicken breast in a cream sauce that includes spinach and parmesan cheese over fettucini, for $7.50. At dinner, go for fresh salmon, marinated in white wine and other ingredients, then grilled and served with tomato chutney, $13.95. Spagio is open until 10:00 p.m. Mon.-Wed, and Thursday, until11:00 p.m. on Tuesday, and until midnight Fri.-Sat., closed on Sunday.

Tony's Italian Ristorante, 16 W. Beck St. at the corner of High St., Columbus, tel. (614) 224-8669, a locally popular place serving lunch and dinner. Tony's serves lunch Mon.-Fri. and dinner Mon.-Sat. Popular at either meal is his fettucini, priced early at $7.95 and late at $12.95. Other dinner items atop the menu include veal, priced at about $15.95 for one of several dishes. Closed Sunday.

INFORMATION AND SERVICES

Emergencies

Dial 911 for fire, police, sheriff, emergency medical service or for the Ohio Highway Patrol in the Columbus area. The non-emergency number for Columbus police is (614) 645-4545. There are quite a few hospitals; **Columbus Community Hospital** can be reached by calling (614) 445-5000. The main **post office** is at 850 Twin River Dr.

Visitor Assistance

The **Greater Columbus Convention and Visitors Bureau** is at 10 W. Broad St., Suite 1300, tel. (614) 222-2489 or (800) 345-4FUN (or tel. 800-345-4386). Visit its Web site at www.columbuscvb.org. The **German Village Information Center** is at 588 S. Third St., tel. (614) 221-

8888. The **Buckeye Lake Tourism Bureau** is at 5192 Walnut Rd., tel. (614) 928-8843.

Things are always happening on campus, especially at a place the size of Ohio State University. Telephone (614) 292-6861 for athletic events; artistic, intellectual, and similar occurrences are at (614) 292-OHIO (or tel. 614-292-6446). On the east side of town, Capital University, 2199 E. Main St., has an art gallery, a school of music, and athletics. Call for events at (614) 236-6801. Franklin University, 201 S. Grant Ave., can be reached concerning events at (614) 341-6237. Otterbein College, in north suburban Westerville, will let travelers in on campus activities if they dial (614) 890-3000.

Newspapers and Magazines

The *Columbus Dispatch,* presented every morning, is the big city's daily newspaper. Entertainment is covered Thursday in the "Weekender" section. Largest and most prosperous of the Columbus free weeklies is the *Other Paper,* published every Thursday. Columbus being a mainstream town, the *Other* covers a lot of mainstream news, at least for what apparently is an alternative paper. But it does have a comprehensive entertainment guide. The *Short North Gazette* is a free, bimonthly tabloid that concentrates on arts activities and the food and nightclub scenes along High Street.

Columbus magazine, printed monthly, is a city periodical. The statewide *Ohio Magazine* is printed here in Columbus and has its own Web site at www.ohiomagazine.com. Travelers also may want to pick up a couple of free tabloids: *Sports and Fitness Columbus,* an informative monthly guide to amateur athletics, with a multisports events calendar, and the locally produced *Midwest Bike Magazine,* a survey of the cycling scene all across the Midwest.

Radio

As for the airwaves, WOSU-AM can be found at **AM 820,** the noncommercial college station broadcasting National Public Radio news, talk shows and locally produced discussion throughout the day. Picking up AM 820 is a snap anywhere in Central Ohio. WOSU-FM is at 89.7 FM. It is the city's only classical music station. A commercial source for news is WBNS, 1460 on the AM dial.

Transportation

Columbus is the largest city in the U.S. not served by passenger rail service. That may soon change, as the state is looking seriously into creating a line with Amtrak between Columbus and Cleveland. Those who have battled traffic up and down I-71 will endorse the rail idea. Meanwhile, Greyhound Bus Lines can be had from the terminal at 111 E. Town St., tel. (800) 231-2222. The public bus service in Columbus is known as the Central Ohio Transit Authority, or COTA. The customer service center is at 177 S. High St., tel. (614) 228-1776. Fares are $1.10 for adults and 55 cents for children ages 7-12. Transfers are a dime. The buses are easy to spot—they're huge, mobile advertising billboards from wheels to roof—including the windows.

COTA has one other service few cities can boast: the transit authority runs trolley service up and down High Street Mon.-Fri. 11 a.m.-2 p.m. Besides reducing the number of cars in the restaurant-gallery-club-shopping area, the 25-cent trolley can move walkers anywhere between the Convention Center at Buttles Street and the south edge of the Ohio State University campus on Sycamore Street. *That's* why visitors see college kids in all the trendy eateries.

Catch a plane at **Port Columbus International Airport,** 2000 Norton Rd., on the city's east side, tel. (614) 239-4000. The facility is accesible from I-670 and is served by these major carriers: America West, American Airlines, Comair, Continental Airlines, Delta Air Lines, Midway Airlines, Midwest Express Airlines, Northwest Airlines, Southwest Airlines, TWA, USAir, and United Air Lines.

SHOPPING

Perhaps because there are large numbers of state employees who work downtown, Columbus offers above-average in-city shopping. Major department stores include the flagship **Lazarus** store at 141 S. High St., tel. (614) 463-2121. There's mall shopping south of the Statehouse on High Street at the **Columbus City Center,** 111 S. Third St., tel. (614) 221-4900 or (800) 882-4900. Major department stores there include **Marshall Field's.** For those who can only shop where there are expanses of parking, look for **Eastland Mall,** SR 317, one mile west of the junction of I-70 and I-270, tel. (614) 861-3232; **Northland Mall,** Morse Road, one mile east of I-71, tel. (614) 267-9258; **Westland Mall,** I-270 and West Broad Street, which is US 40, tel. (614) 272-0012; and the **Mall at Tuttle Crossing,** 5043 Tuttle Crossing Blvd., Dublin, tel. (614) 717-9300. The latter has 130 stores and is Central Ohio's newest large shopping destination.

Bookstores are always pleasant places to cruise, and a couple of Columbus shops are especially addictive. One is the **Book Loft of German Village,** a nicely situated old shop at 631 S. Third St., tel. (614) 464-1774. The Loft offers a free map. One side shows the streets and at-tractions of German Village, while the other displays the aisles, nooks, and crannies of the shop itself. The other bookstore is the **Village Bookshop,** 2424 W. Dublin-Granville Rd., which also is SR 161, tel. (614) 889-2874. Housed in a church that dates from the 19th century, the Village has four million books in stock and discount prices.

Travelers who can't depart Columbus without a college sweatshirt can find a wide selection at **Conrads College Gifts,** 316 W. Lane Ave., tel. (614) 297-0497, across the street from St. John's Arena. The arena is where Ohio State's plays basketball.

COUNTIES AROUND COLUMBUS

NEWARK AND LICKING COUNTY

You won't endear yourselves to most residents if you call it Nurk, UH-hi-uh. Though the cloddish pronunciation can be seen on an occasional T-shirt, laughter about it has long since subsided in this old town. Newark has approximately 44,000 residents, an imposing courthouse square, several large employers, and some of the best-preserved Native American mound systems anywhere.

History
The first natives in this area quickly noted the presence of flint, a special crystalline form of quartz. Used for killing and skinning game, lighting fires, even slaying enemies, specimens of the sharp-edged mineral from Ohio has been found as far away as Louisiana. In pursuit of the very best flint, Indians set up quarrying operations. They knew that flint that had been exposed to the elements cracked easily while substrata flint held its edge. The first Europeans used flint, too; the mineral went into millstones for grinding grain. When US 40, the old National Road, came through here, flint formed the roadbed.

Not everything was mined or sharpened. Both natives and American settlers found it easy to grow crops here—the land was more or less level and the weather moderate. The crops were moved to market via canals. The first shovelful of earth for the portentous Ohio and Erie Canal was turned in Newark in 1825. The lake-to-river project involved 146 locks and 14 aqueducts. Once the canal system was eclipsed by the railroad, Newark became the focus of an 1887 railworkers' strike. Things have calmed visibly since then, resulting in an agreeable town that is a mix of industry, services, and retail shops, just far enough from Columbus to retain its individuality.

The other municipality of significance is time-warpish little Granville, home of Denison University. The school has been sitting since 1831 atop a huge hill, and the bucolic little town, with the big, old houses, surrounds it. This is a walker's dream, enhanced by free handouts at the Granville Public Library, 217 E. Broadway, tel. (740) 587-0196. The tour of the town and the tour of the graveyard will let you know that, next to the Civil War, the most striking event to hit Granville was a flu-like plague in 1834. Unlike the population, the houses survived nicely. Many are on the National Register.

Location and Orientation
The city is 35 miles by car northeast of Columbus via SR 16. A number of residents work in the state capital, though Newark is no late-blooming bedroom community. Come to think of it, Newark may be the largest city in Ohio served by neither an interstate nor a U.S. highway. The stretch of I-70 running west between Columbus and Wheeling,

NEWARK'S LITTLE DRUMMER BOY

Approximately 320,000 Ohio men volunteered for service in the Civil War. They ranged from Gen. George H. Thomas ("The Rock of Chickamauga") to Col. Lorin Andrews, the president of Kenyon College, not to mention the infamous William Tecumseh Sherman. Several generals, such as George B. McClellan and U.S. Grant, were crucial to Union success. But one of the most memorable volunteers proved to be a mere boy. His name was Johnny Clem and he was from a large family of German immigrants who had settled in Newark.

Just nine years old when the South bombarded Fort Sumter in 1861, Johnny told his parents that he wanted to be a drummer boy for the many soldiers departing the state. His parents reminded him of his age and his father said he needed the boy to sell vegetables door-to-door later that summer. Johnny's mother hurried him off to Sunday school, and he did not return. Instead, he hitched a train ride to Columbus and attempted to enlist as a drummer. Too young for the chore, he told the soldiers that he was an orphan and they made him a mascot.

Johnny finally got a drum and helped the men keep cadence on their way to the front. The boy saw action throughout the Tennessee River Valley. In an especially large battle, his drum was damaged by shellfire at Shiloh. From that day on he would be known as Johnny Shiloh. Johnny Clem survived the war, received a service medal, and returned to Newark to finish grammar school.

West Virginia is nine miles south of town and drivers can take either SR 79 or SR 13 north to reach Newark. Travelers heading south out of Newark will cross historic US 40 (the old National Road) just before they reach the interstate.

Newark is the seat of Licking County, which has its share of natural and manmade attractions. Moundbuilders State Memorial (and the Ohio Indian Art Museum, on the same grounds) is on the west side of SR 79 (Hebron Road), exactly where the highway ceases to be limited access on its way to various malls and the village of Heath. Granville is six miles west and Utica is 12 miles north of Newark.

Sights
The **Newark Earthworks,** 900 Cooper Ave., Newark, tel. (740) 344-1919, is most impressive. (Newark is one of the few cities anywhere with important pre-Columbian evidence just off a main street.) The earthworks, some of which measure 1,200 feet in diameter, once were part of the most ambitious such engineering feats in the country. Hopewell people erected them sometime between 1000 B.C. and A.D. 400, yet their purpose remains a mystery. The Moundbuilders Earthworks and the Wright Earthworks are along SR 79, while the Octagon Earthworks are a few blocks away, just north of W. Main St. on Parkview St. The latter two are open during daylight hours year round. On the grounds of the Moundbuilders State Memorial, visit the Ohio

Indian Art Museum, tel. (614) 344-1920, open Wed.-Sat. 9:30 a.m.-5 p.m., Sunday noon-5 p.m., April to October.

The **Dawes Arboretum,** 7770 Jacksontown Rd. S.E., Newark, tel. (740) 323-2355 or (800) 44-DAWES (or tel. 800-443-2937), makes visitors realize just how verdant Ohio really is. Between I-70 and Newark on SR 13, the Dawes Arboretum is set amid gently rolling hills thick with shade. Trees, shrubs, and other woody plants are conveniently labeled and planted so as to be seen to best advantage. There are Japanese gardens, a cypress swamp, and clusters of azaleas, birches, crab apples, hollies, oaks, and conifers. Open dawn to dusk all year round, the arboretum offers a choice of a four-mile auto tour or nearly 10 miles of hiking trails. The visitors center is open Mon.-Sat. 8 a.m.-5 p.m., Saturday and holidays 1-5 p.m.

Blackhand Gorge State Nature Preserve, east of Newark, is located eight miles east of Newark on CR 273. Just east of the preserve, into Muskingum County, is Dillon State Park (see **Southeastern Ohio**). Named for the deposits of blackhand sandstone found there, the gorge offers a 4.3-mile hiking trail through 970 acres of dense wilderness, as well as a bike path. Locks from the Ohio and Erie Canal, plus a tunnel last used by an interurban railway, are overgrown but still discernible. The preserve is open dawn to dusk every day. There are no admission fees.

Buckeye Lake, tel. (740) 467-2690, is a source for largemouth bass, among several game fish species. Recently, the Ohio Department of Natural Resources has stocked the lake with muskellunge, the largest freshwater game fish found in the Midwest. There are a number of things to do here, including hunting, swimming, boating, and snowmobiling. Sprawling over parts of Licking, Fairfield, and Perry Counties, the 3,800-acre lake boasts 32 miles of shoreline, including a fine beach, several lakeside towns, and the national park. Adjacent to the lake is Cranberry Bog, left some 17,000 years ago by retreating glaciers and now a stopover for migratory birds. The lake is just south of I-70; take exit SR 79 south.

Ye Olde Mill in Licking County, is a faithful reproduction of a 19th century working gristmill, located a mile south of Utica and 10 miles north of Newark on SR 13, tel. (740) 892-3921 or (800) 589-5000. It is also the home and the symbol of the Velvet Ice Cream Co. The Lebanese-American Dager family has been making ice cream here since 1914. Visitors here can learn how ice cream has been created down through the years, check out the gristmill, water wheel, and 20 acres of parkland, as well as purchase ice cream treats in the parlor. The mill also is the site of two annual events, an ice cream festival on Memorial Day weekend and a buckeye tree celebration the second Sunday in September.

Museums

From 1895 to 1957, Newark was home to one of America's most dazzling glassmakers. That company is saluted today in the **National Heisey Glass Museum,** Sixth and Church Streets (inside Veterans Park), Newark, tel. (740) 345-2932. There's an international organization devoted to collecting Heisey glassware—including all manner of cups, goblets, plates, and serving utensils—examples of which are on display in this Greek Revival building dating from 1831. Visitors will learn that glass lends itself to experimentation and varying production techniques, resulting in many artistic designs. The museum is open 10 a.m.-4 p.m. Tuesday-Saturday and Sunday 1-4 p.m. Admission is $2, under 18 free.

Neither unusually large nor pretentious, the **Webb House Museum,** 303 Granville St., Newark, tel. (740) 345-8540, houses a number of early 20th-century antiques, heirlooms, and works of art. An inspiring exhibit of paintings features the work of a dozen local women artists. Fame escaped them, though several were exceptionally talented. Their work evokes an era that is gone forever, except in landscapes and portraits like these. The museum is open Thurs.-Sat. 1-4 p.m. and by appointment. Admission is free.

Flint Ridge State Memorial and Museum, tel. (800) 600-7174, is four miles north of I-70 on CR 668. A modern museum straddles one of the flint quarries created by Indians thousands of years ago. In it visitors learn how flint was held in such high esteem that native miners were immune from disagreements while they labored here. Objects made of flint are on display, along with succinct explanations of how ancient people used weapons and other objects to best advantage. Leafy nature trails spread out, heading past wildlife-rich ponds that once were flint quarries. Flint Ridge is open from Memorial Day-Labor Day, Wed.-Sat. 9:30 a.m.-5 p.m., Sunday noon-5 p.m. From Labor Day through October it's open on Saturday 9:30 a.m.-5 p.m. and Sunday noon-5 p.m. There are no admission fees.

The **Granville Lifestyle Museum,** 121 S. Main St., Granville, east of Newark, tel. (740) 587-0373, offers the usual tour of a 19th-century Italianate Victorian home, but it also provides visitors with glimpses of old-time photos, shot by Granville resident Marcus A. Root. Root gained an international reputation, and it's easy to see why—his pictures are wistful and hypnotic. Hours for the museum are Sunday 1-4:30 p.m. Admission is free.

Recreation

More than a dozen public **golf** courses are available in Licking County. Rather than recommend one or two, here's better advice: stop at the Licking County Convention & Visitors Bureau, 50 W. Locust St., tel. (740) 345-8224, and pick up a free brochure describing the various courses. "The Complete Golf Guide for Licking County" provides telephone numbers, directions, and statistics—yet it can be tucked in a shirt pocket.

Licking County is justifiably proud of its **cycling** paradise—32.7 miles of bicycle-pedestrian trails. Existing trails run parallel to SR 16 east out of Newark for about eight miles. Other trails can

NEWARK AND LICKING COUNTY EVENTS

MARCH

Maple Syrup Trail is in Dawes Arboretum, 7770 Jacksontown Rd., Newark, tel. (740) 323-2355. The half-mile trail tells the story of maple syrup, rewarding hikers who trek to the sugarhouse with a sample of syrup.

APRIL

All Heisey Glassware Benefit Auction takes place at the Apple Tree Auction Center, 1616 W. Church St., Newark, tel. (740) 345-2932. Here's a chance for novices to find out what the commotion over this historic glasware is all about (and support the Heisey National Glass Museum with your purchases).

MAY

The **Old Fashioned Ice Cream Festival** in Utica, tel. (740) 892-3463, really does feature an ice cream-eating contest, so begin training now. There are other foods besides ice cream and such diversions as antique gas engines and dogs herding sheep. It all takes place a mile south of Utica at the Velvet Ice Cream Co. and Ye Olde Mill.

JUNE

Land of Legend Bicycle Tour, Newark tel. (740) 788-8484. Visitors and locals alike pedal over scenic, lightly traveled rural roads at distances ranging from 30 to 100 miles.

Historical Crossroads of Ohio, Canal Park, Hebron, tel. (740) 929-2496, salutes a venerable spot in several ways. There is a car show, flea markets and crafts, rides, a parade, a bluegrass jamboree, and gospel music. The four-day event is free.

Granville Garden Tour, tel. (740) 587-4490, gives visitors a chance to see what's growing behind a number of glorious old, well-preserved homes.

Cranberry Bog Annual Open House, Buckeye Lake, tel. (740) 265-6453, gives visitors the opportunity to ride a pontoon boat to an island in the middle of the bog that has rare and fascinating plants.

Wild West/Great Train Robbery, Buckeye Central Scenic Railroad, US 40 about 3.5 miles east of Hebron, tel. (740) 366-2029. Travelers are transformed into passengers and eyewitnesses to "outlaws" boarding and robbing the train. Also in July.

Street Scenes, downtown Granville, tel. (740) 587-4490, is a show and sale by members of a local group known as the Creative Artisans.

Civil War Reenactment, Infirmary Mound Park, SR 37, Granville, tel. (740) 587-2535. Union and Confederate forces reenact camplife and participate in a battle.

JULY

Canal Days Celebration, Cynthia Street Park, Heath, on SR 79 south of the Mound Builders State Memorial, tel. (740) 345-1282, is a free celebration of the original site of the Ohio Canal with a parade, crafts, entertainment, and old-time cars and trucks.

AUGUST

Archaeology Day, Flint Ridge State Memorial, 7091 Brownsville Rd. (CR 668), south of Newark, tel. (800) 600-7174, features a workshop, displays, and demonstrations of prehistoric arts.

Buckeye Lake Area Tour of Homes, tel. (740) 928-1410, features half a dozen showcase homes and can be attended in either a car or a boat.

---

be found in or near Johnstown, Alexandria, Granville, and Heath. A real consideration for travelers are the half-dozen parking lots set alongside the various pathways. For more information, call (740) 349-3863 or pick up a free trail brochure at the visitors bureau. More trails are planned.

In terms of **spectator sports,** Licking County is a center of drag racing. National Trail Raceway, on US 40 near the intersection of SR 37, tel. (614) 587-1005 (on race day call 614-928-5706), plays host to some of the top cars and drivers in the land. There's racing every weekend from late April-Oct., with the National Hot Rod Association Springnationals in June. The cars can cost thousands of dollars, last only a few trips, and cover the quarter mile in four or five seconds. Only after paying the strip a visit will travelers know for sure if such racing is, in fact, a drag.

Arts and Entertainment

Malls and franchises line SR 79 (Hebron Road) between Newark and southwest to the village of Heath. A fun place in Heath is **Blue Moon,**

1314 Hebron Rd., tel. (740) 522-6878, an unpretentious joint that sometimes offers live rock music in a big, insulated room lined with picnic tables attached to the back of the bar. They'll even serve homecooked meals to folks who like the music so much they may have neglected to dine. Another place for tunes in Newark is **The Islands,** 269 Deo Dr., tel. (740) 366-3287. Local standout Matt Avery plays here and elsewhere, and everything from blues/funk to classic rock is scheduled for Friday and Saturday. Farther south in Heath, check out **Chubby's Country Palace,** 565 Industrial Parkway, tel. (740) 522-1303. There's country-western music live Tues.-Sun. evening, with dance lessons 7:30-9:30 p.m. every night but Saturday.

Accommodations

Best Western Newark Inn, 50 N. 2nd St., tel. (740) 349-8411, is a couple of blocks east of the courthouse in the downtown area. It's moderately priced and includes a restaurant and bar. Four facilities are on SR 79 (Hebron Road), which runs between Newark and I-70, nine miles south. They are the **Holiday Inn,** 733 Hebron Rd., tel. (740) 522-1165, the **Hometown Inn** 1266 Hebron Rd., tel. (740) 522-6112, **Howard Johnson Plaza,** 775 Hebron Rd., tel. (740) 522-3191, and the **Star Lite Motel,** 1342 Hebron Rd., tel. (740) 522-3207. Outside of town, **Cherry Valley Lodge,** 2299 Cherry Valley Rd. SE, tel. (740) 788-1200, offers sumptuous, rural splendor in a very expensive resort setting. Amenities include an indoor and an outdoor pool, a golf course, and a restaurant. Back within city limits, look for the **Newark Budget Inn** at 176 W. Church St., tel. (740) 345-9721, or the **University Inn** at 1225 W. Church St., call (740) 344-2136.

There is one bed and breakfast in the immediate Newark area. **Pitzer-Cooper House** is at 6019 White Chapel Rd. SE, tel. (740) 323-2680, between SR 13 and SR 79. For a B&B in Granville, consider the **Porch House,** 241 E. Maple St., tel. (740) 587-1995 or (800) 587-1995. Aptly named, the facility has a wraparound porch and carries a moderate pricetag.

One other accommodation should be noted: the **Pudding House Bed and Breakfast for Writers,** 60 N. Main St., Johnstown, tel. (740) 967-6060, gives a visitor the chance to be a writer or to act like one. This refuge was created for writers, teachers, and others so that they could sit on a jumbo veranda and rock, evidently to get their creative juices flowing. There's a library here, and the absence of children, pets, and smokers should assist concentration. The facility is moderately priced and requires a reservation and a deposit.

Camping can be had at **Hidden Hill,** 3246 Loper Rd. NE, Newark, tel. (740) 763-2750. Look for camping accommodations, too, at **Lazy R Campground,** 2340 Dry Creek Rd. NE, Granville, tel. (740) 366-4385.

Food

The **Buxton Inn,** 313 E. Broadway, Granville, tel. (740) 587-0001, is a wonderfully picturesque place to stay. It's also a good place to dine, with six distinct dining rooms and a tavern. Guests only enjoy the continental breakfast Mon.-Fri. and the full breakfast Saturday or the Sunday brunch. For lunch and dinner, the public is welcome. Luncheon favorites include chicken supreme at $6.95 or seafood Chesapeake at $7.25. At dinner, consider chicken Victoria. It's a fresh breast stuffed with ham and cheese over a bed of rice with a tomato-mushroom-garlic sauce for $12.95. Another evening favorite is a rich seafood combo of crab, clams, and shrimp, baked in a seashell, for $16.95. Last but not least, desserts include a three-layer chocoate mousse cake for $4.25. It's served with real whipped cream.

Just across the street from the Buxton is the **Granville Inn,** 314 E. Broadway, Granville, tel. (740) 587-3333. The same rule applies here: guests only for breakfast, everyone welcome at lunch and dinner. Here, there's a luncheon buffet for $8.75, plus a range of menu items. One popular menu treat is French dip, consisting of shaved prime rib on a portion of French loaf with potato and salad for $8.50. From 5-6:30 p.m. there are four early-bird items every night priced $9.95-11.95. Most popular is the $11.95 prime rib. Later, diners enjoy such standbys as New York strip steak, served with potato, vegetable of the day, salad, and homemade raisin bread for $21.95. Still hungry? Try the walnut pie, $3.50 per slice.

Information and Services

The non-emergency telephone number for the Newark police is (740) 349-6709. Reach the local hospital, Licking Memorial Health Systems, at (740) 344-0331. The Newark post office is at 70 E. Church St.

The **Licking County Convention and Visitors Bureau** is in Newark at 50 W. Locust St., just off SR 16 in the downtown area, tel. (740) 345-8224 or (800) 589-8224. For information about campus activities at Denison University, telephone (740) 587-6266.

Newark stays on top of things through the *Advocate,* published weekday evenings and weekend mornings. The Thursday entertainment section features upcoming events.

LANCASTER AND FAIRFIELD COUNTY

Mount Pleasant, a 250-foot rock outcrop, overlooks Lancaster, a town of about 35,000 residents and dozens of picturesque old houses. Many of the houses are on a free map available from the visitors and convention bureau. The city also can be considered a jumping-off point for the Hocking Hills, which begin less than 20 miles southeast.

Museums

Lancaster has a pair of historic dwellings less than two blocks from each other. The **Sherman House Museum,** 137 E. Main St., tel. (740) 654-9923, is the birthplace of both that scourge of the South, Civil War Union General William Tecumseh Sherman and his younger brother, U.S. Senator John Sherman, sponsor of the 1891 Sherman Antitrust Act. The Sherman dwelling is a squarish, two-story frame structure with a wide front porch. The **Georgian Museum,** 105 E. Wheeling St., tel. (740) 654-9923, is larger, being a multi-columned mansion that dates from 1832. It has been restored so as to show period furnishings to best advantage. Both museums are open April 1 to mid-December, Tues.-Sun. 1-4 p.m. Admission fees are $2.50 for adults ($4 for both) and $1 for students ages 6-18 ($1.50 for both). Tours last approximately 45 minutes.

Accommodations

The **Stratford Inn Tea Room** is a bed and breakfast at 44 E. Columbus St., Lithopolis, south of Canal Winchester, tel. (614) 837-5724. Other B&B destinations include **Barbara's Country Bed & Breakfast and Honeymoon Retreat,** 3705 Crumley Rd., Lancaster, tel. (740) 687-1689, and **Canal View Bed & Breakfast,** 710 Canal Rd., Baltimore, tel. (740) 862-4022 or (800) 683-1999. Barbara runs a large, sumptuous, and expensive-to-luxurious place, while the folks at Canal View offer a separate house at a moderate rate. West of Lancaster six miles is **Butterfly Inn,** 6695 Lancaster-Circleville Rd., tel. (614) 654-7654. The rambling ranch house offers moderate rates.

While there are many camping accommodations south a ways in the Hocking Hills, don't overlook **Lancaster Camp Ground,** 2151 W. Fair Ave., Lancaster, tel. (740) 653-2119. This pleasant destination has nature trails, summer programs, and a swimming pool.

Food

Annie's Cheesecake and Tea Room, 539 E. Main St., Lancaster, tel. (740) 654-3692. Annie's specialties include homemade bread and rolls, soups, and sandwiches served in what is a combination tea room and carryout. Best of all, there are 25 cheesecake flavors—a find a New Yorker might have thought impossible in the heartland. Entrees range from $2.95 to $6.25 and might be any of several sandwiches or salads. Cheesecake prices are $3.25 per slice and either $12 or $23 for the whole thing, depending on whether an eight-inch or a 10-inch cake is specified. The tea room is open Mon.-Fri. 7 a.m.-2:30 p.m. and Saturday 8 a.m.-2:30 p.m. The sandwich shop has the same hours but is open till 6 p.m. during the week.

Shopping

The tiny village of **Bremen,** seven miles east of Lancaster, is the site of the Olde Farm Market, every Fri.-Sat. 9 a.m.-5 p.m. The Mennonite-owned and operated facility located at the SR 37/664 junction sells a raft of goods including pies, jams, jellies, blacksmith wares, furniture, quilts, and more. For information, call (740) 569-9213 or (800) 626-1296. Another nice out-of-the-way place to shop is tiny **Lithopolis,** west off US

LANCASTER AND FAIRFIELD COUNTY EVENTS

FEBRUARY

Antiques Show, Fairfield Career Center, SR 33 at Coonpath Rd., Lancaster, tel. (740) 681-1997, offers folk art, jewelry, prints, and more by 25 new and returning dealers.

MAY

Fairfield Heritage Association Pilgrimage takes place all over the county and involves touring historic and artistic homes and buildings. Call (740) 654-9923 for details.

Lancaster Old Car Club Spring Show, Fairfield County Fairgrounds, 157 E. Fair Ave., Lancaster, tel. (740) 654-8104, will get a visitor's motor running. There are judged antique, classic, and hot rod cars on display, plus a parts swap meet and a steam tractor and engine show.

JULY

Lancaster Festival, tel. (740) 687-4808, takes place at various sites over a 12-day period. Look for art, classical music, guest artists, dance, theater, jazz concerts, and a number of special cultural events for children.

AUGUST

Zane Square Festival, Main and Broad Streets, Lancaster, tel. (740) 687-6651, is an artsy couple of days. It features fine artists and skilled craftspeople showing and selling their works to the tune of live musical entertainment.

---

33 in the northwest corner of Fairfield County. Stores there include antiques dealers, a tea room, a couple of herb sources, and a general store.

Information and Services

In an emergency, call 911. The non-emergency number for Lancaster police is (740) 687-6680. The telephone number for Fairfield Medical Center is (740) 687-8000. The post office in Lancaster is at 204 S. Broad St.

The *Lancaster Eagle-Gazette* comes out weekday evenings and Saturday morning. Entertainment is featured on Thursday.

The **Fairfield Visitors & Convention Bureau** is at 109 N. Broad St. Call them at (740) 653-8251.

CIRCLEVILLE AND PICKAWAY COUNTY

Hopewell Indians were Circleville's first residents. Around A.D. 900-1100, the Hopewell constructed a vast mound and, next to it, a square, fortress-like compound. Within the compound were several smaller mounds. Overgrown but still discernible, this square-circle combination intrigued early European settlers. Circleville was laid out in a circle (hence the town's name), with streets radiating from the mound and encircling it in parallel fashion. By the middle of the 19th century, however, most appreciation of the Hopewell remnants had been lost, and the town was reconfigured in the familiar square-block pattern. This is a community that has served as a rendezvous for farmers growing crops on fertile glacial till soil, particularly west of the city. The Ohio and Erie Canal met the Scioto River near Circleville.

Museums

Ted Lewis Museum, 133 W. Main St., Circleville, tel. (740) 477-3630, is a salute to a vaudeville trouper and the town's most famous son. Ted Lewis was born here in 1890, the son of people who owned a dress shop. He got his showbiz start singing in the local movie house, quickly making the transition to New York City. Along the way Lewis acquired a clarinet and a battered top hat, both of which were used in performing before seven U.S. presidents. The song-and-dance man died in 1971 at the age of 81 and is buried in Circleville. The museum, filled with mementos, has a theater where videotapes of the performer can be seen. It's open Fri.-Sat. 1-5 p.m., and other times by special arrangement.

Green's Heritage Museum and Village, SR 762 and Thrailkill Rd., Orient, tel. (614) 877-4254, is a nice contrast to the salute to Ted Lewis. It's a spacious outdoor re-creation of a number of old-time Ohio endeavors. Included on the property are a smokehouse, a railroad depot, a caboose, a White Castle restaurant building saved from the wrecker's ball, an old-time filling station, and other authentic structures that were moved here. Located a few miles east of I-71, the museum's hours are 9 a.m.-5 p.m.

most days, and the staff tries to accommodate travelers if they're a bit early or late. Admission $2.59 for adults and $1 for children.

Small Town Capital of Ohio Museum, 34 Long St., Ashville, one mile east of SR 23, tel. (740) 983-6367, is housed in the last of the Scioto Valley Railroad's stations to be constucted—the date was 1875. Inside there is an award-winning collection of local history, nostalgia, memorabilia, and downright exaggeration. The famous, the not-so-famous, and the infamous are catalogued, from the dog that voted Republican to a traffic light that helped local drivers anticipate the green. Open Tues.-Fri. 1-3 p.m., Saturday 10 a.m.-3 p.m., April-Nov., the museum is free of charge.

Recreation
Deer Creek State Park, 20635 Waterloo Rd., Mt. Sterling, on SR 207 off I-62, tel. (740) 869-3124, is on Pickaway County's western border. Deer Creek Lake, which covers more than 1,200 acres, was created in 1968 with the completion of a dam; the park opened in 1974. There are 232 campsites, 25 cabins, 1,700 feet of swimming beach, seven miles of hiking trails, 14 miles of bridle trails, and no limit on the size of a boat engine. The big attraction here is the lodge, which has 110 guest rooms. An innovative solar energy system helps heat the resort, which has a restaurant, outdoor pools, a sauna, a whirlpool, an exercise room, and a 350-acre golf course.

The course is open to non-lodge residents and is marked by 10 ponds and 52 sandtraps.

A modest state park with panache is **A.W. Marion State Park,** just northeast of Circleville on SR 188, tel. (740) 869-3124. Overshadowed by nearby Deer Creek State Park, Marion is a nice combination of woods and water totaling 450 acres. This is said to be Ohio's richest land, reason enough for the ancient Adena people to have settled in the area. Today, with Hargus Lake, created by damming Hargus Creek, there's camping, boating, hunting, fishing, hiking, picnicking and 60 campsites.

Accommodations
Deer Creek Resort and Conference Center, a state park facility at 22300 State Park Rd., Mt. Sterling, tel. (800) 282-7275, has 110 rooms, 25 two-bedroom cabins, two swimming pools, and lakeside dining. Prices are expensive. Good bets for motels include **Comfort Inn,** 24571 US 23, Circleville, tel. (740) 477-6116, and **TraveLodge,** 24701 US 23, Circleville, tel. (800) 255-3050. Both are moderately priced.

Several bed and breakfast operations in the Circleville area thrive here. They include **Braeburn Farm Bed and Breakfast,** 6768 Zane Trail Rd., Circleville, tel. (740) 474-7086, south of Circleville and east of SR 23; the **Castle Inn,** 610 S. Court St., downtown Circleville tel. (740) 477-3986, ext. 102; the **Fireside Inn,** 428 E. Main St., Circleville, tel. (740) 474-6640; and **Penguin**

Circleville courthouse

CIRCLEVILLE AND PICKAWAY COUNTY EVENTS

MAY

Deer Creek Dam Days, tel. (740) 986-6535, takes place in Williamsport, eight miles west of Circleville on US 22. Look for parades, a midway, arts, crafts, a flea market, a queen, and food, all on the banks of Deer Creek, which runs through town.

SEPTEMBER

Tofu or not tofu, that is the question. It can be asked at the **American Soya Festival,** held annually in Amanda, 10 miles east of Circleville. Considering the widespread use of soybeans, perhaps it's amazing that this is the only such fest in the entire country. Look for four days of activity, from a queen contest to a bean-spitting event to soybeany foods. For information, write to the festival at P.O. Box 7, Amanda, OH 43102.

Farm Heritage Days, Green's Heritage Museum, 10530 Thrailkill Rd., Orient, tel. (740) 877-4254, is a mix of crafts, wheat threshing, antique carriages and farm machinery on display.

OCTOBER

Circleville Pumpkin Show, tel. (740) 474-7000, is a big deal. The four-day affair is the oldest festival in the state, having observed its 92nd anniversary in 1998. The variety of pumpkin-related food alone is worth a visit, as are all the things one can do with the oversize orange produce. There are several parades, a pumpkin queen, hog calling, and pie eating, with an estimated 400,000 in attendance.

Crossing, 3291 SR 56 West, Circleville, tel. (740) 477-6222 or (800) PENGUIN (tel. 800-736-4846). Braeburn is in the high-moderate range; Castle Inn and Penguin Crossing are expensive to very expensive and offer private baths.

Food

J.R. Hooks Cafe, 115 Watt St., Circleville, tel. (740) 474-2158, has successfully brought Cajun cooking to small-town Ohio. The restaurant's success is due in part to the fact that folks from Columbus have nothing against driving to Circleville for good food. A popular sandwich at lunch is Cajun chicken, which comes with french fries and is $6.29. At dinner, a pulled-pork platter is $8.99. Should there be room, a most pleasing dessert is chocolate chip ice cream with raspberry sauce for $3.49. J.R. Hooks is open Mon.-Thurs. 11 a.m.-11 p.m., Fri.-Sat. 11 a.m.-midnight.

Wittich's, 117 W. High St., Circleville, tel. (740) 474-3313, is the kind of place to take the kids if they've been behaving lately. It's a candy shop with an old-fashioned, 14-seat soda fountain. Besides hand-dipped chocolates and other candies, the nation's oldest family-owned and -operated confectionery (since 1840) creates shakes, sodas, sundaes, cones, and dishes of ice cream. Wittich's is open Mon.-Sat. May-Oct., 9 a.m.-9 p.m.; Nov.-Dec., 9 a.m.-6 p.m.; and Jan.-April, 9 a.m.-5 p.m.

Media

The *Circleville Herald* greets readers weekday evenings and Saturday mornings.

MADISON AND UNION COUNTIES

This is farm country, among the state's best. The eastern edges of these counties are fast becoming developed by Columbus residents who want more room for children, a dog, or a garden.

For recreational opportunities, **Madison Lake State Park,** 4860 E. Park Dr., London, tel. (740) 869-3124, is an unassuming little place with a fishing lake and a swimming beach. The phone rings at Deer Creek State Park, which gives an idea that this is not heavily used. Only electric motors are permitted on the 106-acre lake, and the most in-demand facility is one of two fancy shelters, used by folks enjoying their family reunions. If it appears that there are lots of people out and about on a warm weekend, Madison Lake would be a good park in which to stop.

Accommodations and Food

Winchester House Bed and Breakfast, 122 N. Main St., London, tel. (740) 852-0499, has a sauna, hot tub, and jacuzzi and is moderately priced. The town of London is located at the junction of US 42 and SR 38.

Der Dutchman, 445 S. Jefferson Ave., Plain City, at the junction of US 42 and SR 161, tel.

(614) 873-3414. Travelers seem to have learned of this Amish-style restaurant via a vast word of mouth. It's always packed, with many of the diners going for the broasted chicken dinner, quite a buy at around $6. The breakfast menu is a complete one and the combination lunch-dinner menu also offers such standbys as ribs and meat loaf. The desserts are many and varied, with several kinds of pie always available. Hours are Mon.-Thurs. 6 a.m.-8 p.m., Fri.-Sat. 6 a.m.-9 p.m., closed Sunday.

Media
London reads the *Madison Press,* on sale weekday evenings.

MADISON AND UNION COUNTY EVENTS

JULY

Collector Toy Show, American Legion Hall, Marysville, tel. (740) 826-4201, stars farm toys, trucks, banks, Hot Wheels, racing toys, and other items for show and sale.

Honda Homecoming, US 33, Marysville, tel. (800) 846-0422, brings cycles from all over back to the plant where they were made. There are factory tours, demonstrations, and a parade.

AUGUST

London's **Marigold Festival,** tel.(740) 852-9499, takes place the weekend prior to the Labor Day Weekend at the Madison County Fairgrounds. This salute to the "friendship flower" consists of a baby contest, queen contests for kids and for adults, the naming of a Miss Marigold, a 5K run, free entertainment, and expanses of food.

SEPTEMBER

The **West Jefferson Ox Roast,** tel. (614) 879-7373, has been firing up in Garrett Park for half a century and includes a kiddie tractor pull, the obligatory parade, a queen contest, rides, concessions, a car show, and free entertainment. The unfortunate oxen produce hearty sandwiches, sold only on Labor Day Monday. They must be good—West Jefferson peddles 7,500 pounds of meat (almost four tons!), which is cooked underground.

DELAWARE AND DELAWARE COUNTY

The town of Delaware has a delightful downtown—picturesque, with prosperous antique and other stores and well-kept buildings. Not surprisingly, it's on the National Register of Historic Places.

Two state parks and two reservoirs encourage lots of water sports. The larger park is **Alum Creek State Park,** 3615 S. Old State Rd., Delaware, tel. (740) 548-4631. There are 3,387 acres of lake for anglers, boaters, swimmers, and skiers, plus some of the state's better off-road bicycle trails. Take US 36 east out of Delaware to the main entrance. **Delaware State Park,** 5202 SR 23, Delaware, tel. (740) 369-2761, has a 1,330-acre lake for all sorts of water activities and is about six miles north of town. Hoover and O'Shaughnessy Reservoirs both are reachable by dialing (614) 645-3305 and offer boating, fishing, and sailing. Hoover Reservoir is south of Sunbury, east of SR 3; O'Shaughnessy is southwest of Delaware, east of US 42.

Accommodations
The Delaware area has a couple of locally owned, nonfranchise motels, plus these franchises: **Amerihost Inn,** 1720 Columbus Pike which is also US 23, Delaware, tel. (740) 363-3510; **Hampton Inn,** 7329 SR 36 at I-71, Sunbury, tel. (740) 363-4700; **Super 8,** 1251 Columbia Pike, which is US 23, Delaware tel. (740) 363-8869); and **TraveLodge,** 1001 US 23 North, Delaware tel. (740) 369-4421. The downtown area has a large hotel, the **Delaware,** 351 S. Sandusky St., tel. (740) 363-1262 or (800) 837-1262.

Food
The **Branding Iron,** 1400 Strafford Rd., Delaware, tel. (740) 363-1846, is where diners longing for an occasional hit of western atmosphere with their beef will be accommodated. Various steaks and barbecue ribs are the house specialties. Half a rack of ribs is $9.95, a full rack is $18.95, and a filet mignon, which is 10 ounces, goes for $14.95. (All prices are for complete dinners.) Good food, fun atmosphere. Hours are Mon.-Thurs. 5-9:30 p.m., Fri.-Sat. 5-10:30 p.m. and Sunday noon-8 p.m.

Carrie's Cafe & Coffees, 26 N. Sandusky St., tel. (740) 369-4076 is located in the "Heart of Beautiful Downtown Delaware." Open every day, this is a good spot for a continental breakfast. Besides espresso and other gourmet coffees, there are danish and muffins for $1.25 each. At lunch, head for the deli section. There's a choice of turkey, pizza, or ham *panini* sandwiches for $5.95 (half is $3.95), plus such standbys as a classic Reuben or a build-your-own sandwich for $4.95. The soup is homemade and is $2.50 per bowl or $1.95 per cup. Save room for a milkshake or a malt ($2.50 or $2.75, depending on size), or a slice of cake or pie ($2.75 to $3.50). Carrie's people will even pack a box lunch; ask to see the menu.

Bun's Restaurant & Bakery, 6 W. Winter St., Delaware, tel. (740) 363-3731. Once you're on Winter Street, Bun's is hard to miss. The restaurant's sign dangles above the middle of the street, grandfathered to stay where it is from before strict zoning laws went into effect. Inside, there's a full breakfast menu which includes monster pecan rolls for $1.45. At lunch, the best-seller is chicken salad at $5.75. Dinners each evening might be Swiss steak, turkey, or the extremely popular ham loaf, offered at $8.95. It all tastes homemade in this Delaware landmark, which is open Tues.-Thurs. 7:30 a.m.-9 p.m., Fri.-Sat. 7:30 a.m.-10 p.m., and Sunday 11 a.m.-8 p.m.

Information
The **Delaware County Convention & Visitors Bureau** is at 44 E. Winter St., tel. (740) 368-4748 or 888-DEL-OHIO (or tel. 888-335-6446), across the street from the new library with the shiny green roof.

DELAWARE COUNTY EVENTS

MAY
Delaware Arts Festival, downtown Delaware, tel. (740) 368-4748, includes a juried show of handcrafted, original fine arts and crafts, as well as food and entertainment.

JUNE
Cycling Classic bicycle races, downtown Delaware.

Country Craft Show, 4297 US 42, Delaware, tel. (740) 369-7252, showcases 250-plus artists and crafters in a farm setting.

JULY
Cruise-In, Village Green, Sunbury, tel. (740) 965-5622, displays antique cars, motorcycles, and farm tractors. There's a pig roast, too.

Antique Show & Flea Market, 236 Pennsylvania Ave., Delaware, tel. (740) 363-3353, goes down at the Delaware County Fairgrounds.

SEPTEMBER
Hot Air Balloon Festival, Delaware County Fairgrounds, Delaware, tel. (740) 368-4748.

Little Brown Jug Harness Race, Delaware County Fairgrounds, Delaware, tel. (740) 368-4748. Held during the county fair, this is one of the most well-known harness events in the country.

NOVEMBER
The **Castle Arts Affair,** Delaware County Cultural Arts Center, Delaware.

NORTHEASTERN OHIO

Three of Ohio's seven largest cities—Cleveland, Akron, and Youngstown—lie in the northeastern segment of the state, separated by stretches of refreshingly rural farmland and by a network of streams and rivers. Cities large and small here are connected by various national, state, and local highways. Much of this part of Ohio saw glaciers wallow in from the northwest some 15,000 years ago. The wall of ice stopped about as far south as the northernmost point of the Ohio River, near the Ohio-Pennsylvania line. The entire region, but for a stretch of lake plains near the North Coast, is considered the Allegheny Plateau.

One American in three lives either here or within a day's drive of this area. And despite what's been said about the Rust Belt (some consider Cleveland the buckle), there's an enormous amount of vitality and productivity here. Those who believe in Yankee ingenuity might ascribe northeast Ohio resiliency to the fact that it once was part of Connecticut. But in truth, area history stretches much further into the past.

History

This region has always been quite a place. In the old days it was crisscrossed with animal trails (which also served Native Americans as pathways). Fish were thick in what are now called the Cuyahoga, Grand, Muskingum, and other rivers. Beaver, muskrat, raccoon, deer, bear, and buffalo roamed here. Winters were no bargain, but with preparation, the rich soil, abundant precipitation, and an assortment of wildlife allowed a skilled tribe to survive. That began to change for the Iroquois, the Shawnee, the Tuscarora, and others when the first Europeans, who probably were French fur traders, showed up in the mid 1600s. Before settlers arrived in droves—at the end of the Revolutionary War—colonial, English, and French factions dealt with the area's natives by bribing, fighting, converting, or infecting them, ultimately changing their lives.

Part of the postwar influx of Americans who replaced the departed English poured in from Connecticut, whose boundaries originally stretched from the Atlantic Ocean past the Cuyahoga River. Though Connecticut was soon reduced to its present size, federal lawmakers set aside the Western Reserve—a sizeable chunk of northern Ohio—for Connecticut patriots who had helped defeat the British. Pioneers arrived, appreciated the abundance of cheap land, fenced in what they wanted, and put down roots.

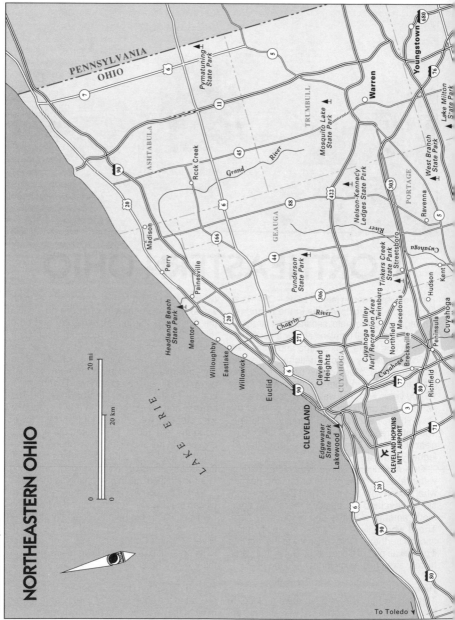

© MOON PUBLICATIONS, INC.

NORTHEASTERN OHIO

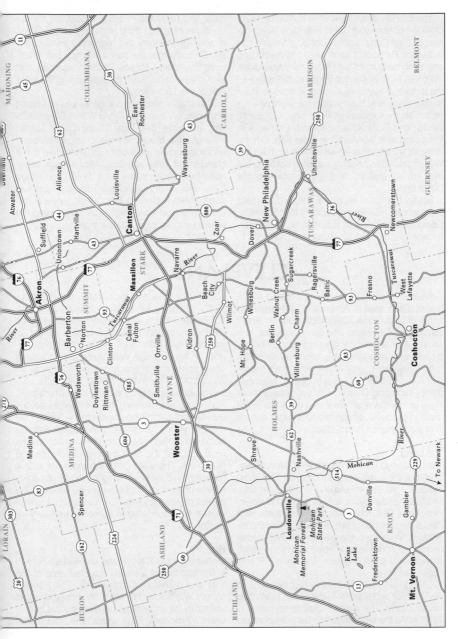

The Erie Canal, completed to Buffalo by 1825, provided northeastern Ohio with more direct access to East Coast markets for its grain and raw materials. Residents soon began to create and ship everything from farm machinery to wooden matches. Neither central England, birthplace of the Industrial Revolution, nor Germany's Ruhr Valley, were any busier than the Buckeye dynamo. Names including Firestone, Goodrich, Gould, and Rockefeller vied with Carnegie in Pittsburgh and Vanderbilt in New York City for America's industrial attention. When the Civil War struck, Ohio not only supplied soldiers, but also armed, clothed, and fed members of the Union army.

But for the usual economic glitches, the area experienced stunning prosperity for 150 years. Generations of central Europeans, Appalachian whites, and African-Americans labored in mills and factories in order to join the middle class, sending their sons and daughters to Ohio's dozens of colleges. So respected were northern Ohioans that the nation elected four Buckeyes President—Hayes, Garfield, Harrison, and McKinley—in quick succession during the latter part of the 19th century.

The state's sense of prosperity and well being started to unravel after World War II. Cleveland's filth became the butt of municipal jokes, Youngstown bred criminals in large numbers, and riots rocked inner cities as whites fled to the blander but safer suburbs. After several especially lean years in the early 1980s, industries large and small retrenched. Today, a variety of companies including Goodyear, several automakers, and small high-tech shops keep the area's productive reputation intact.

CLEVELAND

Cleveland is a big place: the Cleveland-Akron metropolitan area is America's 14th-largest in terms of population. Cuyahoga County, which consists of Cleveland and some suburbs, had some 1.4 million residents at last count. The city proper, with approximately slightly over half a million residents, was where America's Industrial Revolution pretty much began. No other place, including Detroit, has processed more kinds of raw material, created a wider variety of finished products, or conceived a larger quantity of wonderful technical ideas.

The Land

The Cuyahoga River divides metropolitan Cleveland, but there are other landmarks. The most obvious is the rise of land on the city's east side, an area that the glaciers could not grind down. From here, Ohio rolls pleasantly eastward until it meets the low mountains of Appalachian Pennsylvania. Westward, the glacier-flattened terrain resembles Indiana or Illinois, where elevation changes are small and rare. The city is 777 feet above sea level.

Lake Erie keeps Cleveland slightly cooler in the summer and warmer in the winter than cities farther inland. The average July temperature is 72°F, while the temperature in January bottoms out at 25°F. Record temperatures range from 104°F to -19°F. June is the wettest month, with 3.7 inches of rain, and January the driest, with 2.0 inches of precipitation. A total of almost 37 inches of rain falls on the city in a 12-month period. In an average year there are 149 days when some sort of precipitation falls—snow on 23 of them. The average wind velocity is 10.5 miles per hour, slightly windier than Chicago.

Geology has blessed Ohio with the prosperous business of salt mining, thanks to the Salina Formation, which geologists believe was formed some 430 million years ago when an ocean covered much of the area between Michigan and New York. There are mine entrances not all that far from the downtown's nightclubby Flats area, where dozens of workers harvest some of the purest mineral known. The salt is used everywhere, from the table to icy roads to heavy industry.

History

General Moses Cleaveland showed up here in 1796 and found a thickly forested area of big hills and a spacious river valley. The Revolutionary War soldier laid out a city, hoping it would someday be as large as his Connecticut hometown, Wyndham. Four years later, just seven

The six-story silver dome of the Omnimax theatre at the Great Lakes Science Center is a landmark on the Lake Erie coastline.

people called themselves residents; one was a hardy pioneer named Lorenzo Carter. Carter dealt with the Ottawa and Seneca Indian tribes, killed game when it was needed, and generally kept the undergrowth from reclaiming the freshly platted site.

The first Lake Erie steamboat paid a call in 1818, and the city adopted the current spelling of its name in 1832, several years after goods began to come and go on the Erie Canal. The masthead of a local paper, *The Cleaveland Gazette and Social Register,* was one letter too long to fit on conventional newsprint. So a printer dropped the first "a" in the title and thus was Cleveland born.

Unlike the masthead, the city began to expand. Not only were East Coast needs addressed, but trade between this Lake Erie site and Cincinnati on the Ohio River made for frantic commerce. English visitor Charles Dickens called Cleveland a "beautiful town" in 1842. The Cuyahoga River port greeted increasing numbers of German and Irish immigrants. Rail service further intensified activity, particularly since rails were made of steel and steel was milled in the area in vast quantities. Ohio coal, limestone, and water met local iron ore and the results were, among other things, weapons that helped Abraham Lincoln hold the Union together.

Famous "bloodless Baptist bookkeeper" John D. Rockefeller opened an oil refinery in Cleveland in 1863, uncannily anticipating the discovery of large amounts of oil in western Pennsylvania a few years later. Oil soon clotted the Cuyahoga River, spoiled butter at the dairy, and made the beer taste funny. But, boy, did it make Rockefeller rich! He bought up railroads and other refineries, laid pipelines to the oil fields, and by 1879, his Standard Oil was doing 90% of the nation's refining.

The mix of arriving newcomers became more interesting with the new century—as newcomers from 80 ethnic groups: African-Americans from the South, Czechs, Greeks, Hungarians, Italians, Poles, Russians, Slovaks, Slovenes, Ukrainians, and small but vital numbers of Albanians, Arabs, Armenians, and Lebanese brought traditions such as Greek coffeehouses and Slavic social halls, both of which exist here to this day. With these new laborers came political viewpoints that were tried and, if found valid, used by the municipality.

Ohio was second only to Michigan in auto production prior to the Depression, and in the 1920s, the well-to-do moved away from such industry—to "America's most prosperous suburb," Shaker Heights (founded by "Shaking Quakers" in 1889), on the east, and Lakewood on the west, and commuted to the city to work. Meanwhile, the Great Depression hit industrial Ohio hard. Cleveland was the nation's fifth-largest city, and the population of 900,400 included many ordinary families. People lined up at the Red Cross for food and clothing, schools closed for lack of funds, and only soup kitchens and make-work projects prevented actual cases

CITY OF A MILLION (MORBID) STORIES?

Something odd almost always seems to be in the news in Cleveland. Here are a few examples.

- The basis for the David Janssen TV series and the Harrison Ford–Tommy Lee Jones movie *The Fugitive* was the case of a physician accused of murdering his wife in the posh Cleveland suburb of Bay Village. The year was 1954, and Dr. Sam Sheppard was convicted and sent to prison. Retried and acquitted after spending 10 years under lock and key, Sheppard died in 1970. But the case resurfaced in the spring of 1996, when a by-now-elderly man allegedly admitted to a nurse in 1983 that he had killed Marilyn Sheppard. The nurse notified the authorities, who added her statement to the still-unsolved case. Matters were further complicated in March 1998, when DNA evidence apparently indicated that the blood on Sheppard's clothing at the time of the crime was neither his nor his wife's—lending credence to the doctor's story that he had struggled with an intruder.

- It's not an urban legend—the Cuyahoga River, which rises east of Cleveland before swinging south through Akron and heading north toward downtown and Lake Erie, really did self-combust, in 1972. Because the unfortunate stream broadened through an industrial valley just before reaching Lake Erie, it served as a receptacle for all sorts of toxic and hazardous effluvia. Hence the fire. The river nowadays is less sluggish but far from pristine as it flows past revelers in the Flats and empties into the Great Lake.

- What's worse than a burning river? How about a flaming mayor? George Perk was the fellow's name, and the member of the GOP served the city in the 1960s for a single term. He once was asked to open a metalworking convention by cutting a steel ribbon with a torch. A spark from the torch landed in the mayor's handsome shock of hair, which went up in flames. He was not badly hurt, and to this day Perk is a good sport about the incident.

- One of the great tragedies to occur in America took place in Cleveland in 1908. The Collinwood School fire killed 172 children, many of whom died under piles of classmates at exits that became clogged with bodies. Parents, including numerous immigrants, arrived at the school to find their children hopelessly trapped. Unable to extricate them, they could only comfort the burned or injured youngsters as they died. This and other disturbing stories can be found in *The Maniac in the Bushes* (subtitled "And More Tales of Cleveland Woe"), by John Stark Bellamy II. The book is a successor to the local historian's earlier tales of murder and mayhem, *They Died Crawling*. The school tragedy points up the crowded conditions experienced by Clevelanders during the boom times early in the 20th century.

- Eliot Ness may have made his name in Chicago, but the U.S. Treasury Department employee actually spent more of his career in Cleveland, arriving in 1934 and departing, under a cloud, in 1942. As city safety director, Ness broke up much of the gambling that plagued the town. He did so by winnowing crooked cops from the force. His major error came late one night when, driving back to the Lakewood boathouse where he lived, his car was involved in an accident. Ness apparently had been drinking, and he fled the scene. He claimed that he drove his wife, who had the wind knocked out of her, to a hospital. The good people of Cleveland didn't buy that story. When he returned to town in 1947 to run for mayor, their votes for rival Tom Burke resulted in Ness departing Cleveland for the last time.

---

of starvation. Want went away as America began to rearm in the late 1930s.

Cleveland once again became an industrial behemoth, but at a price. In 1944, the explosion of a big dockside gas tank took 135 lives. Organized crime infiltrated unions and began to suck money away from working people by offering them gambling and prostitution that left pay envelopes empty and families destroyed. The Old "Millionaire's Row" of grand homes along Euclid Avenue fell into disrepair—the stretch from East 9th to East 55th Streets became a shooting gallery. Riots flashed through the east-side African-American ghetto called Hough in the 1960s, and a succession of politicians tried in vain to combat the problems.

Gradually, white flight peaked. The city was where even the folks in the suburbs had to come to see professional sports, hear symphonies, see big-time auto racing, experience urban nightlife, view an exhibit of precious art, or hear the din of enshrined rock musicians. In what old-time Cleveland residents view as a real irony, people now pour into the city (which celebrated its 200th anniversary in 1996) from their suburban nests to have a good time.

Further buoyed by a rejuvenated Indians baseball team playing in Jacobs Field downtown, the place that made Rockefeller rich and U.S. goods world famous now gets a lot of positive press. (Yes, the professional football Cleveland Browns slunk out of town after the 1995 season, but they left the team name for the new Browns stadium and franchise in 1999.) One indication that Cleveland is no longer a subhuman industrial hell is that it now has its own environmental magazine. *Eco City* keeps tabs on effluent of all sorts, while monthlies such as *Cleveland* and *Northern Ohio Live* advise folks on where to eat, what to wear, and where to be seen. And the Forest City's magnificent parks, strung like emeralds on a necklace circling the town, can make big-city living not only bearable but downright nice.

Orientation

Cleveland is farther east than Atlanta, farther west than Toronto, and about as far north as New York City. The nearest large out-of-state cities are Detroit, Michigan—170 miles to the northwest—and Pittsburgh, Pennsylvania, 135 miles southeast. Cleveland is served by Interstate Highways 80, 90 and 480 running east and west, and Interstate Highways 71, 77, and 271 running north and south. By car, the city is 470 miles west of New York City, 350 miles east of Chicago, Illinois and 340 miles southwest of Toronto, Canada. Inside Ohio, Cleveland lies 110 driving miles east of Toledo, 140 miles northeast of Columbus, 250 miles northeast of Cincinnati, and just 40 miles north of Akron. It is served by Amtrak, Greyhound, and 10 major airlines. Except for sightseeing boats, there is no passenger boat system into or out of the city, though there's always talk of linking downtown Cleveland to a Canadian site on Lake Erie's opposite shore by regularly scheduled ferry.

Just as there are two sides to every story, there are two sides to Cleveland—east and west. Officially, the split is along Ontario Street, which runs south from the **Cuyahoga County Courthouse** on Lakeside Avenue, past **Gund Arena**

(home court of pro basketball's Cavaliers and a leading venue for touring entertainers) and **Jacobs Field** (home of the Cleveland Indians), and beneath the freeway viaduct's inner belt. Unofficially, however, the mouth of the **Cuya-**

CLEVELAND AREA HIGHLIGHTS

CLEVELAND:

    Cleveland Museum of Natural History
    Cleveland Orchestra
    Cleveland Public Theater
    Cleveland San Jose Ballet
    the Flats entertainment area
    Galleria at Erieview shopping and dining
    Glidden House Inn
    Great Lakes Science Center
    Gund Arena
    Jacobs Field
    Karamu House theater
    Metroparks Zoo
    NASA Lewis Research Center
    Old World church architecture
    Playhouse Square Center
    Public Square
    Rock and Roll Hall of Fame and Museum
    Tower City Center shopping and dining

CLEVELAND NEIGHBORHOODS:

    African-American Memorial Museum
    Cleveland Botanical Gardens
    Cleveland Children's Museum
    Cleveland Institute of Art
    Cleveland Museum of Art
    Cleveland Museum of Health and Hygiene
    Cleveland Play House
    Dunham Tavern Museum
    Lake View Cemetery
    Little Italy
    Shaker Square
    West Side Market
    Western Reserve Historical Society

EAST OF CLEVELAND:

    Cleveland-Style Polka Hall of Fame
    Shaker Historical Society
    Shaker Nature Center

SOUTH OF CLEVELAND:

    Gardenview Horticultural Park

WEST OF CLEVELAND:

    Trolleyville USA

THE UPS AND DOWNS OF THE CLEVELAND BROWNS

Cleveland isn't the birthplace of professional football, but it's not all that far from the sport's mecca, Canton. So when Art Modell, owner of the Browns National Football League team, decided to move his guys to Baltimore following completion of the 1995 season, there was a furor. After all, weren't the Browns the team that commanded such fan loyalty that it had even given rise to the Dawg Pound—the bunch of crazies who sat half-naked in the end zone and acted stupid for TV cameras whenever the game turned boring?

In fairness to Cleveland, the Browns franchise lost money through mismanagement while most other franchises were taking large sums to the bank. In fairness to Modell, he had been asking the city to replace crumbling, lakeside Municipal Stadium for quite some time. The football venue was said to be so aged that some VIPs were abandoning their boxes in favor of viewing the game at home. Baltimore offered Modell a spacious new stadium where he could make more money, and he took it. This prompted Mayor Michael White and others to meet with the NFL in February 1996. City fathers extracted a promise that the league would lend them $48 million for a new stadium.

Modell is bitter at the deal given the city of Cleveland, but fans are apparently more bitter at Modell. Those fans had supported the Browns through thick and thin—and the final two or three seasons had been predominantly thin. Modell wasn't even able to attend the team's final home game because threats had been made on his life. Some no doubt see the Browns' exit to Baltimore (where they are known as the Ravens) as a slap in the face to a city that's on a roll of late. The pennants and jerseys lie in mothballs awaiting an expansion franchise, in a new stadium, with an old name (they will play as the Browns). The city is preparing to back a Modell-free expansion football team in the fall of 1999. For up-to-date info on the new Cleveland Browns, try the team Web site at www.clevelandbrowns.com.

---

hoga River separates this town, which sprawls in the shape of an inverted fan for miles along Lake Erie. The river weaves its way toward the lake through a vast, low, old industrial park, marked by sooty, monochromatic steel mills and is spanned by flaking bridges. It passes the Flats, where Cleveland nightlife is centered, before emptying into Lake Erie.

The center of town is **Public Square.** It is bisected by Ontario Street and Superior Avenue and is flanked by Frankfort Street and Euclid Avenue, both of which run east-west. The city's most visible landmark, **Tower City,** is still called **Terminal Tower** by many of the locals. It is on the southwest corner of the square and remains one of America's classic big buildings. The 708-foot, 52-story building once was the tallest skyscraper outside of New York City, and its huge presence helps keep newcomers oriented. The rapid transit station is at the foot of the tower, as is lots of shopping. Only Key Center, the 948-foot, 63-story bank building at 127 Public Square, looks down on Tower City.

To get a spectacular view of the city as a whole, hit the tower's 42nd floor **Observation Deck,** tel. (216) 621-7981, Sat.-Sun. 11 a.m.- 4:30 p.m. from April through Sept., slightly shorter hours the rest of the year. Tickets are $2 for adults and $1 for children. If the weather is clear, you can see that the area west of downtown flattens out markedly, while the east side is made up in part of a vast and stony bluff. Addresses in Cleveland Heights, Garfield Heights, or Shaker Heights are, naturally, on the city's more elevated east side.

SIGHTS

Downtown

The three most important downtown landmarks are the Rock and Roll Hall of Fame and Museum, on Lake Erie; Jacobs Field; and the Flats area at the mouth of the Cuyahoga River. They create a triangle about 10 blocks to a side that encompasses the heart of Cleveland. Public Square is in the middle of the triangle, and many of the following are within a 10-minute walk from the square.

The **Rock and Roll Hall of Fame and Museum,** 1 Key Plaza (9th Street and Erieside Avenue), just off the Cleveland Memorial Shoreway on the lake, tel. (216) 781-7625 or (800) 493-ROLL (or tel. 800-493-7655) for recorded information, opened on Labor Day 1995 and is frequently so crowded that reservations are needed. The $84 million project, majestic in places and delightfully cheesy in others, has a sunburst made of famous drummers' sticks, a wall where one-hit wonders croon to the curious from their side of shellac in the golden grooveyard, bedazzling costumes of the rich and tuneful, dangling automobiles, perpetual filmclips, and a cantilever stairway to the hall itself, atop this big I.M. Pei-designed pyramid, where the immortals are enshrined. Best time to show up is May, when each year's new inductees are announced. Any time of year there's a chance that Little Richard or a similar notable will be on hand, perhaps to perform, perhaps just to profile. There's a restaurant and a gift shop with a wide selection of costly compact discs, posters, prints, clothing, and souvenirs. Admission is $14.95 adults and $11.50 children and persons over age 55. Visitors can become a museum member, which will admit them to the facility at no charge. Cost of membership ranges $35-2,500 per year; membership is good for unlimited access. For details, call (800) 349-7625. Hours from Memorial Day to Labor Day are Mon.-Tues.10 a.m.-5:30 p.m., Wed.-Sun. 10 a.m.-9 p.m. From Labor Day to Memorial Day, the facility is only open on Wednesday 10 a.m.-9 p.m., closed Monday. No cameras allowed. Preview everything by dialing up the *Plain Dealer*-sponsored site, www.rockhall.com.

Jacobs Field, 2401 Ontario St., tel. (216) 241-8888, is the home of the Cleveland Indians and is known locally as "the Jake." Visitors may think up other names when they learn that all tickets for every baseball game are sold and that they will have to pay a huge premium to a ticket agent for a seat at the ol' ball park. An option is to tour the facility when the Indians are elsewhere. Cost of the tour is $4 for adults and $2 for children and covers 60 minutes of trivia related to the $169 million yellow-brick, steel, and concrete facility. Tours begin on the hour, 10 a.m.-2 p.m., May-September. Be sure to ask if the space-age scoreboard will be activated for your tour. The park is surrounded by Carnegie Avenue, Ontario Street, Bolivar Road, and East 9th Street and is six blocks south of the Public Square. Note: It is illegal to buy tickets from street-side scalpers anywhere in Cuyahoga County, though the so-called ticket agents really perform the same function.

The Flats, an area on either side of the Cuyahoga River's mouth, is some seven or eight blocks west of the Square, immediately west of the galleryish Warehouse District. Besides offering music primarily for late-blooming boomers and Generation X, the area has several restaurants, pub-type bars, and spots where all sorts of entertainment take place. There are parking lots just off Front Avenue on the east side of the river. Streets are narrow and, after dark, it's

the Rock and Roll Hall of Fame and Museum, designed by famed architect I.M. Pei

sometimes tough to figure out how to drive or walk to the opposite bank, much less find the way out. Before going, check out the free *Scene* entertainment tabloid, available at record stores and elsewhere, to see which band is playing where. Some restaurants and a number of popular musicians require reservations or advance tickets, respectively.

Luxury hotels and transportation facilities are within the downtown triangle, as are **City Hall,** at East Sixth Street and Lakeside; the **Cleveland Public Library** at 325 Superior Ave. NE, tel. (216) 623-2800; **Dillard's Department Store,** 100 Public Square, tel. (216) 579-2580, a part of the Tower City Center complex; and **The Avenue** shopping complex, 50 Public Square tel. (216) 771-0033, also at Tower City Center. The latter also is the site of casual dining and a commuter rail station, all under an attractive 19th century English-style glass dome.

By the way, before leaving the immediate area a traveler may want to visit the new-in-'97 **Great Lakes Science Center.** There are more than 300 hands-on exhibits, plus an Omnimax theater that makes science come screamingly alive. Typical screen fare is *The Living Sea,* or, in contrast, a trip across the Serengeti Plain. The tariff for the Omnimax theater is $6.75 adults and $4.50 children. A ticket for both the theater and the science center is $9.95 adults and $7 children.

Beyond the triangle but still nearby is **Cleveland State University** tel. (216) 687-2000. The school has approximately 17,000 students and is on Chester and Euclid Avenues from about 21st to 25th Streets, east of downtown. On West 25th Street at Detroit Avenue in Tremont City eight blocks south of the lake is the **West Side Market,** a huge and imposing yellow brick building where area growers hawk fresh produce, meats, and handmade edibles. There's a small restaurant in the back serving coffee, milk, tea, and soft drinks. Soft drinks also can be had over the counters at Frank's and Frank's II. Best route from downtown is via the recently reopened Veterans Memorial Detroit-Superior Bridge. (Look for the clock tower atop the market.) There is a Greater Cleveland Regional Transit Authority (RTA) stop less than a block from the facility.

Other near-downtown attractions include the **Galleria at Erieview,** 1301 E. 9th St., tel. (216)

861-4343, a recently renovated retail center with 60 shops and restaurants; **Playhouse Square Center,** with its four stately old live-stage theaters between Chester and Euclid Avenues on E. 13th Street; the **Greyhound Bus Station,** tel. (216) 781-0520, Chester Avenue and E. 13th Street; upscale hotels such as the **Radisson** and the **Wyndham;** the **YMCA;** and, as the downtown continues to expand, more.

Two big, new sports venues, one completed a few years back and one almost ready, also are found downtown. **Gund Arena,** home of the National Basketball Association Cavaliers, the Lumberjacks International League hockey team, and other events, is next door to Jacobs Field. The Gund holds more than 20,000 fans in its pro basketball configuration. The new home of the National Football League Cleveland Browns, a $248 million, 72,000-seat, natural-grass, open-air structure, is being completed at W. Third Street and Erieside Avenue, north of the Shoreway, in time for the 1999 introduction of the expansion team to the city.

Cleveland Metroparks Zoo, 3900 Brookside Park Dr., tel. (216) 661-6500, about four miles southwest of the downtown area, is set on 165 acres of shady, rolling terrain. A real attention-getter is *The Rainforest,* a lush, two-acre exhibit that includes 600 animals, 7,000 plants, and a 25-ft. waterfall. Zoo hours are daily 9 a.m.-5 p.m., with extended hours through 7 p.m. Memorial Day through Labor Day. The Rainforest is open daily 10 a.m.-5 p.m., Wednesday till 9:00 p.m. Admission to the zoo is $7 for those over age 12 and $4 for children ages 2-11. Admission to the Rainforest is included with general admission except on Monday mornings and Wednesday after 4:30 p.m. when admission is $5 for adults, $3 for children ages 2-11. From downtown, exit I-90 at either W. 25th Street or Fulton Road and go south. From the Ohio Turnpike, take exit 10 (I-71) and head north. The zoo's Web site is www.clemetzoo.com.

Speaking of untamed, that's what the city can be; take care when walking in an unfamiliar area after dark. Ask hotel or motel personnel or consult a police officer.

Churches

The most vivid noncommercial, historic, and artistic show in all of Cleveland may be just

an onion-dome church on Cleveland's west side

across the thresholds of the city's numerous venerable churches. Ethnic groups from central and eastern Europe came here years ago and built solid houses of worship beneath onion domes or towering spires, with shimmering interiors. Among the most interesting is **St. Elizabeth of Hungary Church,** 9016 Buckeye Rd., tel. (216) 231-0325. Also worth visits are the **Pilgrim Congregational Church,** 2592 W. 14th St., tel. (216) 861-7338, and **St. Theodosius Russian Orthodox Cathedral,** 733 Starkweather Ave., tel. (216) 861-5363, both in Tremont City. The former was built around lots of Tiffany-designed stained glass, while the latter is rich with icons and served as atmospheric backdrop in the Oscar-winning 1978 film, *The Deer Hunter.* For a study in contrasts, walk around the block at St. Theo's and take in the sprawling, smoky view of the still-industrial Cuyahoga River valley. It's hardly an exaggeration to state that anything with a saint in its name or an onion for a dome will offer impressive viewing. Look for towering clues to church locations amid the trees while driving the city's freeways and major arteries. To visit a church, call first or ask around in the immediate neighborhood.

University Circle

Within a square mile on Cleveland's East Side, University Circle is the site of wonderful museums, portions of the city's very generous parkland, galleries, and **Case Western Reserve University.** Dial (216) 368-4440 for campus ac-

tivities that may be of interest, or check www.cwru.edu for a calendar of events.

Culture flourishes here, perhaps because visitors can comfortably walk from any one attraction to another past venerable, pleasant shops and student and other housing. Consider stops at any or all of the following:

The **Cleveland Center for Contemporary Art,** 8501 Carnegie Ave., tel. (216) 421-8671, collection consists of retro, trippy, avant-garde, and bizarre art on consignment. There are five galleries showing items in all kinds of media. Ask about the ongoing lecture series. The Center's hours are Tues.-Thurs. 11 a.m.-6 p.m., Friday 11 a.m.-9 p.m., Sat.-Sun. noon-5 p.m. Free; donations encouraged.

At the **Cleveland Children's Museum,** 10730 Euclid Ave., tel. (216) 791-8838, visitors can splash in the water, go over and under a bridge they just built, or purchase an exhibit-related item. Other neat stuff includes a mobile news van and a computer for manipulating the look of human faces—sort of a way to preview plastic surgery. Kids can come and visit daily 10 a.m.-5 p.m. Admission is $5 for persons over 16 and $4 for children and seniors.

Parklands are all over, but the **Cleveland Botanical Gardens,** 11030 East Blvd., tel. (216) 721-1600, may be a visitor's best initial experience. The free site nurtures 3,000 species of trees, shrubs, and perennials in six gardens. Experts here will give advice on what grows well in visitors' backyards, no matter where they may reside. The grounds are open from dawn to dusk, the building is open Mon.-Sat. 9 a.m.-5 p.m., Sun. noon-5 p.m. There's no admission charge. Adjacent to the gardens, at 12316 Euclid Ave., is **Lake View Cemetery**, which is no ordinary graveyard. Besides being tranquil, scenic, and offering west-facing views of the city, Lake View is the somewhat overdone burial place of and memorial to President James A. Garfield. John D. Rockefeller's remains are here, too. Wade Memorial Chapel on the grounds has a sumptuous Tiffany-glass interior. The grounds are open daily 7:30 a.m.-5:30 p.m. Admission is free and there are guided tours from April to around Thanksgiving. Call (216) 421-2665 for details.

The **Cleveland Museum of Art**, 11150 East Blvd., is here, too. Call (216) 421-7340, or look up www.clemusart.com. Some 34,000 stunning permanent and traveling exhibits are shown here, the former always free of charge. There are 70 separate galleries inside this classic building, the structure alone being worth the visit. The museum must be popular—more than 500,000 visitors come calling each year. Do phone ahead, as there are many programs for all ages. The museum is open Tues.-Sun. 10 a.m.-5 p.m., till 9:00 p.m. Wednesday and Friday. An easy way to find the museum is to ask the whereabouts of Wade Lagoon. This picturesque pond is the center of the University Circle area and is located where Euclid Avenue meets Martin Luther King Jr. Dr.; the museum is just north of the water, between King Dr. and East Boulevard.

Cleveland Museum of Natural History, 1 Wade Oval Dr., tel. (216) 231-4600, will bring tears of nostalgia to the eyes of those who were high school nerds. We're talking serious vertebrate and invertebrate paleontology. Here travelers learn what Ohio was like not only prior to Europeans, but prior to human life. For laughs or for frights there's a *faux* tarantula 15 feet across. The museum is open Mon.-Sat. 10 a.m.-5 p.m., Sun. noon-5 p.m. Sept.-May the museum is open till 10 p.m. on Wednesday nights. Admission is $6.50 adults, $4.50 students and seniors. Best bet? From 3-5 p.m. Tuesday or Thursday, when everyone gets in free.

Western Reserve Historical Society, 10825 East Blvd., tel. (216) 721-5722, offers tours of a 1911 mansion and the opportunity to see one of the finest costume collections in the country.

Original clothing rotates in and out of display constantly—there's that much of it. In contrast, the Crawford Auto-Aviation Museum is part of the society, and there's all sorts of cultural artifacts, highbrow and low, old and quite recent. The library houses what is said to be one of the best genealogical collections in the eastern U.S. The society is open Mon.-Sat. 10 a.m.-5 p.m., Sunday noon-5 p.m. Admission $6.50 adults, $5.50 seniors, and $4.50 children ages 6-12.

There are other museums and attractions hereabouts, within a short distance. Consider visiting the all-volunteer **African-American Museum**, 1765 Crawford Rd., tel. (216) 791-1700, Web site www.ben.net/aamuseum, open Tues.-Fri. 10 a.m.-3 p.m. and Saturday 11 a.m.-3 p.m. ($4 adults, $3.50 seniors, $3 ages 17 and under). The second- or third-oldest African-American museum in the country, it boasts the largest collection of African artifacts in the region outside of the Cleveland Art Museum. Rooms are devoted to African-American scientists and inventors, the civil rights movement, the Middle Passage, and more. The Africa room even houses a full-size, culturally correct hut. The **Dunham Tavern Museum**, 6709 Euclid Ave., tel. (216) 431-1060, open Wednesday and Sunday 1-4 p.m. ($2 adults, $1 children), also makes an intriguing stop. It's a living-history museum housed in an old stagecoach stop (Cleveland's oldest building on its original site).

Little Italy

A pungent area of restaurants and apartments, visitors can meander into most any bistro and taste authentic fare from Northern and Southern Italy, and Sicily. Just east of University Circle, Little Italy is patronized by pasta- and pizza-crazed students during the academic year. You may also hear the area referred to as Murray Hill. That's the traditional name for this section of town, which also boasts a number of galleries and cute shops. An especially intriguing time of year to be here is in August for the Feast of the Assumption, when Italians turn a part of Cleveland into a dazzling religious parade, complete with swaying statuary, Old World garb, and, afterward, tables heavy with food and drink.

Ohio City and Tremont

Ohio City begins on the west side of the Cuyahoga River. A separate municipality for many years, the area's most noticeable landmark is the **West Side Market,** 1995 W. 25th St. at Lorain Avenue, tel. (216) 281-6200. The market is open Monday and Wednesday 7 a.m.-4 p.m., Fri.-Sat. 7 a.m.-6 p.m. Tremont, also on the near west side, is a section of contrasts. The first place many ethnic groups established toeholds in the New World, this longstanding municipality is marked by Orthodox churches, Old World hole-in-the-wall coffeehouses, and just-opened taco stands. The avant-garde set discovered this atmospheric district a few years back, resulting in lots of new faces living in renovated Victorian homes. The heart of Tremont is Lincoln Park, which is bounded by 11th, 14th, Kenilworth and Starkweather Streets.

Both neighborhoods are characterized by a mix of mediocre and revived housing and narrow, occasionally brick, streets in need of patching. For ethnic atmosphere these areas are the real thing. All of Tremont City has been designated a historic district, making it a Cleveland landmark. The more visitors look, the more they see. For example, a handsome red-brick building at 11th and Auburn Streets, now a private business, was constructed in 1927 as the Ukrainian Labor Temple. Neighborhoods are not yet sufficiently gentrified to support any kind of official tour, but consider the following route an informal tour of the area.

Cutting west-southwest from here is Lorain Avenue (SR 10). It's worth a slow drive because remnants of virtually all 80 ethnic groups that called Cleveland home can still be found hereabouts. Most often they're evident in restaurants and taverns, but there are other storefronts where the wedding gown styles or handmade sausages or the destinations featured by travel agencies are reminders of the city's heritage. And the number of antique shops—from the 4100 through the 7900 blocks—totals at least 35. Lorain Avenue is a snap to find; it's the east-west street passing the West Side Market at 25th Street.

Shaker Heights

Once an oh-so-posh eastern suburb, Shaker Heights today is accessible to all. Shaker Square, for example, is an open, pleasant area of nice shops, surrounded by apartments, condos, and homes, and is serviced by public transit from Cleveland. A must-see is the **Shaker Historical Society and Museum,** 16740 S. Park Blvd., tel. (216) 921-1201. This facility is on land once owned by the North Union Colony of Shakers, a furniture-makin' bunch of folks who lived communally in the 19th century. Besides crafting chairs and such, the Shakers were clever tinkerers and inventors. If these artifacts look familiar, it's because Shaker style and ingenuity have been widely copied. The museum is open Tues.-Fri. 2 p.m.-5 p.m., Sunday 2-5 p.m. No admission is charged for the museum or for the placid **Shaker Nature Center** at 2600 S Park Blvd. (about a mile west of the museum), tel. (216) 321-5935. Ponds surrounded by cattails invite the presence of migrating and year-round resident birds, muskrats, frogs, and even an occasional deer.

Miscellaneous Sights

Cleveland has several improbable sights, not the least of which is **Dead Man's Curve.** This 35-mile-an-hour, 90-degree turn sits astride I-80 just east of downtown. The reason for such a permanent and precipitous piece of roadwork isn't clear.

The **National Cleveland-Style Polka Hall of Fame,** at 291 E. 222nd St., Euclid, tel. (216) 261-3263, has been overshadowed by its rock and roll counterpart but is a link to the rich Slovenian heritage shared by a number of Clevelanders. It's open Monday and Thurs.-Sat. 10 a.m.-2 p.m., Tuesday 3-8 p.m., closed Sunday and Wednesday. Call ahead to make sure it's open.

The **Cleveland Museum of Health and Hygiene** is at 8911 Euclid Ave., tel. (216) 231-5010, and is among the more bizarre such institutions around. Long before mothers harped at their kids, this place was extolling the virtues of a healthy lifestyle. The most popular item here is Juno, a transparent female with a circulating circulatory system and major organs. Only Juno and what's billed as the World's Largest Tooth remained after a 1998 renovation—all other exhibits are new or have been updated. The five-building complex has 100,000 visitors each year, many of them schoolchildren. It's open Mon.-Fri. 9 a.m.-5 p.m., Saturday 10 a.m.-5 p.m., Sunday noon-5 p.m. Admission is $4.50 for adults, $3 for seniors and children.

LOLLY THE TROLLEY

Visitors committed to lakefront travel but with an urge to see more of Cleveland can do so on Lolly the Trolley. A one- or two-hour trolley tour begins at the Powerhouse in the Flats; that's on the west side of the Cuyahoga River, downtown. There's ample public parking nearby. Everything from the Cleveland Indians' Jacobs Field to the once-opulent homes of 19th-century millionaires is included in the tour. The two-hour version includes a stop at the city greenhouse.

The tour guide informs passengers not only about the various points of interest but about Lolly, as well. The trolley seats 38, is heated and air-conditioned, and was custom built for Trolley Tours of Cleveland in 1985. Its large red presence is a familiar sight to local residents, running weekends only from November through April and every day during warmer months.

The two-hour tour takes in the artsy, *nouveau* Warehouse District; Public Square's big buildings; ethnically interesting Ohio City, including the West Side Market; the Cleveland Museum; Playhouse Square; the Cleveland Clinic; Millionaires' Row; Jacobs Field; Gund Arena; and the future home of the Browns' fledgling NFL team on the lakeshore. Lolly also buzzes up and down the waterfront, catching the Rock and Roll Hall of Fame and Museum and the Great Lakes Science Center. In all, 20 miles are covered in the longer junket.

Cost of the two-hour trip for adults, seniors, and children ages 2-18, is $11, $10, and $7, respectively. The one-hour tour fares are $7, $6, and $5. No child under five is allowed on the two-hour version. For more information, and to make required reservations, call (800) 848-0173.

NASA Lewis Research Center, 21000 Brookpark Rd., tel. (216) 433-4000, is the only place north of Florida or Texas where the National Aeronautic and Space Administration has a public facility. Subjects covered include developments in aircraft propulsion, satellite communications and aerospace technology. There's no charge to visit the center, which is just west of Cleveland Hopkins International Airport. It's open Monday and Wed.-Fri. 9 a.m.-4 p.m., Saturday 10 a.m.-3 p.m., Sunday 1-5 p.m.

Every suburb has some sort of attraction, and southwest suburban **Strongsville** is no different. **Gardenview Horticultural Park** was built by hand by a local named Henry Ross. A human dynamo, Ross spent almost 50 years digging out ponds and then lining them with concrete he mixed and transported in a wheelbarrow. The facility is most vivid in May, when some 500 crabapple trees explode into bloom. Gardenview is at 16711 Pearl Rd., just south of the Ohio Turnpike (I-80). Dial (216) 238-6653 for information.

You may also want to pay a visit to the **Gerald E. Brookins Museum of Electric Railways, Inc.,** also known as **Trolleyville, USA,** at 7100 Columbia Rd., tel. (216) 235-4725. In an unincorporated area near Olmsted Falls, this museum will familiarize visitors with the interurbans and other trolley conveyances that were popular in the first four decades of the 20th century. Weekends only, Nov.-April. Admission is $5 for adults, $4 for seniors, and $3 for children ages 3-11.

MUSIC

Cleveland Orchestra, is at 11001 Euclid Ave., tel. (216) 231-7300. Under the baton of gifted conductors such as George Szell, Lorin Maazel, and now Christoph von Dohnányi, the Cleveland Orchestra has gained a worldwide reputation for excellence. So accomplished is the Cleveland Orchestra that people in classical circles refer to it simply as "The Cleveland." There is no better collection of musicians in the United States, and there may be no better collection on the planet. Those who can secure a ticket to a Severance Hall performance will be transported. The orchestra plays summers at Blossom Music Center, near Akron, returning to its home in September.

Equally seasonal is the **Cleveland San Jose Ballet,** which performs from September through Christmas at Playhouse Square, 1375 Euclid Ave. Call (216) 621-3634 to reach the box office. Perpetually pinched for money, this company of dancers has been in Cleveland since 1976 and has been a co-venture with the California city since 1986; the dancers and artistic staff live and rehearse in Cleveland, travelling periodically to San Jose for performances. The season highlight for most fans is Tchaikovsky's *The Nutcracker,* but there are half-dozen other classic and contemporary ballets every fall and early winter.

Orchestra, chamber aggregations, and dancers aside, visitors can well imagine that Cleveland is a rock 'n' roll town. Country devotees most often travel to the suburbs to hear their music and to dance. A popular spot for those who wear hats inside is **Boot Scoot'n Saloon II,** 38929 Center Ridge Rd. in west suburban North Ridgeville, tel. (216) 353-0999. Open Wed.-Sat. nights (Sunday is alcohol-free teen night), the Boot offers line dance lessons at 8 p.m. every night but Wednesday. The original Boot Scoot'n Saloon is in Cuyahoga Falls, outside Akron. There are a couple of good local country bands, including Al's Fast Freight and the Curtis Brothers. Both play throughout the metro Cleveland area.

The home of the blues—plus occasional zydeco—in Cleveland appears to be **Wilbert's Bar & Grille,** though the blues, like country, can be heard in a number of joints on any given evening. Wilbert's is at 1360 W. 9th St., tel. (216) 771-2583, just up the hill to the east from the Flats in the Warehouse District. Nationally known folks such as Robert Cray, the Fabulous Thunderbirds, and Lonnie Brooks blow through here regularly. Besides great tunes, the former garage prepares spicy Southwestern cuisine. Other houses that may offer blues include the **Euclid Tavern,** 11629 Euclid Ave., tel. (216) 229-7788, and the **Riverwood Cafe,** 18616 Detroit Ave., Lakewood, tel. (216) 521-1529. The former is filled with college kids, the latter has a slightly older crowd. If musicianship matters more than the kind of music, hit the **Barking Spider,** 11310 Juniper Rd. in University Circle, tel. (216) 421-2863. Folk, blues, jazz, and gospel all are taken in here by a knowledgeable clientele.

Jazz matters, too. Hear it done well at **Nighttown,** 12383 Cedar Rd., Cleveland Heights, tel. (216) 795-0550. A bit closer to downtown is **Club Isabella,** 2025 Abington Rd., University Circle, tel. (216) 229-1177. Isabella may remind a visitor of Greenwich Village—even if he or she never has been near New York City. The music ranges from predictable to avant-garde.

But back to rock 'n' roll. The phrase was first used here by radio disk jockey Alan Freed, who probably copped it from black musicians. The tradition has been kept alive by Ohio rockers from the Isely Brothers to Chrissy Hines to Marily Manson, as well as by legions of fans. The music as it was meant to be played can be heard at these places:

Agora Theatre, 5000 Euclid Ave., tel. (216) 881-6911. After a night at the Agora, rock fans will know the difference between musty and funky. They also will be part of a crowd that is almost as loud and energetic as one of the nationally known bands that come to town and play here.

Fagan's, 996 Old River Rd. in the Flats, tel. (216) 241-6116, serves up seafood, karaoke, DJ's spinning records, and live bands. One or another sort of music occurs Wed.-Sat.

The **Grog Shop,** 1765 Coventry Rd., Cleveland Heights, tel. (216) 321-5588, hosts alternative music, and an alternative crowd. Typical bands might include the Swagger Kings, the Atomic Fireballs, or any of dozens more. Never heard of any of 'em? Well then, they need fan support.

Mirage, 2510 Elm St., is in the Flats, tel. (216) 348-1135; rap music fans and those who like to dance will find a home here. This is the best place in town in which to spot a professional baseball or basketball star out of uniform.

The **Odeon,** 1295 Old River Rd., tel. (216) 732-5331, is another alternative music haven. This popular place plays host to nationally known bands and musicians.

Peabody's Down Under, 1059 Old River Rd., tel. (216) 241-2451. For the just-over-21 set and those with high pain threshholds, Peabody's lays the latest tunes from MTV on its patrons who appreciate alternative music. Mirage, Odeon, and Peabody's all are in the Flats.

Additional listings for music venues in outlying Sagamore Hills and Lyndhurst can be found in the Western Reserve—section.

THEATER

Four theaters—The Allen, The Ohio, The Palace, and The State—make up what is known collectively as **Playhouse Square,** tel. (216) 241-6000. When Clevelanders think of the stage, they think of these houses. And they should, since nationally known stars appear in perennially popular productions like *The King and I* or *Annie.* Playhouse Square also is the home of the Great Lakes Theater Festival, which features plays such as *Most Happy Fella* and Noel Coward's *Fallen Angels.* Not to be overlooked are the stars of the **Cleveland Opera** and the **DanceCleveland** modern dance company, who perform here, too.

There are other stages and theaters, with local talent turning in some remarkable performances. **Cleveland Play House,** tel. (216) 795-7000, the nation's first and longest running regional theater, is at 8500 Euclid Ave. Besides new, contemporary, and classical plays, it offers a children's festival. **Karamu House,** 2355 E. 89th St., tel. (216) 795-7070, emphasizes the promotion of new African-American artists. The alternative scene is covered by **Cleveland Public Theater,** 6415 Detroit Ave., tel. (216) 631-2727, which emphasizes local work and runs festivals of works in progress.

NIGHTLIFE AND ENTERTAINMENT

The Flats, that one-time industrial area on either side of the Cuyahoga River downtown, is Cleveland's nightlife scene at its most intense. Bars, nightclubs, and restaurants cater to a crowd that skews well below middle age and enjoys its music loud. If visitors are club-hopping, there's only one frustration—no matter which side of the river they're on, the opposite bank looks and sounds livelier.

The biggest production has to be **Nautica Entertainment Complex,** a pierlike structure flanked by two jackknife bridges on the west bank of the Cuyahoga River in the Flats. Several buildings are here, including the Powerhouse, a century-old dynamo that has been renovated and now houses restaurants, a comedy club, and a couple of bars. Hard by the waterfront is an outdoor stage for special events. Another building is the Sugar Warehouse, where visitors can eat, shoot billiards, or hit on each other. Happily, one of the facilities here is the dock for the **Holy Moses Water Taxi,** tel. (216) 491-0061). It shuttles those in a partying mood back and forth across the river.

There is more, all over the city. Up the hill from the Flats is the Warehouse District. A popular spot here is **Liquid Cafe,** 1212 W. 6th St., tel. (216) 479-7717. Relax on a couch in your coat and tie after work or dress down in jeans on weekends as you sip or chug amid *"Friends"*-type folks. A different kind of rendezvous just down the block is **Sixth Street Under** at 1266 W. Sixth St., tel. (216) 589-9313. This is a traditional nightclub with live jazz and drinks served to an over-30 crowd.

Close to Jacobs Field is **Pete and Dewey's Planet,** 812 Huron Rd., SE, tel. (216) 522-1500. This is Indians country, and we don't mean there's cactus in the background. Rather, the garb here year round is professional baseball regalia. The beer flows, the pizza is gourmet, and the best way to fit in is to extol the virtues of the local team.

On the seamy side, Cleveland may have more exotic-dancer venues per resident than anywhere in the United States. Sometimes called gentlemen's clubs, they are more numerous than McDonald's near the airport, particularly along Brookpark Road. Should you want to learn before doing, E.D. Publications, Post Office Box ED100, Cleveland, OH 44115-1890 offers a directory, *Exotic Dancer,* that sells for $19.95 on newsstands or $24 by mail. No bargain, and neither are many of these joints, which are heavy on vinyl, smoke, and boredom.

ACCOMMODATIONS

Private Lodgings, Inc., tel. (216) 321-3213, offers apartments, houses and bed and breakfast accommodations in private homes in the Cleveland area. Rates and amenities vary.

Hotels and motels in Cleveland tend to be in groups. There are numerous downtown accommodations, the airport is ringed with motels, and there are clusters of places to stay at various freeway exits. The following overview is just that; don't dismiss an accommodation simply because it isn't listed. Best bet on an unknown site is to take a look at a room and nail down the price. Reservations may access you to money-saving weekend packages or to food or other discounts.

Downtown

What with free continental breakfast and a pool, the **Comfort Inn Downtown,** 1800 Euclid Ave., tel. (216) 861-0001, is a moderately priced bargain.

All of these downtown hotels are very nice and very expensive. The **Embassy Suite Hotel,** 1701 E. 12th St., tel. (216) 523-8000, provides an indoor pool, restaurant, lounge, and entertainment. **Glidden House Inn,** 1901 Ford Dr., tel. (216) 231-8900, is a nice counterpoint to modernity. On the National Register of Historic Places, this oversize (60-room) bed and breakfast hotel is housed in a former paint-family mansion in University Circle. **Holiday Inn,** 1111 Lakeside Ave., tel. (216) 241-5100, has an indoor pool, restaurant, and lounge. **Marriott Society Center,** is at 127 Public Square, tel. (216) 696-9200. Restaurant, lounge, and indoor pool.

Other city hotels that fall in the expensive-to-premium category include the cushy **Omni International Hotel,** 2065 E. 96th St., University Circle, tel. (216) 791-1900. There are three restaurants and a lounge with entertainment. Then there's the **Radisson Plaza Suite Hotel,** 1701 E. 12th St., tel. (216) 523-8000. It offers a restaurant and a lounge with entertainment. **Sheraton Cleveland City Centre,** 777 E. St. Clair Ave., tel. (216) 771-7600 or (800) 321-1090, has two restaurants two lounges, and entertainment.

Luxury hotels include the **Ritz-Carlton,** 1515 W. Third St., tel. (216) 623-1300. Indoor pool, two restaurants, and a lounge with entertainment are highlights. **Renaissance Cleveland Hotel,** 24 Public Square, tel. (216) 696-5600. The Queen Mother of Cleveland hotels, the former Stouffer property is wonderfully located and has a trio of restaurants. **Wyndham Hotel,** 1260 Euclid Ave. (Cleveland Square), tel. (216) 615-7500. The business traveler's dream, with data telephone access and voice mail in every room and an indoor lap pool.

Elsewhere

The east and southeast sides of the city have scores of hotels and motels, many at far lower cost than their downtown counterparts. They fill up fast on warm-weather weekends, primarily for their proximity to Sea World and similar attractions in nearby Geauga County. There are many good values to the south. For example,

ask about weekend rates at hotels and motels in the vicinity of Cleveland Hopkins Airport. Most facilities here, and some of those to the west, offer free airport shuttle. A number of discount motels line Pearl Road. Close to the city to the west, look for motels on the far side of the airport and along limited-access highways.

FOOD

Upscale

Let's get the great food, cost-is-no-object places out of the way, shall we? A Cleveland diner's club, without an ax to grind, rates **Sans Souci,** year after year, the city's best restaurant. This Renaissance Hotel facility at 24 Public Square features savory Mediterranean cuisine in a French country atmosphere. Dress nicely and you'll be rewarded with a memorable dining experience. Two signature dishes are lobster bouillabaisse at $19.50 and lemon pepper angel-hair pasta with lobster basil cream sauce, $15.95. Salads and pasta dishes are a la carte. Call (216) 696-5600 several days before you want to show up.

Other top-shelf choices with similar prices include **Johnny's** for great selections of pasta, beef, and veal dishes. There are a pair of Johnny's locations—Johnny's Bar is at 3164 Fulton Rd., tel. (216) 281-0055, while Johnny's Downtown is at 1406 W. 6th St., tel. (216) 623-0055. The former is more clubby, the latter more reminiscent of Italy, from which most recipes originated. Favorites here include the roast beef filet meal, with three side dishes, at $25.95, and a pasta dish with an X-rated name and ingredients that include bell peppers, pepper flakes, cheese, and heavy cream. Zagat diners called the Fulton Road restaurant "outstanding."

Watermark is in the Flats at 1250 Old River Road on the west side of the river, tel. (216) 241-1600. There's shipboard decor, an emphasis on fresh, quality seafood and more, at less than $20 per entree, plus patio dining in warm weather. **Sammy's** has two locations, in the Flats at 1400 W. 10th St., tel. (216) 523-5560, and near Gund Arena at 100 Gateway Plaza, tel. (216) 420-2900. Both feature a jazz trio, the places are elegant yet casual, and they offer everything from seafood Napoleon at $25 to pan-seared ostrich with an artichoke timbale for $27. Besides an intelligent variety of domestic and foreign wines, local micro-brewed beers can be had.

Marlin, 1952 E. Sixth St., tel. (216) 589-0051, is an atmospheric bistro with upscale American food. The most popular menu item is beef tenderloin, which goes for $19 a la carte. The dessert for which you should leave room is the flourless espresso chocolate torte.

American

Bubba's-Q, 2756 Van Aken Blvd., tel. (216) 295-111, is a soulful site owned by Al ("Bubba") Baker, a former member of the original Cleveland Browns. Locals like what the big guy does to ribs by the rack and buffalo wings by the dozen. Other specialties include shredded beef, pork, or chicken sandwiches, plus a side of collard greens and red velvet cake for dessert. Very moderate prices—a family of four can eat for about $30.

The **Flat Iron Cafe,** 1114 Center St., tel. (216) 696-6968, is one of the better sources of beer and sandwiches in the Flats. The most popular sandwich is the Lake Erie yellow perch at $7.95. The sandwich comes with chips and a pickle, and is worth every cent. With a beer, it's a great —if not well-balanced—meal. One other thing: the low noise level encourages conversation.

Gateway Sports Club and Eatery, 727 Bolivar Rd., tel. (216) 621-6644, is in the shadows of Jacobs Field and Gund Arena. Try pasta, cheeseburgers, or chicken breast smothered in Swiss cheese, mushrooms, and bacon. A sandwich with fries is $5-8. Gateway is clogged to the point of insanity following nearby sporting events.

Max & Erma's is a Columbus-based operation. They're highly recommended for their many hamburger variations. A typical burger with fries is $7. Located at 1106 Old River Rd. in the Flats, tel. (216) 771-8338, Max & Erma's restaurants also can be found on the east at 33675 Solon Rd. and on the west at 30105 Detroit Rd. Phone numbers there, respectively, are (216) 349-3006 and (216) 899-8686.

No snap to find, the **Oriole Cafe** is at 294 N. Rocky River Dr., tel. (440) 243-8809, in northwest Berea (from downtown Cleveland, take I-71 south to the airport, exit, and take SR 237 south into Berea; the cafe's at Bagley and N.

Rocky River Dr.). This is an unpretentious, sports-oriented bar with better-than-usual food. Lunches include a choice of four kinds of Caesar salad, burgers, or chicken breasts, plus daily specials that range from meat loaf to lake perch—the latter served all day Friday. By night, look for homemade pasta or a deal on crab legs. Figure $5 plus drinks for a sandwich at lunch, and two to three times that for dinner. The bar stocks 80 brands of beer and the Indians are on TV here whenever they're on TV anywhere.

Pier W, 12700 Lake Ave. at Winton Place, Lakewood along the water west of downtown Cleveland, tel. (216) 228-2250, is a public restaurant attached to condominiums. It is known for its Sunday brunches ($18.95 for adults, $6.95 for kids) and stunning view of the city. Fresh seafood takes center stage here, with Lake Erie walleye, salmon in parchment, and coconut shrimp meals all going for $19.95. Should you be in Cleveland on July 4th, reserve a dining table on the deck and eat burgers and hot dogs for $9.95 per person while the night sky explodes in color above the lakefront.

Ruthie & Moe's Midtown Diner, 4002 Prospect Ave., tel. (216) 431-8063, consists of a pair of silver dining cars where unusually good food is dispensed. The facility serves real, handmade milkshakes and everything from the usual diner specials to an occasional exotic, authentic Indian curry. Desserts are worth saving room for, and prices are reasonable—another lunch spot where $5-6 goes a long way. Ruthie and Moe offer breakfast, too. Open weekdays only.

Finally, for the most basic of foods, head for **Steve's Lunch,** 5004 Lorain Ave., tel. (216) 961-1460. Steve's son operates a smallish diner where $1 chili dogs are crafted. The chili sauce is ground-beef based and delicious. On the other side of downtown, try a dog at **Pat's Delicatessen,** 5204 St. Clair Ave. The chili dogs here are embedded in a sauce that involves Campbell's tomato soup, ground beef, onions, green pepper, and secret seasonings. Cost of the concoction is $1.50.

Asian

Don't be put off by the obscure location. **Nam Wah,** at 392 W. Bagley Rd., tel. (216) 243-8181, in a Berea shopping center southwest of Cleveland, dishes up savory Vietnamese and Chinese dishes to kids from nearby Baldwin-Wallace College and enthusiastic locals. The spring rolls are a delight, soups such as *pho* are revelations, and the Singapore-style noodles have enough spice to maintain a diner's attention. A typical meal is less than $10. Nam Wah also does a brisk carryout business. Chances are you'll be served by a Vietnamese immigrant being aided toward citizenship by the civic-minded owner.

The salmon curry for $6 and the duck *choo chee* for $5.95 make **Thai Orchid,** 5136 Mayfield Rd., in the town of Lyndhurst, east of Cleveland near the junction of SR 175 (Richmond Road) and US 322, tel. (216) 461-8266, quite a food value on the far east side. The menu is extensive and everything on it seems available. The decor is soothing, despite the fact that the facility is part of a small strip mall. Enter at the side.

West suburban Lakewood has become something of a melting pot, and the restaurant lineup is one indication. **Szechwan Garden,** 13800 Detroit Ave., tel. (216) 226-1987, is a small but worthwhile stop, offering 10 house specials every day. Included are orange beef, spicy shrimp, lemon chicken and other main courses. The $10.95 price also gets a diner soup and steamed rice. The food is Chinese regional, with spices adjustable to the individual diner's taste.

Breakfast

There are more than a dozen **Arabica Coffee House** locations scattered around the city, and all offer consistently strong and tasty brews, plus muffins, sticky buns, and similar edibles for a satisfying continental breakfast at about $3. Competing for the pastry purchase are the city's innumerable bakeries. Good ones include the **Stone Oven Bakery Cafe,** 2245 Lee Rd., Cleveland Heights, tel. (216) 932-3003, which dishes out hearty goods, as does **Michael's Bakery,** 4478 Broadview Rd. in Fairview Park, tel. (216) 351-7530. Michael's opens early—at 6 or 7 a.m., depending on the day—and creates a variety of danish and donuts.

Travelers seeking more than a warm beverage and pastry can visit **Chuck's Diner** at 2194 Lee Rd., in Cleveland Heights, tel. (216) 321-9911. Breakfast specials weekdays may include things like pancakes, two eggs, and a choice of bacon or sausage, all for $2.95. "And the pancakes are *big,*" a waitperson points out. Open from 7 a.m., Chuck's goes round the clock on weekends and tends to be busy no matter when you show.

Another interesting breakfast spot is the **Big Egg,** 5107 Detroit Ave., tel. (216) 961-8000. This establishment recently was named Best Place to Blow Your Diet at 3 a.m., Restaurant with the Most Entertaining Regulars, and Best Dive by a local newspaper critic. Eggs are the mainstay, with more than a dozen omelet variations. Omelet ingredients can be anything from bacon to spaghetti, and a Hawaiian omelet (ham, onions, pineapple) is a mere $3.75. A trio of hotcakes goes for $1.99.

Brewpubs

Groovy T-shirts or an interest in brewing aren't the only reasons to visit the **Great Lakes Brewing Company,** 2516 Market St., tel. (216) 771-4404, on the city's near-west side. The food here is yummy, ranging from sausages and ribs to calamari, plus chicken and pasta. Those who know say Great Lakes brews some of the very best beers and ales in the country. And entrees like pretzel chicken, at $10.95, go well with a brew. The brewery/restaurant also offers outdoor dining. It's on a side street, one block west of the massive West Side Market. If this isn't the place by which brewpubs are judged, perhaps it should be.

There are two downtown **Diamondback Brewery** locations, both of which serve food as well as drink. They are at 724 Prospect Ave., tel. (216) 771-1988 and around the corner at 703 Huron Rd. The locations create their brews on the premises. Popular main dishes include blackened mahi-mahi at $18.95, flour tortilla lasagna at $15.95, and barley ravioli with smoked chicken, also $15.95. As for quenching thirst, order a Black Diamond Pale Ale, which goes for $3.25 per pint. Perhaps incongruously, the Diamondback also serves great pastries—the chef turns out to-die-for desserts such as cranberry linzer torte.

Eastern and Central European

Annie's is a Slovenian restaurant with a pleasantly rustic exterior north of Russell Road at 8430 Mayfield Rd. (SR 322) in Chesterland west of Cleveland, tel. (216) 729-4540. Besides the owner's intriguing accent, one of the nice things about this somewhat dressy place is that the most popular dinner dishes also are available for lunch. Flavorful chicken paprikash is $9.95 of an evening but just $7 at noon; Wiener schnitzel, with its crunchy coating, is $11.95 every night but $7.95 a few hours earlier. Items such as dumplings and mashed potatoes taste distinctly homemade. It's hard to leave Annie's with an empty feeling, especially when dessert strudel beckons.

Also to the east is **Dubrovnik Garden Restaurant,** 34900 Lakeshore Blvd., in Eastlake northeast of Cleveland off I-90, tel. (216) 946-3366. The building looks like it belongs on a golf course and it houses the American Croatian Lodge and Museum. The public is welcome to the interesting mix of foods that once were the pride of Yugoslavia. The meal most in demand is the $9.95 Dubrovnik grill—kebabs made of beef, veal, and pork. Similar and equally flavorful are the sausages, which have a nice taste unlike anything you're apt to find at a freeway exit. Desserts are yummy, too.

Parma Pierogies, 7707 W. Ridgewood Dr., tel. (440) 888-1200, is a great and inexpensive fast-food way to introduce children to ethnic dining. Pierogies have been called Polish ravioli. Stuffings range from spinach to mozzarella, making a buttery pierogi irresistible—even for vegetarians. Besides dessert pierogies, look for stuffed cabbage, noodles, potato pancakes, and *kielbasa,* a succulent sausage. No credit cards, but prices are low. A family of four should be able to eat for $25 or less. (P.S. Pierogies are deceptively filling.)

East Indian/Vegetarian
Saffron Patch, 20600 Chagrin Blvd., Shaker Heights, tel. (216) 295-0400, is a medium-priced East Indian/American establishment offering food such as chicken tandoor at $9.95 for half a chicken, $14.95 for a whole. Diners and help are well dressed and the interior can be described as tasteful and pretty in this suburban slice of South Asia. Saffron Patch's menu includes many rice dishes and curries. A hit with adults and kids is a sweet and tangy yogurt drink called *lassi.*

Tommy's, 1824 Coventry Rd., Cleveland Heights, tel. (216) 321-7757. Meat is available but more popular are moderately priced vegetarian entrees such as spinach pie at $2.95. Other vegetarian hits include a zippy sandwich (toasted cheese, sunflower seeds, more) for $3.95 and a tempeh burger (fermented soy) with all the traditional hamburger fixin's for $3.15. Locals keep this place constantly busy.

Italian
Anthony's is in southeast suburban Solon at 6372 S-O-M Rd., tel. (440) 349-4975. A worthwhile breakfast stop, the restaurant serves many different kinds of coffee and delicious pastries, frequently delivered to the table on classy china, oozing strands of just-applied vanilla sauce. Figure $4-5 for gourmet coffee and a muffin. Lunch and dinner include traditional pasta and other dishes, plus meals such as grilled salmon for $18, grilled long-bone veal chop for $25, and Tuscan tenderloin of beef pie for $16. The wine bar carries an absorbing variety of Italian vintages.

Longo's, tel. (216) 461-1700, 6379 Mayfield Rd., Mayfield Heights, just a block west of I-271, serves up a medium-sized thin-crust pizza with lots of toppings for less than $10. The sandwiches and wings are tasty and competitively priced, too. Primarily carryout, there are nevertheless two plastic tables with chairs for dining in. In the opposite direction, check out a Lakewood establishment by the name of **Angelo's Pizza,** 14019 Madison Ave., tel. (216) 221-0440, which does a white pizza that gets rave reviews. **Angie's Pizza,** with five suburban locations, earns uniformly high marks from area residents, as does **Ohio City Pizza,** 1881 Fulton Rd., tel. (216) 281-5252. Ohio serves pizza with a choice of 15 toppings, plus spaghetti and Buffalo wings.

Back downtown, there's a lot to like at **Frank and Paulys,** tel. (216) 575-1000, in part because there's a lot to eat. The guys serve moderately priced Italian food family style downtown at 200 Public Square (Superior Avenue). A lunchtime serving of pasta is eight ounces, while it's twice that at dinner. Share whatever's ordered, whether it's chicken breast, veal, a 16-ounce New York strip steak or a 20-ounce filet. Evening meals average about $12-15.

Latin/Spanish
Luchita's, a modest, red-brick tavern at 3456 W. 117th St., tel. (216) 252-1169, creates some

of the most authentic Mexican food anywhere north of the border. The rookie Mexican diner quickly learns that chocolate makes a delicious mole sauce for chicken and that cactus is a great ingredient in a numbere of dishes. Prepare to spend $5-7 for lunch and maybe $10 at most for dinner. Both price quotes include a Bohemia beer, which is Mexican despite its name. Luchita's also has several vegetarian dishes. More a restaurant than a bar, it's closed from the end of lunch to the beginning of dinner. The simple stucco interior seems to be populated largely with regular neighborhood visitors.

In the opposite direction, look for **Lopez y Gonzalez** at 2066 Lee Rd., tel. (216) 371-7611, Cleveland Heights. Fancier than Luchita's, this bright, betiled spot has a wider range of dishes and higher prices than its west-side counterpart. The favorite dinner here is paella, a rich seafood dish that includes shrimp, clams, mussels, chicken, and sausage, accompanied with saffron rice, for $18.95. Bête noir is a sinfully rich dessert, billed as flourless chocolate cake but coming across like premium fudge. The coffee here is equally rich and there are several kinds of Mexican beer from which to choose.

Piccolo Mondo, 1352 W. Sixth St., tel. (216) 241-1300, is casual yet upscale. This restaurant in the Warehouse District downtown serves a combination of Italian and South American food that includes tapas, the dainty and addictive Spanish hors d'oeuvres. The most popular meal is a toss-up between traditional paella at $16.95 and Atlantic salmon Wellington at $16.50. Both dishes are served a la carte.

Mediterranean

The **Greek Express** has at least three things going for it. The little restaurant is quite inexpensive, it's inside the glamorous Arcade at 401 Euclid Ave., downtown, and the gyros are as good as you're apt to find. Lunch-hour diners, about to experience onions, yogurt sauce, and contentment, stream away from the Express to sit and munch beneath the skylight in the indoor shopping facility. All for about five bucks.

Nicely located, **Nate's Deli & Restaurant,** 1923 W. 25th St., is a West Side Market neighbor and a counterpoint to some of the *nouveau* dining sites that have sprung up nearby. Nate has hot dogs, pastrami, and other kosher sandwiches, but the Middle Eastern vegetarian dishes are worth the wait—which takes place most noons. A meal with everything from garlicky hummus spread to exotic fava beans is around $6 with a soft drink. Virtually anything can be packed to go.

Seafood

If you can make it to the rock and roll museum you can make it to **Hornblower's Barge & Grill,** moored at 1151 N. Marginal Rd., tel. (216) 363-1151, on the lakefront. Hornblower's is known for oceanic delights at fair prices. Besides crab cakes, salmon steaks and vegetarian entrees are popular. So are burgers. There's no deep frying, and location and variety make it a hit with kids. The most often ordered meal of an evening is salmon steak, which is $14.95.

Another seafood restaurant, this one with a saltwater accent, is **Sweetwater's Sausalito Cafe** at 1301 E. 9th St., tel. (216) 696-2233. Favorites include paella, scallops florentine, various fresh filets, and salmon steaks. Side dishes are especially interesting, featuring anything from okra to whatever is local and freshly grown. Sweetwater's regulars most often order the pasta special, which can vary in price from $9.95 to $14.95. A pianist soothes weekend diners.

Taverns

Don't shrug off the plethora of bars that serve food. While eats may be an afterthought at many places, others pride themselves in serving up meals, sandwiches, and snacks that are the equal of any restaurant in town. The area's best fish fry, for example, can be found at the **Gray Wolf,** 4761 State Rd., tel. (216) 741-1330. Served Wednesday noons and Friday evenings only, the Atlantic cod with cole slaw and fries is but $6. Another place, both friendly and willing to sell you a pizza from next door, is **Edison's Pub** at 2373 Professor Ave., tel. (216) 522-0006, Tremont City. Small— there are about a dozen bar stools—the facility stocks nearly 100 brands of bottled beer and also dishes out items such as turkey chili, hummus, and assorted sandwiches. "The Shame of the Flats" is **Dick's Last Resort,** a raucous spot at 1096 Old River Rd., tel. (216) 241-1234. Dine here on wings, buckets of chicken, sandwiches and more as live bands play every night of the week.

CLEVELAND AREA EVENTS

Note: Information on events without a telephone numbers is available from the Greater Cleveland Convention & Visitors Bureau, tel. (216) 621-4110 or (800) 321-1004.

JANUARY

Winter Expo, Cleveland Metroparks Chalets, tel. (216) 261-6600. All sorts of sports and other activities take place in the city's "emerald necklace," which usually is dusted in white at this time of year.

MARCH

Cleveland International Film Festival, Theater District (also April). If a visitor's favorite film is obscure enough, perhaps he or she will see it here.

APRIL

Tri-C Jazz Fest, Cuyahoga Community College and elsewhere. This jazz buffet lures lots of musicians and their fans

MAY

Cleveland Marathon, Cleveland State University, tel. (330) 425-9811, ext. 2364. More than 10,000 runners from virtually every state and 20 foreign countries make this a major stop on the marathon tour.

Cleveland Performance Art Festival, Colonial Arcade. Performance artists impress with their originality in the downtown landmark.

Rock and Roll Hall of Fame Induction Ceremony, Rock and Roll Hall of Fame and Museum. The stars show up and get humble as their holograms are put on the museum's walls.

JUNE

Great American Rib Cookoff, Burke Lakefront Airport. With an offshore breeze, this event can be whiffed for miles.

Clifton Art & Musicfest, Clifton Boulevard at 117th Street, tel. (216) 228-4383, includes a fine arts and crafts show, live entertainment, and children's activities.

Senior Celebration Day, Cleveland Metroparks Zoo, tel. (216) 661-6500, includes free admission for anyone over 55. Seniors are entertained and mix with animals of all ages.

Pro Beach Volleyball, Nautica Complex in the Flats, tel. (216) 861-4080. The world's best two-woman volleyball teams compete here.

Parade the Circle Celebration, University Circle. Call this a salute to the cerebral as Cleveland pays homage to its several universities and other intellectual institutions.

JULY

Festival of Freedom, Edgewater Park, tel. (216) 623-1105, is a July 4th salute, with fireworks.

Zoo Blooms is a special tour of Cleveland Metroparks Zoo gardens, tel. (216) 661-6500. A highlight is the release of 10,000 ladybugs.

River Expo, Docks 20 and 22, Port of Cleveland. A glorified boat show is a great way to celebrate summer.

Grand Prix of Cleveland, Burke Lakefront Airport. Open-wheel Indy Cars perform on a course laid out across the runways.

AUGUST

Family Fun Fest, Cleveland Metroparks Zoo, tel. (216) 661-6500, offers live musical entertainment, sidewalk chalk artistry, and characters in costumes.

Heritage and Cultural Celebration, Western Reserve Historical Society, tel. (216) 721-5722, includes food, entertainment, hands-on activities, and educational programs.

Feast of the Assumption, Italian Village. The east side of Cleveland takes on an Old World look, highlighted by a colorful religious procession.

SEPTEMBER

Taste of Cleveland, Nautical Complex, tel. (216) 247-4386, in the Flats. Signature dishes from a number of restaurants are available for sampling.

Cleveland National Air Show, Burke Lakefront Airport. This annual event is a spectacular setting for a flying exhibition.

Head of the Cuyahoga Rowing Regatta, Cuyahoga River. The next thing one knows, they'll be drinking from the Cuyahoga.

NOVEMBER AND DECEMBER

Downtown Holiday Lighting Program, Public Square. Big cities look their cheeriest with all the lights on, particularly all the holiday bulbs.

RECREATION

Cleveland Metroparks offer 19,000 acres of biking, golf, hiking, hayrides, nature centers, swimming, picnicking, and more. The 14 sites, termed reservations, are nicely spaced across the area. One of the more unique opportunities, far to the south near Hinckley, is climbing at Whipp's Ledges. There's a permit system which must be requested in advance and climbers must be insured, but the farflung site and the unusual activity indicate there's something for almost everyone. To find out which parks most appeal you, call (216) 351-6300, where you can tal to a Metroparks staffer around the clock.

Golf

There are more prestigious places to play golf than on Cleveland Metroparks courses, but prices are nice and there's a certain pleasant informality. The two best are **Manakiki Golf,**

Terminal Tower, built in 1930, was the tallest building in the world outside of New York City until 1955.

North Chagrin Reservation, 35501 Eddy Rd., tel. (216) 942-2500, and **Sleepy Hollow,** Brecksville Reservation, 9445 Brecksville Rd., tel. (216) 526-4285. Both charge $10.50 for nine holes or $19 for 18. The four others are **Big Met,** Rocky River Reservation, 4811 Valley Pkwy., tel. (216) 331-1070; **Little Met,** Rocky River Reservation, 18599 Old Lorain Rd., tel. (216) 941-9672; **Mastic Woods,** Rocky River Reseration, 19990 Puritas Rd., tel. (216) 267-5626; and **Shawnee Hills,** Bedford Reservation, 18753 Egbert Rd., tel. (216) 232-7184. Greens fees at the latter four are $6-8.50 for nine holes.

Horse Racing

Those who enjoy sports gambling can do so legally in Cleveland at **Thistledown,** the horse track at 21501 Emery Rd., tel. (216) 662-8600, on the city's southeast side. There's no admission charge to wager and watch 14 live races plus dozens of simultaneous telecasts go off each day. Gates open at daily at11:30 a.m. and the season runs from mid-March to mid-December. The facility also has a Web site, www.thistledown.com.

(For beachfront activities, see the **Lake Erie** section that follows.)

TRANSPORTATION

The **Greater Cleveland Convention and Visitors Bureau,** tel. (216) 621-9500 will answer queries concerning bus and rapid transit schedules and routes. Look for the two-tone orange logo, which marks where to catch Regional Transit Authority (RTA) vehicles all over the city. A bus ride costs $1.25 or $1.50, depending on the route. Downtown loop buses are a bargain at 50 cents when you find yourself some distance from your parked car.

The **Rapid Transit System** buzzes electrically between Tower City Center and Hopkins Airport, and between the tower complex and near-in eastern suburbs such as Shaker Heights. Cost of a one-way ticket is $1.50.

For a succinct way to see city highlights, go to Burke Lakefront Airport. Eschew a plane and instead catch one of the **Trolley Tours of Cleveland.** This historic city tour covers 20 miles and more than 100 points of interest. The bright red trolleys have even been known to schedule a tavern stop. Telephone (216) 771-4484 for reservations, which are required. Cost of the tour is $6 for adults, $5 for seniors and $4 for children ages 5-18 for the one-hour tour. Special tours for groups of 20 or more are available. The lakefront airport is a couple of blocks east of the Rock and Roll Hall of Fame, north of I-90. Exit East 9th Street.

INFORMATION AND SERVICES

Reach the **Greater Cleveland Convention and Visitors Bureau** by dialing (216) 621-4110 locally or (800) 321-1004. **Cleveline** is at (216) 961-1996, providing recorded information concerning the city's calendar of events, acquiring tickets, bus and rapid transit use, weekend packages, and other visitor information. There is also a **Cleveland Activity Line,** tel. (216) 899-9448.

There are five **Visitors Information Centers** located around town, each with its own hours and telephone. They include Tower City Center, tel. (216) 621-7981; Cleveland Hopkins International Airport, tel. (216) 265-3729; Powerhouse at Nautica Entertainment Complex, tel. (216) 623-4494; Nautica Boardwalk in the Flats, tel. (216) 623-4442; and the Terminal Tower Observation Deck, tel. (216) 621-7981.

Dial 911 for emergencies requiring the police. The police non-emergency number is (216) 623-5000.

For medical care, the Cleveland Clinic has an excellent reputation and is at 9500 Euclid Ave., tel. (216) 444-2200.

Post office customer service is (216) 443-4199.

Media

The *Plain Dealer* not only is the sole daily newspaper in the city, with a circulation of 386,256, it's the largest-circulation newspaper in Ohio. Best places to find local attraction information are in the "Friday Living" tabloid and in Sunday's "Arts" and "Living" sections. Cleveland is indeed a one-newspaper city, but only when speaking in daily terms. Sun Newspapers serve 78 communities in five metropolitan area counties via 23 weekly newspapers. They're sold at supermarkets and pharmacies and are a great source for very local, proximate events.

Several free periodicals are worth consideration. *Free Times,* is an alternative weekly available all over town and keeps Cleveland abreast of entertainment, food, music, and the usual. *Downtown Tab,* subtitled "Cleveland's Urban Biweekly," gives a nice slant on what's up in music, politics, shopping, and more.

Cleveland magazine employs a slick, formulaic approach to covering the big city ("Favorite restaurants," "Top doctors") and is available monthly for $2.95 at newsstands. *The Times of Your Life,* subtitled "The First Newspaper for an American Generation," is one of the few graphically exciting, intelligently written freebie tabloids for seniors offered anywhere. One issue wondered if heaven meant eternal choir practice and contained a story on pro sports nicknames down through the years. Pity it's only published every other month.

Another nice freebie is *North Coast Sports,* a tabloid monthly that covers Cleveland-area backpacking, basketball, canoeing, cycling, fishing, golf, hiking, rowing, rugby, running, sailing, skating, skiing, skydiving, swimming, tennis, and volleyball (whew!). Especially valuable are schedules of upcoming races and other events. Competing for the active reader is *Sports & Fitness Cleveland,* also a free, monthly tabloid—though it's published in Columbus. *Scene,* a free monthly tabloid obtainable at record stores and some nightspots, covers rock 'n' roll and other entertainment all across northeast Ohio. And for those of the C&W persuasion, check out *Cleveland Country Magazine,* a free monthly tabloid.

There are several worthwhile Web sites for trip planning. Pull up one or more and benefit from the most current information this side of a visitors' bureau laser printer. The official destination is the Greater Cleveland Web site at cleveland.oh.us where the mayor makes visitors welcome, and they receive nice overviews of sights and attractions. Cleveland Live at www.cleveland.com is sponsored by the daily newspaper, *The Plain Dealer,* and has a great many of the kinds of facts a newcomer needs to thrive. Another good address is General Electric's Cleveland Net at www.cleveland.net/cleveland/index.html.

Souvenirs

What bespeaks Cleveland? Here are several suggestions. Perhaps most visibly, any time of year, is Indians clothing and paraphernalia. Shirts, hats, pennants, bumper stickers—all such baseball items are widely available. You know the locals are whacked on the team when you can bellow "Go Tribe!" anywhere and be welcome. One source for sporty Cleveland stuff is **Daffy Dan's,** 2101 Superior Ave., tel. (216) 621-3336. Other wearable sellers include the **Rock Museum** or the **Great Lakes Brewing Company** brewpub-restaurant. Speaking of museums, the gift shop in the **Cleveland Museum of Art** has an array of neat, though not necessarily Cleveland-oriented, merchandise.

For an edible souvenir, venture to **Euclid Meat and Sausage** at 821 E. 222nd St., tel. (216) 261-9006. German, Hungarian, Irish, Italian, Lithuanian, Mexican, and Slovenian sausages are crafted here and shipped worldwide. Send links to friends or reward yourself with wurst by mail. In contrast, the ultimate souvenir is free and flowing in the Flats. Approach the **Cuyahoga River** warily, dip a container into the infamous body of water that once self-combusted, seal tightly, and head for home.

LAKESIDE CLEVELAND

This stretch of waterfront, comprising Lake and Cuyahoga Counties, is blessed with a number of nice beaches. In between are restaurants, hotels and motels, and various other rendezvous. A range of somewhat rural and extremely urban, the two counties also are a mix of civilization and nature at the water's edge.

Lake County is the smallest of Ohio's 72 counties. Yet it's chock full of people and attractions. Cuyahoga County is the Cleveland metropolitan area.

History

The Iroquois dominated this area for a number of years before and after the arrival of Europeans in North America. They were a powerful tribe, moving back and forth at will as less warlike tribes deferred to them. Pioneers, many of whom were from Connecticut, used the Indian trails to reach their destinations. By 1800, the 3.8-million acre Western Reserve, as it was known, had 1,300 white settlers. The land was given to Connecticut in exchange for the state renouncing other claims, and a great variety of people migrated to

the lakeshore. Finns, Hungarians, Slovaks, and Slovenians showed up after the English, the Germans, and the Irish settled in. The lakeside area east of Cleveland became known for its nurseries, vineyards, and orchards—in contrast to the industrialization going on next door in Cuyahoga County.

Orientation

Interstate 90 runs roughly parallel and quite close to the lakefront in these counties, continuing up east to the Western Reserve and Pennsylvania, and to the west just into Cleveland. US 6 and 20, and SR 2 all parallel the Lake Erie coastline, with US 6 staying the closest to the coast all the way west. State Route 2 runs concurrently with I-90 through Cleveland; SR 2 splits from I-90 in east Euclid and stays closer to the shore. Lake County has about 20 miles of shoreline, while Cuyahoga County has approximately 30.

Sights

Arguably the state's best beach, and certainly its longest, **Headlands Beach State Park.** 9601 Headlands Rd., Mentor, tel. (440) 881-8141 is a picturesque revelation. Beach and sand grasses nod in the wind, there's a lighthouse, the area seldom is crowded, and a stiff offshore breeze can create waves of surprising intensity. A heavily used Iroquois Indian trail once ran along here In Lake County, Ohio's smallest county. Opened in 1953, the beach was closed for the 1957 season due to the potentially deadly undertow that year. Besides swimming, visitors can picnic, hike, or fish from the federal breakwall for various bass species, plus perch, bluegill, walleye, coho salmon, and carp.

The park itself offers two separate, spacious parking lots. Just north of either lot, through stands of trees, is the beach. It stretches for a mile and tends to be more gravel than sand in some areas. The eastern end of the facility is made up of the breakwall, the lighthouse, the northern terminus of the Buckeye Trail (see **North Country Scenic Trail**), and the limited-access Headland Dunes State Nature Preserve. Bordering the park on the south is Mentor Marsh State Nature Preserve, a 644-acre marsh with a five-mile hiking trail usable during daylight hours. To reach Headlands, drive north on SR 44 (Heisley Road) from SR 2. Fairport Harbor is the nearest town; the beach is about 30 miles east of downtown Cleveland.

Cleveland Lakefront, tel. (216) 881-8141, is a single state park with half a dozen different sites. Three of the six—Wildwood, Euclid Beach, and Edgewater Park—have swimming areas. One of Ohio's newer retreats, the park came into being in 1977 when the city of Cleveland leased its four lakefront parks to the state. The four parks became known collectively as Cleveland Lakefront State Park in 1978, and in 1982 the Euclid Beach area was added to state park property. Each venue has slightly different amenities.

Wildwood, the easternmost beach in the park, has a six-ramp boat launch and picnic areas. Two long rock breakwalls give anglers access to rich walleye potential, and in the spring the anglers crowd Euclid Creek here to get at spawning coho salmon. Wildwood is accessible by driving north on Neff Road from Lakeshore Boulevard.

Euclid Beach has a 650-foot-long swimming beach, but there also are picnic areas and an observation pier. Euclid Beach is just east of East 156th Street and north off Lakeshore Boulevard.

Gordon Park is virtually in the shadow of the massive Cleveland Electric & Illuminating Company nearby. CE&I discharges lots of warm water, which lures steelhead and salmon in the winter. The site also has half a dozen boat-launching ramps. The park is at East 72nd Street, north of the East Shoreway (I-90/SR 2).

East 55th Street Marina has 335 seasonal rental docks; water and electrical hookups are available. A 1,200-foot fishing platform points westward from a spit of land, creating a U-shaped harbor. This marina is north off the East Shoreway.

Edgewater Park actually is a pair of facilities. There's an upper and a lower park, connected by a paved bicycle path. The upper beach has restrooms, playground equipment, and a statue of Conrad Mizar. It's fitting (no pun intended) that Mizar, a tailor, stands in the park; he promoted summer band concerts in Cleveland parks in the late 19th century. Mizar's likeness is one of the oldest monuments in Cleveland. The view of the city skyline to the east is memorable. The lower park has a 900-foot swimming beach, a concession stand, and a fishing pier. Both sites are accessible from the West Shoreway (SR 2).

Yacht clubs and marinas dot the downtown Cleveland lakefront. A state brochure shows 10 such facilities. The closest to downtown is North Coast Harbor, just west of Burke Lakefront Airport, within walking distance of the Rock and Roll Hall of Fame and Museum, and about nine blocks due north of Jacobs Field, home of the sold-out Cleveland Indians major league baseball team.

Indian Museum of Lake County is on the Lake Erie College campus, 319 W. Washington St., Painesville, tel. (440) 352-1911. The museum was established by the local chapter of the Archaeological Society of Ohio and therefore is scrupulous about what it shows. Artifacts from 10,000 B.C. are on display, and there is an exhibit of the Whittlesey Culture. These prehistoric people lived in the area and may have been killed off by Seneca Indians in a clash over furs. Also shown are native arts and crafts from 1800, gathered from all across North America. Hours are Mon.-Fri. 10 a.m.-4 p.m. and Sat.-Sun. 1-4 p.m. during the school year. In the summer, weekend hours also are 10 a.m.-4 p.m. Closed major holiday weekends, the museum charges $2 for adult, $1.50 for senior, and $1 for student admissions.

Steamship William G. Mather Museum, 1001 E. 9th St. Pier, Cleveland, tel. (216) 574-6262, is a preserved ore boat that has been turned into an exhibit. The 618-foot long boat with the riveted hull was built in 1925 and carried millions of tons of iron ore, stone, coal, and grain. Visitors can see the boat's cavernous (14,000-ton) cargo holds and tour the surprisingly elegant staterooms, the crew's quarters, and the pilot house. A forward cargo hold chronicles the history of Great Lakes shipping. The boat is open Mon.-Sat. 10 a.m.-5 p.m. and Sunday noon-5 p.m., Memorial Day-Labor Day. In May, September, and October, its hours are Fri.-Sat. 10 a.m.-5 p.m. Admission is $4.50 for adults, $3.50 for seniors, and $2.50 for students.

The **U.S.S. Cod,** 1089 Maringal Rd. (off East 9th Street), Cleveland, tel. (216) 566-8770 or (800) 321-1004, is another water-oriented museum. This vessel is a submarine that sank more than a dozen Japanese ships in the Southwest Pacific during World War II. Visitors can look into a torpedo tube, experience the tight fit of a seaman's bunk, or sit in the captain's chair in the ward room. The facility is open The facility is open daily 10 a.m.-5 p.m. May-Labor Day and September weekends. Admission fees are $4 for adults and $2 for children.

Farther east, check out the **Fairport Harbor Museum,** 129 Second St., Fairport Harbor, tel. (440) 354-4825. This historical site consists of a well-preserved lighthouse and the lighthouse keeper's dwelling beside it, both dating from 1871. The conical tower was constructed in 1825. It's 60 feet high, has 69 steps that spiral upward toward the light, and contains a light that could be seen 17.5 miles out into Lake Erie. Besides keeping ships on the straight and narrow, the light marked a terminal for the Underground Railroad prior to the Civil War. Today, the dwelling is filled with maritime exhibits. Hours are Wednesday and Sat.-Sun. 1-6 p.m. from the Saturday prior to Memorial Day through Labor Day. There is no admission charge.

Wineries
Just west of the Ashtabula-Lake county line, look for **Chalet Debonne Vineyard** at 7743 Doty Rd., Madison, tel. (440) 466-3485. Debonne produces about 50,000 gallons of wine each year, the most popular being their Riesling at $8.98 per bottle and River Rouge at $6.23. When it opened in 1971, Debonne was the Western Reserve's first new winery since before Prohibition. Now the facility markets its 23 different kinds of wine in more than 400 Ohio stores and restaurants. Open year round, the facility greets visitors Tuesday, Thursday, and Saturday noon-8 p.m. and Wednesday and Friday noon-11 p.m.

Recreation
Grand River Canoe Livery is at 3825 Fobes Rd., Rock Creek, tel. (800) ME-CANOE (tel. 800-632-2663). Those who paddle the Grand downriver will head west out of western Ashtabula County, pass beneath two covered bridges, and head generally westward. The river empties into Lake Erie at Fairport Harbor, north of Painesville.

The **YMCA Outdoor Family Center** at 4540 River Rd., Perry, tel. (440) 259-2724, charges a small fee for cross-country skiing. Perry is east of Painesville and between US 20 and I-90. There are several other cross-country venues farther inland in Lake County, including the **Chapin Forest Reservation,** 10373 Hobart Rd., Kirtland, tel. (440) 256-2255.

Travelers don't have to hire a charter service in order to test their **fishing** luck. The Chagrin River offers public access at Woodland Park and Lake Shore Boulevard in Eastlake, as well as near the Old St. Clair Bridge, in Gilson Park, and around the Daniels Park Dam in Willoughby. In the Grand River area, try the breakwall from Headlands State Park in Mentor or off the end of Water Street in Fairport Harbor. Arcola Creek in Madison Township has public access at the end of Lake Road. Those who would like to get out on the lake for a day of fishing should contact the Lake County Visitors Bureau for a list of boats and their home ports.

Cleveland Metroparks contain a number of nice **golf** courses. In Lake County, look for **Erie Shores Golf Course,** 7298 Lake Rd., Madison Township, tel. (440) 428-3164. This 18-hole, par-70 facility charges $9.50 for nine holes and $16 for 18 holes on weekends, with weekdays slightly lower. Cart rentals are $5.50 for nine holes and $11 for 18. Also a Metroparks course is **Pine Ridge Golf Club,** 30601 Ridge Rd., Wickliffe, tel. (440) 943-1010. Greens fees are around $18 for nine holes and $33 for 18 (including cart rental). Weekdays are less.

Painesville Speedway, 650 Fairport Nursery Rd., tel. (440) 354-3505, is home to that sport of sports, figure-eight auto racing. On weekend evenings when drivers aren't intentionally running into each other there are various kinds of stock-car races.

Entertainment and Culture
Muldoon's on Vine, 32911 Vine St., Willowick, tel. (440) 944-5082. Music Friday and Saturday at this friendly place is strictly rock 'n' roll. But on Sunday evenings the decks are cleared for a polka band. The usual cover charge is $2.

Two different sites come to mind when talking about **theater** or stage performances in Lake County. **Wickliffe Civic Theater,** 900 Worden Rd., tel. (440) 944-7788, offers a range of adults and children's performances in the 250-seat auditorium at the Wickliffe Civic Center. **Mad Hatter's Comedy Theatre** is at 1697 Mentor Ave., Painesville Township, tel. (440) 354-1HAT (tel. 440-354-1427). Nationally known comedians are booked into Mad Hatter's on Friday and Saturday nights throughout the year.

LAKESIDE CLEVELAND EVENTS

FEBRUARY

Annual Lakeland Jazz Festival, Lakeland Community College Performing Arts Center, tel. (440) 953-7105.

MARCH

Annual Bike Expo, Lake Metroparks, Kirtland, tel. (440) 585-2800 or (800) 669-9226.

APRIL

Dressage Competition, Lake Erie College team, Humphrey Equestrian Center, Concord, tel. (440) 352-3393.

Spring Public Tour, Mooreland Estate, Kirtland, tel. (440) 953-7306.

Annual Grand River Canoe Race, tel. (440) 256-2126, begins at the Harpersfield Dam in Ashtabula County and ends in Hidden Valley Park, Madison.

MAY

Annual Fly Fishing Mini Conclave, Penitentiary Glen, Kirtland, tel. (440) 951-6637.

Yankee Promo Antique Show, Lake County Fairgrounds, Painesville, tel. (440) 354-3339.

B&O Metric Century Bike Ride, Lake Metroparks, Concord, tel. (800) 669-9226.

JUNE

Annual Hot Air Balloon Festival, Chalet Debonne Winery, Madison, tel. (440) 466-3485.

Summer Concerts, Amphitheater at Civic Center Park, Mentor, tel. (440) 974-5735.

Cleveland Open golf tournament, Quail Hollow Resort, Concord Township, tel. (440) 352-6201.

Summer Baseball Fest—1860s, Lake County Historical Center, Mentor, tel. (440) 255-8979.

Kirtland Strawberry Festival, Kirtland High School, tel. (440) 256-1181.

JULY

Vintage Ohio Annual Wine Festival, Lake Farmpark, Kirtland, tel. (800) 366-FARM (tel. 800-366-3276) or (800) 227-6972.

Historic Downtown Willoughby Arts Festival, tel. (440) 942-3433.

North American Walleye Anglers and Harbor Days, Lakefront Park, Fairport Harbor, tel. (440) 256-2126.

Little Mountain Folk Festival, Lake County History Center, Kirtland Hills, tel. (440) 255-8979.

AUGUST

Annual Ohio Wine Festival, Lake County Fair-

Accommodations

Hotels and motels in Lake County are perhaps 5-10% less expensive than comparable facilities in Cleveland proper. It's also true that the farther travelers stay from an interstate highway, the more apt they are to find a room—and a thrifty one at that. There are about 20 motels, a couple of bed and breakfast accommodations, and two campgrounds. The most common motel site is along SR 306, near I-90, in Mentor. Facilities there include a **Days Inn,** tel. (800) 325-2525; a **Knight's Inn,** tel. (440) 953-8835; and a **TraveLodge,** tel. (440) 585-1900. Wickliffe and Willoughby also offer several motels near the interstate.

Among the more unique B&B propositions in Ohio is **Rutherford Boatel Bed and Breakfast,** 311 River St., Grand River, tel. (440) 352-8122. Another option is staying at the **Rider's Inn,** 792 Mentor Ave., Painesville, tel. (440) 354-8200, which is known for its food and drink. Both are in the moderate price range.

Campers will want to check out **Polebridge**

Campgrounds, 4045 S. Ridge Rd., Perry, tel. (440) 259-2702, or the cabins in Lake Metroparks' Hogback Ridge, 4700 Emerson Rd., Madison Township, tel. (440) 256-7275.

Food

You have to admire a place that boasts of its greasy french fries. **Brennan's Fish House,** 102 River St. in Grand River, tel. (440) 354-9785, also is proud of its fresh seafoods, to include Lake Erie yellow perch, oysters, and walleye. The decor is nautical, the fireplace crackles in cold weather, the gazebo lights blaze into the night, and a fresh fish meal such as walleye can be had, complete with french fries and cole slaw, for $11. A perch dinner, also with fries and slaw, is $15. Nautically atmospheric and friendly, you may learn here that the walleye and perch taste good because they are related.

George's Famous Dinner Bell Diner, 1155 Bank St., Painesville Township, tel. (440) 354-3708, offers good food at good prices. For break-

grounds, US 20, Painesville, tel. (800) 227-OWPA (or tel. 800-227-6972), lets vintners show off their wares as continuous rock, reggae, jazz, and blues puts everyone in a laid-back mood.

Johnnycake Jog, Lake County Fairgrounds, Painesville, tel. (440) 354-3339.

Annual Downtown Willoughby Corn Fest, tel. (440) 975-1776.

Lake Metroparks Lighthouse Triathlon/Biathlon, Lakefront Park, Fairport Harbor, tel. (440) 256-1404.

SEPTEMBER

Oktoberfest, Lake County Fairgrounds, Painesville, tel. (440) 354-3339, is said to be the "original American Oktoberfest." If so, how come they got the month wrong? This Labor Day event draws 60,000 people.

Concord Community Days, Concord Township, tel. (440) 354-3003

Perch Fest, which includes a 5K run, is in Lakefront Park, Fairport Harbor, tel. (800) 368-LAKE (tel. 800-368-5253) or (440) 354-2424.

Fall Leaf Trail, Holden Arboretum, Kirtland, tel. (440) 946-4400.

Fall Harvest Festival, Lake Farmpark, Kirtland, tel. (800) 366-FARM (or tel. 800-366-3276).

Annual Pedal the Parks Bike Ride, Lake Metroparks, Painesville, tel. (800) 669-9226 (helmet required).

Northeastern Ohio Rose Show, Mooreland Estate, Kirtland, tel. (440) 953-7306.

City of Mentor Arts Festival, Memorial Junior High School, Mentor, tel. (440) 974-5735.

OCTOBER

Wildlife Festival, Lake Metropark Penitentiary Glen Reservation, Kirtland, tel. (440) 256-1404

Corn and Pumpkin Days, Lake Farmpark, Kirtland, tel. (800) 366-FARM (tel. 800-366-3276) or (440) 256-2122.

NOVEMBER

Quilt Auction, Wildwood Cultural Center, Mentor, tel. (440) 974-5735.

Autumn Leaves Five-Mile Cross Country Run, Quail Hollow Resort, Concord Township, tel. (440) 352-6201, ext. 3507.

Farmpark Country Lights, Lake Farmpark, Kirtland, tel. (440) 256-2122 or (800) 366-FARM (tel. 800-366-3276).

DECEMBER

Annual Christmas Display and Crafts Sale, Wild-

---

fast, ordering Alexander the Great will get a diner steak tips, eggs, hash browns, and toast, all for $6.25. Also popular is a Greek omelet at $4.95. Steak tips also are popular at lunch atop noodles for $5.95. In the evening, especially good values are a half slab of baby back ribs or an eight-ounce prime rib; either is just $7.95. Soups here are homemade and cost $2 per cup. "A cup here is as big as a bowl," says an employee. George's is open Mon.-Sat. 8 a.m.-9 p.m. and Sunday 8 a.m.-8 p.m.

The **Riders Inn,** 792 Mentor Ave., Painesville, tel. (440) 354-8200, once was a stagecoach stop and, simultaneously, an Underground Railroad station during the mid-19th century. Today it's a restaurant that specializes in serving fish and game. The owners also have some dishes derived from ancient recipes found in the attic. Among the most popular is the inn's potato-leek soup, available at lunch or dinner. Orange roughy is popular at either meal, offered at $5.95 for lunch and $13.95 in the evening. Another dinner

favorite is prime rib encrusted in herbs that were grown just outside the door. Open every day for lunch and dinner, Rider's also sets out a 31-item Sunday brunch available 10 a.m.-3 p.m. The brunch is $12.95.

The **Old Tavern,** SR 84 at County Line Road, Unionville, tel. (440) 428-2091 or (800) 7-TAVERN (tel. 800-782-8376), is on the National Register of Historic Places. It was also a stagecoach stop and an Underground Railroad station. These days, luncheon favorites include such items as chicken a la king. Dinner may be seafood pasta, old-fashioned Swiss steak, or one of several steak or lake meals. Lunches are less than $10 and evening meals average about $15. Tuesday nights there's a country buffet for $6.95 and on Thursday diners can order a prime rib meal and a glass of wine for $9.95. Sunday is highlighted by a brunch that begins at 9 a.m. The Old Tavern, which keeps the air fragrant with its corn fritters, is closed Monday.

Shopping

Mall shoppers will enjoy their experience at **Great Lakes Mall,** 7850 Mentor Ave., Mentor, tel. (440) 255-6900. The facility, which is between Mentor Avenue and SR 84, off SR 306, has dozens of stores, including Dillard's, JCPenney, Kaufmann's, and Sears.

Mentor boasts what is billed as the world's largest art gallery. **Gallery One,** 7003 Center St., tel. (440) 255-1200 is sure to have a piece of art to match the couch. Seriously, the works of internationally known artists are commonplace here, as are special exhibits, scheduled appearances by artists, and renowned lecturers.

Amid all those vineyards travelers will find a number of large and diverse nurseries. The growing season is longer than one might suspect, and the vicinity of Perry in particular has garden centers that retail their flora.

Transportation

The best way to view lakeside downtown Cleveland may be from the water, and the best excursion may be on the *Goodtime III.* The ship is moored at the 825 E. 9th St. Pier, tel. (216) 861-5110, next door to the Rock and Roll Hall of Fame. The boat has a 1,000-passenger capacity, an open deck, a semi-open deck, and a deck that's heated and air-conditioned. From June 15 through Labor Day, the boat offers two-hour Lake Erie/Cuyahoga River tours that shove off daily at noon and 3 p.m., on Sunday there's an extra cruise at 6:00 p.m. In September the *Goodtime* leaves port Fri.-Sun. at noon and 3 p.m. only. The cost is $12.50 for adults, $11.50 for seniors, and $7.50 for children. The tours are narrated and soft drinks, hard drinks, and snacks are available. The *Goodtime III* also offers other cruises, like a "rush hour" cruise on Friday, various nighttime cruises, and a daily luncheon cruise available by reservation only.

A sweet deal for folks who want to move around the downtown waterfront is available on the **RTA Waterfront Line.** This Cleveland Regional Transit Authority route begins at the Tower City Center station, on Prospect Avenue, travels north along the east bank of the Flats entertainment area, heads east to North Coast Harbor and ends at South Harbor Station in the East 12th Street municipal building. Buses run 4 a.m.-1 a.m. and the fare is $1.50. Passengers also receive passes that are good for three hours of travel between Tower City and South Harbor. Call (216) 621-9500 if there are questions.

Count on **Laketran** for public bus service throughout Lake County on both fixed routes and dial-a-ride runs, which, with reservations 24 hours in advance, provide door-to-door service on a schedule you create. Fares are 75 cents on fixed routes, $3 for dial-a-ride service. For more information, call (440) 354-6100.

Information and Services

The Coast Guard is in charge of problems that occur on or in the water. Call them at (216) 522-4413.

The **Convention and Visitors Bureau of Greater Cleveland** is downtown at 50 Public Square, Suite 3100, tel. (216) 621-4110 or (800) 321-1001. The **Lake County Visitors Bureau** is at 1610 Mentor Ave., Room 2, Painesville, tel. (440) 354-2424 or (800) 368-5253. Lake Erie College will reveal campus happenings to those who telephone (440) 942-3872 or (800) 533-4996.

The mighty *Plain Dealer* is Cleveland's daily newspaper, published every morning. Entertainment is covered on Thursday. Willoughby stays current by reading the *News-Herald* every morning. Entertainment is covered in Friday's "TGIF" tabloid section.

AKRON

Once the world's rubber manufacturing center, Akron remains an important polymer source and the home of America's largest rubber company—Goodyear. One or more of the tiremaker's blimps are tethered here when they're not hovering above televised sporting events. Akron itself was named for the Greek word *"akros,"* meaning high place; the city sits astride the watershed between Lake Erie and the Ohio River in Summit County (naturally). Water running north eventually exits the continent via the Great Lake and the St. Lawrence River, while water running south flows down the Ohio to the Mississippi River and into the Gulf of Mexico.

History

The first visitors to this area were Native Americans, toting canoes and supplies as they made the eight-mile portage between the Cuyahoga and Tuscarawas Rivers. At one time their path was so worn it was used to mark the western boundary of the United States.

The first people of European descent founded the village of Hudson, some 12 miles north, in 1799. Farmers began to clear land in earnest 10 years later. By 1820 the locals were wondering where the proposed Ohio and Erie Canal would run, and by 1825 General Simon Perkins and others were founding and laying out what would become the city of Akron at the high point of the proposed canal. Approximately 300 lots were defined, in time for the opening of the canal in 1827.

State of Ohio, a low and spacious canal boat, departed Lock No. 1 for Cleveland on July 3, 1827, assuring Akron a long run of production and prosperity. Grist mills, blast furnaces, lumber mills, and more greeted the coming of the first railroad in 1852, and the city helped the Union arm, feed, and clothe its soldiers. Benjamin Franklin (B. F.) Goodrich was lured to town in 1870 by a group of boosters who bought stock in his fledgling rubber plant. Once the horseless carriage showed up in the 1890s, the city's success was assured.

Besides a number of vast tire companies, Akron in the early 1900s was the home of dirigible technology, Quaker Oats—and people intent on work. Between 1910 and 1920, the population soared from 69,000 to 209,000, as everyone from thousands of Appalachian whites to a few hundred Russian Cossacks migrated toward Ohio's puffing smokestacks. The city burst its seams annexing nearby towns and reached a population of 350,000 before sliding into the depression of the 1930s. In contrast to Cleveland or Youngstown, many of the new Akron residents were southern whites. Among other things, they joined the Ku Klux Klan in record numbers.

World War II and the decade that followed

AKRON AREA HIGHLIGHTS

AKRON:

   Akron Art Museum
   Akron Civic Theater
   Akron Zoological Park
   Canal Park (baseball stadium)
   Cuyahoga Valley National Recreation
   Area
   Goodyear World of Rubber Museum
   Hower House
   Inventure Place
   Stan Hywet Hall and Gardens
   University of Akron

SUBURBAN NORTH:

   Blossom Music Center
   Hale Farm and Village

SUBURBAN SOUTH:

   Goodyear Hangar
   Portage Lakes State Park
   Quail Hollow State Park

SUBURBAN EAST:

   Chapel Hill Shopping Mall
   Kent State University
   West Branch State Park

SUBURBAN WEST:

   Portage Hill Vineyards
   Wolf Creek Vineyards

were good to Akron. War machines, farm tractors, trucks, and cars needed tires in all sizes. The prosperity has been interrupted since then, due first to the invasion of foreign cars (and foreign tires) and then to periodic car-sales slumps. Nowadays, Firestone is owned by a Japanese tiremaker and tires made by Akron-based companies are virtually all manufactured elsewhere before rolling off auto assembly lines on cars of American and Japanese heritage alike. With 220,000 residents (and 530,000 in all of Summit County), Akron "never looked better than it does now," according to George W. Knepper, a retired University of Akron history professor and author of a comprehensive history of the state.

"When you consider that 35,000 of the best-paying jobs in the world departed in the 1970s and 1980s, this city has recovered in a dramatic way," Dr. Knepper says, adding that there are few signs nowadays of many residents' Appalachian heritage. Most of the oldest and ugliest manufacturing buildings have been razed, while others have been rehabilitated for use by the growing polymer industry. Not among the nation's first-echelon towns in terms of the arts, Akron nevertheless has become more tidy and more liveable than anyone a quarter century earlier might have imagined.

The city has had its share of well-known people down through the years, from fiery abolitionist John Brown to Alcoholics Anonymous founder Dr. Bob, to rock Pretender Chrissie Hynde. So perhaps it's all right that the only tires still made in Akron are racing and experimental models crafted by Goodyear.

Orientation

Attached umbilically to Cleveland via the Cuyahoga Valley National Recreation Area, Akron is served by I-77 running north to Cleveland and south through Canton, the Tuscawaras Valley and eventually to West Virginia. Interstate 76 runs through Akron, east to Youngstown and Pennsylvania and west to join with I-71, which in turn links Akron to Cleveland and Columbus. Other major roads include east-west U.S. 224 and several important state highways. The commercial airport is just off I-77 to the south, midway between Akron and Canton. Within the metropolitan area are the municipalities of Barberton, Cuyahoga Falls, Fairlawn, Kent, Stow, and Tallmadge,

plus the south end of the Cuyahoga Valley National Recreation Area, which runs north from here for about 20 miles into Cuyahoga County (metro Cleveland).

SIGHTS

Cuyahoga Valley National Recreaton Area represents all the best that Ohio has to offer. The area between Akron and Cleveland has been preserved from the ravages of industry and residential development, and the result is a stretch of lovely country on either side of the Cuyahoga River. There's no fee to drive through here or to stop and take advantage of hiking trails, a spectacular view of Brandywine Falls, a farm visit, or any of the programs devised by federal personnel. The area totals more than 30,000 acres and there are tours that point up the subtlety and natural beauty of the place. Happy Days Visitor Center is on SR 303 between SR 8 and the village of Peninsula. The Canal Visitor Center is two miles south of Rockside Road on Hillside Road in the village of Valley View. Area headquarters is at 15610 Vaughn Rd., Brecksville, tel. (330) 650-4414 or 800-433-1986. The site is of course open every day of the year and shows what Ohio was like before the Industrial Revolution. On weekdays, it's hardly ever crowded, except for deer, which came to visit and decided to stay and multiply.

"A Cooperstown for Gadgeteers and Tinkers," the *Wall Street Journal* called it, and **Inventure Place**—the National Inventors Hall of Fame—is that and more. A great stop between, and in perfect contrast to, Canton's Pro Football and Cleveland's Rock and Roll halls of fame, the $38 million downtown Akron facility salutes people every bit as fascinating as athletes or musicians. Inventure Place is a wonderful destination for kids or adults, raucous in all the right spots, and with a bunch of touchy-feely exhibits that put many other alleged hands-on museums to shame. Also, ask about the Institute for Inventive Thinking, a recent wrinkle in the fabric of ingenuity. If your reaction to Nikola Tesla is to wonder which position he played or to decide if his album went platinum, you need Inventure Place. It's the shiny half-arc of a building at 221 S. Broadway, tel. (330) 762-4463. If all you want to do is browse the museum's interesting shop, there is a new row of 30-minute parking meters intended just for that purpose. (Locals find the cafeteria especially tasty and reasonable and they may overrun it at lunch.) Otherwise, you can visit Wed.-Sat. 9 a.m.-5 p.m., Sunday noon-5 p.m. Admission is $7.50 for adults, $6 for seniors and children under 13.

The **Akron Art Museum,** 70 E. Market St., tel. (330) 376-9185. Art museums in Cleveland, Toledo, even Youngstown sometimes get more attention than this one, and that's unfortunate. The downtown Akron museum is housed in the former post office, a wonderful red-brick Italian Renaissance Revival structure built in 1899 that is on the National Register of Historic Places. The permanent collection includes representative works by everyone from turn-of-the-century landscape artists to Andy Warhol. The photo collection is mesmerizing and extensive, and a new temporary exhibit shows up every 10 weeks. Hours are Tues.-Fri. 11 a.m.-5 p.m., Saturday 10 a.m.-5 p.m., Sunday noon-5 p.m. Admission is free and parking in the lot is $2 for two and a half hours or less.

Akron Zoological Park, is at 500 Edgewood Ave., tel. (330) 375-2550. This nonprofit facility has 300 animals, a picnic area, pony rides, and more. Several intriguing aspects are entirely new or freshly renovated. They include Tiger Valley, a $1.7 million walk that takes visitors from Asia to Africa, past flamingoes, crocodiles, lions, a Sumatran tiger, and a Malaysian sun bear before ending up in a Borneo longhouse. The reptile area has several new and endangered species, such as the Dumeril's ground boa, and Nature's Place is a 100-foot hoop house that starts with an endangered species maze and ends with a place for kids to dress like zookeepers and operate their own puppets. Admission is $6 for adults, $5 for seniors, and $4 for children ages 2-14. The park is open from mid-April to mid-October, Mon.-Sat. 10 a.m.-5 p.m., Sunday and holidays until 6 p.m. Dial up www.neo.rr.com/akzoo on the Web for information on special programs, such as the zoo's Halloween festivities.

At the **Goodyear World of Rubber Museum,** 1144 E. Market St., tel. (330) 796-7117, there is replica of Charles Goodyear's workshop, a collection of racing cars, and a display of tires that have rolled on the moon, among other things, at this free site. Open Mon.-Fri. 9 a.m.-3 p.m., the museum also explains the rubber-making process from plantation to tire.

Hale Farm and Village, 2686 Oak Hill Rd., Bath, tel. (330) 666-3711. A Western Reserve Society property, Hale Farm is billed as a living museum, which is quite accurate. Visitors here see how pioneer families survived, plowing with huge oxen, making their own glass and candles, and relying on craftspeople such as blacksmiths, sawyers, and others skilled at rustic self-sufficiency. Besides a statuesque colonial brick farmhouse and outbuildings, there are authentically costumed guides and a visitors' center stocked with handcrafted items, snacks, and soft drinks. Admission is $9 for adults, $7.50 for persons over the age of 60, and $5.50 for children ages 6-12. Signs are posted on Interstate Highways 77 and 271 leading visitors to the farm. Hale Farm opens in late May and remains open through late October, Tues.-Sat. 10 a.m.-5 p.m., Sunday noon-5 p.m., closed Monday. There are special events scheduled throughout the season (including maple sugaring in February and early March) and in December.

Stan Hywet Hall and Gardens, 714 N. Portage Path, tel. (330) 836-5533. Near the south end of the Cuyahoga Valley National Recreation Area, this stunning 65 room mansion with its spacious grounds plays host to many local cultural events. The landscape really is worth a tour when things are green, as time was spent creating Japanese and other gardens that seem to flow from the many rooms looking out on them. There are flower festivals, antique shows, and exhibits held here, mostly outside and therefore mostly in warm-weather months. Stan Hywet means "stone quarry" in Welsh; the home was owned by Frank Sieberling, who got Goodyear Tire & Rubber rolling. The huge dwelling is a majestic presence on the edge of the Cuyahoga Valley. Admission for a tour is $8 for adults, $7 for seniors and $4 for children (there are many special events held here, and fees for admission will vary). The hall is open daily10 a.m.-4:30 p.m., and the grounds from 9 a.m.-6 p.m., from early April to early January. Both are closed Monday. (Ask about "Pass 2 History," a discount ticket deal that allows visitors into both Hale Farm and Village and Stan Hywet Hall and Gardens.)

Goodyear Hangar is the place to see one of the famous blimps in captivity. The Akron hangar has been sold, but the original hangar, which dates from 1916, frequently houses a blimp at 841 Wingfoot Lake Rd. in suburban Mogadore. If you want to see a huge airship—and a building so large the condensation in it sometimes results in rain—head east out of Akron on SR 224. Turn south on SR 43 and, in less than three miles, a sign on the right will note the Goodyear hangar. Turn right on Wingfoot Lake Road and stop along the road for a view. For information on the occasional tour, call (330) 796-3127.

Kids enjoy laughing at the fads of their parents and ancestors, and the **Kent State University Museum** offers them a real opportunity. This facility has nine galleries devoted to fashions down through the years, and nothing could be more ludicrous than the garb of the 1960s and '70s. Besides constantly changing displays there are occasional international exhibits, plus paintings and examples of glass, silver, and porcelain. The museum is in Rockwell Hall, located at East Main (SR 59) and South Lincoln Streets, tel. (330) 672-3450. Hours are Wednesday, Fri.-Sat. 10 a.m.-4:45 p.m., Thursday 10 a.m.-8:45 p.m., and Sunday noon-4:45 p.m. Suggested donations are $3 for adults and $2 for seniors. Students with ID card admitted free.

Kent State also is the site of the killing of four students and the wounding of eleven by National Guard troops in 1970. Tucked behind classroom buildings, the knoll with its rectangles of marble is neither easy to find nor particularly moving to see. Perhaps a sign of the times is that today's typical Kent State student may not know the location. The **May 4 Memorial,** as it is known, is on the north side of campus, behind Taylor Hall. Those who seek it out can find help by calling (330) 672-2727, which also is the source of news about latebreaking campus activities. The KSU Web site, which covers events and archives, is www.kent.edu.

Speaking of higher education, the **University of Akron** is an important part of the town. The institution has cranked out more people handy with polymers than virtually any place on earth, and the Zips teams, as they're called, recruit athletic kids from the area's high schools. There's no telephone number for on-campus events at the moment, but the general number is (330) 972-7111. Webwise, try www.uakron.edu.

Hower House, 60 Fir Hill, tel. (330) 972-6909. An 1871 Second Empire Italianate-style Victorian mansion, the 28 rooms are furnished with treasures from around the world. It's like being inside a big wedding cake, which tells visitors how 19th-century industrialists and their families lived. On the University of Akron campus two blocks west of SR 8, the mansion, mercifully, is air-conditioned for those taking summer tours, Wed.-Sat. noon-3:30 p.m., Sunday 1-4 p.m. Admission is $4, seniors $4, children and students with ID $2.

The **Akron Civic Theater,** 182 S. Main St., tel. (330) 535-3179, built in 1925, is listed on the National Register of Historic Places for its nostalgic atmosphere. This is a venue for many different groups in need of a stage, such as the Cuyahoga Valley Youth Ballet. Ticket information for any kind of performance here can be had at (330) 253-2488. Tours of the building are intended for 25 or more persons, so most visitors can only admire the facade.

Several nearby state parks deserve mention. **Portage Lakes** is a 3,520-acre collection of multiple bodies of water south of Akron. Located at 5031 Manchester Rd., tel. (330) 644-2220, the park offers fishing, waterfowl hunting, swimming, hiking, picnicking, snowmobiling and other winter sports, and camping. Considering Akron's industrial history, these are pretty clean waters. Another state park, **Quail Hollow,** is at 13340 Congress Lake Ave., Hartville, call (330) 877-6652. Southeast of Akron and just northeast of Hartville, Quail Hollow's boggy waters are evidence of the visitation of glaciers more than 12,000 years ago. Hiking, biking, and winter sports are featured at this 698-acre facility. Like all state parks, admission is free. **West Branch State Park** at 5708 Esworthy Rd. east of Ravenna off SR 5, tel. (330) 296-3239 has a 2,650-acre lake for fishing and all other watersports.

Vineyards

Wolf Creek Vineyards, 2637 S. Cleveland-Massillon Rd., Norton, tel. (330) 666-9285. Here's a novel approach to an Akron-area meal: Find a carryout facility, choose the food, and bring it to this vineyard. You'll be able to unpack your morsels, enjoying them with one or more of 11 red or white Wolf Creek wines as you take in the scenic and bucolic rows of grapes. Wolf Creek

kids having a ball at Inventure Place

began making wine in the early 1980s, opening a tasting room in 1987. Today the vineyard produces 6,000 cases annually, most available at area retailers. The most popular wine at the moment is a 1997 Seyval, a white wine with a somewhat sweet and fruity taste. Several varieties of red and white grapes are grown here, and all wines feature Wolf Creek grapes or those grown nearby. A visit is free, and there are sodas, bottled water, and juices for children. No one under 21 is allowed after 6 p.m. on Friday and Saturday, and there are snack baskets here and pizza-delivery telephone numbers for those who forget food.

Another winery worth a visit is **Portage Hills Vineyards,** 1420 Martin Rd., Suffield, tel. (330) 628-2668 or (800) 418-6493. Set in the middle of its lush vineyards, this winery has a tasting room with snacks and a gift shop. Fifteen different wines are created here and, the last time we checked, 13 were available for taste and purchase. Portage Hills by the bottle is available at beverage shops in Akron and Mogadore. For the do-it-yourselfer, there are beer and wine-making supplies for sale. Open all year, the hours are Tues.-Thurs. noon-6 p.m., Wednesday noon-10 p.m., and Fri.-Sat. noon-11 p.m. Portage Hills is just south of I-76, near SR 224. The Web site is www.portagehills.com.

Metropolitan Akron

Suburban Akron residents in the vicinity of Sanford Road complained recently because noises from gas and oil pumps were disturbing their peace. The general area is said to contain the biggest such deposit in the state, so it's no wonder the pumps operate with vigor. But there's more to greater Akron than oil, gas, and complaints. The towns hereabouts generally are attractive and cognizant of their history, be it the date of the departure of the first canal boat or the arrival of the first buzzard in Hinckley. Here is a look at a few municipalities:

On the map **Barberton** appears to be an ordinary southwest Akron suburb, but it's not just a bedroom community. An older industrial town, it has a couple of claims to fame, not the least of which is that it has been dubbed the world's Chicken Capital. Some 7,500 tons of chicken are consumed here every week in eight chicken houses—restaurants that list chicken as their most-served dish. Two of the restaurants, Belgrade Gardens and Milich's Village Inn, are detailed below. Equally important, the annual Chrysanthemum Festival in late September has 20,000 plantings and one million blooms on display, courtesy of Yoder Brothers growers. This is the largest such bouquet between Florida's Cypress Gardens and the Imperial Palace in Japan.

Cuyahoga Falls is one of the larger Akron suburbs, boasting a pedestrian mall downtown. That's where Oktoberfest, an annual rib burnoff, and several warm-weather ethnic festivals take place. The Falls, as the locals call it, is the place to pick up food prior to attending a Blossom Music Center event (see below).

Hartville midway between Akron and Canton, is known for a couple of good small-town places to eat (see **Food**). One of the restaurants, Hartville Pantry, once served as a stop on the Underground Railroad. Even more historic are the bones of a woolly mammoth discovered by a local farmer who was draining a swamp. The beast's bones are believed to be 28,000 years old and are on display at the McKinley Museum in Canton. A huge flea market takes place on SR 619, west of downtown, on Monday and Thursday.

Hinckley Township is where the buzzards are said to return each year on March 15 to a park known as Whipp's Ledges. **Buzzard Day** takes place in the local Cleveland Metropark and involves a ranger who is the official buzzard spotter. On the first Sunday after he sees one of the beautiful soaring birds, as many as 7,000 folks repair to Hinckley Elementary School, 1586 Center Rd., to enjoy a breakfast of pancakes and sausage and to view art and other exhibits. The official spotter threatens to resign each year, so stop in Hinckley before he does. (A spokesperson, tongue in her cheek, says those who see a buzzard in Hinckley before the official sighting are shunned by the citizenry.) For more information, call (330) 278-2066, which is the Hinckley Chamber of Commerce. The township is three miles east of I-71 on SR 303.

The town of **Hudson,** founded in 1799, is the most New England of Ohio villages, nestled amid little whoop-te-doo hills that were gravel piles left by melting glaciers. A wealthy resident willed the town a lot of money in the 1900s so that the locals could bury their utility lines. One result is that the pretty downtown and the ancient and shady campus of the Western Reserve Academy prep school can be seen unimpeded. Hudson is served by SR 303, running east-west, and SR 91, running north-south. West a scant two miles, past busy SR 8, is the tranquil Cuyahoga Valley.

Ravenna, east of Kent on SR 5, has a historic downtown worth strolling. It's noted, too, for a number of antiques stores and for the Ohio's Traders' Market, a large (108,000 sq. ft.) indoor flea affair at 645 S. Chestnut St., tel. (330) 296-7050, that takes place on Wednesday, Friday, and Saturday.

All the roads of **Tallmadge** seem to lead to the center of town, Tallmadge Circle, which was planned by the Connecticut founders at the intersection of eight different streets. One result is a nice area for a public event, but another is slow-moving traffic. The town itself is mostly residential, with large lots and lots of trees. The annual event with the largest draw is the arts and crafts show on the Circle in June.

MUSIC, CULTURE, AND ENTERTAINMENT

Blossom Music Center, 1145 W. Steels Corners Rd. outside Cuyahoga Falls, is a big-deal outdoor site for famous entertainers, primarily musicians. It's a bit out of the way, west of SR 8. Recent visitors to Blossom have included Jimmy Buffett, the Cleveland Orchestra, Hootie & the Blowfish, Sting, James Taylor, and Wynonna Judd. The season runs from late April to late September. Performers play on stage under a large, permanent canopy while the crowd sits on blankets on the grass. Feel free to bring food but not beverages. No bottles or cans—or cameras, for that matter—are allowed. Charge-by-phone numbers are (216) 241-5555 in Cleveland and (330) 945-9400 in Akron.

The city has a more-than-respectable symphony orchestra. The **Akron Symphony** holds forth at E.J. Thomas Hall on the University of Akron campus, 198 Hill St., tel. (330) 972-7595, offering classical, pops, and educational concerts. The season begins in September and runs into the

AKRON AREA EVENTS

There are annual events all over the place here, from the whimsical (Hinckley Township Buzzard Day) to the mobile (the national Soap Box Derby) to the fragrant (the Barberton Mum Fest). Best bet for more information about any area event or site is to call the Akron/Summit County Convention and Visitors Bureau, tel. (330) 374-8900 or (800) 245-4254.

JANUARY

Peninsula Jazz Festival, Peninsula Library, 6105 Riverview Rd., Peninsula, tel. (330) 657-2291, the Rubber City Retreads join jazz bands from around the country for a series of performances (also in April, July, and October).

MARCH

Buzzard Day, Hinckley Township, SR 303, tel. (330) 278-2066. When you're out of buzzards, you're out of town.

Sugaring Days, Hale Farm and Village, 2628 Oak Hill Rd., Bath, tel. (330) 666-3711.

APRIL

Professional Bowling Association Tournament of Champions, Akron.

Stitchery Showcase, Stan Hywet Hall, 714 N. Portage Path, Akron, tel. (330) 836-5533. Major regional needlework exhibit with workshops, lectures, and demonstrations. All in a great setting, of course.

MAY

Cherry Blossom Festival, Lake Anna Park, Barberton, tel. (330) 848-6739.

May Garden Mart, Stan Hywet Hall, Akron, tel. (330) 836-5533.

Rockin' on the River, Chagrin Falls.

JUNE

Irish Festival, Chagrin Falls.

JULY

AA Founder's Day Celebration, Dr. Bob's Home, 855 Ardmore Ave., Akron, tel. (330) 864-1935.

Italian-American Festival, Chagrin Falls.

Summit County Fair, Tallmadge.

AUGUST

All-American Soap Box Derby, Akron.

Crooked River Fine Arts Festival, Chagrin Falls.

NEC Invitational, Firestone Country Club, Akron.

SEPTEMBER

Lions Club Rib Burnoff, Chagrin Falls.

Chrysanthemum Festival, Barberton.

Western Reserve Academy Antique Festival, Hudson.

OCTOBER

Stan Hywet's Wonderful World of Ohio Mart crafts festival, Akron.

Oktoberfest, Chagrin Falls.

NOVEMBER

Madrigal dinners, Stan Hywet Hall, Akron.

DECEMBER

Christmas at Stan Hywet, Stan Hywet Hall, Akron.

Victorian Christmas open house, Medina.

---

following July. In addition to the orchestra, there are performances by the Symphony Chorus and by the Youth Symphony.

Ballet is performed in Thomas Hall, too. The **Ohio Ballet,** 354 E. Market St., tel. (330) 972-7900 is a professional company performing regularly here and at the Ohio Theatre in Cleveland. A real treat is to watch the ballet outdoors in the summer. Performances are scheduled all over Northeast Ohio, in different settings, during warm months. Phone for a schedule of events.

Carousel Dinner Theater, is at 1257 E. Waterloo Rd., on Akron's south side, tel. (330) 724-

9855 or (800) 362-4100. This is the largest professional dinner theater in the country, seating up to a thousand guests on a packed night. Casts are brought in from New York City for six different musicals, each of which runs six to eight weeks. A typical show might be *South Pacific*. Cost of a meal and the theater ranges from $32 to $39.50 per person. You can check its Web site at www.carouseldinnertheatre.com for the upcoming season schedule.

Four other organizations devoted to the stage are worth noting. The **Weathervane Playhouse** offers mainstage and children's productions directed by professionals year round. It's at 1301 Weathervane Lane in Akron tel. (330) 836-2626. The **University of Akron Theatre** performs four to six shows each year in Guzzetta Hall, which houses a couple of theaters. For information, call (330) 972-7890. **Porthouse Theater,** is a Kent State University endeavor, tel. (330) 672-3884; during summer months, dial (216) 929-4416. It's a covered pavilion at Blossom Music Center. Comedies, musicals, and classics are performed June through August. And don't forget the **Hudson Players,** estimable actors who present six different plays on Friday and Saturday evenings every year. They perform at the Barlow Center, across from the police station in the middle of the village. Reach the box office by dialing (330) 655-8522.

Cuyahoga Falls is the place for country music. The **Boot Scoot'n Saloon I** has the largest dance floor in Ohio, where the line-dance lessons begin at 8 p.m. and one of several good area bands rips it up an hour later. This original Boot is open Wednesday, Friday, and Saturday, with teen night Sunday until midnight. It's at 4193 State Rd., tel. (330) 929-7123.

Live music that sounds heavy and metallic goes down on Friday and Saturday, at the very least, at **Ron's Crossroads.** Ron's is at 153 E. Cuyahoga Falls Ave. in Akron, tel. (330) 384-0749. Show up and listen to bands such as Underture or Cows in the Graveyard. Wednesday is karaoke night, and there may be bands scheduled on other weekday evenings.

J.B.'s on the second floor at 246 N. Water St., Kent, tel. (330) 678-2774, features live music on Friday and Saturday, and it may be anything from blues to reggae to rock to metal. The usual cover charge for the predominantly college crowd is $3-4.

The **Dusty Frog,** at 1272 Weathervane Lane, Akron, tel. (330) 865-5666, has a split personality—a DJ and dancing on one side, a live band and dancing on the other. The DJ plays modern rock for a younger crowd, whereas the band may be a 1980s tribute, a modern rock bunch, or disco, attracting dancers and listeners of varying ages. Cover averages around $2.

Annabelle's, 784 W. Market St., Akron, tel. (330) 535-1112, is the place to go to hear swing bands or folk artists. New owners recently put in a larger dance area downstairs, making this bar

with its neighborhood feel even more popular with the mostly post-college set.

Crawdads, 1099 E. Tallmadge Ave., Akron, tel. (330) 630-1386, features blues and jazz, strains of which waft through this bar and restaurant on Thursday and Saturday, competing with the heady whiff of Cajun cuisine. Burgers and seafood also are popular at this all-ages place, and the kitchen will make it without meat if that's the way you like it.

Northside, 111 N. Main St., Akron, tel. (330) 434-7625, books performances Tuesday through Saturday. This is another blues and jazz place, and it serves yummy food. Besides bar bites such as chicken fingers and breaded buffalo wings, try Gulf shrimp quesadilla or fresh spinach salad as the music plays. There are other salads, beer cheese and several soup varieties, grilled sweet potatoes, even several decadent desserts. Dance afterward if you're able.

ACCOMMODATIONS

What with its interstate highways, Akron has a number of convenient places to spend the night. There are clusters of accommodations where I-77 meets SR 18, northwest of the downtown area, and a similar idea at the junction of I-77 and State Routes 241 and 619, south of the inner city. Though neither is near an expressway exit, the **Hilton Inn at Quaker Square** and the **Cuyahoga Falls Sheraton** will prove interesting. The Hilton, 135 S. Broadway tel. (330) 253-5970, Akron, is encased in a cluster of golden grain elevators once owned by Quaker Oats. It's no exaggeration to state that guests have replaced oatmeal in this oddly attractive downtown structure. There's a shopping mall adjacent. The Sheraton, 1989 Front St., tel. (330) 929-3000 is built so close to the Cuyahoga River rapids that the water is sometimes audible inside the hotel. Other upper-range choices include the **Hilton Inn West,** 3180 W. Market St. (SR 18 Exit 137A), tel. (330) 867-5000, which has two pools, and the **Radisson Inn,** 200 Montrose West Ave., tel. (330) 666-9300.

There are a couple of colleges in the area, and they always seem to have competitively priced and clean places for visiting parents to stay. Especially nice is the moderately priced

University Inn, 540 S. Water St. (SR 43), Kent, tel. (330) 678-0123. The inn is tidy and has an outdoor pool. Cities and towns away from the interstate highway, such as Hudson and Twinsburg, also have good local motels, though they may be booked in the summer when there's a rush toward Sea World just to the north in Geauga County. Call ahead.

Bed and Breakfast

Bed and breakfast operations are common, especially in the vicinity of the Cuyahoga Valley. Prices tend to be inexpensive on weekdays and during the off season, and moderate to expensive during peak periods. Many are located in the town of Peninsula, which is located off SR 303 west of I-271 in the middle of the Cuyahoga National Recreation Area. B&B havens include **Hart & Mather Ltd. Bed and Breakfast,** 1343 Sharon-Copley Rd., Sharon Center, tel. (330) 239-2801; **Inn at Brandywine Falls Bed and Breakfast,** 8230 Brandywine Rd., Sagamore Hills, tel. (330) 467-1812; and **Cassidy Country Inn,** 6374 Waterloo Rd., Atwater, tel. (330) 947-2500, which offers occasional mystery weekends. **Centennial House Bed and Breakfast,** 5995 Center St., Peninsula, tel. (330) 657-2506; and **Tolle House Bed and Breakfast,** 1856 Main St., Peninsula, tel. (330) 657-2900.

There are yet more bed and breakfast operations. They include **Edison House Bed and Breakfast,** 141 Columbus St., Kent, tel. (330) 673-5544; **Fleder's Bed and Breakfast,** 5964 Center St., Peninsula, tel. (330) 657-2284; **Helen's Hospitality House Bed and Breakfast,** 1096 Palmetto Ave., tel. (330) 724-7151; **O'Neil House Bed and Breakfast,** 1290 W. Exchange St., tel. (330) 867-2650; **Peninsula Bed and Breakfast,** 5964 Center St., Peninsula, tel. (330) 657-2284; and **Portage House Bed & Breakfast,** 601 Copley Rd. (SR 162), tel. (330) 535-1952.

Campgrounds

These, too, are numerous. They are of uniformly good quality and may represent the last bastion of low-budget travel. Typically, primitive camping may be $15 per night, while camping with all the amenities can run $25 or more. Check out the following:

Cherokee Park Campground, 3064 SR 43, in Brimfield, just south of I-76, tel. (330) 673-1964

Countryside Campground, 2687 SR 43, in Suffield, about two miles north of US 224, tel. (330) 628-1212

Hidden Cove Resort Campground, 1115 Edgewater Blvd., Deerfield, tel. (330) 584-3695

Hillside Park Campground, 2534 W. Comet Rd., Clinton, tel. (330) 882-5678

Honey-Do Campground, 6794 Avon Lake Rd., Spencer, tel. (330) 775-7122

Mar-Lynn Lake Park Campground, 187 SR 303, Streetsboro, 216-650-2552

Pine Valley Lake Park Campground, 4936 S. Arlington Rd., in Green, tel. (330) 896-1381

Shawnee Lake Park Campground, 6464 Congress Rd., Spencer, 216-648-2577

Stow Silver Springs Park, 5328 Young Rd., Stow, tel. (330) 688-8238; Tamsin Park Resort Campground, 5000 Akron-Cleveland Rd., Peninsula, tel. (330) 650-0579

Woodside Lake Park Campground, 2256 Frost Rd., Streetsboro, tel. (330) 626-4251.

FOOD

Inexpensive

Hartville Kitchen, 1015 Edison St. in Hartville at the junction of SR 43 and SR 69, tel. (330) 877-9353 serves homestyle food in a vast (440-seat) dining room 11 a.m.-8 p.m. except Wednesday and Sunday. A popular evening meal at the moment is roast beef, with three side dishes, for $7.95. Should a diner find room, any of 15 varieties of pie can be ordered for $1.65 per slice. There's parking for 600 vehicles. Nearby is more home cookin' at the **Hartville Pantry,** 101 N. Prospect St., tel. (330) 877-9661. Open daily for breakfast, lunch, and dinner, this restaurant in a building dating from 1829 serves omelets for $3.95-4.25. Evenings, try creamed chicken over biscuit for $5.25 or surf 'n' turf for $9.95.

Belgrade Gardens, 401 E. State St., tel. (330) 745-0113, and **Milich's Village Inn,** 4444 S. Cleveland-Massillon Rd., tel. (330) 825-4553, are both in Barberton. The restaurants are two of the eight chicken houses that bolster this town's claim to being the world's Chicken Capital. Belgrade serves up a back, a breast, a leg, and a wing, along with side dishes of hot rice, cole slaw, and french fries, for $6.95. The fried-chicken dinner at Milich's is a mere $5.10. Both restaurants also offer fish, beef, and other things, and Belgrade serves a Yugoslavian specialty on Tuesday—*sarma*, which is cabbage rolls and sausage—for $6.50.

Dan's Dogs, 111 W. Liberty St., Medina, tel. (330) 723-3647, is a 1950s-style diner. Besides offering hot dogs 35 different ways, Dan serves up chicken, burgers, and fries. Dan's Famous Dog includes mustard, relish, onion, jalapeño peppers, cucumber pickles, and celery salt for $1.90. The Top Dog, with cheese and bacon, is $1.85, a chili dogs is $1.80. Milkshakes, topped with whipped cream and almonds, are $1.80. Diners have the option of eating in or taking food with.

You may have been told that a place has food to die for, and that's hardly an exaggeration at **Grammy's Ribs and Sandwich Shop,** 8012 Ridge Rd. (SR 94), tel. (330) 335-4726 in Wadsworth, 15 miles west of Akron off I-76. Owner George Gillespie was working in the restaurant basement a while back when a stranger confronted him, charged George's wife, who is the restaurant's cook, with stealing his chili recipe, and threatened that harm would befall her if she continued to make and serve her chili. She is fine, and the chili, which goes for $6.50 a bowl and has no tomatoes but plenty of meat in it, is a local favorite. So are rib dinners, which start at $5.75 and include french fries, fried bread, and a side dish.

Pizza is on the menu at **Luigi's,** 105 N. Main St. in downtown Akron, tel. (330) 253-2999. These pies have been judged prizewinners by local folks, and Luigi's also offers antipasto, lasagna, ravioli, and spaghetti. A large pizza with three toppings is $11.75 and should feed a family of four. With four sodas, that's less than $4 per person before tax. Dine in or carry out, as you choose.

St. Bernard Church Hall, 47 E. State St., tel. (330) 253-5161, serves only one meal a week, and it's worth attending. Hispanic parishioners at this downtown Akron church make enchiladas, tacos, tostadas, and other Latino delights that draw a Friday lunchtime crowd of sizeable proportions. The dishes can be had a la carte or as part of a complete meal. Prices are righteous —if you spend more than $5, you're overeating —and the food is all homemade.

Yours Truly Restaurant, 36 S. Main St., Hudson, tel. (330) 656-2900. Breakfast is generous here and is available all day. Favorite post-breakfast foods include a Caesar salad with chicken for $6.40 and a special-delivery hamburger, with Swiss cheese, sauteed onions, mushrooms, and sour cream for $4.95. The average check is just $5.90, so there may be money left for the homemade brownies, carrot cake, or apple pie with cinnamon ice cream (the latter priced at $3.05).

The **Zephyr Cafe,** 106 W. Main St., Kent, tel. (330) 678-4848, is both a vegetarian venue and a popular place. Home fries with the works combines diced potatoes, veggies, and cheese. Check out any of a dozen rollups, omelets, or pancakes. The rollups are stuffed with vegetables, rice, and cheese, among other things. A meal here is $5-10, and items such as pancakes are two for $2.50 or three for $3.25. The entire menu is available all day long. Closed Monday.

Moderate

Liberty Brewing Company, 1238 Weathervane Lane, Akron, tel. (330) 869-2337, is a combination brewpub and restaurant, offering half a dozen lagers, porters, stouts, or ales on tap at any given moment. There's bar food and the menu is modern American with a southern nod— popular dishes include jambalaya at $9.95 and pan-seared Gulf shrimp for $12.95. The restaurant is two blocks off Merriman Road.

Is it the ambience or the wine list? Regardless, the **Loyal Oak Tavern,** 3044 Wadsworth Rd., Norton, tel. (330) 825-8280, is a warm and satisfying place. The menu leans toward steaks and seafoods, with filet mignon at $16.95 and Boston strip at $14.95 the diners' favorites. Seafood is priced strictly according to the market; patrons consistently favor shrimp or scrod stirfries. The wine list includes selections from all over the globe, and the bar is a quiet, friendly place to pass time. Once a stagecoach stop, the tavern's interior now is done in wormy chestnut and is small, aged, tasteful, and inviting.

Visitors can kill two birds with one stone by dining at the **Mill Street Tavern,** 135 S. Broadway, tel. (330) 762-9333 in downtown Akron. They can satisfy their hunger in the former Railway Express Agency Building before they shop at the adjacent Mall at Quaker Square. The food here is Midwest regional, emphasizing steaks and seafood. The house special is prime rib at $14.50, and there's a children's menu. Weekday lunches feature a carving board and an all-you-can-eat buffet for $6.50. Weekends include a prime rib and crab leg buffet, accompanied by live jazz.

Papa Joe's, has a wine list of astounding size, which you can check out at 1561 Akron-Peninsula Rd., tel. (330) 923-7999, the facility may be better known as Iacomini's among the locals. Lunch and dinner menus each have more than 100 items, and there are daily specials for both meals. Typical luncheon fare might be a charbroiled swordfish sandwich or a marinated, charbroiled pork chop, either for $6.95. Evenings, look for fish, steaks, or perhaps the 1932 Express: chicken livers and mushrooms cooked in sherry, atop capellini, for $8.95.

The **Winking Lizard,** 1615 Main St. (SR 303), Peninsula, tel. (330) 467-1002, is an atmospheric place for a beer and a burger while seeing what the Cuyahoga Valley has to offer. Two cheeseburgers, two orders of steak fries, and two beers totals about $15. There are additional Winking Lizard locations, one in Macedonia and the other in Cleveland, but this is the only one set in a former nightclub. If thirst is your only consideration, there's a basement bar.

After wandering south through the Cuyahoga Valley, dinner will be ready at the nearby **Bangkok Gourmet,** located at 1614 Merriman Rd., in Akron, tel. (330) 630-9790. Open Mon.-Sat. 5-9:30 p.m., this tangy Thai restaurant is a nice counterpoint to apples, cider, and other farm fare. Nine curry dishes, from mild to combustible, can be had with different meat or seafood. Red curry with basil is addictive, as is drunken stir-fry with its hint of whiskey. Prices for the two dishes are $10.95 and $9.95, respectively. Cool off with Thai iced tea amid area Asian college students who always make up part of the crowd.

Expensive

Jackets for gentlemen, please, at **Lanning's,** 826 N. Cleveland-Massillon Rd., tel. (330) 666-1159, in suburban Bath. Fresh seafood and beef,

particularly the filet mignon, are popular here. The filet is $24.75, the walleye $19.50. Dinners include baked potato or rice pilaf, salad, rolls, and coffee, as well as tasty soups that vary from day to day. Appetizers can be as extravagant as oysters Rockefeller and desserts are homemade. Hours are Mon.-Fri. 5:30-11 p.m., Saturday 5 p.m.-midnight.

Tangier, 532 W. Market St., Akron, tel. (330) 376-7171, serves Continental meals around a fountain that can be admired by diners seated on two levels. Dinners feature steaks, seafood, or rack of lamb, while lunches can include salads or sandwiches. Lamb is the most-ordered evening meal at $22.95, and the Mideast platter, at $5.95 per person, is the top appetizer. Side dishes are fresh and carry hints of Lebanese spices. Hours are Mon.-Fri. 11:30 a.m.-2 p.m. and 4-10 p.m., Saturday 4-11 p.m., and Sunday 11:30 a.m.-3 p.m. Tangier also has big-name entertainment in its cabaret; call the number listed for details.

RECREATION

Bicycling

The Cuyahoga Valley National Recreation Area is a pleasant place to ride a bike, though there is only one stretch of asphalt designated for bicycles. That's the Akron Railroad Bikepath along Highland Road, a two-laner that heads east out of tiny Jaite (about 12 miles north of town along Riverview Road). The entire route is 17 miles and runs between Sagamore Hills and Kent. Riders can stop if they choose at Dover Lake Park, between the valley and I-271. An equally pleasant but shorter ride includes parking the car in the vicinity of Stan Hywet Hall and following Riverview Road approximately six miles north before turning right into the valley on SR 303. The route takes riders past Hale Farm and Western Reserve Village as it parallels the west side of the Cuyahoga River. Return along Akron-Peninsula Road on the river's west side. Weekday vehicular traffic is quite manageable.

One place to rent a bike for a tour through the valley is **Century Cycle,** 1621 Main St. (SR 303) in Peninsula, tel. (330) 657-2209. Dan and his friends have mountain bikes that appear to be in good repair.

Bowling

Bowlers will go for the galactic lanes in nearby Norton. Stonehedge Place, 580 E. Cuyahoga Falls Rd., tel. (330) 633-8104, is one of only a few alleys in Ohio that lights up in an eerie manner for a lunar kegling experience.

Golf

Just because visitors can't play at the private Firestone Country Club doesn't mean they can't have an enjoyable golfing experience. There are approximately 50 courses in the area that are available to travelers. Among the best are **Good Park** at 530 Nome Ave., tel. (330) 864-0020, which was designed by the same person who designed Firestone, and **Raintree Country Club,** 4340 Mayfair Rd., tel. (330) 699-3232. Both are 18-hole courses. Good Park is a par 71; weekday greens fees for nine and 18 holes are $9.50 and $18, respectively. Raintree, which is par 72, charges $35 for 18 holes on weekdays, which includes use of a motorized cart.

Hiking

Drive to the national recreation area, park the car, don a daypack, and take a fragrant, if brief, 2.5-mile hike along the **Towpath Trail.** Passing through a pine forest, the trail is flat and scenic, heading north from the trailhead on Pine Hill Road. A more extensive trail system can be found in another part of the valley, at **Virginia Kendall Park.** Passing among rock ledges, woods, meadows, even a cave, the trails vary from easy to tough. Towpath Trail is between Brecksville and Macedonia, just off SR 82. Virginia Kendall Park is about two miles east of the village of Peninsula on SR 303.

If hiking for you means ambling through a small town, stop at the Peninsula Library, 6105 Riverview Rd., in Peninsula, tel. (330) 657-2291. Pick up a map of the village and then walk wherever, checking out this picturesque place with its numerous 150-year-old dwellings.

Skiing

The Akron area stands tall, so it's only logical that it's the site of a pair of downhill ski facilities. **Boston Mills** and **Brandywine** ski resorts are a few miles north of downtown Akron, and only three miles apart, in the Cuyahoga Valley National Recreation Area. Owned by the same folks, the resorts let skiers purchase a single pass and ski on both sets of hills. Both use snow-making equipment and have special programs for beginning skiers, snowboarders, those who like to slip down a slope inside inner tubes, and more. Between the two resorts the lifts can accommodate 16,000 skiers an hour. The 18 slopes are divided equally among beginner, intermediate, and advanced. Boston Mills is on Riverview Road, just north of Interstates 71 and 80 (the Ohio Turnpike). Brandywine can be reached by continuing north on Riverview Road and making a right turn on Vaughn Road. The season runs from about mid-December to mid-March each year. For details, call (330) 655-6703 if in Akron, or (216) 656-4489 from Cleveland. Farther away, dial (800) 875-4241.

Cross-country skiing courses are even more common, but one place shines. Brookledge Golf Club, 1621 Bailey Rd., Cuyahoga Falls, tel. (330) 971-8416, is lighted for night skiing. A nice site for daytime nordic skiing is West Branch State Park, east of Ravenna.

Professional Sports

The **Akron Aeros,** may have the most delightful ballfield in the entire country. Their season stretches from early April to early September and runs a total of 142 games, in dazzling Canal Park at 300 S. Main St. The Aeros seat 9,000 and are the AA minor-league affiliate of the Cleveland Indians. The Akron team set an Eastern League attendance record their first year in town, so telephone (330) 253-5151 plenty early for tickets and information. They charge $8 for adults and $6 for seniors and children. It's all quite like what major league baseball once was.

There are other heavy hitters in town, and they show up each year for the **NEC Invitational,** formerly the World Series of Golf, at the Firestone Country Club, 452 E. Warner Rd., Akron. The course is private, so the only way visitors can get on it is as spectators. The invitational is the last week in August each year (but for 2001, when it will be played at another course not yet named), and tickets usually are sold out before the event. Spectator admission prices are staggering, ranging from $130 to $4,500. On the other hand, ordering tickets prior to mid-August is considered pre-season and therefore fees are cut in half. A number of events are held in conjunction with the invitational, from a 5K run, a golf clinic, and a pro-am tournament. To secure a place in the gallery, call (330) 241-6000 or (800) 765-6048.

Northfield Park, 10705 Northfield Rd., Northfield, tel. (330) 467-4101, is the site for year-round, live harness racing, seen from behind glass-enclosed stands. Reservations are required. Once here, visitors can bet on the race they see or on any of dozens of simulcast thoroughbred or harness races from around the country. Those who fail to pick a winner may want to visit the on-site microbrewery, which offers a lager, a stout, and a couple of ales, as well as seasonal specialties. Admission is $1.50 grandstand and $3 clubhouse, with parking ranging from $1 to $3. Admission and parking are free on Tuesday and Thursday. Racing takes place every day except Dec. 24-26 Check out the steeds at www.northfieldpark.com.

SHOPPING

Chapel Hill Mall is the Akron area's biggest shopping facility, boasting 80 stores at Howe Avenue and Brittain Road, just east of SR 8, between Cuyahoga Falls and Tallmadge, tel. (330) 633-7100. The vicinity of SR 18 east of I-77 in northwest Akron includes Summit Mall, tel. (330) 867-1555, and a number of strip shopping centers, movie theaters, and restaurants. Another major mall is Rolling Acres at 2400 Romig Rd., Akron, off I-77, tel. (330) 753-5045. Mulitplex movies are close by.

An amusing place to find something fascinating is **Bumpas Emporium** at 10 Tallmadge Circle in Tallmadge, tel. (330) 633-4911. This venerable drug store with Victorian decor is a huge haven for collectible gifts, crafts, candy, and all else within the bounds of decency and decorum. Notice, too, the antique drugstore fixtures and memorabilia.

The largest assortment of wicker in Ohio can be found at the **Wicker Company,** Towne Center Plaza, 1664 Norton Rd. (at SR 91), Stow. A total of 17,000 square feet is devoted to the lattice look. For directions or information, tel. (330) 656-1317.

Grazers should head for **West Point Market,** 1711 W. Market St., (330) 664-2151 in Akron.

This is a supermarket to the tenth power, dispensing vast quantities of cheese and cheese spread, plus lots of wine, chocolates and baked goods. It's an unconventional place to compose a picnic lunch or to pack a few things for the trip home.

TRANSPORTATION

Metro Regional Transit Authority covers Akron, Summit County and Richfield. For route and schedule information, call (330) 762-0341. The Greyhound Bus Station is at 781 Grant St., tel. (330) 434-9185.

One of the best and most varied ways to see the Cuyahoga Valley is to hop a train. The **Cuyahoga Valley Scenic Railroad** runs 1939 and 1940 Chesapeake & Ohio diesels, pulling passenger cars, up and down through the national recreation area Wednesday through Sunday. For prices ranging from $11 to $20, an adult can be dropped off wherever he or she intends to bike, hike, shop, or explore. One way with a bike for an adult is $7; round trip amounts to $10. The train makes lots of stops—there are at least eight places designated as station locations. Special events, such as fall color, mean added runs and shuttles. For more information, call (800) 468-4070. Catch a train in Independence at the north end of the valley on Old Rockside Road.

Another way to see the Valley is behind a horse. Carriage Trade offers tours that include Brandywine Falls. Cost of a ride is $85, which includes a gourmet picnic and "two hours of pure romance," according to the owner. The stable is at 8050 Brandywine Rd., Northfield, just east of I-271; reservations are a must. From Akron, call (330) 650-6262; from Cleveland, call (216) 467-9000.

INFORMATION AND SERVICES

In an emergency dial 911; the non-emergency number for police is (330) 375-2181. The Akron Police Department is at 217 S. High St. The post office in downtown Akron is at 98 N. Main St., tel. (330) 650-1993; 5Akron City Hospital is at 525 E. Market St., tel. (330) 375-3000.

For general touring information try the **Akron/Summit County Convention and Visi-**

tors Bureau, 77 E. Mill St., tel. (330) 374-8900 or (800) 245-4254 or the **Medina County Convention and Visitors Bureau,** 124 W. Lafayette Rd., Medina, tel. (330) 722-5502.

The Beacon-Journal, which is a morning/Sunday paper serving Akron since 1839, covers Akron, Summit County, and beyond. Check out Thursday's "Enjoy" section for entertainment. The newspaper's Web site is www.ohio.com.

CANTON, MASSILLON, AND STARK COUNTY

All other Stark County attractions pale in comparison to the Pro Football Hall of Fame. Playing football for money got its start here when, in 1919, rough and rugged sons of rough and rugged industrial workers first pulled on uniforms and leather helmets for pocket money. Times have changed since the best pro team was the Canton Bulldogs, and national television advertising and exposure now adds considerably to the hoopla that surrounds inductees to the Hall every summer. But there's more to the area than big-bankroll athletics.

Stark County is a mix of urban and rural, of down-at-the-heels industrial settings and farmers who make a living from the stubborn soil. Some locals can trace their roots to Amish pioneers, to Appalachian whites, to African-Americans who boarded the Underground Railroad, and to immigrants who sailed from Europe. This mix has resulted in a renewed effort to be industrially productive, to rehabilitate the old, and to find out what's new.

There are approximately 375,000 residents in the county. Of that total, 84,000 live in Canton, 31,000 reside in Massillon, and 23,000 call Alliance home. The fastest-growing portion of the county is the area in and around North Canton and Canal Fulton; the latter has a population of 4,200.

Location and Orientation

Some 60 miles southeast of Cleveland, 23 miles south of Akron, and 125 miles northeast of Columbus, the towns of Canton and Massillon are separated by a seven-mile stretch of US 30. The cities are served by I-77, which runs north-south through the middle of Canton, and by east-west US 30. Canton and Massillon are approximately halfway between Mansfield and the Pennsylvania state line on US 30, which also is known as the Lincoln Highway. US Highway 62 enters Massillon from the Amish country and Columbus to the southwest and exits Canton toward the towns of Youngstown and Warren to the northeast. (South of US 62 the terrain is unglaciated and, therefore, more rugged and less fertile.) Other cities and towns of interest in Stark County include Alliance and Canal Fulton.

History

Originally the property of Delaware Chief Turtle Heart, the area now called Canton was deeded to English and French traders in 1784. The first permanent U.S. settlers arrived in 1805, and in 1806 Bezaleel Wells platted the town. By 1815 the area had a newspaper, *The Repository,* which is published in Canton to this day. A dozen years later, in 1827, a Canton resident named Joshua Gibbs greatly improved the design of the metal plow. The city quickly became a leading source for moldboard plows in the 19th century, with as many as six companies manufacturing reapers at one time.

Over Massillon way, a pair of Quaker ministers settled the area in 1812. When the Ohio-Erie Canal was completed in 1828, area commerce expanded. The railroad arrived in 1852 and the city was incorporated a year later. Speaking of railroads, the Underground Railroad ran through here, delivering slaves to freedom. A few older homes are connected via tunnel, a memento of that dramatic pre-Civil War era. Alliance grew in part because two railroads crossed there. The "alliance" of a couple of smaller town resulted in a suitable name for the expanding city.

Major William McKinley mustered out of the Union Army and arrived in Canton in 1867, having passed the bar. While he served clients, the steelmaking business caused his practice and the city to boom. Local coal and limestone were teamed with iron ore from Minnesota via the port of Cleveland in several plants. One product made from steel was roller bearings; Henry H. Timken opened a factory to produce these automotive necessities in 1898. The facility soon became Canton's largest employer.

McKinley served Ohio as its governor from 1892 to 1896 and then was elected President. Following his assassination in 1901 he was buried locally in a memorial tomb purchased with the donations of more than one million

The McKinley National Memorial is Ohio's solemn tribute to the 25th President of the United States.

Americans. Because McKinley loved red carnations, they were named the state flower. But the 25th President was not to be the city's only martyr. Canton, at its steelmaking height, had a notorious underworld. The 1920s saw every form of vice, with only one public figure consistently standing up to it. That person was a newspaper editor, Don Mellett. Mellett pointed his finger at local thugs in print and was murdered for his efforts in 1926. The editor's death so shocked the citizenry that various crooks were immediately arrested and tried or run out of town.

Most of the criminals have vanished and so have many of the big old industries. The mills have been replaced by smaller, leaner operations that fabricate a variety of metal products. The people have changed, too. Instead of gathering to gamble, to hold a union meeting, or to watch the first professional football team—the Canton Bulldogs, starring legendary athlete Jim Thorpe—they congregate at Canton-Massillon high school football games or hoist a beverage at one of several watering holes on Canton's north side.

Massillon lies on both banks of the Tuscarawas River, about eight miles west of Canton. It sprouted in 1826 from a couple of smaller communities in response to the coming of the Ohio and Erie Canal. Farm products in particular rolled into the growing town, to be loaded onto canal boats (called packets) for the trip to Cleveland. The discovery of coal nearby in 1855 accelerated an industrial binge spearheaded by the producers of iron and steel. Republic Steel was founded here and currently employs 1,500 persons.

If Stark County residents share one thing, it is a love of high school football. In 1994, the 100th meeting of Massillon and Canton McKinley high schools was covered by *Sports Illustrated*. The Massillon Tigers won a seesaw battle 42-41 that night before a crowd so large it overflowed Massillon's stadium's 17,000-seat capacity. The winning tradition had been solidly established by coach Paul Brown, who compiled a record of 80-8-2 at Massillon High between 1932 and 1940. Brown went on to coach the Cleveland Browns and Cincinnati Bengals professional teams.

Stark County may be proof that what goes around does indeed come around. The venerable Ohio and Erie Canal's path through here is being restored as a 25-mile-long recreational trail. Besides the presence of hikers and bikers, portions of the route may be set aside for horses. Horsepower (or mulepower), after all, was what pulled the weighty canal boats back and forth, on their way to Cleveland going north or to Zoar heading south.

SIGHTS

The **Pro Football Hall of Fame,** 2121 George Halas Dr., tel. (330) 456-8207, is by far the area's most popular destination. The museum is just west of I-77 on the north side of Canton; the football-shaped roof is easy to spot, immediately north of Fawcett Stadium. Visitors are greeted by a seven-foot bronze statue of Jim Thorpe, the immortal Native American pro football player from the early years. Past Thorpe's likeness is the Exhbition Rotunda, where the history of the National Football League is recounted and where many valuable mementos are on view. Other parts of the museum include Game Day Stadium (featuring a turntable theater), Professional Football Today, the Pro Football Photo Art Gallery, the Adventure Room, the Enshrinee Memento Room, and the Leagues and Champions Room. This is a multimedia experience, with movies, slides, and tape recordings running constantly. The Hall is open 9 a.m.-8 p.m. from Memorial Day to Labor Day, 9 a.m.-5 p.m. the rest of the year, and closed Christmas Day. Admission is $10 for adults, $6.50 for persons 62 and up, and $5 for children ages 6-14; there's a family rate $25. The Hall can be reached by dialing (330) 456-8207. For recorded information, call (330) 456-7762.

Events connected to the annual **Pro Football Hall of Fame Festival** actually begin in May with the crowning of a queen. The remaining excitement takes place in late July and includes everything from a drum corps competition to a 10-kilometer race to a fashion show. There's even a football game, the season's first exhibition National Football League contest, next door in Fawcett Stadium. The teams differ every year and they began evening play in 1998 so as to be nationally televised. The game follows a parade and enshrinement of the new inductees. July events take place over eight days. Festival offices are at 229 Wells Ave. NE. Call them at (330) 456-7253 or (800) 533-4302.

The federal **President William McKinley Memorial Site** is composed of three divisions: the McKinley National Memorial, the McKinley Museum of History, Science and Industry, and the Hoover Price Planetarium, 800 McKinley Monument Dr. NW, tel. (330) 455-7043). The memorial, a dramatic dome, houses the remains of the man who was president from 1897 to 1901, and those of his family. It was built on Canton's highest point, offering those who trudge up the long, wide flight of eastward-facing stairs a panoramic city view. The museum is down the hill and to the south of the memorial about 50 yards. It includes everything from Indian artifacts to the reconstructed bones of a mastodon found in an area bog. The planetarium, which displays night sky reproductions in keeping with the season, is inside the museum. (Not to be confused with an observatory, the planetarium projects views of the sky onto a domed ceiling.) Celestial programs are offered without charge on Saturday at 2 p.m., on Sunday at 2 and 3 p.m., and on weekday afternoons in the summer. Summer hours are Mon.-Sat. 9 a.m.-7 p.m., Sunday noon-7 p.m. Closing hours are 5 p.m. the rest of the year. The facility is closed major holidays and closes for maintenance in January. Admission is $5 for adults, $4 for those ages 60 or more, and $3 for children ages 3-18.

Glamorgan Castle, looms at visitors from across a long front yard at 200 Glamorgan St. in Alliance, tel. (330) 821-2100. Constructed for an engineer who invented the overhead crane, this palatial stone home is now the property of the Alliance School District. It's no ordinary massive mansion—the walls in places are more than a foot thick, constructed with 96 boxcars of Vermont marble and 100 tons of structural steel. The home was completed in 1909 and stayed in the family until 1939, when it became an Elks Lodge. Tours are offered weekdays at 2 p.m. The cost is $3 for adults and $1 for children 12 and under.

Older and equally impressive is **Five Oaks Mansion,** 210 Fourth St. NE, tel. (330) 833-4896, in Massillon. Completed in 1894, the 25-room stone building is a decorator's delight, with Moroccan leather-covered walls, original Tiffany lamps, and acorn and oak tree motifs all over the place. Tours are offered in July and August, Thursday, Sat.-Sun. 1-4 p.m. Admission is $4 for adults and $1 for students ages 6-17.

Harry London Candies, tel. (330) 494-0833 is a popular tour with children and chocaholics. London was a steelworker who decided in 1922 to concoct Christmas candy. It was so eagerly consumed that he went into the business. Today, a modern factory produces 3,000 chunks of candy every minute at 5353 Lauby Rd. in North Canton. Five hundred varieties of chocolate, including such yummies as Mocha Melts, await those who patronize the company store at the end of the visit. Tours are offered every hour Mon.-Sat. 9 a.m.-4 p.m., Sunday noon-3:30 p.m.; the store is open Mon.-Sat. till 6 p.m., Sunday till 3:30 p.m. The store is free, but the tour costs $2 for adults, $1 for children for youths ages 6-18.

Visitors in the Massillon area around Christmas time should drive to North Lawrence, a village about six miles northwest of Massillon (head west on Wooster Street, then turn north on Alabama Avenue). There they will be able to motor through a gauntlet of holiday illumination. The **Ohio Holiday Festival of Lights** art gallery features 200,000 glittering bulbs at 13190 Patterson Rd., which is the address for Clay's Park. Ice sculptures are in the spotlights, and there are carriage rides and a gift shop.

In the opposite direction, 20 miles northeast of Canton on Stark County's eastern edge on US 62, **Alliance** is something of a contrast to Canal Fulton, being an old industrial town. Yet it is not without its attractions. **Mount Union College,** 1972 Clark Ave. has a 109-acre nature center that is free and open to the public. It's a quiet, shady place on the small, pretty campus in a nice part of town. Call (330) 823-2878 for a rundown on campus activities or hit the college Web site at www.muc.edu.

Museums

The giant sucking sound you hear isn't jobs leaving the Rust Belt but is instead the many vacuum-cleaner models on display at the **Hoover Historical Center,** 2225 Easton St. NW, Canton, tel. (330) 499-0287. This was the boyhood home of William H. Hoover; the restored Victorian farmstead is not entirely devoted to cleaning—the gardens are every shade of green during the warm months, thick with herbs planted and maintained by volunteers. Special programs include storytelling for children, 1860s baseball games, tea parties, and more. There's no admission charged for this attraction, which is owned by The Hoover Company (a Canton institution). It's open Tues.-Sun. 1-5 p.m.; the herb gardens are open June-September.

Canton Classic Car Museum, 555 Market Ave. SW, tel. (330) 455-3603. How tough a town was Canton? The police department's 1937 Studebaker, on display here, was armor plated! Look, too, for cars belonging to everyone from Amelia Earhart to Queen Elizabeth, and rarities such as a 16-cylinder 1931 Marmon and the only existing Benham, a 1914 model. Peek into the restoration shop of this former Ford dealership to see what a classic looks like before it has been restored. The entire museum is open daily10 a.m.-5 p.m. Admission is $5 for adults, $3 for persons 65 and above, and $2.50 for children ages 6-17.

Massillon has a pair of museums, the **Massillon Museum** and the **Ohio Society of Mili-tary History Museum.** The former is at 121 Lincoln Way E (US 30), having moved recently into its own building. The latter is two blocks away at 316 Lincoln Way E. Reach the Massillon Museum by dialing (330) 833-4061; the Military History Museum answers (330) 832-5553. The pride of the Massillon Museum may well be a first-floor gallery that displays the works of top Ohio contemporary artists. Other attractions include a photo gallery and a fascinating collection of circus memorabilia donated by a city resident. Equally authentic are such military items as one of the few complete Red Cross packages given to U.S. prisoners of war after their release following World War II, and a library with materials from as far back as the Spanish-American War. The Massillon Museum is open Tues.-Sat. 9:30 a.m.-5 p.m., Sunday 2-5 p.m., admission is free. The Military History Museum is open Tues.-Fri. 10 a.m.-5 p.m., Saturday 10 a.m.-3 p.m., the Society of Military History accepts donations.

Canal Fulton is as close as a visitor will come to seeing an unrestored, unspoiled Ohio Canal town. Ten miles northwest of Massillon, off SR 21, the village has a pleasant and well-preserved old downtown area and, right behind it, an authentic stretch of the Ohio and Erie Canal. Boat rides on the *St. Helena III,* a freighter pulled by sturdy mules, can be had in warm weather. Year round, visit the **Heritage House & Old Canal Days Museum,** 103 Tuscarawas St., tel. (330) 854-3808. A boat trip lasts an hour and costs $5 for adults, $4 for seniors, and $3 for children. A canal ride can be had on weekends in May and daily beginning in June, but only from 1-3 p.m. in either case. Depending on when you show up, you can visit the museum before or after the boat ride. It's free with a boat ticket.

CULTURE, ENTERTAINMENT, AND MUSIC

They belly up to the bars in and around Belden Village, a shopping area north of Canton that's just west of I-77. Several sites offer entertainment (also see restaurants, below), including these spots:

Rock and roll tops the live-music menu at **Sadie Rene's,** 7200 Whipple Rd. in North Canton, tel. (330) 499-8246. Downward Spiral, The Goz, and

THE ANNUAL MASSILLON CRUISE

It's enough to make you stay out after curfew. Each year on the Saturday prior to Father's Day, Massillon stages the **Cruise On In and Dance Party** in the downtown area. A stretch of Lincoln Way (old US 30, now SR 172) is blocked off as more than 650 antique, classic, and custom cars are put on display by loving motorheads from several states. Simultaneously, dozens of food vendors cook up everything from hot dogs to haute cuisine as perhaps 125,000 people mill good naturedly around the machinery and each other.

A cooperative effort of the Massillon Area Car Club and the Massillon Downtown Association, the free annual event also features a live-music stage with talent from noon to approximately 10 p.m. Framed by a bridge over the Tuscarawas River, the festivities feature every kind of automobile and most kinds of people. Magically, it all disappears between 10 p.m. and midnight. However, there's a reprise each Saturday evening until the end of September as a five-block area is shut off and folks get in their cars and slowly drive around, being cool.

Cruise On In and the Saturday evenings that follow mark their 10th anniversary in 1999. It's the largest outdoor car show in Ohio.

bands of that ilk hold forth every evening but Monday, accompanied by orders of wings served by the dozen. Sadie has her own Web site at sadierene .com.

B.B. McLain's, 4675 Munson St. NW, Canton, tel. (330) 499-8577. Top 40 or dance music rattles on weekend evenings through the facility, which was remodeled in 1998. Devotees must be 18 years of age or older.

In contrast to the rocking ways of Belden Village, the **Cultural Center for the Arts Complex,** 1001 Market Ave. N, Canton, tel. (330) 452-4096, offers entertainment of a slightly higher brow. Herein are the Canton Museum of Art's galleries, tel. (330) 453-7666; the Canton Ballet, tel. (330) 455-7220; the Canton Civic Opera, tel. (330) 455-1000; the Canton Symphony Orchestra, tel. (330) 452-2094; and the Players Guild Center for Public Theater, tel. (330) 453-7619. All of these institutions have been around for a long time—the opera

since 1939—and the quality of performances belies the modest size of the metropolitan area.

Carnation City Players have been presenting musicals, dramas, and comedies since 1960 at the Firehouse Theater, 450 E. Market St. (reach the box office at 330-821-8712) in Alliance. Recent hits have included *Man of La Mancha* and Neil Simon's *God's Favorite.* There's an **Alliance Symphony Orchestra,** too. The ensemble has about 65 members ranging in age from the teens into the eighties, and they play in several different spots. Call (330) 823-9500 to find out when the orchestra puts on its madrigal dinner at Glamorgan Castle.

ACCOMMODATIONS

The majority of hotel-motel franchises are in the vicinity of Belden Village, north of Canton. Another area with numerous accommodations is the stretch of US 30 between Canton and Massillon. Any given motel along the latter length of road is less likely to be a franchise and therefore may carry a more modest price. Among the snazzier places to stay are the expensive **Hilton,** at 320 Market Ave. S., Canton, tel. (330) 454-5000, and moderate **Sheraton Inn,** 4375 Metro Circle NW (I-77 Exit 109), Canton, tel. (330) 494-6494. The former has an indoor pool, the latter both an indoor and an outdoor pool. **Best Suites of America,** 4914 Everhard Road NW, tel. (330) 499-1011, Canton, is moderately priced. It offers a wet bar, microwave oven, refrigerator, free breakfast, free evening cocktails, indoor pool, and an exercise room.

At the economy-minded end of the scale, there is a **Motel 6** with an outdoor pool at 6880 Sunset Strip NW (I-77 Exit 111), Canton, tel. (330) 494-7611, and a trio of **Super 8** facilities. The Canton Super 8 is at 3950 Convenience Circle NW (I-77, Exit 109), Canton, tel. (330) 492-5030; the Massillon Super 8 Motel is at 242 Lincoln Way West, tel. (330) 837-8880; the third is in Alliance at 2330 W. State St., tel. (330) 821-5688. The Canton Super 8 has an outdoor pool and some units offer kitchenettes. A **Red Roof Inn** can be found at 5353 Inner Circle Court NW (I-77 and Everhart Road), tel. (330) 499-1970. All are inexpensive, though prices seem to fluctuate almost from one week to the next.

Bed and breakfast destinations are plentiful, particularly if travelers bear in mind that this area is only a few miles north of the historic village of Zoar, with its four B&Bs. Canal Fulton has a pair of such accommodations, **Canal House Bed and Breakfast** at 306 S. Canal St., tel. (330) 854-6229, and **Pleasant Hill 1845** at 451 E. Cherry St., tel. (330) 854-0551. Each is moderately priced and has two separate rooms to let for visitors. A bit farther out, look for the **Main Stay** at 1320 E. Main St. in Louisville, tel. (330) 875-1021, and the **Herb Nest,** 13642 Navarre Rd. SW, Beach City, tel. (330) 359-5087. The Main Stay has three rooms for guests, the Herb Nest has two.

Campers will like what they find here, from a franchise such as **Bear Creek KOA Campground,** 3232 Downing St. SW, Canton, tel. (330) 484-3901, to **Baylor Beach Park,** 8777 Manchester Ave. SW, Navarre, tel. (330) 767-3031. Friendly places like **Pine Valley Lake Park Campground,** 4936 S. Arlington Rd., Uniontown, tel. (330) 896-1381 offer hayrides and have a general store. Other campgrounds include **Cutty's Sunset Camping Resort,** 8050 Edison St., Louisville, tel. (330) 935-2431, **Hillside Park Campground,** 2534 W. Comet Rd., Clinton, tel. (330) 882-5678), and **Paradise Lake Park Campground,** 6940 Rochester Rd., East Rochester, tel. (330) 525-7726. Prices are in the $12-25 range, depending on what travelers need in the way of hookups and such in order to spend an enjoyable evening. One more campground is at **Clay's Park Resort,** 13190 Patterson Rd. NW, North Lawrence, tel. (330) 854-6691, where the $19.95 campsite fee includes admission to the water park. The camping season typically runs from mid-April to mid- or late October.

FOOD

Lending a note of deserved (if perhaps a bit dubious) distinction to the city's reputation, a 1998 survey of 200 U.S. cities indicated that Canton was the third-least-expensive place for business travelers to eat in all America. Only Wheeling, West Virginia, and Macon, Georgia, were cheaper.

Inexpensive

Continental breakfast seems assured at **Ruth Marie's Coffee & Teas,** 3226 Cleveland Ave. NW, Canton, tel. (330) 492-7177. This attractive place has a coffee bar seating 34 and an array of bagels, brownies, croissants, gingerbread, and muffins. Ruth Marie is open Mon.-Fri. from 7:30 a.m. and Saturday from 9 a.m. She even has a Web site at www.ruthmaries.com/store.htm.

West of the bright lights of Belden Village, look for **Chubby's Treats,** 5326 Fulton Rd. NW, tel. (330) 966-3038. Chubby's is easy to spot, residing as it does inside a two-story, Dairy Queen-like fiberglass cone. Part-owner Mrs. Wingerter and friends offer good fast food: hot dogs, coneys, sloppy joes, malts, shakes, sun-

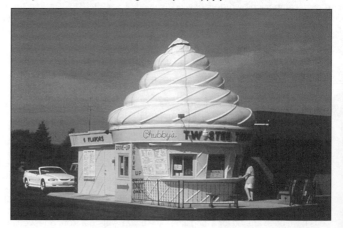

Chubby's Treats

daes, etc. They're open daily 11 a.m.-9:30 from April 1 to Halloween, with extended hours to 10:30 p.m. in hot weather.

Fifteen miles southeast of Canton is little Waynesburg, the home of **Cibo's Restaurant.** When the Mohawk Theater went the way of many small-town movie houses, Rena Rugani opened a retro-priced restaurant there, at 134 W. Lisbon St., tel. (330) 866-3838. Food consumed throughout the former theater ranges from Italian and American specialties to pizza and sandwiches. Specials include all-you-can-eat spaghetti dinners on Thursday for $4.99, all-you-can-eat rigatoni or gnocchi dinners for $4.99 on Friday, and a choice of either roast beef or turkey dinners on Sunday for $6.25 (large serving) or $5.25 (regular serving). Cibo's is open for lunch and dinner Thurs.-Sun.

Open only Mon.-Fri.10 a.m.-5 p.m., the **College Inn,** 715 W. State St., Alliance, tel. (330) 823-3332, is nevertheless highly recommended. There's a long list of sandwiches and a vegetarian menu accompanied by soft drinks only. A reuben sandwich is $4.75 and a vegetarian garden burger is $3.25. The restaurant is heavily patronized by the students from nearby Mount Union College.

If breakfast is what you crave, try **D.D. Stutz's Restaurant,** 4508 Lincoln Way E., Massillon, tel. (330) 477-2525. Lots of stuff here is made from scratch, so it would be a shame to think only of the generous breakfast buffet, which is $5.28. A popular lunch item is broiled scrod at just $5.88, while barbeque ribs in the evening are $9.88 for half a slab and $12.98 for the whole thing.

Haunted by what passed for food at your old high school? **A Centre Place** may make you think again. This restaurant, at 800 N. Market Ave., Canton, tel. (330) 430-2050, is one of several businesses inside the former McKinley High School. Besides offering a spacious outdoor dining area in warm weather, A Centre Place lists many sandwiches; for example, a chicken salad on croissant is $3.75. Taco salad is only $3.95, while chicken parmigiana is $4.75. Open Mon.-Fri. 11 a.m.-2 p.m., you can check out its Web site at www.acentreplace.com.

Moderate

Burkhardt Brewing Company, 3700 Massillon Rd., Uniontown, tel. (330) 896-9200. This brewpub specializes in ales; seven different and distinct varieties, all made on the premises, can be had at the tap. Food matters here, too. A popular appetizer and a pungent counterpoint to the rich brew is sauerkraut balls at $5.95. Chicken breasts come at least two ways, in Anaheim and raspberry configurations. The former is a rolled, breaded chicken breast hiding cheese and covered with hot sauce. The latter is a breaded breast with raspberry sauce. Either meal is $10.95. Lunch or dinner is available every day but Sunday, when dinner only is served.

Vegetarians will want to head for **Mulligan's Pub,** 4118 Belden Village St. NW, Canton, tel. (330) 493-8239. While the pubsters serve burgers, ribs, steaks, and seafood, they also offer a changing vegetarian menu that may feature garden burgers, meatless chili, or a huge burrito. Named "Best Watering Hole in Stark County" in a survey, one of the tavern's most popular luncheon items is a filet steak sandwich at $6.99. Later in the day, the vegetarian Monster Burrito is $6.95. Always busy.

Ricky Ly's, 4695 Dressler Road NW (Thursday's Plaza), Canton, tel. (330) 492-5905. Belden Village is the site of this restaurant, which offers diners exposure to Hunan, Mandarin, or Szechuan dishes. The two most popular main dishes both involve chicken. General Tsao chicken at $9.95 is deep-fried and spicy, with a rich garlic sauce; Hunan chicken at $7.95 is stir-fried with veggies and also is somewhat combustible. Mr. Ly says he can prepare Peking Duck ($23.95) without advance notice. The facility serves lunch and dinner seven days a week.

The **356th Fighter Group Restaurant,** 4919 Mt. Pleasant Rd., North Canton, tel. (330) 494-3500, looks for all the world like a World War I allied outpost in rural France. It's situated just south of the Akron/Canton Regional Airports, serving lunches and dinners six days a week, plus a Sunday brunch. Marinated sirloin for $7.50 is a big lunch item, as is the cajun chicken cheddar sandwich at $6.50. All-you-can-eat deals abound in the evening, with crab legs for $21.95 on Monday and prime rib for $12.95 on Friday and Saturday. What's billed as "50 feet of gourmet food" constitutes the $9.95 Sunday brunch. Top 40 live dance music can be heard every Friday and Saturday and, at times, on Wednesday or Thursday.

Expensive

Kurt's Inn is at 4104 Lincoln Way E. in Massillon, tel. (330) 478-2548. The unique thing here is the number of continental dishes prepared at tableside. Open from 4 p.m. except on Sunday, popular dinner items include Wiener schnitzel at $15.95 and prime rib at $16.95. Specials are featured only for a few consecutive days before they are changed. The signature dessert is baked Alaska, with cherries jubilee and crêpes suzettes also in demand. Located midway between Massillon and Canton, Kurt's Inn is expensive but not prohibitive.

The **Stables Restaurant and Hall of Fame Grille,** 2317 13th St. NW, Canton, tel. (330) 452-1230 is even larger than its name. The facility is situated in a round, domed brick building that once was, in fact, where a rich guy kept his horses. The former stable today is fragrant with steaks, seafood, burgers, and pasta. A popular lunch item here is named after owner and pro football player Chris Spielman: It's the Spielman Burger at $6.75. Included are sauteed mushrooms, onions, bacons strips, and provolone cheese. Dinnerwise, the top choice is honey barbecue ribs, $12.95 for half a rack and $14.95 for a whole rack. There's a bar amid the greenery and a 10,000-pound football sculpture carved from redwood.

RECREATION

Canton claims, with justification, to be Ohio's golf capital. A good-looking 36-hole course that caters to the public is **Tam O'Shanter,** 5055 Hills & Dales Rd., tel. (330) 477-5111 or (800) 462-9964. Tam O'Shanter is open from March through December. Greens fees are a bargain on weekdays before 11 a.m.: 18 holes are $17, or $25 in a motorized cart. Senior citizens can play 18 holes for just $12 and $20, respectively. On weekends, prices for all are $25 to walk and $35 to ride for 18 holes. Another nice local course that welcomes tourists is the **Legends** in Massillon at 2700 Augusta Dr., tel. (330) 830-4653. This 18-hole facility is a mile west of SR 21, just off US 30. It opened in 1995 and charges $42 and $35 greens fees (with cart) on summer weekends for rounds of golf before and after 1 p.m., respectively. Ask the Canton/Stark County Convention and Visitors Bureau for a brochure on the various area courses.

Pedestrians can achieve their high on a leg-pleasing 1.5-mile, off-red, rubberized running and walking track that winds its scenic way past the McKinley Memorial at the McKinley Memorial Site. The only wheeled contraptions allowed on the surface surface are strollers, so take your Rollerblades and skateboards elsewhere. Massillon has a nifty and safe place to run, too. North Sipple-Reservoir Park, off Hanikins Rd. NE, has a trail that heads south for more than a mile before ducking under old US 30 and continuing on into South Sipple Park. Like the Canton version, only feet are permitted.

The public park with the most opportunity is in Alliance. Fifty-three acre **Silver Park** at 2930 S. Union Ave., has half a dozen tennis courts, a lighted basketball court, a sound stage, a sledding hill, and a lake.

Clay's Park Resort, 13190 Patterson Rd. NW, North Lawrence, tel. (330) 854-6691 is less inhibiting—and less costly—than larger attractions near Cleveland or Sandusky, this water park is the kind of place the kids usually love. There are slides, paddle boats, and miniature golf, with food and refreshments available. Admission is $5.95 weekdays and $8.95 weekends. The park is open for fun from Memorial Day to Labor Day, and for camping May 1-Nov. 1. Camping for water buffs is a good deal: the $19.95 per-couple price includes water park admission.

SHOPPING

For shopping as a diversion, Canton offers a fairly busy downtown, with various storefront businesses. **Belden Village Mall,** just west of I-77 north of Canton, is the largest such place in the county. In addition to many of the big national chain and department stores, there are movie theaters and a number of local and regional goods and services. For more information, telephone (330) 494-5490. On Canton's west side is **Canton Centre Mall,** 4000 Tuscarawas St. W, tel. (330) 830-0028. Anchoring the facility are JCPenney and Kaufmann's department stores.

Massillon's contribution to malldom is **Meadows Plaza** at 2008 Lincoln Way E. There is a respectable shopping center in Alliance, **Carna-**

CANTON, MASSILLON, AND STARK COUNTY EVENTS

JANUARY

McKinley Day Celebration takes place in Canton and pays homage to the assassinated president's date of birth on January 25, tel. (330) 455-7043.

MARCH

Antiques in Canton antique show and sale happens the first weekend in the Canton Museum of Art, tel. (330) 453-7666.

APRIL

Big Band Annual Celebration Concert, Canton Palace Theatre.

MAY

Spring Fest, provides a good chance to view the canal and environs in Canal Fulton's Village Park, tel. (330) 854-3808.

JUNE

St. Haralambos Greek Summerfest taks place at the Greek Orthodox Church of the same name, Canton, tel. (330) 454-7278.

Cruise On In and Dance Party, downtown Massillon, features 650 cars on display and a six-figure crowd, many of whom remember the 1960s—and before, tel. (330) 833-4061.

Italian-American Festival, Stark County Fairgrounds, Canton, tel. (330) 494-0886.

JULY

Community Picnic and July 4 Display, Stadium Park, Massillon, tel. (330) 833-2233.

Olde Canal Days Festival, Canal Fulton, tel. (330) 854-2805. Come watch the towpath mules get a workout.

Pro Football Hall of Fame Festival, including the Induction Ceremony and Game, Canton, tel. (330) 456-8207. Need we say more?

AUGUST

Carnation Festival, Alliance, tel. (330) 823-6260. Alliance is the "Carnation City," so named by the Ohio legislature. President William McKinley per-

petually wore a red carnation. Eerily, he plucked the flower from his buttonhole to give to an admirer moments before being hit by an assassin's bullet in 1901. Happily, there's play but no gunplay as ribs, pancakes, and ice cream are consumed, people parade, there are dances, and the athletic enter a triathlon.

Stark County Fair, Canton, tel. (330) 454-0621. Yes, it's fresh-faced kids and their animals, plus rides and exhibits. The fairgrounds event is seven days and spills over into September.

SEPTEMBER

Yankee Peddler Festival, Clay's Park Resort, Canal Fulton, tel. (330) 239-2554. Everyone sells everything on the first three full weekends in September.

Glamorgan Castle Marketplace, Alliance, tel. (330) 821-2100. More sales, one Saturday only.

OCTOBER

Is it chilly in October? Indeed it is if you're talking about the **Chili in October** in Canal Fulton, tel. (800) 435-3623. Attendees ride aboard the authentic *St. Helena III* canal boat prior to partaking in a heartening chili supper. There are only two dinner rides on one Saturday, so make reservations.

Algonquin Mill Fall Festival, Carrolton, tel. (330) 627-5910. Learn what was done with the harvest in days gone by.

NOVEMBER

Craftspeople come out of the woodwork for Canton's annual **Christkindl Market,** usually held the second weekend in November. There are foods, fashions, and more at Canton's Cultural Center for the Arts, 1001 Market Ave. N, tel. (330) 453-7666. Admission is $3 in advance or $4 at the door.

DECEMBER

Big Band Christmas Music, Canton, tel. (330) 454-8172. Yule tunes meet the swing era.

tion Mall, at 2500 W. State St., tel. (330) 821-4447. Besides an assortment of retail stores, the mall has a library branch and a five-screen cinema. There's also a genuine outlet store in town—Carnation Basket Company's **Olde**

Country Basket Shoppe, 112 Prospect St. The store offers 30% off on second-quality baskets, 10% off on first-quality baskets, and has special 50% off sales twice a year. Call them for sale dates at (330) 823-7231.

INFORMATION AND SERVICES

Dial 911 in Canton or Massillon for police emergency. The Canton Police Department is in City Hall, 221 Third St. SW, Canton, tel. (330) 489-3131. The Massillon Police Department also is in City Hall, 1 James Duncan Plaza, Massillon, tel. (330) 832-9811. Medical services in Canton are available at Timken Mercy Medical Center, 400 Austin Ave. NW, tel. (330) 489-1000. In Massillon, the Massillon Community Hospital, 875 Eighth St., tel. (330) 832-8761, provides such services. The post office in Canton is at 2650 Cleveland Ave. NW, while the Massillon post office is at 333 S. Erie St.

Virtually next door to the Pro Football Hall of Fame is the **Canton/Stark County Convention and Visitors Bureau.** It's at 2141 George Halas Dr. NW, just north of the Hall of Fame, and can be reached locally by telephone (330) 452-0243. Actually, the latter site is a satellite office, more convenient than the main office, which is located downtown at 229 Wells Ave. NW, Canton, tel. (330) 454-1439.

The *Canton Repository* is a weekday evening and weekend morning newspaper. It offers an entertainment section, "Ticket," in each Friday's edition. The *Massillon Independent* is published Mon.-Sat. afternoons. A useful entertainment section, "One-Day Trips," comes out on Friday. A weekly newspaper, the *Free Press,* hits the streets on Sunday and is sold throughout Stark County. In Alliance, look for *The Review* weekday evenings and Saturday mornings. The *Free Press* offers a Thursday entertainment section called "Let's Go!"

WOOSTER AND WAYNE COUNTY~ AMISH COUNTRY

Wayne County today has about 101,000 residents and covers about 557 square miles. It's the state's top producer of milk, oats, and hay, and has the largest number of cattle, chickens, and sheep. Approximately 25,000 Amish folk live in Wayne and nearby counties. The city of Wooster's present population is about 24,000, while Wayne County has approximately 110,000.

Regarding persons of Amish faith, reminders are necessary, the most important of mortal interest. The roads in this area are used every day by slow-moving horse-drawn buggies, by children on foot, and by bicyclists. If you are in a hurry, or if you are unheeding of the disparity in speed between your vehicle and nonmotorized travel, visit somewhere else. Locals in restaurants, motels, and information centers warn visitors of the dangers of speeding, noting that a teenage driver killed half a dozen young Amish pedestrians here in 1991.

The only other advice is to be judicious with cameras and camcorders. The Amish sincerely feel that taking their pictures is a religious affront. If you visit an Amish home, a cheese factory, a furniture plant, or anywhere else, leave the camera in the car. If you feel a photo or taped footage is a must, ask permission and defer to the wishes of any Amish adults or children present. Sweeping views of farms, fields, storefronts, and animals should provide most photographers with what they need in the way of visual souvenirs.

Orientation

Sixty miles southwest of Cleveland and 95 miles northeast of Columbus, Wooster is an unofficial gateway to the world's largest Amish settlement. A city of about 22,500, the Wayne County seat slopes upward toward the north from Killbuck Creek. Wooster is 30 miles east of I-71, 30 miles west of I-77, and is served by US 30 and 250 and by State Routes 3, 83, and 585. The area's rolling terrain mixes pasture, woodland, and fields of corn, soybeans, alfalfa, and potatoes.

History

Delaware and Wyandot Indians were the area's first inhabitants. The Delaware, among the least warlike of tribes, migrated westward after Europeans began to intensively farm their tribal homeland in Pennsylvania. Wayne County, named for Indian fighter General "Mad" Anthony Wayne, was surveyed between 1805 and 1807 and quickly settled by farmers, who paid $2 per acre for 100-acre plots.

The city itself was named after a Revolutionary War general, David Wooster, and incorporated in 1817. More widely revered is August Imgard, a German immigrant. Newly arrived in Wooster in 1847, Imgard was disappointed at the austere way in which Christmas was celebrated. He cut down a small spruce tree, rigging a metal star to its tip and bedecking the branches with paper decorations. The Christmas tree custom spread across Ohio and the country.

SIGHTS

Liberty and Market Streets form downtown Wooster's main intersection. The **Wayne County Courthouse,** with its columns carved to resemble classic Greek figures, is on the northwest corner. Unlike many 19th-century Ohio courthouses, this facility sits close to the street and takes up only a portion of a block.

Freedlander's and **Everything Rubbermaid** are downtown landmarks. Freedlander's is a large, traditional, multistory department store just west of the courthouse at 125 W. Liberty St. Everything Rubbermaid is a red- and blue-trimmed, four-story stone building at 115 S. Market St., a block south of the courthouse. Wooster is home to Rubbermaid, Inc. Shoppers come here to stock up on 3,000 different items at this "I-can't-believe-it's-all-rubber" retail destination.

Driving up the hill on Market, the street becomes Quinby Avenue. About a dozen blocks north of the courthouse is Wayne Avenue, an east-west street serving the **College of Wooster.** Dense with shady trees and marked by attractive yellow-brick buildings, the college was founded in 1866 and is home to the **Ohio Light Opera,** an internationally known resident professional company that performs eight different operettas every summer in Freedlander Theater on campus.

Vivid costumes, striking voices, and orchestral accompaniment make such productions as *The Pirates of Penzance* or *The Mikado* come alive. Adding to the enjoyment are free pre-performance commentaries every Friday and Saturday evening and two orchestra-only concerts each summer. Operettas are staged from about mid-June to mid-August and frequently sell out. Performances take place virtually every summer day, and there are numerous matinees. Tickets are $25 for adults

and $12.50 for children and for students under 25. For a brochure, dial (330) 263-2090.

The college's **Ebert Art Center,** which underwent recent renovation, houses a permanent collection of American, Asian, and European works, plus Persian decorative arts. Student work also is featured in the same building.

Details concerning late-breaking college lectures or sporting events are available at (330) 263-2566. That's the information desk in the **Lowrey Student Center,** where a staffer will scroll through a computerized list of activities for now or for when you come to town. The College of Wooster can be found on the Web at www.wooster.edu.

Heading back in the direction of town, turn left onto East Bowman Street. At 546 E. Bowman is the **Wayne County Historical Society,** tel. (330) 264-8856, showing a collection of military memorabilia, mounted birds and animals, Indian artifacts, and more. Open Tues.-Sun. 2-4:30 p.m., the society is housed in the 1817 red-brick home of General Reasin Beall. Admission for adults is $1, high school students $0.50, and children are free.

Wayne Center for the Arts, 237 S. Walnut St., tel. (330) 264-2787, open weekdays 9 a.m.-5 p.m. and Saturday 9 a.m.-noon, offers free, fascinating exhibits, which can include everything from pottery to photographs.

Weather and season willing, there are at least three outdoor sites worth a visit. Two are the **Ohio State University Agricultural Technical Institute** and the 2,100-acre **Ohio Agricultural Research and Development Center** (OARDC) where research on plants and livestock goes is conducted on behalf of state agribusiness. The OARDC is at 1680 Madison Ave. (SR 302), tel. (330) 263-3779, heading south out of town. It offers self-guided tours and includes Secrest Arboretum and a three-acre Garden of Roses of Legend and Romance—showing 500 rose varieties. Admission is free, though the school charges for its annual spring garden preview in February. The Agricultural Technical Institute is at 1328 Dover Road (SR 83), tel. (330) 264-3911, which branches to the left just south of the OARDC. The institute has theme gardens and a small Victorian conservatory. Admission is free.

The third green site is **Quailcrest Farm,** tel. (330) 345-6722, six miles north of Wooster on SR

the Ohio Light Opera's summer production of Christopher Columbus at the Freedlander Theatre in Wooster

83, then west on to 2810 Armstrong Road. The air here in greenhouses and amid display gardens swims with the fragrance of more than 400 herb and other plant species. Set high on a hill, the farm is a good choice in any warm-weather month, and there are large selections of garden books, cookbooks, pottery, and other items. From March-Dec., its hours are Tues.-Sat. 10 a.m.-5 p.m., plus Sunday 1-5 p.m. in May and December.

AMISH TOWNS

Once in the country, several towns beckon with varying degrees of Amish flavor or influence. From north to south they include:

Doylestown. This tiny place, northeast of Wooster on a short stretch of CR169 off SR 585, used to be "the toughest damn spot in the whole United States." Miners in the 1870s, fueled by drink, waylaid innocent farmers along the road, which was a hellish alley of coal mines and taverns. These days, the area is rural and relaxed, the sounds of picks, shovels, and confrontations long gone. Doylestown also has survived the fact that it is the hometown of Frankie Avalon!

Rittman. You're in Johnny Appleseed country, so you might want to visit **Bauman Orchard,** tel. (330) 925-6861), 161 Rittman Rd. Open all year, you can pick your own at the facility, which also features a fruit market.

Smithville. The local historical society opens the old **Mishler Weaving Mill** for tours by ap-

pointment, and there are several shops at **Buchanan Place,** (tel. 330-669-3911) on SR 585.

Orrville. The home of Smucker's jams and jellies, which offers tours, Orrville also houses a **Toy and Hobby Museum,** tel. (330) 683-8697, 531 W. Smithville Rd., and the **Orrville Railroad Museum,** tel. (330) 683-2426, 145 S. Depot St. The toys can be seen on Saturday noon to 6 p.m., and Monday or Friday 6:30-9 p.m. The former Pennsylvania Railroad depot is open Saturday10 a.m.-4 p.m., May-Oct.

Kidron. This hamlet has several claims to fame: a fascinating **Amish livestock auction** beginning at 11 a.m. every Thursday at Kidron and Emerson Roads (CR 52 and CR 79), and an absolutely retro hardware store. **Lehman's,** tel. (330) 857-5757, One Lehman Circle, is a warren of cookware, tools, non-electric lights and small appliances, crockery, kegs, signage, and non-electric refrigerators and stoves. This Lehman's can be overrun with tourists; try the smaller store a few miles south in Mount Hope (in Holmes County; get directions at the Lehman's in Kidron or from Kidron head south to US 250, then east to SR 241 and south to Mount Hope). South of US 30 and just north of this crossroads village, also on CR 52, is **Nut Tree, Inc.,** tel. (330) 857-7685. One of numerous area stores selling handmade furniture, the log cabin-style facility is full of items created by Amish and Mennonite craftsmen who work in a shop next door.

Shreve. This tiny village on SR 226 south of Wooster has a number of cute and quaint shops.

There's also **Kister Water Mill,** 3936 Kister Rd., tel. (330) 567-3500, where a huge waterwheel powers everything from a sawmill blade to a cider press. Hours are Tues.-Sat. 10 a.m.-5 p.m. and Sunday noon-5 p.m. Admission is $3 for persons over 18 and $1.50 for ages 7-18.

Birds flock to watery glacial remnants such as **Brown's Lake Bog** west of Shreve, where there are ongoing efforts to weed out non-native flora and to restore rare local varieties such as pitcher plants and cinnamon ferns. The Nature Conservancy of Ohio opened a pleasant boardwalk trail around the lake in 1990. Caution— wandering off the boards will make for a muddy hike! If your license and gear are in the car, try your fishing luck at **Shreve Lake,** a 228-acre pond just west of the village. The farther south in Wayne County the more rural and Amish things become, and Shreve is only a mile from the Holmes County line.

ACCOMMODATIONS

The **Wooster Inn,** 801 E. Wayne Ave., tel. (330) 264-2341, college-owned, offers 16 rooms in a quiet and atmospheric place, with fine dining, $90-100. In the middle of downtown is a **Best Western,** 243 E. Liberty St., tel. (330) 264-7750, moderately priced and with a pair of restaurants and a lounge. Inexpensive accommodations can be had at the **EconoLodge,** 2137 E. Lincoln Way (US 30), tel. (330) 264-8883, which also features an indoor pool/spa. There's a moderately priced **Hampton Inn** in Wooster at 4253 Burbank Rd., tel. (330) 345-4424. Both the **AmeriHost Inn-Wooster North** at 789 E. Milltown Rd. (SR 3 and 83), tel. (330) 345-1500, and the **AmeriHost Inn-Wooster North** at 2055 E. Lincoln Way (US 30), tel. (330) 262-5008, offer moderate rates. Both have indoor pools and offer free continental breakfasts. The **Super 8** motel at 969 Timken Rd. has inexpensive rates, from $40-48, among the best rates in the city.

East of Wooster in Orrville is the **Royal Star Motel,** 11980 Lincoln Way, tel. (330) 683-7827 or (888) 711-8110, $54-78. Forty-eight rooms, cable TV, air conditioning, restaurant, new in 1997. Also in Orrville is the **Orrville Inn,** 10355 Lincoln Way E. (US 30), Orrville, tel. (330) 682-4080, $35-45.

Bed and Breakfast

In the Wooster area there a number of lovely bed and breakfast options, making it entirely possible to base your visit at a B&B in Wooster and explore the Amish country during day trips. The following are in order by lowest price, though be on the lookout for weekend specials.

Gasche House Bed and Breakfast, 340 N. Bever St., Wooster, tel. (330) 264-8231, $40-50. Four rooms, one with private bath. Children 12 and over only.

The **Crawford House Bed and Breakfast,** 42 N. Main St., Rittman, tel. (330) 925-1977, $50-60. Three guest bedrooms and an executive suite. Porch swing, telephones with data port hookups.

The **Leila Belle Inn Bed and Breakfast,** 846 E. Bowman St., Wooster, tel. (330) 262-8866 or (888) 430-7378, $50-70. Four rooms, private baths, central air and heat. No children under 12. Visit the Web site at www.wooster-bnb.com.

Millennium Classic Bed and Breakfast, 1626 Beall Ave., Wooster, tel. (330) 264-6005, $55-95. Four combinations of suites and single rooms, private baths, several sitting areas in a post-Victorian home.

Historic Overholt House Bed and Breakfast, 1473 Beall Ave., Wooster, tel. (330) 263-6300, $60-70. Three rooms, one a two-bedroom suite.

Harbor Hills Black Squirrel Inn, 636 College Ave., Wooster, tel. (330) 435-4155, $65-85. Four rooms, one with two-person jacuzzi, private baths, Victorian decor.

Land Gate Bed and Breakfast, 3519 Mechanicsburg Rd., Wooster, tel. (330) 345-6176, $70. Four guest rooms, private baths, central air, 19th-century Victorian brick decor.

The following bed and breakfast options are in outlying towns for more of a "get out of town" ambience.

Smithville Bed and Breakfast, 171 W. Main St. (SR 585), Smithville, tel. (330) 669-3333 or (800) 869-6425, $45-62. Private baths, TV, breakfast in a solid cherry dining room.

Grandma's House Bed and Breakfast, 5598 Chippewa Rd., Orrville, tel. (330) 682-5112, $55-90. An 1860 farmhouse, no credit cards. Featured in several regional and national publications.

Moyer Place Bed and Breakfast, 398 N. Market St., Shreve, tel. (330) 567-5930, $55-

65. Three guest rooms, central, TV with VCR, pet boarding, outdoor pool.

Campgrounds
Beck's Family Campground, Friendsville Road (CR 6), four miles north of Wooster, off SR 83, tel. (330) 264-9930, $12-16. Swimming, hiking, fishing, open April-Oct.

Meadow Lake Park Campground, 8970 Canaan Center Rd., Wooster, tel. (330) 435-6652, from $17. Two lakes, open April 1-Nov. 1.

Lake Wapusun Campground, 10787 Molter Rd. (SR 3), Shreve, tel. (330) 496-2355, $15. Five lakes, open mid-April to mid-October.

Whispering Hills Recreation Campground, SR 514 South, Shreve, tel. (330) 567-2137, from $14.50. Olympic-size pool, open April 15-Oct. 15.

FOOD

Amish food in all its homemade glory is widely available throughout Wayne County. Local cooks stoke families who perform heavy manual labor virtually every week of the year, so an Amish meal can be a table-straining affair.

Inexpensive
Wooster residents don't live by Amish food alone, however. Those in search of coffee varieties will find them at **Seattle's Coffee House,** 131 N. Market St., tel. (330) 262-2998. For further contrast, pizzas are popular at the **East of Chicago Pizza Company** franchise, 801 Lincoln Way West, tel. (330) 264-3278, and at the **Miami Restaurant,** 503 E. Liberty St., tel. (330) 263-4400. The latter serves beer and wine, and both also offer submarines sandwiches and fresh salads. The usual franchises are in Wooster on Beall Street and along Burbank Road (SR 83) on the north edge of town.

A burger and a beer are a short order at **C W Burgerstein Great Sandwich Works,** 359 W. Liberty St., tel. (330) 264-6263. Upstairs is **TJ's,** (330) 264-6263, where prime rib is a specialty. Cantonese, Mandarin, and Szechuan Chinese are presented by **Hong Kong Restaurant,** 2241 Benden Dr., tel. (330) 262-2958, and **Buehler's Towne and Market Cafe** inside Buehler's Fresh Food Market, 334 N. Market St., tel. (330) 264-6797, is populated most days from 6 a.m. Ribs

are a specialty at **Olde Jaol Brewing Company,** 215 N. Walnut St., tel. (330) 262-3333, in the former lockup.

Moderate
Great Amish food can be had at the **Dutch Heart Family Restaurant,** 690 W. Main St. (US 250) in Apple Creek, tel. (330) 698-7400. Hours are Mon.-Sat. 7 a.m.-8 p.m. Choose from broasted chicken, liver and onions, or creative daily specials. Like many such tasty places, the waitstaff admonishes to save room for desserts such as peanut-butter pie. The **Barn Restaurant,** 877 W. Main St. (SR 585), Smithville, tel. (330) 669-2555, offers comfort food, as does the **Dutch Essenhaus Restaurant** at 176 N. Market St. (SR 226) in Shreve, tel. (330) 567-2212. And don't forget **Das Dutch Kitchen** at 14278 Lincoln Way E. (US 30) in Dalton, tel. (330) 683-0530. Any given rural restaurant should serve an intimidating amount of good food for not a lot of money. Not many are open on Sunday.

Expensive
For a gourmet lunch with a historical tie, visit the **Granary,** 4374 Shreve Rd. (SR 226), four miles south of Wooster, tel. (330) 264-1014. The restaurant provides crêpes, quiches, baked goods, sandwiches, and a variety of wines. The site is part of a Christmas tree farm, no doubt a tribute to the 150-year-old legacy of August Imgard.

The **Wooster Inn,** 801 E. Wayne Ave., tel. (330) 264-2341 on campus serves elegant meals in a fancy setting. Breakfast might be eggs Benedict, Belgian waffles, or homemade granola, while lunch may feature angel-hair pasta in pesto sauce or a brie-bacon-and-tomato sandwich. Dinner could include locally raised rainbow trout, free-range chicken, or New York strip steak. Hours are daily 7-11 a.m. for breakfast, 11 a.m.-2 p.m. for lunch, and 6-8:30 p.m. for dinner. The entire inn is closed from New Year's Eve through Jan. 10 each year.

NIGHTLIFE AND ENTERTAINMENT

Don't expect a surfeit of nightlife in a part of the country where electricity is sometimes considered an abomination. **Digger's Sports Bar Night Club,** 1865 Beall Ave., tel. (330) 264-7775, sets Wednesday and Friday aside during the school year for live music and dancing. Wednesday is devoted to reggae and college or alternative rock, while Friday can be anything from blues to mainstream rock 'n' roll. The club is on the north end of the College Hills Plaza shopping center, down a flight of exterior stairs. **Becky's Gemini Lounge,** 981 Grosjean Rd., tel. (330) 263-4411, frequently has a loud and metallic band on Friday or Saturday night and a slightly older, less collegiate, crowd than at Digger's. Gemini is in a one-time machine shop behind the Super 8 motel on Timken Road.

RECREATION

Bicycle riding on city pavement isn't great; streets are narrow and traffic is constant. In contrast, county and township roads await, particularly since local drivers watch their speed. Be careful, though—berms and shoulders seem unusually narrow. Good off-road riding can be found in Wooster's **Spangler Park.** From the courthouse, go west on Liberty Street, branching left onto Lincoln Way West (SR 302). Past the fairgrounds, take Silver Road left. You will see a parking lot on the park's edge at the first stop sign. Maps are posted and the trail is a loop, so there's no getting lost. "The 'No trail bikes' sign doesn't mean anything," says a local rider.

Runners and joggers are welcome at **Severance Stadium,** the all-weather college track, but should always make way for students and their activities. The facility is between University Street and Wayne Avenue, one-quarter mile west of Beall Avenue. **Maurer Field,** the old high school football venue, has nice grass and a mediocre track. It's on Bowman Street west of Grant Street. **Christmas Run Park** on Park Boulevard east of Woodland Avenue is the site of a designated fitness trail, while **Wooster Memorial Park** offers 300 acres crossed by footpaths. From downtown, get on US 250 headed north at Lincoln Way East (old US 30) and look for park signs.

Public golfing can be found at the **Spruce Tree Golf Course,** 5854 Cleveland Rd. (SR 3) north of Wooster, tel. (330) 345-8010; at the **Hawk's Nest Golf Club,** at 2800 Pleasant Home

WOOSTER AREA EVENTS

Wooster's newspaper, the *Daily Record,* tel. (330) 264-1125, is a sponsor of the annual **Book Fair** in late September that gets people reading and brings in widely known authors such as former Associated Press reporter and Beirut hostage Terry Anderson.

The **Ohio Mennonite Relief Sale and Auction,** tel. (330) 359-5385, is held in Kidron the first Saturday in August. This traditional fundraiser by the Mennonite Central Committee aids the hungry, homeless, and ill in 57 countries. More than 125 large Amish and Mennonite quilts, plus wallhangings, crib quilts, and wood items are sought by a crowd that fills Central Christian High School. Admission is free, as are other festive activities

The **Wayne County Fair,** the state's largest Junior Fair, runs for six days beginning the Saturday after Labor Day. The fairgrounds are on Lincoln Way West (SR 302), 10 blocks west of the courthouse. Call (330) 262-8001 for grandstand tickets.

Rd. in Creston, tel. (330) 435-4611; and at the **Riceland Golf Course,** 1977 E. Lincoln Way (US 30) in Orrville, tel. (330) 683-1876. You can smack away indoors at **Full Swing Indoor Golf,** at 149 E. Liberty St. in downtown Wooster, tel. (330) 264-4700.

Less active travelers will find the **Movies 10** complex at 4108 Burbank St. on the north side of the city. Check for low-priced children's matinees during the summer. Bookstores include the college's **Wilson Bookstore** in the Lowry Student Center on campus, **Hidden Pearl** at 114 N. Buckeye St., and **Wooster Book Co.** at 205 W. Liberty St. **Books in Stock,** 140 E. Liberty St., buys and sells used and rare books, offering a sizeable inventory of used paperbacks.

Auto-racing fans should head east of Wooster nine miles on US 30, then turn left (north) on CR 84. This will bring them to **Buckeye Speedway,** tel. (330) 264-3131, where stock and sprint cars run every Saturday night, April-Sept. Adults are $8, seniors $7, children under 12 free.

INFORMATION, SERVICES, AND TRANSPORTATION

In an emergency dial 911. The post office is at 153 E. South St., tel. (330) 262-0861. Wooster Community Hospital is at 1761 Beall Ave., tel. (330) 263-8100.

Greyhound serves Wooster. The station is at 155 S. Market St., tel. (330) 262-0341.

Four sources for tourist info in Wooster and Wayne County are the **Apple Creek Chamber of Commerce** (located in the Apple Creek Bank), Box 37, Apple Creek, OH 44606, tel. (330) 698-2631; the **Orrville Area Chamber of Commerce,** 132 S. Main St., tel. (330) 682-8881; the **Rittman Area Chamber of Commerce,** 8 N. Main St., tel. (330) 925-4828; and the **Wooster Convention and Visitors Bureau,** 377 W. Liberty St., tel. (330) 264-1800 or (800) 362-6474.

The *Daily Record* is Wooster's hometown evening newspaper. Weekly newspapers are produced in several of Wayne County's smaller towns.

HOLMES COUNTY~THE AMISH HEARTLAND

From *60 Minutes* to the federal Department of Health and Human Services, everyone admires the Amish. Their commitment to religion and family, and their patience with an intruding outside world have won them widespread support. Such warm thoughts have not always the case.

No Amish communities anywhere are as large, authentic, and accessible as the ones in this vicinity. Nearly 150 congregations live here, and their numbers are growing. (Don't look for churches—Amish congregations worship in private homes.) Because of stagnant produce prices and a population that doubles almost every twenty years, the Amish can't always rely on a completely agricultural life. Evidence of this can be seen along any rural road, where hand-lettered signs offering furniture, baked goods, quilts, vegetables in season, even farm tours, are common. Some visitors may find such promotion distasteful. But for travelers who want to learn, support, and not offend these admirable people, there are opportunities as never before to view the unique culture. Holmes County is where it can best be done.

History

The strict Christian group originated in Europe, where followers of an elder named Jakob Ammann broke off from the 17th-century Swiss Mennonite Church. The Amish may have invented tough love—the most conservative sects advocate strict shunning of persons excommunicated from the church. Excommunication can be imposed on everyone from fibbers to those who flirt with other religions. Ammann also insisted that members dress plainly and that males leave beards untrimmed.

The Swiss harassed the Amish, who also believe that the Bible teaches not to take up arms. Some paid additional taxes rather than go to war, while others moved from Switzerland to Germany to France. William Penn, the English Quaker and founder of Pennsylvania, recruited Amish families and members of several German peace churches; the plain people came to the New World in four waves, beginning about 1736. Here, too, they found folks eager to solve things in battle. The pacifist believers sometimes were simultaneously abused by colonists and by Indians. The largest Amish migration to North America, which involved about 3,000 adults, took place between 1817 and 1860. Many of these people ended up in the Holmes County area, where the first Amish began to farm as early as 1808.

Orientation

Not many other northeastern Ohio counties have so few residents (32,000), with only two towns (Millersburg has 3,200 people; Berlin, 1,000) large enough to be listed in the *Rand McNally Road Atlas* index. The Amish actually form the majority in several tiny villages, though for every stretch of road with a buggy, tourists may outnumber residents. Because of the high proportion of horse-and-buggy traffic, Holmes County has no four-lane highways, interstate or otherwise.

The Amish are simple, not stupid—they tend to avoid heavily traveled US 62, which cuts across the county from northeast to southwest.

The vicinity became a county in 1824, about the time persons of Swiss descent began local cheesemaking operations. Millersburg, the county seat, was incorporated in 1835. It's 80 miles northeast of Columbus, 85 miles south of Cleveland, and about 35 miles southwest of the Canton-Massillon area. The city is on Killbuck Creek, 20 miles downstream from Wooster. It is served by US 62 and by State Routes 39, 60, and 83. The county nowadays is a mix of truck farming and other agriculture, manufacturing, clay and coal mining, lumbering, and tourism.

SIGHTS

Rather than offering stunning natural scenery or huge manmade attractions, Holmes County favors the wanderer. Those who choose to meander will be rewarded with an array of tidy farms, cheese houses, country stores, craft and gift shops, demonstration farms, furniture retailers, restaurants, and specialty shops. The main streets of villages such as Charm or Berlin are a shopper's gauntlet.

Yet the best way to see how the Amish live is to follow one of the many hand-lettered signs posted where a farmhouse lane meets a highway. Whether the sign says "Quilts," "Wooden Chests,"

or "Foods in Bulk," odds are an Amish mother and her daughters are peddling their wares from a cool, dark house without television or electricity. (The men and boys are in the fields.) The house can smell like anything from milk fresh from the barn to whatever's for lunch, but it will be very simply furnished and clean, with hand-washed clothing billowing on an outside line.

If you're shy, there are two demonstration farms showing the Amish way of life. **Yoder's Amish Home,** 6060 SR 515, north of Walnut Creek, tel. (330) 893-2541, offers a house preserved since 1866 alongside a modern Amish residence. The visit can include a buggy ride or a petting session on this working farm. Open mid-April through October, closed Sunday. **Amish Farm** is a mile east of Berlin on SR 39, tel. (330) 893-3232. The tour includes a buggy ride and a slide show, and the home is filled with furniture in the style of the Old Order Amish. There are farm shops and a petting area.

Should you want to delve more deeply into Amish history, stop at the **Mennonite Information Center,** 5798 CR 77, Berlin, tel. (330) 893-3192. A rather intense 265-ft. mural depicting the history and heritage of the Mennonites and the Amish is featured, as is a slide presentation. This is the place to search for a treat in the gift shop, which specializes in objects made in the Third World. Open Mond.-Sat. 10 a.m.-5 p.m. Less structured is the **Amish Flea Market,** half a mile west of Walnut Creek on SR 39, tel. (330) 893-2836. The

Amish farms are easy to spot—there are no electric or power lines. The picturesque, yet functional, farms are worked by hand with the assistance of draft animals, in keeping with time-honored religious beliefs.

40,000 sq. ft. attraction observes daylight hours Thurs.-Sat., April-Dec., closed Jan.-March. The market is a good source for handmade furniture, as well as a mix of trash and treasures.

Victorian House is at 484 Wooster Rd., four blocks north of the square in Millersburg, tel. (330) 674-1576. A lovely old 1902 Queen Anne home with some 28 rooms houses antiques contributed by generous and proud local residents. Open May-Nov., Tues.-Sun. 1:30-4 p.m., the facility charges $3 for adults and $1 for students age 12-18 (under 12 is free), all of whom are taken on group tours. One other thing—Victorian House is meticulously cared for, lending credence to all those Swiss-Amish cliches. The **Killbuck Museum** on Front Street (just off US 62) in Killbuck shows fossils and Native American artifacts. Call (330) 377-4572 for hours.

Mills of different kinds, in various states of repair, can be found hereabouts. Two of the best are **Rastetter Woolen Mill,** 5802 SR 39, Millersburg, tel. (330) 674-2103, and **Baltic Mills,** 111 Main St., Baltic, tel. (330) 897-0522. The woolen mill weaves and sells rugs, while the mills at Baltic produce flour and feed. Rastetter also sells name-brand knitted wear at a discount, while Baltic offers a guided tour and has a gift shop.

Finally, to view the variety of homespun stuff available, stop by the **Gallery of Crafts,** 75 E. Clinton St., Millersburg, tel. (330) 674-5300. Open year-round, this former supermarket is 12,000 sq. ft. of Amish and local crafts, paintings, florals, stained glass, statuary, woodcraft, fabrics, jams, and jellies. Its hours are Mon.-Fri. 9 a.m.-5:30 p.m., Saturday 9 a.m.-8 p.m., and Sunday noon-5 p.m.

Tours through Amish Country

Tours of the county are available through the **Ohio Central Railroad** at 111 Factory St. in the town of Sugarcreek on SR 39, tel. (330) 852-4676, which operates steam and diesel excursions out of Sugarcreek and other Amish country towns. Starting in 1999 the Ohio Central Railroad was planning to scale back its passenger excursions, but continues offering them on a limited basis. The railroad puts out a schedule featuring its planned excursions, some more than 100 miles, along with special Thanksgiving and Christmas season runs; write to P.O. Box 427, Sugarcreek OH 44681, for a current

copy, or check out its Web site at www.ohiocentralrr.com. Adult fares start at around $10 for a one hour ride up to $85 for an all-day round-trip Fall Foliage excursion featuring a picnic style meal. For top of the line travel, rail fans can look into reserving a posh, private Pullman car for any of the excursions. Travelers would be wise to call ahead to confirm scheduled excursions.

Country Coach, Inc., at the Berlin House Restaurant, US 62 and SR 39, tel. (800) 619-7795, Berlin, runs van tours ranging from one to three hours Tues.-Sun. Reservations are requested but walk-ons are welcome. The tours, which also can be joined at the Carlisle Inn on SR 39 in Walnut Creek, are $12 for adults leaving the inn and $10 for adults leaving the restaurant, with children half price on either trip.

ACCOMMODATIONS

In contrast to more urban settings, inns and bed and breakfast facilities far outnumber hotels and motels. A couple of places stand out: the **Inn at Honey Run** is almost startlingly contemporary, yet it complements the Amish way of life. It and such places as **Gilead's Balm Manor** are sure to bring out the romantic in even the most flinty visitor. Both are expensive and worth it.

If you don't feel like spending time on the phone, make one toll-free call to (888) 606-9400. Amish Country Reservations operators will go through their information, finding you the right place at the right price with the right amenities. The service takes bookings for 45 Holmes County destinations. The accommodations below are listed by price, with the least expensive first.

Bed and Breakfast and Inns

Town House Bed & Breakfast, 3 N. Market St., Berlin, tel. (330) 893-2353, $55. No credit cards, prices vary.

Amish Country Inn, SR 39 and State St., Berlin, tel. (330) 893-3000, $43.95-115. Health club next door. Deluxe rooms offer patio or balcony. Swimming pool.

Das Daudy Haus, 3035 CR 600, Millersburg (no telephone, book through Amish Country Reservations), $50-65. A working Amish farm.

Tina's House, 6521 CR 189, Millersburg, tel. (330) 674-6268, $50-55. Nineteenth-century cottage with full kitchen, bath, two bedrooms, air conditioning, queen beds, deck.

Indiantree Farm Bed & Breakfast, 5488 SR 515, Walnut Creek, tel. (330) 893-2497, $50-85. Hiking, cross-country skiing. No children under 8, no credit cards.

Welcome Tree Plantation Bed & Breakfast, 4880 Township Rd. 257, Millersburg, tel. (330) 674-2609, $54-104. Two cottages, two farmhouse suites, two lodge suites; hiking trails, fishing.

Cape Cod Bed & Breakfast, 6192 Township Rd. 362, Millersburg, tel. (330) 893-2225, $55. Three guest rooms, one with kitchenette, built in 1996.

Marbeyo Bed & Breakfast, 2370 CR 144, Sugarcreek, tel. (330) 852-4533, $55-75. Three rooms with private baths on a working Amish-Mennonite farm.

Raber's Tri-County View Bed & Breakfast, US 62, Wilmot, tel. (330) 359-5189, $55-85. Private baths, refrigerator, microwave, queen beds, central air.

Peaceful Valley Bed & Breakfast, 1879 CR 144, Sugarcreek, tel. (330) 852-2388, $58. A Mennonite farm; each room has private bath.

Always Welcome Inn, 4892 Township Rd. 257, Millersburg, tel. (330) 674-2609, $59-109. This 1832 farmhouse offers cottages, lodge suites, and a fellowship center.

Bed and Breakfast Barn, CR 70, Sugarcreek, tel. (330) 852-2337, from $59.95. Fourteen barn rooms, seven cabins.

Lighthouse Bed & Breakfast, 331 US 62, Millersburg, tel. (330) 893-3341, $60. Queen beds, valley view.

Quiet Country Bed & Breakfast, 453 Township Rd., Nashville, tel. (330) 378-2291, $60. Ninety-eight acres, well off highway, no TV.

Sommerset Tourist Rooms, 5094 CR 359, Millersburg, tel. (330) 893-3130, $60.

Travelers Country Loft, 5580 SR 557, Berlin, tel. (330) 893-2134, $60. Three rooms, kitchens with microwaves, no breakfast.

Troyer Farm Guest House, no phone, 3998 CR 168, Millersburg, working Amish farm. $60.

Jake 'n' Ivy's Bed & Breakfast, 5409 Township Rd. 356, Berlin, tel. (330) 674-3215, $65. Newly built, three guests rooms, each with private bath, deck, kitchenettes.

Donna's Country Bed and Breakfast, 5523 Township Rd. 358 (East Street), Berlin, tel. (330) 893-3068, $65-75 for rooms, $125-150 for cottages. Two bed-and-breakfast rooms, three honeymoon/anniversary cottages, one with waterfall.

Garden Gate Get-A-Way, 6041 Township Rd. 310, Berlin, tel. (330) 893-3999, $65-75. Four guest rooms, each with private bath, private entrance, TV, air conditioning.

Grapevine House Bed & Breakfast, 2140 Main St., Winesburg, tel. (330) 359-7922 or (888) 901-8411, $65-75. Six rooms, private baths, TV, air conditioning, spacious back porch, gift porch.

Rose Arbor Inn, 4933 N. Main Street, Berlin, tel. (330) 893-4167, $65-75. Four rooms with private baths, TV, VCR, gardens.

Pomerene Tourist Rooms, 5396 Pomerene St., Berlin, tel. (330) 893-2216, $65-80. Two suites, one with jacuzzi, one with two bedrooms and kitchen. TV, VCR, air conditioning.

Breitenbach Bed & Breakfast, 307 Dover Rd., Sugarcreek, tel. (330) 343-3603, $65-85. Evening refreshments, television, air conditioning, private baths.

Overnite Getaway Bed & Breakfast, 5053 Main St., Berlin, tel. (330) 893-2529, $65-85. One room, with or without attached kitchenette.

Countryview Inn Bed & Breakfast, 3334 SR 557, Charm, tel. (330) 893-3003, $65-95. Make reservation when traveling with children.

Fields of Home Guest House, CR 201, Berlin, tel. (330) 674-7152, $65-125. Five guest rooms, each with its own bath in this log home. Also, whirlpools, kitchenettes, fireplaces.

Das Dunkel Haus Inn, 5335 CR 626, Berlin, tel. (330) 893-2276, $69-79. Three guest bedrooms; whirlpool, cable TV, air conditioning, full breakfast.

Das Gasthaus Bed & Breakfast, 4821 CR 207, Millersburg, tel. (330) 893-3089, $69-79. Private baths, central air. No credit cards.

Guggisberg Swiss Inn, 5025 SR 557, Charm, tel. (330) 893-3600, $69-79. Children allowed on first floor only.

Bigham House Bed & Breakfast, 151 S. Washington St., Millersburg, tel. (330) 674-2337, $70-75. Victorian-style home, four guest rooms, private baths, British hosts.

Down on the Farm Bed & Breakfast, 3836 SR 39, Sugarcreek, tel. (330) 852-4283, $70-80. Stay on an Amish horse farm owned by the Sugarcreek blacksmith; queen beds, bedtime snacks, full breakfast.

Flowerbed & Breakfast, 241 Walnut St., Millersburg, tel. (330) 674-7662, $70-80. Private cottage with own bath, queen bed up and sofa bed down.

Mel and Mary's Cottages, 2972 Township Rd. 190, Baltic, tel. (330) 893-2695, $75-85. Open March through December, fishing and hiking nearby.

Carriage House Inn of Berlin, 5453 East St., Berlin, tel. (330) 893-2226, $75-95. TV, air conditioning, continental breakfast.

Valley View Inn of New Bedford, 32327 SR 643, Fresno (Coshocton County), tel. (330) 897-3232, $75-105. Ten rooms, no children under 10, no TV.

Hasseman House Inn, US 62, Wilmot (Tuscarawas County), tel. (330) 359-7904, $79-110. Four guest rooms, one of which is a honeymoon suite. Open all year, children over 12 only.

Inn at Honey Run, 6920 CR 203, Millersburg, tel. (330) 674-0011, $79-275. Closed first two weeks of January. Children allowed only in main building. Wooded, secluded.

Blue Moon Bed & Breakfast, 47 N. Crawford St., Millersburg, tel. (330) 674-5119, from $80. This is a restored carriage house with living room, kitchen, two bedrooms, bath and screened-in porch. "Primitive country" decor.

Miller Haus Bed & Breakfast, 3135 CR 135, Walnut Creek, tel. (330) 893-3602, $85-105. No children under 5, 20-acre site, dessert each evening, full breakfast.

Swan Lake Cottage, 11667 SR 39, Millersburg, tel. (330) 674-7029, $85. Accommodates four adults, overlooks a lake.

Watchman's Cottage Bed & Breakfast, Charm, tel. (330) 893-3602, $85. Private bath in an adult-sized doll house. Price includes dinner and breakfast.

Hannah's House Bed & Breakfast, CR 201, Berlin, tel. (330) 893-2368, $85-125. Victorian home with four guest rooms, each with private bath, including a honemoon suite. Pool, steam room, sauna.

Oak Ridge Inn, Township Rd. 403, Walnut Creek, tel. (330) 893-3811, $85-150. Opened in 1997, the inn has decks, hot tubs, and fireplaces.

White House Inn, 209 N. Washington St., Millersburg, tel. (330) 674-4311, $95-110. Full breakfast, wakeup tea, evening snacks, suites with private baths.

Cricket Hill Cabin, 6109 Township Rd. 310, Millersburg, tel. (330) 674-1892, $95-115. New log cabin with fireplace, jacuzzi, loft, porch, air conditioning.

Main Street Bed & Breakfast, Main Street, Berlin, tel. (330) 893-1300, $95-115. Waterfall jacuzzi, queen beds, private baths, satellite TV, kitchenettes, authentic furniture.

Port Washington Inn Bed & Breakfast, 4667 Township Rd. 312, Millersburg, tel. (330) 674-7704, $95-135. English Tudor style home, five guest rooms with private baths, indoor heated pool.

Katelynn's Cottage Bed & Breakfast, CR 203, Berlin, tel. (330) 874-9006, $100-125. Rooms feature king beds and luxury baths, jacuzzi and satellite TV.

Gilead's Balm Manor Bed & Breakfast, 8690 CR 201, Frederickburg, tel. (330) 695-3881, $105-165 per night. Four suites attached to manor house, each with fireplace and jacuzzi, satellite TV. Cabinetry crafted by the owner.

Hotels and Motels

Hotel Millersburg, 35 W. Jackson St., Millersburg, tel. (330) 674-1457, $30-85. Guests must be able to use stairs. Rooms feature Amish quilts. Restaurant, tavern.

Comfort Inn of Millersburg, 1102 Glen Dr., Millersburg, tel. (330) 674-7400, $69-89. Part of a large chain, this motel opened in the spring of 1997.

Inn at Walnut Creek, 4869 Olde Pump St., Walnut Creek, tel. (330) 893-3599, $55-90. Seventeen rooms, four suites, cable TV, Shaker furniture throughout.

Carlisle Village Inn, SR 515, Walnut Creek, tel. (330) 893-3636, $84-167. Luxurious Victorian hotel, valley view.

Dutch Host Inn, SR 39 E., Sugarcreek, tel. (330) 852-2468, $59.95-69.95. Twenty-two rooms, TV, air conditioning.

Berlin Village Inn Motel, junction of SR 62 and SR 39, Berlin, tel. (330) 893-2861, $65-75. Cable television, air conditioning. Sunday by reservation only.

Inn at Amish Door, 1210 Winesburg St. (US 62), Wilmot, tel. (330) 359-7996, $89-173. A 50-room hotel, new in 1997, the motif is Victorian and there is an indoor pool.

Campgrounds

Amish Country Campsites, US 62 East, Winesburg, tel. (330) 359-5226, $14. RV and tent camping, open all year.

Baylor Beach Park, SR 93 and US 62, Wilmot, tel. (330) 767-3031, $15. Campsites, dump stations, hot showers, swimming, wilderness tent camping, open all year.

Whispering Hills Campground and RV Park, SR 514, Nashville, tel. (330) 567-2137, $16-20. Electric or primitive camping, 300 sites, Olympic-size pool, nature lodge, hiking trails, fishing, restaurant.

Scenic Hills RV Park, CR 367 (Hiland Road), off SR 39 East, Berlin, tel. (330) 893-3258. Open April 1-Oct. 31, rates vary.

FOOD AND DRINK

Restaurants vary from tiny storefronts to gymnasium-size halls. Quality is consistent, prices reasonable, few serve anything alcoholic, and most are closed Sunday.

Inexpensive

Should you want informal eats, Holmes County has a couple of franchises. **McDonald's** is at 1586 S. Washington St. (US 62) on the south side of Millersburg. Cheeseburgers there feature Swiss cheese. For a sampling of local trail bologna, locally made cheese, and other delicatessen treats, head for **Yoder's Market,** 187 E. Jackson St. (US 62) in Millersburg. In addition to hot and cold deli items, beer and wines are available.

A smaller place for lunch might be the **Winesburg Restaurant,** 2096 U.S. 62, Winesburg, tel. (330) 359-5110. Desserts one recent day included apple, Dutch crumb apple, blackberry, black raspberry, blueberry, cherry, Dutch crumb cherry, peach, red raspberry, and strawberry-rhubarb pies—as well as cream pies, cakes, puddings, and ice cream! Equally good but a contrast in size is **Mrs. Yoder's Kitchen,** 8103 SR 241, tel. (330) 674-0922, a spacious restaurant in minute Mount Hope.

Moderate

Several bed and breakfast places in Berlin rely on the **Boyd & Wurthmann Restaurant** on East Main Street, tel. (330) 893-3287 to fill their guests

each morning. It is, the owners claim, "where the locals head for lunch." A larger spot, capable of feeding 500, is **Der Dutchman of Walnut Creek,** just off SR 39 and 515, tel. (330) 893-2981, which says it is "the original and largest Amish restaurant in Holmes County." Like several others, Der Dutchman offers either menu or family-style dining. Just east of the county in Wilmot is another good-eats facility, the **Amish Door,** 1210 Winesburg St., tel. (330) 359-5464, an oversize Amish house that features both a salad and a dessert bar. Two other out-of-county considerations are the **Dutch Valley Restaurant,** on SR 39 in Sugarcreek, tel. (330) 852-4627 which also offers a daily breakfast buffet, and **Miller's Dutch Kitch'n,** at 2 N. Market St., tel. (330) 897-5481 in Baltic.

Expensive

For non-Amish fare, detour to Ragersville, six miles southeast of Sugarcreek in Tuscarawas County. The **Good House Saloon and Restaurant,** on County Hwy. 46 is south about five miles off SR 39, tel. (330) 897-4000. It's staffed by big-city people experienced in contemporary cuisine. Popular lunch or appetizer fare includes a sandwich-sized portobello mushroom in wine sauce with red onion, Swiss cheese and Roma tomatoes. Fresh salmon arrives twice a week, flown in for dinner. Lunch is served Wed.-Sat. 11:30 a.m.-2:30 p.m., dinner is served Tues.-Sat. 5-9 p.m. Make a reservation and bring cash; the Good House won't take plastic.

Nightlife

Hotel Millersburg, 35 W. Jackson St., tel. (330) 674-1457, is in downtown Millersburg, half a block west of the courthouse on the south side of the street. It has a handsome oak and brass bar that's open in the evenings Tues.-Sat. until 1 a.m. or so. It also serves dinner Tues.-Sun. The hotel formerly offered karaoke but it has been yanked, apparently for lack of interest. So much for nightlife in Holmes County.

RECREATION

Walking is a great way to see any of the dozen villages, each of which can be covered on foot with ease. Hills are common, and there aren't always sidewalks, but on weekdays there's not much traffic. Virtually any road lends itself to running or jogging. Give horses plenty of space if you're on foot. Most wear blinders, but sudden movement in front of them could cause excitement.

The **Briar Hill Golf Course,** at 7732 SR 39 east of Millersburg, tel. (330) 674-3921, is the county's only public links. A Millersburg-area public high school, **West Holmes,** offers exercise possibilities. The facility, at 10901 SR 39, has an open all-weather track, tennis courts, and, behind the school, a couple of basketball hoops.

INFORMATION AND SERVICES

In an emergency dial 911. For medical concerns the Joel Pomerene Memorial Hospital in Millersburg is at 981 Wooster Road (SR 83), tel. (330) 674-1015. The post office in Millersburg is at 56 S. Washington Street.

For travel information, the **Berlin Area Visitors Bureau,** P.O. Box 177, Berlin, OH 44610, tel. (330) 893-3467 or the **Millersburg-Holmes County Chamber of Commerce,** 91 N. Clay St., tel. (330) 674-3975 can both provide assistance in trip planning.

The *Holmes County Hub,* tel. (330) 674-1811 is Millersburg's newspaper, published on Thursday.

HOLMES COUNTY EVENTS

Want to see how things used to be? Show up for the **Amish Country Jubilee,** a three-day summer gospel music concert at Alpine Hills Resort, tel. (800) 241-7493, three miles east of Sugarcreek in Tuscarawas County. Alpine Hills Resort is on CR 139, just north of SR 39. Folks gather at 7 p.m. each of three evenings in late June to hear sacred music, eat Amish pies, and take buggy rides. Admission each evening is $9 for adults, with children 12 and under free.

The **Holmes County Fair** is in mid-August for five days every year. The fairgrounds are on SR 39 west of Millersburg.

The **Ohio Haiti Benefit Auction** in Mount Hope, tel. (330) 852-4855, is the first Saturday in September. This is a cooperative effort among several churches. Items for sale include furniture, quilts, and animals. Breakfast begins at 6 a.m. and there is food all day.

For a stirring time, visit **Yoder's Amish Home,** tel. (330) 893-2541, SR 515 north of Walnut Creek, held on three Saturdays in October. Apple butter will be cooking and there will be sampling opportunities during a time of year when the county's many hardwoods are at their most colorful.

MOUNT VERNON, LOUDONVILLE, AND KNOX COUNTY

Mount Vernon and Loudonville aren't much alike. The former is an impossibly pretty little city of about 15,000 with several streets paved in brick and with sumptuous old, well-maintained homes. Loudonville has fewer than 3,000 residents and an almost jumping-off-point feel, since folks come from throughout Ohio and beyond to canoe or otherwise enjoy the Mohican River. If Mount Vernon is "Ohio's Most Livable City," as it was named by *Ohio Magazine* in 1994, Loudonville is the capital of campers and paddlers. Outdoors people frequently show up for a Loudonville weekend with $10 and a pair of socks and are reluctant to change either. That would account for the less gentrified air on the river. Knox County's rural areas are marked by rolling hills, tidy farms, and picturesque villages.

History
Founded in 1805, Mount Vernon once was the home of John Chapman, otherwise known as Johnny Appleseed. Despite his wanderlust, Champman once owned property here. Also a native was Victoria Clafin Woodhul (1838-1927), the first woman to run for president. A composer, Daniel Decatur Emmett, also is a native and has an equally interesting story. Emmett was a gofer in a local newspaper when, at the age of 15, he wrote a popular song known as "Old Dan Tucker." The teenager joined a traveling show, starring in a pioneering minstrel performance. He wrote another tune while on the road and it brought down the house when it was sung in New Orleans in 1861. That tune was "Dixie."

Emmett eventually returned to Mount Vernon to eke out an existence selling copies of his famous songs.

White settlers began to show up all across Knox County during the first two decades of the 19th century. In Danville, Roman Catholics, Methodists, and Dunkards (German Baptists) farmed and started up small businesses. The hilltop location of Gambier (gam-BEER) was peopled by Englishpersons who founded Kenyon College in 1824. Early farmers were unusual in that they were as likely to raise sheep as any other animal. Loudonville, just north of Knox County, is on two forks of the Mohican River in some of the state's prettiest land. Charles Kettering, the inventor of everything from the carburetor to the iron lung, was born on a farm north of town in 1876. No doubt he canoed the forks of the Mohican, which by the time he was a teenager had seen European settlers for nearly a century. Today the town's economy relies primarily on visitors, who come here in warm weather in quantity.

As for the nice homes and pleasant shopping in the county seat, Mount Vernon has long been a prosperous rural trading center, producing steel and other commodities. There have always been a number of intellectuals and persons of differing religious faiths. From its beginning, Mount Vernon has been a place where it was possible to meet a radical, an anarchist, a secessionist, and an arch-conservative in a single walk around the block. The seat of Knox County is home to a maker of electrical parts for public utilities, a canning company, and manufacturers of automotive parts. The area is thick with dairy and beef cattle, swine, and poultry, and fields are most often planted either in corn or soybeans.

Location and Orientation

The city of Mount Vernon is approximately 50 miles northeast of Columbus along US 36/SR 3; continuing north on SR 3 another 23 miles or so, past Mohican State Park, brings the traveler to the small town of Loudonville. Interstate 71 north from Columbus provides an alternative route to the two towns via several state highways and small roads. Loudonville finds itself approximately equididstant from Mansfield to the northwest, Wooster to the northeast, Coshocton to the southeast, and Mount Vernon to the southwest. Knox County villages include Danville, Fredericktown, and Gambier.

SIGHTS

The village of **Gambier** is so dreamy in appearance visitors will think it slid off the canvas of an Impressionist painter. (In reality, village growth has been carefully managed.) Atop a huge, treelined hill, the village exists because Paul Newman's alma mater, **Kenyon College,** is there. It's a liberal arts institution for men and, more recently, for women. It's also the oldest private college in Ohio, in business since 1824. Besides a couple of stores, restaurants, and places to stay, there isn't a lot here. Yet strolling the campus is visually enriching. Imposing in its grandeur is Kenyon's first building, **Old Kenyon.** The structure is the earliest example of collegiate Gothic architecture in the United States. Ask for directions to Kenyon's 600 acres of woodlands, ponds, and meadows, which is on Laymon Road. For more information on Kenyon College try its Web site at www.kenyon.edu.

The **Knox County Historical Society Museum,** at 997 Harcourt Rd., Mount Vernon, tel. (740) 393-5247, has a store of Dan Emmett documents, plus such diverse attractions as 19th-century dolls and steam-powered farm tractors. Its hours are Tues.-Thurs., and Sat.-Sun. 2-4 p.m. The **Dan Emmett House,** at 501 S. Main St., has no regular hours or fees, but the historic **Woodward Opera House** at 101 S. Main St. can be toured on Saturday 10 a.m.-1 p.m. from spring to fall. The Woodward Opera House is not named after actress Joanne Woodward, but after Dr. Ebenezer Woodward, an entrepreneur who raised funds for its construction in 1853, an example of 19th-century combination public-use building, which houses not only the Opera House, but also a barber shop, a men's clothing store and other merchants. The Woodward is one of America's oldest pre-Civil War theaters. Call the Knox County Convention and Visitors Bureau for more information. The museum and the opera house each ask for $2 to visit.

Anyone who has ever watched *This Old House* will want to be invited into a preserved or restored 19th-century home. Not everyone can return for

*a bed and breakfast
in the quaint hilltop town
of Gambier*

the Mount Vernon annual Christmas Walk in November, so one solution is to contact Sunny O'Neill. She lives in a historic home at 600 N. Main St. and she offers **Mount Vernon home tours** from early September through mid-December. Everything is authentic and the emphases are on decorating with flowers and decorating for the holidays. For details, call Sunny in advance, tel. (740) 393-2400. Tours are $5 per person.

Kokosing Gap Trail

This onetime Penn Central Railroad bed that runs between Danville and Mount Vernon, passing Gambier and a wealth of lovely, bucolic scenery. It stretches for 13.3 miles. Expect walkers, runners, roller bladers, and bicyclists, but nothing motorized except wheelchairs. The path is 10 feet wide, level, and paved, making things predictable underfoot. Eventually, the trail will continue east past Danville into parts of rural Knox and Holmes Counties and their Amish populations. There's a move under way to build a covered bridge where the trail spans the Mohican River, south of Danville.

Mohican State Park and Mohican State Forest

Both of these preserves lie on SR 3, just south of Loudonville, offering a shady mecca to persons traveling by canoe, the park features Clear Fork Gorge cutting through soft shale and sandstone, which is where smallmouth bass and other game fish loiter. Nature trails surround the gorge, named after the Mohican River's Clear Fork.

There are two falls, Big Lyons and Little Lyons, named for a pioneer who lost his life while aiding a neighbor. Riders and pedestrians can get a good look at things, since bridle and hiking trails can be found in the adjacent Mohican Memorial State Forest. An ancient stagecoach trail, used before 1820, once connected Mount Vernon and Cleveland and evidence of the trail still remains. Rental cabins and campgrounds were renovated in 1996 and can be reserved by calling park officials at (419) 938-5411. Look for the covered bridge near the picnic area. The resort dining hall affords a panoramic view, as well as good food. Birders like it here, too. They can find several species of thrush, plus grosbeaks, evening wrens, red-breasted nuthatches, and white-throated sparrows. All in all, Mohican is one of the state's most attractive parks.

Postscript: Teenagers may want to head for Fredericktown, north of Mount Vernon. Once there, they can snoop to find the boyhood home of *Beverly Hills 90210* star and movie actor Luke Perry.

ACCOMMODATIONS

There are some swell places to stay hereabouts, from the **Kenyon Inn** at 100 W. Wiggin St., Gambier, tel. (740) 427-2202, which is both moderately priced and sumptuously appointed, to the **Accent House,** 405 N. Main St., Mount Vernon, tel. (740) 392-6466. On the National Register of Historic Places, this 1840s gingerbread Gothic Revival brick home has been faithfully restored and is an expensive overnight treat. Another nice spot is the **Dan Emmett House Hotel,** which is large, new, moderately priced, and, at 150 Howard St. in Mount Vernon, tel. (740) 392-6886 or (800) 480-8221, centrally located. For other Mount Vernon accommodations, look to the moderate **Curtis Motor Inn,** 12 Public Square, tel. (740) 397-4334 or (800) 934-6835. Several chain and independent motels are sprinkled around the county and in Loudonville.

Bed and Breakfast

A number of bed and breakfast operations exist in Knox County—prices vary, but most fall below the $85-per-night expensive threshhold. In picturesque Gambier, the **Gambier House,** 107 E. Wiggin St., tel. (740) 427-2668, provides a full breakfast in an 1845 home encircled by a cast-iron fence. Also in Gambier is **Woodside Bed & Breakfast,** 401 Chase Ave., tel. (740) 427-2711 or (888) 427-2711, which features architecture from the 1860s.

Several nice options can be found in Mount Vernon, such as the **Heritage House,** 307 N. Main St., Mount Vernon, tel. (740) 392-9301, just north of downtown on SR 3. The 1851 dwelling is on the National Registry of Historic Places. The **Russell-Cooper House Bed & Breakfast,** 115 E. Gambier St., Mount Vernon, tel. (740) 397-8638, is a landmark High Victorian in the city's historic district. Its Web site is www.russell-cooper.com, which is important because discounts are announced on the site from time to time. The **Tuck'er Inn,** 12059 Tucker Rd., Mount Vernon, tel. (740) 392-5659, was constructed in 1969 as a colonial country manor. Also very nice is the **Mount Vernon House**, 304 Martinsburg Rd., tel. (740) 397-1914, which dates from 1870 and has seven rooms, each with private bath.

In nearby Danville travelers can find both the **Red Fox Country Inn,** 26367 Danville-Amity Rd., Danville, tel. (740) 599-7369, a restored 1830s inn on 15 rolling acres, and the **White Oak Inn,** 29638 Walhonding Rd., Danville, tel. (740) 599-6107, which offers wooded acreage, a porch swing—and educational weekends devoted to things like wildlife or archaeology.

Seven miles north of Mount Vernon on SR 13 is the village of Fredericktown, home of the

Heartland Country Resort, 2994 Township Rd. 190, tel. (419) 768-9300. Besides overnight accommodations, this expensive to luxurious rural retreat has a heated pool and a riding stable. In Loudonville, the moderately priced **Blackfork Inn,** 303 N. Water St., (419) 994-3252, has six rooms for guests, each with its own bath, plus a pair of luxury suites. There are a number of guest houses and rustic cabins in the area, too.

Campgrounds

Don't forget the campsites, cabins, and lodge at **Mohican State Park.** Call (800) AT-A-PARK (282-7275) or (419) 938-5411 for details and to make reservations. Half a dozen campgrounds serve Knox County and twice that number can be found in the vicinity of Loudonville.

FOOD

Franchise food in all its predictable glory lines Coshocton Avenue (US 36) on the east side of Mount Vernon, and there's a McDonald's on SR 3 on the south side of Loudonville. For those who crave variety, check out the following:

The **Alcove Inn,** 116 S. Main St., Mt. Vernon, tel. (740) 392-3076, offers a mostly American menu with a few diversions. The sought-after luncheon sandwich is salmon foccacia at $6.25, while the prime rib dinner at $13.95 is the overwhelming favorite each evening. The Alcove has a regional following. Closed Sunday.

Antiquiteas at 100 E. Ohio St., Mt. Vernon, tel. (740) 393-3323 is a nice idea. It's a vintage home filled with antiques, collectibles and gifts where lunches and afternoon teas are served. Lunches are $5.95 and might be quiche, ham-and-chicken lasagna, or creamed chicken with mushroom over a scone. Included are two sides, such as soup and salad. Weekdays, drop in for afternoon tea, which also features coffee and pastries. Closed weekends but for Saturday if there are reservations for parties of four; closed January, July, and August.

The **Gambier Deli,** 110 Gaskin Ave., Gambier, tel. (740) 427-4324, is open early and late and has a sandwich menu that just won't quit. It serves everything from turkey on wheat toast with bacon, mayo, and more for $4.95, to Coach Steen's (the college swim coach) Belly Smacker, a veggie concoction that includes cream cheese, roasted peppers, and lettuce in a pita for $4.50. Breakfastwise, there are 20 coffee varieties, plus muffins and pastries. The Deli delivers and even offers bicycles for rent!

Jody's 109-111 S. Main St., Mt. Vernon, tel. (740) 397-9573, is a top spot for breakfast or lunch. There are four breakfast specialties from $2.99 to $4.99 daily, plus a breakfast buffet weekends. As an alternative to the Mon.-Fri. luncheon buffet, many diners order Jody's baked chicken dinner for $5.50. Two of the homemade desserts that sell out early are apple cake and apple pie, both served with warm vanilla sauce and priced at just $2 a serving.

Pirates' Cove on Brooklyn Street in Gambier, tel. (740) 427-2152 is the place for pizza. An 18-incher with cheese, sauce, and three toppings is $12-13.50. Besides big pies, its pastas, salads, strombolis, and submarines are inexpensive and readily available. So are microbrewed beers. The Cove is open daily 5 p.m.-1:45 a.m.

Rader's Restaurant is on the righthand (west) side of SR 3 as you drive south out of Loudonville, (419) 994-5155. It's where those about to canoe can eat a hearty breakfast, or satisfy their hunger after all day outdoors. Hotcakes are $2.39, or $3.39 with bacon, ham, or sausage. From Mother's Day through September, diners can opt for the weekend breakfast buffet. For lunch or dinner, baked chicken and two sides total $5.99. Throw in a wedge of black raspberry pie ($1.69 plain, $1.89 with ice cream), and this family place will take you some distance up or downstream.

Red Door Cafe, 100 Wiggin St., Gambier, tel. (740) 427-5105, bills itself as the county's only true coffeehouse. Besides Starbucks coffee, look for baked goods, fruit smoothies, fresh juice, and lots of Kenyon College students in varying degrees of repose.

Stevens Java Hut Express in the Mt. Vernon Shopping Plaza, 855 Coshocton Ave., tel. (740) 392-5292, is a quick breakfast stop. Try the Yellow Jacket, a latté emboldened with vanilla syrup, honey, and whipped cream for $2.25, or order something simpler and add a roll or muffin. The Hut also stocks juice, tea, bottled water, and non-breakfast snack items.

The **Village Inn,** 102 Gaskin Ave., Gambier, tel. (740) 427-4131), is a nice lunch or dinner stop, with a tavern attached. This is straight-ahead American food done carefully and well. Lunch might consist of a Cobb salad or a Reuben sandwich with fries and colonial cole slaw; either is $4.95. A typical evening special could consist of chicken parmesan with a side of fetuccini and a house salad for $8.25—the price of each night's special. Closed Monday.

ENTERTAINMENT AND NIGHTLIFE

With the musical heritage of Dan Emmett ringing in their ears, the folks at **Uncle Dan's Playhouse Tavern** offer an assortment of blues, jazz, classics, plays, and musicals on Friday and Saturday nights and, occasionally, on Sunday. The facility is part of the Dan Emmett House Hotel and Conference Center on Howard Street in Mount Vernon, tel. (740) 392-6886 or (800) 480-8221.

If the play's the thing, it's available twice over. The **Mount Vernon Players** put on a musical every summer, plus several dinner theater presentations at the Alcove Restaurant. Ask the visitors bureau for details. The **Ohio Festival Theater,** 922 1/2 W. High St., Mount Vernon, tel. (740) 397-2040), offers Shakespeare and contemporary plays outdoors each summer.

RECREATION

The two major areas for outdoor recreation in Knox County and vicinity are the Kokosing Trail between Mount Vernon and Danville for riding, walking, jogging, or skating and the Loudonville area for a canoeing, kayaking, tubing, or rafting expeditions.

On the Water

The **Loudonville Canoe Livery Inc.,** tel. (419) 994-4161 is next to the bridge at 424 Main St. (SR 39) in Loudonville. It offers a choice of kayaks, tubes, or rafts and recommends the nine-mile ride down the Mohican River for first-time paddlers. There's the opportunity, too, for an upriver put-in for a less-crowded float back home. This facility and most others operate April 15-Nov. 1.

Lake Fork Canoe Livery, 14765 SR 3 S, tel. (419) 994-5484, is four miles north of Loudonville. The firm is on the Mohican River and recommends taking the Lake Fork branch to view wildlife. Trips can run from two hours to three days. Their brochure offers four one-day trips and three overnight cruises.

Other liveries include the area's largest, **Mohican Canoe Livery and Fun Center** on SR 3 S, tel. (800) MOCANOE (or tel. 800-662-2663). They offer go-karts and amusements for children, too. **Pleasant Hill/Mohican Park Canoe Livery,** is on SR 39 in nearby Perrysville, tel. (419) 938-7777, while **Mohican Valley Campground and Canoe Livery,** tel. (419) 994-5204 is also on SR 3 S. The **Blue Lagoon Canoe Livery,** 1597 SR 97, in the town of Butler at the junction of SR 95 and 97, tel. (419) 883-3888, features waterslides and horses. Farther down the Mohican, in Knox County, look for **Mohican Wilderness Camp & Canoe,** 22462 Wally Rd., Glenmont, tel. (740) 599-6741.

Not all of the canoe people service the Mohican. To paddle up or down the Kokosing River, inquire at **Kokosing Valley Camp & Canoe Livery,** 25860 Coshocton Rd. in Howard (right on US 36 east of Mount Vernon), tel. (740) 599-7056. It's the only such service directly on the Kokosing.

On the Land

Golf on the area's rolling terrain is a pleasant way to pass time. There are several nice sites, including **Chapel Hill Golf Course,** five miles southwest of Mt. Vernon on US 36 in the village of Bangs (dial 740-393-3999 or 800-393-3499). Eighteen holes and par 72 greet players; greens fees Mon.-Wed. are $18 or $25 to ride; other weekdays are $19 and $30; weekends and holidays, set aside $23 and $34 for playing privileges. There are six ponds and the fairways are narrow and wooded. Another challenging venue is **Apple Valley Golf Course,** east of Mt. Vernon four miles on U.S. 36. It's also 18 holes and par 72. Greens fees are $29 weekdays and $34 weekends, with prices representing half a cart. The course is part of a resort. Turn into the facility at the sign and take the T-intersection to the left about two miles to the clubhouse.

Improbably, the **Gambier Deli,** 110 Gaskin Ave., Gambier (call 740-427-4324), rents bikes to

MOUNT VERNON, LOUDONVILLE, AND KNOX COUNTY EVENTS

FEBRUARY

Annual Raccoon Dinner, Danville.

MARCH

Kenyon Chamber Singers' Spring Concert, Gambier.

APRIL

Kenyon College/Mount Vernon Nazarene College Combined Concert, Gambier and Mount Vernon.

MAY

Dogwood Trail Tours, throughout Knox County.

JUNE

Danville-Howard Turkey Festival, Memorial Park, Danville.

Dan Emmett Festival and Civil War Encampment, Loudonville.

Mohican Ultra 100-Mile Run, Loudonville.

First-Knox Classic Bicycle Race, Mount Vernon.

JULY

Knox County Fair, Mount Vernon.

AUGUST

Knox County Quilt Show, YMCA, Mount Vernon

Dan Emmett Music and Arts Festival, Mount Vernon.

SEPTEMBER

Fredericktown Tomato Show.

Mohican Bluegrass Festival, Loudonville.

OCTOBER

Tour de Knox bicycle trip, Loudonville.

NOVEMBER

Annual Christmas Walk, Mount Vernon.

DECEMBER

Gambier Craft Sale, Westheimer Field House, Kenyon College.

Kokosing Trail riders by the hour or by the day. Rates are by the hour and change each year.

Do you fish? Do you hunt? Top spots for fishers in Knox County include Apple Valley Lake, east of Mount Vernon about 11 miles on US 36, or Knox Lake, just east of SR 95, north of Fredericktown. Hunters can take aim in the Mohican Wildlife Area, just west of the Knox County-Holmes County line on US 62. Or, try the Knox Lake Wildlife Area near Fredericktown.

SHOPPING

Because it's a prosperous place, Mount Vernon has several downtown stores worth visiting—and the parking is free. Travelers may want to stash their vehicles in the vicinity of the courthouse and check out any of six antique shops, all of which are within two blocks. Explore for yourself by orbiting the courthouse square in ever-larger arcs, or ask the Visitors Bureau at 236 S. Main St. for the"Heart of Ohio Antiques" brochure.

Farther from the courthouse, **Clayborne's Amish Furniture, Inc.,** 18350 Hopewell Rd. (dial 740-392-2805), is a popular destination. Open seven days a week, the store features wood craftsmanship, including incongruities such as Amish-made entertainment centers. Many items are available in oak, walnut, or cherry. In contrast, **Homewood Farms,** 19520 Nunda Rd. in the little village of Howard, sells unusual herbs and perennials—the kinds of plants you seldom find in the local garden center. Head north from Mount Vernon on SR 3 for 10 miles to Nunda Road, then turn left (west).

In Gambier, the place to shop is the **Kenyon College Bookstore,** in Farr Hall on Gaskin Avenue, tel. (740) 427-5410. More books per capita are sold in Gambier than anywhere on earth, and

this funky store takes full responsibility. They also stock a lot of other items, from toys to games to vitamins, and they're open every day of the year, 7:30 a.m.-11 p.m. Another worthwhile stop is the **Weather Vane,** 103 Scott Lane, tel. (740) 427-3636. This boutique carries not only an array of mostly young women's clothing, but economically priced jewelry and local arts and crafts, as well.

INFORMATION AND SERVICES

Call 911 for police emergency in Mount Vernon (or practically anywhere in the U.S.). The nonemergency Mount Vernon police number is (740) 393-9559. For medical attention, head to Knox County Community Hospital, 1330 Coshocton Rd., tel. (740) 393-9000, Mount Vernon. The Mount Vernon post office is at 236 S. Main St.

The **Knox County Visitors Bureau** can be reached at (800) 837-5282 or locally at (740) 392-6102. It's at 236 S. Main St. in Mount Vernon and offers an unusually comprehensive batch of printed materials. Loudonville area attractions can be studied by contacting the **Mohican Country Tourism Association** at (800) 722-7588. The **Mohican Area Tourist Information Center** is at 138 N. Water St. in Loudonville, tel. (419) 994-5225. To access **Kenyon College** doings, call (740) 427-5158.

The *Mt. Vernon News* is the local daily newspaper. It comes out Mon.-Sat. Several villages have weekly papers that usually appear on newsstands each Thursday. In contrast, check out the *Kenyon Review,* one of America's outstanding literary journals. Studded with authors who either are well known or should be, the annual *Review* is a one-volume introduction to where creative writing in this country may be headed.

COSHOCTON AND VICINITY

Coshocton County has just 36,000 residents, with 12,000 of them living in the county seat of Coshocton. The city is a larger, busier, and more intensely promoted municipality than is nearby Newcomerstown, population 4,000. The Coshocton "suburb" of Roscoe Village is the only completely restored canal town in the entire state. Coshocton and its downtown area, called Towne Centre, aren't in the least pretentious. Rather, downtown is a disarming mix of the mandatory courthouse square, brick walks, park benches, refurbished buildings, shady nooks, and adequate parking—all efforts to keep shoppers headed into rather than away from the city. The main highway in the county, US 36, skirts both Coshocton and Newcomerstown, which accordingly feels much less a destination and much more a quiet country town.

That doesn't mean you should drive past Newcomerstown at top speed. The town has several claims to fame, among them that iron-armed baseball pitcher Cy Young is from here. A monument to the winningest pitcher so far is in a park named in his honor. Other sights include the boyhood home of the late "Woody" Hayes, Ohio State University football coach; Turtle Monument, a tribute to a Delaware Indian clan; the Old Stone Fort, which may be Ohio's oldest building; and Temperance Tavern Museum, a building that dates from 1841 and is owned by the Newcomerstown Historical Society.

History
What better way to start a city history than with a little dish? In the 1730's a European female named Mary Harris was captured in New England and brought to the Coshocton area by Chief Eagle Feather of the Delaware nation. Enchanted by her beauty, the chief declared her his squaw and they settled in, rearing a couple of children. All went well until the chief returned with another female captive, this one apparently younger and better looking than Mary. The chief turned up dead one morning and Mary, who had fled to a nearby village, was returned to her village and executed. Whitewoman Street in Coshocton's Roscoe Village commemorates Mary Harris, a woman spurned.

Coshocton may have meant "union of waters," since the Walhonding and Tuscarawas Rivers meet on the west side of the city to form the Muskingum. The confluence was the site of at least one pre-Revolutionary War battle between natives and the British, who were backed up by colonists. The good news about the area was that the Ohio and Erie Canal came through Coshocton in 1830 on its way south. The shallow ditch put Roscoe Village, just west of Coshocton, on the map as a busy canal port. When the railroads made canal use obsolete, the village went into slow but inevitable decline. The canal closed for good in 1913. Problems were compounded by disastrous floods that hit the area that year and in 1935, necessitating nearby Wills Creek and Mohawk dams, part of the extensive Muskingum Watershed Conservancy District.

A local couple, Edward and Frances Montgomery, were interested in the Greek Revival buildings so they started a foundation bent on renovation. Restoration of Roscoe Village began in 1968. Edward, once an engineer for Firestone, perfected a process by which fabric could be coated with rubber. The gloves he conceived allow hands all over the world to safely handle caustic substances. Meanwhile, Roscoe Village has gone from being a decaying eyesore to a marvelous, year-round mix of history, craftwork, dining, and retail.

Newcomerstown is older than Coshocton, having served as the capital of the Delaware Indian nation from 1764. The first Protestant sermon west of the Alleghenies was preached here in 1771 by David Zeisberger, a Moravian minister. *Trumpet in the Land,* the amphitheater drama staged in New Philadelphia each summer, actually is about some 90 peaceful Christian Indians who had been converted by Zeisberger. They lived near Newcomerstown and were slaughtered by English soldiers. Besides pacifism, teetotaling was popular. Newcomerstown's Ohio Canal stopover was called Temperance Tavern. It served food but nothing alcoholic. Today, for better or worse, the tavern is a museum.

Location and Orientation

U.S. Highway 36 links Mount Vernon to Coshocton on the west and Newcomerstown and Uhrichsville to the city on the east. SR 16 ties Newark to the city from the southwest, while SR 83 serves to unite Coshocton and Wooster from the north. The county seat is some seventy-five miles east-northeast of Columbus, 113 miles south of Cleveland, about eighty miles northwest of Wheeling, West Virginia, and 110 miles west of Pittsburgh. Newcomerstown, on the north bank of the Tuscarawas River, is sixteen miles east of Coshocton, just off Hwy. 36. The nearest interstate highway is I-77, approximately 19 miles east of Coshocton and two miles east of Newcomerstown. But for a four-mile stretch of Hwy. 36 and two miles of SR 16, there are no four-lane highways in Coshocton County.

SIGHTS

Coshocton's premier visitors' offering is **Roscoe Village,** tel. (740) 622-9310 or (800) 877-1830, a skillfully restored 19th-century town with shops, restaurants, and nine living-history buildings, including a blacksmith shop, a schoolhouse, and a printing office. A local fellow who got rich making industrial-strength rubber gloves helped underwrite the restoration of this once-crumbling old canal village; results have been gratifying to Coshoctonites and fascinating to history buffs. Though wandering up and down the brick walkways along Whitewoman Street is free and encouraged, the living history tour gains visitors access to restored interiors. Everyone is in costume and furnishings are handmade, either years ago or more recently by Amish artisans. Shops and buildings are open daily 10 a.m.-5 p.m., tours are offered until 3 p.m. Cost of the tour is $9.95 for adults and $4.95 for children ages 5-12.

Roscoe Village is just across the Muskingum River to the west of Coshocton. The main street of the restored area is Whitewoman Street, which runs parallel to SR 16, one block east of the village. The village is built on and around a hill, and a vigorous hike might involve walking up High Street, looking out over the village and the city, and returning to the other end of Whitewoman Street via High Street. The visitor center and main parking area are at the north end of the village. It is from this point that tours begin and

where visitors can briefly follow the towpath to see the old canal boat. One of the more amazing features of the village at the time was a flume that carried canal boats over and above the nearby river.

A nice way to absorb old-time canal atmosphere is to take a ride on the *Monticello III,* a replica of the traditional canal boat but with a sturdy steel hull and comfy seating. The low, cream-colored vessel with its tan-and-brown trim holds 100 passengers. Boat rides take place every hour on the hour each afternoon between Memorial Day and Labor Day, 1-5 p.m. Catch the horsedrawn boat at 23253 SR 83, tel. (740) 622-7528. Cost of the trip is $5 for adults, $4.50 for seniors, and $2.50 for children.

Ten miles northeast of Coshocton is the village of Fresno, home of **Pearl Valley Cheese,** tel. (740) 545-6002. If you savor Swiss, it's worth a special trip—Pearl Valley purveyors recently were named Grand Champions among all Buckeye Swiss cheesemakers. From Coshocton, head east on US 36 to SR 93, then north on SR 93 to the intersection of Township Rd. 90.

What's cheese without wine? Link the two with a visit to **Rainbow Hills Vineyards,** 26349 Township Rd. 251, Newcomerstown tel. (740) 545-9305. Dinner and dessert wines are featured here, and the tasting room is open year round. Hours from July 1 to October 1 are Mon.-Thurs. 1-6 p.m., Fri.-Sat. 11 a.m.-9 p.m. The later weekend hours are devoted to cookouts. Tours begin in the vineyard, proceed through the winemaking process, and end with sit-down tastes of various vintages. The vineyard's most popular wine is Drumming Grouse, a blend of Concord and Fredonia grapes that comes out semisweet red. An intriguing dessert wine is Sassafras. The wines mentioned are $7.75 per bottle.

Another winery, this one new in 1997, is **Shawnee Springs,** 20093 CR 6, west of Coshocton, tel. (740) 623-0744. These friendly people make four varieties at the moment, the biggest seller being Midnight Mist, a sweet Ohio Concord selling for $6 a bottle. There's a tasting barn and crafts and ironwork are for sale. Weather permitting, visitors are encouraged to bring a picnic and enjoy it with a bottle of wine.

Travelers who didn't leave a farm to vacation might like to visit one. **Schumaker Farms,** 52441 CR 16, West Lafayette, east of Coshocton, tel.

(740) 622-8915, is a working farm that caters to visitors. There are hayrides, corn roasts, produce freshly picked or still in the field for a you-pick experience, baked goods, bulk food, assorted gifts, and such meaty favorites as "whole hog" homemade bulk sausage, hams, Amish-made trail bologna, plus cheese. Depending on the time of year, tourists can harvest their own sweet corn, melons, or pumpkins. Call to see what's on the vine.

Baskets in all shapes and sizes, from ancient Asia and Native America, are on display at the **Johnson-Humrickhouse Museum,** 300 N. Whitewoman St., tel. (740) 622-8710 in Roscoe Village. So are pricey and priceless vases, samurai swords, and suits of armor. Closer to home, artifacts left by area moundbuilders have been accumulated. The Johnson brothers, bachelors both, roamed all over in search of all sorts of artwork, then willed the treasures to their hometown. The museum's hours are daily noon-5 p.m., May-Oct.; 1-4:30 p.m., rest of the year. Donations are happily accepted in exchange for admission.

Ohio once was a world-renowned source of pottery. Visitors can tour a working pottery by paying a visit to **Three Rivers Pottery,** 1435 S. Sixth St., Coshocton, tel. (740) 622-4154. Feeling artistic? **Liberty Pottery Studio,** 419 Main St., Coshocton, tel. (740) 622-9991, lets travelers paint their own pottery before it is fired by the experts. Liberty Pottery can also ship your you-paint works for those who may not have time to hang around while the kiln does its job. For visitors who don't want to get anything on themselves, finished examples of Three Rivers work is for sale at **Main Street Station,** 235 Main St., Coshocton, tel. (740) 622-6767. Other locally produced items at the Station include birdhouses and throws—small blankets used to keep warm while sharing a loveseat.

ACCOMMODATIONS

A **Super 8** motel is within walking distance of Roscoe Village. There also are a variety of independent motels locally and in the county. Visitors seeking atmosphere may want to consider the **Valley View Inn of New Bedford,** between Coshocton and New Bedford on SR 643, tel. (330) 897-3232. There are 10 rooms, no chil-dren under 10, no TV, a player piano, and a fireplace. The expensive facility is authentic rather than spartan. Persons intent on staying a night in Roscoe Village can look into the **Roscoe Village Inn,** 200 N. Whitewoman St., tel. (740) 622-2222. A restored historic site, the inn has a restaurant, offers an exercise room, and is expensive.

Other interesting lodging sites include the **Carriage House,** 455 Hill St., Roscoe Village, tel. (614) 622-1329. The Carriage House offers rooms with fireplaces, whirlpool tubs, wet bars, refrigerators, and is a very expensive place to stay. More moderately priced are **Butler Mill House Bed & Breakfast,** 17845 SR 60 South, north of Dresden, tel. (740) 327-7965, featuring four bedrooms, each with its own bath, and a separate two-bedroom suite; and **Highland Farm Guest House,** 25304 Township Rd. 251, which is off SR 751, tel. (740) 545-9337.

This is a pleasant part of the country in which to camp, though city folks who show up in the summer should be prepared for mosquitoes and the chance that a campground is downwind from a farm where the hogs are on full feed. The upside, of course, is that staying outdoors costs only a fraction ($12-27 nightly) of a stay in a motel or B&B. Recommended places include **Forest Hill Lake Campground,** 52176 CR 425, Fresno, tel. (740) 545-9642, where group, tent, and RV camping takes place; **Lake Lila Campground,** 18223 Linton Township Rd. 121, tel. (740) 498-8452; **Lake Park Campgrounds,** 74131 SR 83, tel. (740) 622-7528; **Paradise Valley Campgrounds,** 74131 Plum Rd., Newcomerstown, tel. (740) 498-9260); **Roscoe Colonial Camp Grounds,** 24688 Co. Rd. 10, tel. (740) 622-1695; and **Whispering Falls Campground,** US 36, tel. (740) 545-5069.

FOOD

Good locally made pizza is always a treat, and **Fantilini's** at 306 S. College St., Newcomerstown, tel. (740) 498-5600, is more than adequate. Diners can choose between thick or thin crust and an array of toppings. Also on the menu are submarine sandwiches, salads, and desserts. A large (14-inch) pizza with three toppings goes for around $12, while a foot-long sub will sink most any hunger for a mere five bucks.

Robson's Restaurant, 442 Main St., tel. (740) 622-8262, a Coshocton mainstay, offers solid food at all three meals. Dinners feature steaks, seafood, chicken, and Italian dishes. Whatever the meal, Robson's will prepare orders to go. Popular at lunch is the grilled chicken salad, six ounces of which is a chicken breast, for around $5. Seafood fettuccini with a side salad at $11.95 is a popular evening choice. Hours are Mon.-Thurs. 7 a.m.-10 p.m., Fri.-Sat. 6 a.m.-11 p.m., Sunday 8:30 a.m.-9 p.m.

There are several nice places in Roscoe Village for meals, with the **Roscoe Village Inn** this area's tribute to fine dining. Lunches and other fare are available there inside **King Charley's Tavern,** 200 N. Whitewoman St., tel. (740) 622-2222. Luncheon menus are the same in the tavern and the dining room and feature a club sandwich or one of three big salads for $7.25. Dining room patrons each evening can choose from angel-hair pasta with meatballs, steaks, tuna steak, rack or lamb, and any of five specials that change each week. Meal prices range from $10.95 to $17.95, with rack of lamb $1 more. The **Olde Warehouse Restaurant,** 400 N. Whitewoman St., tel. (740) 622-4001, is the place to be on Friday if you like fish. In addition to a fish sandwich and french fries special for $5.95 at noon, there's an all-you-can-eat fish fry in the evening for $7.95. Look, too, for steaks, chicken, chops, pasta, and other kinds of seafood. **Captain Nye's Sweet Shop,** 365 N. Whitewoman St., tel. (740) 622-7732, is a kid-friendly destination for ice cream and related treats. The **Roscoe Village Bakery,** 101 N. Whitewoman St., tel. (740) 623-6530, stocks rolls, cookies, and other oveny snacks. Open daily from 6 a.m. (7 a.m. on Sunday), the site is picturesque, fragrant, and has coffee and other drinks as accompaniments.

CULTURE, ENTERTAINMENT, AND NIGHTLIFE

Pomerene Center for the Arts, 317 Mulberry St., Coshocton, tel. (740) 622-0326, is a serendipitous place, offering art exhibits, a music series, and lots of cultural doings related to such local annual events as the Dogwood Festival in May. Should travelers have the time, there are workshops that could hone creativity they never knew they had.

As for live music, examine the **Riverfront Supper Club,** 51 Pine St., Coshocton, tel. (740) 622-6298. On Thursday there's free karaoke, and Saturday, for a $3 cover charge, visitors have a choice of dancing to country upstairs or rock 'n' roll one floor below. There's a buffet dining special Saturday evenings, and the bands play from 10 p.m. to 2 a.m.

RECREATION

Several golf courses accommodate visitors. Close to Coshocton is **Hilltop Golf Course** at 23253 SR 83 just north of the city, tel. (740) 622-8083. The 18-hole, par 70 greenery charges $22.50 for 18 holes and half a cart; $16 for seniors and half a cart; $16 for everyone with half a cart on Friday; and $24.50 on weekends and holidays, again splitting a cart. East of town, check out **Hickory Flat Greens Golf Course,** 54188 Township Rd. 155, off SR 93 S, tel. (740) 545-7796. This 18-hole course is a par 72, and greens fees are $9.75 and $16 to walk nine and 18 holes, respectively. A bit farther east, look for **River Greeens Golf Course,** 22689 SR 751, tel. (740) 545-7817. Scratch golfers hit 72 on 18 of this facility's 27 holes. Greens fees are $18 weekdays and $20 weekends, or $26 and $31, weekdays and weekends, respectively, with a cart.

Runners or bicyclists will find that one of the very nicest ways to get some early-morning exercise is to traverse the **Roscoe Village** area. Prior to 8 a.m. there's hardly any traffic, so the narrow streets should present no problems. A trip up and over a couple of hills can be rewarded with a substantial breakfast nearby.

Pheasant hunters should trudge the fields of **Schumaker Farms,** 52441 CR 16, West Lafayette, tel. (740) 622-8915, Oct.-April. Another hunting venue is **Woodbury Wildlife Area,** south of US 36 on SR 60, west of Coshocton. Those who enjoy stream fishing will want to check out Darling Run near where it passes beneath US 36 between the villages of Warsaw and Nellie, about 12 miles west of Coshocton. There also are said to be smallmouth bass in the Walhonding River nearby. Ask a local resident.

The county is a pretty nice place to bike. The roads appear to be in good repair, not many of the hills are steep, and there are several logi-

ROSCOE VILLAGE AND COSHOCTON COUNTY EVENTS

Roscoe Village provides some sort of attraction frequently, as the following calendar indicates.

FEBRUARY

Ice Carving Festival, Roscoe Village.

MAY

Canal Quilters' Quilt Show, Coshocton.

Dogwood Festival, Pomerene Center for the Arts, Coshocton.

Dulcimer Days, Roscoe Village. The dulcimer is a stringed instrument, played here for enjoyment and as part of the Mid-Eastern Regional Dulcimer Championship.

Summerfest historical activities, workshops, sales, Roscoe Village (weekends, Memorial Day-Labor Day).

JUNE

Hot Air Balloon Festival, Coshocton County Fairgrounds.

Strawberries & Cream Festival, Roscoe Village.

Art Show/Sale and Rose Competition, Roscoe Village.

Cox Classic Bicycle Race (part of Tour of Ohio), Coshocton.

JULY

Blacksmith's Ring of the Anvil, Roscoe Village.

AUGUST

Canal Festival, Roscoe Village. Entertainment, juried arts and crafts, several runs, a parade, and more, in the village and in Coshocton.

SEPTEMBER

Old Time Music Fest, Roscoe Village, features instruments from the 19th century and performances by barbershop quartets.

OCTOBER

Fall Foliage Tour, Coshocton County.

Haunted Hayrides, Schumaker Farms, West Lafayette.

NOVEMBER

Winterfest, Johnson-Humrickhouse Museum, Coshocton (also in December).

DECEMBER

Christmas Candlelightings, Roscoe Village.

cal destinations from either Coshocton or Newcomerstown. For example, there's a seldom-seen covered bridge south of Coshocton. Ride out of town for about four miles on SR 83, then turn right just before crossing Wills Creek. Take the first left to Hamilton Farm Bridge. Another out-of-the-way covered bridge can be found by heading north out of Coshocton on SR 83 for approximately three miles. Turn left onto Township Rd. 405 and continue on it to Helmick Bridge. Riders who are allergic to hills will want to aim more toward either the northeast or southwest parts of the county.

INFORMATION AND SERVICES

Dial 911 for police, fire or similar emergency. The non-emergency number for the Coshocton police is (740) 622-2411. Coshocton County Memorial Hospital can be reached by dialing (740) 622-6411.

Coshocton County Convention & Visitors Bureau accepts mail at P.O. Box 905, Coshocton, OH 43812, and can be reached by phone at (740) 622-4877 or (800) 338-4724. For information about Roscoe Village, dial (740) 622-9310 or (800) 877-1830.

Coshocton's daily newspaper is the *Tribune,* published Mon.-Sat. mornings.

THE TUSCARAWAS VALLEY

This is the Tuscarawas Valley, so named by Native Americans. Evidence of long-ago people exists in the vicinity of Bolivar, midway between New Philadelphia and Canton. Ancient people buried their dead in mounds that remain visible. These pre-Columbians also may have contributed to the name of the river: Tuscarawas supposedly means open mouth. That may have to do with the Tuscarawas River, which rises to the north, toward Akron. Fed by innumerable creeks and streams, it passes Dover, New Philadelphia, and Newcomerstown to Coshocton, where it joins the Walhonding to form the Muskingum. New Philly, as it's called hereabouts, is the Tuscarawas County seat. It has a traditional, fortresslike courthouse in the middle of a busy and attractive downtown. Known primarily as a staging area for forays into Amish country to the west or the Muskingum Watershed to the east, the valley is nevertheless a pleasant place to spend some time.

History

History hereabouts seems to be made up of various attempts by persons of European descent to create a perfect society for themselves or for Native Americans. Ohio's oldest town, Gnadenhutten, was settled in 1772 by Chief Joseph, who was an Indian converted to Christianity and, literally, among the last of the Mohicans. Following the massacre of its peaceful residents by a vengeful Pennsylvania militia, Gnadenhutten was resettled by persons of European descent in 1789. Though it did not grow as quickly as several neighboring towns, Gnadenhutten holds an important place in Ohio history.

So does the village of Schoenbrunn ("Beautiful Spring" in German), a tiny island of tranquility in a sea of turmoil as colonists began to farm Indian land. Founded as a Moravian mission in 1772, the town was a harmonious mix of pious natives and colonists and quickly displayed 60 new homes. Missionaries taught native children in the state's first schoolhouse, and they showed Indian adults how to perform metalwork and carpentry. But the mission was soon abandoned, leaving Schoenbrunn to silently revert to woodland.

New Philadelphia was founded in 1804 by a Pennsylvania deer hunter who liked what he saw and bought some land. Dover was platted in 1807; both towns are laid out on a precise grid system. The industrial revolution made Dover-New Philadelphia a popular place, with the latter designated the county seat.

Meanwhile, 200 German peasants settled in at Zoar. They decided to live communally, renouncing all private property. Both men and women worked digging the Ohio and Erie Canal. Soon, the community had enough money to purchase 9,000 acres and build a hotel, tannery, iron mill, saw mill, flour mill, and more. The group remained together until 1898, when too many of its young people wanted to have a look at the rest of the world. Canals were washed away in the disastrous floods of 1913, though they had ceased to be a means of moving goods long before that.

Little Dennison, 10 miles south of New Philadelphia on SR 800, was a beneficiary of locomotion. It grew in importance as the Pennsylvania Railroad added more tracks and facilities. The Dennison depot's tiny canteen served homemade food to 1.5 million GI's going to and from World War II aboard various steam and diesel trains. Sandwiches, donuts, and coffee were provided round the clock to an astonishing 13% of all Americns in uniform during more than three years of conflict. The small town was nicknamed Dreamsville for the warm reception it gave to men in uniform.

Location and Orientation

Dover and New Philadelphia are on SR 250, which runs parallel to I-77 about a mile east of the major north-south highway. Cleveland and Lake Erie are about 80 miles north on I-77. The I-77/70 junction is approximately 40 miles south, just south of Salt Fork Lake State Park. The Wooster area is connected to Dover-New Philadelphia by US 250, which continues to the southeast to Wheeling, West Virginia. The drive to Columbus is approximately 110 miles southwest via a combination of interstate, U.S., and state highways, but no direct route, though I-77 south to I-70 west is probably the fastest route. The Ohio-Pennsylvania border is only 60 miles to the east and Pittsburgh is 30 miles east of that. The Dover-New Philadelphia area is roughly in the center of Tuscarawas County.

SIGHTS

For more than a quarter of a century, summer crowds have thrilled to *Trumpet in the Land,* a vivid outdoor re-enactment of Moravian attempts to practice pacifism while spreading the Gospel amid warring British, colonists, and Indians. The nighttime show features a state-of-the-art sound system and lots of torches and other fiery effects, all in an amphitheater. Staged from late June to late August every night but Sunday, the production is $13 for adults and $6 for children. (Persons over 55 get $2 off on Wednesday, and families receive two free children's tickets when they buy two adult admissions on Monday.) There are no refunds, so if skies look gloomy, decide whether you will be able to use a raincheck. Schoenbrunn Amphitheatre is on University Drive in New Philadelphia. Depart I-77 at Exit 81, then travel east less than a mile on SR 250, tel. (330) 364-5111 or (800) 282-5393.

Schoenbrunn Village State Memorial, East High Avenue (SR 259), New Philadelphia, tel. (330) 339-3636 or (800) 282-5393, is an authentically reconstructed 18th-century Ohio frontier village. In 1923, when such things weren't common, a dedicated group read old diaries in order to replat and revive Schoenbrunn. Today there are 17 reconstructed log buildings, plus the original cemetery, planted crops, a museum, a gift shop, and picknicking facilities. Volunteers in Revolutionary War-era dress re-enact domestic activities. Tours of the village take an hour or less and are self-guided. The village is maintained by the Ohio Historical Society and from Memorial Day to Labor day is open Mon.-Sat. 9:30 a.m.-5 p.m., Sunday noon-5 p.m.; from Labor Day into October the museum is open Saturday 9:30 a.m.-5 p.m. and Sunday noon-5 p.m. Admission is $5 for adults and $1.25 for children ages 6-12.

Ohio's only Revolutionary War fort is **Fort Laurens,** a stockade constructed in 1778 at what is now 11067 Fort Laurens Rd. NW, just west of the junction of I-77 and SR 212, in Bolivar, tel. (330) 874-2059. Today a museum and memorial, this site still shows signs of the original fort's foundation, where colonist-soldiers died fighting both British and Indian forces. The Tomb of the Unknown Patriot of the American Revolution holds the remains of one of the unknown defenders of Fort Laurens who was laid to rest with full military honors by the Ohio National Guard in 1976. Fort Laurens is also the site of Revolutionary War reenactments and demonstrations. The Fort Laurens State Memorial and Museum grounds are open daily from 9:30 a.m.-dusk. From Memorial Day to Labor Day the mu-

Many town squares in Ohio feature classic courthouses like this one in New Philadelphia.

seum is open Wed.-Sat. 9:30 a.m.-5 p.m., Sunday noon-5 p.m.; after Labor Day through October the museum is open Saturday 9:30 a.m.-5 p.m. and Sunday noon-5 p.m. Admission to the park is free; for the museum, adults are charged $3; children ages 6-12 are $1.25.

Described as a Dover industrialist, J.E. Reeves in 1900 built a home that proves business back then was very, very good. Actually, Reeves bought a farmhouse and reconfigured it, sacrificing a hunk of forest for enough oak to build the interior of the **J.E. Reeves Victorian Home and Museum.** Stairways, paneling, sideboards, and entryways show handcrafted elegance inside the big house at 325 E. Iron Ave., tel. (330) 343-7040. Out back, the carriagehouse museum has a military exhibit, a couple of rare old cars, the Reeves family sleigh, and more. Everything is accessible—no rooms are roped off. The facility is open from Tues.-Sun. 10 a.m.-4 p.m. from mid-May to mid-September. Admission is $4 for adults and $2 for children to age 18. Call for other events. (This Dover Historical Society attraction also has its own Web site at web.tusco.net/tourism/reeves.)

Gnadenhutten is on SR 36, ten miles east of I-77, tel. (614) 254-4143 or (614) 254-4756, is Ohio's oldest existing village, settled in 1772 by Delaware Indians converted to Christianity by Moravian missionaries. These industrious folks constructed as many as 60 cabins, complete with glass windows, artwork, and other items rare to the frontier. Gnadenhutten (ja-NA-den-hooten, meaning "Huts of Grace" in German) residents in 1782 were accused unjustly of raiding Pennsylvania villages. The Native Americans were afforded a night of prayer before some 90 men, women, and children were gunned down by a Pennsylvania militia. The victims were buried here in a mass grave that has never been disturbed. From June 1 through Oct. 31 its hours are Mon.-Sat. 10 a.m.-5 p.m. and Sun. noon-5 p.m. From November 1 to May 31 its hours are Saturday 10 a.m.-5 p.m. and Sunday noon-5 p.m. There is no admission charge, but donations are welcomed.

This area has its share of teetotalers, so it may be up to tourists to patronize **Breitenbach Wine Cellars** at 5934 Old SR 39 NW in Dover, tel. (330) 343-3603, where a dozen grape, fruit, and berry wines greet visitors, and local cheeses, smoked meats, and gifts are available. Tastings take place Mon.-Sat. at the facility, which is just west of I-77. The wine most sought after here is Frostfire, which is priced around $7 per bottle and is a white semisweet vintage made from a variety of American grapes.

Few of us have the time or talent to carve, which makes a visit to the **Warther Museum,** 331 Karl Ave., Dover, (330) 343-7513, all the more worthwhile. The late Ernest Warther was an exacting hand carver of wood, ebony, and ivory, reproducing miniature steam engines, an 18th-century steel mill, and other memorabilia. The museum is set amid a small but lovely Swiss garden. For those who want to see a Warther offspring in Amish country, visit **David Warther Carvings,** 1387 Old SR 39, Sugarcreek, tel. (330) 852-3455. David specializes in reproducing America's historic ships. The Warther Museum is open every day, March-Nov. 9 a.m.-5 p.m.; 10 a.m.-4 p.m. the rest of the year. Admission is $7 for adults and $3 for children. David Warther asks $4 for adults and admits students under 18 for free. David carves ivory, but don't get riled—he legally purchases examples of it from various institutions. None of his carvings are for sale, but there are carvings by Warther's apprentices in the gift shop. His museum is closed on Sunday.

Zoar Village

No place is more unique than **Zoar Village,** 10 miles north of Dover on SR 212. The mix of somber and colorful old buildings is a reminder that something historic and heartwarming went on here. German immigrants settled in Zoar beginning in 1817 on 5,600 acres purchased from the federal government. The name of the village means "sanctuary from evil" and is taken from the Bible in reference to the town Lot found refuge in. The immigrants made their living in the usual ways—as blacksmiths and bakers, farmers and weavers. Aware that the community would age, the Zoar Society decided to take care of elderly members. A Christian communal society was formed in 1819, and for the next 80 years everybody looked after everybody else. It was, to borrow a modern phrase, socialism with a human face.

Zoar has several sights worth a visit. There's a twelve-block **historic district** devoted to restaurants, shops, places to stay, and homes. For at least half the year, the village centerpiece is a block square formal garden where Main and Fourth Streets intersect. Don't miss the house of the group's leader, Joseph Baumeler, one of several handsomely preserved dwellings. There are a total of eight Ohio Historical Society buildings available to tour. Tours are $4 for adults, and children ages six-twelve are $1. Planning an area wedding or reunion? The Zoar Community Association rents out **Zoar School,** which can seat 100 and is a nostalgic backdrop for any sort of social gathering.

MUSIC, ENTERTAINMENT, AND NIGHTLIFE

The **Tuscarawas Philharmonic** celebrated its 62nd season in 1997-98, giving concerts of symphonic, pop, or Christmas music in the Dover High School Auditorium, 520 N. Walnut St. (call the orchestra at 330-864-1843). An average of about 65 members performs in October or November, December, February, March, and May. Admission is $8.50 for adults, $7.50 for seniors, and $4.50 for students. Critics have given the philharmonic, which can include a chorus and a children's chorus, high marks.

Bentley's, 120 N. Tuscarawas Rd., New Philadelphia, tel. (330) 364-9852, is a musical counterpoint to the philharmonic. Besides serving meals, the club offers either a live band or a disk jockey every Thursday, Friday, and Saturday night from about 9:30 p.m. Classic rock is distilled, with occasional nods to contemporary rock and modern country. Cover charges are $2 per person on Thursday and $3 Friday and Saturday. The **Gathering Place,** 205 N. Tuscarawas Rd., Dover, tel. (330) 364-3424, presents live music twice a week, on Thursday and Saturday. There's no cover at this restaurant, where tunes tend to be mellow 1960s and '70s hits on Thursday and more contemporary and rockin' sounds on Saturday. The music begins at about 9 p.m.

ACCOMMODATIONS

There are a half-dozen attractive, moderately priced, bed and breakfast operations in Zoar, a 19th-century time trip if ever there was one. They include **Assembly House Bed and Breakfast,** 117 E. Third St., tel. (330) 874-2239; **Cider Mill Bed and Breakfast,** 198 E. Second St., tel. (330) 874-3240, offering a full breakfast, fireplace, and private baths; **Cobbler Shop Bed and Breakfast,** 121 E. Second St., tel. 330-874-2600; **Cowger Manor Bed and Breakfast,** 9 Fourth St., tel. (330) 874-3542; **Garden Gate Bed and Breakfast,** 6 Fourth St., tel. (330) 874-2693; and the **Zoar Tavern and Inn,** 1 Main St., tel. (330) 874-2170.

You don't have to stay in Zoar to stay in a B&B. Here are a couple of moderately priced facilities in Dover: **Brandywine Bed and Breakfast,** SR 39, tel. (330) 364-5023, and **Olde World Bed and Breakfast,** SR 516, tel. (330) 343-1333. The latter has fireplaces, a hot tub, and provides a full breakfast.

Not the bed and breakfast type? Several good-looking independent motels can be found in the immediate vicinity of Dover-New Philadelphia, just off I-77. Franchises in the area include the moderately priced **Comfort Inn,** 2020 SR 39 NW, Dover, tel. (330) 364-8881, with continental breakfast, indoor pool, and exercise facilities; **Holiday Inn,** 131 Bluebell Dr. SW (I-77 Exit 81), New Philadelphia, tel. (330) 339-7731, has free local calls, indoor and outdoor pools, indoor recreation center, and jacuzzi/sauna. Others include Days Inn, Knights Inn, and Motel 6.

There are a couple of other options, both of them attractive. West of Dover and New Philadelphia, the **Atwood Lake Resort,** SR 542, Dellroy, tel. (330) 735-2211 or (800) 362-6406, is an expensive stay that features guest rooms, attractive lakeside cottages, or campgrounds. **Clendening Marina,** 79100 Bose Rd., in Freeport, tel.(330) 658-3691, is moderately priced and on Muskingum Watershed Clendening Lake in nearby Harrison County, southeast of New Philadelphia off SR 800. The **Schoenbrunn Inn** was completed in 1995 at 141 McDonald's Dr. SW, New Philadelphia, tel. (330) 339-4334 or (800) 929-7799. The inn contains a pub which features sandwiches and finger foods, just next door to the Tuscarawas County Convention and Visitors Bureau. The campground closest to the center of things in the county is **Alpine Hills Resort Campground,** SR 39, in Dover, tel. (330) 364-3244.

FOOD

Lots of locals head west a bit to sample the many Amish restaurants on the western edge of Tuscarawas County and on into Holmes County. In contrast, they like their ribs at **Texas Roadhouse,** a chain restaurant that sprang up recently at 131 Bluebell Dr. SW in New Philadelphia. The following places also are popular.

Depot Canteen Restaurant, 400 Center St., in Dennison, south of New Philadelphia on SR 800, tel. (740) 922-6776. This is the place that fed all the railroad-ridin' GI's during World War II. Nowadays, the emphasis is on home cooking for lunch or dinner six days a week and for a meal on Sunday 11 a.m.-3 p.m. Especially popular Friday and Saturday is a beer-batter fish dinner, available in three sizes: $4.45, $5.45, and $6.45. A beer-batter fish sandwich is a mere $3.75. Other specials range from salmon patties to pasta, and the hamburger platter with fries and a side keeps 'em happy at $3.95. After a meal, check out the gift shop and stroll the picturesque little station.

The **Goshen Dairy** has seven area outlets. What a find for the mikshake- and sundae-deprived! This modest chain serves up quality ice cream and related snacks. Goshen has two locations in New Philadelphia and one each in Dover, Bolivar, Gnadenhutten, Sugarcreek, and Uhrichsville. The prices are as cool as the treats.

Grandma Zifer's Boulevard Pizza, 726 Boulevard, Dover, tel. (330) 364-4611. A recent poll indicated that Grandma produces the area's favorite pizzas. A large with three toppings costs $9.70, yields eight slices, and measures 12 inches in diameter. Other items on the menu, which is available to dine in or to go, include spaghetti and salad. The restaurant opens at 4 p.m. every day but Tuesday.

Lam's Oriental Cuisine, 347 Tuscarawas Ave., NW, New Philadelphia, tel. (330) 343-9141, is open every day for lunch and dinner. This is a buffet restaurant, with buffets going for about $4.75 for lunch and $7.95 for dinner ($9.95 on the weekend). Popular standbys include moo goo gai pan and sweet-and-sour pork. Locals rely on Lam's for their introduction to Asian food.

Uncle Primo's 435 Minnich Ave. NW, New Philadelphia, tel. (330) 364-2349, has a smorgasbord of hours, but don't be put off—this is consistently good food. Lunch is served Wed.-Fri., 11 a.m.-2 p.m. Dinner is served Monday 4-9 p.m.; Tues.-Thurs. 4-10 p.m.; and Fri.-Sat. 4-11 p.m. A luncheon fave is lasagna, which comes with garlic bread and a salad, for $5.95. Evenings, try the strip steak dinner at $14.95 or the filet mignon meal for $15.95. The filet, incidentally, recently was judged the best around by the *Cleveland Plain Dealer* daily newspaper. Locals like it here, too.

Limby's Restaurant, 109 N. Wooster Ave., Dover, tel. (330) 343-2731 is an unpretentious place for a beer and a burger. Locally popular, the restaurant offers inexpensive steakburgers for $1.95. Soups and stews are on the menu, too, with chili going for $1.50. The bar-restaurant is open daily for lunch and dinner.

Penso's Pizza Shop, 201 E. Front St., Dover, tel. (330) 343-0516, or 923 E. High Ave., New Philadelphia, tel. (330) 343-0506, is a local favorite. It's been here in one form or another since 1936 and by now the pies are pretty much foolproof. Specify thick crust or thin and either eat in or be prepared to pick up since there's no delivery. A large pizza with three toppings costs around $12.50. Penso's has a full menu that range from chicken, shrimp, or fish dinners to sandwiches, spaghetti, and rigatoni. Open at 4 p.m., the two sites are closed Wednesday.

Zoar Tavern & Inn, 1 Main St., Zoar, tel. (330) 874-2170 or (888) 874-2170, caters to the many tourists who visit Zoar Village, and does so well. For lunch, try the No-Name Burger, two ground steak patties with tomato, lettuce, and a choice of cheese, plus a secret sauce to die for. All burger variations are ground from steak here, and there also are several salad offerings. In the evening, the Davey Filet, a major steak meal, sells briskly at $15.99. Open for lunch and dinner seven days a week, the restaurant has a garden where patrons can dine in good weather.

RECREATION

Muskingum Watershed is a vast spread of 14 reservoirs completed in 1938 that was designed to subdue annual flood waters in a large area of the state. Atwood, Leesville, and Tappan Lakes all are just a few miles east of the Dover-New

Philadelphia area. Atwood and Tappan are by and large developed, while Leesville is not. The largest undeveloped watershed lake is Clendening in Harrison County. It is 1,800 acres in size and has 41 miles of shoreline. Many of the reservoirs are heavily fished. Bass, catfish, and panfish are common catches, and there are boat ramps on all of the major bodies of water. For more information, contact the Muskingum Watershed Conservancy at (330) 343-6647.

One canoe service can be found in Bolivar. **NTR Canoe Livery** is on SR 212, just east of the I-77 offramp, tel. (330) 874-2002. Canoeing, kayaking, and tubing take place on the Tuscarawas River in a stretch of stream that retains its level all summer because it's ... dams. Shuttles head upstream every ... the hour from 10 a.m., seven days a week. ... also are moonlight canoe rides. Staci and h... mother also operate the Northeast Ohio Animal Rehabilitation Center here, nursing injured animals back to health and then releasing them. For more information, check the Web site at www.great-river.com/ntr.

INFORMATION AND SERVICES

Dial 911 for emergency calls in Tuscarawas County. The non-emergency number for the

---

TUSCAWARAS VALLEY ANNUAL EVENTS

FEBRUARY
Romance Your Valentine dinner in the Depot, Dennison.

MARCH
Hog Roast, Baltic.
St. Patrick's Day Parade and Celebration, New Philadelphia.

APRIL
Annual Depot Ball, Dennison.
Midvale Speedway Auto Racing, Midvale, through-out spring, summer, and early fall.
Moravian Easter Sunrise Service, Schoenbrunn Village, New Philadelphia.

MAY
Canal Festival, Dover.
Elderberry Line Excursion train ride, Carrollton, through October.
Spring canal hikes, Zoar to Bolivar.

JUNE
Children's Day, Schoenbrunn Village.
National Clayweek Festival, Uhrichsville.
Cows and Curds, Zoar.
Living History Weekend, Gnadenhutten.
Amish Country Jubilee, Dover.
Revolutionary War encampment, Ft. Laurens State Memorial, Bolivar.
Trumpet in the Land, Schoenbrunn Amphitheater, New Philadelphia (through late August).

JULY
First Town Days Festival, New Philadelphia.
Corn Fest, Franklin Park, Strasburg.
Train/Riverboat Cruise, Dennison Depot (also August).

AUGUST
Annual Harvest Festival, Zoar.
Italian-American Festival, New Philadelphia.
Pioneer Days, Gnadenhutten Historical Museum.

SEPTEMBER
Frontier Essentials: 18th Century Tools and Survival Skills, Schoenbrunn Village.
Putting Things By, food preservation demonstrations, Zoar.
Tuscarawas County Fair, fairgrounds, Dover.

OCTOBER
Ohio Swiss Festival, Sugarcreek.
Fall canal hikes, Zoar to Bolivar.
Fall foliage shuttle, one-hour train ride, Dennison.
Living History Weekend, Schoenbrunn Village.
Wonders in Wood, woodcarving show, Dover Middle School.

NOVEMBER
Lights by the Water, Atwood Lake Park (through New Year's weekend).

DECEMBER
Christmas in Zoar Village.
Indian Christmas drive-through display, Gnadenhutten.

...eriff is (330) 339-7743. ...ne number for Timken ...ew Philadelphia is (330) ...adelphia's post office is at .... The Dover post office is at ...

Tusca... ...ounty Convention and Visitors Bureau, is at 125 McDonald's Dr. SW, New Philadelphia, tel. (330) 339-5453 or (800) 527-3387.

Transportation
Greyhound Bus Lines has a terminal at 303 N. Tuscarawas Ave., Dover, tel. (330) 343-1011. The nearest commercial airport of any size is the Akron-Canton Regional Airport, approximately 35 miles north of Dover on I-77.

The *Times Reporter,* New Philadelphia, is the only county daily. It comes out every morning and runs an entertainment section, "Arts and Leisure," each Friday. Several villages have weekly newspapers.

Shopping
In this state there are more "Ohio's largest antique malls" than there are professional wrestling world champions. Nevertheless, antiquers will want to visit **Riverfront Antique Mall,** 1203 Front St. SW in New Philadelphia, tel. (330) 339-4448 or (800) 926-9806. The facility has 350 dealers among its 84,000 square feet and is open from 10 a.m. seven days a week. The worthy Warther carvers mentioned above also have examples of their work for sale.

The area's largest shopping center is **New Towne Mall** at 400 Mill Ave. SE, New Philadelphia. Major stores include Elder-Beerman and JCPenney.

YOUNGSTOWN, WARREN, AND VICINITY

There's nothing covert about Youngstown—the one-time industrial dynamo—wears its age and cares out front, for everyone to see. Whereas Cleveland razed its empty factories and Akron converted them to facilities for polymer research, Youngstown merely left its decaying furnaces and foundries out in the open, visible even from an interstate highway. On the other hand, work has sprouted in the area in the last few years, not the least of which is the General Motors assembly plant in Lordstown. Once a troubled facility, the site now is a place where reliable people produce reliable cars. Warren, just north of Youngstown, is in better repair, though it began to lose industry back in 1956, when Packard stopped making cars there. Smaller towns, though equally aged, are tidier, if less ethnic and with fewer juicy stories. City, town, or country, this side of the Appalachians has a number of fascinating sites and attractive byways.

History
John Young, logically enough, founded Youngstown. The Connecticut resident came west after purchasing more than 15,000 acres—an entire township—from the Western Reserve Land Company. Most Native Americans had moved farther west by 1797, so Young and friends staked their claim. Youngstown residents looked toward the future with optimism in 1820 with the opening of the Pennsylvania and Ohio Canal. Other villages along the busy Mahoning River also began to grow.

The area might have remained a string of riverside villages had it not been for the discovery of iron ore locally in the early part of the 19th century. One blast furnace was built, then another, and another. The Industrial Revolution was in full swing as furnaces were fed ore plus local coal and limestone, both of which proved plentiful. The area boomed: agents scoured the docks of New York City for immigrant labor and the hills of West Virginia for Appalachian help. The county seat was established in Youngstown in 1876 and by 1890 the city boasted more than 33,000 residents.

With the 20th century, Youngstown took on the look of an oversize company town—which is what it was. Republic Steel, Youngstown Sheet & Tube, and others constructed vast, smoky, glowing mills up and down the Mahoning River. In their shadows they built housing, most of it adequate though nondescript. The Great Depression and labor strife made the 1930s a grim time before the country called on Youngstown to help it rearm for World War II.

Following the war, Youngstown's reputation took a dive. A fellow from Duluth in the 1950s mailed a letter to a friend in Youngstown, including only the friend's name and "Murder City, U.S.A." for an address. The letter arrived promptly. *Newsweek,* in 1961, labeled a local car bombing "Youngstown roulette." The violence was due to organized crime, which featured plenty of gunplay and other forms of violence. Happily, the city has cleaned up much of its act, if not its streets.

Steel continued to pour out of Youngstown until the recessionary 1980s. Most mills closed or downsized and the area began to leak population. From 1980 to 1990, the Youngstown area declined from 115,000 to 95,000 residents (though many of the departed stayed within Mahoning County, which nowadays has 260,000 people). Once dominated by the production of basic steel, the area now relies on automobile assembly in nearby Lordstown, plus small manufacturing and metal fabrication. There are a number of places worth visiting in and around this historic old mill city.

Location and Orientation

Youngstown is strategically placed for those on wheels: The Ohio Turnpike (I-80) cuts just south of the city, and I-76/80 passes to the north. Major roads such as US 224, US 422, and SR 11 also serve Mahoning County. The city is 76 miles southeast of Cleveland, 178 miles northeast of Columbus, 92 miles north of Wheeling, West Virginia, and 68 miles northwest of Pittsburgh, Pennsylvania. Youngstown is two miles from the Pennsylvania state line, where the Ohio Toll Road becomes the Pennsylvania Turnpike.

Interstate 680, a business loop, connects the south and west sides of the city, making a tight circle around the downtown area. Important north-south landmarks south of the city center are Main Street (SR 7) and Mill Creek Park; the park lies on either side of the Mahoning River. Meander Creek Reservoir, west of the city and north of the Ohio Turnpike, is just east of the junction of the Ohio Turnpike and I-76. Suburbs ringing Youngstown include Struthers, Boardman, and Canfield to the south, Wickliffe and Austintown to the west, Niles, Girard, and Churchill on the north, and Hubbard and Campbell to the east. Youngstown and Warren are connected by Warren-Youngstown is US 422, known locally as "The Strip.

SIGHTS

Most impressive indoor place in Youngstown? It may well be the **Butler Institute of American Art** at 524 Wick Ave., tel. (330) 743-1711, adjacent to the Youngstown State University campus. This striking marble structure is on the National Register of Historic Places and houses an art collection that is literally All-American. Edward Hopper, Winslow Homer, Frederic Remington, John Singer Sargent—these artists and others are well represented. More than 100,000 visitors come here each year to view 10,000 pieces of art. It's hard to imagine anyone leaving unimpressed. Hours are Tuesday, Thurs.-Sat. 11 a.m.-4 p.m., Wednesday 11 a.m.-8 p.m., Sunday noon-4 p.m. Admission to the Butler is free.

One block north is the **Arms Museum,** 648 Wick Ave., tel. (330) 743-2589, housed in Greystone, the former home of the Wilford P. Arms family. Hours are Tues.-Fri. 1-4 p.m., Sat.-Sun. 1:30-5 p.m. Adults are charged $3 and children $1 to see Arms finery and the powerful and tumultuous history of the Mahoning Valley. Old-time photos, clothing, antique toys, even a scale-model reproduction of a steel mill make a visit most interesting.

One of many things visitors can learn in the **Youngstown Historical Center of Industry and Labor** is why and how this inland city ultimately took a back seat to other steelmaking locales. Equally important, the transition from iron to steel, now more than a century old, is covered. The graphic black-and-white photos alone are worth a visit, as is the story of the futile struggle to keep aging mills running. It's all here at 151 W. Wood St., tel. (330) 743-5934; admission is $5 for adults, $4.50 for seniors, and $1.25 for children ages 6-12. Admission to the archives only is free.

Maybe **Mill Creek Park,** 816 Glenwood Ave., tel. (330) 702-3000, is an attention-getter because it is such a contrast to the rest of Youngstown. Everyone in town knows the place. It is 2,500 wooded acres and cuts through several neighborhoods as far south as the suburb of Boardman. It is more than a mere park, since it also houses **Fellows Riverside Gardens.** The

...GSTOWN AND ORGANIZED CRIME

...g Ohio cities, Youngstown has
...an economic renaissance in the
...lem must be attributed to a histo-
ry of crime ... city. Fred W. Viehe teaches a class
at Youngstown State University on the history of organized crime. He notes that there was a local organized crime element early in the century before it
was taken over by the national syndicate beginning
in the late 1930s. The national *mafiosi* were thrown
out in the early 1950s, and the consequent power
vacuum resulted in a number of killings.

"Once there's peace, it indicates that one group
has attained power," Viehe says, adding that
Youngstown has been fought over between criminals from Cleveland and from Pittsburgh. They are almost exclusively Mafia figures and they want the lu-
crative illegal gambling trade that goes on here. The
last major war between mob factions took place in
1979 when 10 contract killings took place. There continue to be periodic "hits," however, such as the shooting death of a mobster named Joey Naples in 1991.
The low point of such conduct may have taken place
in 1962, when a hood named "Cadillac Charlie" Cav-
allaro was blown up in his car. Sadly, his two young
sons also were victims of the car bombing. This use of
the so-called "Youngstown ignition" was a common
means of erasing rivals.

Viehe attributes part of the city's problems to the
departure of the middle class for suburbs such as
Boardman, Canfield, and Poland. "There has been a
lack of public outcry," the history professor says,
over crime and corruption. Latter-day scrutiny of
criminal conduct has ranged from the 1997 gam-
bling-related federal probe of native son Edward
DeBartolo, Jr., whose father built many of the nation's
shopping centers, to the $500 million swindling of
shareholders in Phar-Mor, a Youngstown-based
drugstore chain. The stock deal involved question-
able accounting practices by Phar-Mor co-founder
Mickey Monus and others. Monus became obsessed
with the World Basketball League in the late 1980s
and funneled corporate dollars into its formation.

The historian's class is popular, having been taken
by more than one underworld figure. Viehe doesn't
dwell excessively on local aspects of organized
crime, he says, because "I want to stay alive."

---

gardens have a different address, 7574 Colum-
bia-Canfield Rd. and can be reached at (330)
740-7116. Several vantage points allow visitors
to view gritty downtown Youngstown from the
gardens, and there are lakes and hiking trails
that are little used, at least on weekdays. And
don't forget the park's Lanterman's Mill, an awesome, water-powered grist mill that was restored
in the 1980s. The gift shop sells grain that mill
guides will grind as visitors watch.

The **National McKinley Birthplace Memorial,** 40 N. Main St., Niles, tel. (330) 652-1704,
features a 232-by-136-foot Greek Classic marble
building that was completed in 1917. It houses a
library and a museum honoring the Civil War
veteran and President cut down by an anarchist's bullet after serving less than a year of his
second term. The large and somewhat somber
edifice is in the very middle of the downtown
area and admission is free.

The last remaining **covered bridge** in Trumbull County is in Newton Falls, just four miles
from Exit 14 of the Ohio Turnpike (I-80) on SR
534. The bridge spans the east branch of the
Mahoning River and has a pedestrian walkway.
This is a nice place to canoe or to idle and watch
paddlers who have started at the Trumbull
Canoe Trails Park just upstream and are headed
to a spot just above the dam. Total canoe time is
about two hours. Below the dam, which is just
west of the local McDonald's franchise, kids feed
bread to the ducks on the west bank. Newton
Falls is lighted at night.

Youngstown State University's buildings
loom over the north edge of the downtown area.
A part of the state university system since 1967,
YSU has more than 13,000 students. Dial (330)
742-3575, the student activities desk, to find out
if there are special campus events. The school
address is 410 Wick Ave., also the address for
the **McDonough Museum of Art.** Student and
faculty works are shown here. Call (330) 742-
1400 for hours and for information about what is
on display. Admission is free.

Speaking of museums, one more is worth noting. The **Packard Car Museum,** 197 W. Market
St., in nearby Warren, tel. (330) 394-8484, is
where visitors learn among other things how the

folks at Packard helped get the Soviet Union back on its feet after World War II. A few of the cars are so large that a visitor could get lost in the back seat. The facility is open Wed.-Sat. 11 a.m.-3 p.m., Sunday 1-4 p.m. Admission is $2 for adults and $1 for seniors and students.

MUSIC, CULTURE, AND ENTERTAINMENT

Amy's Campus 2000, 901 Elm St., tel. (330) 743-4099, is a place where the young—and the young at heart—can hear rock, folk, and alternative music. Closed Mon.-Thurs. in the summer, this YSU hangout has bands on Friday in the summer. During the school year, there's a DJ Wednesday and Thursday and live tunes Friday and Saturday. Those who enjoy jazz or the blues can visit **Frieda's,** 381 W. Rayven Ave., tel. (330) 746-9003. The band gets to it at 10 p.m. on Friday, and there's a jam session from 5 p.m. on Saturday. Country devotees should look up the **Rebel Lounge,** 5335 76 Dr., Austintown (just west of Youngstown), tel. (330) 799-7453, where bands begin Thurs.-Sat. at 9 p.m.

The **Ohio Brewing Company,** 5790 Youngstown-Warren Rd., Niles, northwest of Youngstown on SR 46, tel. (330) 505-0061, also believes in live music. Thursday, hear acoustic talent; Friday and Saturday, listen to either jazz or blues. The brewpub, which has six of its concoctions on tap, also hires an occasional ethnic band. It then matches the music with appropriate food, be it Greek, Italian, or some other variation. There's no cover charge and the music begins at 9 p.m., ending on Friday and Saturday at 2:30 a.m.

Travelers who would rather watch dancers than perform can attend **Ballet Western Reserve,** tel. (330) 744-1934. These rising stars dance with the local symphony and in large stage productions. Speaking of the stage, **Easy Street Productions,** 27 1/2 Federal Plaza West, tel. (330) 782-6770, is the area's only professional stock theater. Recent presentations have included *Pump Boys and Dinettes, Annie,* and original productions. For a complete list of area amateur theater, consult Youngstown/Mahoning County Convention & Visitors Bureau publications.

Those whose tastes run to classical music can take comfort in the **Warren Chamber Orchestra,** which performs on a regular basis at Champion High School, 5976 Mahoning Ave. NW, call (330) 856-5441 for details. The **Youngstown Symphony Orchestra** recently celebrated its 70th season. Their music is presented several times a year at Powers Auditorium, 260 Federal Plaza West. Call the symphony at (330) 744-4269; reach the auditorium at (330) 774-0264. For variety, try the **Columbiana Summer Concert Association,** tel. (330) 482-2978. These musicians present concerts from June through August at 2905 Middleton Rd.

the National McKinley Birthplace Memorial in Niles honors the 25th president, native son William McKinley

ACCOMMODATIONS

Because all roads seem to meet in or around Youngstown, every conceivable hotel and motel franchise on earth appears to be here. Actually, Youngstown is halfway between New York City and Chicago for cross-country drivers. Look for accommodations on Market Street (SR 7), at I-80 exits along the north side of the city, and at Ohio Turnpike exits on Youngstown's west and south sides. Care to shy away from the jumble of neon? There are alternatives. One is the **Park Hotel,** 136 N. Park Ave., in Warren, northwest of Youngstown, tel. (800) 397-7275. A conventional full-service hotel, the Park offers free continental breakfast and is inexpensively priced. Another non-franchise with appeal is the **Wick-Pollock Inn,** 603 Wick Ave., Youngstown, tel. (330) 746-1200. Victorian decor enhances this in-town site, where accommodations vary from moderate to very expensive. Surprisingly affordable is the moderate to expensive **Avalon Inn & Resort,** 9519 E. Market St., Warren tel. (330) 743-4000. Guests there have course privileges to play at two nearby golf courses, among other amenities.

Bed and breakfast operations in pleasant towns around Warren and Youngstown are another alternative to a franchise sleepover. Consider **Hidden Hollow Bed and Breakfast,** 9340 SR 5, Kinsman, north of Youngstown near the Pennsylvania border, tel. (330) 876-8686; **Inn at the Green Bed and Breakfast,** 500 S. Main St., Poland, south of Youngstown, tel. (330) 757-4688; and **Quando S. Viaggio Bed and Breakfast,** 763 SR 7 NE, Brookfield, north of Youngstown off SR 82, tel. (330) 448-6561. In Warren, travelers can choose from two pleasant accommodations, **Shirlee's Chambers Bed and Breakfast,** 535 Adelaide St. NE, Warren, tel. (330) 732-1118; **Twin Maples Bed and Breakfast,** 736 Mahoning Ave. NW, Warren, tel. (330) 399-7768. All veer toward the moderate side of the economic scale.

There's no shortage of campgrounds in the area. All offer basic overnight accommodations for about $15. They include **Homestead RV Sales and Campground,** 1436 SR 7, Hubbard, off US 62 east of Youngstown, tel. (330) 448-2938; also in Hubbard is **Lor-El's Park and Campground,** 6486 Chestnut Rd. SE, tel. (330) 534-2352; **Ridge Ranch Campground,** 5219 SR 303 NW, Newton Falls, southwest of Warren off SR 534, tel. (330) 898-8080, group, tent, and RV camping, May 1-Oct. 15; **Timashamie Family Campground,** 28251 N. Georgetown Rd., Salem, southwest of Youngstown at the junction of US 62 and SR 14, tel. (330) 525-7054; and **Western Reserve Lake Campground,** 10580 W. Western Reserve, Canfield, tel. (330) 533-5274, camping, swimming pool, baby pool, LP gas, full hookups.

FOOD

Armadillo's has two locations, West at 3031 Mahoning Ave., Youngstown, tel. (330) 793-5060, and East at 277 Boardman-Canfield Rd., Boardman, tel. (330) 758-6250. Open from 11 a.m., these places with their Southwestern accents serve shredded pork or beef sandwiches with sides of beans for $5.25. There are daily lunch specials for $4.99. Baby back ribs go fast here, and there's a New York strip/ribs combination for $16.99. An Angus steak is $12.99, and the tuna and blue marlin is fresh daily. There's a children's menu, too.

Is that Jack Kerouac over by the espresso machine? Travelers might think so at **The Beat,** 215 Lincoln Ave., tel. (330) 743-4227, a 1950s coffeehouse with good, inexpensive food. Hard by Youngstown State University, the Beat offers homemade baked goods for breakfast and such lunch or light dinner vegetarian items as red-pepper-and-pesto or marinated eggplant sandwiches. A bowl of soup and a roll are $2 and are typical of big flavors and small prices at this rendezvous. Art on the walls is locally created, regularly rotated, and for sale. A folk band plays every other Wednesday evening.

Brothers Pizza Italian Restaurant can be found at 760 E. Market St. in Warren, tel. (330) 392-6000. Pizza choices include New York, Sicilian, Old World, Chicago, vegetarian, white, and gourmet. There are hot and cold subs, pasta dinners, veal parmigiana, chicken parmesan, calzones, and strombolis. Prices are righteous at this colorful, modest place, with a 14-inch New York Brothers Special going for $9.95, and linguini with red or white clam sauce just $7.95. The carryout menu is extensive and delivery within Warren is free.

YOUNGSTOWN AND WARREN AREA EVENTS

JANUARY
Ice Bowl Disc Frisbee Golf Tournament, Warren.

FEBRUARY
Packard Band Concert, Packard Music Hall, Warren (also held in March and April).

MARCH
Trumbull Town Hall Lecture Series, Packard Music Hall, Warren.

APRIL
The Barbershopper's Concert, Packard Music Hall, Warren.

MAY
Springfest, Youngstown.
Walk on Wick Art Festival, Youngstown.
Murder Mystery Train Ride, Dennison.
One Day in the Life of a Civil War Soldier, Youngstown.
Hot Rod Super Nationals, Canfield.
Great American Art Auction, Youngstown.

JUNE
Noon in the Park performances, June through August, Warren.

JULY
LPGA Classic Golf Tournament, Avalon Lakes, Warren.
Packard Car Show, Warren.
Trumbull County Fair, Warren.

AUGUST
Italian-American Heritage Festival, Warren.
Canfield Fair, Canfield (runs into September).

SEPTEMBER
Youngstown-Warren Regional Air Show.
Antiques in the Woods, Columbiana.
Children's History Club, Youngstown.

OCTOBER
Atwood Area Fall Festival, Dellroy.

NOVEMBER
Lots of towns do some sort of Christmas fest, but few are more pleasant than **Christmas in the Village** in Columbiana. The holiday card-like setting puts visitors in the mood in time to shop all over Ohio for special gifts.

Abruzzi's Cafe 422, 4422 Youngstown Rd. SE, Warren, tel. (330) 369-2422, is one of those rare, family-owned places where both the pasta and the pie are homemade. Lunch may be breaded pork tenderloin or eggplant parmigiana; either is priced at $5.50. The prime rib at dinner is $13.75. It and other meals are accompanied by delicious bread and pasta. Desserts are homemade, too, and include killer coconut cream pie for $2.25 or fresh strawberry pie (in season) for $2.50. Noisy but nice.

Tavern by the Green, 1 American Way, Warren, dial 330-856-8450. Overlooking the Avalon Lakes Golf Course, the Tavern offers indoor or patio seating in order to enjoy breakfast, lunch or dinner every day from 6:30 a.m. Each meal has daily specials, with a variety of grilled sandwiches, salads, and a fresh fruit plate for lunch. The signature evening dish is spinach ravioli in red-pepper cream sauce for $12.95. Diners need not play golf—or even care about it—to dine at this pleasant spot.

Moonraker, 1275 Boardman-Poland Rd., Poland, south of Youngstown off US 224, tel. (330) 726-8841, has been around for 15 years, though it recently underwent a major menu revision, now serving more seasonal meals with increasingly elegant presentations. The menu changes with the seasons and fresh seafood shows up daily. A lot has changed, but count on a side of pasta in a part of Ohio that knows its pasta well. Dinners are served Tues.-Sat., and don't be alarmed at a full parking lot—this is a popular place for wedding receptions.

Springfield Grille, 7413 S. Tiffany Rd., Poland (dial 330-726-0895), serves a varied American menu. Lunch items could include a portabella mushroom sandwich, marinated and covered with provolone cheese, for $5.95. The crab cake sandwich contains lots of jumbo lump crab and is $8.95 with a salad. Later in the day, sign on for a Zing chicken dinner, a spicy concoction teamed with bow tie pasta and Alfredo sauce (small is $10.95, large is $12.95). Rolls, breads, and desserts are made here every night. A torte is $4.95 for all seven of its layers. Look for the fence atop the building.

Janos Family Restaurant, 6620 Tippecanoe Rd. (SR 224), tel. (330) 533-1929, is a reasonable, pleasant family restaurant with a lofty green sign. Located between Boardman and Canfield, Janos has many breakfast specials and serves homemade rice pudding with the soup-and-sandwich special at lunch. Dinners are the usual, but the cooking is exceptional. Favorites include stuffed cabbage or meat loaf, and the Wednesday menu includes a Greek or an Italian entree. Any of the pleasingly filling dinners is $5-7.

Niki'z Eatery & Pub, 754 Youngstown-Warren Rd., Niles, between Warren and Youngstown off SR 46, tel. (330) 544-6100, serves lunches and dinners, with the adjacent pub open into the wee hours. Lunch amounts to an Italian buffet that includes pizzas, submarine sandwiches, and salads, all for $4.89. Among many entrees, chicken parmesan at $7.99 each evening is very popuar. Order it grilled or fried. NIkI'z Is a frequent destination of the locals.

Ye Old Main Ale & Chowder House, 40 S. Main St. (SR 46), Niles, tel. (330) 652-2300, is built on the site where President William McKinley was born. Open from 8 a.m. for breakfast, lunch, and dinner, the Chowder House serves up solid breakfasts such as ham-and-cheese omelets with home fries and toast for $4. At lunch, a hot sausage sandwich and fries fills diners for $4.50. A popular dinner item is chicken strips for $5.50. On Friday, try the haddock dinner with cabbage and noodles, also $5.50. The kitchen stays open until 8 p.m. weekdays, later on weekends.

RECREATION

South out of Youngstown some 25 miles on the way to Columbiana, look for **Everly's Ranch,** 40157 SR 164, tel. (330) 482-9317 (out-of-state call 800-293-8946). Here's where to temporarily trade a bucket seat for a saddle. Everly's most popular offering is a ride-eat-ride deal that is a trail ride punctuated by some cowboy cookin'. The facility also has boat rides on its own horseshoe-shaped lake, hayrides, party sites, and tent camping. Periodic horse sales take place here,

too. A one-hour ride is $15 and a two-hour ride is $25 plus the cost of a meal. Reservations are advised. Closed Monday.

This is a golf course-rich environment. For example, the Trumbull County Convention & Visitors Bureau has a brochure detailing 22 courses, their hours, addresses, and degrees of accessibility. By many accounts, the top links are at **Avalon Lakes,** 1 American Way, Warren, tel. (330) 856-8898. Just east of the city on SR 82, this facility is part of a resort complex; the easiest way to gain access to a tee is to stay at the resort. The course is taken over by Ladies Professional Golf Association (LPGA) players for a couple of weeks of tournament play in July. Greens fees seven days a week for 18 holes with cart total $55; costs drop to $35 after 4 p.m.

South of Newton Falls lies **Lake Milton State Park,** 16801 Mahoning Ave., tel. (330) 654-4989, a modest but pleasant body of water offering fishing, boating, and a spacious swimming beach. I-76 cuts the lake in half; travelers on the super highway who want to visit the park should exit at SR 534 and follow the signs. There are 1,000 acres of land and 1,685 acres of water here.

The only thing not to like about **Mosquito Lake State Park** is the name. Approximately a mile wide and seven miles long, the lake is a haven for waterfowl and a frequent destination for campers, swimmers, and fishers. Fishing is said to be best toward the northern end of the lake, near Mosquito Creek Wildlife Area. The latter is a popular spot with hunters. To reach the park, turn west off SR 11 onto SR 305 and continue about three miles to the park entrance, 1439 SR 305, Cortland, tel. (330) 637-2856. By the way, the beech-maple belt that runs through here is made possible by the large number of cloudy days and by winter snows that are heavier than in most of the rest of Ohio.

INFORMATION AND SERVICES

Dial 911 in Warren or Youngstown for police or fire emergencies. The non-emergency number for police in Warren is (330) 841-2505; in Youngstown, call (330) 742-8900. Reach Trumbull Memorial Hospital in Warren at (330) 841-9011.

The **Trumbull County Convention and Visitors Bureau** is at 650 Youngstown-Warren Rd.

(US 422), slightly closer to Warren than to Youngstown, tel. (330) 544-3468. The **Youngstown /Mahoning County Convention and Visitors Bureau** is at 101 City Centre One, in downtown Youngstown. Look for the tall, mirror-finish building next to the YMCA, tel. (330) 747-8200).

Youngstown's newspaper is the *Vindicator.* Weekend entertainment is previewed in Section C, "Where to Go," each Thursday. The daily newspaper in Warren is the *Tribune Chronicle.* It hits the streets weekday afternoons and Saturday and Sunday mornings. The *Ticket* magazine insert lists weekend entertainment every Thursday.

Transportation

The Western Reserve Transit Authority (WRTA) provides bus service in the Youngstown area. All bus routes stop downtown at the Federal Station. Cost of a ride on one of the green, blue, and white vehicles is 85 cents for adults and 65 cents for children (kids under the age of three ride free). For more information, call (330) 744-8431. Greyhounds pull into town nearby at 340 Federal Plaza West. The local number is (330) 743-4141.

Youngstown-Warren Regional Airport is at 1453 Youngstown-Kingsville Rd. (SR 193) in Vienna. The facility is east of SR 11 and north of SR 82, about a dozen miles due north of downtown Youngstown and six miles east of Warren. Carriers serving the area include Northwest, United, and USAir.

Shopping

Those who collect tchotchkes will want to visit the **Hummel Gift Shop** on Garfield Road in New Springfield, tel. (330) 549-3728, (800-223-2602 inside Ohio or 800-354-5438 outside the state). Besides the namesake item, look for Disney Classics, Lladros, Precious Moments, Royal Doultons, and year-round Christmas items.

Additional fare can be found at shopping centers such as **Southern Park Mall,** 7401 Market Street at US 224, tel. (330) 758-4511 on the Youngstown-Boardman line. Stores include Dillard's, Kaufmann's, JCPenney, Sears, and 120 other retailers. Another center is the **Shops at Boardman Park,** 255 Boardman-Canfield Rd. (US 224)—one mile west of I-680—in Boardman, tel. (330) 726-8188.

THE WESTERN RESERVE

This is one of the places Clevelanders go when they want to get away from it all. The towns and villages get smaller and less crowded the farther east from the city a traveler moves. The modest population centers survive on a mix of tourism and on the kinds of enterprise that prop up rural America these days: farming and farm services, real estate and insurance, grocery stores and drugstores, schools and local government. Expect this corner of Ohio, with its heavy winter snows and deep-green summers, to continue slow but inevitable growth as more and more people come calling.

History

Everybody talks about it, but no one will say exactly where it is. The Western Reserve, officially and historically, is all or part of 13 northeastern Ohio counties bounded on the north by Lake Erie and on the east by the Pennsylvania line. Around 1650, King Charles II of England granted the colony of Connecticut all lands between America's 41st and 42nd parallels "from sea to shining sea." This area of Ohio is part of that grant.

Following the Revolutionary War, Connecticut gave to the United States its farflung holdings but for three million Ohio acres, which were *reserved* as compensation for damages Connecticut suffered during the conflict. What is now Northeast Ohio became known as New Connecticut or Connecticut's Western Reserve. Yankees really did colonize the area, as preserved saltbox houses and place names make evident. The area west of Cleveland, known as the Firelands, was set aside for those Connecticut residents whose homes had been torched by the Redcoats.

Among other things, the Western Reserve was the most rabidly abolitionist area of the United State prior to the Civil War. Small wonder John Brown successfully raised money here or that local cemeteries show a number of weathered stones belonging to former members of the Grand Army of the Republic.

Today, the Connecticut influence on the area may best be seen in small towns like Hanover or Hiram, Mesopotamia or Middlefield. These municipalities often feature large frame houses surrounding a town square or commons area. Public buildings and churches also show a distinctively New England look.

Location and Orientation

For our purposes, the Western Reserve is an area bounded by I-90 on the north, the Pennsylvania-Ohio state line to the east, US 30 on the south, and the eastern suburbs of Cleveland to the west. There are no major cities hereabouts, but that doesn't make for a vacuum of activity. The little New England towns and villages are as resourceful as they are picturesque. Few, if any, have a population approaching 5,000, making them nice contrasts to the lines awaiting good times at Sea World, Geauga Lake, and elsewhere.

A network of interstate highways makes this corner of the state accessible, as does another limited-access highway, SR 11. Ashtabula (ashta-BOO-la), Lake, Geauga (jee-AUG-uh), and Trumbull Counties generally feature hills and valleys that run in a north-south direction. Consequently, east-west highways such as US 322 or 422 go gently up and down almost constantly. This is nursery country and horse country, a land where gentleperson farmers are numerous—some the products of white flight from Cleveland over the last couple of decades. The southern edge of the area is marked by reservoirs that have helped curb flooding and have been turned into public parks or nature reserves.

SIGHTS

Ashtabula, Carson & Jefferson Scenic Line Railroad, is in Jefferson, tel. (440) 576-6346. On Saturday and Sunday from mid-June through October, climb aboard ol' diesel No. 107 for a one-hour, 12-mile round trip that starts and ends at the depot here. The track has some history to it, as coal moved along the line in the 19th century and New York Central passengers hustled north and south later on. Tiny Carson, the northern end of the ride, was a staging area for materials shipped out of the Ashtabula harbor. Cost of the round trip is $6.50 for adults, $5.50 for seniors, and $4.50 for children ages 3-12. Best time to ride is October, as the train moves past fragrant, freshly harvested fields and woods afire with color. Reservations at that time are recommended.

The views along the **Ashtabula County Covered Bridge Tour** don't include a *National Geographic* photographer resembling Clint Eastwood, but the do include lovely old wooden spans from a simpler time. The tour starts wherever a driver spots a Tour sign with a covered bridge emblem and winds through picturesque farmland and villages for a total of 14 bridges. There are two tours, one with nine covered bridges in 69 miles, one with five covered bridges in 66 miles. A most pleasant intermission on the latter trip is to rent a canoe in tiny Harpersfield. At 234 feet, the Harpersfield Bridge is the longest covered bridge in Ohio; it was built in 1868 and graciously spans the Grand River, thanks in part to restoration work completed in 1992. Those who show up on the second weekend in October can avail themselves of the Fall Foliage Tour, which includes entertainment, a quilt show, contests, and food, all at the Ashtabula County Fairgrounds in Jefferson. For more information, call the Ashtabula County Covered Bridge Association at (440) 576-3769, or send for a brochure and map at 25 W. Jefferson Street, Jefferson, OH 44047. There is also a gift shop at that location.

Mesopotamia, a little village at the junction of SR 87 and SR 534, has an oval green several blocks long surrounded by quaint old houses. Forty miles east and a century removed—or so it would seem—from Cleveland, the tiny town boasts the **End of the Commons General Store,** 8719 SR 534, tel. (440) 693-4295. The store may be as close as it's possible to get to a real 19th-century small-town source for provisions. Treats range from muffin mixes to exotic soft drinks to foods in bulk. Adults and children should have fun looking around—the aged wood floor has a nice pitch-and-roll to it. After purchasing birch beer or a natural fruit drink, retire to the commons and witness Amish teenagers using a pay telephone.

Geauga County Historical Society Century Village is at 14653 E. Park St., Burton, tel. (440) 834-4012. This 65-acre site on south side of the village park has 22 renovated or recreated historical buildings. Open from Memorial Day through October Tues.-Sun. 1-5 p.m., tours leave weekdays at 10:30 a.m., 1 p.m., and 3 p.m., and on weekends at 1 and 3 p.m. The main house, library, and store are open Mar.-Nov., Sat.-Sun. 1-5 p.m. Admission is $5 for adults, $2 for children 6-12. The village also is where several annual events are held, among them a delicious Apple Butter Festival each October. For information on other local doings, consult the folks in the log cabin, beneath the water tower, in the middle of the village park.

covered bridge north of Jefferson, in Ashtabula County

Holden Arboretum, at 3,100 acres, is the largest arboretum in the United States. It's at 9500 Sperry Rd., Kirtland, tel. (440) 946-4400. Green thumbers who make a habit of viewing various gardens say this is the state's best. It assuredly is the largest. Visit here and see azaleas and rhododendron varieties before they're released for retail. Or kick back and, in season, look for incredibly varied birdlife along 20 miles of interpretive trails. Area devotees (the arboretum is only 23 miles east of downtown Cleveland) come here with each change of season. The fields, forests, ponds, and gardens are a nice change from the raucous amusement parks in Aurora. Admission is $4 for adults, $3 for seniors, and $2 for children.

Lake Farmpark, 8800 Chardon Rd. (US 6), Kirtland, tel. (440) 256-2122 or (800) 366-3276. Go on a haunted hayride or watch your pizza grow in this open-air science and cultural center. Aimed at city dwellers, the facility lets visitors milk a cow, ride in a horse-drawn wagon, and generally find out what life is like on the farm, at least for a day. Lake Farmpark is part of the Lake County Metropark System. It's open from Tues.-Sun. 9 a.m.-5 p.m., Jan.-March; also open Monday 9 a.m.-5 p.m., April-Dec. Admission is $6 for adults, $5 for seniors, and $4 for children ages 2-11.

Twinsburg, just off I- 480, which links I-271 and I-80 (the Ohio Turnpike), is famous far past its size. Since 1976, the village of 9,600 has staged the Twins Days Annual Festival. Identical and fraternal twins (and triplets, quadruplets, and so on) from all over show up, some dressed alike, to share what life is like with someone who looks suspiciously like yourself. The scientific and sociological communities descend on this Cleveland-Akron bedroom community on the first Saturday and Sunday of August, but so do many others who are looking for an enjoyable weekend. For details, call the Twins Days Festival Committee at (330) 425-3652. You can also check out the Web site www.twinsdays.org.

State Parks
Punderson State Park, 11755 Kinsman Rd. (SR 87), Newbury, tel. (440) 564-9144. There aren't many natural lakes in the Buckeye State, so when one turned up they built a state park around it. Actually, Punderson is unique in that

the lovely old inn here was first a spacious and atmospheric Tudor-and-stone private residence, but is now a 31-room lodge. It overlooks Ohio's largest and deepest (90 acres and 75 feet, respectively) souvenir pool of the glaciers. Trails here are soft with pine needles and inviting for walks in the summer and for cross-country skiing in the winter. There's a golf course, a campground, and gardens thick with butterflies in warm weather.

Nelson-Kennedy Ledges State Park, SR 282, Newbury, tel. (440) 564-2279, is a modest-sized day park, but don't write it off. Visitors can snake between mossy, wooded, glacier-deposited boulders the size of houses without being overrun by fellow hiking enthusiasts. While the kids squirt through narrow gaps in the rocks, adults will get a tranquil feel for the landscape and fauna of ancient Ohio. Before departing, check out Cascade Falls at the park's north end. Behind the falling water is a small cave.

Tinkers Creek State Park, 5708 Esworthy Rd., Ravenna, tel. (330) 562-5515, was once privately owned, but is now part of the state park system. This 740-acre facility is just three miles south of Aurora. There's a small, manmade lake for swimming and short hiking trails can be followed through an adjacent nature preserve. Birdwatchers and folks who want to glimpse the occasional beaver or muskrat can take the boardwalk path through a boggy area.

West Branch State Park is located midway between Akron and Youngstown, south of SR 5 and north of I-76, tel. (330) 296-3239). The 2,650-acre lake takes up half of the total park acreage, running in an east-west direction. It is bisected by Rock Spring Road, which runs north out of the park alongside the Buckeye Trail. The branch in the title represents the west branch of the Mahoning River. For boaters, one of the nice things about the big reservoir is the number of inlets in which one can get utterly lost. For campers, there are 103 sites on a peninsula on the north side of the lake. Opposite the camping area is a 700-ft. swimming beach, and to the east is the Army Corps of Engineers dam that caused all this river water to stay put.

Boaters may be of two minds about putting in here, since one end of the lake is a no-wake zone and the other is open to unlimited-horsepower craft. On the other hand, a large cove on

WESTERN RESERVE EVENTS

JANUARY

Winterfest, Chesterland.

MARCH

Sugarbush tours, Kirtland.

APRIL

Geauga County Maple Festival, Chardon.
Plant and Tree Fair, Kirtland.

MAY

Horsefest, Kirtland.

May Country Festival, Fairview Farms, 2497 SR 6, Rome, tel. (440) 563-4922, is an arts-and-crafts festival on the lawn of a working dairy farm. There's also rural entertainment and country food at this spot east of Cleveland and south of Ashtabula.

Quilt Show and Sale, Century Village, Burton. Amish, antique, and contemporary quilts are sold in this restored village. Adults are charged $4 to get in; children are free.

Civil War Encampment, Century Village, Burton. Camp life and battle maneuvers are enacted here as Johnny Rebs and Union soldiers show up in costume. Adults $4, children free.

JUNE

Chardon Square Market, Chardon.
Fiberfest, Kirtland.

The **Great Geauga Antique Market** sets up shop from morn to night at the county fairgrounds in Burton. Some 500 dealers display their wares, rain or shine. Admission from before dawn to 9:30 a.m. is $20; after that, it's a mere $4. Children under age 13 are free. A similar event takes place in mid September.

JULY

Dressage (horse show), Chagrin Falls.
Little Mountain Folk Festival, Kirtland Hills.
Native American Pow-Wow, Century Village, Burton Square. Dances, crafts, and food, courtesy of Native Americans dressed authentically. Admission is $4 for adults, and children are free.
Revolutionary War Encampment, Burton.
The **Americans Crafts Festival** takes place each year on two July weekends at Aurora Premium Outlets in Aurora.

AUGUST

Arts Festival, Chardon.
Vintage Ohio, Kirtland.

The **Great Geauga County Fair,** at the Burton Fairgrounds, is Ohio's oldest. Admission is $4 weekdays and $5 on Saturday and Sunday. The five-day fair is held in late August and has been drawing exhibitors and fans since 1822.

SEPTEMBER

Antiques of Chester Show, Chesterland
Country Days, Austinburg.
Fall Harvest Festival, Lake Farmpark.
Historic Civil War Encampment, Kirtland Hills.
Village Peddler Festival, 1408 CR 307 W., Austinburg. An outdoor marketplace that also features food and music. On the shore of Buccaneer Lake between Austinburg and Jefferson. Adults $3, students and seniors $2.50.

OCTOBER

Amish Backroad Bicycle gives visitors the opportunity to tour farm roads surrounded by Plain People on a conveyance in keeping with the area. Reservation for riders (bikes and helmets are a must) takes place at 10 a.m. on a mid-October Saturday at 16004 Hayes Rd., Middlefield, call (440) 285-2222 for more information.
Ashtabula County Covered Bridge Festival and Fall Foliage Tour, Jefferson.
Century Homes Tour, Geauga County.
Great Renaissance Christmas exhibits, Malvern.

NOVEMBER

Quilt and Craft Auction, Chesterland.
Vision of Sugarplums, juried arts and crafts fair, Eastlake.

DECEMBER

The Creative Coalition of Ravenna presents **Christmas Stroll,** a chance to visit several houses and a business or two tarted up for the holidays. The visitation is $6, while a preview night, with entertainment and refreshments, is $15. For more info, call (330) 296-9750.

the south side of the lake has been reserved for those who enjoy swimming off their anchored boats. Fishing goes on year round, as does small-game hunting in season. There are 12 miles of hiking trails, with remnants of a vast beech-maple forest that once stretched from Mansfield into Pennsylvania still evident. Horses and snowmobiles have their own trails, though riders of either must provide their mounts.

Pymatuning State Park is a mile east of Andover in Ashtabula County, with its main entrance just south of SR 85 on Gibbs Road, tel. (440) 293-7360. The spacious lake forms part of the Ohio-Pennsylvania border, with the west bank in the Buckeye State. SR 85 crosses the big reservoir into Pennsylvania via a causeway, becoming Pennsylvania SR 285 on the eastern shore. The park is 23 miles south of I-90 and nine miles east of limited-access SR 11. With 3,500 acres of land and 14,000 acres of water, there's plenty of room.

The park offers 60 cabins, 373 campsites, 30 seasonal campsites, a swimming beach just south of the causeway, marked hiking trails, five boat-launch ramps (the horsepower limit is 10), plus ice boating and other winter sports. Snowmobiles are welcome on the Pennsylvania side of the lake, and boaters can move from one shore to the other. Note, though, that to fish from the bank of a state requires a license from that state. In other words, don't get out of the boat and throw in a line from the eastern shore if all you have is an Ohio fishing license.

This part of Ohio was somewhat slow to develop, pocked as it was by bogs and wetlands. Nowadays, the remaining glacier-created ponds and marshes support everything from beaver to the occasional bald eagle. In fact, bald eagles nest and are routinely visible on the Pennsylvania side of the reservoir. Another phenomenon that takes place is the sight of ducks standing on fish at the spillway. Tourists toss wads of bread to the ducks, and this brings schools of carp, as well. The mallards literally step from one big fish to another in pursuit of the crumbs.

ENTERTAINMENT

The **Neon Moon Saloon,** 8389 Mayfield Rd., Chesterland, near the junction of US 322 and SR 306, provides country fans the opportunity to hear such area bands as Damon Pallay & Dry Country, Kid Lonesome, or Last Chance. The kitchen, which serves up buffalo wings and more, is open Sun.-Thurs. until midnight, Fri.-Sat. nights until 1 a.m. Learn to line dance Wed.-Sat. at 8 p.m. This tuneful facility is in the Maywood Centre Plaza. Call (440) 729-7443 for more information.

Scalpers Bar & Grille, 5718 Mayfield Rd. (US 322), Lyndhurst, tel. (440) 442-4212, has occasional live bands, plus laser karaoke on Wednesday and a disk jockey on Thursday.

Just southeast of metro Cleveland is the bucolic village of Sagamore Hills. Rock and roll occurs at **Larry's Tavern,** which is in a small shopping plaza on Old SR 8, tel. (330) 467-8869. Larry books blues or rock bands like Custard Pie to play on a regular basis, usually Saturday nights. The cover charge is $2 for the 10 p.m. show, but patrons who arrive before 9 p.m. see the band for free. The hills also are alive with the sounds of techno at least one night a week, as the **Hideaway Nightclub & Grille** at 10070 Old SR 8, (330) 467-6902, features a DJ with lights and sound. The music begins at 10 p.m. and there is no cover charge. Other kinds of music are spun Wed.-Fri. evenings for a young crowd.

For travelers a bit higher of brow, look in on the **Fairmont Fine Arts Theater** in the southeast corner of Geauga County at 8400 Fairmount Rd., in the town of Novelty, tel. (440) 338-3171. A trio of performing groups are in residence here, putting on concerts, recitals, exhibits, and youth theater. Speaking of theater, **Chagrin Valley Little Theatre,** 40 River St., Chagrin Falls, tel. (440) 247-8955, has been putting on plays for some 70 years. Among its most engaging works is a mystery each September that includes cocktails, dinner, and an original "Whodunit," that includes fanning out through the village on foot in search of clues! There are eight other plays throughout each season.

ACCOMMODATIONS

There are many, many motels within a few miles of the Sea World-Geaugua Lake vicinity. The following accommodations are for travelers who may prefer non-franchise rest and relaxation. There are several options in the expensive category that are worthwhile checking out. There's **Bass Lake Inn,** 400 South St. (SR 44), Chardon, near the junction of US 7 and SR 44, tel. (440) 285-3100. It has a dozen tasteful rooms set amid tall pines on Bass Lake. An expensive stay, the inn has a restaurant next door (see review, below). The **Punderson Resort and Conference Center,** 11755 Kinsman Rd., Newbury, tel. (440) 564-9144, is expensive, but for the tariff travelers stay in an English tudor manor overlooking Punderson Lake in the state park. Finally the **Quail Hollow Resort and Country Club,** 11080 Concord-Hambden Rd., Concord, tel. (440) 352-6201, offers indoor and outdoor pools, whirlpool, sauna, golf course, tennis, and bicycle rentals.

There are also several expensive-to-luxury priced combination inn and B&B accommodations available. The **Aurora Inn Bed and Breakfast,** 30 E. Garfield Rd. (junction of SR 306 and SR 82), Aurora, tel. (330) 562-6121, is luxury-priced. Built in 1927, the inn has an air of old New England in its 69 rooms and dining and meeting facilities. **Aurora Woodlands Resort,** 800 N. Aurora Rd., Aurora, tel. (330) 562-9151, is a very expensive stay, offering a restaurant, a lounge, and an indoor pool.

Campers can choose from among a number of quality sites, all of them quite inexpensive and open from May 1 to mid-October or later. They include Country Acres **Campground**, 9850 Minyoung Rd., Ravenna, tel. (330) 358-2774, **Heritage Hills Campground**, 6445 Ledger Rd., Thompson (northwest Geauga County), tel. (440) 298-1311; **Kool Lakes Campground**, 12990 SR 82, Parkman (southeast Geauga County), tel. (440) 548-8436; **Paradise Beach Park Campground**, 11149 Old State Rd., Chardon, tel. (216) 285-2140; **Sea Lake Resort Campground**, 250 Treat Rd., Aurora, tel. (330) 562-4423; Tri-County Kamp Inn Campground, 17147 US 6, Montville (northeast Geauga County), tel. (440) 968-3400; **Windrush Hollow Camp**, 15560 Mayfield Rd., Huntsburg (northeast Geauga County), tel. (440) 635-5050.

Bed and Breakfast

There are many excellent, moderately priced options for travelers who prefer bed and breakfast luxury to chain motel uniformity.

The **Chamomile Bed and Breakfast,** 6458 Ledge Rd., Thompson, tel. (440) 298-9794, is moderately priced and provides a full breakfast

and campfire facilities with a pond as a backdrop. The lovely **Lily Ponds,** Hiram, tel. (330) 569-3222 or (800) 325-5087, features not one but two lily ponds to greet guests, who can while away time on a screened-in porch or hike in 20 acres of woods. Mrs. Spencer doesn't mail it in, breakfastwise. Rather, her food is delicious and pleasing to the eye. Lily Ponds is moderately priced and among the more widely recommended B&B's in the entire state. The **Old Stone House Bed and Breakfast,** 8505 SR 534, Mesopotamia, tel. (440) 693-4186, is a modest, out-of-the-way spot near an Amish village. Finally, the **Walker-Johnson Inn Bed & Breakfast,** 15038 S. State Ave., Middlefield, tel. (440) 632-5662, is a lovely Victorian home with antique furnishings and four guest rooms. A full breakfast is served.

Also recommended is **Rider's Inn Bed & Breakfast,** 792 Mentor Ave., Painesville, tel. (440) 942-2742, which falls into the expensive category, but who can put a price on breakfast in bed?

FOOD

Bass Lake Tavern, 426 South St. (SR 44), Chardon, tel. (440) 338-5550, consists of pleasant people adept at providing good food. The soup-sandwich combination changes daily, with other lunch options being baked lemon-tarragon chicken salad at $6.95 or grilled turkey sandwich with portobello mushrooms, $7.25. How about roast duck with field greens for dinner at $10.95? Or an elk striploin at $21.95? Care for a Cajun-barbecue Atlantic salmon filet at $17.95? Travelers need not stay at the adjacent inn to enjoy the food. Lunch is served Mon.-Sat., dinner is served every day.

Belle's Restaurant, is a busy, homey spot at 14609 W. Park St., Burton, tel. (440) 834-8812, on the west side of the village park. Locals like the list of sandwiches, such as the Belle deluxe chicken breast, served with cottage fries, for $5.49. Seafood platters, with cottage fries and cole slaw, are popular for dinner and cost just $7.29. Also $7.29 is the mushroom steak, offered with a choice of potato and a tossed salad. Fruit pies are homemade and disappear in a hurry at $1.79 per slice. Open all day, every day.

There are five casual **Brown Derby Roadhouse** restaurants in the Cleveland area; among the best is the site at I-90 and SR 306 in Mentor, tel. (440) 951-0574. The woodfired steaks are good, and the bar has an endless peanut supply. Open for lunch Sat.-Sun. and for dinner seven days a week, the facility is about 100 yards south of the busy interstate highway on the right (west) side of the road. Several meals are in the $10-12 range.

Clay Street Inn, 2092 SR 45, Austinburg, tel. (440) 275-5151, presents a menu that is an intelligent mix of Asian, Italian, Southwestern, and other cuisines. Two in-demand sandwiches at lunch are the veggie melt with steak fries for $3.95 and the Philly cheese steak with mushrooms and peppers for $5.95. Later in the day, folks order a 14 oz. prime rib for $14.95, catfish for $11.50, or seafood platter for $12.95, all with the choice of two side dishes. Clay Street is open for lunch Mon.-Sat. and every evening for dinner.

Cranberry Station, 68 Public Square, Andover, tel. (440) 293-6651, is one mile from Pymatuning State Park. The emphasis here is on homemade breakfasts, lunches, and dinners, seven days a week. A breakfast favorite is scrambled eggs, seasoned home fries, and sausage or ham, for $3.95. At lunch, try the cold roast beef sandwich on toasted rye, topped with cream cheese and tomato, for $3.45. Evening favorites include roast turkey for $6.75 or pork ribs for $6.25. The dessert tray overflows with good stuff, including slices of coconut cream or cranberry-apple pie.

Market Square Bistro, 16725 Chillicothe Rd. (SR 306), Bainbridge, tel. (440) 543-5115, prepares New American fare. A luncheon meal ordered frequently is the romano crusted chicken breast at $10.95, while a popular dinner is wild mushroom-and-veal meatloaf at $14.95. Save room for multilayered tiramisu, which is $5.50. The wine list is comprehensive. Lunch is served Tues.-Fri.; dinner is served every day but Monday.

Mary Yoder's Amish Kitchen, 14743 N. Old State Rd. (SR 608), Middlefield, tel. (440) 632-1939, is a reminder that there are good Amish cooks outside of Holmes County. Breakfast can be the Saturday-only buffet or an omelet filled with everything; the latter is $4.95. Hot luncheon items include roast beef or turkey sandwiches with mashed potatoes and gravy for $5.75. At night, try the Mary Yoder sampler plate, which has beef, chicken, ham, and two sides for $9.50.

Save room for the date pudding ($2.25 plain, $3.20 with ice cream) or one of a slew of pies. Breakfast is served Monday, Friday, and Saturday, and lunch and dinner are served Mon.-Sat.

A fixture in well-to-do Chagrin Falls since 1972, **Raintree,** 25 Pleasant Dr., tel. (440) 247-4800, makes diners in sweaters or formal wear comfy, serving everything from salmon horseradish to Georgia pork tenderloin. "Dublin lawyer" is a savory lobster casserole that's priced at $9.95 at lunch and $18.95 each evening. Regulars like beef brisket, $7.95 and $12.95, and the English standby, bangers and mash (sausages and potatoes), also $7.95 and $12.95. The help modestly call the place a chop house, and it is that at least. Lunch and dinner are served every day, with Sunday dinner from 4 p.m.

Another good Chagrin Falls restaurant is **Stix,** at 8377 E. Washington St., tel. (440) 543-7849), where barbecue tops the menu, ranging from pork ribs to beef brisket and chicken to steak. Portions are large and diners can choose from a sweet, mild Kansas City sauce or a house variety with more spice to it. Luncheon sandwiches include pulled pork or beef brisket with fries for $6.95. Evenings, try beef ribs at $14.95 or a full rack of pork back ribs at $18.50. Lunch is served Saturday only; closed Monday.

Welshfield Inn, 14001 Main Market Rd., Burton, tel. (440) 834-4164 or (800) 882-1144, offers gracious country dining. The tablecloths are sparkling white, there are fresh-cut flowers on each table, and delicious lunches and dinners are served every day but Monday. At lunch, try chicken pot pie with a fruit salad topped with homemade dressing, all for $6.95. Favorites in the evening include Swiss steak for $10 and lamb shank for $13.95. The original, 150-year-old stagecoach stop, this atmospheric place is regionally popular.

RECREATION

Vacationers may have heard that the Cuyahoga River once was the most miserable body of water on earth. But that was the lower Cuyahoga; the upper Cuyahoga has always been a placid and tidy stretch of stream. The **Green River Tavern and Restaurant,** 13468 Main Market Rd. (US 422), Burton, tel. (440) 834-4337, rents canoes so travelers can investigate woodlands by water. The portage takes canoeists upriver three miles. That could work up an appetite for the restaurant's food, which ranges from sub sandwiches to surf 'n' turf. Paddlers who break a sweat can dine at any of a dozen picnic tables in the covered pavilion. The tavern-restaurant is east of LaDue Reservoir and west of the village of Wellington.

A pair of public golf courses, one each in Chardon and in Chesterland, welcome travelers. **Chardon Lakes Golf Course,** 470 South St. (SR 44), tel. (440) 285-4653, is an 18-hole, par 71 facility where visitors can rent clubs if necessary. The 18 holes at **Orchard Hills,** 11414 Caves Rd., tel. (440) 729-1963, wind in and out of an apple orchard, and there is a picnic area. And don't forget the links at pretty **Punderson State Park** on SR 87 in Newbury, tel. (440) 564-5465. Greens fees at Chardon weekdays are $22 to walk and $32 to ride; weekends are $32 to walk and $40 to ride. Orchard Hills is semiprivate, which means travelers pay a $5 out-of-town fee before ponying up $20 (weekdays) or $23 (weekends) for an 18-hole round. Punderson fees are $31 weekdays and $38 weekends with a cart for the par 72 facility. Seniors receive a reduced weekday rate of $25.

While your mate is playing golf, why not improve your kitchen skills? The **Loretta Paganini School of Cooking** is at 8613 Mayfield Rd. (US 322), Chesterland, tel. (440) 729-1110. The school offers numerous two- to three-hour courses with tantalizing names like "Let Them Eat Dessert!" and "Techniques of French Cooking." The school recruits noted chefs from Cleveland and beyond for these sessions, which are offered at various times most days of the week. Should you be in a consuming rather than a creating mood, the school has a monthly international dinner that may feature Hungarian cuisine one month and Thai the next.

Amusement Parks
Geauga Lake Amusement Park, 1060 Aurora Rd., Aurora, tel. (330) 562-7131 or (800) 843-9283, is close to mega-attraction Sea World. The water park lets kids act like some of the fish they just saw down the road. Best place to portray a surfer is in the wave pool's six-foot breakers. Smaller children will enjoy Butch Hightide's

Play Park, a sandy, castle-and-storybook playground. There's also a formidable roller coaster called the Big Dipper, a carousel, live entertainment, and restored, Flash Gordon-like silver rocket ships from before World War II—more than 100 rides and attractions in all. Admission is $25.99 for persons 48 or more inches high. Those shorter than four feet get in for an admission fee of $12.99.

Hiram, midway between Cleveland and Youngstown at the SR 82/700 junction, is the home of pretty little **Hiram College.** Though the village is only five miles north of the Ohio Turnpike (I-80), the nearest turnpike entrance/exit is 15 miles southeast, near Newton Falls. Should you happen through Hiram, call (330) 569-3211 to learn of late-breaking college lectures, exhibits, sporting events, etc. Its Web site is www.hiram.edu. President James A. Garfield was a student and the college president here; it's hard to believe that the village has changed much since then.

Pioneer Waterland Wet and Dry Fun Park, 10661 Kile Rd., Chardon, tel. (440) 285-0909, has three different areas for visitors. There's Water FunLand, with a three-acre pool that includes areas for watery volleyball and basketball, SportsLand, with everything from miniature golf, to hoops, and KidsLand, a play area. Highlight of the park for young motorheads is the Grand Prix Supertrack, a quarter-mile roadracing facility. Admission is $11.95 for persons more than 40 inches high and free for those who can pass beneath the 40-inch bar. There also is a spectator admission fee of $8.95 for parents who merely want to keep an eye on the kids. Open daily from 10 a.m.-8 p.m. mid-June through August and Labor Day weekend.

Sea World, SR 43, Aurora, tel. (330) 562-8101 or (800) 637-4268, is the home of those fun lovin' killer whales, Shamu and Namu. It's also the place where visitors can feed and frolic with blue-nose dolphin, ride a moving walkway through a shark tank, or bask in the spray of regularly scheduled shows several times a day. The place is educational as well, introducing the dry-land Midwest to wildlife from exotic rivers, faraway lakes, and distant oceans. Special animal guests in the past have included the Anheuser-Busch Clydesdale horses. After dark, look for laser and fireworks shows. The attraction is open from

Memorial Day through Labor Day every day and on weekends through September. Early and late in the season, the park closes at 7 p.m.; the rest of the summer it shuts at 11 p.m. Admission is $30.95 for adults and $2.95 for children ages 3-11, plus a $5 parking fee. All shows are included in the admissions prices.

INFORMATION AND SERVICES

Dial 911 in the event of police, fire, or other emergency. To reach the Geauga County Sheriff's non-emergency number, dial (440) 285-2228. Non-emergency numbers for sheriffs' departments in other counties are as follows: Ashtabula, tel. (440) 576-0055; Lake, tel. (440) 350-5531; Portage, tel. (330) 678-7012; and Trumbull, tel. (330) 675-2500. There are hospitals in Akron, Ashtabula, Chardon, Conneaut, Geneva, Mentor, Painesville, Ravenna, and Warren.

Try these helpful folks: **Ashtabula County Convention and Visitors Bureau,** Jefferson, tel. (440) 275-3202 or (800) 337-6746; **Geauga County Tourism Council,** Chardon, tel. (800) 775-8687; **Lake County Visitor Bureau,** Mentor, tel. (440) 354-2424 or (800) 368-5253; **Portage County Convention and Visitors Bureau,** 173 S. Chillicothe Rd. (SR 306), Aurora, tel. (330) 562-3373; and **Trumbull County Convention and Visitors Bureau,** 650 Youngstown-Warren Rd., Niles, tel. (330) 544-3468 or (800) 672-9555.

Cleveland, Akron, Youngstown, Warren, Mentor, and Willoughby daily newspapers cover all or parts of the area. A number of villages have weekly or semiweekly newspapers that are excellent for covering local music and other entertainment events.

This corner of Ohio is somewhat of a no-man's land for those without private transportation. The best bet to tour the area is to rent a vehicle in Cleveland, most likely at Hopkins Airport, where there are a number of agencies from which to choose.

THE LAKE ERIE SHORELINE

Lake Erie totals 9,910 square miles of surface. It is 241 miles long and averages 57 miles wide. The lake is 570 feet above sea level and has a maximum depth of 210 feet. Shallowest, fourth largest, and the last of the five Great Lakes to be discovered and sailed upon by Europeans, Erie today has more traffic than any other lake, thanks in part to the completion of the St. Lawrence Seaway in 1959. Cleveland, Toledo, and smaller ports play host to vast ships hauling raw materials and finished goods to and from the United States and Canada. Cleveland, Lorain, and Toledo rank 42nd, 43rd, and 44th, respectively, among America's 50 busiest ports. Cleveland's tonnage totals 15.4 million, followed by Lorain with 14.96 million tons and Toledo with 14.07 million tons. A total of seven Ohio counties border the big lake.

Early sailors noted that the water appeared yellow in places. That was because roiling waves kept the sandy bottom in constant motion. They complained that the wind never blew from the same direction twice and they told of storm-tossed seas revealing momentary, terrifyingly bare stretches of the very bottom. The lake has been a killer down through the years, devouring an estimated 1,000 sailors a year, year after

year, as well as goods and money that today total $1 billion. The only upside to such tragedy and loss is that Lake Erie has become a rich environment for recreational diving.

In 1813 a truly memorable historic event took place here. Residents of Cleveland on the sunny day of Sept. 10 looked up from their work at what they thought was the sound of distant thunder. They quickly realized that Commodore Oliver Hazard Perry and his U.S. Navy fleet had engaged British warships some 70 miles to the west, near what is now Put-in-Bay. A crowd gathered on the shore as unseen cannon boomed across the water. Eventually, Perry's nine hastily prepared vessels sank or captured the six English ships. The victory helped confirm that the vast Northwest Territory and the upper Mississippi Valley would belong to the United States.

What was the lake like nearly 200 years ago? Scientists say it was one of the earth's richest ecosystems. Today it still produces more fish per cubic mile than any other Great Lake, despite what heavy use it has been put through. There once were so many fish that early travelers saw white bass and pike clog the mouths of rivers. Huge sturgeon were around in such numbers that steamships burned them for fuel. On a

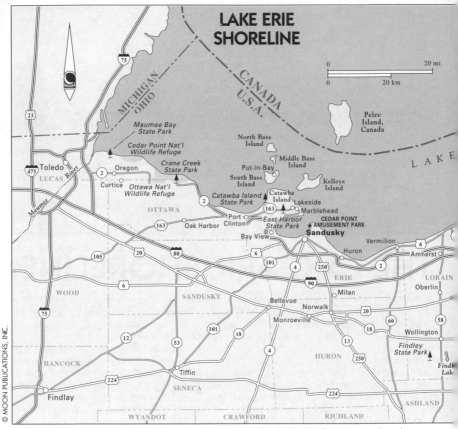

warm, calm day, the lake was a huge, clear, and inviting swimmin' hole.

For the first half of the 19th century, folks were much more taken with Niagara Falls, created by departing Lake Erie water, than with any of the Great Lakes. The British ships captured by Perry and other battered vessels would be sent over the falls from time to time—for the amusement of onlookers. The natural wonder of the falls even overshadowed the opening of the Erie Canal in 1825. The canal allowed people and cargo to float to and from New York City to Buffalo, then onto Lake Erie. Two years later, the *State of Ohio* canal boat glided into Cleveland from Akron, signifying the opening of the first section of the Ohio and Erie Canal. From about that time, the Industrial Revolution played to ever-increasing crowds of Buckeyes, with Lake Erie seated front-row center.

That meant human and agricultural wastes washed into the lake and were soon followed by toxic chemicals. Sulfuric acid from steel mills mixed with DDT from farms and calcium chloride from table-salt refineries. By the mid-1960s there was no life whatsoever in Cleveland's Cuyahoga River, and many parts of the lake were so dirty as to be unfit for bodily contact. The water stunk of sulfides and the bottom had turned a slick, thick black from decaying algae. Happily, these and related problems began to be vigorously addressed following the 1992 Great Lakes Water Quality Agreement.

Some problems remain, among them shoreline erosion and siltation from runoff, which often manifests itself in destruction of shoreline marshes. Fisheries also remain in jeopardy, while some bacteria and refuse continue to enter the lake. And phosphorus, toxic materials, and generating stations take their toll on fish. Solutions are being studied and improvements to a large and vital stretch of the country's North Coast are under way.

THE NORTHEAST COAST

The towns of Conneaut (pop. 13,000), Ashtabula (pop. 22,000), and Geneva (pop. 6,600) hold down the extreme northeast corner of Ohio. In fact, the eastern limit of Conneaut (CON-nee-ut) is the Ohio-Pennsylvania state line. It and Ashtabula traditionally had lake-based economies. Ashtabula in particular had an active harbor area, now thoughtfully preserved and as aimed at recreation as work. The Geneva area is a mix of summer tourism venues and vineyards. Little Geneva-on-the-Lake is a vacation swirl every summer, featuring a main street "strip" with all sorts of food, trinkets, and attractions.

History

Conneaut sits astride an important Indian trail, as do many of the cities along the lake. Natives moved back and forth along the shore, going places and hauling in fish. Later, the amount of ship traffic required creation of the West Breakwater Light here, a warning beacon that resembles a lighthouse. It's white with a thick black band and sits to this day at the end of a long, rough stone breakwater. The light is at the tip of a thin shaft. It greeted Finns, among others, who settled in Conneaut in the 19th century. They are remembered in the renovated Kilpi Hall civic center. It is the former Finnish temperance hall and is now where free summer concerts are presented, as in years past. Conneaut is 27 square miles and has two rare, octagon-shaped dwellings (both private homes, not open to visitors). Kids ice skate inside the breakwater on the smooth sheltering ice found there each winter.

Ashtabula wasn't always the benign place it is today. Moses Cleaveland, founder of the big city just to the west, found Seneca Indians here prior to 1800 who were none too pleased with the appearance of Europeans. Later on, Ashtabula became a hotbed for the abolition of slavery and a stop on the Underground Railroad. In the 1920s, the local sheriff found so many bodies beneath the wharf that he stopped counting. Seafarers and their murderous friends are gone now, replaced by weekend sailors and fishing charters. Not all of the action in Ashtabula is along the water—the city is inland a mile or so from the historic Harbor District. The rest of Ashtabula County has 15 covered bridges in good repair. They are the focus of an October bridge-visiting fest each year.

Geneva-on-the-Lake has for decades been a funky, mostly blue-collar vacation destination. Nothing is pretentious, with sun and sand and water by day and food, drink, and noise each

THE GIANTS OF CONNEAUT

Down through the years, rumors have persisted of an ancient race of giants who lived in the Conneaut area. Stories tell of vast burial grounds containing human skulls so large they could be slipped over the entire head of a normal-sized individual. In Newark, too, there were rumored to be one or more stone tablets showing mysterious letters, but the Conneaut Stones employ the Roman alphabet. Perhaps because no one ever gave Indians much credit, these long-gone giants were reputed to be a race of pre-Columbian caucasians.

Local histories really do make repeated references to ancient burial mounds similar to those found throughout the Ohio Valley. A study published late in the 18th century described a big mound within present-day Conneaut limits, as well as many smaller mounds. A mound excavated in 1815 for a roadbed allegedly turned up a big jawbone with a false tooth. The tooth was said to be metallic, much like present-day silver or other metal fillings. Caskets made of stone also were reported to have been dug up.

Notes under the care of the Western Reserve Historical Society tell of early settlers routinely unearthing gigantic human bones. The stories lose some credibility on reading that the bones were black with age and, invariably, "on exposure to the air crumbled to dust." So the whole race-of-giants story may well have been a hoax, or the bones were those of mammoth, bison, and other long-gone species once common to the area. Still, the thought of the pioneers slipping freshly exhumed, oversized skulls over their heads to run around scaring each other is just goofy enough to be true.

ERIE WRECKS

That's the name of a book by Georgann and Michael Wachter of Avon Lake, Ohio, recounting 98 shipwrecks in the big lake. Ninety-eight would seem to be plenty, but the book covers only selected sinkings in the central and western parts of the water. "There are many hundreds, as many as 2,000-3,000," Georgann reports. She and her husband investigated wrecks in eastern Lake Erie in 1998 so as to bring out a companion volume to their 1997 book, which retails for $24.95 in area dive shops, marine stores, maritime museums, and bookstores.

The eastern end of the lake may have the best-preserved wrecks. The water there, particularly north of Erie, Pennsylvania, is as much as 210 feet deep. A ship that sinks in shallow water often breaks up rather quickly. The Wachters have discovered well-preserved shipwrecks in 150 feet of water, which is the approximate limit for conventional diving equipment. Georgann notes that a number of important ships all over the lake have yet to be found. Many are time capsules—they are as valuable to historians

as they might be to anyone seeking to profit from recovery.

Lately, recovering anything from a wreck has become complicated by the law. Canada and several Great Lakes states, including Ohio, have passed regulations stating that nothing may be taken from a wreck without a permit, obtainable from the Ohio Department of Natural Resources. Casual divers cannot haul so much as a plate or a porthole to the surface. Happily, a number of dive shops take divers to wrecks on summertime charters. The customers, who must carry a diving certification card, can dive in and around a wreck to their hearts' content. Divers and swimmers who find property not on or near a sunken ship can keep it if they recover it by hand. If it appears to be worth $10 or more, the finder must file a written report with the Ohio Historical Society.

Divers, historians, and the curious can order *Erie Wrecks* from Corporate Impact, 33326 Bonnieview Drive, Avon Lake, OH 44012. The cost is $30, which includes tax and postage.

---

evening. Not even a riot in 1965 involving beer drinkers caused folks to book other holiday destinations. Erosion has claimed much of the original stretch of pristine beach at what has been called a "quirky little spa," yet people return each year to stay in one of dozens of locally owned cottages and have a great time all summer long. For travelers before Memorial Day or after Labor Day, leading sources of interest may be the area's numerous wineries, Geneva State Park, or a charter fishing expedition. The city of Geneva has a larger year-round population and is comparatively calmer, a good destination for retail needs

SIGHTS

The **Great Lakes Marine & U.S. Coast Guard Memorial Museum,** 1071 Walnut Blvd., Ashtabula, tel. (440) 964-6847, sits just above Ashtabula's historic harbor in the former home of a lighthouse keeper. The facility, which asks for a donation but does not otherwise charge, displays scale models of iron-ore loading machinery and boats, plus photos, artifacts, paintings, and an actual pilot's house from a Great Lakes ore ship. A view of the

harbor makes a picnic here a pleasant experience, with swimming, fishing, and boat-rental facilities nearby. Hours for the museum, which has a gift shop full of neat souvenirs, are noon-6 p.m. from Memorial Day to Labor Day and 1-5 p.m. during the months of May and September.

Railroad Museum, 342 Depot St., tel. (440) 599-7878, is housed in the former New York Central depot, just off Broad Street, downtown. A steam locomotive, the Nickel Plate Railroad's *Old Iron Horse 755,* stands majestically beside the museum on a siding. Behind the locomotive is a caboose, a mesmerizing vehicle for young visitors. Inside, the museum is filled with the memorabilia of early railroading, and mannequins are decked out in official railroad uniforms. Hours are noon-5 p.m. daily, Memorial Day-Labor Day, closed the rest of the year. Donations are welcome.

The **Ashtabula Historic District,** along Bridge Street, features a drawbridge over the nearby river, plus a stretch of two-story brick storefronts. There's lots of antique and nostalgia shopping here, as well as places to eat and sip a cool drink—outside on a deck if weather permits. Separated by a low area from the rest of the city, the district sits just below the maritime museum.

Only two of Ashtabula County's 13 **covered bridges** are north of I-90. They can be seen by exiting the interstate highway at SR 7, heading north into Conneaut. Turn left (west) onto US 20 and continue west about three miles. Look for the covered-bridge tour sign, which will direct you off the highway left (south). The second bridge is south of Ashtabula on Dewey Road, just north of Plymouth Ridge Road. For more information, call the Ashtabula County Covered Bridge Association at (440) 576-3769, or send for a brochure and map at 25 W. Jefferson Street, Jefferson, OH 44047. There is also a small gift shop at that address.

Geneva State Park on Padanarum Road, Geneva, tel. (440) 466-8400, is one stunning state park. The facility features a marina abob with pricey boats, a 300-foot swimming beach within walking distance of the Geneva-on-the-Lake strip, a multi-lane boat ramp, a fishing pier, camping facilities, a golf course, a few cabins with nothing but beach between the occupant and the lake, and it's all crisscrossed with pleasant walking trails. If walking is a bit slow, visitors can rent bikes here, or they can climb on that summer abomination, the personal watercraft. Bikes are $3 per hour, Wave Runners are $45. There's still more—in contrast to the oompah of the nearby resort, visit peaceful freshwater marshes and estuaries. In the fall, these idle wetlands become stopovers for migrating birds.

One of the oldest remaining houses in the Western Reserve is **Shandy Hall,** 6333 S. Ridge Rd., Geneva, tel. (440) 466-3680. The exterior is modest, and the interior contains 17 rooms devoted to cooking in the cellar or dining while surrounded by wallpaper that was imported from France in 1815. Devotees of old-time, handmade furniture will find a visit especially rewarding. Hours are Tues.-Sat. 10 a.m.-5 p.m.; Sunday noon-5 p.m. Fees are $3 for adults and $2 for seniors and children.

ENTERTAINMENT AND CULTURE

The Kilpi Dixieland Band is typical of the kind of entertainment found on the lawn of the **Conneaut Community Center,** 1025 Buffalo St.,

Conneaut, tel. (440) 593-5888 or (440) 593-4222. There's usually a free concert at 7 p.m. each Sunday. For those who like things more raucous, head to the **Cove Nite Club,** 5326 Lake Rd., Geneva-on-the-Lake, tel. (440) 466-8888, which offers live tunes on Friday and Saturday. The musicians may be of the rock, metal, or even classic persuasion. The cover charge averages about $3. Other Geneva-on-the-Lake entertainment destinations include the **Swiss Chalet,** 4870 Lake Rd., tel. (440) 466-8650, and the **Pavillion Restaurant,** 5276 Lake Rd., tel. (440) 466-3283. The Chalet has free light rock Fri.-Sun. evenings and the Pavillion offers rock on Saturday evenings. The **Dry Dock,** 1118 Bridge St., in Ashtabula's Historic District, tel. (440) 964-9909, offers live music Friday and Saturday evenings, thanks to local bands. There is no cover charge.

The arts survive in the **Ashtabula Arts Center,** 2928 W. 13th St., Ashtabula, tel. (440) 964-3396. This place is home not only to the Straw Hat Theatre in the summer outdoors and community theater indoors the rest of the year, it also offers visual art exhibits that change monthly. Hours are Mon.-Thurs. 9 a.m.-9 p.m., Friday 9 a.m.-7 p.m., and Saturday 9 a.m.-5 p.m. Another place worth visiting is **Rabbit Run Theater, Inc.,** 5648 W. Chapel Rd., Madison, tel. (440) 428-7092. Four summer plays are staged in a converted barn that seats 300.

RECREATION

Fishing
This information was gleaned from a charterboat owner. It holds true for pretty much any Lake Erie port where folks shove off to search for walleye, the tasty pike game fish that can grow to a length of more than two feet. Currents and temperature affect fish location. Walleye like warm water when it's cold and cool water when it's hot. Lure color makes a big difference, but there's no telling what color will be the right one from one day to the next. Good equipment will result in more walleye pulled into the boat. Charter patrons should look over the tackle being furnished them; spinning reels with 6- to 8-pound test line on a five-foot, medium-action rod seems to work best. Prices for charter fishing vary but

are approximately $350 for eight hours of walleye fishing for one to four persons. Bass and perch fishing will be slightly less, and some charter-boat captains offer special rates for expeditions that begin after 4 p.m. weekdays. Bag limits for walleye are 10 fish daily on Lake Erie. As for the season, it runs April-Sept. for walleye and April-Oct. for perch.

Golf

Conneaut Shores Golf Course, 726 Whitney Rd., tel. (440) 593-5403, is a pretty nine-hole, par 36 facility fronting Lake Road. Fees are $7 on weekdays and $9 on weekends. A cart costs $9. **Village Green Golf Course** in North Kingsville. **Geneva-on-the-Lake Municipal Golf Course,** Al Mraz Dr., tel. (440) 466-8797, is an 18-hole

course, par 72. Weekend fees are $9 for nine holes and $16 for 18 holes. Seniors receive the following discount: $6.50 for nine holes and $13 for 18 holes. A cart costs $11 per person. **Hemlock Spring Golf Club,** 4654 Cold Springs Rd., Geneva, tel. (440) 466-4044, is among the longer courses in the area. It totals 18 holes and is par 72. To play, figure $33 with a cart and $23 without.

Beaches

Conneaut offers a swimming beach adjacent to Township Park on SR 531 (Lake Road). Lake Shore Park, north of US 2, west of Ashtabula, is wedged between the Perry Nuclear Power Plant on one side and a gravel repository on the other. There's a small beach, which is breakwall protected, and visitors can rent personal watercraft.

LAKESHORE AREA EVENTS

MAY

Nest with the Birds by showing up at the Municipal Building on Kelleys Island, tel. (419) 746-2360. This is a weeklong nature camp that includes guided bird walks.

Port Clinton Walleye Festival takes place over four days, giving anglers plenty of time to pull in those succulent perch relatives. On shore, there are food vendors, a parade, rides, games, arts, and crafts. For information, telephone (419) 798-1243.

Walleye Festival, Water Works Park, Port Clinton, tel. (419) 732-2864, salutes the game fish with fresh walleye sandwiches. There are other treats, plus entertainment, crafts, rides, a parade, and a flea market, all over four days.

JUNE

Waterfront Arts & Crafts Show, takes place in Port Clinton, tel. (419) 732-3831, over two days. Artists and crafters line downtown streets to show and sell original artwork.

Ten-K & Five-K Kick takes place in Memorial Park on Kelleys Island, tel. (419) 746-2360. This event occurs all along the scenic lakefront—a good spot to run or to cheer on a competitor.

Arts & Crafts Fair is set for East Harbor State Park in the Lakeside-Marblehead area, tel. (419) 734-4424.

JULY

National Matches, SR 2, Port Clinton, tel. (703) 267-1450, happens at Camp Perry. This is an an-

nual national shooting championship for pistol, rifle, and muzzleloader.

Lakeside Tour of Homes, tel. (419) 798-4065, features six to eight Lakeside homes each year and a Women's Club crafts show.

Christmas in July, East Harbor State Park Campground, Lakeside-Marblehead, tel. (419) 734-4424, includes a visit by Santa. Other incongruities include best holiday decor at a campsite and holiday-season movies.

Islandfest, Memorial Park, Kelleys Island, tel. (419) 746-2360, sets the rock rockin' with street dancing, a parade, a crafts market, entertainment, and food.

OCTOBER

The oldest operating lighthouse on the Great Lakes is in Marblehead, reason enough for the **Autumn Lighthouse Festival.** The light has been shining since 1822, so join the crowd to check out arts and crafts, take in entertainment, and soak up history. For details, call (800) 441-1271 or go to www.lake-erie.com on the Web.

Port Clinton hosts a **Harvest Festival** at about the same time. This street fair also offers live entertainment, plus a food court, crafts, and farmers market. Call the same toll-free number as above and consult the same Web site for more information.

CONNEAUT AREA EVENTS

MAY

Blessing of the Fleet, harbor area, Ashtabula, tel. (440) 224-1554, takes into account the fact that commercial fishing is a dangerous business.

JUNE

Northeast Ohio Polka Fest, happens at the Old Firehouse Winery, 5499 Lake Rd., Geneva-on-the-Lake, tel. (800) 862-6751. The free event features live polka bands and Chicago, Slovenian, and Polish dance styles. There is ethnic food and wine, of course.

JULY

Ribs on the River, SR 531, Ashtabula, tel. (440) 964-3050, is set in the historic harbor area. They cook, they eat, they witness a full day of entertainment.

SEPTEMBER

The **Geneva Area Grape JAMboree,** tel. (440) 446-JAMB or (440) 446-5262, lets visitors taste freshly squeezed grape juice, wine, and other grape products. There is, of course, a display of grape stomping, which can be witnessed at no charge. Other activities include a pair of parades, amusements, and ethnic foods. In downtown Geneva.

Antiques, Crafts & Art Sale, Recreation Park, 5536 Lake Rd., Geneva-on-the-Lake, tel. (800) 862-9948, is free at this popular vacation spot.

OCTOBER

Halloween Happenings, Great Lake Medieval Fairgrounds, 3033 SR 534, Geneva, tel. (888) 633-4382, includes haunted hayrides, a spooky castle, and a ghost walk.

Look for a playground, too. Neither of these beaches charges an admission.

There are beaches at Geneva State Park and, logically enough, at Geneva-on-the-Lake.

WINERIES

Wineries come thick and fast in this region, where lakeshore breezes prolong the growing season. Because wine preference is such a personal thing, travelers may disagree with any given endorsement. There are a few here, but sip a sample before buying a case. To further avoid argument, the wineries are listed in approximate east-to-west order.

Markko Vineyard, South Ridge Rd., Conneaut, tel. (440) 593-3197 or (800) 252-3197, isn't just people with money who always wanted to be in the winemaking business. Rather, the 14-acre vineyard has been earnestly crafting wine since 1968, producing quality products with good distribution. The best red at the moment is a soothing and superior 1993 Cabernet Sauvignon that retails for about $20 and can be found in good shops as far away as Dayton. Hours for tours are Mon.-Sat. 11 a.m.-6 p.m.

Buccia Vineyards, 518 Gore Rd., Conneaut, tel. (440) 593-5976, is rustic and family owned, has a bed and breakfast facility on site, and features an arbored picnic table, tasting, and sales rooms surrounded by vineyards and an orchard. A popular wine here is Maiden's Blush, priced at $5.90 per bottle. It and other Buccia vineyards are available in local stores. Open Mon.-Sat. all day long. "We're a family-operated place; I can't be more specific about hours," says an employee.

Rolling Hills Winery, 768-69 S. Parish Rd., Conneaut, tel. (440) 599-8833, is another small, family-run operation. It produces seven varieties, the most popular being Niagara at just $4.50 per bottle. There are tours and a tasting room. Hours are Mon.-Thurs. 4:30-6 p.m., Friday 4:30-8 p.m., and Saturday noon-6 p.m.

Old Mill Winery, 403 S. Broadway (SR 534), Geneva, tel. (440) 466-5560, is a winery that also is a bar. The winery produces 17 different vintages, the most popular at the moment being Geneva Blush, which sells for $7 per bottle. Rock bands perform on Friday and Saturday nights; there are no cover charges. Summer hours are Tues.-Thurs. and Sunday 1-9 p.m., Fri.-Sat. 1 p.m.-1 a.m. In the winter, it's Tues.-Thurs. and Sunday 1-6 p.m., Fri.-Sat. 1 p.m.-1 a.m. Old Mill wines also are available in local stores.

Harpersfield Vineyards, 6387 SR 307, Geneva, tel. (440) 466-4739, sells five wine varieties, four white and one red. The most popular offering are the chardonnays, available at $16-20. Personnel here say their 1995 vintages were the best ever. Harpersfield wines also are available in Cleveland restaurants and retail outlets and in wine shops in Columbus and Cincinnati. The tasting room is open Wed.-Fri. 2-8 p.m., Saturday 2-10 p.m.

Old Firehouse Winery, 5499 Lake Rd., Geneva-on-the-Lake, tel. (440) 466-9300 or (800) 862-6751, is quaint and popular with tourists. A patio and gazebo overlook Lake Erie, making for a great setting where travelers can sample vintages and enjoy food from the winery's full-service restaurant. Tours are available. A Firehouse favorite is frosty peach, a dessert wine, at $6.99 per bottle. The Firehouse is open only in summer, weekends only in May, daily through September. Live music is scheduled every evening in July and August, with acoustic folk being typical fare.

Among the more venerable vineyards is **Ferrante Winery & Ristorante,** 5585 SR 307, Geneva, tel. (440) 466-VINO or (440) 466-8466. Some 17 wines were offered here at last count, from Rosso at $5.99 to Cabernet Sauvignon at $12.99. Besides the airy tasting room, the restaurant is a nice place to sample Ferrante vintages by the glass. For kids, there's either red grape juice or white. Hours are Mon.-Tues. noon-5 p.m.; Wed.-Thurs. noon-9 p.m.; Fri.-Sat. noon-11 p.m.; and Sunday 1-7 p.m. Ferrante wines are available in numerous shops in Cleveland, too.

ACCOMMODATIONS

A delightful place to stay is **Warner-Concord Farms,** half a mile east of Unionville (or about three miles west of Geneva) on SR 84, tel. (440) 428-4485. The 8,000 sq. ft. barnlike structure has a pair of guest rooms and several fireplaces. Prices are moderate to expensive and include a bottle of locally produced wine. Conneaut B&B facilities include **Buccia's Vineyard,** Gore Rd., tel. (440) 593-5976, where each of four rooms has its own six-person hot tub; **Bridgeview Bed & Breakfast,** 1920 Bridgeview St., tel. (419) 593-6767; **Campbell Braemer Bed & Breakfast,** 390 State St., tel. (440) 599-7362; **Homestead Bed & Breakfast,** 263 Daniels Ave., tel. (440) 599-2237; and **Liberty Inn,** 353 Liberty St., tel. (419) 593-6767.

There are several chain motels convenient to I-90. The moderately priced **Days Inn,** is located at 600 Days Blvd., Conneaut, tel. (440) 593-6000. In Ashtabula there are three facilities at the junction of SR 45 and I-90. They include the **Hampton Inn,** tel. (440) 275-2000); the **Holiday Inn,** tel. (440) 275-2711; and **TraveLodge,** tel. (440) 275-2011.

The Geneva area is an accommodations-rich environment: in Geneva-on-the-Lake there are 31 sets of cottages, six campgrounds, 14 motels, and a trio of bed and breakfast operations. Virtually all of the facilities are on or near SR 531, Geneva-on-the-Lake's commercial strip. It's also possible to rent an entire house, which may sleep as many as a dozen vacationers who know each other. Ashtabula's contribution to B&B comfort is **Michael Cahill Bed & Breakfast,** 1106 Walnut Blvd., tel. (440) 964-8449.

As for prices, they are seasonal but for the chain operations near the interstate highway. Bed and

anglers can take advantage of charter fishing all along the Erie coastline

breakfast facilities tend to fall within the moderate price range, and so do cottages in and around Geneva-on-the-Lake when rented by the week.

FOOD

A real find whether with kids or not is the **Covered Bridge Pizza Parlor & Eatery,** 6541 S Main St. (SR 193), tel. (440) 224-0497, just a few feet south of US 20 in North Kingsville between Conneaut and Ashtabula. The pies are mildly but subtly flavored and will please children and adults alike. Quality food, low prices (figure $5 per person), and the fact that the restaurant once really was half a covered bridge make up for the fact that credit cards aren't accepted. Hours are Sun.-Thurs. 11 a.m.-midnight and Fri.-Sat. 11 a.m.-1 a.m. The same folks also operate a carryout-only pizza site at 341 Center St., Ashtabula, tel. (440) 992-8155.

Doxsie Deli Eatery, 1001 Bridge St., Ashtabula, tel. (440) 964-9888, gives diners a view of the Ashtabula harbor lift bridge. Open 8 a.m.-4 p.m. every day, the restaurant's most famous offering is its formidably sized corned-beef sandwich, priced at $4.85. Lots of folks like to order the breakfast special, which consists of two eggs, sausage or bacon, home fries, and toast for $3.25. They then enjoy it and several cups of coffee as they watch the lift bridge go up and down.

Moy's Special Occasion Restaurant, 2339 West Ave., Ashtabula, tel. (440) 964-6877, is another of those very satisfactory Asian places one can find in many Ohio towns. This one has a slight twist, adding a couple of Japanese dishes to the menu and offering such American standards as broiled walleye. Spicy Szechuan and mellow Cantonese cuisines are the standbys of Moy's menu, however. Try kung pao chicken at $7.25, Cantonese hong shue shrimp at $9.75, or press duck at $8.50. Japanese items include teriyaki steak at $11.75 and tempura shrimp at $10.50. The walleye is $8.50 and includes a choice of American or Asian sides. Moy's is open every day for lunch and dinner.

El Grande Steakhouse, 2145 W. Prospect St., Ashtabula, tel. (440) 998-2228, has been cooking under the same owner for 35 years. Luncheon favorites include a steak or chicken kabob salad or an open-faced steak sandwich.

The latter is $7.85. In the evening, dinners range from spaghetti with a choice of meatballs or sausage for $6.95 to a big sirloin steak at $15.75. It's open Tues.-Thurs. 11 a.m.-9 p.m., Friday 11 a.m.-10 p.m., and Saturday 4-10:30 p.m. One reason for El Grande customer loyalty is that folks can show up at closing time, and they will go away later, fed.

White Turkey Drive-In, 388 E. Main Rd., Conneaut, tel. (440) 593-2209, flies in the the face of all restaurant success stories. Its menu is limited, it's only open seasonally, and it doesn't break the bank on advertising and promotion. What it does do, very well, is serve up turkey sandwiches and root beer to locals and to visitors who are aware of its existence. The sandwiches are thick, juicy, and sell for only $2.50. Root beer comes in two sizes, one for slightly less than a buck, one for slightly more. The drive-in is open for lunch and dinner from Mother's Day weekend through the weekend after Labor Day.

INFORMATION AND SERVICES

In Conneaut and Ashtabula, call police or medical assistance in an emergency by dialing 911. In a non-emergency, call (440) 593-6291. Medical services in Conneaut are available at Brown Memorial Hospital, tel. (440) 593-1131. The Conneaut post office is at 268 State Street.

In Ashtabula the police can be reached at (440) 998-1141. Medical services are available at the Ashtabula County Medical Center, tel. (440) 997-2262.

The **Conneaut Board of Tourism** is at 289 Main St., tel. (440) 593-2402. The **Ashtabula County Convention and Visitors Bureau** is at 36 W. Walnut St. in Jefferson, tel. (440) 576-4707 or (800) 337-6746. The **Ashtabula Area Chamber of Commerce** is at 4366 Main Ave., Ashtabula, tel. (440) 998-6998. The **Geneva Area Chamber of Commerce** is at 866 E. Main St., Geneva, tel. (440) 466-8694. The **Geneva-on-the-Lake Convention and Visitors Bureau** is at 5536 Lake Rd., tel. (440) 466-8600.

Ashtabulans read the *Star-Beacon* every morning. There a helpful entertainment section published each Friday.

The **Ashtabula Mall** is on US 20, just east of SR 11. A good place to shop for locally produced wines is the **Wet Your Whistle Stop,** 6663 N. Ridge Rd., Ashtabula, tel. (440) 428-5339. With its large marina, you'll find nautical items for sale in Ashtabula's Harbor District.

The Ashtabula County Transportation System operates buses in the area. Cost of a ride varies. Within the same township, a one-way fare is $1. Between townships, on a one-way trip from Ashtabula to Conneaut, for example, the fare is $1.50. Call (440) 992-4411 or (800) 445-4140 for details. Greyhound Bus Lines stops in Ashtabula at 1819 E. Prospect Rd. The local terminal can be reached by telephone at (440) 992-7550.

LORAIN COUNTY

Lorain County is a mix of industry, agriculture, suburban sprawl, and small-town living. A traveler can find a modern, bustling Ford assembly facility in Avon Lake just a few miles away from a rustic corner store at a county crossroads; it's hard to believe the two are only a few miles apart. Lorain has slightly more than 70,000 people who call the lakeside city home, while Elyria lists a total of about 57,000 residents. Avon Lake dwellers total 15,000, Vermilion's population exceeds 11,000, Amherst has more than 10,000, Oberlin's population totals 8,200, and Wellington has 4,100 citizens. One of the county's biggest get-togethers, Lorain's International Festival each June, accurately mirrors the dozens of nationalities who became Americans and local residents.

History

Native Americans once were plentiful here, but in 1805 a treaty was signed that made this area west of the Cuyahoga River accessible to settlers, who quickly started up towns such as Lorain and Elyria, the Lorain County seat. Both were settled shortly after Ohio became a state in 1803. New Englanders and others crossed the Cuyahoga River and continued westward, finding fertile, if low-lying, land along the lake. By 1820, large ships were calling at the port of Lorain, braving treacherous storms that were to make Erie infamous among the country's big northern lakes. By 1830, Elyria had Ohio's first true high school; citizens there weren't content with children learning only the basics. Meanwhile, anti-slavery sentiment was growing among religious faculty and students at Oberlin College in Oberlin. They and several local citizens, including former slaves, turned the county into one of the busiest routes on the Underground Railroad.

Lorain came into its own as a shipbuilding center in the 20th century. Many of the huge freighters carrying ore, coal, and grain were crafted here by a rich stew of ethnic laborers. Besides shipbuilding, the county puts together a vast number of Ford cars and vans. Lorain and Elyria in recent years have attempted to clean up municipal governments, improving downtown areas that at one time were little but boarded-up buildings. The city of Lorain also has undertaken restoration of the Jewel of the Port, a picturesque lighthouse visible from the local waterfront. Vermilion has little or no industry, relying instead on tourism for much of its well-being.

Oberlin at present is an unpretentious, quiet, Bohemian village. The editor of a local newspaper once called it "Lorain County's Greenwich Village," which still seems accurate. Picturesque Tappan Square is the center of town, and Oberlin College is the center of activity. The school has a lot of musicians and students interested in equality and progressive living in a part of the country that sometimes values other things. Nine miles south of Oberlin, Wellington is worth a visit because three-fourths of the downtown district is on the National Register of Historic Places. New England's rich influence on the architecture is evident. The town is in the middle of the state's dairyland and was the hometown of Archibald M. Willard, the fellow who painted the classic "Spirit of '76." Several Willard originals hang in the town library at 101 Willard Memorial Square, tel. (440) 647-2120.

Location and Orientation

Lorain County is the first county west of Cleveland. Bounded by Lake Erie on the north, the area is served by east-west running I-80 (the Ohio Turnpike), which merges with I-90 just west of Elyria. Other major east-west roads include SR

VALOR IN OBERLIN

Slave catchers from outside Ohio could, under federal law, conduct their dirty business anywhere. Sometimes, they openly grabbed free black people off Ohio streets, taking them south for a life of misery. Yet even when the slave catchers carried valid papers, they often were run out of northern Ohio towns. No village objected to the capture of runaway slaves more strongly than Oberlin, where a number of peace-loving and slavery-hating young men attended college. Oberlin became known as "the town that started the Civil War" following a confrontation over a captured resident.

John Price, a fugitive slave, was taken off an Oberlin street by a federal marshal on a late-summer day in 1858. In order to move the captive south, the lawman had to first get himself and Price south to Wellington to catch a train. Oberlin students, faculty members, and town residents, black and white, pursued the marshal and worked with people from Wellington to free Price. A grand jury quickly indicted 37 men from the two towns, charging them with violating the federal Fugitive Slave Law. Two men, Simeon Bushnell, who was white, and Charles Langston, who was black, were convicted and sent to jail. Others were held in custody for varying lengths of time.

State courts were approached with appeals, despite the fact that the pair had been convicted of breaking federal law. Strong and determined abolitionists staged rallies in Cleveland and elsewhere that brought thousands of people into the streets. The case reached the Ohio Supreme Court, where the Fugitive Slave Law was judged constitutional on a 3-2 vote. But by then the sentences imposed on Bushnell and Langston were nearly served. They emerged as martyrs and the charges against the remaining 35 were dropped. A "grand gathering" was held in Oberlin to celebrate their freedom.

2, which is a divided highway, US 20, and SR 18. North-south highways include State Routes 57, 58, and 83. There is an entrance-exit to I-80 (Ohio Turnpike) at SR 57 on the north edge of Elyria. Elyria, which is also the county seat, is about 30 miles southwest of Cleveland, 90 miles east of Toledo, and approximately 125 miles northeast of Columbus (all figures are highway miles). Vermilion lies just beyond the western boundary of Lorain County, near SR 60.

SIGHTS

Don't confuse **Findley State Park,** SR 58, tel. (440) 647-4490, with the city of Findlay. They are spelled differently and the city is some 90 miles west of the state park. Some 20 miles south of Lake Erie along SR 58, Findley State Park lies atop the world's thickest deposit of sandstone. The former state forest harbors deer, fox, beaver, raccoon, and various reptiles, including turtles, amid its 838 acres of land and 93 acres of earthen-dammed stream. Several hiking trails and one multipurpose trail have been laid out under pines and hardwoods such as red maple, white ash, and wild black cherry. Given the right time of year, the display of wildflowers on the forest floor and in the meadows can be spectacular. Camping, boating, hunting for migratory waterfowl, fishing, swimming, and picnicking are popular activities, though only electric motors are allowed on Findley Lake. Nearby natural destinations include **Wellington State Wildlife Area,** just across the highway to the west, plus Wellington and Old Woman Creek State Nature Preserve to the north. South of the park are Ashland and Spencer Wildlife Area and Fowler Woods State Nature Preserve. Findley is two miles south of Wellington.

The lowslung **Weltzheimer-Johnson House,** 127 Woodhaven Dr., Oberlin, tel. (440) 775-8665, was architect Frank Lloyd Wright's first attempt at "Usonian" design (which Wright defined as "useful for the average citizen") design in the Buckeye State. On the west side of town, set back from the road in a grove of trees on one side and a cul-de-sac on the other, the college-owned, brick-and-wood home has a very low, flat roof, red concrete floors, and other unique Wright touches. It's open for tours on the hour from 1-5 p.m. on the first Sunday and third Saturday of each month. Admission is $5 per person.

There are a couple of wineries in this immediate area. They include **John Christ Winery,** 32421 Walker Rd., Avon Lake, tel. (440) 933-9672; and **Klingshirn Winery,** 33050 Webber Rd., also in Avon Lake, tel. (440) 933-6666. Neither offers tours, but their wines are available during normal busines hours, Mon.-Sat. 10 a.m.-6 p.m. Klingshirn Winery has been making wines since 1935, currently offering 16 different wines and three champagnes. Klingshirn's popular wines include White Riesling and Chancellor, but the biggest seller is a vin rosé for only $3.87. Tastings takes place at the counter, and fresh grape juice is available in the fall for drinking or for home winemaking.

The Black River is spanned by an intriguing drawbridge in downtown Lorain. The facility is the world's longest **bascule drawbridge,** measuring 333 ft. and completed in 1940. For those who are unfamiliar with the design, a bascule bridge is counterweighted. The floor of this drawbridge rises because there's a comparable weight being lowered. Boats sail beneath the suspended floor once an adequate height is reached. The bridge is on US 6 (West River Road).

Tours

The state's best self-guided tour runs all around Oberlin. The **African-American Heritage Driving Tour** takes visitors past a number of sites that harbored former slaves in their trip to Canada on the Underground Railroad. Besides actual houses there are memorials to the slaves, to the Oberlin Anti-Slavery Society, and to local people who gave time, money, and their lives to keep the Union together. The most striking is

White-tailed deer are commonly found in Lorain County's state parks and nature preserve.

the most literal: the Underground Railroad sculpture is a pair of iron tracks, crossed by railroad ties, that juts out of the ground on the Oberlin College campus. Tour maps are available without charge; call the Oberlin Area Chamber of Commerce, tel. (800) 9-OBERLIN or (800) 962-3754, to find out where to pick up a map. Those who would like a guided tour should contact the Lorain County Visitors Bureau, tel. (440) 245-5282 or (800) 334-1673. Cost of the guided version is $50 for groups of 12-50 persons. Tour times are flexible.

The *Mystic Belle,* offers harbor tours in the town of Vermilion, tel. (440) 967-5025. In vivid contrast to the big passenger haulers in Sandusky and Port Clinton, this little sternwheeler with a capacity of 28 chugs the Vermilion River and Lagoon every hour on the hour, 1-9 p.m., in the summer. It's docked at 5150 Liberty Ave. (US 6). Fares are $5 for adults, $4 for seniors, and $4 for children 12 and under.

MUSEUMS

Allen Memorial Art Museum, 87 N. Main St., Oberlin, tel. (440) 775-8665, contains an astounding 14,000 works of art—making it one of the nation's most complete college art museums. The big stone building on the east side of the street houses examples by Turner, Matisse, Warhol, and many other familiar names. Hours are Tues.-Sat. 10 a.m.-5 p.m. and Sunday 1-5 p.m. There is no charge here, though the museum is pleased to accept a $2-per-person donation.

Other museums in this area include the **Inland Seas Maritime Museum,** 480 Main St., Vermilion, tel. (440) 967-3467. Among several fascinating exhibits is one on the *Edmund Fitzgerald,* the Great Lakes freighter that broke apart in a Lake Superior storm in 1975. The *Fitzgerald* also can be seen on a video presentation here. Hours are 10 a.m.-5 p.m. every day except major holidays, when the facility is closed. Admissions are $5 for adults, $4 for seniors, $3 for students under 16, and $10 for a family of two adults and unlimited children.

Smaller museums, most of which have weekend hours, hold fascination for history buffs. Consider the **Benjamin Bacon Museum,** the **Hickories Museum,** and the **Spirit of '76 Museum.**

LORAIN COUNTY EVENTS

FEBRUARY

African American History Festival, 1875 Lorain Blvd., Elyria, tel. (440) 366-5656 takes place inside the local Holiday Inn.

APRIL

Arts, Crafts, & Collectibles Show & Sale is at Commodore's Place, 995 State St., Vermilion, tel. (440) 967-4262 or (440) 967-7737.

MAY

Military Items Exhibit, Spirit of '76 Museum, 201 N. Main St., Wellington, tel. (440) 647-3674, includes displays from the Civil War to the Vietnam War.

Antique Show, Lorain County Fairgrounds, SR 18 West, Wellington, tel. (440) 647-3245, is put on by the Southern Lorain County Historical Society.

Firemen's Festival, Willow Park, Grafton, tel. (440) 926-2428, includes the usual firefighters' water fight and other related activities, including crafts, games, and food.

JUNE

Festival of the Fish, tel. (440) 967-4477, salutes the sleek Lake Erie dwellers with activities in Vermilion's Victory Park. Look for crafts, food booths, children's rides, entertainment, and a parade during the three-day fête.

Oberlin College Conservatory of Music, tel. (440) 775-8200, gives workshops and performances, mid-June through early August, featuring faculty members and guest artists.

Model Shipbuilding Show & Competition, Inland Seas Maritime Museum, 480 N. Main St., Vermilion, tel. (800) 893-1485, includes displays and how-to seminars. There's also a free antique wooden boat show at the city docks.

Ohio Scottish Games Weekend, Oberlin, tel. (440) 442-2147, observes these Scottish traditions: piping, drumming, and parade of tartans, among many.

Lorain International Festival tel. (440) 282-6263, takes place over three days and features 55 distinct nationalities. The fun includes a princess pageant, a parade, an international breakfast, and music ranging from the sacred to the obscure. If travelers fail to find food they like here, they're missing lots of unusual treats. Great costumes, too.

JULY

Afro-American Festival, 1825 Lorain Blvd., Elyria, tel. (440) 366-5656, is a celebration of culture. The event is held at the local Holiday Inn.

Old Time Jamboree, Amherst, tel. (440) 988-5329, is a two-day, community-wide event. Besides a parade there are line dancers and street dancers, as well as food, entertainment, and crafts.

Aircraft Past & Present, 44050 Russia Rd., Elyria, tel. (440) 323-4063, flies into the Lorain County Regional Airport. Military and civilian aircraft are on display, along with classic cars.

AUGUST

The **North Ridgeville Corn Festival** gives guests a choice of corn prepared Amish style or roasted. Admission and entertainment are free and there are carnival rides, games, 5- and a 10-K race, a horseshoe tournament, and various corn contests. Call (440) 327-3737 for more.

OCTOBER

The **Woolybear Festival,** tel. (800) 334-1673, proves no one knows what will catch on. This Vermilion funfest is reputed to be one of the state's largest one-day events. It includes a seemingly endless parade, radio and TV personalities, food, crafts, kiddy rides, and a contest where humans try to look like the woolybear caterpillar.

South of Vermilion, the Bacon Museum is a Greek Revival mansion honoring a prominent local family and early pioneers on Vermilion Road south of I-90, tel. (440) 458-5121 or (440) 967-7310. The Hickories Museum, 509 Washington Ave., Elyria, tel. (440) 322-3341, is also the Lorain County Historical Society. Much of the original written and photographic record of Lorain County is here. As for the Spirit of '76 Museum, 201 N. Main St., Wellington, tel. (440) 647-4367, it salutes native Archibald Willard. He portrayed three Revolutionary War heroes in the painting for which the institution is named.

ENTERTAINMENT AND CULTURE

Artstown, 33491 Lake Rd., Avon Lake, tel. (440) 933-2617, is something more towns should have. What appears to have been a down-at-the-heels office complex has been turned into a hopeful cluster of artists' studios. There's a gallery on the first floor and studios with artists working in various media on the second. Artists being artists, they keep their own hours. Yet visitors can wander through here on any given day and watch local talent at work. Even better, they may be able to find the artwork or sculpture of their dreams. The facility is close to a massive electric generating plant on the opposite (lake) side of the street.

In a very different medium, there is live and recorded music at **Chances,** W. 39th St., which is off Broadway in Lorain, tel. (440) 233-7363. The bar has a Web site at www.en.com/users /3rdear/chances. Techno records and tapes are played every Tuesday and occasionally a blues band will show up. **Coolers,** 37399 French Creek Rd., Avon, tel. (440) 934-9225, has music on Friday and Saturday. Sometimes the tunes are live, sometimes a DJ orchestrates things, and no cover is charged in either case.

Check the playbill at the restored **Lorain Palace Civic Center,** 617 Broadway, tel. (440) 245-2323. The grand old theater has been refurbished and offers live stage shows, movies, and private-use rentals amid spiffy splendor. Call first to see if there's anyone to show travelers around.

RECREATION

Bicycling

A pair of bicycle trails are worth noting. The shorter of the two runs diagonally across Oberlin, to Pyle Road (which leads north to South Amherst). It is entirely paved, measures 3.2 miles and eventually will be part of the North Coast Inland Trail. The other is a longer, east-west route that cuts across the county on paved roads from Grafton Eastern Road in the east, through Oberlin, exiting the county in the west on Garfield Road, just south of SR 113. The bikeway, which eventually will run between Cleveland and Toledo, is signed for cyclists. The run across the county from east to west takes riders through the transition from metro Cleveland to farm country.

Golf

A nice public facility is **Forest Hills Golf Course,**

41971 Oberlin Rd., Elyria, tel. (440) 323-2632. The par 70 course charges $9 for nine holes and $13 for 18, with fees reduced slightly on weekdays. Cart rental is $5 for nine or $10 for 18 holes.

Fishing

Virtually anywhere a fisher sees a breakwater, fishing is permitted (with a current state license). There's a just-completed fishing pier at Miller Road Park in Avon Lake, tel. (440) 933-6333. It's off Lake Road (US 6), between SR 301 and SR 83. In Lorain, Lakeside Landing, off Colorado Street, one block north of US 6, tel. (440) 204-2269, is a popular angling spot. Charters abound in Lorain County. Call the Lorain County Convention Bureau, tel. (440) 245-5282 or (800) 334-1673 for an impartial list, or try Lorain's Central Basin Charter Boat Association, tel. (800) 686-4702. A fishing report is broadcast daily during the season on WEOL radio at 930 AM.

Hiking

Walkers and hikers will be pleasantly surprised at the quality and quantity of paths here. Two Falls Trail, Lake Avenue, tel. (440) 365-7101, in Elyria is a 3.5-mile route along two branches of the Black River. It's an opportune place to see birds—depending on the season, the lowland area plays host to ducks, woodcocks, kingfishers, and buntings. Another neat place to walk in Elyria is Cascade Park, at West River Road and Furnace Street, tel. (440) 365-7101. Hiking trails in this 155-acre plot pass waterfalls, picnic areas, and playgrounds. Most of the other good hiking trails are in Lorain County Metroparks. They include Caley National Wildlife Woods, West Road, Pittsfield Township; French Creek Reservation, Colorado Avenue in Sheffield Village; or Vermilion River Reservation, Vermilion Road in Brownhelm Township. The telephone number for the Metroparks is (440) 458-5121.

Swimming

The beaches here aren't as spectacular as a couple of stretches east of Cleveland, but they are perfectly acceptable. Try Lakeview Park beach in Lorain, tel. (440) 244-9000, just off US 6 between SR 57 and SR 58, or Sharod Park beach in Vermilion, west of the downtown area. Neither charges for swimming or sunning.

ACCOMMODATIONS

The junction of the Ohio Turnpike (I-80/90) and SR 57, near Elyria, is thick with motels, most of them franchises. Smaller clusters of accommodations in the county can be found in North Ridgeville and Vermilion. A couple of non-franchise places to consider are the resortish **Aqua Marine,** 216 Miller Rd., Avon Lake, tel. (800) 335-9343, with accessible golfing, and **Spitzer Plaza,** 301 Broadway Ave., Lorain, tel. (800) 446-7452. Another is the **Oberlin Inn,** 7 N. Main St., Oberlin, tel. (800) 376-4173. All are in the expensive range.

FOOD

Locals and visitors both like **Foxgrape Cafe & Catering,** 19 W. College St., Oberlin, tel. (440) 774-1457. Open for breakfast, lunch, and dinner Mon.-Sat. and lunch and dinner Sunday, this is a popular place for all three meals. Start the morning with corn jacks, which are corn pancakes bearing apples or blueberries or chocolate chips, for $3.95. On the menu for breakfast or lunch is a veggie-egg tart, resembling a quiche, for $5.95. Other luncheon goodies include a tarragon walnut chicken salad for $6.95 or a barbecue chicken salad for a dollar less. Evenings, look to the shrimp, garlic, and veggie stir-fry for $15.95, or one of several steaks.

Much of Elyria's small retail area has moved to suburban malls, leaving a good place to eat like **Moss's Prime Rib and Spaghetti House** a singular attraction downtown at 209 Broad St., tel. (440) 322-8611. Open lunch for Tues.-Fri. and for dinner Mon.-Sat., Moss's lunches include a number of homemade specials for $5.95. On a given day that could be a triple-deck turkey club sandwich with soup, chicken parmesan, or crab cakes. In the evening, there's a petite prime rib for $11.95 and an expansive prime rib for $22.95. The evening menu also includes steaks, pastas, salads, and more. It all looks and tastes deliciously homemade.

Even if a visitor stays elsewhere, he or she might want to sample the dining room in the **Oberlin Inn,** 7 N. Main St., Oberlin, tel. (800) 376-4173. Open every day for all three meals, the restaurant dishes up an expansive breakfast special: two eggs, bacon or sausage, pancakes, and hash browns, all for $5.95. At lunch, a French dip roast beef sandwich, priced at $5.75, is popular. In the evening a popular choice is lightly breaded walleye at $11.95. The staff appears post-collegiate and is most friendly.

Those who can't wait around for the county's big International Festival in June can sample excellent Old World fare at **Old Prague Restaurant,** 5586 Liberty Ave. (US 6), Vermilion, tel. (440) 967-7182. This landmark serves Czech and other Central European foods in an authentic atmosphere. At lunch, consider fragrant cabbage rolls, $4.75. In the evening, roast duck at $12, served with red cabbage, is wildly popular. Other dishes range from various dumplings and Wiener schnitzels to chicken paprikash and goulash. Don't overlook either the soups or the strudels, both of which are radiantly filling and made on the premises. The bar is complete, too, with eight Czech beers and a range of European wines. Old Prague is open for lunch and dinner every day March-Oct., and Fri.-Sun. Nov.-Feb.

Yala's, 3352 Oberlin Ave., Lorain, tel. (440) 282-5169, sells very good carryout-only pizzas. The price is right: a 12-inch pie, cut into 12 slices and carrying three toppings, is a mere $8.95. There are other variations, but the pizza is the thing here. No alcoholic beverages, but diners can luxuriate in either Coca-Cola or Pepsi. Yala's also operates a takeaway pie place in Vermilion at 4676 Liberty Ave., tel. (440) 567-1099. Hours are Tues.-Sat. 11 a.m.-11 p.m. and Sun.-Mon. 3-11 p.m. Carry the pie and sodas to the Black River Wharf Boat Launch, off East 14th Street at Broadway Avenue (SR 57) in Lorain. There's a sheltered picnic area with a nice view of lakefront activity.

SHOPPING

More than 120 stores can be found inside **Midway Mall,** between West River Road and SR 57, tel. (440) 324-5749, on the edge of Elyria. There are several strip malls in the same vicinity, near I-80/90 (the Ohio Turnpike).

There are several alternatives to the megamerchants. They include Apple Barrel Country Place, 40981 SR 18 East, Penfield Township, tel. (440) 647-3323, a good place to stop for plants and baked goods; Durkee's General Store, 919

Main St., Grafton, tel. (440) 926-3488, which has oiled wood floors and sells nostalgic items; and McQuaid's Mercantile, 654 Grand St., Vermilion, tel. (440) 967-7989, selling a mix of nautical, Christmas, and other items.

At least three places in Oberlin are worth a visit. One is the independent Co-op Bookstore, 37 W. College St., tel. (440) 774-3741. The Co-op stocks lots of text and other books, sheet music, and souvenirs. Dave's Army-Navy, 29 S. Main St., tel. (440) 774-3283, sells camping gear, footwear, and the kinds of clothing college kids sometimes like to be seen in. The third site is the East of Oberlin Flea Market, 43433 Elyria-Oberlin Rd., tel. (440) 774-4312. Nearly 50 vendors show up here to peddle food, antiques, collectibles, and crafts.

INFORMATION AND SERVICES

For emergency police and medical assistance dial 911. For non-emergency assistance or information, the Lorain County Sheriff Department can be reached at (440) 244-0373.

The **Lorain County Visitors Bureau** is at 611 Broadway, Lorain, tel. (440) 245-5282 or (800) 334-1673. The vistors' bureau Web site is at www.lcvb.org. The **North Ridgeville Visitors Bureau** can be found at 7307 Avon Belden Rd., tel. (440) 327-3737. The **Oberlin Area Chamber of Commerce** can be reached at (800) 9-OBERLIN or (800) 962-3754. The general number for Oberlin College is (440) 775-8121. The Oberlin Inn, 7 N. Main St., tel. (440) 775-8100, has calendars of college events available fresh each Friday.

Visitors can choose between a morning and an evening newspaper when visiting Lorain County. The earlier daily is the *Morning Journal,* produced every day of the week in Lorain. It runs a Sunday entertainment section, "Arcade." The *Elyria Chronicle-Telegram,* available evenings and Sunday mornings, offers entertainment news in its "Encore" section every Thursday.

Amtrak has a train station and makes regular stops in Elyria. The station is on Buckeye Street, near the intersection of East Bridge and East River Streets, tel. (800) 872-7245. **Greyhound** pays calls to Elyria at 401 Lake Ave., tel. (440) 322-0000. Local bus service is provided by **Lorain County Transit,** tel. (440) 949-2525 or (800) 225-7703. Fares are $1.25 for adults and 60 cents for children.

SANDUSKY~OHIO'S LAKESIDE PLAYGROUND

Though Native Americans knew for centuries about the area that points toward the Lake Erie islands, it was not until about 1750 that Europeans visited. Lake commerce was brisk in the 19th century but peaked and then subsided in the immediate area, so Sandusky and the lakefront evolved into a leading North Coast tourist destination.

History

The French established a fort near an Indian village named Sandusky on Lake Erie in the middle of the 18th century. They realized that conflict with Great Britain might soon take place and they wanted to be ready. In fact, it could have been from this spot, where the Sandusky River flows into the big lake, that a band of French and Indians mustered prior to heading south to sack British Fort Pickawillany, near present-day Piqua. Little else is known until the European-American town of Sandusky was developed in the first decade of the 19th century.

The town grew, populated by the large sailing and steamships that called along the shoreline. Despite being promised a canal that never materialized, Sandusky did well enough, shipping large quantities of coal to other sites on the Great Lakes. A bit later, in 1838, Sandusky and the Mad River Company laid 16 miles of railroad track to Bellevue. By 1848, the line reached all the way to Springfield.

Early on the city manufactured a number of items, including aircraft parts only a few years after the Wright brothers' first flight in 1903. A bit later, progressive elements in the town opted for a city manager form of government. From the 1920s onward, Sandusky became recognized as the gateway to the Lake Erie islands and a vacation destination in its own right. Today, with a permanent population of approximately 22,000, Sandusky is all but overrun in the summer by visitors to Cedar Point and the surrounding area.

As for nearby towns, Milan (MY-lun) is known as the birthplace of Thomas A. Edison, the consummate American inventor. But it was known earlier for having a short canal that allowed farmers to more quickly get their grain to market. The wheat shipping bonanza lasted only until the mid-1850s, when the Lake Shore Railroad was completed. Vermilion, east along the lake, began as a fishing village near the Lorain-Erie county line. Nowadays, it's a picturesque place with a historic downtown area. Huron, between Vermilion and Sandusky, is a resort town on a smaller scale. Norwalk and Bellevue, both inland, depend on a mix of agriculture and industry for their ongoing prosperity.

Location and Orientation

Erie County stretches along the lake for a distance of almost 30 miles. Sandusky is located in the western half of that expanse of lakefront. Milan, population 1,500, is a dozen miles southeast of Sandusky, while Norwalk, population 14,700, is three miles south of Milan. Both are accessible via US 250. West of Norwalk 14 miles on US 20 is the city of Bellevue (pop. 8,100). The Ohio Turnpike, I-80/90, cuts across the county between Sandusky to the north and the towns Milan, Norwalk, and Bellevue to the south. US 20 runs parallel to I-80/90 a couple of miles to the south. Limited-access SR 2 enters the county near Vermilion and departs for Port Clinton after swinging around just south of Sandusky. Major north-south highways include US 250, which goes to Ashland, and SR 4, to Bucyrus (bu-SIGH-rus). Sandusky is 65 miles west of Cleveland, 60 miles east of Toledo, and 110 miles north of Columbus.

SIGHTS

The **Thomas Edison Birthplace,** an almost fairytale red brick cottage at 9 Edison Dr., Milan, tel. (419) 499-2135, lies on the east side of this blissful little town. Edison's daughter once was a director of this site, so rest assured that the artifacts are genuine. The home is covered with the help of tour guides. Hours are from Tues.-Sat. 10

a.m.-4:30 p.m. and Sunday 1-4:30 p.m. from Memorial Day to Labor Day. Hours the rest of the year are Tues.-Sun. 1-4:30 p.m. Access costs $5 for an adult, $4 for a senior, and $2 for children ages 6-12.

The **Firelands Winery,** at 917 Bardshar Rd., Sandusky, tel. (419) 625-5474 or (800) 548-9463, is the largest winery associated with Lake Erie. It was begun in 1880 and currently produces two dozen wines, including Firelands, Cabernet Sauvignon, Chardonnay, Riesling, Gewurztraminer, and Pinot Noir. Best sellers are Chardonnay at $9.99 and Cabernet Sauvignon at $10.49. Besides a tour and a multimedia presentation, there is an opportunity to pick grapes for home consumption. A cooking school takes place here Nov.-June. Its hours are May-Sept. Mon.-Sat. 9 a.m.-5 p.m., Sunday 1-5 p.m.; Oct.-Dec. it has the same hours but is closed on Sunday; Jan.-May it's open Mon.-Fri. 9 a.m.-5 p.m., Saturday 10 a.m.-4 p.m., closed on Sunday.

Cedar Point

Ohio's mega-amusement park pulls them in from all over. A map on a brochure for the facility gives pinpoint directions from as far away as Toronto and Indianapolis. No wonder—the park on the peninsula, north of US 250, has a dozen roller-coasters, more than anywhere else on earth. With names like Magnum, Mantis, and Raptor, the devices should be off limits to anyone

with a bad heart. Other thrill rides, of which there are 59, include Power Tower, where visitors are hauled to a dizzying height atop a multistory, Erector Set-like contraption, then dropped, screaming all the way. Snake River Falls and Thunder Canyon are two more rides calculated to scare the starch out of paying customers. For those with small children, there are rides aboard everything from swans to oldtime cars, all safely on some kind of track or planned pathway.

Additional attractions include Challenger Park and Soak City, both of which are next door. The former has a grand prix racetrack, two 18-hole miniature golf courses, and RipCord, which sends tethered consumers plummeting toward the ground from a height of 15 stories. Soak City is a waterpark with a wave pool. It has every kind of slide save Kodachrome—speed slides, enclosed slides, tube slides, body slides, and additional slides in nearby play areas. Less stressful fun at the Point includes plays and live entertainment, as well as nighttime laser-fireworks shows that bring a raucous end to a raucous day.

Prices are multi-leveled and complex, but generally Cedar Point gate fees are $31.95 for persons who are 54 inches or taller and ages 4-59. Age four and older between 48 and 54 inches cost $27.95. Age four and older but under 48 inches slide through the gate for $16.95. Children three and under are free, while seniors (60 and up) pay $16.95. Separate fees for the RipCord,

Thomas Edison Birthplace, Milan

miniature golf, and the grand prix raceway are $24.95, $5.95, and $5.50, respectively. Cedar Point is open every day from mid-May through Labor Day, then open weekends to mid-October. Soak City opens later in May and closes on Labor Day. For more information, call (419) 627-2350 or consult the Web site at www.cedar-point.com.

Museums
The **Follett House Museum,** 404 Wayne St., Sandusky, tel. (419) 627-9608, is a nice reminder of what the area was like before it took on the Disneylike atmosphere. The limestone Greek Revival home was built in the 1830s and houses an interesting collection of apparel, antique furniture, wooden tobacconists' figures, artifacts from several wars, quilts, Indian relics, and a one-of-a-kind plate and music box. Admission is free and hours are 1-4 p.m. every day June-Labor Day. Hours are Sunday, Tuesday, Thursday 1-4 p.m. April-May and Labor Day-December. The museum is always decorated for the Christmas holidays, and there's a nice view of the city from the third-floor widow's walk.

There are several other area museums of note. They include the **Firelands Historical Society Museum,** 4 Case Ave., Norwalk, tel. (419) 668-6038, which tells about the special "fire lands" hereabouts, given to Connecticut veterans of the Revolutionary War whose homes were burned by British soldiers. The museum is open Tues.-Sun., noon-5 p.m. all summer long; weekends only noon-4 p.m. April-May and Sept.-Oct. Admission is $2 for adults and $1 for children ages 12-18.

The **Mad River Railroad Museum,** 233 York St., Bellevue, tel. (419) 483-2222, contains the usual memorabilia and is open 1-5 p.m. every day all summer, plus weekends in May and September-October. Donations are appreciated. Sandusky's **Merry-Go-Round Museum,** 279 E. Market St., tel. (419) 626-6111, contains a full-size county-fair carousel, has a restoration area, and schedules special exhibits such as armored horses. Hours are Mon.-Sat.11 a.m.-5 p.m. and Sunday noon-5 p.m., Memorial Day-Labor Day. The rest of the year, the facility observes the same hours but is closed Monday and Tuesday. Admission is $4 for adults, $3 for seniors, and $2 for children ages 4-14.

Across the street from the Thomas Edison Birthplace in Milan is the **Milan Historical Museum,** 10 Edison Dr., tel. (419) 499-2968, is a complex of buildings, including a general store, a blacksmith shop, the several 19th century homes, including the main building, originally a doctor's home, built 1846, as well as peaceful gardens and grounds. The museum is open in April, May, September and October, Tues.-Sun., 1-5 p.m.; in June, July and August, Tues.-Sat. 10 a.m.-5 p.m., Sunday 1-5 p.m.; the museum is closed Nov.-March, and on Monday throughout the year.

RECREATION

Bicycling
What with the summer traffic headed to and from Cedar Point, there are better places than Sandusky to ride a bike. Those who are determined should head for the town of Huron, 10 miles east of Sandusky on US 6. The town offers the **Milan Canal Bikeway,** a 27-mile loop that begins in the city park on Ohio Street. The level ride to and from Milan travels through wildlife sanctuaries and features several historic sites. A free trail map produced by Erie County is available from local tourism offices.

Canoeing
This is best accomplished on the Huron River, between Milan and Huron, a paddling distance of about seven miles. There are spots in both places in which to park and launch, but rental spots in the area tend to concentrate primarily on lake boats and lake fishing, so if you're really intent on canoeing, you're best advised to bring your own craft.

Fishing
The Ohio Department of Natural Resources has a toll-free fishing report (tel. 800-945-3543) that will let prospective Lake Erie anglers know what can be caught. While there are a number of fishing piers and promontories, most success is realized on a charter boat. Costs for walleye, perch, bass, and other fish average about $50-60 per person for a day on the water. Many boats will not take more than their normal capacity, which typically is six anglers.

THE ORIGINAL FOR SHERWOOD ANDERSON'S WINESBURG

Clyde, Ohio (population 5,800), seems a nice enough small town. Southwest of Sandusky on US 20, it is a mix of agriculture-related business and industry, with a smattering of retail thrown in. The residents are unremarkably Ohioan and American. That may be good enough for most of us, but it rubbed Sherwood Anderson (1876-1941) the wrong way. Born in Camden, Ohio, southwest of Dayton, he was an executive in a paint company located in Clyde. Anderson found small-town life in Clyde so stifling and devoid of intellectual rigor that he left his family, fled to Chicago, and established a bohemian literary life.

Clyde showed up in Anderson's third book as the book's namesake, *Winesburg, Ohio*. A fraction of its present size, Clyde/Winesburg takes a beating because it is shown as a stunted place, without much hope. People who live there are ground down to a level free of optimism or positive expectation.

Winesburg, Ohio, is a series of sketches involving different townspeople. Without beginnings or endings, these stories come at readers almost as if they stumbled across the characters on the sidewalk or in a cornfield. It has not been out of print since it was first published in 1919. Millions of college students have read it and been struck by the fact that the characters are similar to Mark Twain's, but without Twain's sense of humor. Anderson in turn influenced a number of writers, including Thomas Wolfe and William Faulkner. After Faulkner read Anderson, he immediately went home to write *Soldier's Pay,* marking the beginning of his incredible career.

Today a town actually named Winesburg lies a couple of hours east, in Holmes County. It's about the same size as was Clyde early in the century, but that's where the similarity ends. Regarding Sherwood Anderson, none of his six other books ever approached *Winesburg, Ohio,* in popularity.

Golf

The **Lodge at Sawmill Creek,** tel. (419) 433-3800, has a golf course at the water's edge that is among the state's most dazzling. The 18-hole, par-71 facility is available to golfers not staying at the lodge. Costs are $30 and $58 for walking nine and 18 holes, respectively. A cart is an additional $7.50 for nine or $15 for 18 holes.

Hiking

Milan is among the very nicest places to walk in all the state. From the Thomas Edison birthplace, head south 10 blocks or so, through pleasant, shaded neighborhoods, into a an undeveloped, little-used public woods. The town square also lends itself to pedestrians—there are a number of retail stores and places to stop for a snack or a cold drink. The square is a few blocks west of the Edison edifice.

Swimming

Believe it or not, there are places besides Lake Erie in which to swim. **Surf's Up Aquatic Center,** Meigs and Water Streets, Sandusky, tel. (419) 627-5806, has a big wave pool. Admission charges for the facility, which is open 10 a.m.-8 p.m. Memorial Day-Labor Day, is $4.50

for adults and $3.50 for children. The center also offers sand volleyball, and there are lockers where swimmers and spikers can store their gear.

Those who insist on being hit by nature's waves should check out these beaches: Nickelplate Park and Beach is along the downtown lakefront; the city charges $2 per car for use of the facility. Cedar Point beaches are for use only by Cedar Point patrons, Soak City patrons, and by guests of Cedar Point Resort. Vermilion's Main Street Beach, two blocks north of the downtwon 1837 Historic District, is small, clean, and pleasant.

ENTERTAINMENT AND CULTURE

A total of five plays and musicals are offered each summer at the **Huron Playhouse,** Ohio Street, Huron, tel. (419) 433-4744. Presented in McCormick School, productions range from Agatha Christie mysteries to Broadway-type musicals, comedies, and melodramas. This is Ohio's longest-running summer theater, indicating that the quality of presentations is uniformly good. The curtain parts Tues.-Sat. at 8 p.m. from late

June to early August. Tickets are $9 for adults, $8 for seniors, and $5 for children.

With all the excitement, some may want to retreat to a movie. **Cinema World 8** is behind the Sandusky Mall on SR 250. Telephone (419) 625-3334 to find out what is playing. Huron shows a free movie one evening a week from mid-June to mid-August in its movies-by-the-river program at the boat basin.

Travelers who like their music live and after dark should head for Bourbon Street, 202 Columbus Ave., Sandusky, tel. (419) 624-1288. This downtown spot serves up rock music Wednesday, Friday, and Saturday evenings. The Lodge at Sawmill Creek Resort, SR 2, Huron, tel. (800) SAWMILL (or tel. 800-729-6455), has regularly scheduled live music on most weekends. It ranges from country-western groups such as Kentucky Thunder to the musical version of Charles Dickens' *Christmas Carol*. Those who want to hear Sawmill music do not need to be guests to do so. **Bucko's,** at the corner of SR 2 and SR 6, tel. (419) 433-6112, also in Huron,

offers rock and roll devoid of cover charges on Friday and Saturday nights.

Spectator Sports

A pair of auto-racing ovals are nearby. **Sandusky Speedway** is close to Cedar Point at 614 W. Perkins Ave., tel. (419) 625-4084. Trucks and stock cars race virtually every Saturday night of the summer on this half-mile paved oval. **Norwalk Race Park,** 1300 SR 18, Norwalk, tel. (419) 668-5555, offers racing on Wednesday and Fri.-Sun. evening, April-October.

ACCOMMODATIONS

The Sandusky area has lots of hotels and motels, both privately owned and corporate endeavors. Prices are higher than the rest of the state all summer long. For assistance, contact the Sandusky/Erie County Lodging Locator service, tel. (800) 255-3743. The toll-free service keeps extended hours all summer and can help find ac-

---

SANDUSKY AREA EVENTS

MAY

Cedar Point Chausee Tour of Homes, Cedar Point Road, Sandusky, tel. (419) 626-1641, is a visit to an exclusive beachfront community. Visitors who believe this city is nothing more than a tourist stop should sign on.

Strawberry Festival, Norwalk, tel. (419) 663-2219, is a street fair with a strawberry theme. There are crafts, more shortcake than ever, other foods, and entertainment.

JUNE

Village Green Art Show takes place in Milan, tel. (419) 499-2300, the home of Thomas Edison. It's an idyllic setting for an art event.

JULY

Riverfest, Huron Boat Basin and Amphitheater, tel. (419) 433-5000, ext. 308. Boats participate in a parade of lights and there are lots of fireworks—the weekend following July 4.

Cold Creek Celebration takes place in Castalia, just west of Sandusky, tel. (419) 684-9321.

There are three parades, contests, bands, dancing, a 5K run, a tractor pull, food, and games, all over three days.

SEPTEMBER

The **Milan Melon Festival,** tel. (419) 499-2766 or (419) 433-5700, pays homage to the melons said to be the most flavorful melons in Ohio. Antique cars are displayed, there's a 10K run, a tractor pull, arts and crafts displays, and entertainment.

OCTOBER

Settlers Day is at the Milan Historical Museum, 10 Edison Drive, Milan, tel. (419) 499-2968. Living history presentations and lively music highlight this afternoon event for the entire family.

Antique Cars, Old Time Music & Flea Market, is at Historic Lyme Village, SR 4, Bellevue, tel. (419) 483-6052. In addition to the cars, the tunes, and the buys, there are tours of village buildings.

commodation by area and price. Travelers should be aware that prices for accommodations remain high all summer. One authority on the matter says that Erie County facilities are at least 20% more expensive than accommodations anywhere south of US 20.

Hotels and Motels

Chain offerings in Sandusky include **Best Western,** 1530 Cleveland Rd., tel. (419) 625-9234; **Comfort Inn Maingate,** 1711 Cleveland Rd., tel. (419) 625-4700; **Days Inn,** 4315 Milan Rd., tel. (419) 627-8884; **Econo Lodge,** 1904 Cleveland Rd., tel. (419) 627-8000; **Fairfield Inn,** 6220 Milan Rd., tel. (419) 621-9500; **Friendship Inn North,** 1021 Cleveland Rd. (US 6), tel. (419) 626-6852; **Friendship Inn South,** 3309 Milan Rd., tel. (419) 626-8720; **Holiday Inn Express,** 5513½ Milan Rd., tel. (419) 624-0028; **Holiday Inn Holidome,** 5513 Milan Rd., tel. (419) 626-6671; **Howard Johnson,** 1932 Cleveland Rd., tel. (419) 625-1333; **Howard Johnson,** Milan Road and Parkland Drive, tel. (419) 626-3742; **Radisson Harbour Inn,** 2001 Cleveland Rd., tel. (419) 627-2500; **Ramada Inn,** 5608 Milan Rd., tel. (419) 626-9890; **Rodeway Inn,** 2590 Milan Rd., tel. (419) 625-1291; and **Sheraton,** 1119 Sandusky Mall Blvd. North, tel. (419) 626-6280. The rates can vary from moderate to luxury, even for a no-frills chain, depending on time of year.

Near Sandusky proper, the following chain accommodations are also available in Milan, **Comfort Inn,** 11020 US 250 North, tel. (419) 499-4681; **Days Inn,** 11410 US 250 North, tel. (419) 499-4961; **Hampton Inn,** 11600 US 250, tel. (419) 499-4911; **Super 8,** 11313 Milan Rd., tel. (419) 499-4671 or (419) 499-4753.

South of the immediate Sandusky area in Bellevue, try the **Best Western Resort Inn,** 1120 E. Main St., Bellevue, tel. (419) 483-5740; and in Norwalk, there is **Econo Lodge,** 342 Milan Ave., Norwalk, tel. (419) 668-5656.

Farther afield, Vermilion has a trio of locally owned motels and a **Holiday Inn Express** at 2417 SR 60, tel. (440) 967-8770, Vermilion. Huron's flagship destination is the **Lodge at Sawmill Creek,** an upscale, 240-room resort north of US 6, tel. (419) 433-3800. Sawmill Creek has a championship golf course, its own beach, and it recently underwent a remodeling project that has resulted in an authentic Woodland Indians motif. Sawmill also offers package deals for golfers and nature lovers. Chains in Huron include **Comfort Inn,** 2119 W. Cleveland Rd., tel. (419) 433-5359, and **Clarion Inn Twin House,** 132 N. Main St., tel. (419) 433-8000.

Bed and Breakfast

Bed and breakfast establishments are numerous. In Sandusky three recommended options are the **1890 Queen Anne Bed & Breakfast,** 714 Wayne St., tel. (419) 626-0391; **Red Gable Bed & Breakfast,** 421 Wayne St., tel. (419) 625-1189; and **Tearose Bed & Breakfast,** 218 E. Washington St., tel. (419) 627-2773. Outside of Sandusky, there is **Britannia Bed & Breakfast,** 445 W. Main St., Bellevue, tel. (419) 583-4597; the large and lovely **Captain Montague's Bed & Breakfast,** 229 Center St., Huron, tel. (419) 433-4756 or (800) 276-4756; **Gastier Farm Bed & Breakfast,** 1902 Strecker Rd., Milan, tel. (419) 499-2985; and **Boos Family Inn,** 5054 SR 601, Norwalk, tel. (419) 668-6257.

Campgrounds

And while campgrounds aren't everywhere, Norwalk offers **Le Mar Park,** 263 Whittlesey Ave., tel. (419) 668-0425, Milan has **Trav-L-Park,** 11404 US 250, tel. (419) 499-4627, and in Sandusky, there is **Traveland Family Campground,** 3518 Tiffin Ave., Sandusky, tel. (800) 875-1044.

FOOD

Those who want to savor fresh fish should visit the **Angry Trout,** 505 E. Bay View Dr., Bayview, tel. (419) 684-5900. Billed as a fish and steakhouse, the restaurant has a separate sandwich-salad menu for lunch but offers the same fish, steak, and other entrees at noon and in the evening. The perch dinner, which is a signature dish here, is $14.95. Travelers in the mood for beef may want to try the 24-ounce Delmonico steak, which is $24.95. The Trout is open for lunch and dinner every day May-Oct., and open for dinner only Nov.-April. It's also open on Sunday 11:30 a.m.-9 p.m. every Sunday of the year. The bar is open late any night when food is served.

Berardi's Family Kitchen, 1019 W. Perkins St., Sandusky, tel. (419) 626-4592, offers two seemingly contradictory things that set it apart from every other restaurant in town: an emphasis on low-cholesterol, low-sodium food—and great french fries. The fries come with any sandwich, or a large order is $1.99. Earlier in the day, try one of Donna's omelets. It includes tomatoes, peppers, sprouts, broccoli, mushrooms, home fries, and two kinds of cheese, all for $4.49. Evening specials run around $7 and might be turkey pot pie, chicken cacciatori over rice, chicken marsala, or other meat, fish, or poultry variations. The pie is good, too. Berardi's is open Mon.-Sat. 6 a.m.-8 p.m. and Sunday 7:30 a.m.-1:30 p.m.

DeMore's Fish Den, 302 W. Perkins Ave., Sandusky, tel. (419) 626-8861, is a value-conscious place to try some local favorites. Open for lunch and dinner every day, the Den has perch or pickerel (walleye) sandwiches for about $3, perch or walleye dinners for less than $10, and such standbys as cheeseburgers for about $2. Those who prefer to know exactly how far their fish dollar will travel can purchase cooked perch or pickerel by the pound or half pound. Soup of the day is only about $1.25, and there are numerous accompaniments, from onion rings and french fries to cole slaw and tossed salad.

Jack's Deli, 2350 Cleveland Rd., Sandusky, tel. (419) 626-DELI (or tel. 419-626-3354), is just a mile from Cedar Point. This rendezvous is a good source for either dine-in or take-out food, be it pizza, subs, wings, desserts, beer, or wine. Jack's offers 26 different varieties of submarine sandwiches, hot or cold, for around $5. A large pizza with three toppings costs about $14. The top-selling dessert is cheesecake. Jack keeps the place open 8 a.m.-midnight all summer long and 10 a.m.-10 p.m. the rest of the year.

Margaritaville, 212 Fremont Ave., Sandusky, tel. (419) 627-8903, is on the west side of town, evidently the place where Tex/Mex meets Jimmy Buffett. The lounge offers a waterfall view, the carryout menu is extensive, and the restaurant features chicken, steak, or shrimp fajitas (the latter being $13.50), as well as a half-pound Cheeseburger in Paradise, served with the works and priced at $6.95. Margaritas are many flavored, there's a selection of Mexican beer, and

the help is pleasant. Open Mon.-Sat. 11 a.m.-11 p.m., Sunday 1-10 p.m.

Vanson's Family Restaurant, US 20, in Monroeville, tel. (419) 465-2827, is far enough from the tourist excitement to enjoy being what it is—an informal and popular small-town restaurant. Between Norwalk and Bellevue, Vanson's serves expansive breakfasts and is proud of the quality and size of its omelets. Figure $6 for something like the trucker's omelet, containing ham, green peppers, cheese, potatoes, and onions. At lunch, a half-pound cheeseburger with the works is also about $6. Among many evening selections, a favorite is pot roast with carrots and onions in gravy for $7.50. The restaurant is open every day but Christmas.

INFORMATION AND SERVICES

For a medical or police emergency, dial 911. The non-emergency telephone number for the Sandusky police is (419) 627-5863. The Fireland Community Hospital can be reached at (419) 626-7400. The post office in Sandusky is at 2220 Caldwell St.

Sandusky has a truly superior Web site for visitors at www.buckeyenorth.com. The site details everything from marinas to motels and attractions to restaurants. While tourism-intense places usually have sites, they're seldom this good. Equally helpful is the **Sandusky/Erie County Visitors and Convention Bureau,** 231 W. Washington Row in downtown Sandusky, tel. (419) 625-2984 or (800) 255-3743. There's also the **Lake Erie Information Hotline** at (419) 626-4636. When in Vermilion, contact **Friends of Harbour Town,** 5741 Liberty Ave., tel. (440) 967-4262 for general information on happenings and sights to see. For accommodation assistance in the Sandusky area, contact the **Sandusky/Erie County Lodging Locator,** tel. (800) 255-3743.

Locals stay informed via the *Sandusky Register,* which hits the streets evenings and Sunday mornings. Another area daily is the *Norwalk Reflector,* with editions every evening save Sunday. Southwest of Sandusky, people read the *Bellevue Gazette* weekday evenings and Saturday mornings.

Transportation

Those who want to see it all from the air should contact Griffing Flying Service, Inc., 3115 Cleveland Rd., Sandusky, tel. (419) 626-5161. Located at the Sandusky Airport, Griffing offers rides to and from the nearby islands, as well as scenic rides around the area. Griffing upholds a great tradition: for decades the islands were served by aging but dead-reliable Ford Tri-Motor craft that hauled people, mail, food, and supplies to the hardy souls who chose to stay on the islands through the winter. Nowadays, the planes are newer, but the tradition of reaching the islands by air lives on.

Traveling by water it's easy to become confused due to the number of boats offering passage to and from the islands. All boats listed here depart Sandusky. Boats departing other nearby mainland ports can be found under **Lake Erie Isles.** Among the better values is the *Emerald Empress,* 101 E. Shoreline Dr., Sandusky, tel. (419) 626-5557 or (800) 876-1907. Large (it can carry 600 passengers), modern, and trimmed in green and black, the *Empress* has many kinds of activities: lunch-break and sightseeing cruises Mon.-Tues.; island-hopping cruises Wed.-Sun.; dinner cruises Tues.-Sat.; free worship cruises Sunday; dance cruises on Friday. Final cruise of the year annually is the Halloween Cruise on Oct. 31. Sightseeing cruise fares are $10 for adults, $5 for children six and older, and free for younger children. Call for times.

Goodtime Island Cruises, Jackson Street Pier, Sandusky, tel. (419) 625-9262. For about $21 (with discounts to seniors and children), an adult can leave Sandusky and pay visits to both Kelleys Island and to Put-in-Bay, which is on Lower Bass Island. The 365-passenger craft shoves off at 9:30 p.m. and returns at 6:30 p.m. every day, all summer.

Island Express, Columbus Avenue pier, Sandusky, tel. (419) 627-1500, runs the high-speed *Island Rocket* between Sandusky and Kelleys Island and between Sandusky and Put-in-Bay. The boat leaves every two hours during the day, every day, all summer, and every two hours on weekends in May and September. Cost of the ride on this 70-foot, 2,000-horsepower slingshot is $18 to Kelleys Island and $22 to Put-in-Bay. By the time this book sees print, Island Express should have a big, new, high-speed catamaran running these same routes.

If arriving by bus, the Greyhound Bus Lines visits Sandusky at 6513 Milan Rd., tel. (419) 625-6907. Sandusky has no public transportation.

Shopping

The city has a surprisingly built-up and stable downtown area. The center of the city is seldom crowded, so it isn't unthinkable to spend one day screaming at Cedar Point and the next meandering among retail establishments. Mall shoppers may want to check out the **Lake Erie Factory Outlet Center,** 11001 US 250 (Milan Road) North, tel. (419) 625-4220, or **Sandusky Mall,** US 250 at Strub Road, tel. (419) 626-8574. Those who like their shopping quaint should investigate Vermilion's downtown, known as Harbour District 1837. There are several good places to hang out or to dine, too.

LAKE ERIE ISLES

These islands—North Bass, Middle Bass, South Bass, and Kelleys—are small to the point that they almost seem to have been artificially created. Consequently, their primary use today is as a tourist destination. Included here are Port Clinton, Marblehead, and Catawba Island, which are destinations in their own rights as well as mainland departure points for the isles. The largest island in the cluster is Pelee Island, less than 10 miles due north of Kelleys Island. Pelee belongs to Canada, despite its proximity to Ohio and the U.S.A.

History

The high-water mark, so to speak, of history in these parts has to be Oliver Hazard Perry's victory over the British in the dramatic 1813 sea battle. Perry and his sailors, manning ragtag ships, defeated English military vessels in a day-long battle not far from the islands. Their valor helped end the War of 1812, marking the last serious attempt by the British to regain the lower part of North America. Long before the sea battle, Native Americans found the islands ripe for hunting; pictographs found on Kelleys Island are proof of the bounty. Not long after Perry, settlers began to come here in the summer to absorb the sun and swim in the fresh lake water. They've been at it ever since. And while the demand for alcoholic beverages has risen and fallen, island weather remains ideal for growing rich wine grapes.

Put-in-Bay, the village on South Bass Island, is filled with places to eat and drink. It can be a rowdy affair in the summer as college kids show up on weekends to test their endurance and local patience. Middle Bass Island is mostly taken up with vineyards and a winery, while North Bass Island is little but grapes growing. Kelleys Island has a full complement of tourism services but is more of a family place than Put-in-Bay and environs. South Bass and Kelleys islands have a number of fascinating natural and manmade attractions which are detailed below.

Things calm considerably as the weather turns cool following the grape harvest and the end of tourist season. In Put-in-Bay, for example, the number of residents declines from 1,500 in the summer to just 480 in the winter. The islands receive mail, medicines, and some supplies by air, or by boats that sail year round if the lake fails to freeze over. The Miller car and passenger ferry is most apt to brave wintry waves. South Bass and Kelleys islands are 20-30 minutes from the mainland, depending on the size and speed of the boat or ferry. Incidentally, this part of Lake Erie routinely freezes over for part of the winter. All it takes is a stretch of below-freezing temperatures and calm winds. Boats don't break the ice; nor do they sail when there are large ice chunks afloat.

Orientation

North, Middle, and South Bass Islands, logically, are in a line just above Catawba Island (which really is the mainland). Kelleys Island is north of Sandusky, east of Catawba Island, and southeast of South Bass Island. Catawba Island, Lakeside, and Marblehead are on a peninsula that forms the northern side of Sandusky Bay. Port Clinton is the immediate area's largest town, located 10 miles southwest of Catawba Island. State Route 2 swings past the peninsula, serving Toledo to the west and Sandusky to the east. It is a multilane road only in the easterly direction. State Route 53 is the route most commonly taken to the tip of the peninsula, where travelers can catch a boat to one of the islands.

SIGHTS

Perry's Victory and
International Peace Memorial

Next to Lake Erie itself, nothing is more visible than this 352-foot monument, easily seen from the mainland. Constructed of granite on South Bass Island during between 1912 and 1915, it offers a stunning view of the western end of the big lake. In addition to the monument, which resembles a Greek Doric column, there is a visitor contact center with one of the best collections of War of 1812 material anywhere. Was Oliver H. Perry's victory as important as it seems? Did it turn the tide in an untidy war? Visit and know.

The platform is open daily 10 a.m.-7 p.m. for the summer season from mid-June to Labor Day; the platform closes at 5 p.m. from late April to mid-June, and from Labor Day to late October; in the winter it is open by appointment only, call (419) 285-2184. The only liability here is that there are 37 steps from the monument entrance to the elevator taking visitors to the open-air observation platform. Persons with disabilities may not be able to take in the view from the platform. The elevator costs $3 for adults, free for kids under 17.

Catawba Island and Other State Parks

If lots of people are in line on the mainland at Catawba Point for the ferry boat, a nice nearby spot to while away some time is **Catawba Island State Park,** 4049 E. Moore's Dock Rd., tel. (419) 797-4025. The irony, as noted, is that this 18-acre day park is no island but is instead the tip of a peninsula. There's a fishing pier, a stony beach where visitors swim at their own risk, and boat-launching facilities. Boat traffic is heavy and the view of the islands is vivid in good weather. To reach the park, follow SR 53 up the east side of the peninsula and look for the state park sign. Catawba Island State Park also serves as the main headquarters for the nearby Kelleys Island, South Bass, and Oak Point State Parks.

Kelleys Island is served by ferry boats from Marblehead and Sandusky. The entire island has been designated a National Historic Landmark, and its outstanding attraction is **Kelleys Island State Park,** tel. (419) 746-2546. This 661-acre park offers up a pair of fascinating phenomena: Glacial Grooves State Memorial and Inscription Rock State Memorial. The grooves were gouged into solid rock by ice under enormous pressure during the end of the last Ice Age, as recently as 12,000 years ago. Close examination of the limestone here will reveal fossilized marine life. Inscription Rock was adorned by Erie Indians in the 17th century with drawings of animals, birds, and humans. The park offers a sizeable campground, picnicking areas, boating, and a small swimming beach, plus five miles of hiking trails. Kelleys Island also features a small, picturesque downtown, easily navigated on foot, by bicycle or by electric golf cart.

East of Catawba Island State Park, **East Harbor State Park,** tel. (419) 734-4424, is on the same peninsula as Catawba Island, but is most easily reached by staying on SR 269 north of SR 2. Much the larger at 1,152 acres, East Harbor attractions include fishing, swimming at a large sandy beach, and nearly seven miles of hiking trails (including the Middle Harbor trail with a bird observation blind), as well camping.

South Bass Island has been used as a summer resort for over a century—the remains of the Victory Hotel, which in its day was one of the largest hotels in the world until it was destroyed by fire in 1919, can still be seen. Two

Perry's Victory and International Peace Memorial, Put-in-Bay

other state parks, **Oak Point State Park** and **South Bass Island State Park,** both on South Bass Island are accessbile by ferry from Port Clinton or Catawba Harbor. Oak Point measures just one acre and is primarily a day-use picnic and fishing destination facing Put-in-Bay. South Bass Island is 35 acres and offers boat-launching facilities and a campground. Call (419) 285-2112 for information on the two parks, or try the Catawba Island State Park Headquarters for camping information for South Bass Island.

Perry's Cave
At 979 Catawba Ave., Put-in-Bay on South Bass Island, tel. (419) 285-2405, this cave is said to have been discovered by Oliver Hazard Perry in 1813, the same year as his momentous naval battle. The commodore reportedly stored supplies and held prisoners in the natural limestone cave some 43 steps below the surface. Today, visitors enter the cave from the gift shop area and are treated to an underground lake and various mineral formations. Tours take 20 minutes in the constant 50°F cave. Evening lantern tours are popular; call for a schedule and to make a reservation. Hours are 11 a.m.-5:30 p.m. daily and admissions are $4.50 for adults and $2.25 for children.

African Safari Wildlife Park
Animal lovers should take a look at this park, 267 Lightner Rd., tel. (419) 732-3606, just off the US 2 bypass in Port Clinton. A cageless zoo—animals roam free in a natural setting and including, naturally, many African species, such as ostriches, giraffes, etc. Folks can drive through, stopping at attractions such as the camel ride. Hours are 9 a.m.-6 p.m. from Memorial Day to Labor Day, plus May and September weekends, weather permitting. Admission charges are $14.95 for adults and $9.95 for children.

The Lakeside Association
The perfect antidote to excessive tourism can be found at 236 Walnut Ave., Lakeside, tel. (419) 798-4461. Billed as "the Chautauqua on Lake Erie," Lakeside is the Midwest's largest family-oriented retreat center. It specializes in nurturing family growth and interpersonal relationships for people of all persuasions. If the family is feeling strained after too many days at Cedar Point, Lakeside offers fascinating lectures on everything from Mark Twain to investments, plus a variety of music, outdoor activities, and a nice stretch of beach. There are Christian messages to much of the programming. Admission fees range from $5 for six hours to $210 for the season for an adult. Children and the clergry receive discounts, and there are cottage, hotel, or motel accommodations in various price ranges.

WINERIES

Lonz Winery, Middle Bass Island, tel. (419) 285-5411, opened at the close of the Civil War in 1865. Known at the time as the Golden Eagle Winery, it was by 1875 the largest wine producer in the country. Today, Lonz is situated on the southern tip of the island, next to the ferry dock. The most popular wine currently offered is a pink Catawba to go at $7 or to enjoy on the premises at $8. Highlight of the summer here is the Grape Festival in September. Hours are Sun.-Thurs. 11:30 a.m.-7 p.m., Friday 11:30 a.m.-10 p.m., and Saturday 11:30 a.m.-midnight, from mid-May through September.

Mon Ami Restaurant & Historic Winery, 3845 Wine Cellar Rd., Port Clinton, tel. (419) 797-4445 or (800) 777-4266, has been in operation since 1872. The unusual building is a four-story edifice constructed of limestone. The winery is on SR 53, near the ferries to the Lake Erie islands. Restaurant hours are 11 a.m.-2 a.m. Tours take place at 2 and 4 p.m. Closed Monday and Tuesday in the off season.

Heineman Winery is at the corner of Thompson and Catawba Streets, Put-in-Bay, tel. (419) 285-2811. It's an authentic winery, making and selling 20 varieties on site. Tours take place from May to September at irregular hours, when there are enough people assembled for a tour. There's a tasting room where visitors can purchase Heineman's biggest seller, pink Catawba, for $6.50 per bottle. Tours are $4 for adults and $1.50 for children, including a glass of wine or juice. That fee also includes a tour of Crystal Cave, the world's largest geode and home to the world's largest celestite crystals. The cave lies beneath the winery.

Kelleys Island Wine Company, Woodford Road, Kelleys Island, tel. (419) 746-2678, is open

A CANADIAN VISIT

Few travelers would expect to be able to visit a foreign country from northern Ohio, but alien territory is just a brief boat ride north of Sandusky. From March to around Thanksgiving, daily passenger-vehicle ferry service is available to Canada's Pelee Island. What with great currency exchange rates, Pelee is an inviting destination.

The island is about an hour by boat from the Ohio mainland. Like Kelleys Island, Pelee has a nice display of deep glacial grooves in bedrock, created by the Erie Lobe some 20,000 years ago. These grooves run east-west, a rarity. Other attractions include a large sandstone rock pocked with abraded depressions. Here, as long as 7,500 years ago, native peoples ground corn and other grain into flour.

Other attractions include the second-oldest lighthouse on Lake Erie, a cliff from which an Indian woman is said to have flung herself after learning that her English husband would not return to her, plus several picturesque Anglican churches, and a number of places to fish. Look, too, for bed and breakfast operations such as the **Gathering Place,** tel. (519) 724-2656.

Hauling a vehicle from Sandusky costs $30-60 but the price may be worth it—Pelee is the largest island in this cluster and travelers will appreciate the decent island roads. Fares for individuals one way are $13.75 for persons over the age of 12, $6.75 for children ages 6-12, free for children under 5. All prices are in Canadian dollars. To book a ride to Pelee on either of two boats, call (800) 661-2220. If you feel adventurous, visit Pelee and then continue northward, alighting in either Leamington or Kingsville, Ontario, on the Canadian mainland.

---

10 a.m.-10 p.m. all summer; weekends only through October. No tours are given, but there is a tasting room where half a dozen wines can be sampled. Top seller is the Sunset Pink, similar in taste to a white Zinfandel, at $8.25 per bottle. The firm opened a new building in 1998, an indication that their products are popular.

RECREATION

Bicycling
Travelers who left their bikes at home needn't worry—there are several bicycle rental outlets on South Bass and Kelleys Islands. Hauling a bicycle to the islands is only a couple of dollars on any of the passenger or car/passenger boats. For less mobile visitors, many of the bike-rental outfits also offer electric golf carts as a way around.

Fishing
Like much of the rest of the coast, there are two kinds of lake fishing—from the shore and from a charter boat. The former is less expensive, while the latter produces better results. Fees average $50-60 per person for a charter boat day on the lake.

Swimming
There are two dandy bathing beaches on South Bass Island. The ferry passes one on its swing around into the bay and the dock. This state park beach is at the west end of Catawba Avenue, about six blocks from the downtown area. Another beach can be found just south of Perry's Monument. Those visiting South Bass Island with a heightened sense of adventure can visit Put-in-Bay Parasailing, tel. (419) 285-3703. The facility is just to the right of the public docks on Bay View Avenue. Kelleys Island has a beach on the island's north side, just east of the glacial grooves.

ENTERTAINMENT

The good times roll in several Put-in-Bay taverns on South Bass Island, with live music afternoons and evenings all summer long. They are only a block or two from the ferry dock. On the mainland, a couple of Port Clinton spots come to mind. **Nick's Roadhouse,** 124 Buckeye Blvd., tel. (419) 732-3069, provides a DJ or live music on weekends. Cover charges vary but usually run about $3 for the likes of Danger Brothers and other area rockers. **Z's Tin Goose,** 111 Madison St., tel. (419) 734-6673, provides a DJ on Thursday and a guitar soloist or a small rock band on Friday and Saturday. There are no cover charges. Down the volume scale a notch, **Mon**

Ami, the restaurant-winery at 3845 Wine Cellar Rd., has music almost every evening, all summer long. Usually, it's jazz in an outdoor setting.

ACCOMMODATIONS

The happiest visitors are those who show up with reservations in hand—whether for hotel stays, B&B stays, or camping. Frequently, the reservations are made months in advance, ensuring a spot on one of the islands at the height of the tourist season. One employee of the historic old Park Hotel in Put-in-Bay reports that all weekend rooms for the summer season are booked by the first of April. Folks with reservations in many cases are allowed to haul their cars to the islands (though this is subject to restriction without notice, based on the determination of island authorities as to traffic and crowding. Consequently, call ahead!). The other worthwhile tip is that many island accommodations offer lower rates for single-night stays during the week. Expect to pay about $120 per night for a motel room or for bed and breakfast accommodations, and $1,000 per week for a cottage or a cabin. Kelleys Island has a condominium complex, the **Quarry,** tel. (419) 746-2366, where 2-4 bedroom units are available by the week or for weekend rental.

No matter the time of year, most visitors stay in Port Clinton. There they find chain motels to include **Best Western, Comfort Inn, Days Inn,** and **Fairfield Inn,** plus an assortment of locally owned motels, cottages, and bed and breakfast establishments. Those who insist on overnighting on one of the islands can do so by calling **Kelleys Island Cottage Rentals,** tel. (419) 746-2543 in summer or (419) 626-8779 in winter. Kelleys Island is also the site of the **Rockaway Bed and Breakfast,** tel. (419) 746-2445; **Kelleys Mansion Inn,** tel. (419) 746-2273; and **Lakeview Lane Motel,** tel. (419) 746-2254. Again, reservations are of paramount importance all summer long.

Middle Bass Island has an array of cottages. They include **Beers Cottages,** tel. (419) 285-2314; **Ile De Fleurs House and Cottages,** tel. (419) 285-2130; and **Middle Bass Island Camping and Fishing,** tel. (419) 285-6121. Cottages on Kelleys and Middle Bass Islands usually are

spacious and pleasant. A three-bedroom example on Kelleys recently rented for $195 per night or $900 a week. It provided sleeping accommodations for eight persons. Travelers hoping to get a jump on the season should make reservations because fishing fanatics crowd the bays and beaches at the first sign of spring. Visitors without a place to stay should call the numbers listed below under information and hope for a stray vacancy.

FOOD

There are three concepts at work where dining is concerned. Travelers can order their food to go in a place that's used to putting up picnic-type fare, they can consume bar food in one of the island or mainland taverns, or they can have a solid sit-down meal in one of a number of nice restaurants. Food and drink here can be adjusted to the activities planned.

Cheesehaven, at the junction of SR 53 and SR163, Port Clinton, tel. (419) 734-2611, stocks the raw materials for a sumptuous picnic. The owners boast of 125 kinds of cheese, plus spare ribs, kosher corned beef, roast beef, salami, sausage, exotic wursts, ham, smoked pork chops, and luncheon meats. The help will make carryout sandwiches or suggest ingredients to travelers. Homemade bread, beer, wine, donuts, and ice cream also are available. Figure $3 or so per person for luncheon ingredients and $5 or so for a sandwich made here. Cheesehaven is open Wed.-Mon., 9:30 a.m.-7 p.m.

The **Garden,** Perry and Adams Streets, Port Clinton, tel. (419) 732-2151, is across the street from Waterworks Park. Seafood is in demand here, with a popular luncheon item being the large fish market salad at $7.95. In the evening, fresh Lake Erie catches, particularly perch, are offered at market prices. The Garden is open for lunch and dinner every day Memorial Day-Labor Day, is closed on Sunday in May and September, and closes Sunday and Monday the rest of the year.

Finding a kid-friendly place to eat can be a chore, so **AJ's Deli,** Harbour Square, Put-in-Bay, tel. (419) 285-4AJS or (419) 285-4257, should be a welcome sight. A variety of sandwiches are available on a choice of breads and buns, but more important are a couple of kids' offerings. The "not-so-phonee bolonee" is $1.75 and comprises bologna, cheese, and mayo or mustard on spongey white bread. Another young delight is "jam & slam," a peanut butter-and-jelly sandwich on that same Wonderish bread for $1.25. Adults will like cheddarwurst on a bagel for $3.75 or the substantial Reuben for $5.95. And there are salads, sides, and soft drinks. Order up, carry lunch to a spot overlooking the lake, and dig in. The deli is open for lunch and dinner and until 2 a.m. on Friday and Saturday.

INFORMATION AND SERVICES

The non-emergency telephone number for police in Port Clinton is (419) 734-3121. The telephone number for Port Clinton's Magruder Hospital is (419) 734-3131. The Port Clinton post office is at 121 W. Second St.

The **Kelleys Island Chamber of Commerce** can be reached by dialing (419) 746-2360. The **Ottawa County Visitors Bureau** is at 109 Madison St., Suite E, in Port Clinton, tel. (419) 734-4386 or (800) 441-1271. The **Port Clinton Area Chamber of Commerce** is at 130 Jefferson St., Suite 1-B, tel. (419) 734-5503. The **Put-in-Bay Chamber of Commerce** can be reached at (419) 285-2832.

There's an entertainment section every Friday in Port Clinton's *News Herald,* a Mon.-Sat. evening newspaper.

Souvenirs, ranging from tasteful to tasteless, are available on the island and the mainland. Perhaps the largest variety for shoppers is in Port Clinton, which has a thriving downtown area within walking distance of the *Jet Express* dock and the municipal parking lot.

Transportation

When taking a boat to an island, check on return times. Missing the boat can result in a stay in a pricey room or sleeping in the car. One other admonishment—the sooner the boat ride back from Put-in-Bay the better on Friday and Saturday. The last few departures include drunks and police who annoy each other and everyone else for the duration of the trip. Unless there are unruly passengers, the voyage back and forth usually is pleasant. In rough weather, it seems adventurous.

One of the quirkier ways to get around is offered by **Captain Gundy's Pirate Adventure,** Jet Express dock, Put-in-Bay, tel. (419) 285-4504. The cap'n's craft is a funky, yellow-and-black, piratelike sailing ship. It sails among the Bass Islands for an hour at 2 p.m. every day all summer. In May and September, the boat sets sail at 2 p.m. on Saturday and Sunday only. The vessel is available for private charters and there are over-21 weekend cruises on summer weekend evenings. The crew sings songs of the sea as the sails unfurl. Cost is $12 for adults, $7.50 for children ages 4-12, and is free for younger children.

The Jet Express II *whisks visitors between Port Clinton and Put-in-Bay.*

To get a jump on the festivities, consider departing Port Clinton on the **Island Hopper,** docked at the end of Jefferson Street, tel. (800) 245-1538. This passenger ferry offers folks a full-service bar, DJ music, and a dance floor during a 35-minute trip to Put-in-Bay. Cost of the ride is $7 each way for adults and $1 for children ages 5-12. The *Island Hopper* also offers service between Put-in-Bay and Kelleys Island for the same fares.

The fastest way between Port Clinton and Put-in-Bay is the **Jet Express,** which is docked at 5 N. Jefferson St., Port Clinton, tel. (800) 245-1538. The boat runs late April-Oct., leaving the mainland on the hour and the island on the half hour. There are three decks, two of which are enclosed, and the ride is smooth. The boat makes the trip in less than 30 minutes, obviously, charging one-way adult fares of $8.50 during the week and $10 weekends. Children ages 5-12 are $1 each way, with smaller children free. Bicycles are $2 each way. The *Jet Express* has its own Web site at www.jet-express.com.

A different concept and a different locale highlight the **Miller Boat Line,** Water Street dock, Catawba Island, tel. (800) 500-2421 or (419) 285-2421. This is a passenger and auto ferry to and from Put-in-Bay. The slower-moving, open craft runs from late March-Oct. One-way costs are $4.50 for adults, $1 for children ages 6-12, free for younger children, $2 for bicycles, and $9 for cars, vans, or motorcycles. An island being a finite place, only persons with written proof of accommodation are allowed to take vehicles on weekends. Travelers making same-day roundtrips on weekdays must have their vehicles in line at Catawba by 10:30 a.m. and be prepared to leave Put-in-Bay by 4 p.m. Campers are allowed to take vehicles on board as long as there are vacancies at the state parks on the Bass Islands.

Kelleys Island can be reached from Marblehead aboard the **Neuman Ferry,** Frances Street Dock, tel. (800) 876-1907 or (419) 626-5557. Running from late March through September, this ferry boat, christened *Endeavor,* leaves Marblehead every half hour and Kelleys Island every hour. The Marblehead departure site is two blocks north of SR 163; from the mainland, turn left onto Frances Street at the Marblehead Bank. One-way fares are $9 for adults, $5 for children ages 6-11, free for children under 6, $3.50 for bicycles, and $16 for automobiles. The trip takes about 20 minutes.

WEST TO OREGON

Oregon is where the journey along the big lake ends—not with a bang or a whimper, but with a splash. West of Oregon is Toledo; the larger city shares the mouth of the Maumee River with its neighbor to the immediate east. Between Oregon and Lake Erie lie a number of railroad tracks and a big tank farm. Both facilitate the movement of goods and commodities on the water. East of here is some of the best birdwatching in North America. Travelers can confirm that they are in Oregon by driving past the BP or Sunoco oil refineries at night. Each displays a rolling orange flame, which is excess natural gas being burned off the petroleum products.

History
Oregon dates from 1837, when the largest township in Lucas County was formed to create the municipality. The city's name was chosen for two reasons—a popular novel at the time was *Astoria,* which told of Oregon adventures. And the valiant trip west by Lewis and Clark in 1804-1806 was fresh in American memory. Oregon is a self-sufficient place. It has the normal complement of municipal services and institutions.

Orientation
Interstate 280 cuts across Oregon from northwest to southeast. The highway continues north past the Maumee River and in less than two miles hooks up to I-75, the fastest road to Detroit. US 280 meets I-80/90 (the Ohio Turnpike), about seven miles south of town. Other main roads include east-west SR 2, which connects with Port Clinton to the east and Toledo to the west.

SIGHTS

This retail-industrial city on the east side of the Maumee River is home to **Maumee Bay State Park,** a resort facility the equal of virtually any private hideaway anywhere. Some three million visitors a year pass through Oregon on their way to the park, which is resolutely free of charge. In fact, the only ways to spend money here are to eat, stay overnight, or plunk coins into a clothing-and-valuables locker prior to swimming. US 2 is Oregon's main east-west street, and it's well marked for finding the park. On the east side of Oregon, turn north onto North Curtice Street, which deadends at the resort. To the left is the beach, to the right is the parking lot serving the contemporary, geometric resort building.

Constructed in 1991, the light-gray main building is decorated with rich wood and thick carpet. There are snack bars, pools, lounges, and other amenities visitors simply don't expect in anything owned by the state. Just to the east is a pathway through unspoiled lakeside lowlands for viewing flora and fauna. In an introspective mood? The resort's lakefront is a series of huge concrete steps, perfect for sitting and watching freighter traffic, wheeling gulls, or endless waves. Besides a spacious swimming beach there's a 57-acre inland lake with a sandy floor, great for kids who want to make a quick car-to-water transition. The only sounds you'll hear are the shrieks of delighted children and the occasional pop of devices used to keep the seagulls moving. Other park diversions include golf, bicycling, and fishing.

There is only one winery in the immediate area, **Johlin Century Winery,** 3935 Corduroy Rd., Oregon, tel. (419) 693-6288. "We're a small outfit," the owner reports, adding that the winery offers five or six different varieties at any given time. The most popular Johlin wine is vin rosé, sold in 1.5-liter magnums for $5.50. There's a tasting room and a gift shop on the premises, which is open Mon.-Sat. 11 a.m.-6 p.m., year round.

RECREATION

Bicycling
There's a two-mile bike path that follows city streets along what once was the city's original streetcar path. To make the route along Starr Avenue between Whittlesey Road and Pearson Metropark safe for riders, Oregon thoughtfully widened the street by seven feet, providing 3.5 feet on each side for cyclists' right of way.

Birdwatching
Birdwatching opportunities, from east to west along SR 2 include the following: the 2,600-acre Magee Marsh State Wildlife Area, on the east side of 79-acre Crane Creek State Park, 13531 West SR 2, Oak Harbor, tel. (419) 898-2495; Ottawa National Wildlife Refuge, adjoining the southwest side of Crane Creek State Park,14000 W. SR 2, Oak Harbor, tel. (419) 898-0014; Metzger Marsh State Wildlife Area, west of Crane Creek State Park and north of SR 2; Cedar Point National Wildlife Refuge, three miles east of Maumee Bay State Park; and Maumee Bay State Park, 1400 Park Road No. 1, Oregon, tel. (419) 836-9117 (nature center). All of this area on or near Lake Erie is what remains of the Great Black Swamp, which stretched in the early 19th century from here southwest to Fort Wayne, Indiana. Toledo and Detroit became attractive ports in part because pioneers were unable to penetrate the vast, low-lying swamp. Farmers and other drained the huge bog, and these remnants are what remains.

Experienced birders have their own reference guides, so newcomers will want to stock up on whatever they can find. The parks and wildlife areas have their own literature, much of it showing commonplace flora and fauna. Among the best publications is a simple sheet showing various trails and bird species in Ottawa National Wildlife Refuge. These trails are great places to watch for birds. May is said to be the best time to catch northbound migrations, and the Ohio Division of Wildlife's generous use of boardwalk trails deliver birders deep into the lowlying area. It's said that a skilled birder can tally 30 or more species of warbler alone. Other commonly seen, yet majestic, species include great egrets, great blue herons, ring-necked pheasants, black-crowned night herons, whistling swans, and bald eagles. Best of all, of course, viewing opportunities are entirely free.

Fishing
In addition to opportunities available at the state parks, competitively priced charter services can be hired in Oregon. As in much of Lake Erie accessible from Ohio, the most prized fish are walleye and perch.

OREGON AREA ANNUAL EVENTS

MAY

International Migratory Bird Day, Magee Marsh and Ottawa Wildlife areas, SR 2, Oak Harbor, tel. (419) 898-0960, provides rare birdwatching opportunities. There are also guided tours and a children's program.

AUGUST

German Festival attracts more than 20,000 visitors each year to its site on Seaman Road near Coy Road in Oregon, tel. (419) 698-7029. Food, music, brew, and the urge to *blitzkrieg* the east side of Toledo.

SEPTEMBER

Duathlon by the Bay is at Maumee Bay State Park, 6505 Cedar Point Rd., and involves a run-bike-run sequence calculated to bring out the best in participants. Call (419) 691-3523 for particulars.

OCTOBER

Apple Festival, in Oak Harbor, toasts Johnny Appleseed's best. There's a parade, a bike tour, local talent show, entertainment, food vendors, and many crafters. Call (800) 441-1271 or check out the area's Web site at www.lake-erie.com for more information.

Golf

Fourteen of the 18 holes on par-72 Chippewa Golf Course, SR 579, Curtice, tel. (419) 836-8111, involve a meandering creek. Fees are $13.50 weekdays and $18 weekends, plus $9.75 per person for a cart.

Hiking

Meadow, marshland, and woodland await hikers. Top trails include those at Maumee Bay State Park, which penetrate the otherwise unchanged coastal environment.

Swimming

In addition to the state parks, there are a couple of noteworthy beaches among the many refuges. Check out Howard Farms or Reno Beach, west of Metzger Marsh, and Niles Beach, between Maumee Bay State Park and Cedar Point. Look for public easements to the beach from the nearest street.

ACCOMMODATIONS

Perhaps the motto for proprietors of lodging in the area should be "Drive a few miles away from the turnpike and save!" There are a few nice, moderately priced places to stay hereabouts, from the **Nightingale House** bed and breakfast, 525 S. Wheeling St., Oregon, tel. (419) 698-2263, to the **Comfort Inn—East,** 2030 Navarre St., Oregon, tel. (419) 691-8911, to the **EconoLodge,** 10530 Corduroy Rd., Curtice, tel. (419) 836-2822.

FOOD AND DRINK

Golden Jade, 2745 Navarre Ave., Oregon, serves lunch and dinner every day. The Chinese restaurant specializes in Szechuan and American dishes and offers carryout and delivery. Favorite dishes include almond chicken at $7.95, sweet-and-sour chicken at $7, and seafood fantasia at $11.25. Karaoke music holds forth Thurs.-Sat. 9 p.m.-1:30 a.m. when a number of diners stick around to recall the hits of the last half century.

Grevis' Curtice Inn, 7150 N. Curtice Rd., Curtice, tel. (419) 836-9743, serves "just about everything." Sandwich-wise, a cheeseburger with fries is $4.75. Those who like more beef can wait for the weekend dinner specials, which include 12 ounces of prime rib for $12.95 or 14 ounces for $14.95. Other favorite meals are perch, deep-fried in a light batter for $13.50, which also is the price for either baked or deep-fried pickerel (walleye) with the fixings. In the summer, Grevis' Inn is open Tues.-Sat. 4-10 p.m., Sunday noon-8 p.m. At other times of the year, the restaurant open Tues.-Thurs. 4-9 p.m.; Fri.-Sat. 4-10 p.m.; Sunday noon-8 p.m.

Nightlife

After a day of stomping around the marshes, what better way to celebrate than by stomping to some music? Sites to catch live music are all too few, but visitors who enjoy the country sound will want to head for **Rockin' Rodeo,** 7802 SR 2, about five miles east of Oregon, tel. (419) 836-3022. This place offers bands on Friday and Saturday nights for a cover charge of $3.

INFORMATION AND SERVICES

For emergency aid, dial 911. The non-emergency telephone number for the Oregon police department is (419) 698-7064. St. Charles Hospital in Oregon can be reached at (419) 698-7200. The post office branch is at 3054 Dustin Rd.

The **Oregon Tourism Bureau** is at 5330 Seaman Rd., tel. (419) 698-7029. The telephone number is shared with the city finance department.

The morning *Toledo Blade* carries event and entertainment news of Oregon and vicinity.

NORTHWESTERN OHIO

This area is what many people envision when they think of Ohio. The northwest part of the state is marked by intense farming, meaningful industry, pleasant towns and cities, and no huge centers of population except Toledo. The region has proven to be fertile soil for presidents, inventors, and others who have gone on to great success in a number of different fields. And while not many vacationers spend all of their holidays here, they would be remiss if they avoided the Buckeye heartland altogether.

Cities in this area include Toledo (population 332,000), Mansfield (50,000), Lima (46,000), Findlay (36,000), Marion (34,000), Bowling Green (28,000), Ashland (20,000), Piqua (20,000), Troy (19,000), Fremont (18,000), Sidney (18,000), Tiffin (18,000), Defiance (17,000), Fostoria (15,000), Bellefontaine (12,000), Greenville (12,000), and Van Wert (11,000). Campbell Hill, the state's highest point at 1,549 feet, is approximately two miles east of Bellefontaine.

TOLEDO

For a number of years, Toledo has been the home not only of auto glass but also of the Jeep. There are other ways to make a living in the area, however—notably farming and transporting goods.

Location and Orientation

Few cities anywhere have better locations. At the mouth of the Maumee River, the largest river flowing into the Great Lakes, Toledo also is centrally located. The Ohio Toll Road, otherwise known as Interstate 80/90, runs east from the Toledo to Cleveland, 110 miles away, while the Indiana state border lies due west, about 68 miles. Detroit, Michigan lies to the north 62 miles along I-75, which also runs south Cincinnati, 210 miles away, before crossing into Kentucky. The city of Chicago is about 225 miles aways. Other important cross-town highways are US 20, 23, and 24. Toledo is an important Amtrak passenger stop between New York and Chicago, as well as a Great Lake port of past and present note.

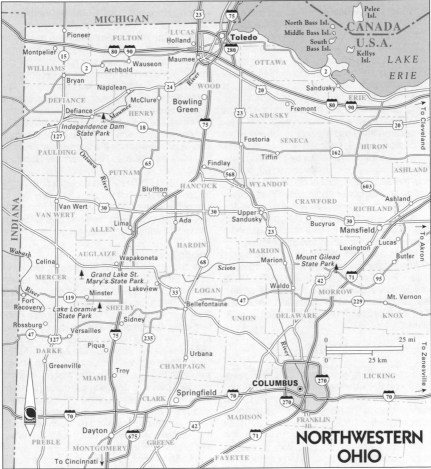

NORTHWESTERN OHIO

© MOON PUBLICATIONS, INC.

History

Toledo traces its beginnings to the construction of Fort Industry, in what is now downtown Toledo, at the end of the War of 1812. The low-lying area—where the Maumee empties into Lake Erie—had been known to pioneers of European descent since 1794, the year "Mad" Anthony Wayne's soldiers defeated a confederacy of Indians in the Battle of Fallen Timbers, just south of the modern metropolitan area. The battle, so named because a violent storm had passed through the area a few days earlier, was of marked importance. It ended 20 years of border warfare, opening Ohio to widespread European-American settlement.

The city was incorporated in 1837, four years after the villages of Port Lawrence and Vistula united to call themselves Toledo. At the time, Toledo was part of the Michigan Territory. Ohio offered to include the lake port in the Buckeye system of canals, and local residents staged a pro-Ohio protest. Troops from Michigan squared off against troops from Ohio, but the matter was peacefully settled in Ohio's favor in 1836 by

President Andrew Jackson. Michigan was compensated for its loss by receiving the Upper Peninsula and admission to the union.

Industrial development, spurred by canals, railroads, and the port, was complemented locally by the discovery of oil and gas in 1844. Glassmaking required a lot of heat, and gas from just south of Lucas County helped get the business going. Glassmaking was introduced in the 1880's by Edward Libbey and Michael Owens, and Toledo became the world's leader in the industrial production of glass, hence its nickname, "Glass City." Other plants were devoted to things automotive; thousands of Jeeps poured out of what was the Willys auto plant during World War II.

Today, this city of about 350,000 is America's 49th-largest municipality and is known as the source of Jeeps plus an array of auto parts, plastics, machinery, and tools. It also has gained a reputation for innovative local government.

Toledo has a number of tall and impressive buildings downtown devoted to diverse administration. They include One SeaGate (1970), 404 ft. and 30 stories; Owens Illinois Headquarters Building (1982), 404 ft. and 30 stories; and the Owens-Corning Fiberglas Tower (1970), 400 ft. and 30 stories.

SIGHTS

Of Toledo's nine Metroparks, the crown jewel has to be **Providence Metropark,** a restored stretch of the Miami and Erie Canal in Grand Rapids, Ohio, tel. (419) 535-3050. This peaceful facility between US 24 and the Maumee River includes the canal, a restored canal boat, the Isaac Ludwig Mill, and a general store. Admission to the grounds is free; visitors pay only for a boat ride if they choose. The park is named Providence because there once was a tiny village called that here, adjacent to lock No. 44 on the canal. Cholera epidemics in 1848 and 1854 and a fire in 1852 destroyed the town, but canal business continued to flourish for a couple of decades thereafter. Hours vary for each attraction but generally all sites are open Wed.-Sat.10 a.m.-4 p.m., Sunday and holidays 11 a.m.-5 p.m., May-October. A boat ride behind two sturdy mules is $4 for adults, $3 for seniors, and $2 for children 12 and under. Crew members dress and act authentically for their guests. The mill features milling

and craft demonstrations, while the general store stocks books, T-shirts, and souvenirs.

One of the more impressive ways to see the town is aboard a TARTA (Toledo Area Regional Transit Authority) trolley that runs through the most historic parts of Toledo every Wednesday morning and Sunday afternoon, June-Sept. Advance tickets for the trolley, which departs from Oliver House, 27 W. Broadway, are advised. For times and fares telephone (419) 245-5218.

Another great way to see parts of the area involves the **Arawanna II,** a stern-wheel riverboat that plies the Maumee River from the Rossford City Marina, 1321 Chantilly Dr., Maumee, tel. (419) 878-2177. Everything from industrial might to posh riverside homes are on display during one of these one-hour, narrated trips. Prices are $4.50 for adults, $4 for seniors, and $2.50 for children 12 and under. Reservations are a must.

Toledo Zoo

This zoo, at 2700 Broad St., Toledo, tel. (419) 385-5721, isn't the largest in Ohio, but it's among the most fascinating—to architectural buffs, among others. The zoo has several Depression-era Works Progress Administration (WPA) buildings. Consequently, the amphitheater, the aquarium, the aviary, the reptile house, the science museum, and the waterfowl pool exude an Art Deco 1930s charm. More recent attractions include an African savannah and a gorilla meadow. Among the most popular spots is a pool with a large expanse of glass for underwater viewing of hippos. There also are formal gardens and an opportunity to dine in a former lion cage at the cafe. In addition to the facilities, the animals themselves look healthy and are fascinating. Admission is $5 for adults and $2.50 for children ages 2-11. Hours are daily 10 a.m.-5 p.m., April-Sept. and 10 a.m.-4 p.m., Oct.-March. The facility is three miles south from downtown on SR 25, along the Maumee River.

Center of Science and Industry (COSI)

Right downtown at Summit and Superior Streets, tel. (419) 244-COSI (or tel. 419-244-2674), if this interactive museum brings to mind cute kids with their hair standing on end due to some static electrical device, you have the right idea. Science is brought exuberantly to life here, as it is at the similar COSI center in Columbus. Can anyone, young or old, resist playing with the Cranium

Troubleshooting Kit or taking the Galvanic Skin Response Test? Hours are Mon.-Sat. 10 a.m.-5 p.m., Sunday noon-5:30 p.m. Admission fees are $6.50 for adults and $5 for children ages 2-18 and seniors. Children under the age of 15 must have an adult chaperone.

Fort Meigs State Memorial
At 2900 W. River Rd. (SR 65), Perrysburg, tel. (419) 874-4121, this is the largest walled fortification in America. It stretches for hundreds of feet along the banks of the Maumee River and is a well-preserved site with plenty of parking and spacious grounds. The fort was used to defend this part of the country during the War of 1812. Structures within the walls are authentic, serving as backdrops for demonstrations or for the self-guided tour. Hours are Wed.-Sat. 9:30 a.m.-5 p.m., Memorial Day-Labor Day; Saturday 9:30 a.m.-5 p.m. and Sunday noon-5 p.m. from the day after Labor Day through October. Admission is $5 for adults, $1.25 for children age 6-12, to get inside the fort.

S.S. *Willis B. Boyer*
Docked at 26 Main St. (International Park), Toledo, tel.(419) 936-3070, once was the largest freighter on the Great Lakes. Now it's a museum ship, docked downtown for all to visit. By any standard the boat is massive. Visitors will be piqued by the captain's snazzy quarters, by the all-stainless steel galley, and by engines that exceed the size of most houses. Most popular place to snap a photo is in the wheelhouse, where visitors pose as pilots. Hours are 10 a.m.-5 p.m. every day May-Sept. and Wed.-Sat. 10 a.m.-5 p.m., Oct.-April. Admission charges are $5 for adults and $3 for students.

Wolcott House Museum Complex
Half a dozen buildings, all faithfully restored in 19th-century garb at 1031 River Rd., Maumee, tel. (419) 893-9602, evoke what life must have been like for the middle class in the Maumee Valley. The inventory of real estate includes the Federal-style Wolcott House, an 1840s Greek Revival home, a log cabin, a saltbox farmhouse, a railroad depot, and a rural church. Hours are Wed.-Sun. 1-4:30 p.m., with the last tour beginning at about 3 p.m. Admission charges are $3.50 for adults and $1.50 for children.

West End District
The city's historic West End District is said to have the largest stock (25 square blocks) of original late-Victorian houses still standing in the United States. Look for great architecture on either side of streets such as Collingwood, west of downtown. Tour the area with a walking-guide brochure in hand. They're available from the helpful folks at the Greater Toledo Convention and Visitors Bureau.

CULTURE AND ENTERTAINMENT

The **Toledo Museum of Art,** 2445 Monroe St., Toledo, tel. (419) 255-8000, is world class. The collection ranges from ancient through contemporary times and is well represented at all stops along the way. Besides paintings, check out furniture and other media. Glass works are especially prominent, in part because the Libbey family underwrote the startup of the museum. That doesn't mean the masters are neglected—Van Gogh, Picasso, Monet, and Matisse are here, with important examples of their work. If this is the only Ohio art museum travelers visit, their time could not have been better spent. Hours are Tues.-Thurs., Saturday 10 a.m.-4 p.m., Friday 10 a.m.-10 p.m., Sunday 1-5 p.m. Admission is free, except for special exhibitions.

The **Toledo Zoo Amphitheatre** at 2700 Broad St. offers big-name summertime entertainment from time to time. Recent Friday or Saturday night shows have included Heart, Bonnie Raitt, the Steve Miller Band, Tragically Hip, and Joe Cocker. All of the shows begin at 7:30 p.m. in this comfy outdoor setting; ticket prices vary but run from about $20 to $30. For more information, call (419) 474-1333.

Southwyck Art Cinema, 2040 S. Reynolds Road, tel. (419) 865-7101, bills itself as the only place in Toledo where you can see non-blockbuster movies. The three-screen house is in the Southwyck Shopping Center. Typical recent movies included *The Governess* and *Clay Pigeons.* Tickets are $4.75 before 6 p.m. and then $7.50 for adults. Children and seniors are $4.75 at all times.

The Toledo Museum of Art also houses good music. From October to May, locals attend a variety of musical and dance performances at the mu-

TOLEDO EVENTS

APRIL

Walleye Derby, Maumee River, West River Road, Maumee, tel. (419) 893-5805, features prizes for adults and children for the longest walleye, a leading game fish.

MAY

The **Great Balloon Chase,** Meigs State Memorial, Perrysburg, tel. (419) 241-4258, features more than 40 of the big, colorful orbs. Besides offering tethered rides, the balloonists compete in several competitions.

Rock, Rhythm, and Blues takes place over the three-day Memorial weekend on the Maumee riverfront, tel. (800) 243-4667. Several big-name stars are booked each year for the event.

Colonial Lost Arts Festival, Seven Eagles Historical Education Center, 16486 Wapakoneta Rd., Grand Rapids, tel. (419) 832-0114, is a family and history event. There are craftspeople, re-enactors, entertainers, and competitors of various sorts.

Garden Fair, Toledo Botanical Gardens, 5403 Elmer Drive, Toledo, tel. (419) 936-2986, includes more than 140 varieties of hard-to-find perennials, plus garden and art supplies.

JUNE

Old West End Festival, Bancroft and Robinwood Avenues, Toledo, tel. (419) 244-1915, puts some history on display. Tours of stately homes are available, as are carriage rides, a juried art fair and antiques show, food, and entertainment.

Taste of the Town, St. Clair Street, Toledo, tel. (419) 242-9587, ext. 107, is only a couple of years old, but the event has the aroma of a winner. The food-music fest has several heavyweight sponsors and its own Web site at www.themetronet.com.

Crosby Festival of the Arts, Toledo Botanical Gardens, 3403 Elmer Drive, Toledo, tel. (419) 936-2986, is Ohio's oldest juried art show. It features more than 200 regional and national artists and crafters, plus children's activities, music, and food.

Jamie Farr Classic, Highland Meadows Golf Club, 7455 Erie St., Sylvania, tel. (419) 241-4653, is a benefit. The Ladies Professional Golf Association (LPGA) event is hosted by the former *M*A*S*H* television show star, who is proud of his Toledo heritage.

JULY

Metroparks Bicycle Tour, tel. (419) 535-3050. This 70-mile junket is a connect-the-dots sort of ride from one Toledo park to another, with the emphasis on scenic history. It's fun and, since the local parks are so nice, visually rewarding.

LaGrange Street Polish Festival, Toledo, tel. (419) 255-8406, happens between Central and Mettler Streets. There are Polish bands, dancers, a polka contest, Polish foods, children's rides, and a crafts area.

Summerfest, Community Park, CR 8, Liberty Center, tel. (419) 533-3901, features polka dancing, a sock hop, food, and beverages. The town is between Bowling Green and Napoleon.

Kaleidoscope of Quilts is at the Franciscan Center, 6832 Convent Blvd., Sylvania, tel. (419) 882-4781. Judged quilts are on display and for sale.

AUGUST

The **Pemberville Free Fair,** tel. (419) 287-3832, isn't a salute to anything but is instead an excuse to have a good time. It's billed as Ohio's premier free fair, taking place in Memorial Park for four mid-August days. Among the highlights are the homemade pies at the American Legion food stand, amusements, exhibits, a kiddie parade, a cow-milking contest, a five-mile run, horse- and pony-pulling contests, and more. Pemberville is east of Bowling Green along SR 105.

The **Northwest Ohio Rib-Off** has nothing to do with Adam's gift to Eve, but is instead a chance to sample regional and national prizewinning barbecue delicacies. There's continuous entertainment, too. Telephone (800) 243-4667 for information.

OCTOBER

Harvest Days, 1031 River Rd., Maumee, tel. (419) 893-9602, is in the Wolcott Museum Complex. The event includes everything from heritage crafts demonstrations to pumpkin decorating.

seum's **Peristyle Concert Hall,** 2445 Monroe St., Toledo, tel. (419) 255-8000. The **Toledo Symphony Orchestra,** Two Marine Plaza, Toledo, tel. (419) 241-1272, is a busy group—it presents as many as 50 concerts between September and May. The symphony also entertains at Peristyle Concert Hall and elsewhere in northwest Ohio. The **Toledo Opera Association,** 1700 N. Reynolds Rd., Toledo, tel. (419) 531-5511, presents a series of operas and touring Broadway productions in various theaters throughout the city.

Speaking of Broadway, the **Toledo Rep,** 16 10th St., Toledo, tel. (419) 243-9277, performs Sept.-June at three locations: the Franciscan Center, 6832 Convent Blvd., in Sylvania, northwest of metro Toledo; Tenth Street Stage, 16 10th St., Toledo; and in Peristyle hall at the Toledo Museum of Art. The **Village Players,** 2740 Upton Ave., Toledo, tel. (419) 472-6817, give Sept.-May performances in their own theater at this address.

Nightlife

Rock and roll takes center stage at a couple of places along Main Street in East Toledo. **Frankie's Inner City Lounge,** 308 Main St., tel. (419) 691-7463, offers conventional and alternative rock, while **Main Event,** 137 Main St., tel. (419) 693-5300, books rock and roll bands on weekends. **Club Nucleus,** across the street from Main Event but without an address or a telephone, may be playing anything from live rock to DJ-spun retro and disco. Expect modest cover charges at these sites.

Recently moved from Perrysburg, the **Citi Lounge,** 209 N. Superior St., downtown Toledo, tel. (419) 243-4446, has a busy lineup. Monday offers swing dance lessons, Tuesday is swing night, Thursday is big-city blues, and Friday and Saturday are live music nights. Cover on the weekends is $3-5. Nationally known acts, such as George Clinton and the P-Funk All Stars sometimes are booked into the lounge, though good local bands such as the Royal Crown Revue can be seen regularly.

Those who ache to dance can do so from early afternoon to early morning Wed.-Sat. at **bretz,** 20th and Adams Streets, Toledo, tel. (419) 243-1900. This gay-friendly bar has a cadre of disk jockeys who spin the latest dance hits, and everybody recovers on Sunday, when a supper is served.

RECREATION

Bicycling

Riders can cruise along the Miami and Erie Canal for six miles, starting or ending up at Providence Metropark (see above). The trail has some coarse gravel, so there may be stretches where bikes have to be walked. Nevertheless, the scenery is 19th-century nostalgic.

Fishing

Charters abound. They are competitively priced and can accommodate visitors, whether traveling solo or in a large group. Reservations are advised, since times of year when the perch or walleye are plentiful make the boats in real demand. To reserve a spot at the rail, call the Lake Erie Charter Boat Information Service at (888) 675-3474.

Golf

Water hazards in this low-lying part of Ohio are a feature of many golf courses. A good example is Detwiler Golf Course, 4001 N. Summit Ave., Toledo, tel. (419) 726-9353. The course is well-located; it's only six minutes from downtown. An Arthur Hills original design, the 18-hole, par 71 facility can be played for $12 plus $7 for a cart (seniors play for $7.50 plus $7).

Spectator Sports

Minor-league baseball has gained lots of fans in the last few years as folks find a relaxed atmosphere, with players eager to greet fans and sign autographs. Such a team is the **Toledo Mudhens,** an International League club playing at Ned Skeldon Stadium, 2901 Key St., Maumee, tel. (419) 893-9438. The 'hens compete from April to September, charging $5 per ticket. After the game, visit the Ohio Baseball Hall of Fame at the same site to learn who starred in the big leagues from the Buckeye State.

Hockey fans can follow the **Toledo Storm.** This minor-league pro team faces off in the Toledo Sports Arena, 1 Main St., Toledo. Telephone (419) 691-0200 for tickets, which range from $7.50 to $9.

Every year, Mid-America Conference **football** teams upend larger schools on the gridiron. To see such a school in action, attend a University of Toledo home football game. The Rockets play such conference foes as Bowling Green State University, Miami of Ohio, Ohio University, and Western Michigan in their Glass Bowl on Bancroft Street. Tickets are a reasonable $13 for adults and $7 for persons under 18. Later in the year, John F. Savage Hall, also on Bancroft Street, is the site for men's basketball games. Tickets are $8 for adults and $4 for children. Telephone (419) 530-2239 for ticket ordering and availability and for details on seeing other sports.

Harness racing, where the jockeys become drivers and sit in a spindly, two-wheel contraption behind the horse, takes place at Raceway Park, 5700 Telegraph Rd., Toledo, tel. (419) 476-7751.

Besides being able to wager on the races in person, you can also bet on simulcast events from around the country. Live racing takes place every Friday and Saturday from 7 p.m. and Sunday from 6 p.m.

ACCOMMODATIONS

There are dozens of motel chains hereabouts, primarily serving drivers headed east, west, north, or south. Among the least expensive is **Motel 6,** 5535 Heatherdowns Blvd., tel. (419) 865-2308. Also thrifty are the Red Roof Inns Holland, Maumee, and Secor. All are hard by limited-access highways, and the Holland facili-

---

THE NORTH COUNTRY SCENIC TRAIL

Until now, America's National Scenic Trails have followed mountain ranges. Soon, a new approach called the North Country National Scenic Trail will cross half the country—and Ohio will play a major part.

The trail begins at Lake Sakakawea in central North Dakota. It heads east through the pines and lakes of Minnesota and cuts briefly across northern Wisconsin before turning east again, across Michigan's Upper Peninsula. The trail crosses the Mackinac Bridge before diving south-southwest through lower Michigan. It turns southeast, entering Ohio just west of Harrison Lake State Park, near the Fulton-Williams county lines. From there the pathway weaves toward Toledo before angling south to a point just east of Cincinnati. The trail moves east along the Ohio River to Shawnee State Park before cutting northeast across the rugged Hocking Hills and through the Wayne National Forest. After that, the path moves north, then east past Beaver Creek State Park, running into western Pennsylvania. The trail cuts through the Allegheny National Forest, seesawing into New York past the Finger Lakes. The North Country journey ends in Adirondack Park, with Vermont in sight, a distance of 4,195 miles.

Due to the new national trail making a sweeping "U" through Ohio, about one-fourth of the total mileage (1,050 miles) is inside Buckeye boundaries. Before unpacking walking shorts, in Ohio or anywhere else, please realize that much of the trail is only proposed. It should also be noted that not all activities are allowed on all stretches of the trail. Walking, hiking, jogging, cross-country skiing, and

snowshoeing are permitted everywhere, while bicycling and horseback riding are approved if the trail has been certified to withstand such use. And because different states pay for trail creation and upkeep in different ways, some stretches require permits by users.

Having noted all that, it should be pointed out that the North Country National Scenic Trail in Ohio follows the Buckeye Trail. The latter has completed stretches in many different parts of the state. One section runs unimpeded from east of Cincinnati to northeast of Dayton, a distance of about 60 miles. There also are long stretches in the vicinity of Grand Lake St. Marys and in the portion of Wayne National Forest northeast of Marietta. The Buckeye Trail association is so grass roots it does not have a telephone.

Those who enjoy access can join organizations dedicated to building and maintaining the North Country Trail in their state. To find out more, contact the North Country Trail Association, 49 Monroe Center NW-Suite 200B, Grand Rapids, MI 49503, tel. (616) 454-5506. In Ohio, contact the Buckeye Trail Association, P.O. Box 254 Worthington, OH 43085.

Trails are where you find them—or where land is thoughtfully purchased, preserved, donated, or otherwise set aside. At the moment, Cincinnati, Columbus, and Cleveland are being tied together via the all-purpose, 325-mile Ohio-to-Erie Trail. Virtually complete from Cincinnati to Xenia and between Akron and Cleveland, the trail will connect to other major trails that run back and forth through the Buckeye State. Completion of the Ohio-to-Erie Trail is set for 2003.

ty, exit 8 east of I-475, tel. (419) 866-5512, sometimes has late vacancies because it's tucked behind a mall. Other motels include the **Cross Country Inn,** exit 8 west of I-475, tel. (419) 866-6565, and the locally owned **Toledo Airport Motel** at 11201 Airport Service Rd., tel. (419) 865-5531.

The vast majority of motels are moderately or expensively priced. The city's splashiest hotel may be the **Radisson Hotel Toledo,** 101 N. Summit St., tel. (419) 241-3000. Attached to the Seagate Convention Center, it's at the corner of Summit and Monroe Streets. Nearby are the **Best Western Toledo Tower,** 141 N. Summit St., tel. (419) 242-2885, and the **Crowne Plaza Hotel,** Two Seagate, tel. (419) 241-1411, next door to the Center of Science and Industry on Summit Street. These big downtown hotels offer very competitive rates, particularly if there are no conventions in town at the moment.

Bed and breakfast spots include **Ghanashia,** 7959 Hill Ave., Holland, tel. (419) 865-6306; **Geer House Bed & Breakfast,** 2553 Glenwood Ave., Toledo, tel. (419) 242-7065, $35-55; and **Mansion View Inn,** 2035 Collingwood Blvd., Toledo, tel. (419) 244-5676.

FOOD

Peel off any of the limited-access highways for the usual lineup of franchise eateries. Look a little farther and you'll come across grass-roots good food that makes hunger rewarding in and near the Glass City.

Two Toledo restaurants, the **Beirut,** 4082 Monroe St., tel. (419) 473-0885, and **Byblos,** 1050 S. Reynolds Rd., tel. (419) 382-1600 serve a choice of Lebanese or Italian cuisine. Both are owned by the same people, with Byblos open for lunch Mon.-Fri. and both available for dinner every evening but Sunday. The kabobs here are high-traffic items, be they chicken, beef, or lamb. The pizzas and the sauce that goes into them both are homemade, and vegetarians will find a number of appetizers and main-course dishes to their liking. Lunch averages about $7, dinner approximately $12.

Cousino's Old Navy Bistro, 30 Main St. in International Park, Toledo, tel. (419) 697-NAVY (or tel. 419-697-6289), is on the east side of the Maumee across from the sports arena. Owned by a former pro football player, the restaurant offers outside dining when weather permits and serves lunch and dinner Mon.-Sat. plus Sunday brunch. Appetizers and alternatives here include a focaccia bread pizza topped with chicken and sun-dried tomatoes at $6.95, or several savory soups for about half that. Burgers are good, and so is the Reuben sandwich, priced at $5.95. Later on, try a hickory-smoked pork chop with banana-ginger chutney for $13.95, pan-fried market fish dinner for about $14.95, or one of several steaks.

North of Toledo, the **Linck Inn,** 301 River Rd., in the city of Maumee, tel. (419) 893-2388, is an attractive place with lace curtains. It serves a lunch buffet for $5.95 that may include chicken, pork chops, Italian beef, and a full soup and salad bar. There are a couple of dinner specials every evening, perhaps salmon patties with peas and cream sauce or meat loaf; either is $7.95. On Friday, look for pickerel (walleye) on special at $9.95. Hours for this suburban destination are Tues.-Fri. 11 a.m.-2 p.m. and Tues.-Sat. 5-9 p.m., plus 11 a.m.-3 p.m. for Sunday brunch.

A great downtown spot is the recently opened **Maumee Bay Brewing Co.,** 27 Broadway St., tel. (419) 241-1253. Housed in a brick building that dates from 1859, the brewpub-restaurant serves up such frothy creations as Fallen Timbers Red Ale and Lost Peninsula Pilsner, plus good pizza, hearty soup, and generous sandwiches—it's better-than-average bar food. A pint and a diner's share of a pizza should total about $10, with the brew and a meal perhaps $15.

Nick & Jimmy's Bar & Grill, 4956 Monroe St., tel. (419) 472-0756, serves all three meals and stays open Sun.-Thurs. until 1 a.m. and Fri.-Sat. until 2:30 a.m. Greek-American cuisine tops a varied menu. Huge hamburgers and cheeseburgers, cherry-smoked chicken and ribs, grilled kabobs, and heaping salads, make the spot locally popular. Nick & Jimmy's is well-attended for breakfast, too. Figure $5 for breakfast, about that for lunch, and maybe $10 for dinner. Even the waitstaff calls this place laid back. It's across from the Franklin Park Mall.

Sourdough Charlie's, 5858 Southwyck Mall, Toledo, tel. (419) 865-0873, serves breakfast and lunch every day. Sourdough pancakes are about $3, biscuits and gravy is also about $3, and corned beef with an egg and an English muffin is $4.50. Lunchwise, go for the salad bar at $4.49, the soup bar at $2.99, or sandwiches such as the blue cheeseburger for $3.49 or the Philly steak for $3.69 (most of the sandwiches show up on sourdough bread). This is a reasonable place to dine while shopping at the adjacent Southwyck Mall.

Tony Packo's Cafe, at 1902 Front St., tel. (419) 691-6054, is a local landmark. The cafe gained fame after Toledo native Jamie Farr (cross-dressing Corporal Klinger) longed for Tony Packo's hot dogs in several *M*A*S*H* television episodes—and for good reason. Teamed with a beer and bowl of chili, it's quite a meal. Live Dixieland jazz is offered after 8:30 p.m. Friday and Saturday. With a new facade out front, this is a happy, busy, visitor-filled joint. Hours are Mon.-Thurs. 11 a.m.-10 p.m., Fri.-Sat. 11 a.m.-midnight, Sunday noon- 9 p.m.

INFORMATION AND SERVICES

In an emergency, dial 911. The non-emergency number for the Toledo police is (419) 245-3340. Medical College Hospitals can be reached at (419) 381-4172. Toledo's main post office is at 435 S. St. Clair St.

The **Greater Toledo Convention and Visitors Bureau** is at 401 Jefferson Ave. Reach them at (419) 321-6404 or (800) 243-4667. **Bowling Green's Convention and Visitors Bureau** is at 163 N. Main St., tel. (419) 353-7945. The **Grand Rapids Area Chamber of Commerce** is at 2415 Front St., tel. (419) 832-1106. To learn of events at Bowling Green State University, call (419) 372-2445. To do the same at the University of Toledo, call (419) 530-2675. For a listing of downtown Toledo doings, call

(419) 243-8024. The citywide events line is (419) 241-111. Visitor information is broadcast on the radio at 1610 AM.

The *Blade* daily newspaper runs an extensive calendar of regional art, music, sports, and special events every Friday, usually in the "Weekend" section. Movie times and capsule reviews can be found in the same section. The *Blade* is published every morning. The *Sentinel-Tribune* in Bowling Green is a Mon.- Sat. evening newspaper with a daily entertainment page.

Transportation

Amtrak stops here at 415 Emerald Ave., tel. (419) 246-0159 on its way east or west. Greyhound picks up and drops off passengers at 811 Jefferson Ave., tel. (419) 248-4665. The Toledo Area Regional Transit Authority (TARTA) operates bus service in the city. To find out how to get from one point to the other, telephone (419) 243-RIDE (or tel. 419-243-7433). Cost of a ride is 85 cents for all passengers, though children younger than five ride free with an adult.

Shopping

Toledo being the Glass City, travelers may want to visit the Libbey Glass Outlet Store, 205 S. Erie St., tel. (419) 254-5000. A different kind of outlet store—one that sells nothing but umbrellas —is Haas-Jordan at 1447 Summit St., tel. (419) 243-2189. It makes and sells more than 500 species of umbrella on the premises. Foodies can visit Erie Street Market, 2375 Erie St., tel. (419) 255-0393, or Farmers Market, Market and Superior Streets, tel. (419) 255-6765, for year-round fresh edibles. Mall devotees can shop at Franklin Park Mall, 5001 Monroe St., tel. (419) 472-7275 or Southwyck Shopping Center, 2040 S. Reynolds Rd., tel. (419) 865-7161.

CENTRAL WESTERN OHIO

This is the heartland, and while folks here don't always take kindly to progressive ideas they do deal sympathetically enough with the average visitor. Populated later than much of the state, the area is most scenic around Bellefontaine and agriculturally productive everywhere. Some of the more picturesque rural areas are sprouting hobby farms and other telltale signs of urban gentry, so visit soon.

History

Native Americans cruised back and forth through here, living off the abundance of wildlife and vegetation and finding it easy to grow corn, squash, and other crops. The French traded implements, blankets, and firearms for furs in the late 17th century. British forces moved in to divide Indian allegiances between the two European powers, succeeding in making friends with the Miami tribe. French and Indian forces punished the Miami in 1752 by destroying their fortification at Pickawillany, near present-day Piqua. For more than a decade afterward, French and British government officials and traders contested this and other parts of what would become Ohio.

Settlers began showing up in earnest here well after statehood. By then the demoralized Indians had drifted west, out of the new state. Pioneers typically were very young, penniless people who wanted to farm or start businesses. They showed up in places like Cleveland or Columbus, found them too confining, and struck out for more remote settlements. An encouraging number were successful. New Jersey residents and Pennsylvanians of English Protestant descent, southern Quakers and Pennsylvania Germans were followed by German, Scotch, and Irish immigrants.

By the middle of the 19th century, Ohio was America's leading producer of corn. Livestock made Ohio first in sheep production, a leader in beef cattle, and the developer of the versatile Poland China breed of hog. Orchards were thick with apples every year. Cities such as Marion prospered by being centers for agricultural plenty—farmers spent their earnings on all sorts of goods. Ohio was a leader, too, in manufacturing capital goods such as wagons, steel plows, farm machinery, fencing, furniture, leather, and more. A labor shortage that lasted for much of the century proved that the state was large and getting bigger. Following the Civil War, even more good fortune was realized.

Northwest Ohio was home to the Great Black Swamp, a watery, forbidding area that covered parts of several counties and was a haven for wildlife. For years settlers near the swamp had hit slimy, apparently useless oil while drilling for water. The gas often found along with the oil, was burned off, largely for amusement. A well drilled intentionally for oil in 1886 near Findlay hit an estimated eight million cubic feet of the substance. The glare from the burning gas pipe could be seen for 40 miles. The heat caused surrounding midwinter grass to green up and the glow could be seen for 40 miles. Many people got rich.

The Great Black Swamp, atop a wealth of oil and gas, was slowly and laboriously drained. When most of the water was gone, farmers discovered the remaining muck to be infinitely suitable for growing crops. They plowed the land from one horizon to the other, realizing hundreds of bushels of corn, and dozens of bushels of oats and wheat, for every acre. To this day, farming forms the backbone of the land—though suburbs across the state are being platted at the alarming rate of 70 acres a day. Eyeing the abundance of this part of Ohio, a fellow in the early 19th century said, "It will be our own fault if we are not the happiest people in the Union."

Mansfield is the largest town in this area, totaling about 50,000 residents. Its history also is representative: it was established on the Mohican River in 1808. A blockhouse was erected here during the War of 1812, the railroad came through here in 1846, and there is a monument to Johnny Appleseed. Virtually every town of any size has one or more claims to fame. Marion was the birthplace and home of Warren Harding, the 29th U.S. president. Harding presided over an administration rocked by the Teapot Dome scandal and by rumors of his womanizing. He died in

1923 after only two years in office. Bellefontaine has tidier bragging rights: it was the site of the very first stretch of paved highway, poured in 1895. Other places are known for a variety of things, from the glitter of glass in Fostoria, to the hiss of skis down snowy slopes in Mansfield.

Location and Orientation

For the purposes of this book, this huge region is bounded on the north by the Ohio Turnpike (I-80/90) and US 20, on the west by the Ohio-Indiana state line, on the south by US 40 and I-70, and on the east by I-71. Both I-75 and US 23 are major north-south highways running between Toledo and Dayton. The latter road, which is four lanes, runs from east of Findlay to and from Columbus, allowing drivers to move directly between northwestern Ohio and the state capital without resorting to two-lane roads. Interstate 75 runs through Lima and Piqua before arriving in Dayton. The area is more than 100 miles from east to west and close to 150 miles north to south.

SIGHTS

Cedar Bog Nature Reserve

At 980 Woodburn Rd., west of US 68 and south of Urbana, tel. (937) 484-3744 or (800) 860-0147, this bog is one of those marvelous incongruities that make Ohio so interesting. Nearly 1,000 feet above sea level, it is in reality a fen—a wetland with upwelling water. The 25-acre memorial is home to rare, threatened, and endangered flora and fauna. A mile-long boardwalk that is handicapped accessible juts far into the site, where a knowledgeable guide points out rare species. Tours seldom are crowded but it's always a good idea to call ahead. Cedar Bog is $3 for adults and $1.25 for children. Hours are Wed.-Sun. 9 a.m.-4:30 p.m., April 1-Sept. 30. In October and March, tours are by appointment only.

Indian Lake State Park

Large and round, Indian Lake, 12774 SR 235 N, near Lakeview, tel. (937) 843-2717, is tucked into the northwest corner of Logan County. There are three beaches, a huge campground, four shelter houses, a playground and three boat-launch ramps. The fish *du jour* is the saugeye, a cross between sauger and walleye. Boat traffic is heavy in warm weather, in part because Indian Lake is a mere 20 miles east of I-75, off US 33.

Malabar Farm State Park

A most unconventional state park, at 4050 Bromfield Rd., in Lucas, tel. (419) 892-2784, Malabar Farm mixes the beauty of farming and the beauty of nature. It is as rich an experience as a traveler is apt to have in any Ohio state park. That may have been what Louis Bromfield (1894-1956), Pulitzer Prize-winning author who was part of the founding staff of *Time* magazine, intended when he began to build Malabar Farm in 1939, a second life after an esteemed literary career. This dream farm was used until 1956 by Bromfield, who entertained here such newlyweds as Humphrey Bogart and Lauren Bacall.

The farm was deeded to Ohio in 1972 and it became a state park in 1976. There is a guided tour of the aptly named Big House, with its 32 rooms, as well as an explanation of Bromfield's philosophy and how he applied it to his haven. Suffice to say that the writer was an active environmentalist long before the term came into vogue. He practiced land and soil conservation, sharing the farm not only with friends and neighbors but with wildlife and the many plants that popped up as a result of his rejuvenation of the land.

In addition to the farm and the stand of pretty trees behind it, there are two trails, each a dozen miles long. One is for hiking, one is for horseback riding. There's also a day-use cabin, a horseman's camp, picnicking facilities, fishing, winter recreation, a restored stagecoach inn with home-cooked meals, and the Malabar Farm Youth Hostel (call 419-892-2055 for information and reservations). All in all, Bromfield wanted Malabar Farm to be 917 acres of the way the rural Midwest ought to be. To see if he succeeded, exit I-71 onto SR 13 heading south, then take an almost immediate left (east) onto Hanley Road. Continue east on Pulver Road, then right (south) on Pulver to Pleasant Valley Road. Turn left (east) onto Pleasant Valley and continue to the park. Malabar Farm is less than 10 miles from the interstate highway. Tours of the Big House are offered year-round, except for holidays. Admission is $3 for adults, $1 for those under 18. Tractor-drawn tours of the farm are offered from Memorial Day through the end of October for $1, under 12 free.

Mac-O-Chee Castle, West Liberty

Mac-A-Cheek Chateau and Mac-O-Chee Castle

Both of these structures, SR 245, West Liberty, tel. (937) 465-2821, were built by the Piatt brothers, two 19th-century gentlemen farmers. The houses are about a mile from each other. The smaller dwelling, Mac-A-Cheek Chateau, is a Norman style country home. The larger residence is a Flemish-style castle. Both are striking, constructed in stone with soaring towers, in sight of a meandering creek. Hours are 11 a.m.-5 p.m. every day, Memorial Day-Labor Day, noon-4 p.m. March weekends, and noon-4 p.m. daily in May and Labor Day-October. Admission to either house is $6 for adults, $5 for students and seniors, and $3 for children ages 3-12. the tours are informative and the interiors are luxurious.

Richland Carrousel Park

This park, at 75 N. Main St. in Mansfield, tel. (419) 522-4223, sets the tone for the downtown area. The park contains 52 animals and a pair of chariots, all of which were hand carved in Mansfield. Hours are 11 a.m.-5 p.m. seven days a week, with hours extended to 8 p.m. Wednesday. There are several carousels here, with no admission charged but for payment in exchange for a ride. A ride is 60 cents, or two-for-$1, or a dozen rides for $5 or 50 rides for $20. The horses, the chariots, and the carousels show workmanship that borders on art.

Caverns

The **Seneca Caverns,** located at 15248 E. Thompson Township Rd. 178, in Bellevue, tel. (419) 483-6711, is a most peculiar cave, being a crack in the earth rather than a hole in the ground. No one knows how this cavern came to be, but there are eight grand rooms with an underground river some 100 feet below the surface. Hours are 9 a.m.-7 p.m. Memorial Day-Labor Day and 10 a.m.-5 p.m. May, September, and October weekends. Admission fees are $7.50 for adults and $5 for children.

Two caves are within a few miles of each other a bit farther south. **Ohio Caverns,** 2212 SR 245 East, West Liberty, tel. (937) 465-4017, is the largest cave system in the state. Hours there are 9 a.m.-5 p.m., April-Oct. and 9 a.m.-4 p.m. the rest of the year, open every day. **Zanes Shawnee Caverns,** 7092 SR 540, Bellefontaine, tel. (937) 592-9592, contain little pools of pearl-like minerals found in only one other cave on earth (in Switzerland). Hours are 10 a.m.-5 p.m. daily (closed Jan.-Feb.). Admission fees are $7 for adults and $4 for children. Cave visitors receive a $1 discount on the usually $6 and $3 admission to another on-site attraction, a museum containing Indian artifacts.

Shamrock Vineyards

Shamrock Vineyards, on Rengert Road, Waldo, tel. (740) 726-2883, is this region's only winery. Located in the southeast corner of Marion County, the site offers 10 wine varieties in a part of the

CENTRAL-WESTERN EVENTS

JANUARY

Toy, Collectible, & Sports Card Show, US 30 and Trible Road, Mansfield, tel. (419) 884-3253, is set for the Richland County Fairgrounds.

FEBRUARY

The **Living History Trade Fair** is at the Sandusky County Fairgrounds in Fremont, tel. (419) 334-8180. Costumed peddlers from Medieval to Civil War times offer their wares.

Evening Owl Walks, Malabar State Farm, SR 603, Mansfield, tel. (419) 892-2784, feature four separate programs followed by guided walks.

APRIL

Collectors Toy & Craft Show, Champaign County Fairgrounds, Park Avenue, Urbana, tel. (937) 826-4201, combines a variety of toys with dolls and crafts.

MAY

Ohio Civil War Collectors Show, Richland County Fairgrounds, 750 N. Home Rd., Mansfield, tel. (419) 289-3120, is a treasure trove. There are 600 tables of military items, plus an artillery show, and a living history encampment.

Volksmarch, Malabar Farm State Park, SR 603, Mansfield, tel. (419) 892-2784, is a six-mile walk. The trek is done at each participant's own pace in Malabar woods, fields, and surrounding areas.

Bluegrass Festival, Country Stage Music Park, CR 1031, Nova, tel. (419) 668-8340, takes place in the northwest corner of Ashland County at the junction of US 224 and SR 511. Besides the music there are camping activities.

Chili Cookoff, Snow Trail Ski Resort, Possum Run Road, Mansfield, tel. (419) 756-1133, lets visitors sample judged chili recipes. Other forms of fun include entertainment and a jalapeño eating contest.

Spring Plowing Days take place at Malabar Farm State Park, SR 603, Mansfield, tel. (419) 892-2784. Teams of draft horses not only plow but snake big logs out of the woods for all to see.

Logan Hills Festival is set for Hall-Fawcett Park, 300 S. Fountain Ave., Zanesfield, tel. (937) 599-3389. Parade, crafters, entertainment, and the "Taloga Outdoor Historical Drama" are scheduled. Zanesfield is on US 33 southeast of Bellefontaine.

JUNE

Marion County Steam & Gas Engine Club Show, Marion County Fairgrounds, Marion, tel. (614) 383-4871, features antique farm machinery in action. Besides a parade of rural equipment there is a salute to antique motorcycles.

Collector Toy Show, Logan County Fairgrounds, Lake Avenue, Bellefontaine, tel. (937) 826-4201. There are farm toys, toy trucks, Hot Wheels, racing toys, banks, and more for show and for sale.

Italian American Festival, downtown Crestline, tel. (419) 683-4466, proves that there are important Italians besides Columbus. Try ethnic dancing, folk music, a spaghetti cookoff, beer gardens, and cultural booths. Crestline is located on US 30 west of Mansfield.

Mad River Steam & Gas Show happens in Urbana at the Champaign County Fairgrounds, tel. (937) 826-4114. Here travelers learn the difference between a Massey Harris and a Minneapolis Moline antique tractor while other old-time power equipment screeches and snorts.

---

state that is less hospitable for grape production than the warmer Lake Erie area. Shamrock's best-selling wines are both Lambruscas: Windfall White and Buckeye Red, both of which are just $4.99 a bottle. Personnel here report that their product is "99% grown here," is available in some Columbus stores, and that 1998 looks to be a vintage year. Hours are Mon.-Sat. 1-6 p.m. all year long.

Mount Gilead State Park

This park, 4119 SR 95, lies about 25 miles southwest of Mansfield. The telephone number, (419) 946-1961, is important because of what takes place in the park. Modest in size and with a smallish lake, this day-use facility nevertheless has a number of especially interesting special programs: Earth Day, a country musicfest, a traditional July 4 celebration, an apple butter fest, even a combination car show and sock hop. For those who would rather do than learn, duck hunting goes on and paddle boats and canoes can be rented. From I-71, travel west about seven miles on SR 95 to the park entrance.

Historic Home and Garden Tour, Urbana, tel. (800) 791-6010. This small city has some snazzy houses, and this is a nice opportunity to see the interiors. There are crafts for sale in some of the homes.

Toy, Collectible & Sportscard Show, Richland County Fairgrounds, US 30 and Trimble Road, Mansfield, tel. (419) 884-3253, features 200 tables for sale or trade.

Summerfest is in Sycamore, in Wyandot County, tel. (419) 927-2432. Activities include live entertainment, a parade, rides, crafts, a flea market, and a chicken-pork chop barbecue.

Tiffin Glass Collectors Club Show & Sale, School of Opportunity, 780 E. CR 20, Tiffin, tel. (419) 447-5505, is a two-day event. Tiffin is located east of Findlay and Fostoria on SR 18.

Home & Garden Tour, Galion, tel. (419) 468-6727, is a chance for this small city west of Mansfield on SR 309 to show off a number of refurbished, classic homes.

JULY

Ohio Lily Society Show, Kingwood Center, 900 Park Avenue West, Mansfield, tel. (419) 522-0211.

Ice Cream Social, Ashland County Historical Museum, 414 Center St., Ashland, tel. (419) 289-3111, is an afternoon event. It includes music and museum displays.

Festival in the Park, City Park, Willard, tel. (419) 935-1654, is a four-day event. It features food and craft booths, nightly entertainment, rides, and a parade.

Heritage Family Fest, Upper Sandusky, tel. (419) 294-3057, is a three-day, citywide affair with a parade and entertainment each evening.

Rib Cookoff, 2441 Kenwood Circle, Mansfield, tel. (419) 755-4838, takes place on the campus of North Central Technical College. Rib chefs compete for cash prizes and local appetites to the tune of various entertainments.

Tree Town Festival, Gormley Park, in the town of Forest (west of Upper Sandusky off US 30), tel. (419) 273-2500, provides shade for a 5K run, a parade, entertainment, and rides.

Fly-In/Camp-Out Air Fair, Upper Valley Pike, Tremont City, tel. (937) 969-8521, takes place at the Mad River Airport. Homebuilt, classic, and conventional aircraft are on display, and there are opportunities for plane rides. Tremont City is located southwest of Urbana off US 68.

Tractor & Engine Show, 1783 SR 60, Ashland, tel. (419) 281-0749, happens at the Ashland County-West Holmes Career Center. Antique tractors and engines are displayed and put through their paces.

NOVEMBER

Tiffin Glass Collectors Club Show & Sale, 780 E. CR 20, Tiffin, tel. (419) 447-5505, occurs in the School of Opportunity. Tiffin glass and other quality glassware are offered for sale. Tiffin is located east of Findlay and Fostoria on SR 18.

DECEMBER

Victorian Christmas Holiday, Tiffin, tel. (419) 447-5866, features horse-drawn carriage rides, a holiday food fair, open houses, a gingerbread house contest, carolers, and Father Christmas.

Christmas at Malabar, SR 603, Mansfield, tel. (419) 892-2784, is a great occasion to visit the state park. The fresh cookies and warm cider alone are worth the trip.

Museums

The **Richland County Museum,** at 51 Church St. in Lexington near Mansfield, tel. (419) 884-2230, is housed in a schoolhouse that dates from before the Civil War. On display here are tools, clothing, toys, furniture, and paintings from the early days of the county. The facility is open weekends 1:30-4:30 p.m., May-October.

The **Wyandot Popcorn Museum,** is a delightful little oddity at 169 E. Church St., Marion, tel. (740) 387-4255. The popcorn poppers on the premises are worth more than half a million dollars and come in every conceivable configuration. The museum operates inside a circus tent. Hours

are Wed.-Sun. 1-4 p.m. and Sat.-Sun. 1-4 p.m., Nov.-April. Admission is free but donations are encouraged. The adjacent Heritage Hall museum, which once was the post office, contains the papers of President Warren Harding.

The **Harding Home and Memorial,** at 380 Mt. Vernon Ave. (SR 95), is located about two miles west of US 23, in Marion, tel. (740) 387-9630. It was from this site that Warren Harding conducted the successful "front porch" presidential campaign. The printer's apprentice who bought the city newspaper at the age of 19 should have stayed in Marion, where he is respected to this day. The Harding Memorial is set in a 10-

acre landscaped park and is a circle of Grecian-style columns made of Georgia marble. The site is open Wed.-Sat. 9:30 a.m.-5 p.m. and Sun. noon-5 p.m. from the Saturday prior to Memorial Day to Labor Day. Admission is $3 for adults and $1.75 for children age 6-12.

RECREATION

Those who like kiddy fun will appreciate **Racing Waters Action Park,** 21254 SR 12, Fostoria, tel. (419) 435-9568. Things to do here include taking on the waterslide, hitting the beach, or driving go-karts, Nascarts, or bumper boats. There are no admission charges; visitors pay for various packages that allow them to pursue the recreations of their choice. The facility is open every day Memorial Day-Labor Day and weekends before and after summer.

Bicycling
Head for North Lake Park off West Fourth Street, Mansfield, tel. (419) 884-3764, to find the head of the **Richland County Bicycle Trail.** The trail heads south out of the city into an underappreciated part of rural Ohio—one that flashes past from the car windows of I-71. This free trail was put together locally, which shows what local government can do when it is motivated. The trail is smooth and, once out of town, delightfully verdant and rural for all of its 18 miles. The **Mansfield Loop** is a 22-mile circle that begins in John Todd Park on Bowers Street, Mansfield, tel. (419) 755-9819. It's an acceptable alternative to the new county trail.

Skiing
Several good downhill ski destinations beckon. One is **Mad River Mountain Ski Resort,** US 30, Bellefontaine, tel. (937) 599-1015, which has slopes that vary in length from 1,000-3,000 feet. The facility includes snowmaking machines, a lodge, a cafeteria, and a bar. Mad River is about five miles southeast of Bellefontaine. Another is **Snow Trails Ski Area,** Possum Run Road, Mansfield, tel. (419) 522-7393. Snow Trails is just east of SR 13, south of town. **Clear Fork Ski Area,** Resort Dr., Butler, tel. (419) 883-2000, is located about 15 miles southeast of town on SR 97.

Spectator Sports
Mid-Ohio Road Racing Course, Steam Corners Road, Lexington, tel. (800) MIDOHIO (tel. 800-643-6446) or (419) 884-4000.

ACCOMMODATIONS

In Bellefontaine, motel chain accommodations include the **Comfort Inn,** 260 Northview Dr., Bellefontaine, tel. (937) 599-6666 and the **Holiday Inn,** 1134 N. Main St., Bellefontaine, tel. (937) 593-8515. In Upper Sandusky, at the junction of US 23 and US 30 travelers will find the **Amerihost Inn, 1726 E. Wyandot, tel. (419) 294-3919 and the** Comfort Inn, 105 Comfort Dr., tel. (419) 294-3891. All are moderately priced.

In Mansfield, there's a nice quartet of moderately priced motels, **Best Western,** 880 Laver Rd., tel. (419) 589-2200; **Comfort Inn,** 500 N. Trimble Rd., tel. (419) 529-1000; **Comfort Inn,** 855 Comfort Plaza Dr., Bellville (five miles south of Mansfield), tel. (419) 886-4000; and **Holiday Inn,** 116 Park Ave. W., tel. (419) 525-6000.

FOOD

Brunches Restaurant, 103 N. Main St., Mansfield, tel. (419) 526-2233, serves breakfast and lunch. Breakfasts include a choice of three omelets ranging in price from $4 to $5. Lunches feature several varieties of quiche, with a muffin, for around $4. Seven-layer salad is an item that should be on more menus; with a muffin and soup it's $5. Known for creating creative club sandwiches, Brunches sells its clubs for $5. Hours at this popular spot are Mon.-Sat. 7 a.m.-3 p.m. and Sunday 9 a.m.-2 p.m. Take the US 30 exit west off I-71.

Grand Central Grill, 320 W. Center St., Marion, tel. (740) 387-8124, recaptures the era of the interurban railway. This atmospheric joint serves lunch and dinner Mon.-Sat., featuring a number of popular gourmet sandwiches at lunch that range from $4 to $5. They include turkey bacon club, Philly cheese steak, and half-pound steakburger. In the evenings, the most popular dishes are the varieties of pasta, from $6.50 to $7.25. Music is featured on the patio on summer weekend nights, and there's a talented acoustic guitar vocalist every Tuesday evening.

MID-OHIO AUTO RACING

Why isn't road racing more popular in the United States? The U.S., after all, has more miles of paved roads than anywhere else. More popular oval racing, which at its worst is like watching fast freeway traffic, is easier to follow. It also offers grandstand seating, from which fans have only to swivel their heads to view most of the track. Ovals may have become America's circuit of choice simply because it was inconvenient to shut down stretches of public road all weekend so a bunch of darn fools could risk their necks. There are a few longtime bastions of road racing, and Ohio is home to one of the best.

The Mid-Ohio Sports Car Course is a 2.4-mile, 15-turn permanent circuit laid out off Steam Corners Road west of Lexington. Less than two hours from either Cleveland or Columbus and about 10 miles southwest of Mansfield, the privately owned track has been in operation since 1962. Each season, half a dozen public racing weekends are held, as well as drivers' schools and amateur events. Fans show up, pay an admission price ranging from $5 general admission to $250 for an up-close photo pass; they park, walk from corner to corner or spread a blanket to view the action. Some turns are slow, others are fast. Speaking of speed, the very fastest cars lap Mid-Ohio in about 70 seconds, a speed in excess of 120 miles per hour.

Events each year generally include the following:

U.S. Road Racing Classic, mid-June. This weekend of sports car racing features everything from Can-Am prototypes to familiar Mustangs and Camaros to open-wheel machines, all in separate events.

Vintage Grand Prix, late June. Yesterday's sports and sports-racing cars take to the track as they did in years gone by. There's also a car show.

Vintage Motorcycle Days, mid July. If old-time cars can orbit the track, so can old-time bikes. Besides the machines on the asphalt there is an off-track motocross contest, a motorcycle show, and a parts swap meet.

Super Cycle Weekend, late July. Streamlined cycles capable of top speeds faster than most cars take to the track in several different classes. Dealers from across the state join their customers to show up here and view the races.

Indy Cars, early August. The fast, open-wheel machines compete in a 200-mile race. Also on the schedule are other classes of open-wheel cars.

Sports Car Club of America Runoffs, mid-fall. This amateur event features 24 classes of cars and tells amateur roadracers all over the country who is the person to beat and what he or she is driving.

For tickets or information, telephone (800) MID-OHIO (tel. 800-643-6446) or (419) 884-4000.

COURTESY MID-OHIO SPORTS CAR COURSE

Carle's Bratwurst, 1210 E. Mansfield St., Bucyrus, tel. (419) 562-7741, produces its own succulent sausages. They offer a bratwurst sandwich on rye bun with a choice of kraut, onions, mustard, or all of the above for $2, and they pack brats to go or to ship back home. Production goes on most weekdays, so visitors can look through a window and see tomorrow's sausages being made. Hours are Mon.-Sat. 8 a.m.-7 p.m. and Sunday11 a.m.-3 p.m. in the summer; Mon.-Sat. 9 a.m.-6 p.m. the rest of the year.

G&R Tavern, 100 Marion St., Waldo, tel. (740) 726-9685, is famous for its fried-bologna sandwiches. Each one is $2.70, and the tavern sells about 800 pounds of bologna in sandwich form every week. There are burgers and other fried foods for the faint of heart. The G&R is open Mon.-Sat. 8 a.m.-10 p.m. Waldo is on US 23, eight miles south of Marion.

Rocky's, 22 S. Park Square, Mansfield, tel. (419) 522-1342, is an atmospheric English pub in the middle of the downtown area. The food is Continental and ranges from steak dinners ($14.95-18.95) to an especially popular vegetarian mushroom pasta ($16.95). Don't overlook the Cuban black-bean soup, which was on the menu when Rocky's opened in 1970 and continues to draw praise. A number of foreign beers and stouts are available. Kitchen hours are Tues.-Fri. 4-10 p.m. and Saturday 5-10 p.m.

INFORMATION AND SERVICES

The **Mansfield/Richland County Convention and Visitors Bureau** is at 52 Park Ave. W., tel. (419) 525-1300 or (800) 642-8282. The **Ashland Area Chamber of Commerce** is at 47 W. Main St., tel. (419) 281-4584. The **Marion Area Convention and Visitors Bureau** holds forth at 1952 Marion-Mt. Gilead Rd., Room 121, tel. (740) 383-1666 or (800) 371-6688. The **Seneca County Convention and Visitors Bureau** is at 84 Jefferson St., Tiffin, tel. (419) 447-5866. When in Upper Sandusky, visit the **Wyandot County Visitors and Convention Bureau** at 108 E. Wyandot Ave., tel. (419) 294-3349.

The **Crawford County Visitors Bureau** can be reached at (419) 562-4205. Bellefontaine is home to the **Greater Logan County Area Convention and Visitors Bureau,** 100 S. Main St.,

tel. (937) 599-5121. The **Fremont/Sandusky County Convention & Visitors Bureau** is at 1510 E. State St., tel. (419) 332-4470 or (800) 255-8070. **Bellevue Area Tourism & Visitors Bureau** can be reached at (419) 483-5359 or (800) 860-4726.

Several colleges are in this expansive area. To find out what sporting event, lecture, exhibit, or other event may be going on when travelers are in town, they should call Ashland University, Ashland, (419) 289-4142; Bluffton College, Bluffton (419) 358-3000; Heidelberg College, Tiffin, (419) 448-2000; Ohio Northern University, Ada, (419) 772-2000; or Tiffin University, Tiffin, (419) 447-6442.

There are a number of daily newspapers hereabouts. Among the largest is the *News Journal* out of Mansfield. The evening paper's entertainment section is called "Weekend" and comes out each Thursday. Nearby, look to the *Times-Gazette* in Ashland Mon.-Sat. mornings. The *Marion Star* is an evening daily that runs an entertainment section in its Sunday morning edition. The *Advertiser-Tribune* is a morning daily news product in Tiffin, while the *Daily Chief-Union* serves residents of Upper Sandusky each evening.

Bucyrus dwellers read the *Telegraph Forum* weekday evenings and Saturday mornings. They read the *Kenton Times* evenings and Saturday mornings in Hardin County, and in Logan County they favor the evening and Saturday morning *Bellefontaine Examiner.* Fostorians enjoy the *Review Times* evenings and Saturday mornings, which runs an entertainment section each Friday.

Finally, look for *Zig Zag,* a free semimonthly tabloid offered in the Bowling Green-Fremont-Tiffin area. The newspaper modestly bills itself as "Northwest Ohio's Premier Free Historical/Cultural Publication," and that may be true. But the value of the giveaway is a rundown of concerts and other events, apparently all across the northern half of the state.

Transportation

Greyhound runs up and down I-71 between Cleveland and Columbus. Catch the bus in Mansfield at 74 S. Diamond St., tel. (419) 524-1111. There's talk in the legislature of creating a passenger rail system between Cleveland and Columbus, but no funds have been set aside.

Shopping
The mall-obsessed can cruise **Richland Mall,** in the Mansfield suburb of Ontario, tel. (419) 529-4003, which is just off SR 309 west of the city.

Safety and Emergencies
In emergencies, dial 911 for police, fire, or medical assistance. In **Mansfield,** police quarters are at 30 N. Diamond St.; their non-emergency telephone number is (419) 755-9724. Hospital facilities are available at Med Central, 335 Glessner Ave., tel. (419) 526-8000.

In **Marion,** find the police at 233 W. Center St., non-emergency tel. (740) 387-0541. Marion General Hospital is at 98 McKinley Park Blvd., tel. (740) 383-8400.

ALONG I-75

If there is commerce anywhere, there is proof of it on this stretch of federally funded, divided highway. Lots and lots of people and goods move back and forth between Toledo and Cincinnati, departing the big road for stops in Lima and Findlay, or to head north to Detroit or south into Kentucky. Not the most scenic drive on earth—or in Ohio—the interstate does what it was designed to do: move quickly among a number of points of interest.

History
Interstate highways follow the paths of least resistance rather than the paths most steeped in history, so I-75 doesn't exactly trace any significant group's wanderings. On the other hand, it passes close by a number of cities that have been around for a while. Findlay and Lima are best known for sitting atop a huge dome of natural gas in the 19th century.

Location and Orientation
Interstate 75 enters Ohio from Michigan at Toledo. From the port city, it heads in a south-southwest direction, passing such Northwest Ohio cities as Bowling Green, Findlay, Lima, Sidney, Piqua, and Troy before crossing I-70, a convenient line to divide the northwest from the southwest.

SIGHTS

Mary Jane Thurston State Park
At 1-466 SR 65, McClure, tel. (419) 832-7662, this park is on the upper Maumee River. The namesake was a Grand Rapids lady who donated the first few riverfront acres so that the park could exist. Its 555 acres are devoted to 35 campsites, a boat-launch ramp, 114 docks that are rented out for the season, several overnight dock rentals for visitors, plus picnic tables and so on. Park personnel indicate that boaters can go 15-17 miles upstream from here, depending on water level and time of year.

Museums
The **Allen County Museum,** at 620 W. Market St., Lima, tel. (419) 222-9426, lets visitors know what a crucial part Lima played in the spread of the railroad across Ohio and the country. A handsome locomotive constructed by Lima Locomotive Works stands just outside the museum in Lincoln Park. The museum itself is filled with railroad and other memorabilia from the 19th and early 20th centuries. Hours are Tues.-Sun. 1-5 p.m. There are no admission fees for the museum itself. The adjacent MacDonell House, which is listed on the National Register of Historic Places and is filled with Victorian furnishings, costs $2 for persons ages 12 and over.

You must makes reservations to visit the **John Dillinger/Sheriff Sarber Memorial Museum,** 333 N. Main St., Lima, tel. (419) 227-3535. Dillinger, a Hoosier who relieved banks of their money all across the Midwest in the 1930s, was held in the local jail for a while. Visitors' questions are answered and they are shown a documentary video that tells how Sheriff Jess Sarber lost his life when Dillinger's gang broke him out of captivity. The tour is free.

The **Neil Armstrong Air and Space Museum,** I-75 at Wapak-Fisher Road, Wapakoneta, tel. (419) 738-8811 or (800) 282-5393, salutes a pioneering astronaut and hometown boy. Armstrong was the first person to set foot on the moon, so there's good reason to erect a dome in his honor and fill it with flight- and space-related

A training jet similar to one flown by Neil Armstrong stands outside the Neil Armstrong Air and Space Museum in Wapakoneta.

items. There are various rockets, planes, and memorabilia here, including items from the history of flight to Apollo mission spacesuits. Hours are Mon.-Sat. 9:30 a.m.-5 p.m., Sun. noon-5 p.m., March-Nov. Admission for adults is $5; seniors, $4; children 6-12, $1.25.

Fort Amanda State Memorial

This park, on SR 198, Wapakoneta, is in reality a memorial noting the former location of a fort built by William Henry Harrison in 1812. Nine miles west of the city, the site has hiking trails, picnic tables, and a shelter. Fort Amanda is open daylight hours only.

Piqua Historical Area

A historic farm dating to 1829 is the focus of this area, on Hardin Road, Piqua, tel. (937) 773-2522. The farmhouse is authentically furnished and there are expanses of green for special events. Hours are Wed.-Sat. 9:30 a.m.-5 p.m., Sunday noon-5 p.m., Memorial Day-Labor Day, plus September and October weekends. Admission is $5 for adults and $1.25 for children. Prices include access to a canal boat ride and other activities. One whole side of this busy town just to the south—the side just west of the river—is filled with Victorian and other picturesque housing. The dwellings are well preserved, in part because of the big levee that has separated them from the Miami River down through the years.

RECREATION

Golf

Among several nice courses, consider Hawthorne Hills Golf Course, 1000 Fetter Rd., Lima, tel. (419) 221-1891. Hawthorne is an 18-hole, par-72 facility with water fairways. Greens fees are $15 weekdays and $17 weekends. A cart is $19, or $9.50 per person.

Hiking and Biking

There's a 5.1-mile path along the Ottawa River that connects Collett Street Recreation Area to Heritage Park, south of Lima. Pick up the path in town on Collett Street south of Northshore Drive, across from Hover Park.

Baseball

"What time is the baseball game?" a visitor asks.

"What time can you be here?" the ticket seller replies.

Happily, quite a few fans follow the **Lima Locos,** a locally owned baseball team that is part of the Great Lakes Summer Collegiate League. Teams from places like Detroit, Toledo, and Dayton sharpen their skills at the Shawnee High School field on Beeler Road, about two miles west of I-75, tel. (419) 991-4701. By the way, the Locos aren't crazy; rather, they were named for the fact that Lima once produced locomotives.

ACCOMMODATIONS

Where there are interstate highways there are motels, and I-75 is no exception. In Lima, the available accommodations include the following: **Best Western,** 3600 E. Bluelick Rd., tel. (419) 221-0114; **Comfort Inn,** 1210 Neubrecht Rd., tel. (419) 228-4251; **Fairfield Inn,** 2179 Elida Rd., tel. (419) 224-8496; **Hampton Inn,** 1933 Roschman Avenue, tel. (800) HAMPTON (or tel. 800-426-7866); **Holiday Inn,** 1920 Roschman Ave., tel. (419) 222-0004; **Quality Inn,** 1201 Neubrecht Rd., tel. (419) 222-0596.

In Piqua, travelers will find two nice choices, **HoJo Inn,** 902 Scot Dr., tel. (937) 773-2314 and **Comfort Inn,** 987 E. Ash St., tel. (937) 778-8100. In Findlay, there is the **Holiday Inn,** 820 Trenton Ave., tel. (419) 423-8212 and the **EconoLodge,** 316 Emma St., tel. (937) 422-0154. Travelers to Wapakoneta can stay at the **Holiday Inn,** I-75 and Bellefontaine St., tel. (419) 738-8181.

PIQUA'S PLACE IN HISTORY

Fort Pickawillany stood near the heart of present-day Piqua. It was a fortified British fur-trading post and Indian village, the westernmost British outpost in a land being contested by the English and the French. Among the Indians who lived there was a Miami chief nicknamed Old Britain. He had earned the nickname due to his close association with the English. The chief was strongly advised by a French military leader to move his people to land that was under French control. But the chief liked the nearby Great Miami River and opted to stay with the British. That would prove to be a costly error.

On June 21, 1752, French and Indian forces from Detroit attacked Fort Pickawillany, capturing the site and killing 13 of Old Britain's people and an English fur trader. The Indians on the French side boiled and ate Old Britain, then destroyed the fortifications. A historical reference work calls the one-sided battle the beginning of the war that eventually saw the defeat of the French and the resulting Treaty of Paris in 1763. The withdrawal of the French to Quebec left the colonists with no enemy other than Mother England.

The Ohio Historical Society is working to purchase the land where Fort Pickawillany once stood.

FOOD

Brown's Restaurant & Catering, 1030 Bellefontaine Ave., Wapakoneta, tel. (419) 738-4013, celebrated its 50th anniversary in 1998, and with good reason. Brown's may be as good a mom 'n' pop restaurant as a traveler can find. Open Mon.-Sat. for lunch and dinner, the facility serves up plates of ham ("Not processed, it's cut right off the bone," a waitress promises.), plus chicken, meat loaf, and many other homemade dishes. Cream pies are a specialty here, and they come out of the kitchen tall and fluffy. For all the attention that goes into the food, none of it is expensive. To spend more than about $6 on lunch or dinner and dessert a traveler would have to eat twice.

La Piazza Pasta & Grill, 2 N. Market St., Troy, tel. (937) 339-5553, is on the town square. The restaurant serves lunch Mon.-Fri. and dinner every day. At lunch, almost everyone heads for the buffet, though menu items also are available. The buffet includes two pastas, two meat dishes, plus salads and more for $6. Later on, visitors clamor for pasta dinners featuring La Piazza's acclaimed tomato-basil sauce. Such dinners are $10-12, and there are chicken, fish, and steak dinners available from a large menu that also offers tangy antipasti.

Old Barn Out Back, 3175 W. Elm St., Lima, tel. (419) 991-3075, really looks like a barn. The signature dishes here are ribs smothered in tangy-sweet sauce and home-style fried chicken. Ribs are available in a $8.95 large portion (which includes soup and salad bar) or a $5.95 smaller portion (which includes soup, but no salad; pie is $1 extra). Similar portions of the chicken run $7.95 and $4.95. The Old Barn is also renowned for its Ho-Ho chocolate cake with hot fudge frosting and cream in the middle. Open for lunch and dinner Tues.-Sun. (closes at 6 p.m. on Sunday).

A drive in the country will take you to the **Red Pig Inn,** SR 65 in Ottawa (west of Findlay on US 127/SR 15), tel. (419) 523-6458. This restaurant emphasizes pork, its most popular plate a slab of ribs at $13.95 (half a slab is $6.95). Other dishes with a porcine connection include grilled country ham dinner, served with red beans and rice, for $8.95, and blackened pork pizza at prices ranging from $6.95 to $9.95, depending on size and toppings. The inn also serves chick-

EVENTS ALONG I-75

APRIL

Country Gathering Folk Art & Craft Show takes place in the Hancock Recreation Center, 3430 N. Main St., Findlay, tel. (419) 655-3160. This is an exhibit by juried crafters.

MAY

Antique Show & Flea Market, Allen County Fairgrounds, SR 309 East, Lima, tel. (419) 228-1050, is a well-attended annual affair.

Trout Derby occurs in the Buckeye Quarry, Bluffton (about 18 miles north of Lima), tel. (419) 358-6911. A ton of trout is stocked in the quarry, with prizes for each tagged fish that is caught.

Gem & Mineral Show, Miami County Fairgrounds, CR 25-A North, Troy, south of Piqua, tel. (937) 773-0545, features dealers and displays. There also is a silent auction.

Spring Four-Wheel Drive Jamboree, Allen County Fairgrounds, SR 309 East, Lima, tel. (419) 228-7141, features more than 1,400 trucks. They compete in several events, including monster trucks.

Arts & Crafts Festival, downtown Bluffton (north of Lima), tel. (419) 358-5675, includes sales of hand-crafted items, a pet show, lots of food, and performing artists.

Buckeye Farm Antiques, Tractor, and Engine Show, Auglaize County Fairgrounds, US 33, Wapakoneta, tel. (419) 738-6615, emphasizes yesteryear. There are old-time tractors and equipment refurbished, on display, and demonstrated.

Textile Demonstration Days is scheduled for the Piqua Historical Area State Memorial. That's at 9845 N. Hardin Rd., Piqua, tel. (800) 752-2619. Costumed folks clean, card, and spin wool, just like in pioneer days.

Go-Kart Grand Prix & Auction is at the Allen county Fairgrounds, Lima, tel. (419) 227-5121. There are go-kart races, pre-1972 hot rods on display, a car and truck show, a parts swap meet, and a nostalgic rock concert.

JUNE

Arts Festival, Riverside Park, 231 McMannes Ave., Findlay, tel. (419) 422-3412, is for adults and children. Artists show how they create as well as offering their works for sale, and there are special children's displays, three stages, and multicultural areas.

Troy Strawberry Festival, Troy City Square, tel. (937) 339-1044, will take travelers by surprise if they have no advance warning. There are more than 200,000 in attendance to pay homage to the strawberry, mostly by eating lots of shortcake and eyeing hot-air balloons, entertainment, a parade, and more.

Pork Rind Heritage Festival, Harrod, tel. (419) 648-2063, takes place east of Lima. Besides freshly popped pork rinds there is a hog roast, a parade, crafts, and live entertainment over two days. Harrod is east of Lima, off SR 309.

Cruise Night, Findlay, tel. (800) 424-3415, features lots of trick cars descending on a peaceful town. It's all in good fun as people profile in their classic machines.

Serving Up the Arts, downtown Sidney (about 10 miles north of Piqua along I-75), tel. (937) 498-2787. Music, visual arts, dance, drama, and a progressive party are scheduled to support the Shelby County Gateway Arts Council.

Randolph Freedom Day is at the Rossville Museum & Cultural Center, 8250 McFarland Rd., Piqua, tel. (937) 773-6789. The event commemorates slaves freed in 1846. There's food, music, and a video on the history behind the celebration.

Trains, Planes & Automobiles Fest, Bluffton Airport, 1080 Navajo Drive, Bluffton (north of Lima), tel. (419) 358-5675, is a free-admission event. It features antique cars, model trains, airplane rides, and skydiving.

Ohio National Championships Motorcycle Races, Allen County Fairgrounds, SR 309E, Lima, tel. (419) 991-8124, is a whirligig of speed and noise as more than 100 riders roar around the fairgrounds dirt oval, but not all at once.

JULY

Midwest Double Century, exit 111, I-75, Wapakoneta, tel. (419) 222-7301, is quite a bike ride. There are 100-kilometer, 100-mile, and 200-mile versions of this event, all over lightly traveled back roads.

Country Concert, 7103 SR 66, Fort Loramie, tel. (937) 295-3000, is set for Hickory Hill Lakes, west of Sidney. The three-day event includes leading Nashville artists, and camping is available on site.

Car Show, Delphos, tel. (419) 692-7361, includes antiques, classic, and collector cars on display, plus a swap meet. Delphos is west of Lima along either SR 309 or US 30.

Taste of Findlay, tel. (419) 422-3313, lets visitors sample the wares of local merchants while sauntering around downtown and listening to live entertainment.

SEPTEMBER

Piqua Heritage Festival, Piqua Historical Area, tel. (937) 339-1044. The Johnston Farm is the scene of an event that salutes both native Americans and pioneers. Demonstrations, foods, and music commemorate a time when Piqua was on the edge of Ohio Civilization.

Tipp City Mum Festival, downtown Tipp City, (937) 667-8425. This town has a prominent nursery, so it only makes sense to devote a weekend of arts, crafts, food, entertainment, and street dancing to one of their prettier flowers. Tipp City is located 14 miles south of Piqua along US 75 at the junction of SR 571.

OCTOBER

Great Outdoor Underwear Festival, Spring Street, Piqua, tel. (937) 773-2765. Piqua once was home to an underwear factory, reason enough for folks to toast their personal garments. Look for food, arts and crafts, a parade, a celebrity underwear auction, and a footrace known as the Undy 500!

Candlemaking on the Farm, 9845 N. Hardin Rd., Piqua, tel. (800) 752-2619, lets visitors watch candles being made by hand from beeswax at the Piqua Historical Area State Memorial. Candles are available for purchase.

DECEMBER

Christmas on the Farm, 9845 N. Hardin Rd., Piqua, tel. (800) 752-2619, takes place at the Piqua Historical Area State Memorial. It consists of an authentic 19th-century holiday, from the traditional mummers' play to the old-fashioned desserts.

en, seafood, and steak, but this is big hog country and the locals support their own. For those seeking variety, Friday night and Sunday noon feature buffets. The Red Pig serves lunch and dinner every day.

Wilson's Sandwich Shop, 600 S. Main St., Findlay, tel. (419) 422-5051. This restaurant has been around for years, making "the best burgers ever," according to locals and visitors fortunate enough to learn of the place. Wilson's grinds its own beef, selling juicy burgers for $1.15 and adding a dime to the sum for a cheeseburger. The shakes are thick and cheap, priced from 80 cents to $1.60, depending on size. Those who show too early for burgers can grab a donut for 50 cents or a teaser (hash browns with an egg in the middle) for $1. Said to be the inspiration for the Wendy's chain, Wilson's is open every day, 9 a.m.-1 a.m.

INFORMATION AND SERVICES

911 is the number to dial for all kinds of emergencies in Lima or Findlay. Non-emergency police numbers in Lima and Findlay are (419) 221-5247 and (419) 424-7150, respectively. The Lima Memorial Hospital can be reached at (419) 228-3335. Call (419) 423-3500 to reach Blanchard Valley Hospital, Findlay. The post office in Lima is at 350 W. High St. The Findlay post office is at 229 W. Main Cross St.

The **Lima/Allen County Convention and Visitors Bureau** is at 147 N. Main St., Lima, tel. (419) 222-6045. The **Hancock County Convention and Visitors Bureau** is at 123 E. Main Cross St., Findlay, tel.(419) 422-3315 or (800) 424-3315. For the **Miami County Visitors and Convention Bureau,** head for 405 S.W. Public Square, Troy, tel. (937) 339-1044 or (800) 348-8993. The **Shelby County/Sidney Chamber of Commerce** is at 100 E. Poplar St., Sidney, tel. (419) 492-9122.

Findlay is served by the *Courier,* published Mon.-Sat. mornings. Entertainment is covered on Tuesday. The *Lima News* keeps folks abreast every morning, offering "Weekend Entertainment" on Thursday. In Delphos they read the *Daily Herald,* published weekday evenings and Saturday mornings. The *Evening Leader* delivers the news weekday evenings and Saturday mornings in St. Marys, and the *Wapakoneta Daily News* hits the streets weekday evenings, emphasizing entertainment on Thursday. The *Sidney Daily News* runs its entertainment section, "Kaleidoscope," on Friday, publishing weekday evenings and Saturday mornings. *Piqua Daily Call* is a weekday evening and Saturday morning effort, with the *Troy Daily News* adhering to the same schedule and publishing a Sunday paper. Troy runs an arts page every Friday.

Transportation

Greyhound buses travel up and down I-75, but they don't stop in many of the small towns along the way. The interstate bus service does maintain a terminal at Market and Jackson Streets in Lima, tel. (419) 224-7781, and at 12906 Deschler Rd., North Baltimore, tel. (419) 257-2098. Allen County Regional Transit Authority offers local bus service based in Lima. For information, telephone (419) 222-2782.

Shopping

The **Lima Mall** is at 2400 Elida Rd., tel. (419) 331-6255. The **Findlay Village Mall** has more than 80 stores and is at 1800 Tiffin Ave., tel. (419) 423-8732. An innovative way to pick up a long-lasting Ohio souvenir is to call Carriage House Lighting in Troy at (937) 339-3364. Joe and Leslie Merle produce handmade colonial-reproduction tin lighting that's in so much demand they won't sell to passersby. But they will tell travelers where the nearest retail outlet may be for one of the 50 lights they ship each week.

Less decorative but more filling is Dietsch Brothers, 400 W. Main Cross St., Findlay, tel. (419) 422-4474. These people make chocolates to die for. Antiquers who find themselves in Findlay may want to visit Jeffrey's Antique Gallery, 11326 Township Rd. 99, tel. (419) 423-7500. And for those who want an outlet-shopping experience, try the U.S. Plastics Factory and Outlet Store, 1390 Neubrecht Rd., Lima, tel. (419) 228-2242. Potentially 13,000 plastic items for home, office, and garden are offered.

OHIO'S WESTERN FLANK

If it's true that Eskimos know 40 words for snow, residents of northwesternmost Ohio must know at least 40 words for flat. Reminiscent of the prairie, this extremely fertile, mostly rural part of the state once was part of the Great Black Swamp. The swamp was so vast, stretching as it did from just east of Toledo almost to Van Wert and then north and west across the Indiana line into the Limberlost region and back to near the Ohio-Michigan line, that it took many years to drain it. The soggy, overgrown area concealed wolves and snakes, and also major deposits of oil and gas, plus land where farmers could grow magnificent crops. The north and west borders today are enterprising areas of tidy farms and picturesque small towns. Modest, lightly traveled, US 127 certainly isn't the fastest way to move up and down the state, but it's a pleasant ride for those who have the time.

History

This is legendary country—just ask anyone who knows 18th-century history. Native Americans defeated the forces of General St. Clair near Fort Recovery in 1791 so decisively that he was replaced by General "Mad" Anthony Wayne. Like St. Clair, Wayne moved up the western edge of Ohio from the Cincinnati area. Unlike his predecessor, who may have been lax, Wayne built a string of forts and carefully trained his troops. That training, together with superior firepower, forced the most warlike Indians to depart what would become Ohio for keeps. They retreated after losing the Battle of Fallen Timbers on Aug. 20, 1794, near the Maumee River just southwest of Toledo. The battle was named for the many uprooted trees in the area, felled by a storm the day before.

General Wayne signed a peace accord with the natives at Fort Greenville in 1795, this document is now known as the Treaty of Greenville. The agreement was a signal that the Ohio area could be safely inhabited and that it was on the way to becoming one of the United States. The pioneers moved in but were forced to veer either north or south to get around the Great Black Swamp, which teemed with wildlife. Among the newcomers were Roman Catholic Germans who inhabited an area south of Van Wert where church spires show their influence to this day. Others came from the East Coast, searching for fertile soil at a good price.

Farm productivity around here took a quantum leap with the Industrial Revolution. Ingenuity supplemented agriculture locally, as a fellow in Ohio City, eight miles south of Van Wert on SR 118, crafted a most remarkable vehicle. In 1891 —five years before Henry Ford—an executive named J.W. Lambert built a three-wheel automobile of his own design and motored around town in it. Lambert friction-drive vehicles were produced for consumers from 1901 to 1916 and were among the very earliest functioning horseless carriages. Nowadays, the contraptions are in evidence all along US 127. Also evident are dozens of manufacturing firms that create items or products known nationally and internationally. Western Ohio, with its farms and factories, is nothing if not industrious.

Location and Orientation

U.S. Highway 127 drops down out of Michigan some 45 miles west of Toledo and about half that distance east of the Indiana line. It moves southwest to Bryan, south to Van Wert, through Celina, and around Greenville before continuing south through Cincinnati and across the Ohio River into Kentucky. All of Ohio's major east-west roads cross this modest national highway. The road spans the Maumee River west of Defiance and it passes close to the source of the westbound Wabash River south of Celina.

SIGHTS

The **Bear's Mill**, at 6450 Arcanum-Bear's Mill Rd., Greenville, tel. (937) 548-5112, was built in 1849. The water-powered millstone still grinds wheat, corn, and rye, with pancake mix from this effort sold on site. The big, restored frame building can be visited Friday and Sunday 11 a.m.-5 p.m., Saturday 9 a.m.-5 p.m. There are no admission fees for the National Register of Historic Places facility, which also sells its own handmade pottery. The mill is east of Greenville and just south of US 36.

The **Van Wert County Historical Museum** at 602 N. Washington St., Van Wert, tel. (419) 238-3226, is housed in an 1890 Victorian mansion. Free and open to the public 2-4 p.m. each Sunday, the big old place includes a children's room and an annex. Herein visitors will find memorabilia that dates from the time of Anthony Wayne's forays, plus a selection of everything from cut glass to farm implements. Restored stores of yesteryear include a barber shop and country grocery.

Sitting nine miles west of Wauseon at 22611 SR 2, in Archbold, tel. (419) 446-2541, **Sauder Village** offers a museum, a farmstead, and a

---

TROUBLE AT THE TRIANGLE

"Teenagers drive trails of drink and death to Ohio cabarets," screamed an *Indianapolis Star* headline on a Sunday morning in the early 1960s. The story lamented the fact that young people from eastern Indiana traveled to Ohio on Friday and Saturday nights, where beer could be purchased and consumed in an oversize, barnlike structure outside Greenville that was noisy, smelly, badly lighted, and a lot of fun. That place was The Triangle.

A large building with a gravel parking lot, The Triangle had a house band that approximated the latest hits while kids from a radius of more than 50 miles danced and swilled beer containing 3.2% alcohol. "Three-two," as it was called, could legally be purchased in Ohio at the time by persons between the ages of 18 and 21. Bartenders and waitstaff could tell the difference between beer for teens and beer for adults by the bottle caps, which were different colors. While "three-two" was less alcoholic than the real thing, large quantities buzzed up teens from Dayton or Springfield or Muncie or Fort Wayne, who then attempted to drive home. Road deaths were common.

Such circumstances were among the reasons the federal government decided in 1986 to withhold federal highway dollars to any state that failed to hike its age minimum for alcohol consumption of any kind to 21. Curiously, Ohio had always been a difficult place to buy liquor. Until 1996, only state-operated liquor stores sold whiskey, vodka, and other spirits. A customer had to enter a state store, find an example of the bottle he or she wanted on display, and copy a serial number onto a pad of paper. The pad and the money for the liquor were turned over to a state employee, who fetched the desired item from the back room. Ironically, between World War II and the 1960s, there also were so-called Blue Laws in the state. Among other things, it was legal to sell beer on Sunday but illegal to sell milk.

Back to the Triangle. It survived the over-21 movement and continues to play music, mostly on weekends. Nowadays, the place alternates rock and country, and it sometimes serves as a performance venue when a well-known musician or band comes to town. The facility is one mile west of town on SR 502 (Vine Street), just west of the water-treatment plant. Don't look for a sign—there isn't any. The telephone number is unlisted.

pioneer village. More than that, the facility books a number of special events every year, such as quilting fairs, fiddling contests, doll shows, even fall butchering (see **Events Along US 127**). Most such diversions take place on weekends, leaving the village very easy to navigate on weekdays. Hours are Mon.-Sat. 10 a.m.-5 p.m. and Sunday 1-5 p.m. Admission charges are $9.00 for adults and $4.5 for children ages 6-16.

AuGlaize Village

Located at 12296 Krouse Rd., three miles west of Defiance and just off US 24, tel. (419) 784-0107, AuGlaize Village recaptures mid- to late-19th century Ohio with 17 reconstructed buildings and four museums. The folks inside the doctor's office, the sawmill, the blacksmith's shanty, and the barber shop all seem to know what they're doing, and they go about it in authentic costumes, using long-ago tools. One yearly special event is the black iron artistry weekend, featuring talented blacksmiths plying their trade. Thank the Defiance County Historical Society for this ambitious attraction, which is open Sat.-Sun. 11 a.m.-4 p.m. early June-Aug. Special event hours are 10 a.m.-5 p.m. Admission charges are $3 for adults during special events and $2 on non-event days, $2 for seniors and $1 for students.

Fort Recovery State Memorial

This memorial at the junction of SR 49 and SR 119, in Fort Recovery, tel. (419) 375-4649, or (800) 283-8920, marks the defeat of colonists by Native Americans on the banks of the Wabash River—a massacre resulting in even more loss of life than Custer's Last Stand. General St. Clair's debacle here in 1791 set the stage for the appearance of General "Mad" Anthony Wayne. A simple white granite monument stands in memory of those who died near what is now a village of 1,300 residents, only a mile east of the Indiana-Ohio state line and a dozen miles west of US 127. There's an atmospheric wooden stockade here, plus life-size dioramas. Hours are noon-5 p.m. every day, Memorial Day-Labor Day and noon-5 p.m. weekends in May and September. Admission fees are $2 for adults and $1 for children.

Garst Museum

At 205 N. Broadway, Greenville, tel. (937) 548-5250, the Garst displays items that once belonged to Annie Oakley, the "Little Miss Sureshot" who became famous for her shooting ability and parlayed a steady hand and a clear eye to immortality via wild west shows. Annie was born near this city in 1860. Other artifacts range from military uniforms and early furnishings to a car built in Greenville to run in one of the first Indianapolis 500 auto races. Admission to the mansion behind the iron fence is free, though donations are accepted. Hours are Tues.-Sat. 11 a.m.-5 p.m., Sunday 1-5 p.m., closed all of January.

State Parks

Grand Lake St. Marys State Park, 834 Edgewater Dr., tel. (419) 394-3611, occupies large portions of Auglaize and Mercer Counties, consisting as it does of 500 acres of land and 13,500 manmade acres of water. The vast lake is bounded on the west by US 127 and the city of Celina. The land portion of the state park is closer to the village of St. Marys on the northeast shore. It's easily reached from I-75 by driving west on US 33 to SR 29, a distance of about 15 miles, then following the signs. This is a major boating and fishing lake; a state hatchery stocks the water with bass, catfish, northern pike, and walleye. No limit is set for boat power, so expect everything from Jet Skis to motor yachts.

Independence Dam State Park, 27722 SR 424, Defiance, tel. (419) 784-3263, lets visitors know where they got all that water for all those canals so long ago. In the case of the Miami and Erie Canal, a dam was created that diverted water into a section of the canal from the Maumee River. This expanse of greenery is an area between the river and the dam. The 600-plus acres are ideal for hiking, camping, or just watching the big river roll northeast toward Lake Erie.

Lake Loramie State Park, 11221 SR 362, Minster, tel. (937) 295-2011, has 400 acres of land and more than four times that in water. There are 14 hiking trails and a campground with 164 sites. Those sites are filled every weekend all summer, with many folks getting early and late camping in each May and September. The showers are turned off Nov. 1, which fails to stop a few hardy, year-round campers. Anglers can expect bluegill and crappie, and the saugeye (a sauger-walleye hybrid) placed in the lake a few years ago are just being caught in big numbers now. The park is in between US 127 and I-75, off SR 705.

RECREATION

Golf

Celina offers a challenging facility in the **Fox's Den,** Irmscher Boulevard, Celina, tel. (419) 586-4919, a Jim Fazio-designed 18-hole course. Fourteen of the 18 holes involve water, and there are more than 50 sand traps. Weekday packages are especially good values, with 18 holes of golf and cart, a motel for the night, and a $15 meal certificate for $65. Accommodations are at the nearby Holiday Inn Express.

South of Greenville and a couple of miles east of US 127 is **Beechwood Golf Course,** 1476 SR 503, Arcanum, tel. (937) 678-4422. The 18-hole, par-72 facility charges $16 on weekdays and $19 on weekends, plus $10 per person for a cart. Eleven of the 18 holes have water hazards.

Running and Walking

Greenville has one of the prettiest places in Ohio in which to exercise. Simply the city park, the facility gives walkers or runners a choice—they can follow the outline of several picturesque, shady ponds, or they can turn right up a little hill

and find themselves at the local track/football stadium. The field has several entrances, all of them open, an all-weather track, and a lush expanse of grass. Except for the usual posted warnings about pets and motorized vehicles, everyone appears to be welcome. Those who exercise during summer's daylight hours can reward themselves afterward with a trip to the park concession stand.

Spectator Sports

America has produced a number of great racing drivers, and many got their start at little bull rings like **Eldora Speedway,** 13929 SR 118, Rossburg, tel. (937) 338-3815. Sprint cars run on the dirt here at frightening speeds, usually in weekend evening programs. The high-bank, half-mile oval also serves as the venue for four days of sprint-car racing that culminates in a 40-lap race paying $100,000 to the winner. Admission varies, from $6 to $32, depending on the importance of the contest. Rossburg is 11 miles north of Greenville and two miles west of US 127.

ACCOMMODATIONS

Greenville seems to have cornered the bed-and-breakfast spots along the highway. Check out **Apple Blossom Inn,** 5842 SR 571 East, tel. (937) 548-1223; **Park Bed and Breakfast,** B and Garst Avenues, tel. (937) 547-1563; **St. Clair Bed and**

Fort Recovery hosts the National Tractor Pull Association finals in July.

WESTERN FLANK EVENTS

The events of this area are mostly along US 127, close to the Indiana border.

MAY

Old-Fashioned Days, Arcanum, tel. (937) 692-5755, lives up to its name with crafters, car and tractor shows, entertainment, rides, and a parade.

Schutzenfest, CR 19, Ridgeville Corners, tel. (419) 267-3490, is put on by the local American Legion. It's a German festival that includes everything from polka music to food to drink to a shooting contest.

JUNE

John Paulding Days, Courthouse Square, Paulding, tel. (419) 399-5215, pays homage to the town founder. Look for a parade, a truck show, a car show, crafters, rides and games, flea markets, and food.

Go-Kart Races & Car Show, Fulton County Fairgrounds, Wauseon, tel. (419) 335-2010, is a place to go fast very close to the ground. The second day of the two-day event includes a classic car show.

Peony Festival, Van Wert, tel. (419) 238-6223, lets visitors go on self-guided tours of various local gardens. Other forms of fun include a parade, a crafts show, and a car show.

Versailles Poultry Days, tel. (419) has been going on for half a century. The small town on SR 47, northeast of Greenville, serves up lots of chicken dinners to go along with a 5K run, ultimate frisbee, rides, music, and entertainment. There's also a Little Miss Poultry.

June Art Exhibit, Wassenberg Art Center, 643 S. Washington St., Van Wert, tel. (419) 238-6837, features artists from northwest Ohio and northeast Indiana. The artworks are juried for this event, which takes place afternoons for six days.

Flowing Rivers Festival, Defiance tel. (419) 782-7946, is held on the site of the original Fort Defiance, beside the river. Look for waterskiing competition, a parade, an art festival, and lots of good food.

Black Swamp Steam & Gas Show, AuGlaize Village, US 24, Defiance, tel. (419) 497-2331, shows what powered old-time equipment. There's a tractor pull, a working sawmill, and various threshers.

Zuma Days happens in Montezuma, which is between Celina and Greenville, tel. (419) 268-2839. Expect volleyball, horseshoe, and waterball tournaments, music, a 5K run, a chicken barbecue, and a hog roast.

Governor's Cup Regatta is on Grand Lake St. Marys at North Shore Park, Celina, tel. (800) 860-4726. More than 150 hydroplanes in several classes compete at speeds that can approach 150 miles an hour.

National Threshers Annual Reunion, Fulton County Fairgrounds, SR 108, Wauseon, tel. (419) 335-6006, should test noise threshholds. More than 30 operating steam engines will chug away, along with 300 working gas tractors.

Breakfast, 224 E. Third St., tel. (937) 548-9533; and the **Waring Bed and Breakfast,** 304 W. Third St., tel. (937) 548-2682. Apple Blossom and the St. Clair offer a bath with each room, while the Waring is an Italianate Victorian home with an in-ground pool. Bed and breakfast establishments aren't all that common elsewhere along this stretch of federal asphalt and concrete.

Neither, for that matter, are franchise motels, though as the population expands so do the amenities to serve it. Hotel/motel facilities include the moderately priced Comfort Inn, 1190 E. Russ Rd., Greenville, tel. (800) 228-5150, and Holiday Inn Express, 2020 Holiday Dr., Celina, tel. (419) 586-4919; A nice place to stay near Archbold is the tudor-look Sauder Heritage Inn at

Sauder Village, SR 2 near SR 66, tel. (419) 445-6408. Deluxe. The expensive but comfy Inn at Versailles, 21 W. Main St. at Center St., Versailles, tel. (937) 526-3020, has 20 guest rooms and a French Country atmosphere.

FOOD

The **Barn,** US 2, Archbold, tel. (419) 445-2331 or (800) 590-9755, proves that the most dangerous foe of a waistline is a restaurant with a bakery next door. This Sauder Village restaurant serves lunch and dinner Mon.-Sat. and a three-meat buffet Sunday 11 a.m.-2 p.m. The facility is housed in a poplar barn that dates from 1875; it

Countryfest, Shrine Grounds, 2291 St. John Rd., Maria Stein, tel. (419) 925-4151, takes place in the most Germanic pa.rt of Ohio. Beware the backseat-driver contest but look forward to the food.

JULY

Darke County Steam Threshers Annual Reunion, Darke County Fairgrounds, Greenville, tel. (937) 692-8215, involves 30 or more machines. The steam-powered units cut wood, thresh wheat, and compete in pulls. Look also for food and entertainment.

Summerfest, Williams County Fairgrounds, Montpelier, tel. (419) 485-4416, takes place in the northwest corner of the state. Hogs are roasted, chickens are barbecued, art is displayed, and locals parade.

Fiddle Contest, SR 2, Archbold, tel. (800) 590-9755, occurs at Sauder Farm & Craft Villages. Fiddlers from Ohio and surrounding states compete for cash prizes and trophies.

Black Iron Artistry & Other Pioneer Skills, AuGlaize Village, Defiance, tel. (419) 393-2662, stars area blacksmiths. They demonstrate the art of shaping iron while crafters display other pioneering skills.

Midwest Summer NTPA Nationals, 2205 SR 49, Fort Recovery, tel. (419) 375-4911, is a tractor pull that takes place in Ambassador Park. This is a bigtime event, with competitors from across the U.S. and Canada in their tractors and trucks.

Children's Summer on the Farm, SR 2, Archbold, tel. (800) 590-9755, is another Sauder Farm & Craft Villages event. The kids can make ice cream and participate in an old-fashioned spelling bee, should they choose.

Annie Oakley Days, Darke County Fairgrounds, Greenville, tel. (800) 504-2995, salutes a local girl. Besides sharpshooting and muzzloading, look for a parade, entertainment, antiques/crafts, and more.

Lake Festival is set for Celina, tel. (419) 586-2219. Following the grand parade, there's a Civil War reenactment, fireworks over the lake, a car show, and a crafts show.

Summerfest, Hamler, tel. (419) 274-7475, includes polk music and German food and drink during three days of fun.

Williams County Antique Tractor Show, Williams County Fairgrounds, Montpelier, tel. (419) 485-4416, is a huge display of antique power. There also are crafts, antiques, and collectibles shows at the same time.

OCTOBER

Butchering Day & Woodcarver Show, Sauder Farm & Craft Village, SR 2, Archbold, tel. (800) 590-9755, lets folks watch expert woodcarvers at work and see farm animals turned into food, if they care to.

Halloween Lantern Tour, AuGlaize Village, US 24, Defiance, tel. (419) 782-7255, provides guides to an allegedly haunted village. Reservations suggested.

NOVEMBER

Top of Ohio Farm Toy Show, Williams County Fairgrounds, Montpelier, tel. (419) 485-4416 or (419) 485-3755.

---

was rebuilt on its present site. Diners need not visit the village in order to satisfy their hunger. A solid choice for lunch is a beef Manhattan sandwich, with gravy and mashed potatoes, natch, for $6.50. Broasted chicken in the evening is a big hit at $6.95. It's served with a choice of two sides. Bakery-made desserts include a number of enticing pies, plus cheesecake.

Riverview Frosty Boy, 1000 W. Riverview St. (SR 424), Napoleon, tel. (419) 599-3830, is a milkshake-and-sandwich nirvana. The sandwiches include beef barbecue or shredded chicken, $1.85, or $3 with a 16-oz. soda and chips. The homemade ("We don't use any beans") sauce that turns a hot dog into a Coney dog is all beef. Two Coney dogs, chips, and a 16-oz. soda

are just $3.25 ($3 for those who pass up a great sauce). Thoughtfully, Riverview also has low-cal sherbet and frozen yogurt, as well as soft-serve ice cream. The rendezvous is open 11 a.m.-9 p.m. March-Memorial Day and Labor Day-Oct. Summer hours are 11 a.m.-11 p.m.

Charlie's Down Under Restaurant, 200 Clinton St., Defiance, tel. (419) 782-2283, is very good and very popular. Open for lunch and then for dinner Mon.-Fri. and for dinner only Saturday, Charlie's wisely offers many of its most popular creations in half portions. At lunch, for example, grilled chicken, steak or shrimp salad is $4.75 petite and $5.75 for a full portion. In the evening, a full filet is $19.50, a petite $4 less. Whitefish and salmon are offered at $10.95/$8.95

and $16.25/$11.95, respectively. Thirty kinds of pie emerge from the kitchen, the most popular being chocolate peanut butter at $1.25 for half a slice and $1.75 for a regular serving. For the ravenous, a whole pie is $9.

The **Inn at Versailles,** 21 W. Main St., Versailles, tel. (937) 526-3020, is a French country destination with food to match. The inn serves lunch every day but Saturday and dinner every evening. Luncheon specials are priced at only $5.49 and usually are four in number: an entree, a pasta, a quiche, and a panini. In the evening, dry-aged New York strip steaks are offered at $14, while *choucroute,* which is sauerkraut with a French accent, comes to the table with potatoes, sliced pork, specialty sausage, and carmelized apples for around $11. The inn, which is 15 miles northeast of Greenville, also has 20 guest rooms and suites.

Jim's Drive-In Restaurant, 100 Martz St., Greenville, tel. (937) 548-5078, is a retro delight. Open only from mid-March to mid-August, Jim's features car hops delivering root beer, Spanish hot dogs, shakes, fries, and more to an ever-changing cadre of vehicles and people. Open daily 11 a.m.-9 p.m., the timeless site should return a bit of change from a $5 bill, no matter how large the diner's appetite.

INFORMATION AND SERVICES

Bryan is the site of the **Williams County Visitors Bureau,** 130 S. Lynn St., tel. (419) 636-1999. Persons visiting Sauder Village may want to call the **Archbold Area Chamber of Commerce** at (419) 445-2222 to see what else is happening locally. The **Greater Defiance Area Tourism and Visitors Bureau** can be reached at (419) 782-0864 or (800) 686-4382. The **Van Wert Convention and Visitors Bureau** is at 118 W. Main St., tel. (419) 238-4390. The **Auglaize and Mercer Counties Convention and Visitors Bureau** is at 112 S. Front St., Suite 2, St. Marys, tel. (419) 394-1294 or (800) 860-4726. In Greenville, call the **Darke County Chamber of Commerce** at (937) 548-2102. Its Web site is www.darkecounty-ohio.com. The Defiance College telephone number to learn more about events on campus is (419) 784-4010.

The *Bryan Times* emerges weekday evenings and Saturday mornings. Defiance receives the *Crescent-News* on the identical schedule and adds a Sunday edition. "Arts and Culture" are covered Wednesday by the Van Wert *Times-Bulletin,* published weekday evenings and Saturday mornings. The *Daily Standard* is read by Celina residents Mon.-Sat. evenings, and in Greenville the *Daily Advocate* covers the news weekday evenings and Saturday mornings. The Saturday edition emphasizes entertainment.

Transportation
Perhaps Mr. Lambert built his motorized tricycle because there were so few forms of public transport. Nary a bus line nor a commercial airport can be found along US 127, though Bryan is blessed with an Amtrak stop. On the north side of town and just a few steps west of US 127, this is one of the few stops between Toledo and Chicago. For more information, telephone (419) 636-5057 or (419) 636-5671.

Shopping
Those who find comfort in shopping locally will be rewarded on US 127. Good buys include baked goods, farm produce, handmade lawn decor, and more. There are no malls of any size, though several towns, such as Defiance, offer pleasant downtown shopping areas. North of the Ohio Toll Road (I-80/90) exit 2, near the Michigan border, look for the Pioneer Anique Mall, 103 Baubice St., in the village of Pioneer, tel. (419) 737-2341. Nearby Montpelier, 10 miles northwest of Bryan, has two antique havens: Cemetery Ridge at 13-805 SR 107, tel. (419) 485-8033, and the Village Trading Post, 123 Empire St., tel. (419) 485-4996.

Safety and Emergencies
In emergencies, dial 911 for police, fire, or medical assistance. For non-emergency assistance in **Greenville,** you can find the police at Broadway and Main Streets, non-emergency tel. (937) 548-1103. Wayne Hospital is at 835 Sweitzer St., tel. (937) 548-1141.

SOUTHWESTERN OHIO

There's a little bit of everything in southwestern Ohio, from big cities to bucolic byways, flat farm fields to rugged uplands, stagnant ponds to rolling rivers. And the people are as varied as the terrain—both the Wright brothers and Larry Flynt have played a role in the history and makeup of the region. Sights vary, too, from over-the-top King's Island to the silent accomplishment that is Serpent Mound. In between are a few million locals going about their lives in all sorts of ways.

History
The initial residents were nomads who moved in after the glaciers receded from the area that would become known as the Miami Valley. They are known for their custom of burying their dead in mounds—the state's tallest example of which is in Miamisburg, near Dayton. Several sets of early people came and went, with the Shawnee and the Miami the dominant Indian tribes prior to the arrival of Europeans. French fur traders did a brisk business here until they were replaced by British soldiers. The English in turn were pushed aside by settlers whose safety was ensured by General Anthony Wayne and his well-trained soldiers. Following statehood in 1803, the biggest impediment proved to be the unpredictable waters of the area's numerous rivers.

Never an industrial juggernaut like the powerhouses of northeast Ohio, the southwest opted for a diverse mix of enterprise, agricultural, and services. Soils varied, from the rich plains around Eaton in the west to the marginal and hard-to-work hills in and near Cincinnati. Most farming was a blend of dairy and hogs, corn and oats. Smart people such as Charles Kettering were lured here by the chance to associate with others who were ingenious, and everything from jet engines to refrigerators, detergents to bicycles, software to hardware, have been produced here.

Today's residents of Southwest Ohio may be descended from Appalachian English and Scots, canal-digging Irish, beer-brewing Germans, former African-American slaves, or newer arrivals such as Cambodians, Mexicans, or Vietnamese. The economic resurgence of the 1990s has expedited the demolition of substandard housing in Cincinnati and Dayton, though there continue to be pockets of need in and out of larger population centers. Through it all, living with weather and several rivers that can get riled, Ohioans in this part of the U.S. believe they have it pretty good. After a restaurant visit in Cincinnati, a plane ride in Dayton, or antiquing in Waynesville, who's to argue?

CINCINNATI

History

Cincinnati's history is longer and richer than that of virtually any other town in Ohio. Admired originally by scouting parties as a pleasant area between the Great and Little Miami Rivers, Cincinnati initially was called Losantiville. Arthur St. Clair, first governor of the Northwest Territory, changed the name to its present designation to honor the Society of Cincinnati—the association of Revolutionary War officers to which he had belonged, named for Cincinnatus, the 5th-century Roman patriot (and consul and dictator).

A fort was constructed in 1789, and the first inhabitants of European heritage were soldiers paid to combat the natives. General "Mad" Anthony Wayne chased the Indians out of the area in a hurry, and a few settlers started to farm on the uplands north of the village of 900 residents. The town was incorporated in 1802, the year before Ohio became a state. Local folks took matters into their own hands, running the town via a council. Nonpolitical people of importance included Dr. Daniel Drake. The Kentucky native helped establish the Medical College of Ohio here. Since the town was a port and a significant stop on the way up or down the Ohio River, celebrities passed through the area. They included James Monroe, Andrew Jackson, the Marquis de Lafayette, and the English novelist and travel writer Frances Trollope. She lived in the town for several years in the 1820s before returning to England to write the famously harshly critical bestseller based on Cincinnati life, *The Domestic Manners of the Americans.*

When the Beecher family moved here from New England—so that Reverend Lyman Beecher could teach theology—everyone from rivermen, prostitutes, and freed slaves, as well as everyday people showed up to greet them. All of Beecher's 13 children would distinguish themselves, but none more so than Harriet Beecher Stowe. She, of course, wrote *Uncle Tom's Cabin,* basing many of the book's anecdotes on tales heard in Cincinnati. Abolitionists were active in the town, despite the fact that Kentucky, just across the river, was a slave state. The city lured folks from Indiana, Kentucky, other parts of Ohio, and elsewhere with a whirlwind of work—on the docks, in slaughterhouses, in retail stores, and in a growing number of industries, such as the furniture industry.

Even Charles Dickens was impressed with the city, which in 1842 had the largest population of any settlement west of the Alleghenies. Starting in 1846 canals linked Cincy with other towns, and the first railroad reached town in 1857. Large

The Miamisburg Mound near Dayton is 68 feet high and covers 1.5 acres—it was built by the earliest inhabitants of the Miami Valley, a people known as the Moundbuilders, and is the largest example of its kind in Ohio.

numbers of Irish and even larger numbers of Germans came to the area and stayed. They and others fell out to defend the city when it came perilously close to enduring a Confederate invasion in 1862 and again in 1863.

Reconstruction was idyllic and industrious. In 1869, the Cincinnati Reds became the first professional baseball team. Shoe- and bootmaking plants, machine-tool making facilities, and concert halls were erected in encouraging numbers. Several industrial expositions were held.

Electric lighting showed up in 1888. In 1895, the hodgepodge that was 37 different street railways lines was consolidated, running punctually thanks to established routes and timetables. Not all was progress, however. There was a section of town nicknamed Rat and Sausage Row, and an area near the public river landing had become blighted with slums.

In the 20th century steamboats and trunkline railroads tied Cincinnati to the rest of the country. Art galleries, opera houses, opium dens,

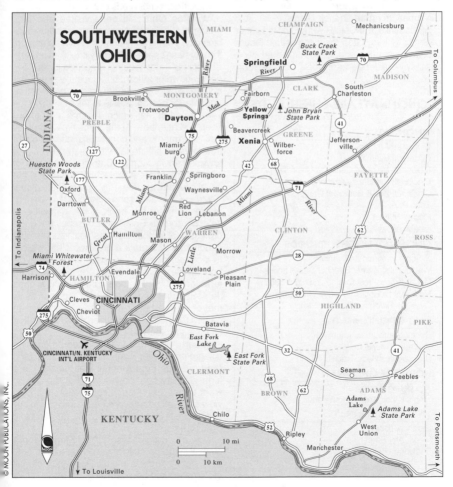

and disorderly houses all flourished, and the highlights of the town were said to be its devotions to art and to misbehaving. The influence of its Germanic citizens lightened considerably during World War I, as public schools ceased teaching the German language and several prominent folks were detained as enemy aliens. Criminal elements were routed with the introductions of the prohibition of alcohol and of clean and efficient local government. Minor criminals either stocked riverboats with booze or found sites in Newport, Kentucky, opposite Cincinnati, to entertain their clients.

All the while, the Ohio River and its tributaries periodically inundated low-lying areas. Floods occurred just often enough to remind residents that they were, for better or worse, in a river town.

CINCINNATI AREA HIGHLIGHTS

CINCINNATI

Cincinnati Art Museum
Cincinnati Ballet
Cincinnati Museum Center at Union Terminal
Cincinnati Symphony Orchestra
Cincinnati Zoo & Botanical Gardens
Eden Park
Findlay Market
Taft Museum

CINCINNATI NEIGHBORHOODS

Clifton's Victorian architecture
Walnut Hills' Harriet Beecher Stowe house
Mount Adams' restaurants and night clubs
Mariemont's English-cottage atmosphere
Over-the-Rhine's nightlife

EAST OF CINCINNATI

Coney Island Amusement Park
Riverbend Music Center
River Downs Race Track

NORTH OF CINCINNATI

The Beach Water Park
King's Island Amusement Park

WEST OF CINCINNATI

Harrison Tomb
Mount Airy Forest
Shawnee Lookout Park

An equally destructive disaster took place in 1918, when huge slabs of ice two feet thick destroyed every boat and barge in the area. The threat of floods declined following construction of dams and reservoirs in the state during the Great Depression, yet the big river has run amok twice recently—in 1990 and 1997. In 1999 a powerful tornado leveled one square mile about 15 miles northeast of downtown in the Blue Ash and Montgomery areas. The tornado packed winds in excess of 200 miles an hour, leading to four deaths and destroying hundreds of homes.

Winston Churchill once visited and pronounced Cincinnati America's handsomest inland city. While many suburbs have sprung up, the city hasn't seen as much white flight as, say, Cleveland. Today much of Cincinnati looks old— not rundown or forlorn, but gracefully aged. The number of storefronts devoted to architecture and interior design attests to the interest in the venerable homes, which demand a lot of upkeep and attention. At the same time, dramatic new apartments and condominiums soar out of tree-studded hills to face the languid river. The town is heavily Roman Catholic, with a mix of African-American, Appalachian white, and the usual new arrivals from many parts of the globe.

Meanwhile, after some municipal blundering, at presstime for this book, a site is now being selected for the Reds' new baseball park; the professional football Bengals' field is under construction; and there's a grassroots effort afoot to increase public park space along the riverfront. Earnest as such efforts are, they are counterbalanced by the facts that talk-show hose Jerry Springer formerly served Cincinnati as its mayor, that a holier-than-thou businessman named Charles Keating turned out to be a major savings-and-loan-scandal crook, and that porn king Larry Flynt and the city have an ongoing disagreement over Flynt's dirty-book newsstand (and dubious First Amendment flagship) in a high-visibility spot downtown. For those who want to get above such commotion, the best view of town on the river's north side is from tiny Milton Street Park in Prospect Hill, at Milton and Boal Streets.

Now a food warehouse, the old **King Records** plant is in the process of becoming a landmark. Fully eight inductees into the Rock and Roll Hall of Fame worked here pressing and packing LPs in the 1950s. They include James Brown (who recorded "Papa's Got a Brand New Bag" and several other hits here), Hank Ballard, Clyde McPhatter, Little Willie John, Jackie Wilson, and Bootsie Collins. The site is at 1540 Brewer Ave. in Evanston, near downtown.

Location and Orientation

Cincinnati rather obviously is served by the Ohio River, but boating isn't the most common way to travel these days. Interstate highways come at the "Queen City" from a number of directions. Interstate 74 slants southwest 110 miles from Indianapolis. From the north, I-75 enters Cincinnati from Dayton, Toledo, and Detroit and crosses over the Ohio River into Kentucky to the south. The run from Columbus southwest to Cincinnati on I-71 is 111 miles. The highway branches from I-75 a few miles south into Kentucky before heading westward for Louisville. A major east-west road is US 50, with US 52 hugging the banks of the Ohio River from the east and US 50 doing likewise to the west. The "Queen City," as Cincy is sometimes called, is approximately as far north as Baltimore, Maryland, or Colorado Springs, Colorado, and about as far west as Lansing, Michigan, or Tallahassee, Florida.

The landmark that's easiest to spot is Carew Tower, Fifth and Vine Streets, completed in 1930 and rising 49 stories to a summit of 574 feet. That won't help visitors who lose sight of the edifice as they move up and down the city's hills. Perhaps the key to navigating Cincinnati is to recall that I-275, though it dips briefly into Kentucky, encircles the metro area. To reach the downtown area, travelers headed clockwise on I-275 should always take a right at freeway exits. Those going the opposite direction should exit and turn left.

Once downtown, the city is a bit easier to figure out. The Ohio River is as close to a south side as Cincinnati gets. Five blocks north of the river is Fountain Square, the heart of the city. Vine Street, the north-south thoroughfare that defines the west side of Fountain Square, divides the city east and west. Facing north from Fountain Square, the Mount Adams and Hyde Park areas are to the east. Western Hills and Bridgetown lie to the south. North are several neighborhoods and such near-in suburbs as

CINCINNATI'S GENIUS OF WATER

The very heart of Cincinnati is Fountain Square. The centerpiece of Fountain Square is the Tyler Davidson Fountain, which features a nine-foot, larger-than-life lady with outstretched arms on an ornate pedestal. From her hands cascade small but relentless sprays of water. In warmer months, legions of sweltering Cincinnatians pass the flowing water and take comfort from it. Trouble is, the lady is slowly clogging up.

The fountain, which represents the Genius of Water and its life-sustaining uses, life-enhancing pleasures, and its industrial utility, was completed in 1871 by German sculptor August von Kreling. Besides providing cool drinks to passersby, it has become a rendezvous at lunch, a place to cavort when the Reds win the World Series, and a widely recognized symbol of the city. Local officials have checked out the bronze statue's inner workings and they report that the pipes and structures that support the woman are badly rusted.

Costs of bringing the lady back to her old, free-flowing self are estimated at $1.5 million. The city has set aside $2.3 million for restoration of the entire square to more closely resemble its original look. The final bill for this undertaking, as well as for reworking the fountain, is expected to be $3.8 million. Cincinnati hopes to raise at least $1.5 million from private sources and to complete work by the fall of 1999. Check out the Online Guide to Public Art in Downtown Cincinnati at www.idioinc.com/oacdocs/oacbin/16tyler.html for more info on the "Genius of Water."

Wyoming, Forest Park, and Montgomery. Many attractions in town are south of the Cross Country Highway which runs east-west about 12 miles north of Fountain Square.

SIGHTS

Cincinnati Zoo & Botanical Gardens

As nice a place as any to begin, this zoo has been called America's finest, at 3400 Vine St., tel. (513) 281-4700. Open all year long, the zoo boasts such rarities as the most gorilla births of any such institution, plus legendary residents like

Komodo dragons, white Bengal tigers, even a priceless black rhinoceros. As competition for visitors' dollars intensifies, the zoo turns up the heat with an authentic-appearing jungle trail-rainforest exhibit and such creepily fascinating attractions as the nation's first insectarium, "Insect World." The **Wings of the World** exhibit features everything from puffins to penguins to tropical birds (among other things, the zoo was the home of Martha, the last passenger pigeon). Consistently spotless, lush, and intriguing, the zoo also is the site of a number of fund-raising events such as Zoo Baby Month (usually June, but occasionally varied by a week or two) that make it heavily used and familiar to local residents. It's even busy around Christmas. Hours are daily 9 a.m.-6 p.m.; once inside the gates, patrons can stick around in the summer until 8 p.m. Admission charges are $10 for adults, $8 for seniors, and $5 for children, and zoo parking is $5. In a state with several fine zoos, this one is the best.

Amusement Parks

Even more popular than the zoo are a couple of destinations in northeast suburban Mason. **Paramount's Kings Island,** visible from I-71, off Exit 25A, tel. (800) 288-0808, bills itself as the entertainment capital of the Midwest. The 350-acre facility has numerous thrill rides and all of the other amusements expected in such a park. In addition to the attractions themselves, Kings Island has accommodations so that families can visit easily on consecutive days. On the opposite side of I-71 is the **Beach Waterpark,** 2590 Waterpark Dr., tel. (513) 298-SWIM (tel. 513-298-7946) or (800) 886-SWIM (tel. 800-886-7946). Two million gallons and 35 acres add up to one of the top five water parks in the country. Both facilities are open every day from Memorial Day to Labor Day and weekends before and after during warm weather. Paramount's Kings Island charges $34.99 for persons ages 7-59, $19.99 for children ages 3-6 and for seniors, while the Beach Waterpark is $19.95 for adults and $10.95 for kids ($5.95 for kids under 48 inches tall).

Coney Island, 6201 Kellogg Ave., Cincinnati, tel. (513) 232-8230, is an amusement park, but its claim to fame is the Sunlite swimming pool. The largest recirculating pool in the country,

Sunlite holds three million gallons of water and covers two acres. Rides vary but include everything from preschool-sized devices to the Zoom Flume waterboggan and the Pipeline Plunge tube water slide. Look for miniature golf and pedal boats, too. The pool is open daily 10 a.m.-8 p.m. Ride hours are 11 a.m.-9 p.m. on weekdays and noon-9 p.m. on weekends. Admission to the pool is $10.95 for adults and $8.95 for children. For pool and rides both, prepare to pay $14.95 for adults and $12.95 for children. An after-4 p.m. price for the pool is $6.95.

Consider, too, a pair of non-corporate recreational facilities. The larger is **Great Time Family Fun Center,** 756 Old SR 74, Cincinnati, tel. (513) 753-6900. Amusements include two go-kart tracks, miniature golf, bump-a-cars, batting cages, video and redemption games, and more. There is no admission charge; as an example of costs, go-karts are $4 for adults and $2.50 for children. The center, a mile east of I-275, is open all summer 9 a.m.-9 p.m. **Eastgate Adventures,** 3232 Omni Dr., Cincinnati, tel. (513) 753-8000, is an amusement facility, but not the pretentious sort many travelers are used to. Rather, it offers miniature golf or go-karts, charging golfing adults $5 and golfers 12 and under $3.50. Go-karters must meet height minimums and pay $4 for a four-minute ride. Clean and nicely landscaped, Eastgate is open all summer, 10 a.m.-11 p.m.

William Howard Taft National Historic Site

An inspiration to all the city's home renovators is this National Park Service historic site, at 2038 Auburn Ave. in the Mount Auburn section of town, tel. (513) 684-3262. East of Vine Street and west of Reading Road, Taft's vivid, yellow and green brick childhood home can be reached on foot from downtown and is worth the few blocks' walk. Upstairs is a self-guided tour that outlines the life of the 27th president, who also served as president of the Philippines and was the only person to serve both as America's chief executive and the chief justice. Downstairs is a 30-minute guided tour detailing Taft family belongings and the great man's era. Admission is free and there is a public parking lot a block away at Southern and Young Streets. The site is open daily 10 a.m.-4 p.m.

Mount Airy Forest

A lovely parklike setting can be found at 5083 Colerain Ave. That's the site of the a bucolic place only minutes northwest of downtown. The Mount Airy Arboretum's **Raraflora Gardens** contain unusual plants nicely terraced around a small lake. The hills are alive with the growth of dogwood trees, azaleas, ferns, lilacs, magnolias, and a number of ornamentals that are at their best in the spring. It's the immediate area's best place to hike or meander on foot, and it's big—at over 1,400 acres, this is America's largest municipal park. From the river, head north on I-75 to I-74 west and the Colerain Avenue exit. Turn left on Colerain to the address. The grounds are open daily 10 a.m.-4 p.m., admission free. For more information, call (513) 541-8176.

Wineries and a You-Brew

A couple of wine sights and an unusual brew rendezvous commend themselves to travelers. **Meier's Wine Cellars,** 6955 Plainfield Pike, Cincinnati, tel. (513) 891-2900 or (800) 346-2941, is the state's oldest and largest winery. The tour here includes a walk through the 1.8-million gallon tank farm, plus a look at the century-old casks. There's a tasting room and a gift shop at tour's end, plus a garden with snacks and wines by the glass. For children and those who prefer nonalcoholic beverages, more than a dozen juice varieties are offered. Wine devotees have dozens of options, from champagnes to Lambruscas. Tours take place every day but Sunday, June-Oct. At other times, appointments are needed. Incidentally, Meier's grapes are grown on a small island in Lake Erie!

A contrast in size and age is **Henke Wine,** 701 E. Epworth Ave., tel. (513) 541-3177. Actually a restaurant, this bistro serves its own vintages and attunes them to the menu. Among the more popular Henke wines is its Riesling, available at $3 per glass or about $10 per bottle, both typical prices. Seven wines are made here, among them Seyval, a "surly" white that drinks like a red, and *vin de rouge,* a popular everyday red. Dinner specials may be a marinated chicken breast or a pork loin, and costs for the meals run between $7.95 and $9.95. Grapes used by Henke, which is open for dinner, are purchased from Ohio, Virginia, and the northeastern U.S.

Brewmaster's Personal Brewery, 9980 Kings Automall Dr., tel. (513) 697-0844, is a brewery where customers can choose their favorite style of beer and then concoct it, affix their name to it, and lug a case home. The equipment, ingredients, and staff are on hand—just show up and choose from more than 100 styles of beer to make. There are also a dozen beers on tap available for those who'd rather spectate.

Sawyer Point and Cinergy Field

These two spots in downtown Cincinnati are impossible to miss when driving close to the river. Sawyer Point is a park used for everything from concerts to exhibits. It's one of the few places flat enough to safely in-line skate, it's a nice place to stroll, and there's plenty of parking. Cinergy Field sits like a huge white puffball on the very edge of the river in the downtown area. It's the home of the National League Reds baseball team and the National Football League Bengals, but perhaps not for long. Like many big-league organizations these days, the Reds and Bengals each want a state-of-the-art stadium, even though Cinergy (formerly known as Riverfront Stadium) was new in 1970.

Tours

Tours by land or by water are plentiful. The only problem with some of the bigger boats available on the Ohio is that they insist on groups of as many as 150! The thriftiest craft for visitors with their families or by themselves is the **Celebration Riverboat,** 848 Elm St., Ludlow, KY, tel. (606) 581-0300. Fares, which include lunch or dinner, are $13.95 and $21.50, respectively. While on the water, check out the half-dozen bridges that connect the city and northern Kentucky. One of the country's longest drawbridges is the L&N Railroad bridge, measuring 365 feet, constructed in 1922.

MUSEUMS

Prepare to be impressed by the stunning **Cincinnati Museum Center** at Union Terminal, 1301 Western Ave., tel. (513) 287-7000 or (800) 733-2077. This faithfully restored train station, just a few blocks northwest of downtown, houses the **Cincinnati Historical Museum and Library,**

The spacious Union Terminal once served train passengers, but now it houses the Cincinnati Museum Center.

the **Cincinnati Museum of Natural History,** the **Cincinnati Children's Museum,** and the **Robert D. Lindner Family Omnimax Theater.** An important part of the city's history, the big crescent of a building is best approached on a sunny morning from the east, down a long walk-way crowded with greenery. The top ticket deal is to purchase admissions for all attractions ($12 apiece for adults, $8 each for children). Any two attractions are $9 and $6, respectively. A single history facility is $5.50 for an adult and $3.50 for a child, while the Omnimax Theater is $6.50 per adult and $4.50 per child. Seniors can deduct $1 from any adult fare or combination. The terminal is open Mon.-Sat. 10 a.m.-5 p.m.; Sunday11 a.m.-6 p.m.

The **Taft Museum,** at 316 Pike St., Cincinnati, tel. (513) 241-0343, is a reminder that the Tafts have been an important family down through the years houses a number of paintings by European masters, plus European decorative arts and Chinese ceramics. Worthwhile exhibits also come and go on a regular basis. The building itself is memorable, being a pristine white, Federal-style mansion constructed in 1820. Admission is $3 for adults and $1 for seniors and children. The Taft is open Tues.-Sat. 10 a.m.-5 p.m.; Sunday 1-5 p.m.

Art Museums

A couple of art museums make the A-list for Cincinnati visitors. They include the **Cincinnati Art Museum,** 953 Eden Park Dr., tel. (513) 721-5204; the **Weston Art Gallery** at the Cincinnati Arts Association, Aronoff Center for the Arts, 650 Walnut St., tel. (513) 621-2787; and **Contemporary Arts Center,** 115 E. Fifth St., tel. (513) 345-8400. All offer changing exhibits, permanent collections, and such quirky goings on as "Think Small," the Art Academy's recent exhibit displaying works no larger than two inches across! For all the grousing about Cincy and conservatism, this city has an estimable number of people who know, care about, and like to share their art and the art of others. The Cincinnati Art Museum charges $5 for adults and $4 for children and is open year round Tues.-Sat. 10 a.m.-5 p.m., Sun. noon-6 p.m., closed Sunday. The Art Museum features free docent-guided tours daily at 1 p.m. The Weston Art Gallery asks for a $1 donation and is open Tues.-Sat. 10 a.m.-5:30 p.m., Sunday noon-5 p.m., closed Monday. The Weston also stays open till 8 p.m. when there is a performance at the Aronoff Center. Admission at the Contemporary Arts Center is free to all on Monday, but otherwise is $3.50 for adults and $2 for seniors and students. The Contemporary Arts Center is open Mon-Sat. 10 a.m.-6 p.m., Sunday noon-5 p.m.

Harriet Beecher Stowe House

At 2950 Gilbert Ave., Walnut Hills, tel. (513) 632-5120, this home was restored in the 1970s and now serves as a cultural center. The modest dwelling has a gift shop where visitors can pick up a copy of *Uncle Tom's Cabin*—a book that has remained in print for more than 140 years. Other interesting items include a map of Ohio Underground Railroad routes. Stowe's home is open Tues.-Thurs. 10 a.m.-4 p.m. No admission is charged but donations are encouraged.

NEIGHBORHOODS AND SUBURBS

Clifton
North of downtown and just northwest of the zoo, this area is the address of lots of good restaurants and other places where the locals like to hang out. It's well located, being close to where I-74 and I-75 meet US 27. Hilly and chock full of nice older housing, including some beautiful Victorians, the enclave is green and urban at the same time.

Harrison, College Hill, and Western Hills
Along with closer-in suburbs on the west side, these spots suffer from a municipal inferiority complex compared to the more upscale east side. Actually, the west side has lovely curvaceous, up-and-down roads with pleasant homes tucked all along, and less traffic and noise than the rest of town. Among the more impressive sites is a vast rail yard at the bottom of Price Hill, perhaps 20 tracks wide, that separates this side of town from the rest of Cincy. Roads pass above it. For a good look at the boxcars and flatcars that come and go, drive along SR 264 (Bridgetown Road). In contrast, the metro area's best place to walk is Mount Airy Forest, which is bisected by I-74 and US 52, some six miles northwest of downtown.

Mariemont
A most idyllic eastern suburb. Ground was broken in 1923 for the carefully planned community, which is a memento of the "garden city movement"—an effort to make American towns resemble leafy English villages. Red brick and Tudor are much in evidence here, as is a real effort to keep things just as they are. The town of only about 3,100 residents was designed by two dozen of America's leading architects at the time. Today, this is a low-key place with not a lot of traffic, despite being served by US 50 (locally, Wooster Pike). Even though there is a real mix of upscale and modest housing, Cincy residents who should know better assume the folks who live in Mariemont are rich.

Mount Adams
Mount Adams is located just east of downtown and southeast of the Over-the-Rhine neighborhood. Reach Eden Park and you will have found Mount Adams' residential area to the south, a spot measuring only about 10 blocks by 10 blocks. As for finding it on a map, consider the neighborhood to be bounded by US 50 on the south, I-71 on the west, and SR 3 on the north. The place is characterized by narrow and hilly streets, pretty places to live, and a couple of cultural attractions. Travelers can get their bearings in the **Mt. Adams Books Store & Cafe,** 1101 St. Gregory Place, tel. (513) 241-9009. The store also houses the **Monastery Wine Bar,** where visitors can ask directions while they sip a house wine for $3.50 that is not only tasty and exclusive to this bar, but also shows a label designed by local artist Wolfgang A. Ritschel.

Over-the-Rhine
This is the original German settlement of Cincinnati. These days, it's a place where people play and live the urban good life on this side of the river. There are restaurants, bars, faithfully rehabbed buildings, coffeehouses, night spots, and various shops. The center of this glitzy part of town can be considered the 1200 block of Main Street. Whimsical touches to the neighborhood include the occasional bocce court. To stroll the area when it's most spruced up, attend the art gallery walk, 6-10 p.m. on the last Friday of every month.

RECREATION

Eden Park, at 1501 Eden Park Dr., Mount Adams, is a pretty place, with sweeping, eastward views of the Ohio River. Visitors who tire of merely admiring the view or watching an artist capture the scenery should try climbing the "Old Reservoir Wall" in the park. To do so legally, obtain a permit from the Cincinnati Board of Commissioners, tel. (513) 352-4080. The only thing wrong with this place is the noise from superpowered sound systems booming from cars driven by teenagers. Mornings, when the kids are still in bed, are most tranquil. Eden Park is also home to the Cincinnati Art Museum.

Golf

First-time visitors to Cincinnati may look at the terrain and wonder if they will ever have a flat lie on the golf course. The answer is probably not, but the ups and downs of area courses make them all the more interesting. Mason, northeast of town off US 42, has two nice golf courses. Swingers should try either of two courses at the **Golf Center at Kings Island,** 6042 Fairway Dr., Mason, tel. (513) 398-7700. One is a championship, par-72 course that costs $45 Mon.-Thurs., $55 on Friday, and $65 on weekends (all fees include a cart). The other is a par 60 facility that costs $10 for nine holes and $12.50 for 18. Also in Mason, **Kingswood Golf Course,** 4198 Irwin Simpson Rd., tel. (513) 398-5252 sets par at 71 and greens fees at $11.50 for nine holes and $18 for 18. A cart is $11 for nine holes and $22 for 18; cart fees may be split with a fellow player.

Somewhat closer to downtown, Cincinnati and Hamilton County maintain a total of 14 courses. To the west is **Miami Whitewater Forest,** 8801 Mt. Hope Rd., Harrison, a very popular and challenging county course with par set at 71. Fees are $11.50 to walk and $17 to cart nine holes; $18.25 to walk and $29.25 to cart 18. Eastward, golfers give the **Vineyard,** 600 Nordyke Rd., tel. (513) 474-3007, high marks. It's an 18-hole, par 71 course charging $15 and $20.75 to walk and to ride nine holes, respectively; fees to walk and to ride 18 holes are $25.50 and $37.

Cycling

Since the **Loveland-Morrow Bikepath** is nearby, paddlers can improvise their own biathlon. A post-contest party could even be held in pretty **Little Miami Scenic State Park.** Equally nice is the Shaker Trace Trail in **Miami Whitewater Forest,** New Haven and Oxford Roads, Harrison, tel. (513) 367-4774. The trail is eight miles long and boasts rental bikes and skates and a golf cart "sag wagon" that supplies water to the weary, patches flats, and provides some other assistance to riders. It's just west of the Great Miami River and north of I-74.

Billiards

An upscale place for pool, snooker, darts, and/or cigar puffery can be found on the second and third floors at 1140 Main St. in the Uptown area. **Westminster's Billiard Club,** tel. (513) 929-4400 is open weekdays from 4 p.m. and Sat.-Sun. from 7 p.m.; it's a good place to wait out a rain. Those who seek more activity than pool but don't want to perspire might consider glow-in-the-dark bowling. It's available at **Colerain Bowl,** 9189 Colerain Ave., in Bevis, northwest of downtown at the junction of I-275 and US 27, tel. (513) 385-8500. Balls, pins, and alleys take on eerie hues in the dark.

Professional and Spectator Sports

Cinergy Field, sits like a huge white puffball on the very edge of the river in the downtownarea. it's the home of the National league Reds baseball team and the National Football League Bengals, but perhaps not for long. Like many big-league organizations these days, the Reds and Benglas each want a state-of-the-art stadium, even though Cinergy (formerly knowm as Riverfront Stadium) was new in 1970.

Everyone thinks of the Reds or the Bengals, when sports are mentioned in Cincinnati. But there are several other noteworthy attractions. Both the University of Cincinnati and Xavier University field quality men's basketball teams. Seeing a game can be like previewing a National Basketball Association lineup. Tomorrow's hockey stars may be on the ice for the Cincinnati Cyclones, an International Hockey League franchise. They and the professional soccer Silverbacks play inside the Crown, 100 Broadway. Professional tennis comes to the Queen City at 6140 Freeway Dr., Mason, site of the annual men's ATP tournament just to the west side of I-71 (look for a towering spire marking the tennis stadium site).

River Downs racetrack, 6301 Kellogg Ave., tel. (513) 232-8000, features live thoroughbred racing from mid-April through Labor Day. Simulcasting from other racetracks can be witnessed from within a climate-controlled clubhouse, and there are food opportunities from snacks and drinks to fine dining. Admission is free. General-admission parking is free, while preferred parking in front of the clubhouse is $3.

The Cincinnati skyline from across the Ohio River

These telephone numbers will let visitors know when and if tickets are available for games or matches: Reds, tel. (513) 421-7337; Bengals, tel. (513) 621-3550; University of Cincinnati, tel. (513) 556-2287; Xavier University, tel. (513) 745-3000; Cyclones or Silverbacks, tel. (513) 421-7825; ATP tennis, tel. (513) 651-0303; River Downs, tel. (513) 232-8000.

CULTURE AND ENTERTAINMENT

The top spot for rock 'n' roll and its several permutations is **Bogart's,** 2621 Vine St., tel. (513) 281-8400. If the following attractions mean nothing to a visitor, he or she will want to go elsewhere for quieter, if no less meaningful, entertainment: Sonic Youth, Reverend Horton Heat, Shawn Colvin, the Skatalites, Ben Folds Five, and Green Day. These nationally known entertainers and many others are scheduled at Bogart's on any day of the week for night-time performances. The crowd appears to be of college age but by no means all students. Lesser known local and regional bands—some showing real promise—open for the headliners. This is a theater-type venue.

Other places to experience live music include Loveland's **Tequila Jack's Saloon,** 126 W. Loveland Ave., tel. (513) 583-1717, which features blues on Friday and Saturday; **Jefferson Hall,** 1150 Main St., Over-the-Rhine, tel. (513) 723-9008, a haven for local and national blues and R&B acts; **Buzz Coffee**

Shop and CD-O-Rama, 2900 Jefferson Ave. (across the street from the University of Cincinnati), tel. (513) 221-3472, where reggae, ska, and alternative rule; the **Leo Coffeehouse,** inside the YMCA in the 200 block of Calhoun Street, a coffeehouse for folkies; and **Annie's,** 4343 Kellogg Ave., tel. (513) 321-0220, an east-side rendezvous where estimable rockers such as Foghat sometimes are featured.

Taft Theatre, Fifth and Sycamore Streets, tel. (513) 721-8883, draws an older audience for attractions such as Beatles tributes or comedian Louie Anderson. Other entertainments include the classic *Peter Pan* and the Broadway hit, *Rent.* Ticket prices range from $15 to $60, depending on the attraction and location of the seat desired. The Taft's season runs from September to May.

What with the popularity of country music, it's perhaps surprising that music from the hills and valleys hasn't made more of an inroad. Look for big-name C&W entertainers like Clint Black, playing downtown at places such as the Crown stadium on Pete Rose Way, tel. (513) 562-4949. Those who enjoy a bit of line dancing can show up at the **Cheyenne Cattle Co.,** Forest Fair Mall, Forest Park, north of downtown just inside the I-275 loopeast of US 27, tel. (513) 671-443, and **Autto's Cadillac Ranch,** 11974 Lebanon Rd., Sharonville, north of downtown on US 42, tel. (513) 563-6007.

Cincinnati residents with long memories celebrated the 1998 reopening of the **Greenwich**

CINCINNATI EVENTS

For a comprehensive, pocket-sized calendar of events booklet for the entire year, call (513) 621-6994 or 800-CINCY-USA (tel. 800-216-2987).

JANUARY

Warehouse Sale of Books and Records, conducted by Friends of the Library at 1621 Dana Ave., for more info call (513) 369-6959.

FEBRUARY

Annual Arts Sampler Weekend, made possible by the local telephone company. Some 75 free arts events are staged simultaneously and without charge all across the metropolitan area.

MARCH

Cincinnati Zoo Celebrity Winter Walks take place throughout the month.

Greater Cincinnati Folk Art and Craft Show features it all, with much more sublime than substandard—in excess of 100 fine craftspeople are featured.

Cincinnati Heart Mini-Marathon involves runs and walks of varying lengths starting at the Convention Center, all to benefit the American Heart Association.

APRIL

The **Great Easter Egg Scramble** takes place at the Cincinnati Zoo.

The **Spring Floral Festival,** also at the Cincinnati Zoo, gets gardeners and floral admirers pumped for blooming weather.

WalkAmerica, head out to Sawyer Point on the river in order to benefit the March of Dimes.

MAY

Jammin' on Main is a multi-stage downtown street music festival sponsored by the Cincinnati Arts Festival.

Taste of Cincinnati, downtown. Here's an efficient way to sample some of the city's many fine restaurants.

House Tour of Historic Wyoming, featuring six houses and offered by the Cincinnati Preservation Association.

Cincinnati May Festival, held at the Cincinnati Music Hall, is the oldest choral festival in the western hemisphere.

Sing Cincinnati is a concert series held at several downtown locations.

Tavern, 2440 Gilbert Ave., tel. (513) 221-1151, known in the past for showcasing jazz talent. Jazz takes center stage once again in a nice atmosphere, enhanced by visual arts on the wall which are for sale, by a new menu, and by a separate cigar lounge that has an exhaust fan so as not to drive the non-cigar-smoking majority out the door. Jazz also is performed at these places, among others: **Local 1207,** 1207 Main St., Over-the-Rhine, tel. (513) 651-1207, a smart place where jazz and blues alternate; likewise, **Stow's on Main,** 1142 Main St., Over-the-Rhine, tel. (513) 684-0080 may offer either jazz or blues artists.

The **Cincinnati Symphony Orchestra,** 1241 Elm St., tel. (513) 381-3300, divides its time between Music Hall and Riverbend Music Center, east of town. The **Cincinnati Ballet,** tel. (513) 621-5219, dances 30 times a year at the Aronoff Center, offering a repertoire that ranges from classical to contemporary dance. The **Cincinnati Opera,** tel. (513) 241-2742, is the second-oldest such company in the country. It is internationally acclaimed and offers four productions during its summer season at the Music Hall, 1241 Elm St. The **Cincinnati Pops Orchestra,** tel. (513) 621-1919, like the symphony, splits its season between Music Hall and Riverbend.

Metropolitan Cincinnati's outdoor entertainment site is **Riverbend Music Center,** 6295 Kellogg Ave., tel. (513) 232-6220. In the summer the Cincinnati Pops orchestra plays here virtually every Friday and Saturday, with admission ranging from $14 (lawn) to $27 (pavillion) to $32 (VIP). On other nights, mega-acts such as Metallica, the B-52's with the Pretenders, and the Doobie Brothers show up and turn up the amps. Rock show prices vary, parking is included in the ticket price, and most music begins each evening at either 8 or 8:30 p.m. Persons who staff the phones are helpful, willing to provide information on events whenever travelers will be in the area. Food can be brought in, but no drinks are allowed except commercially sealed bottles of water.

JUNE

Riverbend Summerfest, early June through late July, is five weekends of concerts featuring the Cincinnati Pops and Cincinnati Symphony orchestras, plus nationally known guests.

Rainforest, Krohn Conservatory, Eden Park, lets visitors sip gourmet coffee as they walk among tropical plants and cavorting butterflies. Through August.

JULY

Queen City Blues Fest takes place at Sawyer Point on the river. Call (513) 684-4227 for tickets, or e-mail gcbs@compuserve.com.

AUGUST

ATP Tennis Tournament, Mason. This is one of nine major international men's tournaments and it takes place each year early in the month.

SEPTEMBER

The *Delta Queen* visits Cincinnati's Public Landing during her cruise on the Ohio River. The *Mississippi Queen* also pays a call in September.

Riverfest takes place during Labor Day weekend at Bicentennial Commons. It's a long goodbye to summer, with food, fireworks, and entertainment.

Cheetah Run is a 2.5-mile zip around the Cincinnati Zoo for runners who can get up and hit the starting line by 8 a.m. Cool down afterward by walking through the botanical gardens.

Oktoberfest comes a bit early to downtown Cincinnati in what has become five blocks of food and entertainment along Fifth Street.

OCTOBER

The **Gold Star Chilifest** takes place on West Court Street and features nationally known country acts, plus chili, natch.

NOVEMBER

Holiday Junction occurs at the Museum Center. It's a tribute to trains and railroading in an impossibly romantic old building that was created originally for people to meet passenger trains.

There are two **Festival of Lights** events, one at the Cincinnati Zoo and one downtown on Fountain Square. Both have been noted by the national media for their holiday splendor. The festivals also run in December.

DECEMBER

Balluminaria is an innovative concept. A dozen hot-air balloons fire up around Eden Park's Mirror Lake. The reflection creates one of the season's most spectacular visuals. Call the Cincinnati Park Board for specifics, tel. (513) 352-4080.

The big town has a number of outlets for live theater. It's hardly an exaggeration to state that a committed buff can find a stage presentation virtually every week of the year. Top notch productions take place at **Playhouse in the Park,** 962 Mount Adams Dr., in Mount Adams at the southern edge of Eden Park, tel. (513) 421-3888, with comedies, dramas, classics, and musicals; the **Broadway Series,** 120 E. Fourth St., tel. (513) 241-2345, features touring companies; **Fahrenheit Theatre Co.,** at various locations for classical theater, tel. (513) 559-0642; and **Showboat Majestic,** foot of Broadway, Public Landing, tel. (513) 241-6550, which is both a National Historic Landmark and a nostalgic place to experience a performance.

ACCOMMODATIONS

There are a number of nice places to stay in the heart of the city. Among the best is the **Cincinnatian Hotel,** 601 Vine St. at Sixth and Vine Streets, tel. (513) 381-3000, (800) 942-9000 outside of Ohio, or (800) 332-2020 within the state. The Cincinnatian is a luxury, eight-story hotel with a restaurant to match (see below). It also offers guests a lounge and an exercise room. Other swell downtown spots include the **Garfield House Suite Hotel,** 2 Garfield Place (I-71 Exit 1C), tel. (513) 421-3355. Rooms range from expensive to luxurious; breakfast is free, there is an exercise room, a restaurant, and a lounge. The **Hyatt Regency-Cincinnati,** 151 W. Fifth St. (I-75 Exit 3), tel. (513) 579-1234, provides rooms from very expensive to luxurious. An indoor pool, exercise room, restaurant, and lounge greet guests. Another popular spot is the **Omni Netherland Plaza,** Fifth and Race Streets, tel. (513) 421-9100. Rates are luxury level and earn guests an outdoor pool, exercise room, restaurant, and lounge at this national historic landmark. Consider, too, the **Westin Hotel,** Fountain Square, tel. (513) 621-7700. A luxury-priced hotel, it has a restaurant, lounge, and exercise room.

Several entirely adequate, lesser-priced downtown hotels and motels exist, most of them franchises. Other areas with a plenitude of rooms include Blue Ash, Mason, and Sharonville. The Kentucky side of the river seems more bed-and-breakfast friendly than metro Cincinnati, but here are a couple of places for those committed to a comfy B&B stay. One is the Italianate Victorian **Prospect Hill Bed & Breakfast,** 408 Boal St., tel. (513) 421-4408. This expensive B&B is in the city's oldest suburb, offering a full breakfast in a setting of fireplaces and antiques. Another is **Victorian Inn of Hyde Park Bed & Breakfast,** 3567 Shaw Ave., tel. (513) 321-3567.

Getting close to Cincinnati, travelers begin to see hotel and motel franchises in large numbers. Typical are the **Days Inn—Cincinnati East,** 4056 Mt. Carmel-Tobasco Rd., tel. (513) 528-3800, and the **Holiday Inn Eastgate Conference Center,** 4501 Eastgate Blvd., tel. (513) 752-4400. Both are very near I-275, which makes a vast circle around Cincinnati. These and other motels charge moderately to expensively for a room.

There are contrasting choices for Kings Island visitors. One is the **Kings Island Inn,** 5691 Kings Island Dr., Mason, tel. (513) 398-0115 or (800) 727-3050. A very expensive family hotel with two pools, the inn puts you close to all the action. For dedicated campers who want to be nearby, try **Yogi Bear's Camp Resort at Paramount's Kings Island,** I-71, Exit 25, Mason, (513) 398-2901. Tent sites range up to $40 for two people, camping cabins with electricity range up to $55 for two. Not for the faint of heart!

FOOD

Good places to eat are everywhere in Cincinnati, and the restaurants serve more different kinds of food than anywhere else in Ohio.

Erie Avenue
For some 20 blocks through the city's posh eastern suburb of Hyde Park, this surface street offers many superior dining experiences.

A bistro with outdoor dining is **Pasta al Dente,** 3672 Erie Ave., tel. (513) 321-7400. Obviously Italian, the restaurant is open for dinner every day and has a lengthy wine list. A bit farther on,

past statuesque housing, there's the **China Gourmet,** 3340 Erie Ave., tel. (513) 871-6612. Its Cantonese and Szechuan dishes have won awards. More big, sumptuous houses loom as the road widens into a boulevard with upscale shopping. This elongated heart of Hyde Park has many choices. The **Echo,** just off Erie at 3510 Edwards Rd., tel. (513) 321-2816, is a popular breakfast, lunch, or dinner spot offering "home cooking without going home." Fifty feet away is the **Melting Pot,** 3520 Edwards Rd., tel. (513) 871-7773, with a choice of more than a dozen fondues. Between the two is **Arthur's,** at 3516 Edwards Rd., tel. (513) 871-5543. Burgers, hors d'oeuvres, salads, and soups are featured at this neighborhood bar-cafe.

Not everything necessitates sitting down. Returning to Erie Avenue, look for a **Graeter's** ice cream store at 2740 Erie Ave., tel. (513) 321-6221. There are 11 such treat-dessert destinations throughout the metropolitan area. Before leaving Hyde Park, diners would do well to visit the **Indigo Casual Gourmet Cafe,** 2637 Erie Ave., on the south side, tel. (513) 321-9952. The fare here ranges from pizza to vegetarian and can be consumed at outside tables in warm weather. **Darci's California Cafe,** 2653 Erie Ave., tel. (513) 871-6167, serves sandwiches and salads, urging customers to save room for dessert. Back on the north side of the square, check out **Awakenings,** 2734 Erie Ave. tel. (513) 321-2525, a coffeehouse offering desserts and live jazz. The last stop in this neighborhood is **Teller's of Hyde Park,** 2710 Erie Ave., tel. (513) 321-4721. Lunch and dinner happen in this former savings and loan building every day. The menu, best described as "slightly gourmet," blends Pacific Rim and Mediterranean dishes to the tune of live jazz or acoustic music. Teller's offers more than 100 different beers, 30 of which are on tap. It also serves up a $6.95 Sunday brunch, tempting diners with such delights as pear-and-pecan pancakes with maple syrup and whipped cream.

East Walnut Hills
Continuing westward, East Walnut Hills presents visitors with a short drive and a lot of great dining choices along Madison Road. **O'Bryon's Irish Pub,** 1998 Madison Rd., tel. (513) 321-5525, dishes up burgers, prime rib, and seafood, and is

a place where kids under 10 eat for free. Less than a block distant is **Chateau Pomije Cafe,** 2019 Madison Rd., tel. (513) 871-8788, a wine bar with an adjacent sales room. The cafe offers a full menu of Mediterranean, Southwestern, and Thai dishes. Still hungry? The **Brick Yard,** 2038 Madison Rd., tel. (513) 321-3953, deals out brews and handmade pizzas. Behind the Brick Yard is the rewarding **Bonbonerie Fine Pastries,** 2030 Madison Rd., tel. (513) 321-3399. A specialty is scones, but visitors can try whatever they like in the bakery's adjacent tea room.

Downtown

All hail the **Maisonette,** 114 E. Sixth St., Cincinnati, tel. (513) 721-2260. If there's any restaurant where a meal is worth $150 per couple, this may be the one. The Maisonette, it's said, is the best French restaurant between New York and San Francisco. The French-Mediterranean menu covers everything from fresh fish to veal to marinated rack of lamb, the side dishes are pleasant surprises, and there's a great selection of wines. Travelers face neither risk nor embarrassment by putting themselves in the hands of the knowledgeable and efficient waitstaff when ordering. Set aside two hours, make reservations a couple of weeks in advance, and spruce up before arriving. The result will be a memorable experience at a place that has maintained its five-star rating for 30 years running. Open for lunch Tues.-Fri., dinner Mon.-Sat.

The **Palace,** Sixth and Vine Streets, tel.(513) 381-6006, has virtually as many awards on the walls as the Maisonette. It's inside the Cincinnatian Hotel, where it serves American regional gourmet cuisine à la carte. A popular luncheon item might be grilled veal medallions with sweet corn flan ($18), or petit filet mignon with risotto cake in a red wine demiglaize ($16.50). In the evening, consider barbecued rack of lamb encrusted in pecans with a barbecue glaze for $32, or fresh pan-seared Chilean sea bass, served over Japanese soba noodles with a a rice wine butter sauce and a salmon egg roll. Soothing live music accompanies the evening meal and may feature a pianist, harpist, or jazz trio. The Palace serves dinner every day, lunches on weekdays only, and asks that men wear jackets in the evening.

Montgomery Inn at the Boathouse, 925 Eastern Ave., Sawyer Point, tel. (513) 721-7427, is one of the places people leave Cincinnati raving about. The house specialty is barbecue porkloin back ribs, available in either half or full rack with Saratoga potatoes (baked sweet potato chips) at $14.95 or $18.95, respectively. Other popular menu items include a pulled-pork sandwich deluxe at $6.50 and barbecue beef at $5.75, both for lunch. Chicken, chops, or steak dinners range from $12.95 to $23.50. Open every day, the Sawyer Point restaurant does not take Saturday reservations. Oh yeah—the view of the Ohio River from here is breathtaking. The original Montgomery Inn is north at 9440 Montgomery Rd., tel. (513) 791-3482.

Guys in skirts can be. . . okay. That's what visitors to **Nicholson's Tavern & Pub,** 625 Walnut St., tel. (513) 564-9111, will think once they sample a hearty ale or consume something from the Scottish/American menu. Whether it's an hors d'oeuvre or merely bar food, a Scotch egg can be addictive. It's an egg rolled in a sausage-bread crumb mixture and baked. At lunch, try authentic fish and chips for $10.50. In the evening, Edinburgh *osso buco* is $12.95. There are 14 ales on tap here, plus 70 single-malt scotches, and 38 imported bottled beers. Nicholson's is open every day for dinner and every day but Sunday for lunch.

Skyline Chili, 643 Vine St., tel. (513) 241-2020, is the most urban of hundreds of restaurants in Cincy that specialize in chili. The locals eat it over spaghetti, topped with onions, or beans, or cheese, or all of the above. There are 80 Skyline restaurants, serving the stuff with pasta in an oblong dish, as a topping for a hot dog, or with crackers in a bowl. It's cheap and hearty, allowing diners to eat and run for about $5. There certainly are other chili choices—Chili Company, Chili Express, Chili Palace, Chili Supreme, and Gold Star come to mind. Ask a local which he or she may favor.

Arboreta, 1133 Sycamore St., tel. (513) 721-1133, was voted Best New Restaurant recently, and it does a couple of things very well. Cincinnati being within an overnight drive of salt water, the sea bass is consistently fresh. Served with pan-fried noodles, braised bok choy, and stir-fried vegetables in a Thai sauce, it's Arboreta's most sought-after meal and is priced according to the market price of sea bass. Other hits include Amish chicken at $16.95, angel-hair pasta at $14.95, and Black Angus filet at $21.95. Patio dining is popular at the restaurant, which is open Tues.-Sun. for dinner and features live music Thurs.-Sat.

If breakfast is the nearest meal, head for the **Inn the Wood Restaurant and Tavern,** 277 Calhoun St., Clifton, tel. (513) 221-3044. This restaurant dishes up an egg-cheese-potato combination that's cheap, filling, and at least mildly addictive. Breakfast is served all day here and can include omelets or pancakes. A main dish and coffee with refills should set a diner back no more than $5-7, with tip. Those who lean toward a weekend brunch should try **Kaldi's,** a coffeehouse with panache at 1202 Main St. in the Over-the-Rhine neighborhood, tel. (513) 241-3070. There are muffins, sticky buns, quiches, fruits, and veggies to suit most tastes and they serve several varieties of coffee.

West

Ohio is some distance from Mexico, but that doesn't mean authentic food isn't available. A nice place is **Don Pablo's Mexican Kitchen & Cantina,** 9455 Colerain Ave., Northgate, tel. (513) 741-0477. Pablo fires up a mesquite grill for flavorful fajitas, handmade enchiladas and tortillas, kicky salsa and chips, fresh frijoles, and a choice of several steaks. The lunchtime favorite is "Don Diego," a chicken and a beef enchilada, for $5.35; evening diners like "El Matador," which includes two crispy chicken flautas, a cheese enchilada, a beef taco, and a chicken enchilada, all for $8.95. Don Pablo's is open for lunch and dinner every day. Also at 11363 Montgomery Rd. in Symmes Township, west of Cincinnati near the junction of I-275 and Loveland Rd. (SR 48), tel. (513) 489-8600.

Regina Bakery, 4025 Harrison Ave. (SR 264 about five or six miles west of downtown), tel. (513) 481-2985, in Cheviot, is the place where a vacationer is most apt to meet Homer Simpson. Why? Because Regina dials out some of the best donuts in town. Popular choices are 44 cents for the unadorned and 55 cents for those with cream or jelly. Coffee, juice, and milk are available. Regina opens her place Tues.-Thurs. 6 a.m.-6 p.m. and Sunday 7 a.m.-1 p.m.

Sebastian's, 5209 Glenway Ave., Price Hill (southwest corner of town, just north of the river), tel. (513) 471-2100, holds up the Greek end of the table rather well by serving wonderful, inexpensive gyros. They're $3.40 apiece and can be had with side dishes such as Greek fries. With a soft drink, a filling meal here is less than $6. Sebastian's is open Mon.-Sat. 10:30 a.m.-8:30 p.m.

Taste of the World Cafe, 4037 Hamilton Ave., tel. (513) 542-2233, once was a mere coffeehouse. Someone knew how to cook, though, and began to offer an occasional, savory dish. Nowadays, Taste of the World serves up Indian and Mediterranean items such as curry, noodles, and hummus. Adventurous folk music is offered on weekends and may be Balkan acoustic or coal mine authentic. For lunch, try the crunchy oriental chicken salad, served with spicy Asian noodles, for $5.25. A bit later, order the baked cod with fresh dill and lemon butter, mashed potatoes, salad, and fresh-baked bread for $7.95. This low-key place is open Mon.-Sat. for lunch and dinner.

North

Anand India, 10890 Reading Rd., Evendale (near the junction of US 42 and SR 126, east of I-75), tel. (513) 554-4040, serves lunch every day but Monday and dinner every day. The luncheon buffet is $6.99 and is a good introduction to the cuisine of northern India. Luncheon menu items range from $4.50 to $7 and may include lamb, beef, fish, or no meat at all. A popular veggie dinner selection is spinach-cheese *saagbaneer,* for $7.99. Tandoori chicken each evening is $8.95, which includes sides such as lentils. It's all "just spicy enough," said one diner.

The **Grand Finale,** just south of I-275 at 3 E. Sharon Rd., Glendale, tel. (513) 771-5925, started out as a strictly dessert destination and responded to the growing clientele with a full menu. Lunch and dinner favorites include ginger chicken and fresh fish dishes. The restaurant's name refers to a meal's fine final morsel, be it chocolate cordial pie, apple-cinnamon cheesecake, white chocolate mousse in puff pastry, or red-raspberry white-chocolate fudge pie. Like youth, dessert is wasted on the young. Be a sensible adult, stop counting calories, and take care of that craving for sweets. Dessert prices range from $3.95 to $5.50, but who cares? Open for lunch and dinner Tues.-Sat. and for Sunday brunch.

Lu Lu's Noodles, 135 W. Kemper Rd., tel. (513) 671-4949, is a handy place for visitors headed to the Tri-County Mall or those who find themselves on the northern stretch of I-275. Open for lunch or dinner, the facility offers rice, ramen, egg, and other noodle varieties accompanying a mostly Asian menu. Luncheon specials may be pineapple chicken, *moo goo gai pan,* or noodles and can include an egg roll or fried rice. With a soft drink, the price is about $5. Later in the day, dinners may be *moo shu* pork or General Tsao chicken, both priced at $6, or pad thai, just $5.25. This is wholesome, tasty food in an area that leans toward food franchises.

There's no such thing as too many pizza places, so here's one more: **Pomi's Pizzeria & Trattoria,** 7880 Remington Rd., Montgomery, tel. (513) 794-0080. A big pizza with three toppings is about $14 here, and it and all other pies are nicely done in a wood-fired oven. The pizza variety is as rich as the sauce, with deep-dish and Sicilian pizzas offered. Not in the mood for a pie? Look to salads, sandwiches, and pastas from a full menu. Pomi keeps the doors open every day for lunch and dinner.

East
Lemon Grass Thai Restaurant, 2666 Madison Rd., Hyde Park, tel. (513) 321-2882. Western palates can rest assured that they will not be overtaxed here: diners can choose the seasoning of their dish on a scale of one to 10. Be advised that eight, nine, and 10 are incendiary. That said, the Lemon Grass serves up traditional Thai food that is the equal of just about any Asian restaurant. Menu items such as chicken, pork, or shrimp curry, *pad thai, satay,* and a number of vegetarian items will cost diners about $10 plus drink, tax, and tip. Open Mon.-Frid. for lunch and every day for dinner.

Hyde Park Chop House, 3159 Montgomery Rd., Landen, tel. (513) 697-0800, is an upscale, atmospheric place featuring thick-cut steaks and chops, plus fresh seafood. Open Mon.-Fri. for dinner only (the bar stays open later), the restaurant's most popular item is steak Oscar—a 10-oz. filet mignon topped with lobster, with a demiglaize beneath and a Bearnaise sauce on top. The dinner is $27.95. Norwegian salmon comes in fresh and sells for $15.95. Most diners show up in business-casual or better attire.

Here's the scoop on two comfort foods, pizza and burgers. **LaRosa's,** tel. (513) 347-1111, with one phone number and more than 40 locations all over metro Cincinnati, is quite popular. Kinds include traditional, pan-style or hand-tossed super crust. A large pizza with three toppings will run about $15. LaRosa's is open every day for lunch and dinner and also offers pastas, hoagies, salads, soups, and side dishes from french fries to garlic rolls. **Zip's,** 1036 Delta Ave., in the Mount Lookout neighborhood in the southeast corner of town, tel. (513) 871-9876, serves burgers and fries the franchises can only dream about. A cheeseburger is $2.50, fries are $1.25, and Zip's makes up for its lack of milkshakes by keeping a complete bar. Hours are Mon.-Sat. 11 a.m.-1 a.m. and Sunday 11 a.m. to midnight.

Brewpubs
There are more cerebral experiences than cruising brewpubs, but Cincinnati has several pubs that should be noted, for their suds if not for their substance. They include **Main Street Brewery,** 1203 Main St., Over-the-Rhine, tel. (513) 665-4677; **Barrel House Brewing Co.,** 22 E. 12th St., Over-the-Rhine, tel. (513) 421-2337; **Holy Grail Brewery & Grille,** 13 W. Charlton St., Corryville, tel. (513) 861-7821; **Watson Brothers Brewhouse,** 4785 Lake Forest Dr., Blue Ash (north on I-71, east on Pfeiffer Rd. [SR 26]), tel. (513) 563-9797; and **Rock Bottom Restaurant & Brewery,** 10 Fountain Square Plaza, tel. (513) 513-621-1588.

Farmers Markets
Cincinnati's food scene would be incomplete without mentioning two additional locations. **Findlay Market,** Race and Elder Streets, just north of the downtown area in Over-the-Rhine, is an open-air market operating on Wednesday, Friday, and Saturday. Folks come from Ohio, Indiana, and Kentucky to sell produce in season, flowers, meat, herbs, and other rural delights. Beneath big wall murals, this is one of the places where they city's chefs shop. The other is **Jungle Jim's International Farmers Market,** 5440 Dixie Hwy. (SR 4), Fairfield (dial 513-829-1919). Jim's is four acres covering more kinds of cheese, mushroom species, produce variations, types of olives, flavors and spices, cigars from everywhere but Cuba, and wine from wherever vines make grapes. Corny, noisy, pretentious, and

crowded, Jim's also is a great place to buy a gift or purchase something like goetta, the meat-like, mushlike, oatmeal-and-pork complement to eggs and toast found on numerous Cincy breakfast tables.

INFORMATION AND SERVICES

In an emergency, dail 911. To reach Cincinnati police in a non-emergency, call (513) 352-3920. The main post office is on the southeast corner of Fifth and Main Streets. For a medical non-emergency call University Hospital at (513) 558-1000.

The **Greater Cincinnati Convention and Visitors Bureau,** 300 W. Sixth St., tel. (513) 621-2142 or (800) 246-2987, carries lots of information for travelers. There's also a local visitors' information telephone line, (513) 746-1040, and a helpful Web site is www.cincyusa.com.

Media
Cincinnati is one of a dwindling number of American cities still served by competing daily newspapers. The popular *Cincinnati Enquirer,* is published every morning. "Let's Go/Weekend" covers entertainment on Friday. The *Cincinnati Post,* on the streets every evening but Sunday, looks at entertainment on Thursday in its "Weekender" section. The *Enquirer* was taken down a notch in 1998 when it followed a lengthy investigation of the Cincy-based United Fruit Company with an apology to Chiquita Banana and all her friends. More than that, the newspaper paid United Fruit $10 million! The stories weren't necessarily untrue concerning overseas bribery and deceit, but much of the material was obtained illegally by an investigative reporter who was subsequently fired. The *Enquirer* is a chastened newspaper in a city that needs periodic investigative work. Check out either the *Enquirer* or *Post* (they're jointly printed) at www.gocinci.net.

Several weekly newspapers enliven the metro area. They are *Cincinnati City Beat, East Side Weekend Magazine,* and *Everybody's News.* The first is published on Thursday, the second on Wednesday, and the third on Friday. *City Beat* and *Everybody's News* contain calendars of events and cover food, the arts, movies, and related matters. *City Beat's* annual "Best of . . ." issue, which emerges in the spring, is a nice capsule guide to the ambience of the town. The east-side tabloid has a restaurant review but runs more to fashion and decorating and less to controversial issues. Also, check out *City Beat's* Web site, www.best-of-cincinnati.com.

Cincinnati Magazine is a monthly that covers the urban scene. It sells for $2.50 on newsstands. The restaurant review issue comes out each March. Recent stories have ranged from a profile of a local minor-league hockey player to the problems of urban sprawl in Warren County, northeast of the city.

WLW, at 700 on the AM dial, is the 50,000-watt overdog among radio stations. Much of the format is either news, contentious talk, or numbing sports talk. An alternative can be found by tuning in WNKU at 89.7 on the FM band. All sorts of music, much of it local, is presented by this college radio station from across the river at Northern Kentucky University. Even more committed to local musicians is WAIF, 88.3 FM. Best place to hear local news remains WLW, which tells the populace what's going at the top of every hour.

Transportation
Virtually every bus that's part of the public Metro system stops within a block or two of Fountain Square. For route and scheduling information, call (513) 621-4455. The MetroCenter office, 122 W. Fifth St., is staffed weekdays 7:30 a.m.-5 p.m. and provides route, schedule, and fare information. Tokens and special fare deals also can be had at the center. Rush-hour is considered 6-9 a.m. and 3-6 p.m. During those times, fares are 80 cents. They drop to 65 cents during non-rush periods. For public transit, that's a bargain. Folks looking to take a bus out of town can rendezvous at the **Greyhound** station, 1005 Gilbert Ave., tel. (513) 352-6020 or (800) 231-2222.

Air travelers may be surprised to learn that the terminal isn't in Ohio. Rather, the **Cincinnati/Northern Kentucky International Airport,** tel. (606) 767-3151, is across the Ohio River and approximately 12 miles southwest of downtown. The facility is served by Air Tran, American Eagle, Comair/Delta, Continental Express, Northwest, Skyway, TWA, United, and USAir. International carriers include British Airways, Lufthansa, KLM, and Swissair. The airport is a major hub for Delta. Expect to pay approximately $12 one way or $16 round trip for an aiport bus ride. Those are JetPort Express prices; reach them at (606) 767-3702. The Airport Taxi Service, tel. (606)

767-3260, advertises that its automobiles run 24 hours a day and that four can ride for the same price as a single passenger.

Shopping

Cincinnati is at least as retail-friendly as any other big town. Carew Tower, for example, is home to 70 shops. Enter at Fourth and Race Streets. Major shopping centers, in addition to the downtown area, include Eastgate Mall, I-275 and SR 32, tel. (513) 752-2290; Forest Fair Mall, I-275 and Winton Road, tel. (513) 671-2882; Kenwood Town Centre, 7875 Montgomery Rd., Exit 12 off I-71, tel. (513) 745-9100; Northgate Mall, 9501 Colerain Ave., (513) 385-5600; and Tri-County Mall, 11700 Princeton Rd., tel. (513) 671-0120.

Strangest place to shop? That title might go to **Hubba-Hubba,** 4181 Hamilton Ave., Northside, tel. (513) 542-7888. This retail establishment sells polyester, go-go boots, Cosmo Kramer-style (à la *Seinfeld*) clothing, and related retro goods and furnishings. It's open Tues.-Fri. noon-6 p.m., Saturday noon-5 p.m.

OHIO RIVER WEST

The Ohio River begins its westward run along the southern Ohio border in East Liverpool; it is only fitting to take one last, memorable glance as it ends its trek westward and heads south between Indiana and Kentucky. This can be done best west of Cincinnati in **Shawnee Lookout Park,** a county park sitting on a ridge between the Ohio and Great Miami Rivers at their confluence near the Indiana state line. To get to the park, take US 50 west from Cincinnati to the village of Cleves, then follow Mt. Nebo Road and look for the signs, or ask a resident for directions. Once inside the park, look for the **Blue Jacket Trail.** This path will spiral downward close to standing water before angling up to a vantage point. Looking west, the traveler can take in the end of the Miami Valley and beyond, particularly at times of the year when there are no leaves. There also is an earthen fort, created by pre-Columbian peoples, down a shorter trail. A map of the park is available at the small museum, which displays native and pioneer artifacts.

History

East of Cincinnati lies a small and fascinating patch of Kentucky bluegrass. This intrusion of prairie, which took place long before there were human inhabitants, can be seen in Adams Lake State Park and away from the main highways in parts of Adams and Brown Counties. The Cincinnati area and environs are part of the Miami Valley—defined by the Great and Little Miami Rivers. Fertile and teeming with wildlife, the valley was a favorite area for prehistoric natives and for the Shawnee and Miami who followed. After Ohio achieved statehood, this part of the state became known for its rampant, pre-Civil War, antislavery activity. That occurred in part because slavery had been outlawed since the creation of the Northwest Territory in 1787. As such, it offered freedom to those in chains.

The little town of Ripley, 60 miles upriver from Cincinnati, saw the Rev. John Rankin and former slave-turned-businessman John Parker risk their lives as conductors on the Underground Railroad. Harriet Beecher Stowe could not have picked a better vantage point than Cincinnati from which to write *Uncle Tom's Cabin.* Since 1865, the riverfront areas east and west of Cincinnati have remained thinly populated, in contrast to the teeming activity along the banks of the big city.

SIGHTS

State Parks

Adams Lake State Park, tel. (740) 544-3927, exists in the shadow of the more renowned Shawnee State Park 20 miles to the east, but this small facility need not be apologetic. There's fishing (electric motors only), boating, and hiking, and everything is adjacent to a nature preserve known as Adams Lake Prairie. The park is 1.5 miles north of the village of West Union on SR 41.

East Fork State Park, SR 125, Bantam, tel. (513) 734-4323, mixes rugged hills and open meadows and, at 8,420 acres, is one of the state's largest parks. It's also among the most diverse. The 2,160-acre lake is designed for boats of unlimited horsepower, and there's swimming,

Ulysses S. Grant was born in this little house on April 27, 1822.

hunting, fishing, 85 miles of hiking trails, 57 miles of bridle trials, and 46 miles devoted to back-packing.

A few miles north of East Fork State Park is **Stonelick State Park,** 2895 Lake Dr., Pleasant Plain, tel. (513) 625-7544. The lake here is 200 acres and only electric motors can be used. Fishing, hunting, swimming, and hiking are popular. Both parks offer large numbers of camp-sites.

North Bend to Ripley
There are a number of pleasant sights to be seen along the Ohio River starting at the Indiana border on US 50, not least of which is Shawnee Lookout Park, described above. East of Cincinnati, travelers can continue to follow the river on US 52.

The **Harrison State Memorial,** tel. (513) 297-2300, high atop a hill, marks the final resting place of William Henry Harrison (1773-1841), the country's ninth president. A Virginian by birth, Harrison had the misfortune to die after only 31 days in office. Perhaps it's ironic that he was laid to rest beneath this traditional obelisk, since the area once was Shawnee country and Harrison defeated a large contingent of Shawnee at Tippecanoe in Indiana in 1811. There is no charge to see the tomb, which is between the Ohio and Great Miami Rivers on the west side of the village of North Bend.

About 15 miles west of Cincinnati, the **Ulysses S. Grant Birthplace State Memorial** is

a small, whitewashed home a few yards from the river in Point Pleasant on US 52, less than 30 miles upriver from Cincinnati. Under the occasional chestnut tree, the small home where Grant was born in 1822 is a nice stop, if for no other reason than that there's a park adjacent to the river, a bridge dedicated to U.S. Grant, and a mom-and-pop convenience store next to the park where soft drinks are available, and rest rooms. The home is open Wed.-Sat. 9:30 a.m.-5 p.m. (closed noon-1 p.m.), Sunday noon-5 p.m., April-Oct. Admission is $1 for adults, 50 cents for children 6-12. For more information call (513) 553-4911.

Adjacent to US 52 in Chilo, **Crooked Run** is a rewarding place to view wildlife. One of the few undeveloped embayments in the area, the Clermont County site was created with the construction of the nearby Meldahl Lock and Dam. Depending on the season, waterfowl show up here in droves. There is no admission fee and the site is open at all times. For more information, call (513) 732-2977.

Finally, just up the hill from US 52 on the west side of Ripley, the **Rankin House Museum,** tel. (513) 392-1627, square foot for square foot, may be the most historically important building in the state. The modest brick dwelling served as the home of Rev. John Rankin, a Presbyterian minister in Ripley and a dedicated abolitionist. As even the shortest visit to the museum will reveal, Rankin's home stood atop a hill shorn of trees above the village. It was illuminated every night for years prior to the Civil War, serving as a beacon to some 2,000 men, women, and children looking to catch the Underground Railroad. The home is said to be the place where Harriet Beecher Stowe heard the story of Eliza, the brave young woman who dashed from one ice floe to another in crossing the Ohio River to freedom. Open late April-Memorial Day, noon-5 p.m. weekends only; Memorial Day-August, Wed.-Sun. noon-5 p.m.; Sept.-Oct. noon-5 p.m. weekends or by appointment.

Loveland

The **Loveland Historical Museum** is a most disarming place to visit, at 201 Riverside Dr., Loveland, tel. (513) 683-5692. Recent attractions have included the photos of a talented local photographer, a weekend of heritage activities such as soapmaking and spinning, and a couple of days devoted to various herbs. The museum is open Fri.-Sun., 1-4:30 p.m., and is free to the public.

Chateau Laroche on Mulberry Street, tel. (513) 683-4686, is a medieval castle quite unlike any other edifice in the state. Harry D. Andrews started building the castle in 1929, and it became his life's work for the next 50 years. The castle made of stone looks for all the world like a French fortification. If the kids enjoy tales of Robin Hood they will be most pleased visiting this remarkable residence just west of the Little Miami River. Chateau Laroche is open daily, 11 a.m.-5 p.m. April 1-Sept. 15. From September to April the castle is open weekends only. Admission is $1 per person, children under five free.

Promont

Along the Little Miami River a bit is this historical society and museum at 906 Main St., Milford, tel. (513) 248-0324. The tall, Italianate mansion formerly served as the residence of a governor. He favored stained glass, marble fireplaces, and a sweeping view of the village. Free of charge, the facility is open Friday and Sunday 1:30-4:30 p.m.

Kabler Farms

Kabler Farms, 4529 Elmwood Rd., Batavia, tel. (513) 732-0501, has a deer herd, a number of elk, and miscellaneous hooved animals just north of SR 32 and east of I-275. Visitors pay $4 for

adults and $3 for children under 12 to help feed and pet young animals, search for fossils along a shady creek, and consult the resident fox. Hours are by appointment only.

RECREATION

Just below that great vantage point listed above is **Shawnee Lookout Golf Course,** 2030 Lawrenceburg Rd., North Bend (telephone 513-941-0120). While parts of it are low lying, that doesn't mean Shawnee is flat or uninteresting.

AREA EVENTS

APRIL

April 25 is the birthday of Civil War general and President **Ulysses Simpson Grant.** Folks take note of the event at the historic figure's birthplace in Point Pleasant and where he attended school in Georgetown. For a more complete schedule, call (513) 553-3661 (Point Pleasant) or (937) 378-6237 (Georgetown).

Frontier Days, 111 Race St., New Milford, tel. (513) 831-2411. Four days of food, a parade, zoo animals, rides, booths, music, and custom cars.

Hoedown in the Park, East Fork State Park main beach, off SR 125, Bethel, tel. (513) 734-4323.

JULY

The **Ohio Tobacco Festival** is a celebration not of the killer weed itself but of those who have made their livelihood from it through the years. The fete takes place in Ripley and includes parades, commercial exhibits, antique displays, a flea market, food, constant entertainment, and a tobacco auction. There's no indication that any of several scheduled contests involve smoking or spitting. To confirm, call (937) 377-6555.

Triathlon and Duathlon, East Fork State Park, off SR 125, Bethel, tel. (513) 734-4323.

AUGUST

New Richmond River Days includes food, rides, arts, crafts, entertainment, and fireworks all along Front Street. Call (513) 553-3101 for details.

NOVEMBER

Victorian Harvest Bazaar, Loveland Historical Museum, Loveland, tel. (513) 683-5692.

Water may influence how close players get to par, which is 70. Greens fees for 18 holes are $15 to walk and $26 to ride.

Canoeing

There are several valid reasons for staying off the Ohio River in a small, private boat. One is the amount of barge traffic, unable to stop for, or sometimes even see, a fishing or power boat. Those who want to negotiate a body of water should travel eastward to Loveland, about two miles east of I-275. There, at **Loveland Canoe Rental,** 200 Crutchfield Pl., tel. (513) 683-4611, they can acquire time in a craft that is responsive to the whims of the Little Miami River.

ACCOMMODATIONS

East of 275 along the river, travelers should look to non-franchise motels, bed-and-breakfast operations, or public or private campsites to take them in. An exception is the Rodeway Inn franchise at 55 Stern Dr., Seaman, tel. (937) 386-2511.

Bed and breakfast accommodations in Adams, Brown, and Clermont Counties include **Bayberry Inn,** 25675 SR 41, Peebles, tel. (937) 587-2221. This moderate facility is 20 miles from the river, but is pleasantly located on the scenic portion of US 41. Another B&B some distance from the river is **Murphin Ridge Inn,** 750 Murphin Ridge Rd., West Union, tel. (937) 544-2263, near Adams Lake State Park. The promise at this moderately priced site is fine dining and a swimming pool. Nearby is **Dogwood Farm,** 7070 SR 125, West Union, tel. (937) 544-5227. Breakfasts show up on the patio in warm weather or by the fire when the cold winds blow outside this moderate accommodation.

There are two B&Bs in the town of Ripley, close to the river, the first is the **Baird House,** 201 N. Second St., tel. (937) 392-4918, adorned with a wrought-iron lace porch and balcony and nine fireplaces; the price is moderate. The second is the **Signal House,** 234 N. Front St., (937) 392-1640, a moderately priced Greek Italianate site on the river that once was home to two Civil War officers. Farther east along the river and in the moderate range is **Three Islands,** 503 E. Eighth St., Manchester, tel. (937) 549-2149. It has four guest bedrooms and serves a full break-

fast on weekends. In Georgetown, look for the **Bailey House,** 112 N. Water St., tel. (937) 378-3087, a moderately priced Greek Revival brick accommodation that is also on the National Register of Historic Places.

Female travelers have one other option, and a good one: with a little planning they can stay at **Grailville,** a conference and education center at 932 O'Bannonville Rd., Loveland, tel. (513) 683-2340. Founded by a nonprofit, nondenominational women's movement, this low-key retreat offers grounds harboring a spacious stretch of the Little Miami River, ponds, art, architecture, and a bookstore. Meals are available in the dining room if it is already feeding a group. Sunny yellow trimmed in white, the huge old farmhouse appears most welcoming. Ask about the "R & R" (rest and reflection) program when making reservations. Prices are $25 per person per night plus meals, which are $4.50 for breakfast, $5.75 for lunch, and $7.75 for dinner, when available.

FOOD

Moyer's Vineyards, Winery, and Restaurant, 3859 US 52, Manchester, tel. (937) 549-2957, is an oasis for those seeking good food and locally made wine, available by the glass in the restaurant and by the bottle to go. Open for lunch and dinner Mon.-Sat., restaurant patrons can look out over its vineyards to the Ohio flowing by. Luncheon selections range from eggs Benedict at $6.50 to pasta with garden vegetables, $6. Later in the day, patrons order meals such as ribeye steak for $14, chicken teriyaki for $9, or scampi for $12.50. Dessert might be grated lemon pie, a $3 item, or raw apple walnut cake, also $3. A dozen wines are crafted here, with reds, whites, roses, and after-dinner wines such as strawberry or raspberry available. Bottle prices range from $5.25 for house red, rose, or white, to $12 for sparkling raspberry. Wines by the glass are only $2-4.

Cincinnati's famed chili parlors have spread their tentacles across half the state, but in case you haven't tried any of the hearty stuff, slide into **Skyline Chili,** 730 Lila Ave., Milford, tel. (513) 831-4611, for typical fare. The chili is served over spaghetti and is topped with a choice of cheese or grated onions. Oyster crackers are in limitless supply, and for $5 each travelers should be able to fill themselves and have a soft drink. Open every day for lunch and dinner.

INFORMATION AND SERVICES

In an emergency if you need police or medical assistance, dial 911. Otherwise, in an Adams County non-emergency, reach the sheriff at (937) 544-2314. Adams County Hospital in West Union can be contacted by dialing (937) 544-5571. The West Union post office is at 117 E. North St. In a non-emergency, dialing (937) 392-4377 connects callers with the Ripley mayor's office or with police. The Ripley post office is at 100 Second St. Call the Clermont Sheriff's Department at (513) 732-7500. Clermont Mercy Hospital can be reached by telephoning (513) 732-7500. The post office in Batavia, the Clermont County seat, is at 575 W. Main St.

Contact the **Adams County Chamber of Commerce** at (937) 544-5454. The **Brown County Chamber of Commerce** can be reached at (888) 276-9664. As for Clermont County, tourism authorities are at the **Convention and Visitors Bureau,** tel.(513) 732-3600.

There's no daily newspaper between Portsmouth and Cincinnati, at least not on the Ohio side of the river.

Shopping

Running into Cincinnati to shop is one answer for the folks who live around here, but it's far from the only answer. Nice places to look for gifts and other amenities include **Lewis Mountain Herbs & Everlastings,** 2345 SR 247, Manchester. This spread of herb plantings and greenhouses is fragrant for much of the year, and there's a gift shop. Lewis Mountain also has an annual festival in October.

Farther from the river, northern Adams County has a number of quaint, rural places to shop. The Amish population is small but growing, with **Keim Family Market,** 2621 Burnt Cabin Rd., Seaman (no telephone), offering many locally made items. They range from baked goods and cheese to crafts, gazebos, gliders, porch swings, picnic tables, and other outdoor wood furniture. The blackberry jam cake at $4 is worth fighting over, while the $5.50 black walnut pie should be pictured in the dictionary where "rich" is defined.

BETWEEN CINCINNATI AND DAYTON

The area between Dayton and Cincinnati is rolling hills, perhaps symbolic of the roller-coaster aspect of the area's economy. In contrast to the boom-and-bust nature of work and jobs in the cities of Hamilton or Middletown, the little towns in the area are smugly secure, subsisting rather well on tourism or higher education or some other specialty. Not long after the Northwest Territory was proclaimed there were people of European descent in this area. They came initially to rid the land of its natives; they stayed to farm or to merchandise along the scenic Great and Little Miami Rivers. Today, this area is home to some of the nicer parks and historic areas in the state.

History

Hamilton and Middletown both were founded in 1791, though under different circumstances. Hamilton began as a supply fort used by General Anthony Wayne's troops while fighting Indians. Middletown, up the Great Miami River 10 miles, was the site where a fellow by the name of Daniel Doty built a log cabin for his wife. Hamilton was named after Alexander Hamilton, the first secretary of the treasury, while Middletown was the name of Doty's New Jersey hometown.

Because of their riverside locations, the towns' prosperity seemed certain. After all, the Miami-to-Erie Canal had linked the Great Lakes and the Ohio River by 1828. Both towns nurtured industry while putting up with periodic high water, sending goods to Union forces that helped win the Civil War. Between 1865 and 1945, Hamilton's population increased from around 7,000 to about 58,000. At one time or another, everything from beer to cake mix, safes to paper, and carriages to aircraft parts were manufactured along this stretch of the river—which has been more docile since federal work in the 1920s and 1930s decreased the chances of floods. Today, Hamilton is the Butler County seat and has a population of 61,000. Middletown has 46,000 residents.

There are several historic small towns in this area of hills and rivers. They include Oxford, the home of Miami University and the place where Professor McGuffey taught college students, be-fore publishing his highly influential series of schoolbooks for young readers in 1836. The *Eclectic Readers* went through many printings and were used as state textbooks until 1920. (He later went on to become president of Cincinnati College and then Ohio University.) Oxford served as a refuge from slavery and, much later, was the staging area for freedom riders who helped desegregate the Deep South in the 1960s. There is Lebanon, a pretty little town that has parlayed its ancient stagecoach stop into a tourism rendezvous. The less visited places, from Darrtown to Red Lion, offer small-town flavor, in contrast to either Dayton or Cincinnati.

OXFORD

Sights

Oxford may be the handsomest town in Ohio. The downtown area has several stretches paved in brick, most notably High Street, and Miami University's various buildings are handsome red brick trimmed in cream. The town is small enough to be explored on foot, one of the reasons few of the 16,000 students need to keep cars on campus. A stroll along the four-block business district with its fresh-faced students, bookstores, and places to eat and drink is enough to make a traveler attempt to enroll for next semester. After the walk, hop in the car or straddle a bicycle and head north out Bonham Road. Besides cruising past the university's handsome football stadium, travelers will see a picturesque covered bridge on their left. This is an indirect route to Hueston Wood State Park; a better highway is SR 732, which runs parallel to Bonham Road on the west.

Hueston Woods State Park, SR 732, tel. (513) 523-6347, north of Oxford, has a nice lake, great hardwoods that make for a colorful fall, a picturesque resort, a golf course, tidy cabins, and a campground. Equally important, the park has a wild animal rehabilitation program responsible for healing injured or orphaned birds of prey. On outdoor display at the 2,971-acre facility north of Oxford are birds, small animals native to the area, and deer. Among the better ways to tour here is on an off-road bicycle along nicely trimmed, bike-only trails. This virgin forest of beeches and maples was saved from the frontier ax because the original developer of the land was also one of the original conservationists—Matthew Hueston set aside an undeveloped portion of his land and so did his descendants. In 1941, the land was purchased by the state, which created Hueston Woods State Park.

Arts and Entertainment

Visual arts have their place, and a good place is the **Miami University Art Museum,** Patterson Avenue, tel. (513) 529-2232. Among many worthwhile permanent and changing exhibits, look for the Charles M. Messer Leica Camera Collection. Other items of interest amid this 7,000 square feet are pre-Columbian and African sculptures. There is just enough locally produced items to give a visitor a feel for this part of the country down through the last two centuries. The museum is free and is open Tues.-Sun. 11 a.m.-5 p.m.

What would a college town be without music? Places to hear live tunes include the **Hole in the Wall Bar,** 19 W. High St., tel. (513) 523-1190, the **Balcony,** 116½ E. High St., tel. (513) 523-4700, and **First Run,** 36 E. High St., tel. (513) 523-1335.

Food

Uptown Bakery, 109 W. High St., tel. (513) 523-0770, is a great place to fight your way past the kids for a morning cup of coffee or tea and a variety of baked goods. A continental breakfast in this small but tidy place is about $2, and it's also open for lunch. Soups, salads, and baked goods share center stage on the chalk menu, and there is a nice selection of exotic sodas, coffee, and tea to wash down the meal. Lunch here should cost no more than $5.

DiPaolo's, 23 Beech St., tel. (513) 523-1541, has evolved from a pizza joint into an upscale continental Italian restaurant. It's the kind of place visiting parents take their Miami University sons or daughters for a great meal. The variety is dazzling and can include a nice variety of pastas, kebabs, rack of lamb, even crayfish. Luncheon fare generally is $5-8, with dinner entrees to around $20. Desserts are deserving, with several imaginative chocolate creations. Open every

day but Sunday for lunch and every day for dinner, the restaurant is just around the corner from High Street, Oxford's clickety-brick main thoroughfare.

First Run, 36 E. High St., tel. (513) 523-1335, is a popular restaurant. As the name indicates, this restaurant is in a redone movie theater. It's a good spot for gourmet pizza, as well as prime rib, steaks, and pork chops. The most popular sandwich at lunch is the Philly steak for $5.95. For an in-demand evening entree, ask for the stockyard prime steak at $8.95. A disk jockey holds forth after dinner Wed.-Sat. evenings, and there is patio dining in warm weather. First Run is open every day for lunch and dinner and until 2 a.m. every night but Sunday.

Mary Jo's Cuisine, 308 S. Campus Ave., tel. (513) 523-2653, is a European-style cafe with a country French menu. Closed the month of July, the stylish, 11-table spot serves from a changing menu based on what's grown locally. *Prix fixe* entrees are served on Friday and Saturday evenings, from $22.95 to $24.95, and may be meat, fish, chicken or vegetarian. Favorites may be as French as *coq au vin* or as down-home as stuffed cabbage leaves. On Thursday, everything is a la carte. Mary Jo calls her cuisine "wine friendly" and says her wines are priced at only twice wholesale. Lunch is offered Mon.-Fri. and showcases salads that may smack of Thai peanut sauce, Aztec sauce, or homemade mayonnaise. Lunch is approximately $10. Desserts are $2.95 and may be bread pudding with fruit and a glaze, lemon and other tarts, pies, a dark-chocolate flourless torte or cheesecake. Reservations are recommended.

LEBANON

Sights

Fort Ancient State Memorial, three miles east of I-71 on Wilmington Road, is seven miles east of Lebanon. The best way to reach this worthy facility is to get off I-71 at Exit 36, then take a quick right and follow Caesar Creek a couple of miles. Here is where travelers will learn fascinating details of prehistoric life in the area. For example, flint for arrows and weapons wasn't lying about but was instead dug up by people who were expert at finding it. The displays cover 15,000 years of American Indian heritage. The displays were refurbished in 1997-98, making the $5 adult ad-

The old town of Lebanon has a colonial look uncharacteristic for the Midwest.

mission and $1.25 for children ages 6-12 well worth it. The gift shop is nice, too, with books, tasteful jewelry, and T-shirts. The campground has all the modern conveniences and 95 sites. Tnrance to the park grounds is $4 per vehicle. Call (513) 289-2095 for more information.

Glendower State Memorial, Orchard Ave. (US 42), Lebanon, tel. (513) 932-1817, is a magnificent historic home open to the public Wed.-Sat. 10 a.m.-4 p.m., Sunday 1-4 p.m. from early June to late October. Dating from 1836, and with a long list of distinguished owners, the red-brick house boasts Ionic columns and the original locks and doorbells, which still work. Glendower is furnished with the personal and household items of more than 400 pioneer families of the community. This site, overlooking downtown Lebanon, is one of the outstanding Greek Revival homes in all of the Midwest. Admission is $3; students with ID, $1.

Morrow, on US 22 a dozen miles southeast of Lebanon, is home to **Valley Vineyard Winery,** 2276 East US 22, tel. (513) 899-2485. The most popular wine among 16 varieties is Vidal Blanc, which recently won a trio of international awards. It sells for $7.75 per bottle. Enjoy it with regularly scheduled steak cookouts and pig roasts here on Friday and Saturday evenings, where the little old winemakers have been busy since 1970. Tasting, tour, and sales hours are Mon.-Sat. 11 a.m.-8 p.m. and Sunday 1-6 p.m.

Turtle Creek Valley Railway offers rides from the train station at 198 So. Broadway in down-

town Lebanon. This is a pleasant way to take in the countryside, with the 14-mile trips offered from May through October on Wednesday and Fri.-Sun. In July and August, ice-cream socials are held in conjunction with the trips, while Santa clambers aboard on the weekends from right after Thanksgiving to mid-December. Costs of a ride behind the well-preserved diesel, in the open-air cars built in the 1920s for the Lackawanna Railroad, are $10 for adults, $6 for children, and $9 for seniors. Call (513) 398-8584 for more information.

Entertainment
In contrast to the Sorg Opera Company's stellar efforts in Hamilton, check out the **Turtle Creek Valley Railway Dinner Theater,** 198 S. Broadway, tel. (513) 896-7553. Playgoers ride the rails from the Lebanon train station, to be surprised by actors who entertain them for the hour-long ride through the countryside. Easing back into the station, the crowd then heads for the Golden Lamb, Lebanon's classy, oldtime inn. There, during a complete meal, playgoers watch bodies fall left and right as the melodramatic final act takes place. Cost of the ride, the performance, and the meal total $49.50 per person. The play is well acted by clever local and regional performers on Friday evenings, and the meal is more than satisfying.

Spectator Sports
Lebanon Raceway, 665 N. Broadway (SR 48),

tel. (513) 932-4936, features harness racing from September to May. The horses take to the track with the post parade at 7:30 p.m., running Monday, Tuesday, Friday, and Saturday. Simulcast racing takes place from August 1-late June, Mon.-Sat. starting at 11 a.m. Admission is $2. Parking is $1 or $1.50.

Golf

When in Lebanon, look for **Shaker Run Golf Course,** 4361 Greentree Rd., tel. (513) 727-0007 or (800) 721-0007. Greens fees for 18 holes Mon.-Thurs. are $65; Fri.-Sun. it's $75. Both fees include a cart.

Food

The **Golden Lamb,** 27 S. Broadway, tel. (513) 932-5065. Celebrities such as Charles Dickens have broken bread in this restaurant, which is inside Ohio's oldest inn. The menu is a tribute to the past, featuring such hearty fare as fresh turkey, skillet-fried chicken, prime rib, swiss steak, salmon, and the widely popular leg of lamb, which is $14.25. Noted desserts include Shaker sugar pie, priced at $2.25, which is sure to give diners a rush. Lunches are lighter, involving salads or sandwiches. Lunch and dinner are served every day of the week in this classy old brick structure, where casually dressed tourists are welcome.

HAMILTON

Sights

The **Benninghofen House,** 327 N. Second St., tel. (513) 893-7111, also serves as the Butler County Historical Society and Museum. A lavish lifestyle is preserved beneath the 13-foot ceilings in this Italianate house, built in 1861. The house is open Tues.-Sun. 1-4 p.m. No admission is charged, but donations are encouraged. Another appealing place is the **Lane-Hooven House,** 319 N. Third St., tel. (513) 863-1389. It's an octagonal home that dates from 1863. The gingerbready home is open 9 a.m.-4 p.m. and by appointment. Nearby is historic German Village, a venerable section of town with a number of nicely rehabilitated older homes. Another historical area is Dayton Lane, where the swells all lived a century ago. All of these sites are

downtown and within walking distance of each other.

Pyramid Hill Sculpture Park and Museum, 1763 Hamilton-Cleves Rd., tel. (513) 868-8336, combines the best of human endeavor and natural surroundings. The place showcases 10 sizeable sculptures in a lovely, 250-acre setting *Atlantic Monthly* has called this ". . . the most beautiful natural setting of any art park in the country." Is that so? Visitors can find out by driving through the park, by hiking the facility on their own or by taking a tour. Look for gardens, a 19th-century stone home, five lakes, an amphitheater, an arboretum, picnic sites, and more. Hours are Tues.-Sun. 10 a.m.-6 p.m. (the exit gate stays open until 7:30 p.m.). Fees are $3 for adults during the week and $4 on weekends; children are charged $1.50 apiece at all times.

Music

Look to **Hamilton Music Theatre,** 509 Main St., (513) 887-0618, where bluegrass and country acts are booked on a somewhat regular basis.

Golf

A clubhouse built in 1831 and a golf course completed in 1997? That's the deal at **Walden Ponds,** 6090 Golf Club Lane, Indian Springs (northwest of Cincinnati on SR4), tel. (513) 785-2999, a par-72 facility with lots of water hazards surrounding its bent-grass tees, fairways, and greens. Greens fees at this site just north of Hamilton are $45 for Monday through Thursday play, and $55 to play Friday through Sunday. Those fees include cart and a bucket of range balls. The best buy may be after 4 p.m., when the tariff drops to $35 for 18 holes plus cart and range balls.

Food

Academy Restaurant, 343 N. Third St. (US 27), tel. (513) 868-7171. The American-Continental menu includes a number of favorites—beef, poultry, and seafood—from $12.95. Piano music accompanies meals, and there is a pretty glass-enclosed garden. Dinner is served Mon.-Sat.

Alexander's Grille, One Riverfront Plaza, tel. (513) 896-6200, is inside the Hamiltonian Hotel. As such, it serves breakfast, lunch, and dinner seven days a week—but don't assume Alexander's takes customers for granted. The food is skillfully pre-

HAMILTON-MIDDLETOWN ANNUAL EVENTS

JANUARY

Lebanon Antique Show, the Warren County Career Center is the locale for this event, tel. (513) 932-1817 for details.

MARCH

Hueston Woods Maple Syrup Festival, Oxford. This state park has lots of original-growth trees, which should make for especially tangy syrup. For a sap check, call (513) 523-6347.

APRIL

The **Annual Greater Hamilton Art Exhibit,** is juried and open to anyone living within 30 miles, held at the Fitton Center.

MAY

Main Street Art Hop and Open House, Hamilton. Local artists display their prowess along Main Street.

JUNE

Spring Antique Farm Machine Show, crops are planted using historic machinery and methods at the Chisholm Historic Farmstead.

Fort Ancient Celebration, 6123 SR 350, Oregonia, tel. (800) 283-8904. All sorts of activities are scheduled, from a tomahawk-throwing contest to an herb tour. Everything has a prehistoric connection at this site where natives are noted.

Summer Sounds Concert Series, held at Sunset and Douglass parks, as well as City Centre Plaza, Middletown. These midweek, open-air concerts also take place in July and August.

Mid-America Truck Jamboree, it ain't all arts and crafts, as this noisy soiree in Hamilton proves.

JULY

All American Weekend, a traditional July 4 celebration on the grounds of Middletown High School.

AUGUST

Ohio Renaissance Festival, in Harveysburg, recreates 16th-century England on weekends and on Labor Day from August through October. Call (513) 897-700 for more info.

SEPTEMBER

Damfest, Hamiltonians put on water skiing and related shows along the Great Miami River.

Indian Heritage Festival, games, food, and entertainment take place in the small town of Trenton, just west of Middletown.

The **Ohio Honey Festival** proves that important things take place besides education in a college town. Oxford is the site of this three-day homage, which includes eats made of honey. The most notorious guy here is the fellow who walks around with 10,000 bees on his chin, calling it the Living Beard. Call (513) 523-8687 for more details.

OCTOBER

Middfest International, features a different country each year, showcasing ethnic foods and authentic arts, crafts, and entertainment in City Centre Plaza, Middletown.

Ohio Sauerkraut Festival, Waynesville. Savor the fragrance of corroded cabbage in this antique-bedecked town, tel. (513) 897-8855.

NOVEMBER

Main Street Music Fest and Open House, Hamilton, features local musicians playing music as they mosey around downtown.

DECEMBER

Blue Christmas, the area's top blues musicians do an annual benefit jam at Middletown's Manchester Inn, tel. (937) 422-5481.

Christmas Glow, features the unique sight of hot-air balloons tethered around the City Centre Plaza in Middletown, their propane burners lighting up the night amid holiday food and entertainment.

During the **Historic Lebanon Christmas Festival and Candlelight Parade,** one of the state's most picturesque towns dresses for the holidays and invites visitors, tel. (513) 932-1100.

Holiday Festival and Tour of Homes, Oxford. Here's a chance to see the homes and the town when the college students are home for the holidays.

Christmas in the Village, Waynesville, tel. (513) 897-8855 for details.

pared and there are such nice touches as a prime rib buffet on Friday night and a brunch each Sunday. The dining is casual for travelers' convenience and, each evening, there's a nice selection of meat and fresh fish entrees, all less than $20.

MIDDLETOWN

Arts and Entertainment
Sorg Opera Company in Middletown puts on four presentations a year. Recently, they've offered *Lucia di Lammermoor, Falstaff, My Fair Lady,* and *The Nutcracker.* Performances take place at the Sorg Opera House, 57 S. Main St., tel. (513) 425-0180. Formed in 1990, the company's reputation has reached the point where performers from outside the U.S. audition for parts. The productions are audience friendly, with songs either in English or with English surtitles. Costs for a ticket range from $15 to $45.

They relax in comfy tables and chairs at the recently opened **Miami Valley Opry,** 1226 Central Ave., tel. (513) 743-9140 or (888) 488-4866. Country music is delivered by local and regional artists each Saturday 7-10:30 p.m. in an alcohol- and smoke-free environment.

Biking
Two bike paths follow the east bank of the Great Miami River through Middletown. The Miami-Erie Canal Bikeway connects a forest preserve on the city's north side with the 3.5-mile Hamilton Bikeway. The latter runs between the Soldiers and Sailors Monument at the High Street Bridge to Joyce Park to the south. Bicycles also are permitted on certain marked walkways near the City Building. Bikes can be rented in Renschler Forest Preserve at the end of Reigart Road, north off SR 4 between Middletown and Hamilton. Riders can cruise along the remnants of the historic Miami-Erie Canal.

Family Fun
Americana Amusement Park, 5757 Middletown-Hamilton Rd., tel. (513) 539-7339, is a family amusement park. It features, among other things, the Screeching Eagle, a classic wooden roller coaster. There's also a mining town called Loggers Run, a swimming pool, shows

and attractions, and a huge picnic grove. The park is open from 11 a.m. every day all summer. Admission is $15.95 for adults and $13.95 for children ages three and older; parking on the premises costs $4. The park is open until 9 p.m., so thrifty travelers might want to consider the after-4 p.m. rate, which is $6.95 per person for both children and adults.

Food
The **Jug,** 3610 Central Ave., tel. (513) 424-1677, has been in business at the same site for 66 years. A 1950s-style drive-in, it features carhops who deliver items such as a double cheeseburger with waffle fries and a soft drink for around $3. Other sandwiches, priced just as competitively, are available, with concoctions like a chocolate shake for around $2. The Jug is open daily 11 a.m.-10 p.m.

Manchester Room, 1027 Manchester Ave., tel. (513) 422-5481, is a hotel dining room with a good reputation. Breakfast, lunch, and dinner are served, with businesspeople from nearby offices enjoying the soup-and-salad bar lunch at $5.95. There is a full menu evenings, with a prime rib buffet for $14.95 on Friday and Saturday. And because it caters to travelers the Manchester Room feeds the casually dressed.

ACCOMMODATIONS

There are several clusters of motels in this area. One is along SR 4 running south out of Hamilton. Another is along I-75 at the SR 73 and SR 122 Exits to Middletown. Both feature a mix of franchises and individual motels. Those who prefer their stay in a traditional hotel have at least two choices: the **Hamiltonian Hotel and Meeting Center,** One Riverfront Plaza, Hamilton, tel. (513) 896-6200, or the **Manchester Inn and Conference Center,** 1027 Manchester Ave., Middletown, tel. (513) 422-5481. Both have snazzy restaurants and offer the numerous services of traditional in-town hotels. A night at either place is in the expensive range, especially at the Hamiltonian, where the top (sixth) floor is called the "executive level" and offers perks such as free newspaper, free continental breakfast, small meeting rooms, hair dryers, and multiple telephones.

Bed and breakfast accommodations in Hamilton are represented by the inexpensive **Eaton Hill Bed and Breakfast,** 1961 Eaton Rd., tel. (513) 856-9552. The Eaton Hill has two guest rooms with shared bath. There's also the **White Rose,** 116 Buckeye St., tel. (513) 863-6818, with two bedrooms and private baths in historic German Village. Oxford has several franchises, including a **Hampton Inn,** a B&B, a state park resort, and a college conference center. The **Alexander House Bed & Breakfast,** 22 N. College Ave. (US 27), can be reached by dialing (513) 523-1200. It's moderately priced, has five rooms with private baths, and is amid the Miami University campus. The **Duck Pond Bed and Breakfast** at 6391 Morning Sun Rd. (SR 732 N), can be reached at (513) 523-8914. It has four rooms, one of which comes with its own bath; rates are moderate.

Vacationers would be foolish to overlook a stay in the recently renovated **Hueston Woods State Park Resort.** There are 94 guest rooms, there's a massive stone fireplace surrounded by a Native American motif, guests have their choice of indoor or outdoor pools, and the food is praiseworthy. A night in the lodge is expensive and worth it.

In the opposite direction, a pleasant rural destination is the **Countryside Inn,** 3802 Dry Run Rd., So. Lebanon, tel. (513) 494-1001 or (800) 905-8576. In Lebanon, there are several motels and the **Golden Lamb Inn,** US 42 at the junction of SR 123 and 63, tel. (513) 932-5065. Lebanon also has a half-dozen bed and breakfast destinations

INFORMATION AND SERVICES

In an emergency in Hamilton or Middletown, call 911 for assistance. The non-emergency number for police in Hamilton is (513) 868-5811. In Middletown it's (513) 425-7701. Fort Hamilton-Hughes Memorial Hospital, Hamilton, can be reached at (513) 867-2000. In Middletown, look to Middletown Regional Hospital, (513) 424-2111. The post office is at Monument and Court Streets in downtown Hamilton and at 320 N. Verity Parkway in Middletown.

The **Greater Hamilton Convention and Visitors Bureau** is at 201 Dayton St., tel. (513) 844-8080 or (800) 311-5353. Lebanon's **Chamber of Commerce** is at 120 E. South St., Suite 201, tel. (513) 932-1100. In Middletown, the **Convention and Visitors Bureau** is at 30 City Centre Plaza, tel. (513) 422-3030. The **Oxford Visitors and Convention Bureau** is at 118 W. High St., tel. (513) 523-8687. The **Warren County Convention and Visitors Bureau** is in Lebanon at 777 Columbus Ave., Suite 2, tel. (513) 933-1138 or (800) 433-1072. Miami University has two methods of alerting travelers to athletic and other events. One is Miami Vibe, the campus informational phone line, tel. (513) 529-6400. The other is an easily seen sandwich board at the intersection of Campus Avenue and High St., where the business district meets the campus.

Hamilton reads the *Journal-News* on weekday mornings and on Sunday. Middletown stays informed with the *Middletown Journal.* It reaches readers weekday evenings and weekend mornings. Entertainment is covered each Thursday. Talk radio takes place in Hamilton on WMOH, 1450 AM, serving the area since 1944. There's a public-radio site with some reach that comes out of Oxford. It's the Miami University station, WMUB, at 88.5 on the FM dial. Another Oxford station, independent as a hog on ice but concerned with music, is WOXY, 97.7 FM. Immodestly, 97X bills itself as "The Future of Rock and Roll."

Transportation
One of the problems of having a big state school in an isolated small town comes into play before and after each holiday as Miami University students try their luck at getting home and back to campus. There are few public transit facilities, though Amtrak's "The Cardinal," running between Chicago and Washington, D.C., passes through Hamilton three times a week. The station, which is unstaffed and has no telephone, is at Martin Luther King Boulevard and Henry Street. Travelers don't need a ticket but they do need a reservation to be welcomed on board. Travelers pay for their tickets after boarding.For reservations or information call (800) 872-7245.

Shopping
Downtown Lebanon has a number of crafts and antique stores. For something more contemporary, look to Forest Fair Mall, tel.(513) 671-2882,

and Towne Mall, tel. (513) 424-3318, the former at the Middletown-Springboro exit and the latter at the Middletown-Franklin exit to I-75. For something much closer to the land, pick up the *Shoppers Guide to Fresh Fruit and Vegetables,* a brochure created by Warren County's 11-member truck-farming organization. The brochure pinpoints locations where travelers can pick or purchase everything from beans to baked goods, blackberries to broccoli, and grapes to gourds. You-pick items available in season include apples, strawberries, and pumpkins.

Flea marketeers will enjoy **Trader's World,** 601 Union Rd., at I-75 and SR 63 just east of Monroe, tel. (513) 424-5708. The sprawling site has more than 1,000 vendors and is open Sat.-Sun. 9 a.m.-5 p.m. all year long. Travelers in search of real craftsmanship may want to visit **Isaacs' Shaker Hill,** 3534 E. US 22/SR 3 in Morrow, east of South Lebanon, tel. (513) 899-2927. Tom Isaacs and his son Tom, Jr. make Shaker and Queen Anne reproductions in their home, which itself dates from 1863. Handmade reproductions include items from tin, pottery, and other substances common some time ago. It's best to call for an appointment.

SPRINGFIELD, YELLOW SPRINGS, XENIA, AND BEYOND

This area, east of Dayton, northeast of Cincinnati, and west and south of Columbus, is most interesting. Springfield, the largest of the three cities, is a post-industrial place served by an interstate highway and within commuting distance of either Dayton or Columbus. Yellow Springs, south of Springfield and closer to Dayton, can't make up its mind whether it wants to be a utopian haven or a tourist destination. Xenia, also near Dayton, is a growing but unpretentious place, as are the several smaller county-seat cities to the south and east. The terrain is surprisingly level and productive around the town of Washington Court House to the east; this part of southwest Ohio appeals to those who want to live out past the suburbs. The more rugged southernmost stretch, along SR 32, is increasingly peopled by Amish families who find northeast Ohio or southeast Pennsylvania too expensive and overcrowded.

History

Springfield arose along Buck Creek. The surrounding valley is "just deep enough to take away the monotony of the landscape," according to *The Ohio Guide,* the federally funded, Depression-era survey of the Buckeye State. Until Revolutionary War hero George Rogers Clark (older brother of William Clark of Lewis & Clark fame) and his frontiersmen showed up, the area from Xenia to Springfield was thick with Shawnee. Clark routed them in 1780 and the town was officially founded by 1818, named for springs that ran fresh and clear out of cliffs near the creek. Those same cliffs are easily seen today along the south edge of Wittenberg University and Buck Creek. The springs have ceased, but waves of bug-eating bats may flap out of the stone crevasses on summer evenings, headed for food in Snyder Park, just to the west.

The National Road (later US 40) came through town in 1838, making Springfield a stop for Ohio Stage Company wagons. Although Ohio's various canals missed Springfield, for years in the 19th century the city was known as the western terminus of the then-named National Pike. Wittenberg was founded on a shady rise in 1845, and the new railroad brought the first students the following fall. Farm-machinery works filled the town with jobs, consolidating ultimately into an International Harvester truck plant, just north of the present-day city.

At one time, early in the 20th century, four magazines with circulations totaling twenty million copies a month were created and printed here. But now even the largest, a weekly named *Collier's,* is gone, and the town now has a smaller population of about 70,000 persons. In contrast, the village of Yellow Springs, eight miles south, has never had many more folks than the current crop of about 4,000. But they have been as individualistic a bunch as you're apt to come across anywhere in Ohio.

Yellow Springs was founded a couple of years before Springfield, in 1804. It was named for the heavy iron content of springs nearby, said to put a healthy skip in the step of those who drank from it. The big news at this one-time health resort, however, was the establishment in 1853 of Antioch College. Horace Mann, the famed educator, was its first president. He came to Clark County intent on running a school that was free from religious influence. Mann died, reportedly of overwork, in 1859.

Arthur E. Morgan, an engineer who would become president of the Tennessee Valley Authority during the Depression, was named college president in 1920. He helped advance learn awhile-work awhile cooperative education, which spread to institutions across the country. Antioch often has attracted bohemian students, drawn as much by its location in a lovely little egalitarian town as by religious objectivity or work-study plans.

Perhaps unfortunately, Antioch recently made headlines in a rather odd way. The school decided in the fall of 1993 that students and staff would have to obtain mutual and specific verbal consent before "each new level of physical and/or sexual conduct or contact." The "campus sexual-conduct rules" got a lot of laughs on late-night talk shows, particularly when it was noted that alcohol made consent invalid.

Xenia was a couple of log cabins in 1804. It became a market center, but the town's importance increased even more in the tense years prior to the Civil War. Freed slaves settled in Greene County in large numbers. The state's most important Underground Railroad route passed nearby; some of today's African-American area residents are descended from runaway slaves. It's no coincidence that Central State University and Wilberforce University, two predominantly black colleges, are just three miles east of Xenia. In fact, Wilberforce University was the first institution of higher education both owned and operated by African-Americans.

Xenia may be the most thoroughly dissected town in Ohio, in more ways than one. In her history *Ohio Town,* the late Helen Hoover Santmyer sifts old Xenia in a manner most delightful. It's safe to say that, thanks to Ms. Santmyer, the city of some 25,000 souls enjoys a quirky renown far beyond its size. She also wrote a highly successful novel, *And Ladies of the Club,* which was published in 1982—when she was 88 years of age.

But the city was also affected when it was hammered by a tornado in 1974 that killed 36 residents and leveled numerous buildings. On April 3, 1974, one of the mightiest tornadoes ever seen hammered the city, bearing winds clocked as high as 318 miles an hour. Paperwork from Xenia living rooms was found as far away as Cleveland—a straight-line distance of about 200 miles. A total of 315 persons died in several states that day, and three dozen of the victims were from Xenia. Because many took for granted the tornado watches and warnings, most residents didn't head for cover until the terrible weather was upon them.

Location and Orientation
Springfield is on I-70, which makes a swing around the city to the south before heading east 44 miles to Columbus or west past Dayton a total of 57 miles to the Indiana state line. Other highways serving the city include US 68, which comes out of Findlay and heads south through Yellow Springs and Xenia, and grand, neglected, old US 40. The old National Road, the ultimate highway in days before multilane interstate roads whisked everyone everywhere, US 40, parallels I-70.

Yellow Springs also is served by SR 343, which is important to remember since it takes visitors out of the village east toward John Bryan State Park and the village of Clifton. US 42 runs around the west side of metropolitan Columbus before heading southwest through Xenia to Cincinnati.

US 35 runs east-west and is Xenia's main route to and from Dayton, a dozen miles west. US 42 runs northeast-southwest, from west of Columbus to Cincinnati. US 68 leads north to both Yellow Springs and Springfield. Southward, US 68 heads for the Ohio River. Pleasant county seats such as Washington Court House, Wilmington, and Hillsboro are placed around this area.

SIGHTS

Parks and Preserves
John Bryan State Park, east of Yellow Springs on SR 343, tel. (937) 767-1274, is a stunning place, featuring steep limestone gorges and seductive greenery along the Little Miami River.

The park welcomes **rock climbers** and rappellers, but those who decide to climb the gorges must register at the ranger station and follow the directions in the climber's display case. No lead climbing is allowed. The gorge runs, under different names, from Clifton to Yellow Springs, a distance of approximately four miles. The locals, who know their way around, say they can hike from one village to the other without ever leaving the close proximity of the river. Visitors are advised to stay on the marked trails and to heed signs that warn of precipices. Just east of the state park is **Clifton Gorge State Nature Preserve,** tel. (937) 964-8794, another place where geology comes alive.

Close to Yellow Springs, where the gorge meets the Antioch University campus, is the **Glen Helen Nature Preserve,** tel. (937) 767-7375, where visitors can find the town's namesake yellow springs. To get to the preserve and the springs, drive as far into the campus as possible, park the car, and amble down a trail to the right for about 100 yards, and have a drink. Don't worry—the water's school bus-orange tinge is caused by iron; the water is cool and refreshing. As for the preserve, it's open to the public and includes 1,000 acres of woods, waterways, prairies, and fields. There is also a raptor center, where wounded birds of prey are nursed back to health. There are no fees for any of these river-related sites.

A gorge that is equally fascinating and much less visited exists in Highland County. **Highland Nature Sanctuary,** 7629 Cave Rd., Bainbridge, east of Hillsboro off US 50, tel. (937) 363-1363, once was part of a privately owned attraction known as Seven Caves. Now, hiking this public, 47-acre site reveals a gorge untouched by the Industrial or any other revolution. There are caves, dolomite cliffs, prairie wildflowers, and trees that are older than the state here. Guided tours are the preferred way to see this isolated place, which is adjacent to **Miller's Nature Sanctuary.** Miller's also has a gorge but is privately owned and requires permission for a visit. For information on visiting the private land, call (937) 544-9750.

Spreading across parts of Warren, Clinton, and Greene Counties is **Caesar Creek State Park,** 8570 E. SR 73, Waynesville, tel. (513) 897-3055. The park is an Army Corps of Engineers project that created an abundant recreational area on a tributary of the Little Miami River. There's swimming, boating, bridle trails, camping, fishing, and more. The lake measures some 7.5 miles, with a water level adjusted by a dam at the south end of the big pond. One of the more fascinating diversions here is to look for fossil trilobites and other ancient creatures. A free permit from the visitor center is all that's needed in order to scour the spillway below the dam for signs of Ordovician life dating from 400 to 500 million years ago. Should no trilobites turn up, explore Caesar Creek Gorge a bit farther downstream. Caesar Creek also was the first park in the state to have off-road bicycle trails.

A naturalist at the Glen Helen Nature Preserve gives a talk about the rehabilitation and recovery of an injured owl from the raptor center.

Off-road bikes can be rented here, at the head of the 1.5-mile beginners' trail. Travelers who go places with their dogs will find a nice training area along the west side of Caesar Creek, paralleling SR 380, and there is hunting in season, primarily for game birds.

Adding to the park-rich environment in this area is **Buck Creek State Park,** northeast of Springfield at 1901 Buck Creek Lane, tel. (937) 322-5284. The home of a 2,120-acre lake created by the Army Corps of Engineers, Buck Creek also is the place to go to check out central Ohio wetlands and meadows. Endangered species here include the spotted turtle, occasionally observable along the 9.5 miles of hiking trails. The sandy beach is close to half a mile long, and there's sometimes excellent walleye and bass fishing. There are 101 campsites are here, as well as some cabins, and the four-lane boat launch ramp assures helmspeople of a spot on the water.

National Afro-American Museum and Cultural Center

It isn't all greenery hereabouts, though. Tiny Wilberforce is the home of this center, at 1350 Brush Row Rd., tel. (937) 376-4944. The museum is a contemporary, gymnasium-sized structure that displays artifacts, manuscripts, and library materials. Those who want to know more about African-American social customs and their influences on U.S. society down through the years would do well to spend some time here, Tues.-Sat. 9 a.m.-5 p.m., Sunday 1-5 p.m. Admission charges are $3.50 for adults and $1.50 for students and children. Also nearby are **Central State University** and **Wilberforce University** attended overwhelmingly by African-Americans. The village is just east of Xenia and north off US 42.

Historic Sites

There are a couple of wonderful prehistoric and historic locales that are off the beaten path. The most auspicious is **Serpent Mound** in northern Adams County, 19 miles south of Hillsboro on SR 73. Open from April to mid-November, this is the largest serpent effigy in North America and is on a hill just east of Ohio Brush Creek. Estimated to have been built about 2,000 years ago, the mound snakes for one-quarter of a mile along the ridgeline. There's a museum here, too, with artifacts left by ambitious engineers from long

ago. Admission is $4 per car. Employees will let visitors take a look at the mound in the off season if the weather is reasonable.

Several buildings are on historic preservation lists in Springfield. Among the larger and more impressive is the **Pennsylvania House,** 1311 W. Main St., tel. (937) 322-7668. This old Federal structure dates from the first days of the old National Road, when a series of inns was needed to house travelers. This example is massive, with more than two dozen rooms. The structure fell into disuse but was saved during the 1940s by its current owners, the Lagonda Chapter of the Daughters of the American Revolution. They've accumulated lots of displays from the 19th century, but the site is open only on the first Sunday of each month. Fees are $3 for adults and $1 for children. When the museum is closed, perhaps the best bet is to park nearby and walk around the exterior of this great old place.

CULTURE AND ENTERTAINMENT

Springfield is blessed with the **Clark State Community College Performing Arts Center.** The performing arts complex, at 300 S. Fountain Ave., offers several forms of entertainment in a season running from October through May. Its primary presentation is the Four Star series, four appearances by performers such as the Nylons or Marilyn McCoo and Billy Davis, Jr. singing from the Duke Ellington songbook. Club Kuss, an informal cabaret, presents performers such as country blues guitar player Guy Davis. The center's Turner Studio Theatre delivers entertainment such as E.B. White's *Stuart Little,* while the Kuss Auditorium's Action Zone series presents a trio of shows that range from *Beauty and the Beast* to touring improvisation. There also are several Springfield Arts Council bookings, such as jazz vocalists Manhattan Transfer and the traveling production of *Grease!* Call the box office at (937) 328-3874 for more information on what's hot. With half a dozen or so Wittenberg University Series stage events, tel. (937) 327-6231, travelers stand a chance of seeing a quality show almost any time during the academic year.

Other Springfield attractions include the **Springfield Museum of Art,** 107 Cliff Park Rd., tel. (937) 325-8100, which signs on anything from traveling

AREA EVENTS

The area east of Dayton offers a nice variety of indoor and outdoor events to attend throughout the year.

FEBRUARY

Black History Month, National Afro-American Museum, Wilberforce, tel. (800) BLK-HIST (or tel. 800-255-4478).

MARCH

How to Make a Gorge is a fascinating hike through Clifton Gorge State Nature Preserve, SR 343, tel. (937) 964-8794.

APRIL

Wildflower Pilgrimage, Clifton Gorge State Park, SR 343, Clifton, tel. (937) 964-8794. The spring wildflowers here await admiration and identification.

MAY

Yellow Springs Community Chorus, Kelly Hall, Antioch College, tel. (937) 767-1696. Schubert's "Mass in A Flat" was a recent chorus selection at its annual concert.

Antique Show and Flea Market Extravaganza, Springfield, tel. (937) 325-7621.

Tour of Historic Homes, Hillsboro, tel. (937) 393-4883.

Wright Memorial Glider Meet, 5385 Elbon Rd., Caesar Creek Glider Port, Waynesville, tel. (513) YEA-SOAR (or tel. 513-932-7627).

Springfield Swap Meet and Car Show, Clark County Fairgrounds, tel. (937) 376-0111.

JUNE

Native American Pow-Wow, Blue Jacket Amphitheater, Xenia, tel. (937) 275-8599.

Yellow Springs Street Fair is a tolerable mix of arts, crafts, food, and entertainment in a tolerant town. This event is also held in October. Call (937) 767-2686 for more information.

Banana Split Festival, Courthouse Square, Wilmington, tel. (937) 382-2737. The banana split allegedly was invented here, so folks return each year to dine, play, and be entertained.

MS 150 Bike Tour charity ride starts in Warren County and overnights at Wittenberg University in Springfield after 75 miles of riding through small towns. The next day, it's back to Warren County, with all funds aimed toward a cure for multiple sclerosis. Call (513) 769-4400 for details.

JULY

The Way It Was, Caesar Creek State Park Pioneer Village, tel. (513) 897-1120.

AUGUST

Meteor Shower Campout, Caesar Creek State Park, tel. (513) 897-2437.

SEPTEMBER

Amish Community Auction, Wheat Ridge. Telephone 513-544-5454 for time and place.

The **Fair at New Boston,** George Rogers Clark Park, SR 4, Springfield, tel. (937) 882-9216, retells the taming of the frontier with exciting re-enactments.

National Storytellers Celebration takes place during the Highland County Fair in Hillsboro. Call (937) 393-4883 for the complete story.

Cars & Parts Magazine **Swap Meet/Car Show,** Springfield, tel. (937) 325-7621.

Old Clifton Days, Clifton.

OCTOBER

Yellow Springs Street Fair, see June listing.

DECEMBER

Clifton Mill's Light Display, Clifton, tel. (937) 767-5501, an already picturesque place becomes more so with the addition of one million holiday lights.

art exhibits to bluegrass musicians; the **Springfield Civic Theatre** ensemble, tel. (937) 325-2668, and the **Springfield Symphony Orchestra,** tel. (937) 325-8100, both of which perform at the Clark State Performing Arts Center. Wittenberg students provide music, drama, or dance at Chakers Theatre, 909 Woodlawn Ave., tel. (937) 327-6231.

Yellow Springs' **Dayton Street Gulch** tavern offers patrons "Clean Gene" on a regular basis. Gene has thousands of rock 'n' roll hits from the 1950s to the 1980s on computerized CDs, allowing quick retrieval for drinkers' requests. "Try a Little Tenderness" by Otis Redding? Not a problem. "The Letter" by the Box Tops? Glad you asked. It's good fun and there's no cover charge. Other live entertainment in Yellow Springs includes periodic concerts by the community chorus and the community orchestra. Both perform in the First Presbyterian Church, 314 Xenia Ave., tel. (937) 767-7751.

A fellow with the improbable name of Marmaduke van Swearingen was wearing a blue jacket more than 200 years ago when he was abducted by Shawnee warriors. The young man grew up to become Blue Jacket, a Shawnee chief who led his adopted people in a vain attempt to preserve their land in this area. Van Swearingen's story is relived in the *Epic Outdoor Drama of Blue Jacket,* 520 Stringtown Rd., Xenia, tel. (937) 376-4318. The show is presented from mid-June through Labor Day, Tues.-Sun. evenings, and there is an occasional matinee. Admission varies—Tues.-Thurs. it's $12; Fri.-Sat., $14 Fri.-Sat.; and Sunday $8; children under the age of 13 are charged $6. Besides being historically accurate, this is vivid good fun, with dialogue punctuated by the occasional cannon!

Finally, a late-breaking item, Hillsboro's infamous **North High Saloon** has been torn down to make way for a new city building. Always difficult to classify (Was it culture? Was it entertainment?), the North High certainly has a place in history. It was the site, a few years back, of a fight in which country-western singer Johnny Paycheck ("Take This Job and Shove It") became riled at a fellow bar patron and shot him (for which Paycheck served a prison sentence).

RECREATION

Cycling

If there's a showpiece public recreation facility in this area, it's the **Little Miami Scenic River Bikeway.** Completed in 1998, it runs as far north as Springfield and as far south as Milford—nearly 70 miles in length—and is slated to extend clear to Buck Creek State Park, north of Springfield. Enjoyed by locals and folks who come from some distance, there's a special lot where visitors can park just north of Yellow Springs. Yellow Springs' just-restored Pennsylvania Railroad station is located alongside the path in Hilda Rahn Park. The station now houses the local chamber of commerce and has public restrooms. Bikes and skates are available to rent in the C&O caboose on the east side of SR 68, opposite Ha Ha Pizza. In Xenia, the trail intersects with pathways to Jamestown, Beavercreek, and Cedarville. Cyclists, joggers, walkers, and skaters

all are welcome in any direction. There is no better route for an introduction to southwestern Ohio.

Golf

To get in the swing of things, try one of these area sites: **Indian Springs Golf Club,** 11111 SR 161, Mechanicsburg (northeast of Springfield), tel. (800) 752-7846, is a lengthy (7,138 yds.) 18-hole facility, with championship tees and par 72. Weekday greens fees are $26, weekend fees are $35; add $10 for a cart. **Locust Hills Golf Course,** 5575 N. River Rd., Springfield, tel. (937) 265-5152 or (800) 872-4918, has an 18 and a nine-hole course, par 72 and par 36, respectively. Fees are $12 weekdays and $17 weekends, with a $15 charge for weekend play that begins after 3 p.m. Carts cost $8 per person. Down Xenia way, consider **WGC Golf Course,** 944 Country Club Dr., tel. (937) 372-1202. The course is par 71 and greens fees are $30 on weekdays, $32 on weekends, and $26 for teeing it up after 3 p.m. All fees include cart use. East of Hillsboro, link up with **Rocky Fork Golf Course,** 9965 SR 124, tel. (937) 393-9004. Par on this 18-hole course is 70. Greens fees are $9 for nine holes and $18 for 18 holes. Carts are $17 for nine holes and $28 for 18.

Jogging

Runners, particularly those in search of a sure-footed cushion, should look into the all-weather track surrounding the football field at Wittenberg University. Besides being easy on the feet, the scoreboard carries the time and temperature—which is a nice way to keep up the pace. The field is just off McCreight Avenue, two blocks east of North Plumb Street (SR 41). Park on the south side of the stadium and enter through the pedestrian gate closest to the fieldhouse. (It only looks locked.) Running in Yellow Springs way may be accomplished on the bike trail or in the nature preserve, the latter being part of the Antioch College campus. It's not advised anywhere near the gorge or on narrow pathways if people are present.

Spectator Sports

Don't be frightened away by the name—**Kil-Kare Speedway and Drag Strip,** 1166 Dayton-Xenia Rd., north of US 35 and west of Xenia, tel. (937)

caution is called for along the gorges in Yellow Springs

426-2764, is open weeknights from 5 p.m. in the summer for "tune and test," where drivers on the three-eighths mile oval or the drag strip pay $10, sign a waiver, and get to scare themselves silly. Spectators can watch for $3. On warm-weather weekends there's actual competition, with an occasional nationally known driver showing up to challenge the local stock car guys. Since it costs more money than most drivers make, calling local car racing a professional sport is a stretch. But the races have purses, which make these neighborhood daredevils professional.

ACCOMMODATIONS

Springfield has a number of national motel chains, most of them just off I-70 on the south side of town. Newer establishments include the **Holiday Inn,** 383 E. Leffel Lane, tel. (937) 323-8631, and the **Ramada Limited,** 319 E. Leffel

Lane, tel. (937) 328-0123. These and others are close to South Limestone Street (SR 72), with signs that can be seen from the freeway exit. Another newer motel is the **Fairfield Inn,** just off the intersection of SR 41 and SR 68, tel. (937) 323-9554, on the city's northwest edge. The Holiday Inn, Ramada Limited, and Fairfield Inn all have indoor pools. A nice place to stay in town is the **Springfield Inn,** 100 S. Fountain Ave., tel. (937) 322-3600. It and the Holiday Inn offer entertainment, primarily on weekends. Look, too, for a **Holiday Inn** in Xenia at 300 Xenia Town Sq., tel. (937) 372-9921. All of these facilities tend to be moderately priced.

There are many bed and breakfast operations in this eastern part of southwest Ohio. They include the recently opened **John Foos Manor,** 810 E. High St., Springfield, tel. (937) 323-3444; **Houstonia House Bed and Breakfast,** 25 E. Mound St., South Charleston, tel. (937) 462-7428; **Morgan House Bed and Breakfast,** 120 W. Limestone St., Yellow Springs, tel. (937) 767-7509; and **Allendale Inn,** 38 S. Allison Ave., Xenia, tel. (937) 372-1856. Between Xenia and Beavercreek, look for **Alpha House Bed and Breakfast** in tiny Alpha, tel. (937) 427-3408 or (800) 337-2852. West of Wilmington, check out **Cedar Hills Bed and Breakfast,** 4003 SR 73, tel. (937) 383-2525. Down Hillsboro way, consider **Deer Run Farm,** 7914 Buckley Rd., tel. (937) 393-4209.

All of the state parks mentioned here have some form of camping, with Rocky Fork offering the largest number of sites, plus cabins, cottages, and motels. Highland County boasts several nice private campgrounds, including **Shady Trails,** 11145 North Shore Dr., Hillsboro, tel. (937) 393-5618, and **Babington Campgrounds,** 11993 Spruance Rd., Hillsboro, tel. (937) 466-2323.

FOOD

Current Cuisine, 237 Xenia Ave., tel. (937) 767-8291, specializes in thick, cold sandwiches and entrees that can be quickly microwaved. A ham-and-provolone is $3.79. With a 16-ounce glass can of juice, lunch comes to less than $5. Dinners are equally worthwhile: Cornish game hen with dried-fruit stuffing and wild rice is $14.95, while spinach pesto lasagna goes for $9.95. Dinners include salad, two veggies, and homemade bread. Current Cuisine is open for lunch and dinner.

Cedar Street, 617 Cedar St., Springfield, tel. (937) 322-5781), is an atmospheric place. Open every day but Saturday for lunch and every evening for dinner, this restaurant offers a conventional American menu. The most popular sandwich at lunch is stacked roast beef and cheddar at $6.75. In the evening, prime rib at $13.95 is a favorite, though the fresh Atlantic salmon at $14.95 also is ordered frequently. Diners with large appetites save room for Black Forest cheesecake, priced at $3.95.

Clifton Mill, 75 Water St., Clifton, tel. (937) 767-5501, serves hearty breakfasts and lunches in a building that really was the village mill many years ago. Sitting above the Little Miami River gorge, the restaurant makes everything from scratch and specializes in homemade breads, rolls, biscuits, and pancakes. A plate of flapjacks at breakfast is approximately $5. Lunches are highlighted by a number of sandwiches, the most popular being chicken salad at $6.99. Open seven days a week for breakfast and lunch, Clifton Mill is a picturesque and tasty stop in this tiny village.

Ha Ha Pizza is at 108 Xenia Ave., Yellow Springs, tel. (937) 767-2131. Driving south into Yellow Springs on SR 68, the first building on the right will be Ha Ha Pizza. Despite the name, this modest-appearing place takes food seriously: pizza crusts are made with organically grown flour and all food is prepared to order. A large (16-inch) pizza with three toppings is less than $12.50 and can be had with such exotic additons as artichoke hearts or smoked oysters. Calzones and subs are many and varied, and there's a salad bar and a wide selection of teas and other soft drinks.

Jo's Drive-In Restaurant, 1355 Detroit St., Xenia, tel. (937) 372-2211. Drive past the new McDonald's on the north edge of town and turn in here. Owner Georgianna (Jo for short) cooks up her own version of a double-deck burger and sells it for $2.95. Other solid choices include a homestyle burger, slightly larger than the predictable version, plus smoked sausage, chicken breast fixed a variety of ways, chili dogs, and more. Breakfast options include a couple of nice touches—fried mush, three big pieces with syrup, is $2.50. Also recommended is the breakfast sampler, which Jo says includes a little bit of everything. No longer a drive-in, Jo's is open weekdays for dinner, and Mon.-Sat. for breakfast and lunch.

Linardo's, 2230 E. Main St., Springfield, tel. (937) 323-3011, offers a Greek-American menu. Open weekdays for lunch and Mon.-Sat. for dinner, the restaurant has a good local following. Luncheon items include a gyros sandwich, moussaka, and other Greek dishes for $8.95. The big hit each evening is a combination sampler platter that provides the diner with many different Greek specialties. It's $12.95 and includes a salad and pastry. Baklava can be had for $2.50. For those with more conventional tastes, there's a full menu of steak and other American entrees.

Mike & Rosy's Deli, 330 W. McCreight Ave., Springfield, tel. (937) 390-3511, keeps college students well fed. The deli's hoagy is the showcase item here, and it's a meal at $4.95. Many other sandwich variations can be made to order, and there's a dining room covered with sports memorabilia for those who want to sit down after collecting their food from the counter. Cinnamon rolls, bagels, coffee, and juice are available mornings. Mike & Rosy's is open daily for lunch and dinner, and weekdays for breakfast.

Samuel Walker's, 64 W. Main St., Wilmington, tel. (937) 383-6664, is a favorite rendezvous of Wilmington College administrators and townsfolk. The American menu varies from casual to upscale, with luncheon favorites including homemade soup and a sandwich for $4.99 or a spinach salad in a honey-wheat bread shell for $6.99. A recently introduced evening entree with a following is trout almondine at $14.95. Like the rest of the restaurants in this list, Walker's is a refuge from franchise sameness. The facility is open for lunch and dinner Mon.-Sat., and for Sunday brunch.

The **Winery,** 2369 Upper Valley Pike, Springfield, tel. (937) 399-2334, formerly produced its own wine but now "imports" it from northern Ohio under the Hafle label. Most popular from among six wines offered is Danielle's Blush at $8.45 per bottle. Wine by the glass, be it red, white, or in-between at this Italian restaurant, is just $2.25. In the summer there's outdoor dining. While Italian dishes are available, the big hits are steak, chicken, and seafood prepared on the grill. In the winter, the Winery's signature dish is baked lasagna at $7.95. It's open Wed.-Sat. from 5 p.m.

The **Winds Cafe,** 215 Xenia Ave., Yellow Springs, tel. (937) 767-1144, is among Ohio's very best restaurants. It's a place where cooks and waitstaff refuse to rest on their laurels—the menu and the wine list change at the start of each month. Recently, the Winds offered intriguing meals such as these: grilled tea-cured salmon with fresh ginger *beurre blanc* and sesame-cashew rice, $18; Indian market platter, $15.75; and grilled beef tenderloin atop a mushroom-cognac ragout, drizzled with arugula pesto, served with potatoes cooked in cream. The highlighted wine was a Carmenet 1995 Dynamite Cabernet at $7 per glass or $25 per bottle. Everything else is equally adventurous, from a Tuscan bread salad appetizer at $6.95 to cocktails made with premium spirits. The Winds is open for lunch and dinner Mon.-Sat. and for Sunday brunch. By the way, the entrance is around the corner on the north side of the building.

Ye Olde Trail Tavern, 228 Xenia Ave., Yellow Springs, tel.(937) 767-7448, is in an ancient building. The menu here features pizza and burgers, though there are other items. Prices here are pretty reasonable, which is why so many pizzas are ordered for pickup. A big pie is around $10-12 depending on accessories. Don't let the dilapidated exterior, small bar, or cramped seating intimidate—this is a friendly place with outside dining in warm weather. Open for lunch Wed.-Sat. and for dinner every evening but Sunday.

Young's Jersey Dairy, 6880 Springfield-Xenia Rd. (SR 68), Yellow Springs, tel. (937) 325-0629, is hard to classify. It's at least two places to eat, and there are diversions such as miniature golf, a driving range, a batting cage, wagon rides, and a gift shop. But back to the food: The faster of the two restaurants is a mecca for milkshakes, sundaes, and other ice-cream treats. This is no ordinary ice cream—it's made from unpasteurized, unadulterated milk from Young's herd of jerseys, which are known for the high butterfat and protein content of their milk. The sandwiches and cold treats are tasty, normally priced, and can be eaten on the premises or taken out. The other food destination serves sit-down meals and is just as popular as the ice-cream place. The **Golden Jersey Inn** opened in 1998 and is known for, among other things, Grandma's meatloaf, which is $7.95 for dinner. The inn is open 7 a.m.-10 p.m. every day.

INFORMATION AND SERVICES

The Springfield/Clark County Convention and Visitors Bureau is at 333 N. Limestone St., Suite 201, tel. (937) 523-8687. The bureau maintains a "What's Happening Hotline," tel. (937) 323-INFO (or tel. 937-323-4636). The Yellow Springs Chamber of Commerce, open weekdays noon-2 p.m., is at 108 Dayton St. tel. (937) 767-2686. The Greene County Convention and Visitors Bureau is at 3335 E. Patterson Rd., Beavercreek (dial 937-429-9100 or 800-733-9109). The Fayette County Travel, Tourism and Convention Bureau can be found at 101 E. East St., Washington Court House, tel. (740) 335-8008. The Highland County Chamber of Commerce is at 128 W. Walnut St., Hillsboro, tel. (937) 393-1111.

Several colleges are in the vicinity, and they have athletic events, convocations, and other happenings that may be of interest to passersby. Contact Wittenberg University in Springfield at (937) 327-6114, or go its Web site at www.wittenberg.edu. Antioch University in Yellow Springs can tell you the scoop at (937) 767-7331. Call (937) 376-6011 for info on events at Central State University in Wilberforce. Adjacent Wilberforce University can provide similar assistance at (937) 376-2911.

Media

The *Springfield News-Sun* keeps readers apprised every morning of the week. It offers an entertainment section each Thursday. The entertainment section in the *Xenia Daily Gazette* also comes out on Thursday. Other dailies south and east of Greene County include the evening *News Journal* in Wilmington, the weekday evening-Saturday morning *Record Herald* in Washington Court House, and the evening *Times-Gazette* in Hillsboro.

Information on Xenia is available from www.ci.xenia.oh.us. Though the site is devoted to bicycling, it provides general information and sources for articles from publications. The weekly *Yellow Springs News* maintains a site that includes a calendar of events. Look for it at www.ysnews.com.

WBLY-AM, 1600, maintains an all-talk format with regularly scheduled news. WYSO, a listener-supported FM station at 91.3 on the dial, offers Pacifica Network News and news features shows such as National Public Radio's *All Things Considered.*

Transportation

The Greyhound Bus Lines terminal in Springfield is at 600 W. Main St., tel. (937) 323-9701 or (800) 231-2222. Springfield City Area Transit (SCAT) can be reached for schedule and route information at (937) 328-7228. Every corner on every route is a bus stop. Passengers need to signal the driver that they want a ride. Fares are 75 cents for adults, 35 cents for seniors, and no charge for children five and under.

Shopping

Antiquing is a big deal in Springfield. Travelers in search of a memento from yesteryear might consider the 200 dealers at AAA-I-70 Antique Mall, 4700 S. Charleston Pike, tel. (937) 324-8448, Springfield Antique Center, 1735 Titus Rd., tel. (937) 322-8868, or Heart of Ohio, 4785 E. National Rd., tel. (937) 324-2188.

A former church, built in 1878, is the site of an antique mall in the tiny village of Clifton, south of Springfield and I-70 about seven miles south on SR 72. The one-time Clifton Presbyterian Church is one of several understated, fun places to look around in this little old town.

In Yellow Springs, an array of crafts and consumer products, many of them made cooperatively, await shoppers. Visit **King's Yard,** a cluster of shops selling everything from shoes to scents, behind Ye Old Trail Tavern, 228 Xenia Ave. Elsewhere, in the summer and fall, look to farmstands for everything from jars of thick sorghum molasses to apples and other fruits and vegetables. Amish farmers and Appalachian craftspeople seem to sell perpetually along SR 32 south of Hillsboro.

For a more orderly shopping experience, try **Ohio Factory Shops,** on US 35 in Jeffersonville (Exit 65 off I-71), tel. (614) 948-9090 or (800) 746-7644. One of two such factory shops in the state (the other is in Lodi, west of Akron), this facility has dozens of apparently sale-priced retailers, most of them related to clothing. Names like Levi-Strauss, Ann Taylor, Eddie Bauer, Nike, and Polo are common. The shopping center is open every day.

DAYTON

Dayton has 180,000 residents, making it Ohio's sixth-largest city. More than that, Dayton is part of a megalopolis that stretches 60 miles, from the Ohio River and Cincinnati to the north side of I-70. The city has a bit of everything, from a namesake university to recently renovated parts of town and a couple of horsey-set suburbs. Vulnerable to the country's economic whims, Dayton in the late 1990s had recovered from much of its Rust Belt past. This is also considered the Home of Aviation, and it is certainly a plane-crazy area. In 1997, a Dayton man with a private plane and a pilot's license decided to fly his single-engine Aeronca one afternoon. He left the plane running on the taxiway and it took off without him. Filled with fuel, the craft flew for about two hours before crashing into a soybean field near Urbana, some 40 miles away! The Wright brothers would have been proud.

History

The first humans hereabouts may have been the Moundbuilders. After all, they left an impressive array of their earthwork here and throughout southern Ohio. They were succeeded by Algonquin and other tribes in the Miami Valley, which was bounded by what would be called the Great Miami and Little Miami Rivers flowing through it north to south. The first European likely was a French explorer named Joseph de Beinville. He proclaimed the area for France but opted to leave metal plaques staking the claim rather than settling in.

English traders in the 1750s were followed by George Rogers Clark in 1780. Clark found Shawnee, Lenni Lenape, and other tribes in the area before a small group that included New Jersey politician Jonathan Dayton acquired land here. Dayton, as the town was to be called, was surveyed and laid out in 1795. The first permanent residents probably rode barges as far west as Cincinnati before alighting and following either of the two Miami rivers to their new homes. Dayton became the Montgomery County seat shortly after statehood was granted in 1803.

The town enjoyed the prosperity that floated along the Miami-Erie Canal, which connected Lake Erie and the Ohio River beginning in 1845. Unlike northern Ohio, there were enough "copperheads," or southern sympathizers, to make the Union's Civil War cause somewhat unpopular. After the conflict, rail traffic helped the city grow, as did the invention of the cash register by local resident John Patterson. His ingenuity was followed by Charles F. Kettering's Delco (Dayton Engineering Laboratories) plant and by the Wright Brothers' successful plane flight in 1903. The period from the Civil War to World War I was a golden one for Daytonians.

Aviation continued to play an important part, both for manufacturers and for flyers. So did electricity and a public library, both of which enhanced the community prior to 1920. But much of the downtown had been marred a few years earlier in the Great Flood of 1913. The Miami Conservancy District was formed, but until dams were built north of the city in the 1920s and 1930s there was little protection from rampaging water. Daytonians weathered the Great Depression and World War II as well as any other Americans, tending to parks and green spaces for themselves and their children while they became more aware of valued aspects of their past. An example encompassing both is SunWatch Archaeological Park, a resurrected village once populated by pre-Columbian natives. Another example is the well-marked Aviation Trail, which guides visitors to Dayton's many pioneering flight sights. Additionally, Wright-Patterson Air Force Base in Fairborn, north of Dayton, is home to the state's largest remaining stretch of prairie. Don't go looking for flowers and grasses, though, as the prairie in its entirety is within the confines of the base.

Location and Orientation

East-west I-70 and north-south I-75 meet just north of Dayton. The two highways also are linked by I-675, which skirts the east side of the city. Several other short expressways within city limits feed the interstates. Dayton is 55 miles north of Cincinnati, 75 miles southwest of Columbus, about 150 miles south of Toledo, and 35 miles east of the Ohio-Indiana line. US 35 enters

Dayton from the west and departs headed southeast. US 40 parallels I-70. The Mad River meets the Great Miami River in downtown Dayton, with the heart of the city being on the Miami's east bank. Dayton's loftiest building is the Kettering Tower (formerly the Winters Bank building), completed in 1970 at 40 N. Main St. It stands 405 feet high and has 30 stories.

SIGHTS

The National Park Service looked around Dayton in 1992, saw several eminent and restorable sites, and combined them to form the **Dayton Aviation Heritage National Historic Park.** The park complex consists of four sites: the Wright Brothers' bicycle shop, a nearby printing plant called Hoover Block, the home of poet Paul Laurence Dunbar, and the Carillon, a park where relocated buildings are on display. The sites are as much as 14 miles apart, so visitors are given maps to get them from one setting to the next. The Wrights' shop is a museum and is in the same neighborhood as the Hoover facility. The only airplane on display is at the Carillon, where a 1905 *Wright Flyer III*—said to be the first craft capable of sustained flight—has been restored. The museum is at 22 S. Williams St., just off West Third Street. Best bet is to exit I-75 onto westbound Third. Admissions are charged at two of the four sites, the Carillon and the Dunbar

home. The former is $2 for adults and $1.25 for children ages 6-17, while the latter is $3 for adults and $1.25 for children ages 5-12. For information on all the sites, call (937) 225-7705.

The **Dayton Museum of Discovery,** at 2600 DeWeese Parkway, tel. (937) 275-7431, has a bit of everything. There's a nice mastodon skeleton, an Egyptian mummy, an indoor zoo with many of the animals native to the area, a planetarium that should align the planets in better mental order, touchy-feely experiments, and adornments for the kids, all in a modern, accessible building. The museum is west of I-75's Exit 57-B. Once the exit is reached, look for posted directional signs. Its hours are Tues.-Thurs. and Saturday 9 a.m.-5 p.m.; Friday 9 a.m.-9 p.m.; Sunday and holidays noon-5 p.m. Admission is $4 for adults, $2.50 for seniors, and $1.50 for children ages 3-16.

The **SunWatch Archaeological Park,** right here in Dayton, Ohio, at 2301 W. River Rd., tel. (937) 268-8199, is the most excavated pre-Columbian village known. A National Historic Landmark, the 800-year-old site in the last few years has yielded more than a million artifacts that help explain the lives of these very early farmers. The reproduced village has thatched-roof houses in their actual spots around what once was a plaza. Globetrotters will be reminded of a remote African village or perhaps a Mayan settlement. Travelers who want to learn how archaeologists do what they do should make a point of showing up here.

United States Air Force Museum, Fairborn

Hours are Tues.-Sat. 9 a.m.-5 p.m. and Sunday noon-5 p.m. Admission is $4 for adults and $3 for children ages 6-17 and seniors. SunWatch is open mid-March through November.

United States Air Force Museum

The oldest and largest military aviation museum in the world is located at Wright-Patterson Air Force Base in Fairborn, tel. (937) 255-3284, displaying more than 200 planes and missiles, plus exhibits ranging from a moon-orbiting space capsule to the personal property of WW I aviation hero General Billy Mitchell. The old planes are swell, but the aircraft in the Modern Flight Gallery are awesome. They range from a Strategic Air Command long-range bomber to a radar-dodging Stealth and many other supersonic craft armed to the gills. Did it take more courage for the Red Baron to climb in his flimsy Fokker, or for Chuck Yeager to strap himself into an early experimental jet aircraft? Set aside at least an entire day here to find out. Hours are daily 9 a.m.-5 p.m. and the entire operation is free.

The Air Force even encourages visitors to shoot photos, noting that even the most powerful flash may not reach from wingtip to wingtip on the biggest planes. The museum also has an IMAX theater showing a stirring IMAX movie that takes visitors through the history of flight. The thundering stereo sound combines with from-the-cockpit footage to deliver a breathtaking documentary. Except for the gift and snack shops, this is about the only place where a visitor has to spend money. Admission to the IMAX presentation, which occurs every hour from 10 a.m., is $5.50 for adults, $5 for seniors, $4 for students age eight to college, and $2.75 for children ages 3-7. For theater details or reservations, call (937) 253-4629.

RECREATION

Golf

Almost all area golf courses are accessible to the public. Typical sites include **Kittyhawk Golf Course,** 3383 Chuck Wagner Lane, tel. (937) 237-5424, on the city's northeast side. Kittyhawk has three 18-hole courses, including the longest one in the area at 6,713 yards. Fees are $12 for nine holes and $18 for 18 holes weekdays,

$20 for 18 holes weekends. **Larch Tree Golf Course,** 2765 N. Snyder Rd., tel. (937) 854-1951, on the northwest side in Trotwood, charges $18 weekdays and $22 weekends, plus $11 per cart. **Yankee Trace Golf Course,** 9860 Yankee St., to the south in Centerville, tel. (937) 438-4653, asks for $35 weekdays and $39 weekends, plus $12 for the use of a cart. All these courses are par 72, with the exception of one 18-hole par 56 course at Kittyhawk.

Parks

Walkers, joggers, cyclists, and runners release their endorphins in Dayton's **Five Rivers Metroparks,** tel. (937) 275-PARK (or tel. 937-275-7275), comprising 14 different expanses of greenery around the city that cater not only to the pedestrian but also to the bike and horseback rider. Three of the larger parks—Englewood, Taylorsville, and Carriage Hill—lie just to the north of I-70. Englewood's hiking trails invite use, Carriage Hills is a reproduced 1880s farm, and Taylorsville is ruggedly bisected by the Great Miami River. Germantown MetroPark, southwest of the city, has 14 miles of hiking trails, a scenic overlook and 500 feet of boardwalk jutting into an unspoiled nature center. **Sycamore State Park,** tel. (937) 854-4452, between Trotwood and Brookville on Salem Avenue (SR 49), is the closest spot to downtown Dayton for primitive camping; it also offers a couple of fishing ponds. None of the parks charge for use. (Since the Wright brothers were in the bicycle business, what better way to salute them than by rolling through a Dayton MetroPark?)

Canoeing

Another neat place is close by: the Little Miami River is a dozen miles east of downtown. Canoe trips on this state and federally designated scenic river are popular. Contact **RiversEdge Outfitters,** which is between Xenia and Waynesville on the east side of US 42 (the river side), slightly closer to Waynesville. The Little Miami presents another opportunity to see what Ohio might have looked like before everyone's ancestors showed up. A 1.5-hour canoe rental costs $21, while the longest trip, running five to seven hours, is $31. Solo canoes and kayaks are available at $16 per trip. RiversEdge is open weekends April-Oct.; the river's disposition may affect whether ca-

ATTRACTIONS BEYOND DAYTON

Several Dayton-area municipalities may be of interest to travelers passing through. Consider a visit to one or more of the following:

Centerville: Perhaps the most fascinating attraction in this suburb south of Dayton is the **International Women's Air & Space Museum**—call (937) 433-6766 for directions. Open by appointment only, the facility showcases early wingwalkers and other stuntpersons, along with such more familiar names as Amelia Earhart and astronaut Sally Ride. The town itself has 21,000 residents and is on SR 48 (Centerville's Main Street), less than 10 miles from the heart of downtown Dayton.

Eaton: Not really a suburb, this Preble County seat on US 35 about 25 miles west of Dayton has 7,500 residents and a couple of highlights. Besides being a pretty place, Eaton is the site of **Fort St. Clair State Memorial** on the west side of town in a glady and uncrowded park. It's easy to envision the 18th-century fortification that once stood here amid the trees. There are half a dozen covered bridges in Preble County, the nearest to Eaton being the 100-ft. **Chrisman Bridge** just north of town on Eaton-New Hope Road and the **Roberts Bridge** on Beech Street. Eight miles southeast of Eaton, just west of SR 122, is the **Preble County Historical Center,** tel. (937) 787-4256. The center's half-dozen historical buildings can be seen without charge 1-5 p.m. on the first Sunday of the month, May-Oct., plus December.

Germantown: Another town just a dozen miles from the downtown, this quiet village of 5,000 residents on SR 725 has managed to preserve much of what is nice about smalltown Ohio's past. There are a couple of good places to eat here, and if you drive a block or so off the main street you're apt to find a restored covered bridge, free of grafitti and apparently as sturdy as the day it was last used in 1963—though the structure's side panels have been removed.

Miamisburg: The locals may take it for granted, but **Miamisburg Mound State Memorial,** the state's largest Indian mound is here. Next to the golf course, it's not only large enough to be impressive (68 feet high), but has a stairway that allows visitors a trip to the top. Once there, the westward view past the factory across the street is quite nice, especially during months when there isn't much foliage. The mound dates from about A.D. 400. Miamisburg has approxmiately 18,000 residents who support a pleasant downtown area. The memorial is open daily from dawn to dusk and admission is free. It's on SR 725, some 15 miles south of downtown Dayton.

Springboro: Once a stopover on the Underground Railroad, Springboro is two miles east of I-75 and about 20 miles south of downtown Dayton. Walking tours that include some 50 historic and restored homes and shops are available, and there is an antique mall in the downtown area.

Trotwood: A railroad once ran from Trotwood to Greenville in Darke County, hauling produce and goods between the Dayton area and the farmlands to the northwest. Nowadays, Trotwood has pretty homes, with 30,000 residents spread across 30 square miles. There are 2,600 acres of parkland, and the 13-mile **Wolf Creek Rail Trail** bicycle path has replaced the steam engines that once were a part of everyday life.

Vandalia: On US 40, Vandalia bills itself as "the crossroads of America." Seven miles north of Dayton and the site of **Dayton International Airport,** Vandalia has 14,000 residents and is home to the **Trapshooting Hall of Fame,** on US 40 adjacent to the airport on the south. This is a good place to investigate various **MetroParklands** to the east and to find out about early 20th-century efforts, particularly around Englewood, to tame area rivers with vast earthen banks and spillways.

Waynesville: Remember the things in Grandma's attic that Mom said were priceless? Here is where they ended up, in what has become the Midwest's antique mecca. Folks come here from all over, not so much to get a bargain as to admire the various antiques and crafts that are inventoried in 70 quaint shops from one end of the village to the other. Waynesville has approximately 2,000 residents, all of whom seem to be in the memorabilia business. The town is about 20 miles southeast of Dayton, where US 42 meets SR 73.

noeing is allowed. Call RiversEdge at (937) 862-4540 or (800) 628-2319 for more information.

CULTURE AND ENTERTAINMENT

Perhaps the best annual event within the city limits, the **National Folk Festival,** is a free, three-day affair that takes place in mid-June. No matter what kind of music visitors might fancy, they're apt to hear it here.

All types of music can be heard here: Master Ge Xiong and the Hmong Culture Reunion from Asia, the legendary Magic Slim and the Teardrops representing down-home blues, Natalie McMaster, all the way from Cape Breton Island, playing fiddle and step-dancing. More than 100 acts perform outdoors, rain or shine, in an eight-block area bounded by First, Fifth, Jefferson, and Ludlow Streets. For more information, call (937) 223-3655.

Those who savor the blues should slide into the **Trolley Stop,** 530 E. Fifth St., tel. (937) 461-1101. Live music by nationally recognized blues players such as North Carolina's Skeeter Brandon is featured on weekends. There's usually a modest ($2-3) cover charge. Other places in Dayton proper where folks play music on a regular basis include **Canal Street Tavern,** 308 E. First St., tel. (937) 461-9343, for rock 'n' roll; and **Gilly's,** Fifth and Jefferson Streets, tel. (937) 228-0414, for rock, jazz, or blues. In nearby Beavercreek (west of Dayton on US 35), **Martino's Bar and Spirits,** 4392 Indian Ripple Rd., tel. (937) 427-3550, offers everything from blues to Grateful Dead tributes to folk.

Up a notch on the culture scale, classical music is available live and without charge in the **Dayton Art Institute's Gothic Cloister,** 456 Belmonte Park North, tel. (937) 223-5277. **Books & Co.,** 350 E. Stroop Rd., in nearby Kettering (the town is south of Dayton on US 48), tel. (937) 298-6540, offers classic quintets and other musical configurations without charge on a regular basis.

Several sites exist for regional and national touring acts. They include **Fraze Pavilion,** Lincoln Park Boulevard at Troyer Road, Kettering, tel. (937) 297-3720, with a full summer season of entertainment. The largest area site for music and other entertainment forms is **Memorial Hall,** 125 E. First St., Dayton.

The playbill is full at the **Victoria Theatre,** First and Main Streets, Dayton, a dazzlingly restored playhouse that serves the following seasons: **Broadway on Main, Theatre for the Young at Heart,** and **Discovery!** The Broadway on Main seasonal offerings include half a dozen traveling productions, from *Grease!* to *Camelot.* The young and the young at heart can see one or more of half a dozen plays intended primarily for children, ranging from *The Snow Queen* to a Laura Ingalls Wilder sampler. Discovery! offers approximately 10 production each season as an outreach program aimed primarily at local schoolchildren. *Heidi* was followed by *Phantom of the Opera* on one recent schedule. For more information, contact the Victoria box office at (937) 228-3630.

The **Dayton Philharmonic Orchestra,** tel. (937) 224-9000, has been performing since 1933. Most concerts are in Memorial Hall, though occasional performances take place a block away at the Dayton Convention Center, 22 E. Fifth St., and in the Victoria Theatre. In addition to classical music, the orchestra offers "Superpops" shows with celebrities such as Doc Severinsen or Gladys Knight, plus casual concerts featuring outstanding local or regional soloists. The **Dayton Ballet,** tel. (937) 449-5060, schedules four different shows during its season, which takes place in the Victoria Theatre. **Dayton Opera** performs a trio of presentations, such as *La Boheme,* at Memorial Hall. The season for all of these classical music and dance presentations runs from October to mid-spring.

Perhaps the most pleasant surprise for culture buffs is the recent, $16.7 million renovation of the **Dayton Art Institute,** 456 Belmont Park N., tel. (937) 223-5277. Redesigned gallery spaces and added visitor amenities make the beautiful sandstone building quite user friendly. The collection is rated "superb" by the American Association of Museums and includes Monet's *Waterlilies,* Edward Hopper's *High Noon,* and Andy Warhol's *Russell Means.* The Asian collection is outstanding, with objects from India, China, Tibet, Japan, Southeast Asia, and Persia. Hours are daily 10 a.m.-5 p.m., with galleries open until 9 p.m. on Thursday. The museum also stays open from 6-10 p.m. several nights a month and adds live jazz or gospel to lure patrons in. There are no admission charges.

DAYTON EVENTS

FEBRUARY

Aviation Classic Film Festival, U.S. Air Force Museum, Carney Auditorium, Wright-Patterson Air Force Base, Fairborn, tel. (937) 255-4704. Whether you admire Waldo Pepper or Van Heflin, there's something for you at these periodic 7:30 p.m. showings. A small admission fee is charged.

APRIL

Sugar Maple Festival, streets of the Old Village, Bellbrook, tel. (937) 848-3236, arts, crafts, concessions, and entertainment welcome spring.

JUNE

Behind the Scene Tour, Wright-Patterson Air Force Base, Fairborn, tel. (937) 255-3286, limited to those ages 12 and older. Visitors learn how venerable planes are brought back to good-as-new condition.

Art and Culture Festival, Main Street, downtown Miamisburg, tel. (937) 866-1914. Look for outdoor performing artists, visual arts demonstrations, and food.

Kids Fest, Lincoln Park Commons, 695 Lincoln Park Blvd., Kettering, tel. (937) 296-2587. Clowns and musicians entertain the youngsters, and there are plenty of games, crafts, and other activities.

JULY

The **United States Air and Trade Show** takes place at the Dayton International Airport, just west of Vandalia, tel. (937) 898-5901. More than a quarter million people turn out to be thrilled by military and civilian pilots and their planes.

Black Cultural Festival, Montgomery County Fairgrounds, 1024 S. Main St., Dayton, tel. (937) 224-1619, a lively celebration of African and Afro-American culture, this annual event showcases music, culture, and dance, with a variety of ethnic foods.

SunWatch Summerfest, SunWatch grounds, I-75 Exit 51, Dayton, tel. (937) 268-8199. Native Americans were here before anyone else, and this prehistoric archaeological site helps recall the times before there were Europeans or Africans around.

AUGUST

Sweet Corn Festival, Community Park, Dayton-Yellow Springs Rd., Fairborn, tel. (937) 878-2860. Between ears, look for Elvis impersonators, cloggers, bluegrass music, a corn-eating contest, and other late-breaking events. Bring floss.

For dinner theater events, try **La Comedia Dinner Theatre** (formerly the Miami Valley Dinner Theatre), SR 73, south of Dayton in Springboro, off I-75, tel. (513) 232-6220. Half a dozen productions, from a Patsy Cline tribute to *Fiddler on the Roof,* are staged annually. Ticket prices start at $32 and go up to $44 for adults; tickets for children under 12 are $19. La Comedia also offers Sunday brunch performances.

ACCOMMODATIONS

Only a couple of large hotels operate in the downtown area, a tipoff to the fact that people don't spend a lot of time there. Look for the **Radisson Hotel and Suites,** Third and Ludlow Streets, tel. (937) 461-4700; the **Dayton Marriott,** 1414 S. Patterson Blvd., tel. (937) 223-1000; or the Crowne Plaza Hotel, Fifth and Jefferson Sts., tel. (937) 224-0800. Rates are in the expensive to luxury range. Lower priced motels and hotels are clustered in Fairborn, around Dayton on I-75, and along I-70, just north of the city.

The Miamisburg area has an assortment of motels near I-75, but some may prefer the atmospheric **English Manor Inn Bed and Breakfast** at 505 E. Linden Ave., Miamisburg, tel. (937) 866-2288. This moderately priced 1924 Tudor-style mansion is filled with antiques and serves up a full breakfast. Other B&B facilities include the moderate **Prices' Steamboat House Bed and Breakfast,** 6 Josie St., Dayton, tel. (937) 223-2444; the **Gunkel Heritage Bed & Breakfast and Antiques,** 33 W. Market St., Dayton, tel. (937) 855-3508; the pleasant, small-town **Yesterday Bed and Breakfast,** 39 S. Main St., Centerville (south of Dayton along SR 48), tel. (937) 433-0785; and a pair of B&Bs in West Alexandria, west of the city 20 miles: **Twin Creek Country,** 5353 Enterprise Rd., tel. (937) 787-3990, and **Twin Creek Townehouse,** 19 E. Dayton St., tel. (937) 839-5974. All fall within the moderate price range and are attractively furnished.

Ladies Professional Golf Association (LPGA) Classic, Country Club of the North, at Factory and Indian Ripple Rds., Beavercreek, tel. (937) 291-4230. This is a six-day charity event, with tickets to watch the pros ranging from $15 to $1,500.

The **Dog Days of Summer Bicycle Ride,** tel. (937) 222-1710, is organized by Dayton folks but takes place west of the city, visiting such sites as General Anthony Wayne's Fort St. Clair State Park in Eaton.

SEPTEMBER

Italian Fall Festa, Bella Villa Hall, County Line Road, Kettering, tel. (937) 258-3600. There's an air of Europe in Kettering—and the heavy aroma of Italian dishes—as everyone who is Italian or who wants to be shows up.

Pork Festival, Preble County Fairgrounds, Eaton, tel. (937) 339-1044. This is big pig country, so the weekend begins with an early breakfast of sausages and progresses to a smorgasbord, along with crafts and exhibits.

The **Dayton-Miami Valley Fine Arts Festival** takes place at the Mall at Fairfield Commons in Dayton, tel. (937) 427-4300. Arts organizations and artisans team up to display various media.

Taste of the Miami Valley, Courthouse Square, Dayton, tel. (937) 226-8211. For a buck or two, visitors can taste individual specialties from 50 area restaurants. Entertainment is continuous and there are cooking demonstrations.

OCTOBER

Ohio Sauerkraut Festival, Waynesville, tel. (937) 897-8855. Briny cabbage is on the menu, but there are no forced feedings. Instead, look for free entertainment and 450 crafts exhibits.

MetroParks Riverfest, Carillon, DeWeese, and Triangle Parks, in the Dayton area. Regattas, boat races and rides, open houses at museums, a half-marathon, and a bike rodeo are among numerous events staged when the rivers are tame and the trees are turning. Call (937) 226-8211 for more information.

DECEMBER

Historic Lebanon Christmas Festival, tel. (937) 932-1100. The largest horsedrawn carriage parade in the state takes place by candlelight in this historic old village. Fueled by warm drinks and hot chestnuts, visitors can see live window displays, crafts, and entertainment.

FOOD

Dorothy Lane Market, 2710 Far Hills Ave., Dayton, tel.(937) 299-3561, is a grocery that's open from 6 a.m. to midnight. The huge deli has a couple of selling points that may make travelers stray from conventional restaurants. Besides great panini sandwiches and 30 dishes prepared daily for picnickers, the market bakes wonderful European bread and shows an estimated 3,000 wine varieties. There's a second location at 6177 Far Hills Ave., tel. (937) 434-1294. Just keep telling yourself: Neither market is on Dorothy Lane, though the Dorothy Lane name is on at least two freeway signs.

The **Breakfast Club Cafe,** S. Main St. at Patterson Blvd., Dayton, tel. (937) 228-2179, is open for breakfast and lunch daily 6 a.m.-3 p.m. Specialties include several intriguing omelet variations, plus pancakes. Omelets range from $4.35 to $6.25; the high-end omelet is a assemblage of steak, cheese, and mushrooms, served with potatoes and pancakes. A typical pancake might be banana-walnut, priced at three for $3.25. The coffee is strong and flavorful and is dispensed to everyone from those who got a good night's sleep to those who have yet to turn in. The decor is sunny and the place is popular—prepare to wait for a table on weekends.

King Cole, 40 N. Main St. (Kettering Tower), Dayton, tel. (937) 222-6771. Coats and ties for gentlemen and dresses, skirts, or dressy slacks for the ladies are the dress code and the norm at this expensive upscale restaurant with a romantic French accent. Seafood arrives from all over the world, and the kitchen prepares seductive sauces for lamb, veal, fowl, and beef. Popular desserts include bananas Foster and cherries jubilee. Expect to spend about $60 per couple, plus drinks and tip. Open weekdays for lunch and dinner and for dinner only on Saturday.

Elsa's, 3618 Linden Ave., Dayton, tel. (937) 252-9635, is the consummate Mexican restaurant. Open every day for lunch, dinner, and beyond, the facility serves homemade salsa, among many other south-of-the-border treats. Customers rave about the black bean soup, which goes for $2.75 per bowl. They also like the ribs, which are $9.75 and $14.50 for a half- and a full-slab, respecitvely. The super burrito, a meal in itself, is $9.25, and there are all the usual Mexican entrees. The margaritas, made with quality tequila, are large, soothing, and not for designated drivers. Besides the East Dayton location, look for Elsa's South at 6318 Far Hills Ave., tel. (937) 439-3817.

Giovanni's is a red-and-green storefront institution in Fairborn at 215 W. Main St., tel. (937) 878-1611. Patronized by Wright-Patterson Air Force Base fly boys and girls and by Wright State University students, the restaurant's award-winning pizza is a clear winner. A 7-inch personal pizza with cheese and three toppings goes for $4.75. Expect to spend about three times that for a large pizza with multiple toppings. Evenings, spaghetti is a favorite. A spaghetti-with-meat-sauce dinner includes roll and salad and sets diners back $8.25. Open for lunch and dinner.

One of the better informal places to eat in the Dayton area is **Wrapsody,** 298 N. Main St. (SR 48), Centerville, tel. (937) 435-1900). The wraps are tortillas filled with an intriguing variety of goodies, from steak tropicana to portobello mushrooms with bleu cheese to grilled veggies. A not-so-jumbo wrap is $2.95, a jumbo $4.95 to $5.45. The not-so is more than adequate for lunch. Accompanying the wraps are homemade chips with a choice of salsas ($1.75), and fruit smoothies or carrot juice blends (either is $2.95). Everything can be made to go and there's outside seating. Open for breakfast on weekends featuring a scrambled-egg wrap, and daily for lunch and dinner.

Kathy's Kitchen, 35 W. Center St., Germantown, tel. (937) 855-7150, is one of those small-town, home-cookin' restaurants travelers always hope to find. Germantown is located southwest of Dayton along SR 4, south of Miamisburg. Kathy is open for breakfast and lunch every day and for dinner every day but Sunday. In the morning, try sausage gravy and biscuits for $2.25 or a breakfast double-decker sandwich (ham, egg, bacon, lettuce, tomato, and cheese) for $4.15. The lunch and dinner menu meals are the same and feature daily specials such as cabbage rolls at $5.99 or a pair of four-ounce,

pan-fried pork chops for $6.25. One visit will confirm that this is where the locals like to dine.

The **Florentine Inn,** 21 W. Market St., also in Germantown, tel. (937) 855-7759, offers Continental meals. Steaks in several configurations are popular, with a New York strip priced at $13.50. Fresh walleye or halibut is $13.95. A pasta dish that sells well is chicken mozzarella with spinach fettucini at $11.95. Desserts are homemade and range in price from $2.95 to $3.95. They might be cream pies, fruit pies, or cake. Housed in a colonial red frame building ornamented with wrought iron, the Florentine is open for dinner Tues.-Sun. for dinner.

The **Tavernette,** 111 W. Main St., Medway, tel. (937) 849-0423, is one of those places where a visitor can relax with a drink, knowing the steak or seafood will be well prepared. Popular steak dinners here are the two sizes of filet mignon, $12.95 or $14.95. The seafood dinner most often ordered is deep-fried walleye at $12.95. The Tavernette is open for lunch Tues.-Sat. and for dinner Mon.-Sat. Tiny Medway is very near I-70/675 junction, northeast of Dayton.

The **Midway Restaurant** on US 40, north of Eaton and just west of SR 503 in Lewisburg, tel. (937) 962-2218, is locally famous for several menu items. The pork tenderloin steak sandwich is $3.50 and is the top selling sandwich in a part of Ohio that savors its pork. The onion rings are homemade and are either $1.50 or $1.95, depending on size. The pies are in great demand, too, selling for $2 per slice. The most popular breakfast item is sausage gravy and biscuits at either $1.75 or $2.50, depending on size. Unpretentious and with a perpetual oldies jukebox, the Midway is open for breakfast, lunch, and dinner every day.

Peerless Mill Inn, 319 S. Second St., Miamisburg, tel. (937) 866-5968. Near the banks of the Miami-Erie Canal, the Peerless has been a restaurant since the 1920s. It's a stylish and comfortable place to have an evening meal or Sunday brunch. The menu's most popular item may well be prime rib at $16.95. There's always a fish of the day: Halibut recently was priced at $18.95. Other meals are priced from $12.95 and can be a New York strip steak, seafood casserole, or duck.

Northeast of the Dayton area, **Thai West,** 6118 Chambersburg Rd., Huber Heights, tel.

(937) 237-7767, is one of a rapidly increasing number of tangy Thai eateries in the Buckeye State. The restaurant is a family-style place, serving electrifying red or green curries, with a choice of pork, beef, or chicken at $8.95 and shrimp at $10.45. Pad thai, the ubiquitous noodle dish fragrant with cilantro, scallions, and peanuts, is $8.95. One of the most overlooked items on a Thai menu are the soups, which are filling without being heavy. A popular soup here is *tom kha gai*, featuring chicken, coconut milk, and mushrooms, for $5.50. Cool it all down with a scoop of coconut ice cream at $3.50. Thai West is open Tues.-Sun. for lunch and dinner.

INFORMATION AND SERVICES

The emergency telephone number for fire, police, sheriff, highway patrol or emergency medical service is 911. The non-emergency number for Dayton police is (937) 222-9511. Miami Valley Hospital can be reached at (937) 208-8000. The main post office in downtown Dayton is at 1111 E. Fifth St., tel. (937) 227-1231.

The **Dayton/Montgomery County Convention and Visitors Bureau** is at One Chamber Plaza, tel. (937) 226-8211 or (800) 221-8234 (within Ohio). To find out what's doing on the University of Dayton campus at 300 College Park on the city's south side, call the student activities information line, tel. (937) 229-4141. Out Wright State University way, at 3640 Colonel Glenn Hwy. in Fairborn, try the general number, tel. (937) 775-3333. The thorough Wright Web site at www.wright.edu, carries current events under "What's New."

The *Dayton Daily News* offers "Go" every Thursday as its entertainment section. The *Daily News* is produced every morning. The *Beavercreek News-Current* is an evening and Saturday morning daily with a Thursday entertainment section. Fairborn reads the *Daily Herald* Mon.-Sat. evenings. For news, weather, and traffic information while at the wheel, tune to WHIO 1290 on the AM dial. Another AM station, WING (1410), broadcasts CNN news round the clock.

Transportation
The **Miami Valley RTA** can provide route and scheduling information to travelers who dial (937)

226-1144. There's a fresh crop of orange-and-yellow electric buses and a ride on either an electric or non-electric bus at the moment costs $1 for adults and 50 cents for children ages 6-12. The pavilion at 22 S. Main St. dispenses tokens and has route information posted. One nice thing about the MVRTA is the bike rack on the front of most buses. For regular fare, bike riders can plop their conveyances in the rack and ride through choking traffic to a pristine path on the other side of town. Those who want to go beyond the immediate area can reach **Greyhound Bus Lines** at (937) 224-1608. The Greyhound station in Dayton is at 111 E. Fifth St.

One of the more unusual ways to view parts of this sizeable city is to take a ride on one of Dayton's ducks. These amphibious vehicles with their blue, yellow, and white canopies ply the Great Miami River, giving passengers a perspective few have of the downtown area. The tours take place at noon, 2, and 4 p.m. on weekends from the Museum of Discovery, 2600 DeWeese Parkway. The cost is $12 for adults, $11 for seniors, and $10 for children 10 and under. For information and reservations, call (937) 275-9156.

A dozen miles north of Dayton, just off US 40 in Vandalia, is **James M. Cox-Dayton International Airport,** tel. (937) 454-8205. Airlines serving the Dayton area include America West, American, Continental, Delta, Northwest, TWA, United, and USAir. Several taxi, van, and limousine services move passengers between the airport and the city. A typical one-way fare is $20 to or from downtown.

Shopping
To shop downtown, or at the mall—that is the question. Elder-Beerman maintains a department-store presence at the Courthouse Plaza, Second and Ludlow Streets in the city, tel. (937) 224-8000. Mallwise, look to Dayton Mall, 2700 Miamisburg-Centerville Rd., tel. (937) 433-9833. This facility is accessible from either I-75, Exit 44, or I-675, Exit 2. The Mall at Fairfield Commons is at 2727 Fairfield Commons, in Beavercreek, tel. (937) 427-4300. Beavercreek is the westernmost municipality in Greene County and is separated from the rest of the Dayton metro area on the west by I-675. There are several especially nice retail areas along Far Hills Avenue (SR 48) in Kettering. An unusual retail emporium can be

found in the Town & Country Shopping Center at Far Hills Avenue and Stroop Road. The Dayton Art Institute has a **museum store** there, apparently for shoppers who want arty items but don't want to go all the way downtown. A bit farther out is **Bellair Country Stores,** 1490 N. Fairfield Rd., Beavercreek, tel. (937) 426-0788. Built around a 100-year-old farmhouse, the complex feature antiques, crafts, and gourmet food, and there's a restaurant on the premises.

ALONG THE OHIO RIVER

In contrast to many U.S. rivers, the Ohio River is the result of two sizeable bodies of water joining each other: the Allegheny and the Monongahela Rivers meet in downtown Pittsburgh, Pennsylvania to form the beginning of the Ohio River. From that point, the Ohio moves generally southwest for 981 miles before emptying into the Mississippi River at Cairo, Illinois. Between western Pennsylvania and southern Illinois lies the Ohio River Basin, home to one American in 10. There are 20 dams and 49 power-generating facilities along its length, and the river provides a minimum depth of nine feet for commercial navigation. More than 230 million tons of cargo go up or down the Ohio each year, and about 70% of that total is coal or some other energy product moving by barge.

Despite the activity, water quality is better than it's been for nearly 200 years. From about 1810, when people migrated to Pittsburgh in some numbers, water quality began to decline. By the 1940s, a combination of industrial pollution, raw sewage, and mine waste created a river virtually devoid of healthy living things. The pH value, a measure of acidity and water quality, dropped to a highly acidic value of 4.0 in the upper Ohio (pure water has a pH value of 7.0), with coliform bacteria population from untreated sewage measuring a scary 20,000 per 100 milliliters of water.

Cleanup began on a large scale in the late 1940s as a result of years of illness from waterborne disease. Sewage-treatment plants were built in encouraging numbers, the 1972 federal Clean Water Act forced industries to clean up discharges, and by the mid-1970s the Ohio had made a striking recovery. Fish populations rebounded dramatically, though species that feed on the bottom of the river continue to be harmed by sediments containing high levels of PCBs and chlordane. Consequently, game fish are safe to eat, but wild-caught bottom-dwellers such as carp and channel catfish should never be consumed. The river is a source of drinking water for more than three million people.

Vacationers can closely follow the twists and turns of the Ohio on roads that are mostly two lane and rarely heavily traveled. The riverside trip from the Pennsylvania state line to Indiana is approximately 475 miles. There are several days' worth of interesting sights along the route, which starts at a point as far north as New York City and dips to a spot farther south than Washington, D.C.

Traveling through Ohio from Pennsylvania to Indiana can be a sobering experience. Refineries, mills, powerplants, locks and dams, and high-tension wires sometimes impede the view, preventing travelers from seeing this broad, brown ribbon for what it once was: a passageway of opportunity for generations of westward-bound traders and settlers. Still, there's a certain muddy charm to the river today, whether it flows past tough small-town kids practicing high school football or their aging steelworker parents resting on the front steps. Both generations may have been chased away from their homes at one time or another by rising water. Despite lives that frequently are hard, the people who live near the river have taken care to preserve the past. And they have backed efforts to improve the quality of the endlessly flowing water.

Orientation

Shadowing the big river from one end of Ohio to the other is a snap. In East Liverpool, catch southbound SR 7. Stay on SR 7 through Steubenville, past Wheeling, and along Wayne National Forest to a point 21 miles west of Marietta. From there, SR 7 continues west and river devotees head south on SR 124. After a 56-mile run on SR 124, the less traveled highway rejoins SR 7, which returns to the north bank for 67 miles, passing Gallipolis before disappearing at a point roughly across the river from Huntingtown, West Virginia. The riverside route becomes US 52, rolling through Portsmouth and several smaller towns before turning northwest in downtown Cincinnati. The final 21 miles of the drive takes place on US 50. (The route west of Portsmouth to the Indiana border along US 52 and US 50 is covered in the **Ohio River West** section in the previous chapter.) Major area interstate highways include I-70, I-71, I-75, and I-77.

UPPER OHIO RIVER

George Thorogood covers a song, "Smokestack Lightning" (cut number nine on the *Born to Be Bad* CD), that may have had as its inspiration a big chimney in tiny Stratton, north of Steubenville. The Ohio Edison smokestack is alive with bursts of warning lights because planes frequent Pittsburgh International Airport, several miles to the east. The smokestack, occasional industry, and a few towns are the only reminders of the 20th century along this stretch of the upper Ohio River between East Liverpool and Marietta. The trip is most intensively bucolic south of I-70, winding several miles through preserved forest before bursting out of the woods and into the pretty riverside clearing that has become Marietta.

EAST LIVERPOOL AND VICINITY

Perhaps the least impressive thoroughfare entering the Buckeye State is Pennsylvania SR 68. It slithers into East Liverpool before becoming SR 39, a narrow, ill-paved small-city street that hooks up with SR 7, then heads south along the Ohio toward Steubenville. East Liverpool is an aged little town of about 13,500, typical of a part of the country where the land, the air, and the water were taxed to their limits to feed

dying—or long-gone—industries. The center of America's pottery business in 1900, with 20,000 residents at the time, this municipality is surrounded by some very pleasant, unspoiled countryside.

Sights

Stop first at the **Museum of Ceramics,** 400 E. Fifth St., tel. (330) 386-6001, a sleeper of an Ohio Historical Society site. Housed in the former post office, the fascinating museum is much more than an old building filled with tired artifacts. Rather, it tells a story in words and pictures of how East Liverpool and vicinity bloomed and then wilted as America's pottery source. The faces that peer out from old photos and the hand-painted designs on the various pieces on display make pottery workers almost eerily alive, despite the fact that few artisans have produced such products here since the Great Depression. At a time in which there were more favorable foreign-trade barriers, 90% of all working persons in the town were part of the pottery business. Besides producing beautiful yellow ware, Rockingham pottery, and bone china, the industry helped raise several substantial downtown buildings and some nice old homes. Museum hours are Wed.-Sat. 9:30 a.m.-5 p.m.,

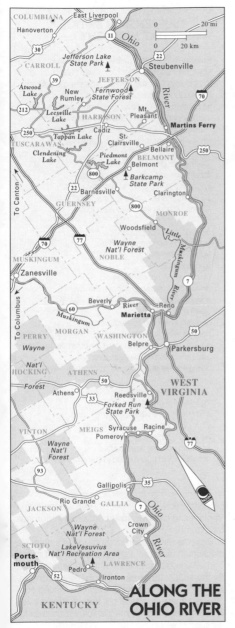

ALONG THE OHIO RIVER

Sunday and holidays noon-5 p.m. Admission fees are $5 for adults, $4.50 for seniors, and $1.25 for children.

In town for the evening? Catch a performance by the **Pottery Players Theatre,** 415 Market St., tel. (330) 385-5400. This small but dedicated band of locals presents five main-stage productions and at least two directors' specials every year. Recently, the repertoire has included *The Music Man, Schoolhouse Rock Live,* and *Steel Magnolias.* The theater is the former phone company and seats only 90 (per the fire code), so call well in advance for tickets. They cost $6 for adults and $5 for seniors and children.

Beaver Creek State Park, 12021 Echo Dell Rd., about 10 miles north of East Liverpool and just east of SR 7, is an extremely attractive place, tel. (330) 385-3091. Sizeable hills, sandstone cliffs, sighing pines, and the state's first stream in the Wild and Scenic Rivers system makes this a most pleasant destination, particularly on weekdays, when it's virtually deserted. Activities include horseback riding, fishing, hunting, hiking, and camping. A restored mill and several renovated buildings also are on the 3,038 acres of land. The webs of hiking and bridle trails are extensive, and Beaver Creek Meadows Golf Course is adjacent for those who thought to bring their clubs.

Guilford Lake, 6835 E. Lake Rd., Lisbon, tel. (330) 222-1712, is a site of considerable historic significance. John Hunt Morgan, the rebel general who cut a swath across southern Ohio in 1863, was captured in the vicinity of this quiet state park. The lake originally was constructed in 1834 as a reservoir for the Sandy and Beaver Canal. The state purchased the site in 1927 and Depression-era labor completed the dam in 1932. The park totals 396 acres (92 of which are water), offering a 600-foot swimming beach, camping, boating, a half-mile hiking trail, picnicking, and fishing for bass, bluegill, crappie, and channel catfish. A marsh, the remains of an ancient glacial lake, formerly occupied the site. Guilford is north of US 30 on SR 172, east of SR 9, about two miles west of Lisbon, and 20 miles northwest of East Liverpool.

Food

There are a couple of restaurants worth consideration before following the river south toward

Steubenville. One is **Yanni's Cafe,** tel. (330) 385-0082, an authentic Italian spot at 105 E. Sixth St. Open six days a week for dinner and weekdays for lunch, the angel-hair pasta with a tossed salad for just $3.99 at lunch is a hit. Spaghetti and meatballs are $5.50 in the evening. Closed Sunday. The other is the **Fifth Street Sampler,** 206 E. Fifth St., tel. (330) 385-7115, a worthy destination that creates delectable soups and sandwiches. Try the crab bisque, a mere $1.50 per cup or $2.50 per bowl, or the large and popular club sandwich, assembled on marble rye for $5.95, with a choice of sides such as pasta, green salad, or fresh fruit in season. The Sampler is open for breakfast and lunch during the week and from lunch until 5 p.m. Saturday.

STEUBENVILLE AND VICINITY

The drive from East Liverpool is four lanes and nice enough, but a more striking way to enter Steubenville is by car from Wierton, West Virginia. That's because US 22 crosses the Ohio River here via an 820-foot cable-stayed bridge that's as glitzy a structure as a traveler is apt to see. A wonder of shiny struts and strands, the bridge was completed in 1990. Once on the west side of the river, the venerable town of about 22,000 residents has a couple of pleasant surprises. The most visual are 26 huge murals painted to recall the city's history. The murals were created by a number of different artists on virtually every hard, vertical, accessible exterior surface in the downtown area. A nice approach to see them all is to meander up and down the city streets, stumbling on them as you come to them (tours of the murals are also available). It's a tribute to Steubenville's character that these murals remain grafitti-free.

History

Steubenville began life in 1786 as a simple blockhouse. It was called Fort Steuben, named after a Revolutionary War hero, but it was little more than a lone building surrounded by wooden fence. The site served as a place where surveyors could rest before or after sizing up the new Northwest Territory. The surveyors abandoned the site, but it was re-established in 1797 by Virginia pioneers. The modest clearing saw

---

SUSPENSION BRIDGE AT MIDNIGHT

Edwina Pendarvis teaches at Marshall University in Huntington, West Virginia. This poem of hers shows that the bridges spanning the Ohio River play key roles in the lives of those who live near them. The following is from *human landscapes,* published in 1997 by Bottom Dog Press, Huron, Ohio. Pendarvis is one of three poets whose work makes up the book.

The new bridge across the Ohio
tapers upward like a white pavilion,
spanning the space between two states.
Slung from steel cables, it's a slender spire
lifting traffic skyward like a song.

No wonder a young drunk
walking home late one night
from Huntington
to Proctorville
lost his sense of direction
on the dark road high above the river—
a single moon overhead,
one in the water below,
two lights burning toward him
then passing him slowly by—
no wonder a sudden longing drew him to the rail,
and he fell like a Chinese poet
diving for the pearly moon beneath the waves.

The mountains here
look like the mountains of China,
and rivers are everywhere the same.
Drunk on rice wine or moonshine,
we all risk drowning,
traveling our wayward path
uncertain and suspended in the singing light.

---

potential settlers pour out of Pennsylvania and Virginia and pass westward into the wilderness for a number of years.

Basic services soon sprang up—a sawmill, a blacksmith, a bank, a general store, and more. The village became known for its woolen mill. By the 1830s, laborers in Steubenville were agitating for better pay and improved working conditions. However, a brief but intense depression in 1837 weakened the mechanics' association for several years. Steubenville citizenry at about this time petitioned the state to be included in the new canal system; promises were made, but no canal was ever constructed.

Nevertheless, immigrants traveled the National Road (now US 40) as far west as Wheeling, then frequently turned right for 26 miles up the Ohio to settle in Steubenville. The steel industry employed many newcomers, making the small city among the most heavily first-generation European in a very ethnic state. To this day, many of Steubenville's churches trace their roots to central Europe. Some who weren't in church were engaged in naughty activities: Prohibition in the 1920s brought not only illegal drink, but gambling and prostitution to the town. The end of Prohibition in 1933 failed to curb organized crime.

After Steubenville's mills gave their all to support the troops in World War II, the city fell on hard times. Steel and other industries declined, their processes outmoded. In the 1970s, these old industries contributed to the federal government's declaration that Steubenville and the Ohio Valley had the nation's worst air. People departed the city not only because there were no jobs but because they tired of seeing what they were breathing—inversion layers sometimes trapped smoke and stench near the ground, killing the infirm and the elderly.

Happily, the surviving industries are cleaning up their acts. No longer does West Virginia threaten to sue Ohio over pollution matters. And while Steubenville depends more on services and less on heavy industry, it is a cleaner and healthier place, with picturesque 19th-century buildings perched high above the passing stream.

Sights

The **Custer State Monument** marks the place where William Armstrong Custer was born in 1839, in New Rumley. This tiny village is on SR 646, 35 miles west of Steubenville. A modest monument in a tiny town, the Custer salute contrasts well with Cadiz, 10 miles to the south on US 22. That's the 1901 birthplace of **Clark Gable,** a Hollywood leading man if ever there was one. His boyhood home, where reconstruction was completed in 1998, is at 103 Charleston St., Cadiz. Free tours are available at varying times since the home is staffed by volunteers. For more information call the Clark Gable Foundation in Cadiz at (740) 942-4989.

The **Welsh Jaguar Classic Car Museum,** 501 Washington St., Steubenville, tel. (740) 283-9723, is another Steubenville surprise. Open noon-6 p.m. Thurs.-Sun. (longer hours in summer), the museum displays a rotating selection of 18 cars. At any given moment, the exhibit can include a dozen Jaguars, a Mercedes-Benz gull wing 300SL, or even the pink Cadillac formerly owned by candy magnate Frank Brach's heiress widow, Helen Brach (née Helen Voorhees, from the Steubenville area), who disappeared under

Murals depicting Steubenville's past are a common sight throughout the city.

CLARK GABLE'S HOMETOWN~CADIZ, OHIO

It started with a telephone call from a disk jockey. A fellow from a radio station in Quincy, Illinois, dialed up the Cadiz, Ohio, post office on February 1, 1984, to ask a postal worker whose birthday it might be. The postal worker had no idea and said so. The DJ reported that it was Clark Gable's birthday and wondered what the late star's hometown was doing to celebrate.

That was the last time no one in this small coal-mining town knew who was born on Feb. 1. In 1985, a women's group organized the first annual "Clark Gable Birthday Celebration." Despite the fact that a terrible ice storm hit the day before, some 300 hardy townspeople and devoted fans showed up to toast the movie idol. Gable was born here in 1901 and spent several boyhood years in nearby Hopedale before eventually finding his way to Hollywood and the silver screen. He died in 1960.

Realization of Gable's roots in Cadiz came along at an opportune time for the town. In the late 1970s, the market for high-sulfur coal, mined nearby, went

away. Cleaner-burning coal from the western U.S. put many Cadiz residents out of work; in 1985 the unemployment rate reached 25%. Community spirit was rekindled in the mid-1980s when the Clark Gable Foundation discovered that the star's birthplace had been torn down. Consequently, the organization's first goal was to erect a monument on the site. Somehow, the foundation and the community raised $7,000 and a handsome stone was dedicated on February 1, 1986.

Since then, the birthday party has attracted several actors who were in *Gone with the Wind*, the Civil War epic that made Gable a superstar for his portrayal of Rhett Butler. Equally exciting, Gable's only son, John Clark Gable, came to Cadiz to toast his dad. In 1998 he helped dedicated Gable's birthplace, which has been reconstructed and opened as a theater/museum. Gable never returned to eastern Ohio, but the mere fact that he was born here has brought attention to the town and enjoyment to residents, fans, and travelers.

---

very suspicious circumstances in February 1977 (and whose story is undyingly popular with unsolved-mysteries TV programs). Uniquely, the cars on display are all also for sale. Museum admission is $1. If you're lucky enough to already own a Jaguar, the on-site **warehouse,** tel. (740) 282-8649, which devotes some 50,000 square feet to Jaguar parts, from the oldest to the newest, may be worth a stop as well.

Fernwood State Forest is a dozen miles southwest of Steubenville, off SR 151. Activities include fishing, hunting, trapshooting, hiking, horseback riding, camping, and an interpretive nature trail; the entire area covers over 2,107 acres. Call (740) 264-5671 to learn more.

Jefferson Lake State Park is approximately 11 miles northwest of Steubenville on SR 1 north off SR 43. Some 945 acres in size, this park is a haven for birds large and small. Wild turkey, ruffed grouse, and other birds call this area home. So do folks who like to fish, swim, picnic, and hike. Though the dammed, artificial lake measures just 17 acres, it contains respectable numbers of largemouth bass, catfish, and others. Besides nearly 100 standard campsites, campers can take advantage of Ohio's swell Rent-A-Camp

program. Show up, pay a few bucks, and enjoy a tent, a dining fly, cookstove, and additional gear. No search for a site, no tent to erect or take down, this is as close to an exertion free night outdoors as travelers are apt to find. Call the park headquarters at (740) 765-4459 for more information on the Rent-A-Camp program as well as other park offerings.

Accommodations
East Liverpool and Steubenville have a number of unremarkable local motels, with Steubenville offering the moderately priced **Holiday Inn,** 1401 University Blvd, tel. (740) 282-0901 and an inexpensive **Super 8,** 1505 University Blvd., tel. (740) 282-4565. The **Twi-Lite Motel,** 1201 University Blvd., Steubenville, tel. (740) 282-9725, has live entertainment Friday and Saturday from about 10 p.m. The house band plays classic rock, blues, and country in the lounge. There is no cover charge.

There are bed and breakfast operations in the area, none more unique than **Granny's Shanty,** 921 Ohio Ave., East Liverpool, tel. (330) 385-7722. Open weekends only, the moderately priced five bedroom facility plays host to Saturday night murder mysteries with period clothing and an elegant dinner. For those who'd rather not look for clues and villains, try **Heavilin's Bed and Breakfast,** 40707 Cadiz-Dennison Rd., Cadiz, tel. (740) 942-3572. Heavilin's has three spotless, moderately priced rooms in a big white Victorian farmhouse. The **Lamp Post,** 372 Canton Rd., Wintersville, tel. (740) 264-0591, may be Ohio's best B&B buy: A double is $46, a single is $36, and those rates include full breakfasts! Book ahead, as others are aware of this value just west of Steubenville. Try the Lamp Post's Web site at users.1st.net/lamppost.

Food

Jaggin' Around Restaurant and Pub, 501 Washington St., Steubenville, tel. (740) 282-1010. Forget the too-playful name (the restaurant is in the same building as the Welsh Jaguar museum, described above) and concentrate on sandwiches, pasta, and steak in this downtown facility. Pleasant fare at lunch includes a steak salad or a mesquite chicken salad; either is $5.95. Pastas come in several varieties each evening and are priced from $6.95 to $9.95. The place is casual, attractive, and open for lunch and dinner.

Spread Eagle Tavern & Inn, 10150 Historic Plymouth St., Hanoverton, tel. (330) 223-1583. Both a restaurant and a place to spend the night, this handsome colonial brick establishment serves fresh seafood and smokes all its own meats. Popular entrees include lobster in puff pastry for $28 and prime rib in several sizes from $22.95 to $28. The chef conjures up three or four daily specials, from tuna to twin tournedos of beef. There's a rathskellar with live piano music

EAST LIVERPOOL AND STEUBENVILLE EVENTS

FEBRUARY

A dinner dance is held every February 1 in Cadiz to salute **Clark Gable's Birthday.** Celebrities who have attended past events include Gable's son and members of the cast of *Gone with the Wind.* For more information call the Clark Gable Foundation in Cadiz at (740) 942-4989.

MARCH

Wellsville's **Spring Craft Show** observes free admission and takes place in the Alumni Center. Call (330) 532-2731 for details.

MAY

A **Victorian Spring Craft Workshop** is held in the Museum of Ceramics, 400 E. Fifth St., East Liverpool. There's a fee for this three-hour learning session. Call (330) 386-6003 to find out more.

19th Century Tea Party, Museum of Ceramics, 400 E. Fifth St., East Liverpool. This is a tea party for kids and moms on Mothers Day. Call (330) 386-6003 for particulars.

JUNE

Dean Martin Festival, Steubenville. The late singer-actor-entertainer's fans prowl his hometown, collecting memorabilia and dispensing anecdotes. Call (740) 283-4395 for a list of scheduled events.

Tri-State Pottery Festival, tel. (330) 385-0845, occurs in downtown East Liverpool. Check the food, rides, displays, and entertainment.

JULY

Summer Fun-Cational Children's Program, Museum of Ceramics, 400 E. Fifth St., East Liverpool. This "day camp" gives children a hands-on view of Ohio history. Call (330) 386-6001 to learn about fees, hours, and activities.

SEPTEMBER

Ethnic Festival, Thompson Park, East Liverpool, tel. (330) 385-0845. Ethnic foods, artists, crafts and crafters, and entertainment take place mid-month here.

The **International Mining and Manufacturing Festival** is set for Cadiz, 26 miles west of Steubenville on US 22. In existence for more than 30 years, the four-day fest has separate parades for industry and for the queen, plus country and jazz music, food, a pizza-eating contest, and lots of huge coal-excavating equipment on display. Call (614) 942-2082 to find out more.

OCTOBER

Carrollton, some 35 miles west of East Liverpool on SR 39, is the scene of the **Algonquin Mill Fall Festival.** This Carroll County Historical Society event commemorates grist milling and features free entertainment, antique vehicle displays, home-cooked foods, and demonstrations. Contact the society at (330) 627-5910 for more information.

on weekends. Lunch and dinner are served every day at the Spread Eagle, which is 25 miles west of East Liverpool, just off US 30.

Information and Services
For police, fire or medical emergencies, call 911. Otherwise, the East Liverpool police can be reached at (330) 385-1234. The non-emergency number for Steubenville authorities is (740) 282-5353. East Liverpool City Hospital is at (330) 385-7200. Steubenville's Ohio Valley Hospital is at (740) 283-7000. The post office in East Liverpool is at 700 Dresden Ave. The post office in Steubenville is at 150 N. Third St.

The **East Liverpool Area Chamber of Commerce** is at 120 W. Sixth St., tel. (740) 385-0845. The **Steubenville Convention and Visitors Bureau** is at 501 Washington St., tel. (740) 283-4935.

East Liverpool's daily newspaper is the *Evening Review,* which offers entertainment listings in the Thursday edition. Steubenville's contribution to daily journalism is the morning *Herald Star,* also covering entertainment every Thursday.

MARTINS FERRY TO MARIETTA

Belmont County is one of those busy places that always seems to grow where one state ends and another begins. There's precious little except 80 miles of scenic highway between the Belmont County area and Marietta. A nice stop might be Sunfish Creek State Forest (see below). Wayne National Forest's easternmost flank begins here, near the village of Sardis. The big forest is detailed below, too. As for Marietta, the first capital of the old Northwest Territory bills itself as "the start of it all." The city of 15,000 is located where the Muskingum River meets the Ohio. It is attractive and well kept, deriving much of its income from visitors.

History
The Belmont County area was in dispute long before the Revolutionary War. Many settlers crossed the Ohio River here, which led to several skirmishes with the resident Indians, and was the subject of some contention in the French and Indian War, when George Washington, a British soldier-colonist at the time, pitched a tent in the vicinity of what is now Powhatan Point on

the Ohio's west bank. The areas that are Martins Ferry, Bridgeport, and Bellaire served as places to take a breath after having been ferried across the Ohio River. The towns evolved into steelmaking centers that were both rugged and productive. Today, interstate commerce accounts for much of the county's activities.

Marietta was founded in 1788 by 48 pioneers who arrived on a flatboat. The city was named after Marie Antoinette, who was seen as something of a heroine at the time. The town was the original headquarters of the old Northwest Territory, which accounts in part for the majestic buildings. As such, it became more of an administrative center and a jumping-off point than a metropolis. Marietta College was established in 1835 and oil and gas were transferred to riverboats here after being discovered farther north along the Muskingum. Today's Marietta is a wonderful example of a preserved town now in its third century of existence.

The second-oldest town in Ohio is Belpre, 13 miles downriver from Marietta and on the riverbank opposite Parkersburg, West Virginia. Its reputation as a historic area is growing, abetted by several wonderful old houses, a few of which date from before 1800.

Location and Orientation
Belmont County is separated from the West Virginia panhandle by the Ohio River. Besides US 40, the area is served by I-70 and by river-hugging SR 7. The county line is approximately 125 miles east of Columbus and about 60 miles southwest of Pittsburgh. Marietta looks also looks across the Ohio to West Virginia; it is less than a dozen miles upriver from Parkersburg, West Virginia. The city is 125 miles southeast of Columbus, 165 miles south of Cleveland, and 235 miles east of Cincinnati. Highways servicing Marietta include I-77, which runs north and south; SR 7, which tracks the river; scenic SR 550 between Marietta and Athens; SR 60 to Zanesville; and SR 26, which winds its way into the city from the northeast, among covered bridges in Wayne National Forest.

Sights
While visiting the village of Belmont, consider a stop at **Dysart Woods.** This dense, 50-acre area of moss-covered trees is exactly what the

Built in 1848, the Castle is a classic Gothic Revival-style mansion, one of many examples of fine architecture in Marietta.

area was like more than 200 years ago, primarily because it has never been logged or otherwise touched. Nor has the substrata been mined, which brings up a controversy. Locals fear that the original-growth stands of white and red oak, beech, cherry, tulip poplar, ash, and sugar maple are in danger. That's because the land beneath the trees, which soar as high as 100 feet and run to four feet in diameter, may soon be mined. Ohio University, which has a campus here, owns the woods. But the Ohio Valley Coal Company could exercise mining rights on a rich coal seam deep beneath the trees. Environmentalists believe that a mine could drop the water table, killing off this patch of forest which was preserved by several generations of the Dysart family before it became university property. At the moment, coal operations are half a mile away. It might be a good idea to see this authentic cluster of pre-European America sooner rather than later. Dysart Woods is some 20 miles west of the river, 4.5 miles east of Belmont, off SR 147.

Travelers who like atmospheric history should visit the **Gay '90s Mansion,** 532 N. Chestnut St., Barnesville, tel. (740) 425-3505 or (740) 425-2926, which serves as Belmont County's museum. The 26-room former home has more wood in its mantels alone than most modern houses have in their entirety. The quality and quantity of craftsmanship in this building is a major reason why it has won awards. It's open Thurs.-Sun. 1-4:30 p.m., May-Oct. Admission is $4 for adults and $1 for children.

Barkcamp State Park is just south of I-70 on SR 149, about 17 miles west of the Ohio River, tel. (740) 484-4064. Small as state parks go, Barkcamp nevertheless offers a bridle trail, hunting, fishing, swimming, and a fishing pier for handicapped persons. The naturalists are especially knowledgeable. Between the park and St. Clairsville, just off the interstate on SR 331, is the Shaeffer-Campbell covered bridge. It's one of the state's most accessible.

Quaker Meeting House State Monument is easiest to reach from Martins Ferry. Once there, catch SR 647 in the middle of town. The road twists and turns for nine miles as it heads northwest to the village of Mount Pleasant. Travelers will find the meeting house at the far end of this gem of a well-kept village. Smaller than many elementary-school gymnasiums, the old brick building somehow accommodated 2,000 members of the Society of Friends, segregated by sex, for important 19th-century confabs. The site is no longer used for meetings, nor is it open regularly for visits.

Sunfish Creek State Forest, in Monroe County just west of SR 7, is a 637-acre site that's not only seldom visited but misleadingly named. The forest's primary recreational activity is hunting; the creek can be too shallow for fishing much of the year. While in Monroe County, consider a side trip to Woodsfield, 18 miles west of the river on SR 78. Besides seeing a pleasant town, visitors can pivot southward in this county seat, reaching Marietta by driving through a sizeable stretch of Wayne National Forest.

Wayne National Forest may first be seen by unfolding a map of the state. Three large and distinct shaded areas indicate where separate parcels of the forest are found—near Marietta, around Athens, and west of Gallipolis. The total forest covers one-quarter million acres of Appalachian foothills. A nice introduction to this vast expanse is the drive from New Martinsville, West Virginia, to Woodsfield on State Routes 536 and 78. Catch SR 26 in Woodsfield and head south, a scenic drive through the forest, following the Little Muskingum River for more than 20 miles. (Do bear in mind, though, that you can go some distance on this drive between towns. Plan ahead, and allow plenty of time.) Once visitors get a feel for this place, they may want to spend more time.

Half a dozen covered bridges greet hikers, along with several nice camping units, a horse trail, and a stretch of the Buckeye Trail, much of which runs between the Little Muskingum and the Ohio Rivers. Amateur botanists who traverse the area at less than highway speeds will see a number of rare forest flowers, and there's always a chance that an endangered animal, such as a bobcat, might be spotted amid the hickory, sycamore, oak, loblolly pine, and other tall trees. For more information plus helpful pamphlets and good advice, visit the U.S. Forest Service's Marietta office, three miles east of the city in the little village of Reno on the south side of SR 7, opposite the Highway Patrol barracks, tel. (740) 373-9055.

Drivers following the Ohio River have a second opportunity to visit Wayne National Forest downstream. The southernmost section covers parts of Gallia, Jackson, Lawrence, and Scioto Counties, nudging up to the big river at Crown City and at a point just west of Ironton. The U.S. Forest Service Wayne National Forest Ironton district office is at 6518 SR 93, tel. (740) 532-3223, within the

THE RUIN OF BLENNERHASSETT ISLAND

Once past the village of Belpre, heading west on SR 7, keep an eye on the river. Close to the West Virginia shore lies Blennerhassett Island, a low, forested strip of land with an intriguing tale behind it. Harmann Blennerhassett was an Englishman with a pocketful of money gained by selling the family estate and sailing to America. Arriving here in 1798, Harmann and his family headed for the frontier. On impulse, Blennerhassett bought this 500-acre island and built a magnificent house on it.

For several years, the Blennerhassett landing was seen as an important stopover on the way west. The family was generous, entertaining lavishly. But in 1805, a year after he killed Alexander Hamilton in a duel, Aaron Burr spent the night and changed Blennerhassett's life—very much for the worse. The former vice president was a smooth talker, and he spoke of buying a marshalling area in Louisiana so that he could invade and conquer

Aaron Burr (1756-1836)

Mexico. Blennerhassett, lanky and almost blind, was caught up in tales of cities filled with gold. He happily bought Burr thousands of dollars in supplies and gave him money to recruit soldiers. Burr headed downriver. Blennerhassett soon learned that not only was Burr's scheme illegal but also that the federal government was actively arresting participants! Finally, troops landed on the island and took control of it. The Blennerhassetts managed to escape, but their abandoned house and grounds were looted, then burned. Only a well and traces of a foundation remain. There's a charge to dock on the island, but the fee does permit campers to stay overnight. Much of the island is planted in crops, and a dam connects the site to West Virginia. A modest marker tells of Blennerhassett's decline and fall, though there is a replica of Blennerhassett's 13-room Palladian mansion that is open for tours. For more information, call (304) 420-4800.

boundaries of the national forest in Pedro. To get there, take SR 93 north from Ironton.

Once in the pretty, red-brick city of Marietta, there are two institutions which put everything in a nice historical context. They are **Campus Martius Museum,** Second and Washington Streets, tel. (740) 373-3750, and the **Ohio River Museum,** 601 Front St., tel. (740) 373-3750 or (800) 686-1545. The former was a fort built between 1788 and 1791. Briefly, it served as the seat of government for the entire Northwest Territory. The modern, Federal-style museum houses the original fortifications, plus every kind of artifact, from maps to wagons. There is information, too, about very early (800 B.C.-A.D. 100) local moundbuilders. The river museum has its own steamboat, the *W.P. Snyder, Jr.,* anchored nearby, plus a number of adventure-related displays from the Ohio down through the years. Admission for either facility is $4 for adults and $1 for children. Both museums close Nov. 30 and reopen March 1.

A couple of what might be construed as factory tours should be considered while in the Marietta area. One is **Rossi Pasta,** 114 Greene St., tel. (740) 376-2065 or (800) 227-6774, where visitors can cruise the place that handmakes pasta sold by the Greenbrier, Harry & David, Williams-Sonoma, and Macy's. The product is for sale in many colors and configurations. Handiwork also is in evidence at **Lee Middleton Original Dolls,** 1301 Washington Blvd., in Delpre (about 12 miles south of Marietta along SR 7), tel. (740) 423-1481 or (800) 233-7479. Employees skillfully paint faces on lifelike dolls, which are for sale. Rossi Pasta is open every day; the doll factory is open weekdays (the outlet store is open Mon.-Sat.). Also in Belpre, **Lloyd Middleton Dolls,** 2005 Washington Blvd., tel. (740) 423-8599 or (800) 845-1845, is open Mon.-Sat. (Aside to the inquisitive: Lloyd and the late Lee were husband and wife before going their separate ways in 1990.)

Culture

Give it up for the **Becky Thatcher Showboat,** 237 Front St., Marietta, tel. (740) 373-6033, where melodramas are presented on a regular basis. Professional actors strut their stuff in the summer and fall, creating an atmosphere not common on the river for more than a century. Shows are scheduled every day but Sunday in July and August. Admission is $15 for reserved seats, $12 for general admission and $10 for students and seniors. Travelers who suspend their disbelief, hissing villains, are in for an enjoyable time. Recent productions have included *Sweeney Todd* and *Mischief in the Magnolias.*

Mid-Ohio Valley Players, Inc., 229 Putnam St., Marietta, tel. (740) 374-9434, stages seven productions in a season that runs from mid-October to late June. Recent offerings have included *Shadowlands* and *Beau Jest.* Two of the seven productions are primarily for children. The curtain parts at 8 p.m. (7 p.m. for children's presentations). Admission is $8 for adults, $7 for students and seniors, and $3 for anyone under 18.

Recreation

Beginning at the west edge of Belmont County and proceeding north are five big **lakes** in the Muskingum Watershed Conservancy District. They are, south to north, Piedmont, Clendening, Tappan, Leesville, and Atwood, and they cover a distance of about 40 miles. All offer fishing and boating, there are a few swimming beaches, and hunters are welcome in season in Leesville Lake's wildlife area. Piedmont Lake is three miles north of I-70 and can be reached by exiting SR 800 north.

What with Queen Anne, Federal, and Colonial architecture all over the place, Marietta is nice to view **on foot.** (Check out the **Castle** at 418 Fourth St. as an example.) Hills rise away from the river, but the downtown area parallel to the Ohio or the Muskingum is of course quite level. The levee is accessible and appears to be where locals bent on everything from airing babies to training for marathons show up. Another scenic and educational site is around Marietta College, 215 Fifth St., with a tree-tour brochure of the campus in hand. Some 45 varieties can be spotted in a walk that should take no more than an hour. (At the right time of year, tree No. 27 yields its buckeyes.) Finally, 40 miles of hiking trails abound in the eastern segment of Wayne National Forest. Obtain maps at the office in Reno.

Got your golf clubs in the car? Check out **Hill and Dale Golf Course,** west of St. Clairsville on the south side of US 40, tel. (740) 695-9018. It is a nine-hole facility. Par is 29 for men, 30 for women, and greens fees are $6. Golfers have a choice of at least two Marietta-area courses: **Lakeside Golf Course,** SR 60, in Beverly (northwest of Marietta along SR 60), tel. (740) 984-4265, and **Oxbow Golf & Country Club,** CR 85, Belpre, tel. (740) 423-6771. Lakeside is a par 70 and sets greens fees on weekdays at $10 and $15 for nine and 18 holes, respectively, and $13 and $18 for nine and 18 holes played on weekends. Carts are an extra $5 per nine holes. Oxbow's par 71 course costs $27 with a cart and $15 without for an 18-hole round Mon.-Thurs. Ante up $32 and $20, respectively, Fri.-Sun. for cart and no-cart play.

With two rivers just on the other side of the levee, **watersports** are a big deal. The only rental facilities in the area are back in Wayne County. Rates vary according to trip length, but the least expensive is $5 for adults and $1 for children for a 45-minute trip. Four different covered bridges span the Little Muskingum within paddling distance. Wingett Run is 20 miles northeast of Marietta along SR 26.

Accommodations

Interstate 70 being a busy place, there are a number of spots in Belmont County that greet the sleepy. Franchises include **Days Inn, Hampton Inn, Holiday Express, Knights Inn, Red Roof Inn,** and **Super 8 Motel,** all within a stone's throw of the big highway. Non-franchise motels are here too, and there are bed and breakfast facilities at strategic points around the county. Consider such B&Bs as **Georgian Pillars,** 128 E. Walnut St., tel. (614) 425-3741, or the **Gingerbread House,** 501 E. Main St., tel. (614) 425-2773, both of which are in Barnesville. Martins Ferry is the locale for **Ivy Inn,** 46 N. Fourth St., tel. (614) 633-3396 evenings or (614) 633-0316 days, and the highly rated **Mulberry Inn,** 53 N. Fourth St., tel. (614) 633-6058 or (800) 705-6171, ext. 3136. Motel prices tend to be moderate, while the B&Bs are a bit less.

Several campgrounds offer accommodations; the ones in western Belmont County, near the Muskingum Watershed lakes, offer good value. Closer to Martins Ferry, campers looking for a nice spot between Belmont County and Marietta can stop at **Crawford's Crawdads,** 51700 SR 78 in Clarington, tel. (740) 458-0206. A couple of miles south of Sunfish Creek, Crawford's fronts on an Ohio River backwater, has new showers, and furnishes fishers and hunters with supplies and advice year round.

The **Lafayette Hotel,** 101 Front St., Marietta, tel. (740) 375-5522, (800) 331-9337 in Ohio, or (800) 331-9336 outside the state, looks out on the Ohio River and is a downtown landmark. The five-story red-brick building with its blue awnings provides 78 traditionally decorated and expensive rooms, plus a restaurant of note (see below). There are seven motel franchises and half a dozen area bed and breakfast facilities. Nearby, the **Best Western** and **Comfort Inn** provide boat dockages for their guests, with the Best Western running a water-taxi service for guests.

Among the more unusual places to stay is aboard the sternwheeler, *Claire E,* 127 Ohio Street, Marietta, tel. (740) 374-2233 or (740) 374-3876. Offering three rooms, the boat serves a full breakfast and asks that children be left at home. Kids are welcome at **Withington Manor,** 316 Fifth St., tel. (740) 374-3556; the **Herb House,** 426 Sixth St., tel. (740) 373-5248, and **B. Tucker Inn,** tel. (740) 374-3733 bed and breakfasts. Others to consider are the new **Hune House Inn,** SR 26 in Wayne National Forest, tel. (740) 473-2039, and the critically acclaimed **Buckley House,** 332 Front St., Marietta, tel. (740) 373-3080. A bed and breakfast establishment in Belpre, **Daydreamer Gardens,** CR 51, tel. (740) 423-4729 or (800) 741-3867, provides kitchen privileges, an outdoor pool, and boat dockage. Bed and breakfast accommodations tend to be moderately priced.

Food

Every Ohio town seems to have a Chinese restaurant, and a good one is **Wen Wu** in the Plaza West Shopping Center on US 40 in St. Clairsville, tel.(740) 695-6688. Locally popular, the facility gives diners lunch and dinner buffets or a daunting menu of made-to-order Cantonese, Mandarin, and related items. The weekday luncheon buffet is $4.99 for adults and $2.50 for kids under 12. Dinner buffets are $6.99 and $3.50, respectively. There are a number of combination platters in the $6-7.50 range, and all meals emphasize fresh vegetables. Wen Wu is open daily for lunch and dinner.

First Ward, 15 S. Fourth St., Martins Ferry, tel. (740) 633-1969, is locally popular because the food is good and inexpensive. Breakfast, served from 6:30 a.m., might include two eggs, home fries or hash browns, bacon or sausage, and toast for around $2. At lunch, homemade pasta is a sought-after special and ranges from $2.95 to $6.95 depending on size and whether a side salad is desired. In the evening, T-bone steak dinners can be had for $13. There's always someone enjoying the food here, but for Sunday, when the facility is closed.

Becky Thatcher Restaurant and Lounge, 237 Front St., Marietta, tel. (740) 373-4130. Don't let the street number fool you—this continental restaurant and lounge is on the second deck of the riverboat and is a separate business from the showboat melodrama (see **Culture** above). As for the street number, that's the parking lot. Once on board, chicken tortellini salad at $6.95 is a big favorite at lunch, with cashew pork at $16.95 the most popular evening meal. Most-requested dessert is Oreo ice cream pie at $2.95. Open year round Mon.-Sat. for lunch and dinner.

The **Blue Onion,** 300 Fourth St., Marietta, tel. (740) 373-4604), is redecorated and renamed. The owner-chef has brought several New Orleans dishes up the river as part of his creative American cuisine. Lunch includes specialty sandwiches and entree salads, an omelet, and there's always a quiche with fresh fruit, priced at $4.50. A roasted, deboned half a duck with shoestring potatoes is $13.95 each evening. New Orleans dishes include crawfish *étoufée* and jambalaya pasta. The restaurant is named for a china pattern, and the decor is a mix of white tablecloths and cobalt antiques. Out front in good weather are four umbrella tables. Open Mon.-Sat. for lunch and dinner and for Sunday brunch 11 a.m.-2 p.m. Carry-in alcoholic beverages are permitted.

The **Gun Room** in the Lafayette Hotel, 101 Front St., Marietta, tel. (740) 373-5522, is an atmospheric yet casual place to enjoy breakfast, lunch, or dinner seven days a week. Luncheon includes choices of several sandwiches or plates. The club sandwich is $4.95, while the Boston scrod plate is $5.75. Beef eaters can indulge themselves in the evening with a choice of either 12 or 14 ounces of prime rib, priced at $15.95 and $17.95, respectively. Various meringue pies, $3.50 per slice, are the most popular desserts.

Levee House Cafe, 127 Ohio St., Marietta, tel. (740) 374-2233, has an international menu and a regional reputation. Situated in the oldest (1826) drygoods store in the Northwest Territory, the restaurant's tin ceilings look down on numerous kinds of pastas for lunch (at about $5)

and pasta, shrimp, chicken, beef, and other dinners which range from $12.95 for chicken dishes to $14.50 for filet. Specials include a different meatloaf every Monday evening for $6.95 and, weather permitting, outdoor grilling of fresh salmon, marinated chicken, New York strip steak, prime rib filet or a huge pork chop each Wednesday evening. There are three dining rooms and dining outdoors in the summer.

Marietta Brewing Company, 167 Front St., Marietta, tel. (740) 373-2739, brews five different beers and ales on site. Thoughtfully, the establishment also makes a pair of nonalcoholic drinks, sarsaparilla and root beer. The various liquids go well with cheeseburgers, steaks, seafood, and more. A popular item for lunch or dinner is a personal-size pizza with a choice of toppings for $5.95. At dinner, diners frequently order the ribeye steak meal for $15.95. The storefront brewery-bar-restaurant is in the middle of the downtown shopping district.

Information, Tours, and Services

For police or medical emergencies, dial 911. The Belmont County Sheriff's Department can be reached by dialing (740) 695-7933. Call the Monroe County Sheriff at (740) 472-1612. The St. Clairsville police are available at (740-695-0123. Contact Marietta police by dialing (740) 373-4141. For medical needs, call Eastern Ohio Regional Hospital in Martins Ferry, tel. (740) 633-1100, or Marietta Memorial Hospital, tel. (740) 374-1400.

The **Belmont County Tourism Council,** is in the Ohio Valley Mall, Unit 485, tel. (740) 695-4359. The **Monroe County Tourism Council** can be reached at (740) 472-5499. The **Marietta/Washington County Convention and Tourism Bureau,** tel. (740) 373-5178 or (800) 288-2577, is in a wonderful old home at 316 Third St. Marietta also staffs a tourist information trolley permanently affixed to the Washington Square Shopping Center on SR 7 at Acme Street. A helpful Web site is www.rivertown.org. To find out what may be happening on the Marietta College campus, call (800) 331-7896. The **Belpre Area Chamber of Commerce,** can advise travelers calling (740) 423-8934.

The largest circulation newspaper in Belmont County is the *Times Leader,* produced evenings and Sunday morning in Martins Ferry. The *Marietta Times* is a weekday evening and Saturday morning daily. It runs an entertainment section each Thursday. WMOA, an ABC affiliate at 1490 AM, airs a 30-minute show at 8:30 a.m. Wednesday morning that details events and interviews locals about what's going on in Marietta and the surrounding area.

The **Valley Gem Sternwheeler** gives boat rides to visitors every hour 1-5 p.m. June-Aug., no service on Monday. In May and September, catch the boat on the hour from 1-4 p.m. on weekends and holidays. The ride takes travelers on a narrated trip down the Muskingum and up a portion of the Ohio on a 300-passenger boat built in 1989. Fares are $4.50 for adults and $3 for children ages 2-12.

Narrated **trolley tours** are an easy way to see Marietta. The vehicle leaves the Levee House Cafe, at Ohio and Second Streets, a couple of times each afternoon and once on Saturday morning during peak periods, Wed.-Sun. Fares are $7.50 for adults, $7 for seniors, and $5 for children. Call (740) 374-2233 for more information.

More conventional transportation is available from **Greyhound.** There are several spots to board in Belmont County, but no terminal exists. Call (304) 232-1500 to reach the Greyhound office in West Virginia for schedule and fare information. There is a Greyhound terminal in Marietta at 224 Putnam St., tel. (740) 373-2237.

Folks come from all over to visit the **Ohio Valley Mall,** just east of St. Clairsville. The nine cinemas and more than 130 shops, plus restaurants and food chains, form a major attraction. In Marietta more than 75 shops—quite a number, given the size of the town—greet pedestrians along Front Street facing the Ohio River. There are antique dealers, galleries, places to eat and drink, and spots to relax and watch the Muskingum and Ohio Rivers roll by. A nice place to visit if in the shopping mode is Kaplan Pottery, Fruit Farm Rd., Amesville, tel. (740) 551-2921. Fruit Farm Road is west of Bartlett on SR 550, between Marietta and Athens.

GALLIPOLIS TO PORTSMOUTH

Gallipolis, 70 miles southwest of Marietta, originally lured French citizens escaping their revolution. A small number of French descendants remain in today's quiet town of 4,800. Portsmouth, with 22,000 souls, is situated at the confluence of the Scioto and Ohio Rivers. It is approximately halfway between Marietta and Cincinnati, west of Marietta 87 miles by river roads and 62 miles via state roads through the southernmost segment of Wayne National Forest. Smaller towns along the riverway include Pomeroy and Ironton. The latter is an especially attractive old place, having been tarted up by people who made big money processing iron ore in the mid-19th century.

History
One of Ohio's most venerable towns, Gallipolis began with a scam. On the eve of the French Revolution, representatives of the Scioto Company went to Paris. There the land speculators convinced nervous members of the middle class that an escape to French utopia awaited them in America for $1.25 per acre. Watchmakers, clothiers, furniture makers, and others purchased 150,000 acres, sailing for their paradise in 1790.

The Ohio River settlement where they ended up was called City of the Gauls.

The French immigrants expected a civilized place and were met with a few log cabins, blockhouses, and swampy ground. Some turned back to America's eastern cities, others sailed down the Ohio and the Mississippi to New Orleans, and a few hung on and were absorbed by Yankee culture. Gallipolis residents earned their livings by shipping coal and produce downriver, a practice that continues to this day.

Like many of Ohio's river towns, Portsmouth was settled early. "Early" in the case of Scioto County means pre-Columbian, as Tremper Mound north of Portsmouth proves. Even before the Shawnee, who greeted the first Europeans, moundbuilders found the area a rich place to farm and hunt. Later on, a town was planned here, where the Scioto River empties into the Ohio, in 1803. From 1832 to 1853, the town of Portsmouth grew because it was a transfer point from canal barges to riverboats. Until the advent of the railroad, Portsmouth was a huge outlet for Ohio goods headed west or south. Farming was rewarding in the low bottomlands

THE COLLAPSE OF THE SILVER BRIDGE

Travelers take for granted that a highway won't buckle or that a bridge won't fall—until such a cataclysmic event takes place. That's exactly what happened in the early evening of December 15, 1967, when the Silver Bridge spanning the Ohio just upriver from Gallipolis, broke apart, carrying 46 people to their deaths.

A retired riverman, Charles H. Stone, now in his 80s, of Point Pleasant, West Virginia, remembers the disaster vividly. Stone spent decades on the Kanawha and Ohio Rivers as the captain of a towboat, passing back and forth many times beneath the Silver Bridge, pushing freight as far upriver as Pittsburgh and as far downstream as Cairo, Illinois. By 1967 he had sold his interest in the towboat service he ran with his father to a man who owned a boat works and marine business on the Ohio side of the river. He was helping the new owner with paperwork at 4:45 p.m. on December 15 when he heard an employee yell, "My God, the bridge is falling!" By the time Stone ran outside, the 700-foot suspension span was down.

"It happened quick," he recalls, adding that he immediately called his father. The elder Stone ran the half-block from his Point Pleasant home to the riverfront and found it to be eerily quiet—with pigeons circling in the gathering darkness and a great deal of debris in the water. Of the people who fell more than 100 feet into the 44° F water, few survived. One was a truck driver who crawled atop his cab and was pulled to safety as the vehicle bobbed in the current. It was a terrible Christmas holiday that year on both sides of the river.

There never was unanimous agreement as to how the structure, which was built in 1927-28, failed. The official inquiry blamed the collapse on the fracturing of an I-bar, along with inadequate inspections. Stone remembers that an employee of the boat works, who passed across the bridge minutes before it fell, saw what he thought was a Volkswagen Beetle hubcap in the roadway. Stone advances the notion that the man saw one of the large nuts that helped hold the bridge together. The span was, after all, made of 20-foot iron beams bolted together and suspended high above the water. "It was strong enough for cars, but I don't think it could carry heavy trucks," Stone says.

The bridge was replaced very quickly. After all, Lyndon B. Johnson was president and one of his cronies was Robert C. Byrd, the U.S. senator legendary for his devotion to West Virginia infrastructure. Johnson said he didn't want studies and designs, he wanted a new bridge. A structure that arched over the Mississippi River at Vicksburg, Mississippi, was copied and put up. It is known today as the Silver Memorial Bridge. While the new bridge was being erected, a bridge similar to the one that collapsed, which crossed the Ohio upriver at St. Mary's, West Virginia, was closed and ferry service initiated.

In a bizarre footnote, people came forward with strange tales of mysterious lights, demons, and a bat-winged Mothman seen around Point Pleasant shortly before the bridge fell. Perhaps the most popular bit of apocrypha was the rumor that the 18th-century Shawnee Chief Cornstalk had cursed the vicinity shortly before he was killed while being held in captivity.

near the rivers, though the chances of a flood each spring were all too real. Expanses of backwater rewarded hunters and fishers, but malarial mosquitoes bred in ponds and ditches. Portsmouth today is, among other things, the world's shoestring capital.

Location and Orientation

Gallipolis is on the Ohio River, midway between the West Virginia cities of Parkersburg and Huntington. It's 108 miles from Columbus, 255 miles from Cleveland, and 155 miles east of Cincinnati. The city is served by US 35 from the northwest, by SR 7 running through the town parallel to the river, and by SR 160 from the north and SR 141

and SR 218 from the west. US 35 continues south into West Virginia, through Charleston.

Portsmouth faces eastern Kentucky. It is only 90 miles south of Columbus, 120 miles southeast of Cincinnati, and 230 miles southwest of Cleveland. US 23 connects Portsmouth to Columbus, and US 52 runs along the Ohio River between Portsmouth and Cincinnati.

SIGHTS

There are several historic buildings in this area, not the least of which is *all* of downtown Ironton. The ironmaking magnates who once lived here created a lasting memorial to themselves in the form of a nice urban area adjacent to the river. Other individual sites include **Our House State Memorial,** 434 First St., Gallipolis, tel. (740) 446-0586, an authentic 1819 river tavern. Our House is open from Memorial Day to Labor Day, Tues.-Sat. 10 a.m.-5 p.m. and Sunday noon-5 p.m. Admission is $3 for adults, $2 for seniors, and $1 for children. The **1810 House,** 1926 Waller St., Portsmouth, tel. (740) 354-3760 or (740) 353-2099, is both a home and a museum. This farmstead has been faithfully restored inside and out. It's open May-Nov. Sat.-Sun. 2-4 p.m.

Bob Evans Farms

The Bob Evans Farm at SR 588, in Rio Grande, is the birthplace of the midwestern restaurant chain, Bob Evans Restaurants. Bob Evans started out more than half a century ago fixing homemade sausage and other food in a modest restaurant. Nowadays, his places are at almost every freeway exit. The farm is different, however. It's where Mr. and Mrs. Evans raised their six kids in a house that was an old stagecoach stop; the house is now on the National Register of Historic Places. the farm is open daily 8:30 a.m.-5 p.m. Memorial Day-Labor Day. Admission is free, and modest fees are charged for horseback rides, canoeing, and more. One of the nicest offerings is an overnight that combines horseback riding and canoeing for $60 per person. Reservations are required, and there are a number of special events each season, so smart visitors call ahead. Crafts and demonstrations of various rural skills take place daily, and there are free wagon tours every day, too. The farm is just east of the village of Rio Grande on the north side of the highway. For more information call (740) 245-5305 or (800) 994-3276.

The Floodwall Murals

These murals stretch for 2,100 feet along Portsmouth's Front Street on slabs of concrete meant to keep the Ohio and Scioto Rivers in their places. The nostalgic scenes were all done by one person—Louisiana artist Robert Dofford. He began the massive project in 1993 and had completed 34 murals by the end of 1997. Visitors

THE TRUE LEGEND OF BEVO FRANCIS

Clarence "Bevo" Francis, playing on the Rio Grande College basketball team in 1952-53, led his team to a 39-0 record—the highest number of victories ever achieved in a single season by a college team. In the process, he set a number of NCAA records: top single-season scoring average (48.3), best two-year average (47.1), and most points in a single game (113). The numbers would have been higher but for the fact that the NCAA does not recognize games between Rio Grande and non–degree-granting institutions.

Rio Grande College was a degree-granting institution—albeit just barely—when Bevo showed up in the fall of 1952. There were only four buildings on the entire campus. One of them was the Community Hall gymnasium, which had neither a shower nor a locker room. Players would dress for practice or a game, then dash through sometimes freezing temperatures to the gym. Despite such hardships, Rio Grande and Bevo Francis systematically beat every team they played, at home or away.

Initially, the six-foot, nine-inch Francis—who was from Wellsville, Ohio—and his fellow Redmen blew out local and area colleges. As the season pro-

gressed, they were invited to play teams with big-time programs such as the University of Dayton and the University of Cincinnati. Despite a schedule that included 17 consecutive road games, Rio Grande finished its very long season with a perfect record. The team exceeded 100 points on 23 occasions and Francis was named an All-American in several polls.

The following season, the Redmen played powerhouses such as Arizona State, Creighton, Providence, and Wake Forest. Though the season wasn't perfect (the team finished 21-7), they packed Madison Square Garden, and Francis scored 113 points against Michigan's Hillsdale College. In a game against Kentucky's Ashland College, Francis scored 55 points in the final 10 minutes of the game!

The bubble burst after only two seasons when Bevo moved on to professional basketball. But for two years, folks in this river county got used to seeing big-city reporters and photographers in their humble college gym. Today, nearly half a century later, Rio Grande has 2,000 students and a gaggle of bright new buildings. And the new gymnasium even has a shower.

The side of an old barn in Wayne National Forest bears a classic old Mail Pouch Tobacco advertisement.

can park near this 0.4 mile stretch of art and either take in the entire run at once or weave back and forth between the floodwall and various shops on Second Street. Subjects range from a view of an old-time motorcycle club to a salute to Portsmouth native and baseball great Branch Rickey to long-ago scenes of downtown. It's all free and rather like an invitation to look through a local family's treasured album.

State Parks and Wayne National Forest

The **Forked Run State Park,** at SR 124, in Reedsville, tel. (740) 378-6206, features a 102-acre lake with an 800-foot beach, plus nearly 200 campsites, four Rent-A-Camp units, areas for hunting and fishing, picnic areas, shelters, and new volleyball courts. Nearby is **Shade River State Forest,** a 2,600-acre reserve crisscrossed with interpretive trails.

Travelers to the Portsmouth area will find **Shawnee State Park** tucked into uplands away from the Ohio River and centered around peaceful Turkey Creek Lake. The park, officially located west of Portsmouth at 4404 SR 125, is surrounded by 63,000 acres of hardwood state forest, which helps create the hazy views of the big river and beyond from one of several ridges. White-tailed deer, turkey, raccoon, and various songbirds are common, and since only electric boat motors are permitted, there is real tranquility. There also is camping for folks on horseback and in vehicles, plus modern conveniences in the big, rustic-looking lodge or in cabins. The park is sit-

uated on Roosevelt Lake and is well-stocked, yielding largemouth bass, catfish, bluegill, crappie, and trout. This is an expansive place—bridle trails alone total 75 miles. Many Buckeye families spend a week or more here, year after year. For more information, call (740) 858-6652. (See **Recreation,** below, for more information.)

The southernmost area of **Wayne National Forest** takes up much of the space between Gallipolis and Portsmouth. Because of its expanse—and because of minimal population—even the main highways are blissfully free of billboards. This is mostly uninhabited country, with names like Greasy Ridge and German Hollow for discernible features. A good introduction is the backpacking trail adjacent to Lake Vesuvius, just east of SR 93 and five miles north of Ironton. In addition to the water, Lake Vesuvius Recreation Area has a restored iron furnace. There's a U.S. Forest Service district office in the town of Pedro at 6518 SR 93, tel. (740) 532-3223, within the boundaries of the national forest. To get there, take SR 93 north from Ironton.

ACCOMMODATIONS

Gallipolis has a respectable number of modest, locally owned motels, plus these franchises: **Best Western, EconoLodge, Holiday Inn,** and **Super 8.** The locals all charge budget or near-budget prices, with the national affiliates a few dollars higher. Bed and breakfast establishments in the area are comparable to the franchises in price.

Portsmouth offers several unique places to stay, three in the city and one in the country. Downtown, there's the **1835 House Bed and Breakfast,** 11 Offnere St., tel. (740) 353-1856, a bed and breakfast with three guest rooms, two of which offer private baths. Moderately priced, 1835 House has a heated outdoor pool and is on the National Registry of Historic Places. Also in town, the **Captain's Quarters,** 529 Sixth St., Portsmouth, tel. (740) 354-6609, provides off-street parking and is within walking distance of major attractions. It's moderately priced and has three guestrooms. The **George Williamson House,** 322 Dry Run, tel. (740) 858-6900, is in West Portsmouth. This B&B is in an 1860s Greek Revival/Italianate home. There are six fireplaces and three guest bedrooms in the moderately priced accommodation. Of course, Portsmouth also offers the usual accommodation franchises, including **Comfort Inn, Days Inn, Holiday Inn, Ramada Inn,** and **Super 8 Motel.**

In contrast to the urban coziness, **Shawnee State Park Lodge,** SR 125, a dozen miles west of the city, is a large and modern facility for outdoor activities. Fishing, boating, swimming indoors or out, golfing, tennis, hiking, horseback riding, and more are available. Fifty guest rooms and 25 cabins, moderate to expensive, are in some demand, so reservations are advised. For more information, call (740) 858-6621 or (800) 282-7275.

FOOD

Le Marquis, 300 Second St., Gallipolis, tel. (740) 446-2345, formerly was known as the Stowaway. Now, with remodeling and an ownership change in the summer of 1998, the restaurant serves several French dishes as well as steaks, prime rib, salads, and sandwiches. Open for lunch and dinner every day but Sunday, Le Marquis has deals like the "Business Special" for lunch, which is half a sandwich and a cup of the day's freshly made soup. In the evening, filet dinners are $14.95 or $16.95, depending on whether the diner wants the six- or nine-ounce cut. Whatever the name, the bistro remains popular with local and area diners.

Two **Shake Shoppe** locations in Gallipolis are worthwile places to stop with the kids for an ice-cream treat. The first location is at 383 Jackson Pike, tel. (740) 446-1611 and the second is at 901 Second St., tel. (740) 446-2682.

C.R. Thomas's Old Place, 124 S. Second St., Ironton, tel. (740) 532-8500, is a busy and popular place. Serving lunch and dinner every day, the restaurant-bar dishes up luncheon items like Cajun grilled chicken breast, smothered with peppers and other treats, for around $6.50. In the evening, a full rack of baby back ribs, zestily sauced, emerges from the kitchen at $12.99 for the meal. The bar stays open until midnight weekends, with the kitchen closing an hour earlier.

Portsmouth offers a number of fine places to dine, starting with the **Boneyfiddle Cafe,** 429 Second St., tel. (740) 354-6900, which is open Mon.-Sat. for lunch and dinner. Featuring a modern American menu, the bistro's biggest seller at lunch is a Veggie Lover's sandwich. It's a stir-fry of eggplant, onions, and more, served in a cream cheese-streaked wheat pita. Two dinner popular entrees are lasagna, priced at $7.95 and made on the premises, and grilled halibut, at $11.95. Popular desserts include chocolate truffle cheesecake at $3.95 and bread pudding for a dollar less.

Up the street from Boneyfiddle, **Mault's Brew Pub,** 224 Second St., tel. (740) 354-6106, one block north of all those murals, is the restaurant portion of the Portsmouth Brewing Company. It offers a full menu. One of America's great drinking values can be found here on Monday, as imbibers can purchase pilsner, Red Bird Ale, Spartan Export, Babe's Brown Porter, or Winter Bock for 75 cents for a 10-ounce glass. If travelers still want food they can order one of several German delicacies such as the Brewmeister's Best sausage dinner, with potato salad and kraut, for $6.95. An 18-inch pizza with three toppings is $11.25, and pepper steak or prime-rib dinners are $14.25 each. Mault's is open Fri.-Sun. for lunch and dinner and for dinner only on Monday.

Rockwell's, 1701 Grandview, tel. (740) 354-6202, serves lunch and dinner seven days a week. Among the more popular luncheon items is grilled boneless chicken breast. Accordingly, the chicken salad lunch is $5.99. In the evening, chicken with pasta and shrimp with pasta are also favorites. The shrimp dinner is $11.99. Favored by locals, Grandview parallels US 52, just to the north.

RECREATION

Shawnee State Forest, say the experts, has the state's best backpacking trails. They're certainly among the longest, allowing hikers to go for as much as a week without retracing footsteps. Once home to the people for whom the forest is named, this area also has seen its share of moonshiners, particularly during the federal Prohibition era. Today, the most dangerous things around are poisonous copperheads and timber rattlesnakes. That's one reason to wear substantial hiking boots. The other is the number of shallow creeks a hiker has to ford during the course of an extended walk. Ohioans refer fondly to this part of the state as the "Little Smokies." Hikers will find out why the first time they crest a big ridge and are afforded a magnificent view, particularly looking toward the Ohio River.

A dozen miles north of Ironton, east of SR 93, is **Lake Vesuvius National Recreation Area.** In addition to the usual recreational activities, experienced and in-shape visitors can try rock climbing. The cliff is above the lake and a climber is sure to attract some attention, since there's a busy ball diamond near the base of the ascent. Call (740) 532-0151 for more information.

Closer to earth, the folks at **Lone Oak Farm,** 30391 Roy Jones Rd., Syracuse, tel. (740) 992-2800, offer **horseback riding** hourly and overnight trail rides. From SR 7 east of Pomeroy, enter the village of Syracuse and turn north onto Bridgeman Street. Bridgeman runs into Roy Jones Road, and Lone Oak is half a mile on up the road.

Those who prefer to ride with a roar can visit Hanging Rock and Pine Creek **off-road** vehicle trails. From Ironton, head north on SR 93 some 23 miles and look for a sign marked Telegraph Trailhead Parking. Turn left onto CR 193 for an eighth of a mile and do as the sign bids.

Those who like river **fishing** should pay close attention to the waters in the vicinity of Racine locks, near the village of Racine on SR 7, east of Gallipolis. This stretch of the Ohio is said to possess some of the best fishing in the entire length of the river. Visitors who prefer to fish in a lake

FISHING IN THE FOOTSTEPS OF MINING

Some of the state's more remarkable fishing holes can be found about seven miles west of Ironton, just north of US 52, off SR 605. Known as the Hanging Rock Area, these 51 fishing ponds are the result of strip-mining in the 1960s and 1970s that left much of the rural, upland area badly scarred. Steep, nearly vertical slopes made so much as walking in the area a hazard. Nowadays, these holes and hazards form ponds where anglers can catch their limit.

Managed by the U.S. Forest Service, Hanging Rock ponds provide opportunities to catch largemouth bass, bluegill, and channel catfish. Fish populations are surveyed and ponds are stocked in cooperation with the Ohio Division of Wildlife. About one-third of the ponds can be reached by car, making fishing by handicapped persons viable. There is a large parking lot midway down the improved access road that puts anglers close to the middle of all the ponds. The area also contains 26 miles of off-road vehicle trails.

Bass and bluegill are more common than catfish, and there are reports of sunfish in at least three ponds. Two ponds have no fish at all. None of the ponds measures more than 2.5 acres, so moving from one pond to another is a snap. To avoid a lifeless pond, pick up the Forest Service's brochure, which includes a chart telling which ponds are stocked. Maps are free at the Wayne National Forest Ironton Ranger District office, 6518 SR 93, Pedro, tel. (740) 532-3223.

might try the body of water at Forked Run State Park, SR 124, Reedsville. The lake is stocked with catfish, bluegill, crappie, largemouth bass, sauger, and trout.

Golfers can look to several local places, including the **Meigs County Golf Course,** 33080 Willows Run Rd., Pomeroy, tel. (740) 992-6312. This nine-hole course sits above Pomeroy in the hills. Par is 34, and greens fees are $8 for nine holes and $10 for 18 holes walking, or $14 and $22 for nine and 18 with a cart. The 18-hole, par 72 course at **Shawnee State Park,** seven miles west of Portsmouth on US 52, is between the highway and the Ohio River, so a hook from the fifth tee is apt to land in the water. Greens

GALLIPOLIS-PORTSMOUTH AREA EVENTS

APRIL

Trout Derby, Shawnee State Park. A sunup to sundown fisheree with an awards ceremony that follows. Anglers must have valid Ohio licenses. Call (740) 858-6652 for details.

MAY

French 500 Flea Markets take place several times each summer at the Gallia County Fairgrounds, 189 Jackson Pike, Gallipolis. All are free. For added info, call (800) 765-6482.

Lake Vesuvius, SR 93, north of Ironton, is the site of an annual **Fishing Derby.** Events include children's fishing and casting contests. To learn more, call (740) 532-3223.

If you're in the area on Memorial Day weekend and you need a hit of patriotism, visit the **Oak Hill Village Festival of Flags,** some 25 miles west of Gallipolis on SR 279. These folks put out 2,000 flags, hire entertainment such as Phil Dirt and the Dozers, and there are rides and food booths on the Memorial Day weekend. Call (740) 682-6301 for information.

JUNE

Bluegrass Competition and Jamboree, village of Rio Grande. The "King of the Cowboys," was from the Portsmouth area, and he's saluted each year at the **Roy Rogers Festival.** There's entertainment, a banquet, and dealers selling Western memorabilia. Call (740) 353-0900 to be better informed.

Battle of Buffington Island Weekend, Portland, commemorates the only true Civil War battle to have taken place in Ohio.

SEPTEMBER

Sorghum plants look like corn and produce a sweet syrup that tastes great and should be more widely used. Sample some at the **Sorghum Festival,** SR 141, Wilgus, about 29 miles south of Gallipolis along SR 141 through Wayne National Forest. The Grange Hall is the setting for tasting, listening to country music, and viewing crafts. Call (740) 643-2196 for details.

Portsmouth River Days, a Labor Day weekend event for four decades, pledges something for everyone. That something includes activities on the river, arts and crafts, midway rides, free live entertainment, sidewalk sales, a queen's pageant, a fish fry and other food, a parade, and fireworks. Call (614) 354-3943 to find out more.

Barnesville's **Ohio Pumpkin Festival** takes place in the downtown area.

OCTOBER

Big Bend Sternwheeler Festival, Pomeroy, includes boat races, a masquerade contest, chili cook-off, casino night, fireworks, a parade, and a queen contest.

Belmont County Rubberneck Tour provides a chance to drive the hills and see the leaves show their color. For more information, call (614) 695-7272.

Sorghum Makin' takes place every year on John R. Simon's farm, 8721 Pond Creek/Carey's Run Rd., Portsmouth, tel. (740) 259-6337. There's no admission charge to see oldtime crafts and hear fiddlin' music, so buy some sorghum!

fees are $10 and $18 for nine and 18 holes to walk, $16.50 and $29.75 for nine and 28 holes with a cart.

CULTURE AND ENTERTAINMENT

Gallipolis and Portsmouth each have an important site for visual arts. The former's cultural rendezvous is the **French Art Colony,** 530 First Ave., tel. (740) 446-3834, a regional multi-arts center presenting a dozen different exhibits throughout the year. There also are classes in visual and performing arts. The facility is open Tues.-Fri. 10 a.m.-3 p.m. and Sunday 1-5 p.m. No admission is charged. In Portsmouth, visit the **Southern Ohio Museum and Cultural Center,** 825 Gallia St., tel. (740) 354-5629. It's open Tues.-Fri. 10 a.m.-5 p.m. and Sat.-Sun. 1-5 p.m. Admission is $1 for adults and 75 cents for children, free admission on Friday. The quantity and quality of changing exhibits here make the facility one of the nicest stops in the area. Local artists, who show promise, exhibit upstairs.

Portsmouth Little Theatre, 1217 Lawson St., tel. (740) 353-5824, marked its 50th year with the 1997-98 season. Recent productions have ranged from *Steel Magnolias* to *Groucho: A*

Life in Revue. The company usually does at least four different shows a year, in September, November, February, and April. Admission is $8 for adults and $7 for students and seniors.

Music is in the air Wednesday through Saturday evenings at the **Ye Olde Lantern** restaurant, 601 Second St., Portsmouth, tel. (740) 353-6638. Jazz piano, classical guitar, acoustical guitar—these and other offerings are available from 6:30 p.m. to dinner guests, to those interested in dessert and coffee, or to anyone with an urge to order something cold and hear music. There is no cover charge.

SERVICES AND INFORMATION

For emergency police or medical assistance, dial 911. In Gallipolis, call police in a non-emergency by calling tel. (740) 446-1313. The Gallipolis local hospital is Holzer Medical Center, tel. (740) 446-5000. The post office in Gallipolis is at 440 Second Ave. The Portsmouth police can be reached at (740) 353-4101. Medical needs in Portsmouth are met at Southern Ohio Medical Center, tel. (740) 354-5000. Mail those cards at the Portsmouth post office, 610 Gay St.

The **Ohio Valley Visitors Center of Gallia County** is at 45 State St., Gallipolis, tel. (740) 446-6882 or (800) 765-6482. Tourist information in for Pomeroy, Reedsville, and Forked Run State Park in Meigs County is dispensed by the park district, tel. (740) 992-2239. The **Portsmouth Convention and Visitors Bureau** folks can be reached at (740) 353-1116.

Pomeroy readers subscribe to the *Daily Sentinel,* produced weekday evenings and Sunday mornings. The *Gallipolis Daily Tribune* is available weekday evenings. The *Ironton Tribune* comes out weekday evenings and Sunday mornings, and the *Portsmouth Daily Times* serves its readers weekday evenings and weekend mornings.

The Greyhound terminal in Portsmouth is at 715 Chillicothe St., tel. (740) 353-2260.

Shopping

The Gallipolis contribution to consumerism is its small but inviting downtown area. Portsmouth boasts something of a rarity these days for a town its size: a downtown department store. Marting's, 515 Chillicothe St., tel. (740) 354-4511 or (800) 533-3550, has been selling clothing, accessories, jewelry, housewares, and more for 125 years. It also has Boneyfiddle Art Gallery, 537 Second St., tel. (740) 353-8689, a pleasant stop just a block from the Floodwall Murals.

SOUTHEASTERN OHIO

The story of this part of the country is the story of a number of ventures that almost worked. Iron, coal, gas and oil, pottery, tobacco and other crops—the silent hills teased residents with promises of wealth which seldom came to pass. Consequently, the people who were born here either left in order to make a decent living or stayed and resigned themselves to a hardscrabble existence. Through it all, those who remained developed a rich culture that is virtually palpable. The culture is evident in the food, which is inexpensive and filling; in the small towns, where everyone knows everyone else; in the arts and crafts, which can be hypnotic or sad or labor intensive; and in the celebrations, which can be exuberant.

Natives are of two minds concerning the tree-studded hills. Most would live nowhere else. If that's so, why do some rural residents abandon cars, appliances, and trash here? An expert says it's a matter of education and prosperity. Education and prosperity have penetrated the hills as never before, yet the love-hate relationship between those who live here and their natural surroundings continues. With a stable or slightly declining population, and with more flatland tourists discovering this part of Ohio each year, the locals may have wider options than ever before.

ZANESVILLE AND THE NATIONAL ROAD

The line designating Appalachia runs north of here, but I-70-US 40 certainly seems like a dividing line. The routes run between Columbus and Wheeling, West Virginia, going from flat, fertile, and uninteresting to hilly, tough, and picturesque only a few miles east of the state capital. Zanesville, Muskingum, and Cambridge derive meaningful income from the highways and

their accessibility. Travelers who whistle past these freeway exits in their zeal to reach more populated places will be missing very attractive parts of the upper Southeast that are dignified with age. Consider this a vote to exit I-70 and roll along old US 40 in its parallel path between West Virginia and central Ohio. Lightly traveled, the old road passes near most worthwhile at-

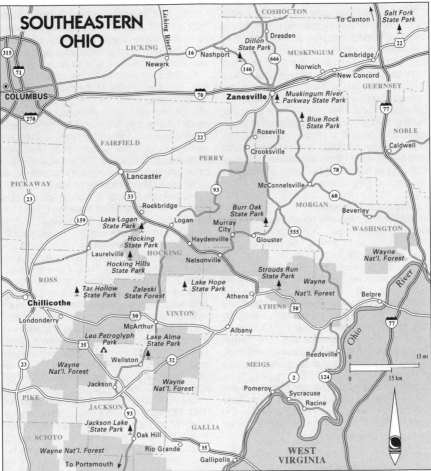

tractions and simply isn't as soulless as the limited-access road that replaced it. The stretch between Zanesville and Cambridge, where pottery and all else seem for sale, is hilly, verdant, and has an almost nostalgic air.

History

Zanesville was founded in 1799 by Ebenezer Zane, an ancestor of Zanesville-born author Zane Grey. The high-quality clay in the area resulted in the production of stoneware and other pottery. The first oil well in Ohio was drilled in 1814 near

Caldwell, about 20 miles south of Cambridge. The fellow drilling the well was looking for brine, which of course contained salt, a valued commodity. He hit oil and plugged the well because it was not what he had in mind. Two years later, a mix of oil and brine was struck nearby. Oil was separated from brine by soaking blankets in the liquid and squeezing out the heavier oil. The raw petroleum was thought by some to be medicinal. Huge deposits of gas were found near McConnelsville, south of Zanesville, in 1830. Coal was found all across southeastern Ohio soon afterwards.

Not that many people got rich. Some turned to the production of pottery, creating dishes, bowls, and other vessels that were sturdy, sometimes breathtakingly beautiful, and increase in value with the passing years. The pottery business could not compete with less expensive foreign china or metal pots and pans, so small manufacturing facilities blossomed, particularly in Zanesville and Cambridge. In New Concord, much of the commerce today pertains to Muskingum College and to the pride in having nurtured the astronaut and former U.S. Senator John Glenn. And in Dresden, basketry and marketing have combined to create a mecca for shoppers and sightseers.

Location and Orientation

Zanesville is 56 miles east of Columbus; 70 miles east of Wheeling, West Virginia; 150 miles south of Cleveland; and 63 miles northwest of Marietta. The major highways through this part of the country run east-west, with I-70 and US 40 being the most frequently traveled. The biggest north-south road is I-77, which passes through Cambridge on its way between Cleveland and Marietta. The terrain here grows increasingly hilly as travelers head east out of Columbus. None of these municipalities are large: Zanesville, which is the Muskingum County seat, has 26,000 residents, making it twice the size of Cambridge, the seat of Guernsey County. Running between Zanesville and Marietta, scenic SR 60 generally follows the Muskingum River and can be an impressionistic painting in the summer or fall; there are other scenic routes through the area as well.

SIGHTS

Parks

Two very different state parks flank Zanesville. South of the city some 14 miles down scenic SR 60 is **Blue Rock State Park,** 7924 Cutler Lake Rd., Blue Rock, tel. (740) 452-3820. It was one of the state's first 10 parks. Created with land purchased in 1936, Blue Rock offers fishing and swimming in 15-acre Cutler Lake, plus 100 campsites and, in the adjacent state forest, bridle and hiking trails. Pets are cool here, and there are several nature-education programs.

In contrast, **Muskingum River Parkway State Park** is headquartered on SR 666, a dozen miles north, and shares the same telephone number, (740) 452-3820. As the name suggests, the parkway includes the river and surrounding area, stretching approximately 85 miles south to Marietta. That's where the Muskingum, swollen by feeder streams, enters the Ohio. It's a momentous voyage, traveling through parts of Ohio that haven't changed all that much since the river was a major source of transport. Boaters can take advantage of 10 locks, completed in 1842, and which are still in operation. Organized unlike any other state facility, this elongated attraction makes for an especially memorable and relaxing jaunt.

Muskingum County is a park-rich environment. A nice one is **Dillon State Park,** 5265 Dillon Hills Dr., Nashport, tel. (740) 453-4377. This big (7,548 acres) facility is only a few miles northwest of Zanesville on SR 146. It is characterized by bedrock that has formed sheer cliffs amid a lush hardwood forest. Dillon Reservoir measures 1,660 acres and was constructed initially for flood control. Nowadays it supports not only swimming, fishing, and unlimited boating, but a wide range of wildlife. White-tailed deer, ruffed grouse, and wild turkey drink from the waters of the reservoir and of Licking River, which meanders into the park from a low area to the northwest. There also are 29 cabins and 195 campsites, good places to headquarter if a really thorough look at Dillon is desired.

Salt Fork State Park, US 22, Cambridge, tel. (740) 432-1508, is Ohio's largest state park, offering 17,000 acres of rural Guernsey County in which to recreate. Hiking, horseback riding, swimming, and fishing are just four of many activities that go on here. Visitors should ask the nearest ranger for directions to Hosak's Cave, which has a waterfall plunging from it, and Morgan's Knob, the park's highest spot and a great vantage point. Naturalists lead an annual foliage hike on one weekend in mid-October that has drawn praise from travelers all across the country. The lodge has 148 rooms and there are 54 cabins. Everything here is well maintained, and there are special weekend events devoted to everything from big bands to Ohio wines to chocolate.

The **Wilds,** tel. (740) 638-5030, is a private park, quite unlike any other. Here, on over 10,000

handsome baskets for sale

acres, roam a worldwide variety of endangered animals. Reticulated giraffes, white rhinoceri, and a host of other rare species from Africa, Asia, and North America are common in the Wilds' hills and valleys. The tours are guided and they include an introductory film, *A Place Called the Wilds.* Here visitors learn that this is reclaimed strip-mine land. That knowledge is reinforced by the sight of *Big Muskie,* a coal-retrieving dragline that is said to be the largest of its kind. The park is at 14000 International Rd., just off SR 146, between Chandlersville and Cumberland. Look for direction signs on I-70. The Wilds is open daily 9 a.m.-6 p.m. from Memorial Day to Labor Day. Tours run from 10 a.m.-5 p.m. In May, September, and October, the park closes at 5 p.m. and the last tour begins at 4 p.m. Admission prices are $8 for adults, $7 for seniors, and $5 for children ages 5-12.

Dresden

North of Zanesville 16 miles on SR 60, this en-tire town is a worthwhile sight. The town is the home of Longaberger Basket Company, a very successful maker of baskets sold via home parties. Where the term "company town" once made miners shudder, this is indeed a happy, modern-day contrast. The firm owns many of the restaurants and other attractions and offers factory tours. It seems to even the briefest visitor that half the town is peddling baskets of one hue or size or another, with the World's Largest Basket at Fifth and Main Streets in the middle of downtown making for a convenient place to meet. That meeting may well take place while peering over a stack of just-purchased basketry, antiques, crafts, and pottery as travelers stagger to their cars under the weight of the accumulation. Free tours of the factory at 95 Chestnut St. are given Mon.-Sat. 8 a.m.-4 p.m., Sunday 1-7:30 p.m., but visitors will have to visit during the week to see the production line in action.

Art Centers

The **Zanesville Art Center,** 620 Military Rd., Zanesville, tel. (740) 452-0741, is an art museum with two kinds of exhibits. One consists of an impressive collection of American, Asian, and European art; the other is said to be the largest public collection of ceramics and glass, for which the area once was famous. The ceramics and glass displays are fair indicators of what people perceived to be beautiful in the late 19th and early 20th centuries. Some items are striking. The center is open Tuesday, Wednesday and Friday 10 a.m.-5 p.m., Thursday 10 a.m.-8:30 p.m., and Sat.-Sun. 1-5 p.m. There is no admission charge.

The **Andrew Kachilla Center for Arts,** 727 Wheeling Ave., Cambridge, tel. (740) 432-2432, accomplishes a couple of things. It salutes Kachilla, a southeastern Ohio native who worked in several mediums, producing "outsider" or "naive" art. Some of the artist's many works also are part of the Zanesville Art Center's permanent collection. The Cambridge facility also shows works by members of the local artists' league. This is a good place to catch the artistic flavor of the region. Hours are Tues.-Sat. 11 a.m.-4 p.m. Admission is free here, too, and there's a gift shop—perhaps the best place in town to find something local and distinctive.

Zanesville's Y-Bridge
This bridge has to be driven to be appreciated. Heading westward on Main Street in the downtown area, visitors will cross the Muskingum River. In midstream, the bridge splits, with Main to the left and Linden Avenue to the right. Complicating matters, the heart of the Y faces the point where the Licking River enters the Muskingum. Why was such a bridge constructed? Because the "Y" configuration let travelers cross either river; they could head northwest, southwest, or east. The current bridge dates from 1902. On the west side of New Concord is a small, brick-paved, S-shaped bridge, no longer used, that has been preserved on the north side of US 40. According to the sign, the S or Z (take your pick) configuration made the bridge stronger and its construction easier.

Art Glass Workshops
Two places, Boyd's Crystal Art Glass and Mosser Glass, Inc., both in Cambridge, offer tours. Boyd's is at 1203 Morton Ave., tel. (740) 439-2077, while Mosser holds forth at 9279 Cadiz Rd., tel. (740) 439-1827. Both offer glassware in the form of animals, paperweights, tableware, and other shapes is available for purchase. Neither facility charges for a tour. Boyd's hours are Mon.-Fri. 7 a.m.-3:30 p.m.; its showroom is open 8 a.m.-4 p.m. the same days. Mosser offers tours Mon.-Fri. 8:30-10:30 a.m. and 12:30-3 p.m. and is closed the first two full weeks in July, the day after Thanksgiving, and the last two weeks of December. The tours are reminders that lots of glass once was made in various parts of eastern Ohio.

MUSEUMS

The **National Road-Zane Grey Museum,** 8850 East Pike, Norwich, tel. (740) 872-3143, presents a nice mix of subjects. This large facility is on US 40, at I-70 Exit 164, some 10 miles east of Zanesville. The museum features a 136-foot diorama depicting the history of the road that begain in Cumberland, Maryland, and stretched to Vandalia, Illinois, in the 19th century. Also here is an original Conestoga wagon, constructed in Pennsylvania of substantial materials to survive the trip west. Author Zane Grey, who grew up in Zanesville, is represented by manuscripts and some of his personal belongings. From May-Sept. its hours are Mon.-Sat. 9:30 a.m.-5 a.m., Sunday and holidays noon-5 p.m. from May to September; March-April and Oct.-November its hours are Wed.-Sat. 9:30 a.m.-5 p.m. and Sunday noon-5 p.m., closed holidays. Admission is $5 for adults, $4 for seniors, and $1.25 for children ages 6-12.

Ohio Ceramic Center, Ceramic Road, Crooksville, tel. (740) 697-7021, covers the history of pottery in the Buckeye State. Each of the five buildings has its own theme. Visitors will be impressed with the look, color, and quality of the pieces. Its hours are Wed.-Sun. 9:30 a.m.-5 a.m. from early May to mid-October. Admission fees are $1 for adults; children are free. Those who want to learn about the history of area pottery would do well to make this their first stop.

This being a historic area, there are a number of smaller museums and private homes travelers may find interesting. Several, such as Zanesville's fascinating **Dr. Increase Mathews House,** 504 Woodlawn Ave., tel. (740) 452-8550, or the **Stone Academy,** 115 Jefferson St., tel. (740) 454-9500, keep brief hours. These sites are open May-Sept. Wed.-Sat. noon-4 p.m. Others keep no regular hours but can be viewed by appointment. For a complete list, contact the Zanesville-Muskingum County Convention and Visitors Bureau, (740) 453-5004 or (800) 743-2303.

RECREATION

Canoeing
Canoe rentals aren't all that common, but there's a prominent source in Nashport, 13 miles northwest of Zanesville. Dillon Lake Water Sports Shop, 6275 Clay Littick Dr., tel. (800) 640-7964, will provide travelers with a craft by the hour, day, or longer.

Golf
A pair of local courses welcome visitors. **Fuller Fairways,** Clay Pike, Zanesville, tel. (740) 452-9830, is an 18-hole, par 70 facility. Fees are $6.50 for nine holes and $12.50 for 18, with a cart costing $5 for nine holes and $10 for 18 holes. The course is east of Zanesville. Take I-70 to

the Adamsville Road exit. Exit right and then take another right onto Clay Pike. **Green Valley Golf Club,** 4420 Dresden Rd., Zanesville, tel. (740) 452-7105, is an 18-hole, par three course. Cost is $7.50. Green Valley is about 10 minutes north of downtown Zanesville.

Walking

Any of these towns offers historic places in which to walk around; Zanesville and Cambridge have organized theirs. Zanesville's Historic Putnam Tour starts where the Muskingum River bends, adjacent to the Sixth Street Bridge. This 16-block area is lined with homes dating from 1805, including Putnam Presbyterian Church, a significant stop on the Underground Railroad. The Cambridge walking area centers around the Guernsey County Courthouse and measures about five blocks by two blocks. Highlights include an Odd Fellows building, a theater, and other structures of varying ages. Contact the visitor center in each town for a free, information-packed brochure on the respective sites.

ACCOMMODATIONS

Interstate 70 is flanked by hotels and motels at virtually every interchange. Zanesville has half a dozen national franchises, including **Best Western Town House,** 135 N. Seventh St., tel. (740) 452-4511; **Comfort Inn,** 500 Monroe St., tel. (740) 454-4144; **Days Inn,** 4925 East Pike, tel. (740) 453-3400; **Fairfield Inn,** 725 Zane St., tel. (740) 453-8770; **Holiday Inn,** 4645 East Pike, tel. (740) 453-0771; and **Super 8,** 2440 National Rd., tel. (740) 455-3124. All offer moderate prices, including the independent **Baker's Motel,** 8855 East Pike, tel. (740) 872-3232. The latter is conveniently located across the highway from the Zane Grey Museum. Cambridge also has several franchise and independent motels.

There are dozens of area bed and breakfast operations. An attractive facility near Muskingum College in New Concord is **Bogart's,** 62 W. Main St., tel. (740) 826-7439 or (740) 872-3514. Each of the four rooms with private baths is moderately priced; the tariff is $10 less Sun.-Thurs. nights than on weekends.

FOOD AND DRINK

Zanesville offers a few nice dining options for either lunch or dinner, or both. **Dumplings Buffet,** 3575 N. Maple Ave. (SR 60), tel. (740) 455-2112, serves lunch and dinner seven days a week. Ham and roast beef are carved daily from 3:30 p.m., and there really are numerous dumpling variations (chicken, beef, and ham; apple, cherry, and peach) on the menu. Adults are assessed about $6 for lunch and around $8 for dinner, while kids are charged according to age—50 cents a year up to age 10. The facility is in the Colony Square Mall. **Maria Adornetto's Restaurant,** 953 Market St., tel. (740) 453-0643 or (800) 343-5026, is popular with locals and interstate travelers. The restaurant serves lunch Sun.-Fri. and dinner every evening. For lunch, lots of guests order sandwiches, the most popular being the build-your-own burger at $4.95. There are a number of plate lunches, too, like the boneless, skinless chicken breast with potato, vegetable, and salad for $6.95. Full lines of steaks, seafood, and Italian specialties are offered evenings. Favorites include fettuccini at $9.95, lasagna at $8.95, and steaks from $14.95.

Picnic Pizza has two Zanesville locations, 1250 Maple Ave., tel. (740) 450-7201, and 3575 Maple Ave., in Colony Square, tel. (740) 452-8451. Both sites offer a fairly complete Italian menu, with the 1250 Maple Ave. location offering beer and wine. A large pie here measures 16 inches; with three items on top it costs $12.25. Pastas, subs, strombolis, calzones, pepperoni rolls, and lasagna carry similar fair prices. Both stores are open for lunch, dinner and later seven days a week, with the Colony Square mall location closing at 6 p.m. on Sunday.

Quality American food is turned out at the **Potting Shed Cafe,** 301 S. Market St. (SR 668), in nearby Somerset, tel. (740) 743-2520, in a gardenlike atmosphere, inside an antique mall. The Potting Shed serves lunch only. A croissant sandwich might be stuffed with turkey and honey dijon dressing for $4.75. Desserts are a big deal; one of the favorites is angel food pie at $2.50. After lunch, check out the only equestrian statue left in Ohio. It's in the town square and it features Civil War General Philip Sheridan. Somerset is located approximately 15 miles west of Zanesville along US 22.

To the east, along US 40, **Old Library Coffee House,** 30 E. Main St., New Concord, tel. (740) 454-2555, is a nice place to stop for lunch, dinner, or a hit of caffeine. The facility is on the National Road, just down the hill from Muskingum College. Daily specials, drink included, range from $3.50 to $4.50 and may be beef and noodles with a side salad or any of a number of homemade soups teamed with a roll and side salad. Baked goods are abundant and go well with a cappuccino, latte, herbal tea, or Italian soda. It's even possible to rent a video here.

Located east of Concord, Cambridge's **Kennedy's Cakes and Donuts,** 875 Southgate Parkway, tel. (740) 439-2800, alleges that it has Ohio's largest display of baked goods. Who cares to argue? This is the place to stop not only for a continental breakfast but for a snack, too. More than one million milkshakes have been made here, too, so the Kennedys are adept at attacking sweet teeth from a number of angles. Open Mon.-Sat. from 5:30 a.m. and Sunday from 7 a.m., the treat place is a couple of miles north of I-70 off SR 209 (take Exit 178).

Nightlife
JR's Saloon, 13665 Era Rd., Mt. Sterling, tel. (740) 869-3078, gets tuneful a couple of nights each week, usually Friday and Saturday, with bands like the Country Drifters. In Zanesville, check out the piano player weekend evenings at Maria Adornetto's restaurant, 953 Market St., tel. (740) 453-0643.

INFORMATION AND SERVICES

For emergency medical or police assistance, dial 911. The non-emergency number for the Zanesville police is (740) 455-0700. The Zanesville hospital, Good Samaritan, can be reached at (740) 454-5000. The Zanesville post office is at 1035 Zane St.

The **Zanesville-Muskingum County Convention and Visitors Bureau** is at 205 N. Fifth St., Zanesville, tel. (740) 454-8687 or (800) 743-2303. The bureau hands out discount cards good at several county attractions. The **Cambridge/Guernsey County Convention and Visitors Bureau** is at 2250 Southgate Parkway, tel. (740) 432-2022 or (800) 933-5480. To find out what's doing on campus at Muskingum College in New Concord, telephone (740) 826-8134, or check its Web site at www.muskingum.edu.

Zanesville is served by the *Times Recorder.* In Cambridge, look for the *Daily Jeffersonian,* published weekday evenings and Sunday mornings.

Transportation
Greyhound stops in Zanesville at 375 Fairbanks St. The telephone number is (740) 454-2901. Z-Bus is the local transportation system. It's part of the Muskingum Area Public Transit, charging 75 cents for adults, 55 cents for students, and 35 cents for disabled and elderly persons. For route information, call (740) 454-8573.

Sternwheelers once paddled up and down the Muskingum River, and the *Lorena,* 375 Muskingum Ave., Zanesville, tel. (740) 455-8883 or (800) 246-6303, is a surviving example. One-hour rides are available daily (weather permitting) at 1, 2:30, and 4 p.m. all summer. Price of the venture is $3.50 for adults and $1.50 for children ages 2-12. A dinner cruise takes place every summer Wednesday and approximately once a month on Saturday. The *Lorena* is a passenger steamboat capable of carrying about 100 persons.

Shopping
Did we mention pottery? It's available in all shapes and sizes here, new and old, some of it so fresh out of the kiln it may still be warm, some of it mixed with locally crafted glass items. Among the fine shops in the Dresden area are several along Main Street, including Dresden Pottery, 721 Main St., tel. (740) 754-3000; Side Street Stoneware, 700 Main St., tel. (740) 754-4438; and Social Supper, Inc., 305 Main St., tel. (740) 754-2451 or (800) 669-5013.

The Zanesville area is also blessed with an abundance of similar stores: Ebenezer's Barn, 510 East Pike, tel. (740) 454-2075; Floriware, 333 Market St., tel. (740) 454-7400; Hartstone, Inc., 1719 Dearborn St., tel. (740) 452-9992; Ohio Pottery West, 1905 W. Main St., tel. (740) 454-2248; Quality Imports, 45 White Rd., tel. (740) 452-2820; and Zanesville Pottery & China, 7395 East Pike, tel. (740) 872-3345 or (800) 860-6456. In South Zanesville shoppers can find Burley Clay Products, 26 Shawnee Ave., tel. (740) 452-3633.

ZANESVILLE AREA ANNUAL EVENTS

MAY

Hopalong Cassidy Festival, downtown Cambridge, tel. (740) 439-6688, welcomes May with a salute to a famous son, actor William Boyd. Check out western entertainment, cowboy eats, and the occasional visiting Hollywood star.

Springfest takes place at Buell Island Park in the village of Lowell, midway between Zanesville and Marietta, tel. (740) 896-2419. There are horseshoe-pitching contests, a parade, a flea market, food, and entertainment.

Muskingum Valley Trade Days & Flea Market happens on SR 78 in Reinersville, tel. (740) 558-2740. Everything from a huge flea market to events devoted to showing off coonhounds takes place here over a five-day span.

Dresden Shopping Basket Factory Express begins in Dennison and ends up in Dresden, Ohio's basket capital, tel. (330) 852-4676. The connection is made possible with a diesel passenger train that waits while folks shop and take a factory tour.

JUNE

Jonathan Bye Days occurs in the City Park, Byesville, tel. (740) 685-2320. The town founder is feted with a flea market, arts and crafts, a dance, a parade, and concessions.

Zane's Trace Commemoration, Zane's Landing Park, Zanesville, tel. (740) 453-0959, toasts Ohio's first long-distance road. The three-day event includes sternwheeler rides, a two-hour parade, arts and crafts, entertainment, and a flea market.

Living Word Outdoor Drama, SR 209 West, Cambridge, tel. (740) 439-2761, portrays scenes from the life of Jesus Christ. There is a cast of 30, and the costumes, animals, and scenes feel authentic.

Cruise-In, downtown McConnelsville, tel. (740) 982-4213, is emceed by a disk jockey who orchestrates both the tunes and the presentation of nearly 150 antique and restored cars and trucks.

National Cambridge Collectors Glass Show & Sale is at the Civic Center, 7033 US 40, in Cambridge, tel. (740) 432-4245. Look, too, for a large glass-only flea market.

JULY

The **Ohio Hills Folk Festival** occurs in Quaker City —where at the SR265/513 junction in the southeast corner of Guernsey County, tel. (740) 679-2954. This gala has been taking place for nearly a century, proving they yearned for the good old days in the good old days. Featured here are parades, a car show, a flea market, craft demos, a 5K run, mud volleyball, and evening entertainment. Shade can be found in a country store, a farm museum, or a Quaker meeting house.

Will it happen in Crooksville or Roseville this year? That's the question concerning the **Crooksville-Roseville Pottery Festival,** which alternates between two villages south of Zanesville. Besides visiting the Ohio Ceramic Center, travelers can view local pottery being made, check out the flea market, participate in 5K and 15K runs, attend pottery exhibits and sales, and eat. Call (614) 697-7323 for details.

Pottery Lovers Show & Sale, US 40, Cambridge, tel. (812) 547-5707, is inside the Pritchard Laughlin Civic Center. The two-day event is for experts and those who would like to be.

Zanesville Pottery Show & Sale, 334 Shinnick St., tel. (740) 452-7687 or (800) 743-2303, is a Secrest Auditorium event. It, too, is a two-day show-sale.

There are a few other stores in other area locations, such as Beaumont Brothers Pottery, 315 E. Main St., Crooksville, tel. (740) 982-0055; Ohio Pottery, 8540 E. Pike, Norwich, tel. (740) 872-3137; and two shops in Roseville—Alpine Pottery, 7674 Ceramic Rd. NE, tel. (740) 697-0075 and Robinson-Ransbottom Pottery Co., 5545 Third St., tel. (740) 697-7355. Interstate 70 is thick with signs beckoning pottery shoppers to exit and buy, buy, buy.

Committed mall shoppers will want to cruise Colony Square, 3575 N. Maple Ave. (SR 60), Zanesville, tel. (740) 454-3255. Anchor stores include Elder-Beerman, JCPenney, Lazarus, and Sears.

THE HOCKING HILLS

Proudly unglaciated, the Hocking Hills were carved by water and wind over millennia to form several magnificent natural lakes, caves, hollows, gorges, and cliffs in Hocking County. Something like an Ohio version of a little Grand Canyon, this area is little known outside the state, yet it offers some of the most scenic places to wander in the entire Midwest (and a great detour for families with little ones getting restless in the back seat).

History

At one time, it was hard to make a living here. Native Amercians and persons of European heritage found the forests thick and the earth leached of many nutrients. So the American settlers began to poke around underground, where they hit rich seams of coal. While there remain large deposits, the fact that the high-sulfur coal doesn't burn clean has made it a marginal commodity. Happily, as the mines were closing, automobile began to haul people out of the cities and into countryside such as this. They discovered places like Conkle's Hollow and Old Man's Cave and they've been showing up ever since. Logan was named for Chief Logan, an advocate of peace between natives and settlers.

Location and Orientation

Logan, population 6,700, is the Hocking County seat. It is approximately in the middle of the county on US 33, which runs from Columbus to Athens. State Route 93 also cuts through Logan, heading north to New Lexington and south to Wellston. A network of state highways run near or into the Hocking Hills, including SR 56, SR 374, SR 664, and SR 678. Logan is 50 miles southeast of Columbus, 18 miles southeast of Lancaster, and 25 miles nothwest of Athens.

SIGHTS

Hocking Hills State Park, off SR 374, tel. (740) 385-6841, carries a Logan address, but that won't help in finding the place. It's in the south-west corner of Hocking County, perhaps as close to Chillicothe as to Logan. It's also the place where a visitor is most apt to wonder, "Can this really be Ohio?" That's because the park is blessed with formations and natural wonders accurately named Ash Cave, Cantwell Cliffs, Cedar Falls, Old Man's Cave, and Rock House. Hocking Hills is a superb place to camp—fragrant with pines, astir with wild creatures, and sculpted over millions of years by wind and water. There are 2,331 acres, 24 different hiking trails, 15 different campgrounds with a total of 170 sites, and enough rugged wilderness to satisfy anyone east of, say, the Badlands. The only sour note is that some state bureaucrat recently approved construction of a water slide adjacent to the lodge.

visitors follow a steep and narrow path in the Hocking Hills

COAL MINING

It's hard to envision, but much of the Hocking Valley once was the center of a booming coal-mining industry. Miners worked long, dangerous hours in the latter part of the 19th century, earning 80 cents per ton of coal extracted. Their peers in other parts of Ohio were paid five to 10 cents more per ton, but that was because other seams were thinner and more difficult to work. The coal seam in the Hocking Valley was as much as 14 feet thick. Its only fault was that two bands of shale and a band of bone coal ran through it, and sorting these inferior materials made for a lot of hard work.

In 1884, the market for coal softened and miners' hours and pay were reduced. They held still for 70 cents per ton, but when the coal companies cut compensation to 60 cents, the miners struck. Apparently anticipating the walkout, the companies brought in hundreds of immigrants, most of them Italian, to harvest coal. The strike had a lasting effect on the Hocking Valley, as armed Pinkerton guards exchanged gunfire with the desperate miners. The immigrant strikebreakers were beaten and some were frightened away; the coal companies ejected strikers and their families from company housing. Many miners left the area.

The wage dispute lasted six months and was the longest work stoppage ever by Ohio coal miners. Down through the years miners continued to strike for a variety of reasons. Between 1952 and 1991 there were 18 major strikes affecting the industry in the state. Spearheading better economic and working conditions was the United Mine Workers of America (UMWA), which formed from two smaller unions as a result of a pact signed in Columbus in 1890. UMWA membership peaked at 375,000 in 1920 but quickly declined to 80,000 by 1929, due to reduced dependence on coal.

Today, the remaining coal operations in the state usually are of the safer open-pit variety. Demand for Ohio coal has continued its decline in part because coal from the western United States is much cleaner burning than the high-sulfur coal from Ohio.

Hocking State Forest, Rockbridge, tel. (740) 385-4402, envelopes the Hocking State Park. The state forest spreads south of the village of Rockbridge, which is on US 33 northwest of Logan. Approved activities include horseback riding, camping, hunting, fishing, and hiking. Check with the ranger about the rock climbing and rappelling area. Another highlight here is the annual fall foliage color tour.

Hocking Valley Scenic Railway, runs rain or shine out of the depot at Nelsonville, US 33, tel. (740) 470-1300. Two trains, one short and one long, leave every day May 23-Nov. 1. The short run goes to Haydenville and back, while the long haul is a round trip to Logan. Mine products once pulled out of here headed north to Lake Erie, so this is an authentic rail line rich in history. The steam locomotive was built in 1916 and the diesel was built in 1952. The individual cars are from the Erie and Rock Island railways. Cost of the short trip, which departs at noon and lasts 75 minutes, is $7.50 for adults and $4.75 for children ages 2-11. The long trip, which pulls out at 2:30 p.m. and returns two hours later, is $10.50 for adults and $7.25 for kids. Since this is vintage equipment, wheelchair access cannot be guaranteed. Nor are there restrooms on the trains themselves.

Lake Logan State Park, CR 3 (Lake Logan Road), tel. (740) 385-3444, is a day-use park. That means there are no overnight facilities. But the fishing here is good, and so long as visitors have their lines in the water—or are engaged in some other recreational activity—they are welcome around the clock. There's more water here than parkland, 400 acres versus 319 acres, so fishing, swimming, and boat rental are popular pastimes. Heading south, just outside Chillicothe, is **Tar Hollow State Park,** 16396 Tar Hollow Rd., Laurelville, (740) 887-4818, has a bit of everything. Amid its 619 acres spread across portions of Hocking and Ross Counties, those who tire of dozens of hiking trails can swim or fish here, and there are nearly 100 campsites for those so inclined.

RECREATION

Canoeing
Hocking Hills Canoe Livery, 12789 SR 664 South, Logan, tel. (740) 385-0523 or (800) 634-

6820, plies the Hocking River, which comes into Logan County from New Lexington in the northeast and heads southeast from here, through Athens to the Ohio River. The livery service operates from mid-April through October.

Climbing

Evidently something that can be taught, rock climbing is covered by Hocking Outdoor Sports (in the same location as the Canoe Livery, above), 12789 SR 664 South, Logan, tel. (740) 385-5312. This is a warm-weather sport—cold can affect one's grip on the rope. Consequently, April through October are the months where these folks take climbers out into the state forests to go up and down the faces of rocks and cliffs. Hock-

ing can be reached by e-mail: adventure@hockinghills.org. Reservations are recommended.

Also check out Hocking State Forest for their approved climbing and rappelling sites.

Horseback Riding

There are two approaches here. Palmerosa Horse Campground, 19217 Keifel Rd., Laurelville, tel. (740) 385-3799, wants travelers to show up with their own horses. Once here, they can saddle up and ride off on hundreds of miles of woodland trails. Or they can hole up in the campground, in a cabin, or in one of two bunkhouses. For more information, check its Web site at www.hockinghills.com/palmerosa. Stone Valley Ranch, 31606 Fairview Rd., Logan, tel. (800) 866-5196 furnishes the horses (or ponies for kids). Both are open year round.

ACCOMMODATIONS

Because this is a rural area, travelers may get the notion that there aren't many places to stay. Nothing could be further from the truth. Hocking Hills accommodations come thick and fast if visitors know where to look. There are approximately 20 bed and breakfast operations, ranging from simple, but spic 'n' span, farmhouses to facilities with hot tubs, swimming pools, private baths, and more. The B&Bs tend to fall in the expensive price range, and most have rural Logan addresses. Chalets, cottages, and cabins can be simple or amenity filled, and campgrounds are commonplace.

Perhaps the most luxurious spot in the area is the **Inn at Cedar Falls,** 21190 SR 374, Logan, tel. (740) 385-7489. The inn has secluded, very expensive, log cabins studded with antiques, and serves gourmet dinners. Another sumptuous place to stay is **Glenlaurel,** 15042 Mt. Olive Rd., Rockbridge, tel. (740) 385-4070 or (800) 809-REST (tel. 800-809-7378). Billed as a Scottish country inn and cottages, this is a very expensive, luxurious retreat in the heart of the Hocking Hills. The Hocking County Tourism Association, tel. (740) 385-9706 or (800) 462-5464, will help visitors secure a place that fits their pocketbooks and their anticipations.

HOCKING AREA EVENTS

JANUARY

Winter walk, Conkle's Hollow State Nature Preserve, Rockbridge, tel. (740) 653-2541.

Annual winter hike, Hocking Hills State Park, Logan, tel. (740) 385-1118 or e-mail artsmall @hocking.net.

FEBRUARY

Annual art auction, Hocking College, Nelsonville, tel. (740) 753-3591.

MARCH

Nature photography workshop, Hocking Hills State Park, Logan, tel. (740) 385-6841.

APRIL

Ohio Spring Classic Bicycle Races, Cantwell Cliffs, Rockbridge, tel. (740) 890-4145.

MAY

Moonshine Festival, New Straitsville, tel. (740) 394-2239, lets visitors see a whiskey still at work. Tune up for fiddle and banjo contests, opry music, and "moonshine" foods at this nostalgic four-day event.

SEPTEMBER

Hocking Hills Indian Run, Hocking Hills State Park Dining Lodge, tel. (740) 385-9706, is a two-day event. There are five-, 10-, and 20-kilometer races both weekend days and a 60-kilometer run on Sunday.

FOOD

Steak is a good idea after a day in the woods, and that's what **Jack's Steak House,** 35770 Hocking Dr. (Old US 33), Logan, tel. (740) 385-9909, dishes up every day from 9 a.m. to midnight. The most popular cuts tend to be sirloin, rib-eye, and T-bone, accompanied by baked potato or home fries, tossed salad or slaw, roll, and butter. Such a steak dinner costs between $7 and $13.95, depending on size and cut. There are a number of sandwiches for lunch, the most popular being a 3.5-oz. ground sirloin, served with a choice of a soup cup or fries for a mere $3.15. Lots of bus tours stop here.

KC's, 34 W. Main St., Logan, tel. (740) 385-0241, opened in the summer of 1998 and serves straight-ahead American food at very good prices. The downtown establishment offers a breakfast special that includes two eggs, home fries, and a choice of ham, bacon, or sausage for $3.15. A number of sandwiches can be had at lunch, including a grilled Reuben for $2.75. In the evening, dinner may be barbecued chicken at $6.95 or ribs at $8.95. The kinks have been ironed out and this is becoming a popular spot with locals and visitors alike.

INFORMATION AND SERVICES

In a medical or police emergecny call 911. The non-emergency number for police in Logan is (740) 385-6866. Telephone Hocking Valley Community Hospital in Logan at (740) 385-5631. The Logan post office is at 80 N. Market St.

The **Hocking County Tourism Association** is in a picturesque building at 13178 SR 664 South, Logan, tel. (740) 385-9706 or (800) 462-5464.

The *Logan Daily News* is sold weekday evenings and Saturday mornings.

Shopping

Rocky Shoes & Boots, Inc., 39 Canal St., Nelsonville, no telephone number listed, the world's largest maker of Gore-Tex water repellant footwear, operates a genuine factory outlet. More than 100 different styles of boots and shoes are offered at discount prices. Hours are Mon.-Sat. 9 a.m.-8 p.m. and Sunday 10 a.m.-6 p.m. In Logan, Artisan Mall, 703 W. Hunter St., tel. (740) 385-1118 is open normal business hours every day and is stocked with Appalachian crafts, antiques, and collectibles. On the south side of town, look for Logan Antique Mall, 12795 SR 664, tel. (740) 385-2061. Some 70 dealers are reputed to sell treasures there seven days a week.

ATHENS AND THE SOUTHEAST HEARTLAND

Ohio University will celebrate its 200th year in 2004, reason enough to visit this pretty town filled with students, hippies, and overeducated people who take menial jobs in order to stick around. This is a serendipitous spot where Appalachia meets higher education; both manage to survive.

History

Because the land around Athens was less fertile, the natives who grew corn, squash, and other vegetables preferred land north and west of here. Yet there is evidence of early Adena and other people: a flat area northwest of Athens served as a burial ground. There was no denying the abundance of wildlife in the area, as members of the exploratory Ohio Company discovered after the Northwest Ordinance of 1787 permitted settling. The ordinance also stated that "schools and the means of education shall forever be encouraged." Ohio University became the first institution of higher learning in the Northwest Territory. The first African-American graduated from the school in 1828, followed by the first woman in 1873. Down through the years, Athens has been seen as a place where the urban child of a Cleveland millworker and the rural child of an Appalachian tobacco grower can meet and learn something of each other's lives. Athens at the moment has 21,000 year-round residents.

THE MILLFIELD MINING DISASTER

The Depression was a year old when catastrophe struck the Millfield Coal Mine in northern Athens County. Mining executives were checking safety equipment on Nov. 5, 1930, when an explosion roared through the mine near Sunday Creek. Rescue workers sifting debris found 82 dead, though nine hours after the blast they discovered 19 men alive—some three miles from the main shaft. The disaster led to enactment of mine safety laws, but they were too late for the victims of the Millfield mine.

The site today is no snap to find. From Athens, head north on US 33 and then SR 13. Turn east off SR 13 in tiny Millfield and meander east. Within a mile there is a stark, red-brick smokestack to the right of the narrow, bumpy roadway. A state historical marker confirms the grisly spot. These days, it's overgrown and virtually devoid of activity. The most incessant sound on a summer morning is the hum of insects.

Because of the number of mines in the state, tragedy has been a constant through the years. The second worst day in Ohio mining took place near St. Clairsville, west of Wheeling, West Virginia, in Belmont County. There, on March 16, 1940, 77 miners died. Just four years later and eerily near, 66 men were killed in a mine disaster near north of St. Clairsville in the village of Belmont. That tragedy took place on July 5, 1944. Both of these disasters could be blamed on the frantic energy needs created by World War II.

Ohio coal has always been of mixed quality. And while no one in the 19th century took notice of pollution, low-sulfur, clean-burning coal was quickly mined out. Today, Ohio coal is retrieved primarily by the open-pit method of excavation in the eastern and southeastern parts of the state. The work is unsightly but infinitely safer than sinking shafts deep underground. Current environmental thinking means the land eventually will be reclaimed.

Location and Orientation

Athens is as close to the geographic center of Southeast Ohio as a traveler is apt to get. The city is 75 miles southeast of Columbus, 25 miles north of the Ohio River, 44 miles west of Marietta, 160 miles east of Cincinnati, and 210 miles south of Cleveland (all figures are highway miles). Athens is served by north-south US 33 and east-west US 50. But for a stretch of a dozen miles through Wayne National Forest, US 33 is a four-lane divided highway between Athens and Columbus.

SIGHTS

Burr Oak State Park, SR 13, Glouster, tel. (740) 767-2112, is a showpiece. Fifteen miles northeast of Athens, the park has a pristine lake, decent fishing, some of the most scenic hiking trails in the state, and a resort and conference center that's dazzling. The center has a huge indoor pool, a quality restaurant, and lots of diversions for children. The best way to approach Burr Oak is from the north on SR 78 via McConnelsville, and the best time is autumn. This "rim of the world" drive shows the park and the fiery trees to best advantage. Those who like their outings unspoiled can investigate nearby Burr Oak Cove in Wayne National Forest, tel. (740) 592-6644. A portion of the North County/Buckeye Trail passes through here and will one day be a part of a 1,200-mile pathway around the state.

Strouds Run State Park, 11661 State Park Rd., Athens, tel. (740) 592-2302, offers the best of the Appalachian Plateau. With more than 2,600 acres, the park boasts a couple of scenic overlooks that give visitors memorable views of this part of the country. More than 15 miles of hiking trails connect the park's numerous highlights, which include 900 feet of sandy bathing beach, a boat ramp, campsites, and picnicking facilities. Dogwood, redbud, and wildflowers make a spring visit here a must for anyone nearby. The south end of the park touches US 50 about five miles east of Athens.

Wayne National Forest covers parts of four counties in the vicinity of Athens. The U.S. Forest Service district office, tel. (740) 592-6644, is at 219 Columbus Rd., in Athens. This patch of the big forest lies primarily northwest of Athens and northeast of Logan. Another sizeable stretch of federal land lies east of Athens. This eastern segment is not heavily populated and is an easy place for an inexperienced hiker to get lost. Burr Oak State Park, about 20 miles north of Athens, is located on the eastern edge of Wayne National Forest.

Lake Hope State Park and **Zaleski State Forest,** SR 278, McArthur, tel. (740) 596-5253, cover a lot of ground. The park is a small part of the forest, which totals 25,000 acres. Both are wild and scenic areas that have recovered from being cut for fuel to fire the iron-smelting industry that once thrived in the vicinity. The heart of the park is, of course, Lake Hope, which curls in a semicircle around adjacent hills. Hope Furnace, a preserved smelting operation, is intact here,

and there are 15 miles of hiking trails. Only electric motors are permitted on the lake, which makes the 600-ft. beach tranquil. Besides a dining lodge, there are more than 60 cabins and 223 campsites. Backpackers must register before going off into the state forest.

RECREATION

Bicycling

Is it possible that the nicest walking, running, or cycling venue in Ohio is dead level, not all that long, and virtually devoid of shade? It is if it's the **Ohio University Bicycle Path,** a curvaceous strip of asphalt that follows the broad sweep of the Hocking River as it passes the OU football stadium, the golf course, and a portion of the campus. The path is atop a levee, and the distance from one major highway bridge to another is only about 1.5 miles. Those who wish to change into running gear will find restrooms on the second floor of the stadium, with plentiful parking just outside. An unobtrusive visitor can change clothes, use the toilet, or get a drink of water, at least during the week.

Farther afield, the **Hockhocking Adena Bikeway** runs between Athens and Nelsonville and includes the aforementioned OU bike path. The 33-mile round trip is amazingly flat, in part because the paved trail runs alongside the Hocking River as it winds through thick forests and beneath rock outcroppings. Other highlights include the Hocking Canal and an old coal-company town. Riders can park in Nelsonville at the Quality Inn on SR 691, or in Athens at the city park on East State Street. The only word of caution involves crossing SR 682. The view of traffic here is extremely limited.

Golf

The **Elm Golf Course,** CR 76, Athens, tel. (740) 594-0130, welcomes the public to its nine-hole, par 35 facility. Fees during the week are $7 to walk and $12 to ride. Add a dollar to both figures for weekend rates.

Horseback Riding

Those who prefer their horsepower living and breathing may want to visit **Smoke Rise Ranch Resort,** just off SR 78, east of Murray City, tel.

LIVING SIMPLY

Have you ever longed for the simple yet meaningful Amish way of living? You may be interested in the Ohio-based Center for Plain Living and its bimonthly magazine called *Plain.* It's produced by a Cleveland native in Chesterhill, a town of 400 residents north of Athens.

Scott Savage was raised a Quaker, though not one of the plain Quakers sometimes found around Chesterhill. Until recently, his day job involved writing grants for the medical college at Ohio University in Athens. Now, he devotes his time to publishing *Plain,* a periodical that, among other things, tells of the Savage family's attempts to live without the curse of modern conveniences and rails against the increasing complexity of society.

For a periodical with no advertising or much of a promotional budget, *Plain* has been receiving a gratifying amount of attention. *The New York Times* ran a lengthy feature on Savage and his center, which serves as a clearinghouse for criticism of technology-driven American culture. Readers write in to encourage the Savages and each other. More or less typical is the writer who revealed that, since his youth, he had been frightened of the noise produced by automobiles as well as of vacuum cleaners and flush toilets.

Savage and his wife and two children live and dress very much like Old Order Amish, in plain, dark clothing devoid of buttons or zippers. Mr. Savage wears a broad-brimmed hat; Mrs. Savage, a small white bonnet. They blend well with the Chesterhill population, though Scott may still be driving his car and his wife may still be wistful for a radio. The family telephone number is unlisted, perhaps in response to media attention.

Should you desire more information, write to the Center for Plain Living, P.O. Box 100, Chesterhill, OH 43728.

115 YEARS AND STILL BURNING~THE NEW STRAITSVILLE MINE

One hundred fifteen years and counting. Amazingly, that's how long an underground coal mine fire has been burning in a rural area southeast of New Straitsville in Perry County.

Once coal was discovered in Ohio, there was a real rush to mine it. By 1880, some 30 counties were shipping bituminous coal to customers in and out of the state. Bituminous coal is also called "soft coal." When burned, it releases a great deal of volatile material. The number of mines made the competition stiff and kept prices low. Mine owners frequently had to squeeze all the work they could out of the miners to keep their facilities profitable. Miners reacted by forming unions and staging strikes.

An especially bitter five-month strike occurred in New Straitsville in 1884. Though no one ever owned up to it, striking miners apparently set fires in five different mines. The seams of coal were as much as 14 feet wide and ran for miles underground; they caught and have never quit. During the Great Depression, the federal Works Progress Administration attempted to douse the fire and failed. There are enough fractures in the subterranean rock to admit oxygen, keeping the flames fed and the fire moving. Around 1940, two companies competed so fiercely to show tourists "The World's Greatest Mine Fire" that armed guards had to be hired to protect the attractions from each other.

The conflagration has continued command attention over the years. A rural schoolhouse got so hot there was talk of abandoning or demolishing it before the fire moved off in a different direction. Locals have found fissures hissing steam and smoke; for laughs, they boil coffee or fry eggs on the hills and in the hollows. Forest Service personnel sometimes see steam vents around streams and creeks, particularly in the vicinity of SR 216. A portion of that road once buckled due to heat from the subterranean blaze.

Doug Crowell, author of *The History of the Coal-Mining Industry in Ohio*, published by the Ohio Geological Survey, says no one can venture a guess on how long the New Straitsville flame will flicker. But it appears visitors have plenty of time.

(740) 592-4077 or (800) 292-1732. This is a working cattle ranch where visitors can view goings on from the saddle. There are trail rides, performance areas, bunkhouse-style cabins, and campsites. Murray City is 15 miles north of Athens. Those who bring horses into the area may want to put up at Chitananda Bed and Breakfast in Wayne National Forest near Burr Oak Lake, tel. (740) 347-4858. Proprietors Bob and Kathy Harty keep a couple of box stalls available so that visitors can ride the nearby state trails at Stone Church. Adjoining Burr Oak State Park, look for Lonesome Dove Trail Riding, 10705 Dock II Rd., Glouster, tel. (740) 767-2170. This outfit offers horses and experienced guides for traversing the wooded state-park pathways.

Off-Roading

Next to skateboarders, the most vilified bunch of folks on the planet may be those who ride off-road vehicles. The U.S. Forest Service has provided at least one nice Ohio run for these citizens, and it's between Athens and Logan, just north of US 33. **Monday Creek,** as it's known, has about 40 miles of trail, five different parking lots, a pair of campgrounds, and four distinct trail areas. Any two-, three-, or four-wheel motorcycle or other vehicle measuring less than 50 inches wide is okay for riding, so long as it's properly registered. For more information, contact the U.S. Forest Service's Athens Ranger District, 219 Columbus Rd., Athens, tel. (740) 592-6644.

Spectator Sports

Among the more unusual annual events around is the **DiDi Mau,** an annual off-road bicycling race held in Nelsonville each May. Officiated by the Vietnam Veterans of America and the National Off Road Bicycling Association, prizes of as much as $1,500 are posted for distance of up to 35 kilometers. The organizers say they chose the Nelsonville area because of its resemblance to parts of Vietnam, mud and all. The theme is, "You don't have to like it, you just have to show up!" For more information, contact the Vietnam Veterans of America, Chapter 100, at P.O. Box 2601, Athens, OH 45701. (*"Didi mau,"* for those not fluent in Vietnamese, is an order that translates roughly as "Leave here quickly!")

ENTERTAINMENT AND CULTURE

A former dairy barn of some size has become the **Dairy Barn Cultural Arts Center,** 8000 Dairy Lane, Athens, tel. (740) 592-4981. The barn, which was saved from the wrecking ball and converted into a 6,500 sq. ft. art gallery, is open Tues.-Sun. 11 a.m.-5 p.m., open on Thursday until 8 p.m. The gallery is closed between shows. Admission charges depend on what is being shown. For example, one recent show, "Beadworks," exhibited the work of 56 artists and cost $5 for adults and $3.50 for students. Calling the center in advance is a good idea, particularly if Appalachian-related art is being displayed. The Web site can be found at www.eurekanet.com/~dbarn.

O'Hooley's Irish Brew Pub, 24 W. Union St., Athens, tel. (740) 592-9686, has a number of attractions. Musically, Friday and Saturday evenings are devoted to Joe Bob Billy & the Texas Aliens and bands of that ilk. To get college and post-college patrons in the mood, the drinking establishment offers seven different tap beers, ales, porters, and stouts, all brewed on the premises. Spinning Hippie Organic Ale, for example, is $2.50 for 16 ounces and could be compared to Newcastle Ale. Thoughtfully, the management has posted the alcohol content of each brew. Domestic and foreign bottled beers are available, all at very low prices (a Rolling Rock long neck is $1.75). Food is basic: hot dogs, chips, and salsa. The music generally begins around 10 p.m. and the cover is $3. For more information, call (740) 592-9686 or go to the pub's Web site, www.frognet.net/~ohooleys.

ACCOMMODATIONS

A most pleasant place to spend the night is the new **Ohio University Inn,** 331 Richland Ave., Athens, tel. (740) 593-6661. It contains a restaurant, a tavern, an outdoor pool, a pretty courtyard, and it's a mere two blocks off campus. The two-story brick structure charges $99 per couple weekends and $89 for two during the week. Athens alternatives include a couple of motels: **Amerihost Inn,** 20 Home St., tel. (740) 594-3000; **Budget Host,** US 50 West, tel. (740) 594-2294; and **Days Inn,** 330 Columbus Rd., tel. (740) 592-4000. The chains tend to be more moderately priced than the Ohio University Inn.

There are a number of interesting overnight

ATHENS AREA EVENTS

MAY

Athens International Film Festival, tel. (740) 593-1330, has been showing flicks like *Bad Girls Go to Hell* and *Ma Vie en Rose* every year since 1973. Artists such as Ned Beatty show up. Call for films and screening locations.

International Street Fair, Court Street, Athens, tel. (740) 593-4330, is a joint efforts by OU students and the community. Visitors will find music, dance, food, arts, and international cultural displays.

Spring Literary Festival, Irvine Auditorium, Ohio University, tel. (740) 593-4181. This free, three-day event involves lectures and readings of nationally known creative writers.

JUNE

Chauncey-Dover Spring Festival, SR 13, Chauncey, tel. (740) 797-3202, takes place north of Athens. It involves three days of entertainment, food, crafts, a flea market, a parade, rides, and games.

Poston Lake Bluegrass Festival, 21344 Potter Rd., Guysville, tel. (740) 662-2051, is a two-day event featuring quality bluegrass music. Guysville is located east of Athens along off US 50 on SR 329.

Country Music Show, Albany Fairgrounds, Washington Street, Albany, tel. (740) 698-6155, is how the local fire department raises money. The benefit always features a Nashville headliner.

AUGUST

The **Parade of the Hills** marches through Nelsonville each August for seven days. Highlights include a carnival and midway, local folks selling a little bit of everything, and the crowning of a Miss Parade of the Hills. Call (614) 753-1006 for more information.

options outside of town. Bed and breakfast places include **Albany House,** 9 Clinton St., Albany, tel. (740) 698-6311; **Carpenter Inn,** 39655 Carpenter-Dyesville Rd., Albany, tel. (740) 698-2450; or **County Line Farm,** 11133 Hooper Ridge, Glouster, tel. (740) 767-4185. The Carpenter Inn offers hot tub or sauna; County Line Farm is a working dairy operation. Prices are moderate, especially during the week. Campgrounds abound, in state parks and elsewhere. One of the more popular spots is **Smoke Rise Ranch Resort,** CR 92, Murray City, tel. (800) 222-1732. Besides campsites, this 2,000-acre ranch offers cabin stays and is open year round.

FOOD

The **Bagel Street Deli,** 27 S. Court St., Athens, tel. (740) 593-3838), is a swell stop beginning at 7:30 a.m. for breakfast. The 90 cent bagels are hefty, the coffee's hearty, and there are enough college kids so that if you order a soda no one will laugh. This is a good stop to pick up a to-go sandwich for later on. Turkey on a bagel with choice of cheese, plus lettuce, tomato, and mayo is $3.25. Vegetarian bagel sandwiches number at least a dozen and include such ingredients as hummus, various cheeses, and a selection of peppers. Look for the red canopy over the door, across from the drugstore.

Burrito Buggy, Court and Union Streets, Athens (no telephone), serves up many different winning burritos to go. The chicken-chili burrito is $3.50 and tastes addictive. There are vegetarian and low-fat choices, side dishes such as red beans and rice, and a choice of either a can of soda for 50 cents or wild berry zinger iced tea for 75 cents to $1.25, depending on size. It's tough to spend more than $5 for lunch at this mobile diner, which is closed on Sunday in the summer.

Casa Nueva, 4 W. State St., Athens, tel. (740) 592-2016, is worker-owned and -operated. It's a casual place with contemporary decor, serving organic Mexican and eclectic food. Breakfasts include eggs or marinated tofu, each with toast and home fries, at $3 apiece; lunch and dinner items include several takes on grilled cheese for approximately $2.50; burritos for around $5; a three-layer stacked enchilada for $6.25; home-

made desserts; and more than 80 beers from around the world. The art on the walls changes frequently and is for sale, and there's sometimes live jazz or bluegrass music.

Farms-A-Plenty is a clever idea. This carryout restaurant at 9449 Clover Lane, Athens, tel. (740) 592-2474, relies almost entirely on locally raised items for its menu. A hot shredded-chicken barbecue sandwich is $2.89, a turkey and smoked cheddar sandwich is $2.99, a ham-and-cheese turnover is $1.50, and none of the 10 or so dessert creations cost more than $1.50—brownies, for example, are just 45 cents, while double servings of blueberry, cherry, or peach pudding are $2.49. There are daily specials, too.

Late Night Pizza, 122 W. Union St., Athens, tel. (740) 592-2008, appears to be the pie of choice among both town and gown. Decide among artichoke parmesan pie, twice-baked potato pie, enchilada pizza, or Gorgonzola pie—$12 for a small and $16 for a large. More conventional pizzas are $7.50 for a medium and $10.50 for a large. Add $1-2 for each topping besides cheese and sauce. For those who can't choose, the calzones are authentic and are priced at $8. Open daily at 4:30 p.m., Late Night Pizza offers free delivery. During the school year, this establishment operates a cart selling pizza by the slice at Court and Union Streets.

Seven Sauces, 66 N. Court St., Athens, tel. (740) 592-5555, creates eclectic evening meals seven days a week and has been well reviewed in big-city daily newspapers. Top choices include grilled or blackened yellowfin tuna ($12.95), Indonesian chicken ($11.95), filet mignon ($13.95), and West Indian vegetable curry ($8.95). Appetizers and desserts look good, and there's a full-service bar. Reservations are appreciated by the chef, who is also the owner.

The slickest tourist aid in all of Southeastern Ohio may well be the **Athens Menu Book,** a magazine-style presentation of the foods served in the city, complete with prices, as well as a map that will aid out-of-towners in finding the restaurant of their choice. The booklet carries a $2 price tag, has a number of food coupons, and can be obtained at Little Professor Book Center, 65 S. Court St., Athens, tel. (740) 592-4418. Coupons in the book will save more than its retail price.

INFORMATION AND SERVICES

In an emergency, police and medical services can be summoned by calling 911. The non-emergency number for Athens police is (740) 592-3315. Reach O'Bleness Memorial Hospital by dialing (740) 593-5551. The post office in Athens is at 5 W. Stimson Ave.

The **Athens County Convention and Visitors Bureau** is at 667 E. State St., tel. (740) 592-18189 or (800) 878-9767. Contact the **Jackson Area Tourism and Convention Bureau**, 159 Broadway St., at (614) 286-2722 or (800) 522-7564.

The *Athens Messenger* is available weekday evenings and Saturday mornings.

Shopping

Southeastern Ohio is light on megamalls but makes up for the fact with a large number of small establishments selling one-of-a-kind items.

Among them: Blue Wren Gifts and Gift Baskets, 8647 Lavelle Rd., Athens, tel. (740) 594-2254, north of West Union Street and west of SR 682; His Own Dog, 10 W. Union St., Athens, tel. (740) 592-4600, carries original-design T-shirts, among other things; Main Street Fibers, 6989 Main St., Guysville, tel. (740) 662-1100, which bills itself as the area's most complete selection of natural yarn and other spinning fibers (Guysville is about 10 miles southeast of Athens, just off US 50/SR 32); and Mountain Leather, 25 S. Court St., Athens, tel. (740) 592-5478, selling everything from pasta to picture frames—plus leather hats, purses, briefcases, wallets, belts, and more.

Antiquers can find neat stuff at the Athens Art, Craft and Antique Mall, 180 Columbus Rd., tel. (740) 594-7199. And for the loyal mall shopper, check out University Mall, 1002 E. State St., Athens, tel. (740) 592-3574. Stores here include JCPenney, Kmart, and Elder-Beerman.

CHILLICOTHE AND VICINITY

Chillicothe (chill-uh-KAW-thee) has just 22,000 residents, somewhat surprising in view of its large and numerous old downtown buildings. The city is built on a line of demarcation—to the west and north is flat and fertile farmland; to the east and south is foothill Appalachia.

History

Before humanity's arrival, the Wisconsin Glacier came to a temporary halt near here, leaving northwestern Ross County flat and southeastern Ross County hilly. Paleo-Indians showed up about 11,000 years ago, creating elaborate ceremonial and burial earthworks. The Shawnee were here when Europeans arrived, and the tribe made the mistake of siding with the British during the American Revolution. One such Shawnee was Blue Jacket, a European settler who was kidnapped as a child while herding cattle and rose to lead his adopted Native American people alongside such warriors as Tecumseh. (The town of Xenia presents Blue Jacket's story in its *Epic Outdoor Drama of Blue Jacket* during the summer.)

Chillicothe was founded in 1796, the name meaning "important town" in Shawnee. From

statehood in 1803 to 1816, the city served Ohio as its capital. While Chillicothe grew and prospered from the usual building of canals and railroads, it also benefited from another activity—papermaking. A paper plant established in the 1890s eventually became the nationally known Mead Corporation. Before pollution controls, the sour odor of the papermaking process permeated the town. Rather defensively, Chillicothe residents told complaining tourists that the ill wind was "the smell of money."

World War I saw the city overrun with soldiers. At one time, there were four men in uniform at nearby Camp Sherman for every town citizen. The campsite later became the location for correctional facilities and for a veterans' hospital. The city today is a regional shopping center that has shown great care in preserving tall, venerable, downtown red-brick buildings and historic homes.

Location and Orientation

Chillicothe, the seat of Ross County, is 47 miles south of Columbus, approximately midway between the state capital and the Ohio River. The city is 112 miles east-northeast of Cincinnati and

100 miles due west of Parkersburg, West Virginia. It's connected to Columbus and to points south by US 23, to Cincinnati by US 50, and to Dayton 81 miles northwest and to the southeast by US 35.

SIGHTS

The **Adena State Memorial,** on Adena Road, Chillicothe, tel. (740) 772-1500, was the home of Ohio's sixth governor and first U.S. senator, Thomas Worthington. It was from this majestic home, constructed in 1807, that state fathers witnessed the sunrise over Mount Logan. The view inspired them to have the hill and the rays of sun affixed to the Great Seal of Ohio. The mansion is furnished with antiques and there are a number of flower gardens and venerable outbuildings on the grounds. Adena is open Wed.-Sat. 9:30 a.m.-5 p.m. and Sunday noon-5 p.m., Memorial Day-Labor Day, plus weekends in May and October. Admission is $2 for adults and $1 for children.

The **Buckeye Furnace State Memorial,** southeast of Wellston, tel. (740) 384-3537, honors the charcoal iron industry that thrived in the hills during the 19th century. This particular furnace, made of native sandstone, was used from 1851 to 1894, producing as much as 12 tons of iron a day. There are iron-making exhibits in the museum. The park portion of the Ohio Historical Society site is open year round during daylight hours. The museum is open Wed.-Sat. 9:30 a.m.-5 p.m.; Sunday and holidays noon-5 p.m. all summer; from Labor Day through October it's open Saturday 9:30 a.m.-5 p.m. and Sunday noon-5 p.m. Admission is $3 for adults and $1.25 for children ages 6-12.

Adena pipe in the shape of a human figure

The 120-acre **Hopewell Culture National Historic Park,** at 16062 SR 104, Chillicothe, tel. (740) 774-1126, tells the story of the prehistoric Hopewell culture who lived here. Their saga is presented in exhibits and a short documentary video, *Legacy of the Mound Builders.* Visitors are permitted to tour a 2,000-year-old Hopewell mound. Artifacts also are on display and there are numerous brochures. Books detailing Hopewell culture are available at fair prices in the gift shop. From Memorial Day weekend through Labor Day, the visitor center is open daily 8:30 a.m.-6 p.m.; at other times it closes at 5 p.m. Closed Thanksgiving, Christmas, and New Year's Day. Admission is $2 for persons 17 and older, with a maximum charge of $4 per private vehicle.

The **Leo Petroglyph Park** on Park Road in Leo, is hard to find, and that's unfortunate. Petroglyphs (designs chipped into the faces of rock) were created by ancient people many hundreds of years ago and 40 of the works of art still exist in their original setting. One of the glyphs that is missing was purloined in the 19th century by a preacher fascinated with the reproduction of an elephant's foot—or was it the foot of a mammoth, which once roamed Ohio? To reach the park, which is free, exit US 35 east onto Davis Hollow Road, some 18 miles southeast of Chillicothe. Take Davis Hollow into the hamlet of Pine Road, then turn right onto Pine Road and look for the park on the left. Or ask in the little village of Leo.

State Parks

From Chillicothe, head south on US 35 to Jackson, then continue south on SR 93 to find **Jackson Lake State Park,** 935 Tommy Been Rd., Oak Hill, tel. (740) 682-6197. This is another of those improbably scenic lakes that bend around imposing hills in southeastern Ohio. Sandstone hills support second-growth forests containing oak, maple, hickory, tulip, and other trees. SR 279 crosses the lake at the south end, near the spillway, which also is the site of a well-preserved iron furnace. Recreation available here includes swimming, fishing for bass and other species, and ice fishing. Among the smaller parks with 92 acres, Jackson Lake has 34 campsites.

Lake Alma State Park, SR 349, Wellston, tel. (740) 384-4474, offers group camping on an island in a 60-acre lake. It also is a site for seasonal hunting, bowhunting, and trapping. Lake Alma originally was a stone quarry on the Jackson-Vinton county line. The lake was intended as part of an amusement park early in the century; it had a dance hall, a merry-go-round, and an outdoor theater. Nowadays, the city of Wellston leases it to the state as a park. The 2.5-mile hiking trail makes a wide arc around the lake. After a hike, there's a choice of two beaches on Lake Alma's north side for a refreshing dip. Bass, catfish, and panfish can be had in this electric motors-only body of water. Campsites total 72.

Farther afield, visit **Paint Creek State Park,** 23 miles west of Chillicothe and just north of US 50, outside Bainbridge, tel. (937) 365-1401. Among several activities in this vast, 9,000-acre facility is rock-climbing, supervised by the Army Corps of Engineers. No permit is required, and there is no lead climbing. Closer to Chillicothe, **Scioto Trail State Park,** Stony Creek Road, Chillicothe, tel. (740) 663-2125 is known for its bridle and off-road biking trails. The park is south of the city and just west of the Scioto River.

Noah's Ark Animal Farm

At 1527 McGiffins Rd., Jackson, tel. (740) 384-3060 or (800) 282-2167, this will be especially appreciated by younger children. Farm and wild animals—bear, bobcats, deer, ducks, llamas, raccoon, zebras—they're here to be admired. There are kiddie rides and train rides, plus miniature golf. Nearby is a Yogi Bear's Jellystone Resort with camping facilities and cabins. The farm, owned by a couple raised as Old Order Amish who conceived and installed church-pew cushions, is open April 1-Dec. 15. Hours are Mon.-Sat. 10 a.m.-6 p.m. and Sunday noon-7 p.m. Admission is $5 for adults and $4 for children ages 3-12.

RECREATION

A sizeable area golf course is available to visitors at **Running Fox,** 310 Sunset St., Chillicothe, tel. (740) 775-9955, has 27 holes and charges $9.50 weekdays or $13 weekends for unlimited play. Carts are $7.50 for nine holes and $12 for 18.

Improbably, there's a ski hill in the vicinity. **Spicy Run Mountain,** tel. (888) 774-2978, about 30 miles southwest of Chillicothe, has the longest run in Ohio and, with snowmaking equipment, keeps its various trails properly snowy. In good weather, reach the hill from Chillicothe by driving south out of town on scenic, seldom-traveled SR 772. This route into Appalachia should be taken as far as the village of Idaho, then turn right or west on SR 124 a couple of miles to Spicy Run. Besides skiing day and night there's snowboarding. Ski and snowboarding packages can be rented, as can individual pieces of equipment. Lift tickets are $25 for adults and $20 for seniors and students, per four-hour session.

ENTERTAINMENT AND CULTURE

Tecumseh! has been called the best of Ohio's summer outdoor dramas. It has been presented from early June to Labor Day since 1973, drawing two million spectators to the Sugarloaf Mountain Amphitheater on Delano Marietta Road, north of Chillicothe and east of US 23, tel. (740) 775-0700. The story of the Indian leader who defied American leaders and tormented Ohio settlers is a moving one, told with a large cast, authentic costumes, and special effects. Prior to the performance, visitors can pay $3.50 for adults and $2 for children under 10 for a behind-the-scenes tour given 2-5 p.m. the same day as a performance. A buffet dinner, $8 for adults and $4.80 for children is set out 4:30-7:45 p.m. The performance itself is held nightly at 8 p.m. and costs $13 for adults Mon.-Thurs. and $15 for adults Fri.-Sat., children being $6 at all times.

The **Pumphouse Art Gallery,** Enderlin Circle (in Yoctangee Park), Chillicothe, tel. (740) 772-5783, has art hows, exhibits, quilt shows, and antique shows throughout the year. The historic brick building, constructed in 1882, also is the site of an art festival in late June and Oktoberfest

CHILLICOTHE AREA EVENTS

MAY

The **Wild Turkey Festival** takes place three days each year in McArthur, midway between Athens and Chillicothe on US 50, tel. (740) 596-5033. Doin's include arts and crafts, amusement rides, contests, food, entertainment, and—oh yes—hunting gobblers. A highlight is the turkey-calling contest; like all the events admission is free.

Feast of the Flowering Moon occurs in May in downtown Chillicothe. This is the celebration of the flowering of plants, a crucial event to Native Americans and to early settlers. There's a juried crafts show, live entertainment, food aplenty, and other contests and events. Call (800) 413-4118 for more information.

JUNE

Canal Days Festival, Waverly, tel. (740) 947-9542, takes place at this village south of Chillicothe on the Scioto River. The five-day affair includes entertainment, arts and crafts, a parade, rides, and games, in or near the local high school.

Western Heritage Days Championship Rodeo, Ross County Fairgrounds, Chillicothe, tel. (740) 773-3675, makes the original Ohio capital come alive. Dancing, separate shows for sheep dogs, Texas Longhorns, and horses are just a few of the activities.

JULY

Happening in the Park happens in Canal Park, Waverly, tel. (740) 947-7640. Appalachian crafters display their wares to children and adults, and there is food and entertainment.

First Capital Post Card Show, at the Comfort Inn (junction of US 23 and US 35) in Chillicothe, tel. (740) 772-2770, features old picture post cards.

SEPTEMBER

The hills are alive with the sounds of apples crunching at the **Jackson County Apple Festival** each year. The apples roll and the cider flows as pies, apple butter, and candy apples are everywhere. Add to this three parades, free entertainment, and rides and games. To find out more, call (614) 286-1339.

The **Ohillco Coal Festival** in Wellston celebrates all things mining—mining displays, coal mining memorabilia, coal art, the Coal Miner Olympics—and offers plenty of entertainment, and food over five days. For details, call (614) 384-5141.

OCTOBER

Rural Ohio Appalachia Revisited, Lake Hope State Park and Zaleski State Forest, McArthur, tel. (740) 596-4938, showcases the natural beauty of Appalachia through crafters and musicians.

Fall Hike, Lake Hope State Park, SR 278, Zaleski, tel. (740) 596-5253, takes place the third weekend in October and is among the best times and places in the state to see the vivid colors of the turning leaves.

---

the last weekend in September. There's a permanent collection of historic art and a gift shop with objects visitors won't see elsewhere in the area.

As for live music, travelers should head for Cross Keys 19 Main St., Chillicothe, tel. (740) 774-4157. Bands such as Chili Sauce play rock and roll, blues, oldies, or boogie woogie on Saturday nights more or less regularly. There is no cover and tunes usually commence around 9 p.m. Goody's Lounge in the Days Inn, 1250 N. Bridge St., Chillicothe, tel. (740) 775-7000, can be counted on for country bands such as Dallas or for standup comedy. There is a cover charge of around $3 for the music.

Spectator Sports

Take the family out to the ball game by watching the Chillicothe Paints at the VA Stadium, SR 104 North, Chillicothe, tel. (740) 773-TEAM. The Single A Frontier League team has an 80-game season that lasts from June through September; half the games are played here. The attraction is billed as professional baseball with a hometown atmosphere, and while the guys on the field may never make the big leagues, they try hard. Admission is $3. The team also maintains a gift shop at 59 N. Paint St. downtown. It's open 10 a.m.-2 p.m. weekdays, May-Oct. Go Paint!

ACCOMMODATIONS

A number of visitors to the *Tecumseh!* performance elect to stay over afterward, and there are several nice places in the city. **Blair House Bed and Breakfast,** 58 W. Fifth St., tel. (740) 774-3140, is on the National Register of Historic Places. There are several other local bed and breakfast operations, too. Chain motels include the **Comfort Inn,** 30 N. Plaza Blvd., tel. (740) 775-3500; **Days Inn,** 1250 N. Bridge St., tel. (740) 775-7000; **Hampton Inn,** 100 N. Plaza Blvd., tel. (740) 773-1616; **Holiday Inn Express,** 1003 E. Main St., tel. (740) 772-5733; and **TraveLodge,** 1135 E. Main St., tel. (740) 775-2500. A popular local motel is **Christopher Inn,** 30 N. Plaza Blvd., tel. (740) 774-6835. It offers a free continental breakfast, an indoor pool, a hot tub, and a sauna. Campers will feel welcome at **Buffalo Trail Camping Area,** 34611 US 50, Londonderry (east of Chillicothe), tel. (740) 887-2031, or at **Sun Valley Campground,** 10105 CR 550 (northwest of Chillicothe on US 35), tel. (740) 775-3490.

FOOD

Grillworks, 649 Center Central, US 50, Chillicothe, tel. (740) 774-6394, serves a little bit of everything. Italian and Mexican dishes, sandwiches, steaks—it's all available for lunch or dinner every day. A favorite luncheon sandwich, besides the usual hamburgers and cheeseburgers, is grilled chicken, served with fries, for $6.95. In the evening, best values include a steak for $7.95 and fajitas for $8.95. An informal spot, Grillworks sometimes has a DJ on weekends to spin a few tunes, and diners can play a satellite-linked interactive trivia game while awaiting their fare. **New York, New York,** 200 N. Plaza Blvd., Chillicothe, tel. (740) 773-2100, brings a bit of Gotham to Ohio. The food is contemporary American cuisine and that can include a wide variety of pasta dishes for dinner, plus several steaks in various sizes. The biggest chunk of beef is an 18-oz. porterhouse for $24.95. Look, too, for fresh fish dishes, which vary in price according to what is available. Those who are less hungry frequently satisfy themselves with soup, salad, and an appetizer, which costs $15 or less. New York, New York is open Mon.-Thurs. 5-10 p.m. and Fri.-Sat. 5-11 p.m.

INFORMATION AND SERVICES

In a medical or police emergency, dial 911. The non-emergency number for the Chillicothe police is (740) 773-1191. Contact medical personnel at Medical Center Hospital, (740) 772-7500. The local post office is on Walnut Street between Main and Fourth Streets.

The **Jackson Area Chamber of Commerce** is at 382 Pearl St., Jackson, tel. (740) 286-2722. The **Ross/Chillicothe Convention and Visitors Bureau** is at 5 W. Water St., Chillicothe, tel. (740) 775-0900. The **Vinton County Chamber of Commerce** is at 114 W. Main St., McArthur, tel. (740) 596-5033.

"Snapshots" is the entertainment section produced each Friday by the *Chillicothe Gazette.* The Gazette is sold weekday evenings and Saturday mornings.

Transportation

Greyhound Bus Lines serves Chillicothe, with tranportation between Columbus and Portsmouth. The local station is at 193 E. Main St., tel. (740) 775-2013. To get around town, check out the buses belonging to the Chillicothe Transit System. For route and schedule information, telephone (740) 773-1569. Fares are 50 cents for adults and seniors, 25 cents for students, and free for children less than school age.

Shopping

Next to City Park in downtown Chillicothe is the First Capital District. This mix of antique emporia, specialty shops, restaurants, and taverns fits in well with the many historic brick buildings. The area is ablaze with decorations from Thanksgiving to Christmas each year. In Jackson, look for the Art & Craft Mall at SR 32 and Burlington Road, tel. (740) 286-8484. All items are handmade and all crafters have survived jury scrutiny. The mall is open Mon.-Sat. 10 a.m.-7 p.m. and Sunday noon-5 p.m.

BOOKLIST

CULTURE

Bernstein, Mark. *Grand Eccentrics.* Wilmington, OH: Orange Frazer Press, 1997. This is a group biography of half a dozen late-19th-century individuals—including Wilbur and Orville Wright, Charles Kettering, John H.Patterson, Arthur Morgan, and James Cox—each of whom left an indelible mark on Ohio (particularly Dayton, where they did everything from financing each other's schemes to trying to run one another out of town), as well as on America and the world.

Vezza, Dianne Wehrs. *In the Weesome Hours.* Wilmington, OH: Orange Frazer Press, 1998. Ms. Vezza discovered an ancient diary belonging to a 19th-century Ohio woman named Mary Lackey Williams and faithfully transcribed it. The Union widow and divorcee will strike the reader as smart, resourceful, and modern in many ways.

DESCRIPTION AND TRAVEL

For the state's own publication (free), *Ohiopass,* is a 160-page magazine-format annual offering full of vivid photos and descriptions; it also includes some 30 pages of discount coupons to everything from horse racing to the Living Bible Museum. Call (800) BUCKEYE (or tel. 800-282-5393) to request the latest edition.

Allen, Hayward. *The Traveler's Guide to Native America: The Great Lakes Region.* North-Word Press, Inc., 1992. This fascinating book begins with prehistory and intertwines the stories of various Native American tribes—explaining in detail Ohio's magnificent mounds, among other things.

Baumann, James A. *Ohio Cum Laude.* Wilmington, OH: Orange Frazer Press, 1997. Thousands of kids from out of state pour into Ohio each year for higher education, joining thousands of Buckeye kids at 54 four-year residential colleges. Those institutions are covered, as are all the other places of higher learning. A college or university often is the centerpiece of an Ohio school town, and this is a nice introduction.

Braftin, Barbara. *Ohio Online.* Wilmington, OH: Orange Frazer Press,1997. This is Ohio's own guide to Internet Web sites. While it probably was dated before it came out, these "yellow pages" remain a nice item for those who like to plan vacations and check out Ohio events via computer.

Groene, Janet, and Gordon Groene. *Country Roads of Ohio.* Oaks, PA: Country Roads Press, 1993. The authors pay 17 arbitrary visits to places in Ohio they like and come away with worthwhile information in pleasant prose. Sites chosen are mostly rural, hence the title.

Groene, Janet, and Gordon Groene. *Natural Wonders of Ohio.* Oaks, PA: Country Roads Press, 1994. This book explains what the authors of the preceding volume *did* on those country roads—checked out flora and fauna. Subtitled "A Guide to Parks, Preserves & Wild Places," the book contains good summaries of public and private destinations.

Particular Places: A Traveler's Guide to Inner Ohio. Wilmington, OH: Orange Frazer Press. A two-volume set that is unfortunately out of print now, this nice collection combines reprints from *Ohio* magazine and freelance contributions in discussing various sites in Ohio (primarily southern and central). Both volumes shy away from the major cities, and the information is good even if the prose is sometimes overwrought.

Taxel, Laura. *Cleveland Ethnic Eats.* Gray & Co., 1995. If one of your goals in any town is to dine with the locals, this "Guide to the Authentic Ethnic Restaurants and Markets of Greater Cleveland" is the book for you. Ms. Taxel's approaches and assessments are generous yet accurate and insightful.

Zimmerman, George. *Ohio, Off the Beaten Path.* Old Saybrook, CT: The Globe Pequot Press, 1993. Zimmerman is the state travel director for Ohio, so he knows whereof he speaks. Precise descriptions of many familiar and overlooked spots, public and private, fill this worthwhile work.

Zimmeth, Khristi Sigurdson. *Ohio Family Adventure Guide.* OldSaybrook, CT: The Globe Pequot Press, 1996. Tilted heavily in favor of travelers with children, this is a nice general guide to the Buckeye State's more popular attractions.

Pulfer, Laura. *I Beg to Differ.* Wilmington, OH: Orange Frazer Press, 1998. Pulfer is a columnist for the *Cincinnati Enquirer* and occasional commentator on National Public Radio. Down through the years, she's distilled lots of good, if opinionated information (the book is subtitled, "Politically Incorrect, Proudly Midwestern, Potentially Funny.")

Roberts, Les. *The Duke of Cleveland.* New York: St. Martin's Press, 1995. Roberts is a recovering refugee from Los Angeles who now makes his home in Cleveland. This mystery is one in a series starring private eye Milan Jacovich. Other books in the series include *The Cleveland Connection, Deep Shaker, Full Cleveland, The Lake Effect,* and *Pepper Pike.* They're geographically accurate and diabolical fun to read.

GOOD READING

Anderson, Sherwood. *Winesburg, Ohio.* 1919. Anderson's collection of short stories should be included in any list of America's dozen or so best books. The work is especially recommended to those who get sentimental over the small-town Midwest life of bygone days. Anderson's Winesburg actually was the north-central Ohio town of Clyde (which is no longer chagrined at its literary portrait).

Frazier, Ian. *Family.* New York: Farrar, Straus and Giroux, 1994. This is a good book by a great writer. Better known for the best-selling *Great Plains* and the hilarious *Dating Your Mom,* Frazier tells the story of his family in America down through the years. Wilderness and suburban Ohio are much in evidence and make for sometimes wrenching contrasts.

McNutt, Randy. *Ghosts.* Wilmington, OH: Orange Frazer Press, 1997. The author takes readers on an eccentric trip to dozens of Ohio ghost towns. Along the way, he introduces you to tattooed chickens, legendary daredevils, swamp ghosts, and a fellow who bit off his mother-in-law's ear. Accompanied by pen and ink illustrations.

HISTORY

Brandt, Nat. *The Town That Started the Civil War.* Syracuse, NY: Syracuse University Press, 1990. Relates the 1858 resistance of a few courageous souls in Oberlin, Ohio, to slavecatchers, despite incarceration, a trial, and other hardships.

Cash, James B. *Unsung Heroes.* Wilmington, OH: Orange Frazer Press, 1998. This is a modern-day appraisal of Ohio presidents and their eras in the White House. The book delves into the triumphs and defeats of the seven Buckeyes who served the country between Reconstruction and the Roaring Twenties—several of them "genuine heroes."

England, J. Merton, ed. *Buckeye Schoolmaster: A Chronicle of Midwestern Rural Life, 1853-1865.* Bowling Green, OH: Bowling Green State University Press, 1997. This book tells in a schoolmaster's own words about the day-to-day life of Ohio in a momentous 12 years in the mid-19th century.

Feather, Carl E. *Mountain People in a Flat Land: A Popular History of Appalachian Migration to Northeast Ohio.* Athens, OH: Ohio University Press, 1998. When industrial Ohio needed workers, it turned to the underemployed in Appalachia. This recounting of hardship and assimilation is fascinating and reader-friendly.

Federal Writers' Project. *Cincinnati: A Guide to the Queen City and its Neighbors.* Cincinnati: Wiesen-Hart Press, 1943. In addition to a thorough history of the city, this book contains several dozen black-and-white photos of places in town that either have been razed or metamorphosed into something no longer easily recognized.

Federal Writers' Project. *The Ohio Guide.* Ohio State Archaeological and Historical Society. 1940. This compilation remains wonderfully fascinating, accurate, and thorough.

Havighurst, Walter. *Ohio, a Bicentennial History.* New York: W. W. Norton and Company, Inc., 1976. Havighurst, an award-winning history professor at Miami University in Oxford, Ohio, was well qualified to write this 200-year salute to his home state. His overviews of various large matters give readers a good sense of how issues such as the Civil War affected Buckeyes and their state.

Knepper, George W. *Ohio and Its People.* Kent, OH: Kent State University Press, 1989. This may be the ultimate Ohio history. It's well written by an academic who is a past president of the Ohio Historical Society, but the starchy stuff is kept to a minimum. Big, attractive, comparatively recent, and informative.

Laffoon, Polk, IV. *Tornado.* New York: Harper & Row, 1975. The timeless tale of tragedy that struck Xenia, Ohio, on April 3, 1974. Laffoon mixes humanity and weather in a moving literary tribute to a resilient little town.

McGovern, Frances. *Written on the Hills: The Making of the Akron Landscape.* Akron, OH: University of Akron Press, 1996. No town in America boomed more than this rubber production center-and this natural and human history tells the tale well.

O'Bryant, Michael, ed. *Ohio Almanac.* Wilmington, OH: Orange Frazer Press, 1997. This Ohio encyclopedia contains more than 100,000 bits of information-everything from annual events to zip codes, as well as lists of wealthy residents and the like, pieces on Ohio's effect on religions (and vice versa), and much more. And the profiles of famous Buckeyes goes a long way toward humanizing historical figures.

Santmyer, Helen Hoover. *Ohio Town.* New York: Harper & Row, 1984. This memoir of Xenia by the late author of *And Ladies of the Club* is what every town history should be: funny, respectful, nostalgic, authentic.

Vonada, Damaine. *Ohio Matters of Fact.* Wilmington, OH: Orange Frazer Press, 1993. This compendium of what sometimes seems to be every conceivable piece of information-trivial and otherwise-about Ohio should be considered indispensable.

Vonada, Damaine. *Ohio Sports Matter of Fact.* Wilmington, OH: Orange Frazer Press, 1995. Similar to the preceding title, with an emphasis on athletics.

Wachter, Georgann, and Michael Wachter. *Erie Wrecks.* Corporate Impact, 1997. Tells about a number of major shipwrecks in this stormiest of all Great Lakes. Not all wrecks are covered (not all have been *discovered*), but the Wachters are working on a sequel. The book is available from Corporate Impact at 33326 Bonnieview Drive, Avon Lake, OH 44012. The cost is $30, which includes tax and postage.

MAPS

1997 Road Atlas. Skokie, IL: Rand McNally, 1996. Still the most legible collection of state maps, the current atlas devotes two pages each to Ohio north and south and is also useful for those needing maps of surrounding states.

Ohioana Ohio Literary Map. This map lists more than 130 Ohio authors in 17 categories and, though intended primarily for use in a classroom, can be used to navigate Buckeye literary landmarks. It can be ordered from the Ohioana Library Association, 65 S. Front St., Suite 1105, Columbus, OH 43215; cost is $7.50, including tax and postage.

Ohio Atlas & Gazetteer. Freeport, ME: DeLorme Mapping Co., 1991. This atlas will show you everything from covered bridges to top fishing spots. For the minutia-minded, or for those who are perpetually lost, every public road in the state is reproduced.

Ohio Tour and Highway Map is free of charge by calling (800) BUCKEYE (or tel. 800-282-5393), the official state tourism source. The map folds into glove compartment size. One side has a busy highway map, the other a less crowded view with major state and private attractions noted.

PHOTOGRAPHY

Albrecht, Eric. *God's Country.* Wilmington, OH: Orange Frazer Press, 1998. West-central Ohio's forests and bogs were no match for determined German settlers in the 19th century. They created 42 parishes in a 22-mile swath of agriculture that has been called "the most concentrated ethnic rural settlement in America." Before the modern world whisked this chunk of history away, Albrecht recorded it all on film.

Images From the Heart. The Emerson Companies, 1997. This book is the Cleveland bicentennial's official commemorative publication. As such, the softcover version costs $24.95 and contains more than 300 photos of what makes Cleveland the unique, 200-year-old place that it is.

Platt, Carolyn V., photography by Gary Meszaros. *Creatures of Change: An Album of Ohio Animals.* Kent, OH: Kent State University Press, 1998. Despite the human onslaught, Ohio has served as the home for an array of animals since the coming of Europeans. This book follows their status and allows the reader up-close looks at the various species.

RECREATION

Combs, Rick, and Steve Gillen. *Canoeing and Kayaking Ohio's Streams.* Rexford, MT: Backcountry Publishing, 1995. This book proves, among other things, that you can find real whitewater in Ohio. There's even a handy list of the fastest and most frightening streams.

Ramey, Ralph. *Fifty Hikes in Ohio.* Rexford, MT: Backcountry Publishing, 1994. Relief maps accompany every suggested hike, though they are in black and white and, of course, one-dimensional. That's about the only limiting factor in this fascinating book, written by an official with the Ohio Department of Natural Resources who is a former nature preserve director.

Van Valkenberg, Phil. *Best Bike Rides Midwest.* Old Saybrook, CT: Globe Pequot Press, 1997. This compact paperback fits most anywhere and details eight day-long rides in the Buckeye State. The work eschews the usual bike trails, taking riders instead on tours of covered bridges, ice cream stores, or big rivers. It offers easily understood maps, details landmarks to the tenth of a mile, and throws in bits of history and geography.

TOLL-FREE TELEPHONE NUMBERS
FOR OHIO TRAVELERS

The following numbers are valid toll-frees within the state of Ohio. Few of them are working numbers beyond Ohio and its neighboring states. Most are intended for reservations.

BED & BREAKFASTS

Albany House Bed & Breakfast, Athens, (800) 600-4941
Amerihost Inn, Logan, (800) 459-4678
Amish Country Reservations, (888) 606-9400
At Home in Urbana Bed & Breakfast, Urbana, (800) 800-0970
Blue Ash Hotel & Conference Center, Cincinnati, (800) 468-3597
Bear Run Inn Bed & Breakfast, Logan, (800) 369-2937
Captain Montague's Bed & Breakfast, Huron, (800) 276-4756
Castle Inn Bed & Breakfast, Circleville, (800) 477-1541
Christopher Inn, Chillicothe, (800) 257-7042
Cobbler Shop Bed & Breakfast, Zoar, (800) 287-1547
Comfort Inn, Boston Heights, (800) 228-5150
Cornelia's Corner Bed & Breakfast, Westerville, (800) 745-2678
The Empty Nest Bed & Breakfast, Logan, (800) 385-5812
English Manor Bed & Breakfast, Miamisburg, (800) 676-9456
Fly Inn Bed & Breakfast, Kelley's Island, (800) 365-2601
Glenlaurel Inn and Spa Bed & Breakfast, Rockbridge, (800) 809-7378
Grand Lake St. Mary's Bed & Breakfast, St. Mary's, (800) 484-8409
Harrison House Bed & Breakfast, Columbus, (800) 827-4203
Hart & Mather Guest House, Sharon Center, (800) 352-2584
Heartland Country Resort Bed & Breakfast, Fredericktown, (800) 230-7030
Hill View Acres Bed & Breakfast, East Fultonham, (800) 365-2601
Historic Overholt Bed & Breakfast, Wooster, (800) 992-0643
Hocking House Bed & Breakfast, Laurelville, (800) 477-1541
Inn Towner Motel, Logan, (800) 254-3371
Joy Harvest Bed & Breakfast, Ada, (800) 851-1255
Kings Island Inn, Mason, (800) 727-3050
Idlewyld Bed & Breakfast, Lakeside, (800) 365-2601
Lansing Street Bed & Breakfast, Columbus, (800) 383-7839
Larchmont Bed & Breakfast, Marietta, (800) 353-3550
Laurel Brook Farm Bed & Breakfast, Hocking Hills, (800) 578-4279
Liberty House Bed & Breakfast, West Liberty, (800) 437-8109
Lily Ponds Bed & Breakfast, Hiram, (800) 325-5087
Main Street Inn Bed & Breakfast, Fort Recovery, (800) 837-1519
Midwestern Inn, Solon, (800) 626-9466
Milennium Classic Bed & Breakfast, Wooster, (800) 937-4199
Ohio State Park Resorts, (800) AT-A-PARK (282-7275)

One Hundred Mile House Bed & Breakfast, Portsmouth, (800) 645-2051
Painted Valley Farm Bed & Breakfast, Hocking, Hills, (800) 223-3397
Penguin Crossing Bed & Breakfast, Columbus, (800) 736-4846
Pitz-Cooper House Bed & Breakfast, Newark, (800) 833-9536
Porch House Bed & Breakfast, Granville, (800) 587-1995
Quail Hollow Resort, Concord, (800) 792-0258
Ravenwood Castle Inn, Hocking Hills, (800) 477-1541
Roscoe Village Inn, Coshocton, (800) 237-7397
Rose of Sherron Bed & Breakfast, Galion, (800) 368-8426
Running W Farm Bed & Breakfast, Hocking Hills, (800) 600-4919
Shaw's Inn Bed & Breakfast, Lancaster, (800) 654-2477
Smithville Bed & Breakfast, Smithville, (800) 869-6425
Spencer House Bed & Breakfast, Rockbridge, (800) 600-0585
Steep Woods Bed & Breakfast, Hocking Hills, (800) 900-2954
Thunder Ridge Cabins Bed & Breakfast, Logan, (800) 600-0584
Timberframe Bed & Breakfast, West Liberty, (800) 232-2319
Travelers Inn, North Ridgeville, (800) 469-5287
Valley View Inn, Fresno, (800) 331-8439
Van Meter Bed & Breakfast, Chillicothe, (800) 365-2601
Village Lodge, Strongsville, (800) 328-7829
Winfield Bed & Breakfast, Ashland, (800) 269-7166
Wolfe's Inn Bed & Breakfast, Newark, (800) 654-5643
Yesterday Bed & Breakfast, Centerville, (800) 225-0485

ATTRACTIONS

The Beach Waterpark, Mason, (800) 886-7946
Carrousel Dinner Theatre, Akron, (800) 362-4100
Clay's Park Resort, North Lawrence, (800) 860-4386
The Cleveland Orchestra, Cleveland, (800) 686-1141
The Columbus Zoo, Columbus, (800) 666-5397
Dover Lake Park, Sagamore Hills, (800) 372-7946
Geauga Lake Waterpark, Aurora, (800) 843-9283
Hale Farm and Village, Bath, (800) 589-9703
Harry London Candies, No. Canton, (800) 321-0444
Inventure Place, Akron, (800) 968-4332
Lake Farmpark, Kirtland, (800) 366-3276
Lake Metroparks, Wickliffe, (800) 254-7275
Moundbuilders State Memorial, Newark, (800) 600-7174
Paramount's Kings Island, Mason, (800) 288-0808
Roscoe Village, Coshocton, (800) 877-1830
St. Helena III Canal Boat & Canal Museum, Canal Fulton, (800) 435-3623
Sea World, Aurora, (800) 637-4268
Wyandot Lake, Columbus, (800) 328-9283
Zoar Village, (800) 262-6194

CAMPGROUNDS AND RV PARKS

Bass Isle Resort & Camping, Middle Bass Island, (800) 837-5211
Camp Toodik Family Campground, Loudonville, (800) 322-2663
Crystal Rock Campground, Sandusky, (800) 321-7177
Cutty's Sunset, Louisville, (800) 533-7965
Dayton Tall Timbers KOA, Brookville, (800) 432-2267
Lake Hill Campground, Chillicothe, (800) 522-9016
Long Lake Park, Loudonville, (800) 662-2663
Mohican Reservation, Loudonville, (800) 766-2267
Mohican Valley, Loudonville, (800) 682-2663
Noah's Ark Campground, Jackson, (800) 282-2167
Pin Oak Lake Park, Berlin Heights, (800) 262-7657
Sauder Village Campground, Archbold, (800) 590-9755
Smith's Pleasant Valley Family Campground, Loudonville, (800) 376-4847
Tomorrow's Stars Music Park, South Charleston, (800) 331-8767
Top O' the Caves, Hocking Hills, (800) 967-2434
Wapakoneta KOA, Wapakoneta, (800) 292-7254
Whispering Hills Camp Ground, Shreve, (800) 992-2435
Yogi Bear's Kings Island Camp-Resort, Kings Island, (800) 832-1133

CANOE LIVERY

Indian River Canoe Outfitters, Canal Fulton, (800) 226-6349
Mohican Canoe Livery and Fun Center, Loudonville, (800) 662-2663
Mohican Reservation, Loudonville, (800) 766-2267
Mohican Valley, Loudonville, (800) 682-2263
Pleasant Hill, Perrysville, (800) 442-2663

EXCURSIONS

Cuyahoga Valley Scenic Railroad, Peninsula, (800) 468-4070
Goodtime I, Sandusky, (800) 446-3140
Great Day! Tours and Charter Bus Service, Cleveland, (800) 362-4905
Greyhound Bus Lines, Cleveland, (800) 231-2222
Miller Boat Line, Put-in-Bay, (800) 500-2421

GOLF COURSES

Deer Lake Golf Course, Geneva, (800) 468-8450
Maple Ridge Golf Course, Austinburg, (800) 922-1368
Tam O' Shanter, Canton, (800) 462-9964
Tannenhauf Golf Club, Lexington, (800) 533-5140
Timber View Golf Club, Marysville, (800) 833-4887

SHOPPING

Lake Erie Factory Outlet Center, Sandusky, (800) 344-5221

TOURISM

Ohio Division of Tourism, (800) BUCKEYE (282-5393)

CENTRAL OHIO

Greater Columbus Convention and Visitors Bureau, (800) 345-4386
Delaware County Convention and Visitors Bureau, (888) 335-6446
Dublin Convention and Visitors Bureau, (800) 245-8387
Fairfield County Visitors and Convention Bureau (Lancaster), (800) 626-1296
Licking County Convention and Visitors Bureau (Newark), (800) 589-8224
Pickaway County Visitors Bureau (Circleville), (888) 770-7425
Union County Convention and Visitors Bureau (Marysville), (800) 642-0087
Westerville Visitors and Convention Bureau, (800) 824-8461
Convention and Visitors Bureau of Worthington, (800) 997-9935

NORTHEAST OHIO

Akron/Summit Convention and Visitors Bureau, (800) 245-4254
Ashtabula County Convention and Visitors Bureau, (800) 3-DROP IN (800-337-6746)
Canal Fulton Chamber of Commerce, (800) 993-9693
Canton/Stark County Convention and Visitors Bureau, (800) 533-4302
Cleveland Convention Bureau, (800) 321-1004
Convention and Visitors Bureau of Greater Cleveland, (800) 321-1001
Coshocton County Convention and Visitors Bureau, (800) 338-4724
Geauga County Tourism Council (Chardon), (800) 775-8687
Geneva-on-the-Lake Convention and Visitors Bureau, (800) 862-9948
Knox County Visitors Bureau (Mt. Vernon), (800) 837-5282
Lake County Visitors Bureau (Painesville), (800) 368-5253
Mansfield and Richland County Convention and Visitors Bureau, (800) 642-0375
Mohican Country Tourist Association (Loudonville), (800) 722-7588
Portage County Convention and Visitors Bureau (Aurora), (800) 648-6342
Greater Steubenville Convention and Visitors Bureau, (800) 859-5333
Sugarcreek Tourist Bureau, (800) 852-2223
Trumbull County Convention and Visitors Bureau (Niles), (800) 672-9555
Tuscarawas County Convention and Visitors Bureau New (Philadelphia), (800) 527-3387
Wayne County Visitors and Convention Bureau (Wooster), (800) 362-6474
Youngstown/Mahoning County Convention and Visitors Bureau, (800) 447-8201

NORTHWEST OHIO

AuGlaize and Mercer Counties Convention and Visitors Bureau (St. Marys), (800) 860-4726
Bellevue Area Tourism and Visitors Bureau, (800) 562-6978
Bowling Green Convention and Visitors Bureau, (800) 866-0046
Darke County Visitors Bureau (Greenville), (800) 504-2995
Greater Defiance Area Tourism and Visitors Bureau, (800) 686-4382
Fremont/Sandusky County Convention and Visitors Bureau, (800) 255-8070

Hancock County Convention and Visitors Bureau (Findlay), (800) 424-3315
Lima/Allen County Convention and Visitors Bureau, (888) 222-6075
Greater Logan County Area Convention and Visitors Bureau (Bellefontaine), (888) 564-2626
Lorain County Visitors Bureau, (800) 334-1673
Mansfield/Richland County Convention and Visitors Bureau, (800) 642-8282
Marion Area Convention and Visitors Bureau, (800) 371-6688
Medina County Convention and Visitors Bureau, (800) 860-2943
Ottawa County Visitors Bureau (Port Clinton), (800) 441-1271
Sandusky/Erie County Visitors and Convention Bureau, (800) 255-3743
Seneca County Convention and Visitors Bureau (Tiffin), (888) 736-3221
Greater Toledo Convention and Visitors Bureau, (800) 243-4667
Van Wert Convention and visitors Bureau, (800) 617-9378

SOUTHWEST OHIO

Greater Cincinnati Convention and Visitors Bureau, (800) 246-2987
Clermont County Convention and Visitors Bureau (Cincinnati), (800) 796-4282
Dayton/Montgomery County Convention and Visitors Bureau, (800) 221-8234
Fayette County Travel, Tourism and Convention Bureau (Washington Court House),
   (800) 479-7797
Greene County Convention and Visitors Bureau (Beavercreek), (800) 733-9109
Miami County Visitors and Convention Bureau (Troy), (800) 348-8993
Middletown Convention and Visitors Bureau, (888) 664-3353
Warren County Convention and Visitors Bureau (Lebanon), (800) 433-1072

SOUTHEAST OHIO

Athens County Convention and Visitors Bureau, (800) 878-9767
Belmont County Tourism Council (St. Clairsville), (800) 356-5082
Cambridge/Guernsey County Convention and Visitors Bureau, (800) 933-5480
Hocking County Tourism Association (Logan), (800) 462-5464
Jackson Area Tourism and Convention Bureau, (800) 522-7564
Marietta Tourist and Convention Bureau, (800) 288-2577
Ohio Valley Visitors Center of Gallia County (Gallipolis), (800) 765-6482
Perry County Development/Tourism Center (New Lexington), (800) 343-7379
Ross/Chillicothe Convention and Visitors Bureau, (800) 413-4118
Zanesville/Muskingum County Convention and Visitors Bureau, (800) 743-2303

AIRLINES

Air Canada/Air Ontario, (800) 776-3000
America West Airlines, (800) 2FLY AWA (235-9292)
American Airlines, (800) 433-7300
American Transair, (800) 225-2995
Canadian Airlines International, (800) 426-7000
ComAir, (800) 354-9822
Continental Airlines, (800) 523-3273

Delta Air Lines, (800) 221-1212
Midway Airlines, (800) 621-5757
Midwest Express Airlines, (800) 452-2022
Northwest Airlines, (800) 225-2525
Southwest Airlines, (800) 435-9792
TWA, (800) 221-2000
United Air Lines, (800) 241-6522
USAir-USAir Express, (800) 428-4322

AUTOMOBILE RENTAL

Alamo Rent a Car, (800) GO-ALAMO (327-9633)
Avis Rent a Car, (800) 831-2847
Budget Car and Truck Rental, (800) 527-0700
Dollar Rent a Car, (800) 800-4000
Enterprise Rent a Car, (800) RENT-A-CAR (736-8222)
Greyhound Rent a Car, (800) 327-2501
Hertz Rent a Car, (800) 654-3131
Holiday Payless Rent a Car, (800) 237-2804
National Rent a Car, (800) 227-7368
Payless Rent a Car, (800) PAYLESS (729-5377)
Thrifty Car Rental, (800) 367-2277
Ugly Duckling Rent a Car, (800) THE DUCK (843-3825)
Value Rent a Car, (800) GO VALUE (468-2583)

BUS TRAVEL

Greyhound, (800) 231-2222

HOTELS AND MOTELS

Amerisuites, (800) 833-1516
Best Western International, (800) 528-1234
Budgetel Inns, (800) 428-3438
Choice Hotels International (Clarion, Comfort Inn, Quality Inn, Sleep Inn), (800) 424-6423
Courtyard by Marriott, (800) 321-2211
Days Inn, (800) 329-7466
Doubletree Hotel Reservations, (800) 222-8733
EconoLodge, (800) 553-2666
Embassy Suites Hotels, (800) EMBASSY (362-2779)
Exel Inns of America, (800) 367-3935
Fairfield Inn by Marriott, (800) 228-2800
Four Seasons Hotels, (800) 332-3442
Friendship Inn, (800) 453-4511
Guest Quarters Suite Hotels, (800) 424-2900
Hampton Inns, (800) 426-7866

Hilton Reservations, (800) 445-8667
Howard Johnson, (800) 578-7878
Hyatt Hotels and Resorts, (800) 233-1234
Independent Motels of America, (800) 341-8000
Inn Suites International Inns and Resorts, (800) 842-4242
Inter-Continental and Forum Hotels, (800) 327-0200
Knights Inn, (800) 843-5644
Lenox House Suites, (800) 445-3669
Marriott Hotels, (800) 228-9290
Motel 6, (800) 466-8356
Nikko Hotels International, (800) 645-5687
Quality Inns, Hotels and Suites, (800) 424-6423
Ramada, (800) 228-2828
Red Roof Inns, (800) THE ROOF (843-7663)
Renaissance Hotels and Resorts, (800) 468-3571
Ritz-Carlton Hotels and Resorts, (800) 241-3333
Rodeway Inns, (800) 228-2000
Sheraton Worldwide, (800) 328-3535
Shilo Inns, (800) 222-2244
Shoney's Inns, (800) 222-2222
Signature Inn, (800) 822-5252
Stouffer Hotels & Resorts, (800) 468-3571
Super 8 Motels, (800) 800-8000
Wyndham Hotels and Resorts, (800) 822-4200

INDEX

AGRICULTURAL EVENTS

AMISH COUNTRY

BREWERIES

CAR SHOWS AND MUSEUMS

CHRISTMAS EVENTS

CONSERVATION AREAS

GARDENS AND FLOWER SHOWS

HIKING

HOME TOURS

Buckeye Lake Tour of Homes: 73
Cedar Point Chausee Tour of Homes: 202
Century Homes Tour—Geauga County: 175
Historic Home and Garden Tours—Urbana: 228
Holiday Festival and Tour of Homes—Oxford: 272
Home & Garden Tour—Galion: 229
House Tour of Historic Wyoming: 256
J.E. Reeves Victorian Home and Museum—Dover: 160
Lakeside Tour of Homes—Conneaut: 187
Mount Vernon Home Tours—Mount Vernon: 147-148
Old West End Festival—Toledo: 220
Tour of Historic Homes—Hillsboro: 279

KID STUFF

LIVING HISTORY SITES

Algonquin Mill Fall Festival—Carrollton: 301

Black Iron Artistry & Other Pioneer Skills—Defiance: 243

Dunham Tavern Museum—Cleveland: 92

Geauga County Historical Society Century Village—Burton: 173

Hale Farm and Village—Bath: 113

Living History Trade Fair—Fremont: 228

Living History Weekend—Gnadenhutten: 163

Living Word Outdoor Drama—Cambridge: 323

Medieval & Renaissance Festival—Columbus: 60

Ohio Historical Center/Ohio Village—Columbus: 58

Piqua Historical Area—Piqua: 234

Providence Metropark—Grand Rapids: 218

Roscoe Village—Coshocton County: 154

Santa Maria—Columbus: 57

Settlers Day—Milan: 202

Tecumseh!—Chillicothe: 335

The Way It Was—Caesar Creek State Park Pioneer Village: 279

Wild West/Great Train Robbery—Hebron: 73

see also reenactments/encampments

NATIVE AMERICAN HERITAGE

NATIONAL PARKS/MONUMENTS

STATE PARKS/MEMORIALS

THEATER/PERFORMING ARTS

UNUSUAL CLAIMS TO FAME

Great Outdoor Underwear Festival: 237
Woolybear Festival: 194
World's Chicken Capital: 115
World's Largest Tooth: 93
World's Longest Bascule Drawbridge: 193

WINERIES/VINEYARDS

ABOUT THE AUTHOR

Writer, editor, and photographer David K. Wright was born in one Midwestern state and has since lived in most of the rest. A native of Richmond, Indiana, he attended college in Ohio and was drafted into the Army in 1966, the day following graduation. After a meteoric newspaper career, Wright turned to freelance writing full time and has produced 38 nonfiction books in 20 hectic years.

At the moment, he is the managing editor of a small press in Minnesota. A disabled veteran, he is grateful to the Moon staff for their patience during an illness and convalescence.

"I think I know what writers have to have in order to do a Moon handbook," he says. "It's the desire, no matter where they are, to be somewhere else. That's an urge I've never been able to shake."

MONICA WRIGHT

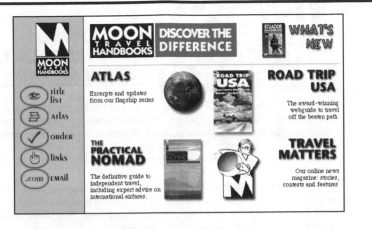

MOON TRAVEL HANDBOOKS

LOSE YOURSELF IN THE EXPERIENCE, NOT THE CROWD

For more than 25 years, Moon Travel Handbooks have been the guidebooks of choice for adventurous travelers. Our award-winning Handbook series provides focused, comprehensive coverage of distinct destinations all over the world. Each Handbook is like an entire bookcase of cultural insight and introductory information in one portable volume. Our goal at Moon is to give travelers all the background and practical information they'll need for an extraordinary travel experience.

The following pages include a complete list of Handbooks, covering North America and Hawaii, Mexico, Latin America and the Caribbean, and Asia and the Pacific. To purchase Moon Travel Handbooks, check your local bookstore or order c/o Publishers Group West, Attn: Order Department, 1700 Fourth St., Berkeley, CA 94710, or fax to (510) 528-3444.

"An in-depth dunk into the land, the people and their history, arts, and politics."
—*Student Travels*

"I consider these books to be superior to Lonely Planet. When Moon produces a book it is more humorous, incisive, and off-beat."
—*Toronto Sun*

"Outdoor enthusiasts gravitate to the well-written Moon Travel Handbooks. In addition to politically correct historic and cultural features, the series focuses on flora, fauna and outdoor recreation. Maps and meticulous directions also are a trademark of Moon guides."
—*Houston Chronicle*

"Moon [Travel Handbooks] . . . bring a healthy respect to the places they investigate. Best of all, they provide a host of odd nuggets that give a place texture and prod the wary traveler from the beaten path. The finest are written with such care and insight they deserve listing as literature."
—*American Geographical Society*

"Moon Travel Handbooks offer in-depth historical essays and useful maps, enhanced by a sense of humor and a neat, compact format."
—*Swing*

"Perfect for the more adventurous, these are long on history, sightseeing and nitty-gritty information and very price-specific."
—*Columbus Dispatch*

"Moon guides manage to be comprehensive and countercultural at the same time . . . Handbooks are packed with maps, photographs, drawings, and sidebars that constitute a college-level introduction to each country's history, culture, people, and crafts."
—*National Geographic Traveler*

"Few travel guides do a better job helping travelers create their own itineraries than the Moon Travel Handbook series. The authors have a knack for homing in on the essentials."
—**Colorado Springs** *Gazette Telegraph*

MEXICO

"These books will delight the armchair traveler, aid the undecided person in selecting a destination, and guide the seasoned road warrior looking for lesser-known hideaways."
—Mexican Meanderings Newsletter

"From tourist traps to off-the-beaten track hideaways, these guides offer consistent, accurate details without pretension."
—Foreign Service Journal

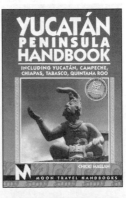

Archaeological Mexico	**$19.95**
Andrew Coe	420 pages, 27 maps
Baja Handbook	**$16.95**
Joe Cummings	540 pages, 46 maps
Cabo Handbook	**$14.95**
Joe Cummings	270 pages, 17 maps
Cancún Handbook	**$14.95**
Chicki Mallan	240 pages, 25 maps
Colonial Mexico	**$18.95**
Chicki Mallan	400 pages, 38 maps
Mexico Handbook	**$21.95**
Joe Cummings and Chicki Mallan	1,200 pages, 201 maps
Northern Mexico Handbook	**$17.95**
Joe Cummings	610 pages, 69 maps
Pacific Mexico Handbook	**$17.95**
Bruce Whipperman	580 pages, 68 maps
Puerto Vallarta Handbook	**$14.95**
Bruce Whipperman	330 pages, 36 maps
Yucatán Handbook	**$16.95**
Chicki Mallan	400 pages, 52 maps

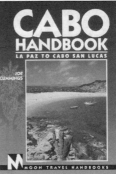

"Beyond question, the most comprehensive Mexican resources available for those who prefer deep travel to shallow tourism. But don't worry, the fiesta-fun stuff's all here too."
—New York Daily News

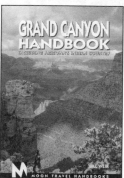

LATIN AMERICA AND THE CARIBBEAN

"Solidly packed with practical information and full of significant cultural asides that will enlighten you on the whys and wherefores of things you might easily see but not easily grasp."

—*Boston Globe*

Belize Handbook	**$15.95**
Chicki Mallan and Patti Lange	390 pages, 45 maps
Caribbean Vacations	**$18.95**
Karl Luntta	910 pages, 64 maps
Costa Rica Handbook	**$19.95**
Christopher P. Baker	780 pages, 73 maps
Cuba Handbook	**$19.95**
Christopher P. Baker	740 pages, 70 maps
Dominican Republic Handbook	**$15.95**
Gaylord Dold	420 pages, 24 maps
Ecuador Handbook	**$16.95**
Julian Smith	450 pages, 43 maps
Honduras Handbook	**$15.95**
Chris Humphrey	330 pages, 40 maps
Jamaica Handbook	**$15.95**
Karl Luntta	330 pages, 17 maps
Virgin Islands Handbook	**$13.95**
Karl Luntta	220 pages, 19 maps

NORTH AMERICA AND HAWAII

"These domestic guides convey the same sense of exoticism that their foreign counterparts do, making home-country travel seem like far-flung adventure."

—*Sierra Magazine*

Alaska-Yukon Handbook	**$17.95**
Deke Castleman and Don Pitcher	530 pages, 92 maps
Alberta and the Northwest Territories Handbook	**$18.95**
Andrew Hempstead	520 pages, 79 maps
Arizona Handbook	**$18.95**
Bill Weir	600 pages, 36 maps
Atlantic Canada Handbook	**$18.95**
Mark Morris	490 pages, 60 maps
Big Island of Hawaii Handbook	**$15.95**
J.D. Bisignani	390 pages, 25 maps
Boston Handbook	**$13.95**
Jeff Perk	200 pages, 20 maps
British Columbia Handbook	**$16.95**
Jane King and Andrew Hempstead	430 pages, 69 maps

Canadian Rockies Handbook	**$14.95**
Andrew Hempstead	220 pages, 22 maps
Colorado Handbook	**$17.95**
Stephen Metzger	480 pages, 46 maps
Georgia Handbook	**$17.95**
Kap Stann	380 pages, 44 maps
Grand Canyon Handbook	**$14.95**
Bill Weir	220 pages, 10 maps
Hawaii Handbook	**$19.95**
J.D. Bisignani	1,030 pages, 88 maps
Honolulu-Waikiki Handbook	**$14.95**
J.D. Bisignani	360 pages, 20 maps
Idaho Handbook	**$18.95**
Don Root	610 pages, 42 maps
Kauai Handbook	**$15.95**
J.D. Bisignani	320 pages, 23 maps
Los Angeles Handbook	**$16.95**
Kim Weir	370 pages, 15 maps
Maine Handbook	**$18.95**
Kathleen M. Brandes	660 pages, 27 maps
Massachusetts Handbook	**$18.95**
Jeff Perk	600 pages, 23 maps
Maui Handbook	**$15.95**
J.D. Bisignani	450 pages, 37 maps
Michigan Handbook	**$15.95**
Tina Lassen	360 pages, 32 maps
Montana Handbook	**$17.95**
Judy Jewell and W.C. McRae	490 pages, 52 maps
Nevada Handbook	**$18.95**
Deke Castleman	530 pages, 40 maps
New Hampshire Handbook	**$18.95**
Steve Lantos	500 pages, 18 maps
New Mexico Handbook	**$15.95**
Stephen Metzger	360 pages, 47 maps
New York Handbook	**$19.95**
Christiane Bird	780 pages, 95 maps
New York City Handbook	**$13.95**
Christiane Bird	300 pages, 20 maps
North Carolina Handbook	**$14.95**
Rob Hirtz and Jenny Daughtry Hirtz	320 pages, 27 maps
Northern California Handbook	**$19.95**
Kim Weir	800 pages, 50 maps
Ohio Handbook	**$15.95**
David K. Wright	340 pages, 18 maps
Oregon Handbook	**$17.95**
Stuart Warren and Ted Long Ishikawa	590 pages, 34 maps

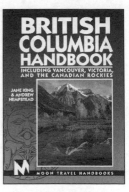

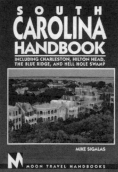

Pennsylvania Handbook	**$18.95**
Joanne Miller	448 pages, 40 maps
Road Trip USA	**$24.00**
Jamie Jensen	940 pages, 175 maps
Road Trip USA Getaways: Chicago	**$9.95**
	60 pages, 1 map
Road Trip USA Getaways: Seattle	**$9.95**
	60 pages, 1 map
Santa Fe-Taos Handbook	**$13.95**
Stephen Metzger	160 pages, 13 maps
South Carolina Handbook	**$16.95**
Mike Sigalas	400 pages, 20 maps
Southern California Handbook	**$19.95**
Kim Weir	720 pages, 26 maps
Tennessee Handbook	**$17.95**
Jeff Bradley	530 pages, 42 maps
Texas Handbook	**$18.95**
Joe Cummings	690 pages, 70 maps
Utah Handbook	**$17.95**
Bill Weir and W.C. McRae	490 pages, 40 maps
Virginia Handbook	**$15.95**
Julian Smith	410 pages, 37 maps
Washington Handbook	**$19.95**
Don Pitcher	840 pages, 111 maps
Wisconsin Handbook	**$18.95**
Thomas Huhti	590 pages, 69 maps
Wyoming Handbook	**$17.95**
Don Pitcher	610 pages, 80 maps

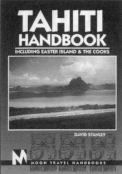

ASIA AND THE PACIFIC

"Scores of maps, detailed practical info down to business hours of small-town libraries. You can't beat the Asian titles for sheer heft. (The) series is sort of an American Lonely Planet, with better writing but fewer titles. (The) individual voice of researchers comes through."

—*Travel & Leisure*

Australia Handbook	**$21.95**
Marael Johnson, Andrew Hempstead,	
and Nadina Purdon	940 pages, 141 maps
Bali Handbook	**$19.95**
Bill Dalton	750 pages, 54 maps
Fiji Islands Handbook	**$14.95**
David Stanley	350 pages, 42 maps
Hong Kong Handbook	**$16.95**
Kerry Moran	378 pages, 49 maps

| Indonesia Handbook | $25.00 |
| Bill Dalton | 1,380 pages, 249 maps |

| Micronesia Handbook | $16.95 |
| Neil M. Levy | 340 pages, 70 maps |

| Nepal Handbook | $18.95 |
| Kerry Moran | 490 pages, 51 maps |

| New Zealand Handbook | $19.95 |
| Jane King | 620 pages, 81 maps |

| Outback Australia Handbook | $18.95 |
| Marael Johnson | 450 pages, 57 maps |

| Philippines Handbook | $17.95 |
| Peter Harper and Laurie Fullerton | 670 pages, 116 maps |

| Singapore Handbook | $15.95 |
| Carl Parkes | 350 pages, 29 maps |

| South Korea Handbook | $19.95 |
| Robert Nilsen | 820 pages, 141 maps |

| South Pacific Handbook | $24.00 |
| David Stanley | 920 pages, 147 maps |

| Southeast Asia Handbook | $21.95 |
| Carl Parkes | 1,080 pages, 204 maps |

| Tahiti Handbook | $15.95 |
| David Stanley | 450 pages, 51 maps |

| Thailand Handbook | $19.95 |
| Carl Parkes | 860 pages, 142 maps |

| Vietnam, Cambodia & Laos Handbook | $18.95 |
| Michael Buckley | 760 pages, 116 maps |

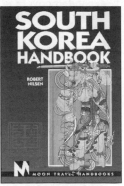

OTHER GREAT TITLES FROM MOON

"For hardy wanderers, few guides come more highly recommended than the Handbooks. They include good maps, steer clear of fluff and flackery, and offer plenty of money-saving tips. They also give you the kind of information that visitors to strange lands—on any budget—need to survive."

—*US News & World Report*

| Moon Handbook | $10.00 |
| Carl Koppeschaar | 150 pages, 8 maps |

| The Practical Nomad: How to Travel Around the World | $17.95 |
| Edward Hasbrouck | 580 pages |

| Staying Healthy in Asia, Africa, and Latin America | $11.95 |
| Dirk Schroeder | 230 pages, 4 maps |

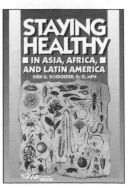

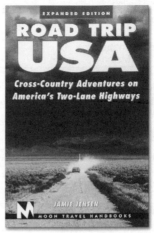

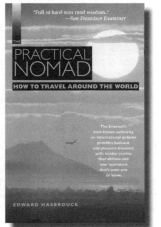

WHERE TO BUY MOON TRAVEL HANDBOOKS

BOOKSTORES AND LIBRARIES: Moon Travel Handbooks are distributed worldwide. Please contact our sales manager at info@moon.com for a list of wholesalers and distributors in your area.

TRAVELERS: We would like to have Moon Travel Handbooks available throughout the world. Please ask your bookstore to contact us for ordering information. If your bookstore will not order our guides for you, please contact us for a free catalog.

> **Moon Travel Handbooks**
> **C/o Publishers Group West**
> **Attn: Order Department**
> **1700 Fourth Street**
> **Berkeley, CA 94710**
> **fax: (510) 528-3444**

IMPORTANT ORDERING INFORMATION

PRICES: All prices are subject to change. We always ship the most current edition. We will let you know if there is a price increase on the book you order.

SHIPPING AND HANDLING OPTIONS: Domestic UPS or USPS priority mail (allow 10 working days for delivery): $6.00 for the first item, $1.00 for each additional item.

UPS 2nd Day Air or Printed Airmail requires a special quote.

International Surface Bookrate 8-12 weeks delivery: $5.00 for the first item, $1.00 for each additional item. Note: We cannot guarantee international surface bookrate shipping. We recommend sending international orders via air mail, which requires a special quote.

FOREIGN ORDERS: Orders that originate outside the U.S.A. must be paid for with an international money order, a check in U.S. currency drawn on a major U.S. bank based in the U.S.A., or Visa, MasterCard, or American Express.

INTERNET ORDERS: Visit our site at: www.moon.com

ORDER FORM
Prices are subject to change without notice. Please check our Web site
at **www.moon.com** for current prices and editions.
(See important ordering information on preceding page.)

Name: _____ Date: _____

Street: _____

City: _____ Daytime Phone: _____

State or Country: _____ Zip Code: _____

QUANTITY	TITLE	PRICE

Taxable Total_____

Sales Tax in CA and NY_____

Shipping & Handling_____

TOTAL_____

Ship: ☐ UPS (no P.O. Boxes) ☐ Priority mail ☐ International surface mail

Ship to: ☐ address above ☐ other _____

Make checks payable to: **PUBLISHERS GROUP WEST**, Attn: Order Department, 1700 Fourth St.,
Berkeley, CA 94710, or fax to (510) 528-3444. We accept Visa, MasterCard, or American Express.

To Order: Fax in your Visa, MasterCard, or American Express number, or send a written order
with your Visa, MasterCard, or American Express number and expiration date clearly written.

Card Number: ☐ **Visa** ☐ **MasterCard** ☐ **American Express**

☐ ☐ ☐ ☐ ☐ ☐ ☐ ☐ ☐ ☐ ☐ ☐ ☐ ☐ ☐ ☐

Exact Name on Card: _____

Expiration date:_____

Signature:_____

Daytime Phone: _____

U.S.~METRIC CONVERSION

1 inch = 2.54 centimeters (cm)
1 foot = .3048 meters (m)
1 yard = 0.914 meters
1 mile = 1.6093 kilometers (km)
1 km = .6214 miles
1 fathom = 1.8288 m
1 chain = 20.1168 m
1 furlong = 201.168 m
1 acre = .4047 hectares
1 sq km = 100 hectares
1 sq mile = 2.59 square km
1 ounce = 28.35 grams
1 pound = .4536 kilograms
1 short ton = .90718 metric ton
1 short ton = 2000 pounds
1 long ton = 1.016 metric tons
1 long ton = 2240 pounds
1 metric ton = 1000 kilograms
1 quart = .94635 liters
1 US gallon = 3.7854 liters
1 Imperial gallon = 4.5459 liters
1 nautical mile = 1.852 km

To compute celsius temperatures, subtract 32 from Fahrenheit and divide by 1.8. To go the other way, multiply celsius by 1.8 and add 32.

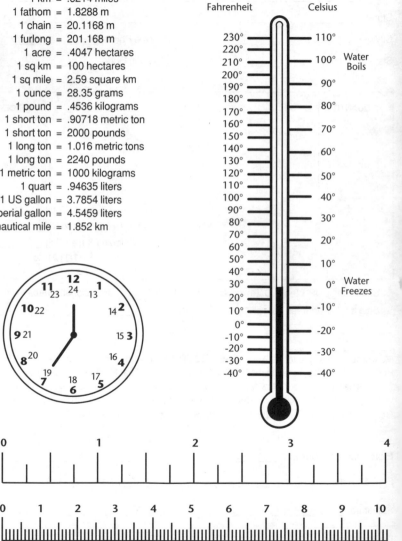